Safari of a Patchwork Pilgrim

For Jem, who survived all this and still encouraged its recapture.

Also, in memory of Mildred Thoko Ndaba

Safari
of a
Patchwork
Pilgrim

A Life

Philippa Rees

Cover Design: Philippa Rees/Biddles
Cover Image: Original: Honoré Daumier.
First Print Edition 2024

Published by:
CollaborArt Books
(collaborartbooks.com)

Copyright © Philippa Rees 2024

ISBN 978-0-9575002-7-3

All rights reserved. No part of this publication may be reproduced, stored in a retrieval system or transmitted in any form or by any means without the prior written permission of the author, nor be otherwise circulated in any form of binding or cover other than that which is published and without a similar condition being imposed on the publisher.

Typeset in Minion 12.5pt

Printed in Great Britain by
Biddles Books Limited, King's Lynn

'It is told that a stranger, visiting Heraclitus and finding him by the kitchen fire, hesitated to enter, 'Come in, come in', he cried, 'the Gods are here too.'

— Aristotle 'On the Parts of Animals'

"I caught him, with an unseen hook and an invisible line which is long enough to let him wander to the ends of the world, and still to bring him back with a twitch upon the thread."

— G.K. Chesterton, Father Brown

'Poets are the unacknowledged legislators of the world'

— Shelley 'The Defense of Poetry' 1821.

Be not afeard; the isle is full of noises,
Sounds and sweet airs, that give delight, and hurt not.
Sometimes a thousand twangling instruments
Will hum about mine ears; and sometime voices,
That, if I then had waked after long sleep,
Will make me sleep again: and then, in dreaming,
The clouds methought would open, and show riches
Ready to drop upon me; that, when I waked,
I cried to dream again.

       Shakespeare. *The Tempest*

GRATITUDE

To Eldred Godson, whose enthusiastic belief in this work sustained its creation.

TABLE OF CONTENTS

Book One. The Voorloper

Prologue: Daimon Urges Renewed Effort.   1

Chapter 1	Marna and Maweni	7
Chapter 2	Yourmother	21
Chapter 3	Heli and Mafeking	33
Chapter 4	Light: Love on Safari	52
Chapter 5	Three Wishes	60
Chapter 6	Brother Paul: Basutoland	74
Chapter 7	Max; and First Loneliness	86
Chapter 8	Judith; Romantic Longing	95
Chapter 9	George Eliot and Raymond, my father	104
Chapter 10	Great Aunt Mary and a Cat	111
Chapter 11	Red Hot Pokers	127
Chapter 12	Max, Milly and Mandela	133
Chapter 13	David: Marriage Knot	146
Chapter 14	Serpents: Handling the Natives	163
Chapter 15	Cassirer: A Perceptive Philosopher	177
Chapter 16	Jessica, Rosalind and Etiquette	198
Chapter 17	Frau Fick: Bavaria	208
Chapter 18	Terry: a Man Who Came to Dinner	228
Chapter 19	Opening Pandora's Box	246
Chapter 20	Snakes and Ladders	251
Chapter 21	Promised Land	266
Chapter 22	Clifford Alloway: A 'Mafioso' Godfather	286
Chapter 23	Cutting the Knot: Exile	298

Book Two. Voetstoots

Caveat Lector. 309

Chapter 24	Margaret and Dick Milford: Hoeing in a Cabbage Patch	311
Chapter 25	Georgina and Combe Cottage	327
Chapter 26	Martin Israel: Storm	341
Chapter 27	Torpedo: Love: Finally	354
Chapter 28	Judas: Galloping Through Fire	372
Chapter 29	Cuckoo's Nest	382
Chapter 30	Adrian: Released	391

Interlude. Distillation: Setting Sail for Integration. 401

Chapter 31	Loose Ends	403

Book Three. Versamel

Disembarkation 421

Chapter 32	John: Toil and Spin	425
Chapter 33	Incubation of a Writer	452
Chapter 34	Hedley Haynes: Skips and Reclamation	461
Chapter 35	Scrapbook: Limits on Loyalty	478
Chapter 36	The Miracle Worker	498
Chapter 37	The Donga Divide	525
Chapter 38	Return: Facts are not Truth	539
Chapter 39	Taeke: Coming Full Circle	550
Chapter 40	Far Fetched	562
Chapter 41	Milly-Polly. Finishing Touches	574
Chapter 42	The Twitch upon the Thread	584
Chapter 43	The Full Picture. Uitspan	606

Afterword: The Refuge 616

Glossary 620
Author's Note 622
Other Works 623

BOOK ONE

Voorloper*

* Forerunner: The one who walks in front to lead the oxen.

PROLOGUE

Daimon Urges Renewed Effort

I can't wait any longer. Maybe I am just going to let the conversation run and invite you to listen in. God knows—and I know God well enough to claim this— that I've tried everything else to get the old woman back to work. We haven't much time left, and she is now so terrified she won't begin in case I take the reins again. I am headstrong when buckled between the shafts.

I mean, look at the ravages of what she still thinks was a failure. Not that it was; not entirely. The timing was out, but to the easy surfer, time is a wave. You catch and skim down the glass wall of its propulsion and swivel back before it breaks. Hang on too long, get catapulted into glorious salt bubbles and end up with a mouthful of grit. She is still spewing sand, so until she gets up and back on board, I'll start this, her chronicle; sooner or later, we can count on her to interrupt. Then, we might manage a tango or a slow and thoughtful sarabande.

Above all. I want to call her back because we Daimons have a thin time when abandoned by our protégée. I also have work to finish but am now reduced to a reedy voice in the deserts of her despair. No need for it, really.

Another reason I am addressing you directly is to correct a profound misconception. Most people, if they acknowledge a Daimon at all, see me as an itinerant peddler, wheeling a cart through a capricious circuit, offering the market specials no one bought: hats, matches or a knife sharpener, useful but inessential offerings. Then, pocketing pennies, I plod off. That belief stems from the fear that if we were welcomed in and given a full-time home, bed and board, we would be found to smell, eat too much, or make strident demands and call for beer and skittles every day. That, or early attendance at meditation, straining the knees in unnatural postures while hoping for enlightenment.

It is quite the opposite. It is our protégées who are the roving peddlers. We are the constant presence, at the head of the bed, behind the chair and sometimes through the eyes—those are the good times—when we take a walk through woodland and cause sun flashes through the trees. Those are the enlightenments, there for the gathering, like mushrooms, just by looking. It is always our hope to foster those. Yes, the looking does the creation. Very few know that.

Some would call me the 'voice of Soul' or the 'quickening Spirit', and both are accurate, albeit insufficient. We Daimons hold the blueprint and select the materials to refine the design. But, like an architect, we have to negotiate with the wild impulses of the unlettered builder, who fancies Gothic for a classical edifice or who fashions irrelevant curlicues or follies. Demolition is frequently necessary! Those are the important lessons.

What I seek to convey is that nothing, absolutely nothing, is irrelevant or incidental, which is a way of saying that only love would have the patient tolerance to take so many detours just to secure the fundamental freedom on which the structure of each life is erected. Until freedom itself makes the choice to accept the blueprint of a life forged as much by its future as its past. We live by one rule: never to impose or interfere, but simply to offer.

My companion of a thousand long nights, who turned to me in the tear-moist sheets, sought me under the moon in the roots of a beech, has wandered away. I cannot bear the loss any longer. Yet I am constrained by our mutual love of liberty; I cannot call her back. Therefore, I will usurp and write the book she is afraid of, dredge her memory and lay out my fine woven nets for all to pluck and mend.

Your nets?

Who else's?

So, I never had any liberty, really. The knots were tied before I arrived?

What you caught with them, where you threw them, how often and with whoever was entirely your domain. Your nature was woven, woven by your past and its intentions in you, but not your liberty to make mistakes...

My nature, as you call it, was moulded by what? It certainly never intended ease or a smooth passage. Are you, at heart, a sadist?

How could I be, since you are not? We are never at odds, merely sometimes alienated, and that's from your neglect and inattention, not mine.

So, if I sign this contract to participate—and I am not saying I will—you are the one wafting a scent of Albertine rose while I will be crawling apologetically through the mud?

I have a better plan. You can tell the stories. You have had a rich life and known some extraordinary people who benefitted and suffered from that stoical determination of yours. Tell us about them. Make small art of episodes. They deserve no less. Their footfalls lead to a destination. It is a destination many seek. Why not tell them how you found it?

The chief obstacle in what you suggest is that the person you are talking to wasn't there!

No, but I was! If you had been present all along there would be no tale to tell, no mistakes or errors of judgement to learn from. Those are the stories; they start with stubbed toes and barked shins. All of them. Pirouetting through life is what birds manage. Humans have other missions to accomplish.

You realise that my 'rich life' only began to reveal its direction halfway through, when we met.

Of course, but our meeting was inevitable. Your early years formed that inevitability. That ardent child was always searching. For me.

And you were always closing doors?

I only closed the fruitless doors until your narrow path delivered you to me. I was always what you sought, but if you want to truly capture your story it needs the stumbles and errors, the innocence. More now than ever.

How so? More than ever?

Because innocence is soon due for extinction. The world cannot afford innocence any longer. Mankind will grow up suddenly and fast. This life, its naïveté, its simple joys, its desolations, are a record of humanity's childhood. And humanity's loneliness. In writing this, you are recording history already. A portrait of emotional innocence and careless weaving will one day be shelved under 'Antiquity: Humanity's searches for meaning'. The equivalent of botanical compendia, primitive and quaint forms before hybrids removed their carbuncles and excess hair. They have their charm, as does your wayward life. Give it due honour. It got us here.

You are suggesting that what lies ahead is devoid of joy and unpierced by disappointments?

Not exactly, but the two are closely intertwined. More that the joy will be self-created, a constant glow, not the effervescent arching toward loss. Joy, once achieved, is already on the wane.

Where would I begin? Just pull it up as it comes, like hair from a plughole?

Not a pretty image! Wherever you like. Perhaps before we met? In the slow-growing light of your search, before you understood what it was you sought.

I'll think about it. The continuous sheet of time we call memory, written to dissolve, like protein in gruel, makes my life instead a thin piece of cardboard which, when I was twenty-nine, God snapped across his celestial knee into two halves, only raggedly left linked.

I'd leave all mention of God for later. He had to knock loudly for you to respond.

He knocked the door down and me behind it. Don't you start exonerating God!

He answered my call. Perhaps it was too loud; I had tried everything else.

∽

Someone recently said, 'While you are going through your life, it feels as if everything is just an assortment of random events, things just happening for no good reason, chaos. But when you look back on your life, it seems like a finely crafted novel.'

My life has come close to being the opposite. There was little chaos or randomness. Instead, unrolling events marched in lock-step towards a mountain summit. That shining peak needed just one more, then another, and yet another Herculean ascent. I have always seen its extraordinary improbabilities as being worthy of a novel, a badly crafted novel; too many repetitive patterns as though the author had forgotten she had written, started again and failed to use 'delete' for one draft or the other.

It launched with such vivid characters but then let them evaporate without justifying such startling idiosyncrasies. It continued with new adventures and a sense of ah at last! Only to fizzle up a blind alley. Yes, looking back, I always felt destined to play a major role in my life, only to perceive others played a bigger one; so not even the principal character stayed principal for long. Was I ever the principal of my life? I truly am unsure.

That's why we are here. To find out.

A journey re-told from its destination is a meal recalled after its digestion. The sharp chillies, the sliced bright cucumber and a chopping board arrayed with colour and a rich variety have been homogenised in the soup of hindsight. It may have a piquant aroma, but uncertainty has boiled away. The remaining gruel is good for toothless gums and lethargic metabolism, but it is not tempting for those who hope to travel rather than arrive.

This is the difficulty with writing memoir. The aged scribe is not the child that set out; the disappointed wife is not the bright-eyed romantic whose dreams were fashioned by heroes and who crept out in the night when hope died. I now realise that the death of false hopes was crucial, and yet the hopes drove all my adventures and the acquiring of necessary knowledge. Each foray down a no-through road returned with a vocabulary, not merely an academic discipline, but an emotional one of failure or illusions shattered. I have learnt most from failure and from paring away. Yet the shavings littered about created the life that remained. Nothing was irrelevant.

So, I must give you the life as it happened, and since I have become a writer, I will employ the resources of a writer's recapture, for writers are storytellers. I will take the liberty to adopt the voices of my characters, better to fracture your view and give each the iridescence of individual sparkle. Nothing they say will be factually untrue, but through them, I will find and give a sheen of recovered surprise.

Bon appétit.

Good. We're away.

CHAPTER 1

Marna and Maweni

'She thought it good for them to see... that a woman with her sleeved tucked up above her elbow might know all about the Subjunctive Mood or the Torrid Zone- that in short, she might possess 'education' and other good things ending in 'tion'...

I will take you first to meet Marna, my grandmother, as she was the first person I met; if 'met' covers the strong arms that lifted and pillowed me against her, the smell of 4711 cologne, the hug that was sustained even as she directed the unloading of the car by which I was delivered. Then the sprinkling of kisses that followed as we navigated the stone steps to a house. That required care. Below her substantial breasts, her invisible feet had to make their own decisions.

All were new: hugs, kisses and breasts. I don't remember anything before them.

From photographs, I have calculated that I was not quite two.

I start with Marna only because she was the monumental galleon that sailed, in her flowered rigging, imperturbably through all the winds and tides that followed. Don't be misled by her imperious carriage or her eyes as sharp as a bird of prey or the nervousness of those about her. They have misjudged her and quake, but I want you to enjoy her. So don't take her seriously. If you make her laugh, she will be your friend forever. You might even be gifted with her silent shaking of delight and even tears. Only Marna cried with laughter. So, no deference is required. Awareness and good manners she does like and a hearty appetite. She will feed you well. Never ask for parsimonious portions. A half cup of tea or a scrape of butter will get you no more than a scrape of attention.

Shall I paint her portrait, this indomitable, seemingly effortless ship-of-state, on her lark-thin legs, with her thin hair, dropping tortoiseshell combs in her wake, and occasionally into the bubbling soup? No, I will let her introduce herself. She will do it better than I could. Besides, you must hear her speak.

As she does, imagine an expressive face with a patrician nose, a wide mouth that is good at the repressed smile when she recalls pleasures, an easily arched brow of incredulity at stupidity, of men in particular, and eyes that seek accuracy by looking upwards to her right while she brings memory into focus. Memory, she cherishes, although for modern tastes, there are sometimes superfluous facts about genealogy and who descended from whom. She won't expect you to remember them; they are just the bones on which her sinewed reflections hang. From fragments dropped over many years, I shall give her voice to our history. She was there, and I was not. Life delivered her into the crosshairs of the 'Cape Colony'. Well before the Boer War, her parents sailed from Europe, one from Rotterdam, one from Liverpool, to meet one another in the Orange Free State, where Boers and Blacks gazed at each other across the veldt, ready for skirmish or wars. Most Europeans settled for the Cape with its vineyards and gracious gables and the hope of occasional post. Not my ancestors!

To understand my grandmother is to begin to understand South Africa, its fierce loyalty, and its contradictions. Her telling tells more of her than history; she is more important than distance can capture. She bequeathed both my inheritance and the flag of freedom from it.

Marna's Story

My full curved handle is Wilhelmina (Minnie) Humphreys Barrett, which hardly lifts the jug of who I am. 'Marna' came about because the author, my granddaughter, early on, could not manage Grandmama. So instead of the pinched 'Minnie' I was gifted with a soft pillow name which stuck. Names are important. Nobody knows my story, and I don't know the whole story either since important forebears died too soon and wars took out the others. I must prick out the canvas without the detail to stitch it fully. If I were George Eliot, I would be permitted to stroll into an unfinished story. dropping a perfumed handkerchief without stopping to retrieve it.

Not many of my generation were as fortunate as I was in general, and not many as unfortunate in the particular. I did not choose my parents but I must take some responsibility for the husbands. I mean, would you, at twenty-three, suppose that your ardent suitor with a fetching moustache and a ready smile, who expressed an interest in this new 'science of aviation', would order long distance, by ship, then ox cart, the components of a French monoplane? It was called a Bleriot, and no sooner unloaded, he set to, connecting struts, blades, propellers, wires and wing-nuts and assigned his young wife, namely yours truly, to do duty on miles of thick rubber-like canvas for the wings. Four-score broken Singer machine needles later, he was set. A few gathered for the maiden flight. It made a great kerfuffle before he hopped a few hedges to great applause. Horses do it more gracefully.

A few months later, he strapped himself in, pulled down the goggles, took off with a 'tootle pip', and flew away. By hop-skip-and-jumps to England from Durban. La marriage? Left in the fumes and dust! So, you see, I know about betrayal of every stripe: personal, religious and political, which is why I steer clear of any dogma or allegiance.

You would not foresee that, would you? You might add to all the 'bleriots' I thought appropriate. I was abandoned with a fatherless boy of three, poverty and disgrace. Mark this well because men doing a runner has been a recurrent pattern in this family, by precipitate death, by passions for other things or just the baser reasons like my granddaughter's father, Raymond, following Rommel out of North Africa with his red-taloned nurse. Raymond was a rotter; I saw that at once. A playboy by inclination, you could see that in every gesture and that too-easy laughter, although I must admit he had a very quick brain. My daughter married him in the hope of medicine. I married Evelyn Driver, the pilot with his appropriate name, to escape my mother, and if you had encountered her, you would understand. Anyway, Raymond left my granddaughter as good as orphaned. See what I mean? About repetitive patterns? None of us escape what came before; we run back into ourselves with barked shins.

Men have never really delivered, which is why I make a fuss about education. Girls need it more than boys do because, on the whole, women deliver— in every sense. We are a tribe of strong women— we've certainly had to be.

I am sure even a paltry education would have set up an image of South Africa in the nineteenth century. I am a product of that century's end: lurching wagons over the Drakensberg, whipped by resolute Afrikaners escaping their hated British overlords; wives in poke bonnets, circled in covered wagons and skirmishes from between the wheel-spokes with the Zulu. A rock on the koppie adjacent to Maweni, our family's farm, bears the carved signatures of the soon to be slaughtered, Piet Retief drinking a final koffie before trusting Dingaan with his life and those with him, all of them ending in a pool of blood.

No, the Zulu does not do anything by halves.

Harrismith, undistinguished in every way—even its name could not be more commonplace! — sits at the navel of the country; all the rivers are sourced from here, so I suppose it is inevitable that everyone passes through it. Perhaps that's why I met them all. From a distance, the picture would be of a rough country tamed by resolve and fortitude. Distance rather smudges things.

Yes, that was all true, but facts and history tell very little. They do not speak of the country's call, a country bigger than any of us; it had its sudden whiplash storms, its savage droughts and more beauty than we deserved. Nothing can ever replace these skies with their rolling cumulus clouds, the sunsets in vermilion and duck-egg blue until the night drops its coverlet of stars as abruptly as a storm cuts out the power. It is a savage beauty and something of that lives in us all. We hunger, we Africans.

What few understand is why we can hardly bear its beauty when present or live without it when we leave. Something critical in us ceases to live. There is some ancient call to those of us raised here; it may indeed be the cradle of mankind, and that might explain it. We were rocked in anthropology, fed from the spoon called origins, and grew up with the singing bush that opened each day and kept singing about deeper time and the wisdom of crickets.

Yet we also knew there was another story, or perhaps only we whites knew that; the blacks had no such disquiet, which is why they will remain when we are long gone. They belong in a way we never can. I remember thinking that in Uganda, watching that languorous loping run of the Maasai, tirelessly for miles, like tempered animals with their bare-chested ribs rippling, their spears oscillating ahead, and those thin muscled legs like racehorses in the surf in the rising dawn. Both are in their natural element.

I must not get carried away, or I shall never get to the meat of this attempt to make you understand what being South African does to us. It twists all of us with the poignancy of the unattainable love, just beyond reach. Even as it grips us, we know it will not reciprocate. It is pulling away even before we embrace it, for we are invaders. I do not mean that politically or racially. I mean, Man is not yet worthy of Africa; a white man is even less so. Whites lumber about in the natural world, absurdly self-important, more so when they carry a gun.

Perhaps that is why we still look to Europe to explain ourselves, as though some claim of its contribution— all that literature, all that history flows in our veins too — will compensate for our failure to be absorbed by Africa. But there is a savage rub: Britain, in the main, does not accept South Africa because it did not form it or grant it condescending independence. We took that for ourselves.

First, the Boers, the rough bunch in the saddle —half my forebears —although some of them were educated, and many noble, and then their dreadful racist descendants like Malan and Verwoerd opting to declare a Republic. A republic to do what? A few productive whites; a mass of black people made hungry! The British all busy pillaging the gold and diamonds to line their pockets, and send the haul mined by the blacks to secure vaults elsewhere. Boer extremism and stupidity were fostered by the British failure to acknowledge them. Afrikaner

Nationalism was created by their sense of disrespect, no respect for their privations, or their journeys into unknown territory with little certainty of food but plenty of tribal enemies waiting to ambush. They had suffered greatly before the British concentration camps sealed up their grievances; those were abominable.

That is why Britain does not acknowledge us; Britain is ashamed of us, ashamed of our voices and our more recent history of questioning its authority. Although we incubated a fair few international statesmen like Gandhi. who I once met soon after he arrived— he was rather a lost figure then, the diminutive in a dhoti with his Jewish features and sad eyes, and darling Jannie Smuts in his modest shack on the Platteland, losing his government while resurrecting the League of Nations. Jan Smuts was almost the quintessential Afrikaner: quiet, unassuming and a very fine botanist. That is what interested him, not politics and certainly not war. How little do people know of what is important to the inner man.

Apart from Percy Fitzpatrick, who had the sense to love dogs more than people (as I do) and darling Jock— now there *was* a dog— the British I met had never emerged as individuals when buttoned into roles and self-importance, like the dreadful Baden Powell, with his Boy Scout obsession, and the arrogant Cecil Rhodes, always with an eye to the main chance, making his millions. His intended railway from 'Cape to Cairo'? What arrogant presumption! Who agreed to that? Did he ask the Egyptians? Or any others along the proposed route? He just assumed they would be grateful to have their resources removed with greater speed!

For Britain, South Africa made a disproportionate contribution. We've never had it acknowledged. Even Churchill cut his teeth here, yet we are held at arm's length like some smelly rag, the disgraced outpost of the lost Empire.

England is more class-prejudiced than any country; ashamed that we do not dissimulate and pretend as it does. Hypocrisy does not easily survive in the noon sun; it breeds like fish-moth behind the drawn curtains of twilight. I confess that I remain proud that we are not hypocritical. Many other things, perhaps, but not that!

I shall tell you a little of who I am, or perhaps more accurately, who I once was. I do hope you will not imagine its purpose is self-aggrandisement, although there are some impressive raisins in the bread of betrayal. My parents could not have been more ill-met, nor I more punished by their improbable marriage, just like my little granddaughter. My father from England, my mother from Holland, they were thrown together in the unlikely tin-roofed dorp of Harrismith in the Orange Free State, a dusty settlement dumped for no reason, a staging post for travel to elsewhere. It signifies. Both I and my granddaughter were born there. The details tell a lot. In 1854, my father, Charles Ashton Barrett, sailed in a ship chartered by his father, Henry Joseph Barrett, from Liverpool to Durban. It was called 'The Palace', and indeed, it must have been palatial for a single family. They played cricket and quoits on the deck with the crew and took a library of classics and volumes of maps in bookcases lashed to the rigging. No doubt, many balls were lost in the ocean.

The Atlantic Ocean was all theirs. Imagine it! For a boy born in Hull to a respectable rich merchant living with a nanny in a grand house of marble tiles and curved staircases with never a sight of the open sea, suddenly in a floating palace cresting the spume waves to the New World! He must have thought he'd become a character in Rider Haggard. Not that Rider Haggard had written yet, nor was my father old enough to read him then. I am not much good at time anymore. I remember things very well, but not always in the right order.

Charles, my father, was six, his aunt Eliza Mary Barrett—she will be important in his tale— was just shy of thirty, and his mother, Henry Joseph's wife, also a Mary, was only twenty-six.

Finally, this 'Palace' docks in Durban, where there is a scattered population of English-speaking immigrants, with Indian servants and steepled Anglican churches. Does Henry Joseph seek out a shady villa amongst the banana and mango trees with a gentle walk to the rolling breakers of the Indian Ocean? Where he might join a club and read a paper? He does not. No, siree. He loads up a piano, the bookcases and the mahogany furniture onto an ox cart and sets out for the interior with his English wife, his sister and small son. He heads for the Orange Free State, where the Boers hold sway. His two women will protect their fair skins with muslin veiling and hope that being white will be enough— when black was the enemy—to obscure the belief that the 'blerrie Engelse' had no business in the Afrikaner Vrystaat.

I cannot imagine they were welcomed. Henry Joseph was no farmer, so why did he head for the one place where only farming or shooting black people was on offer? Perhaps because nobody would be asking questions? Was he escaping? I have a hypothesis. I will deliver it anon.

There, they live for ten years until his wife Mary dies at only thirty-nine years of age. Does Henry Joseph stay to comfort his fifteen-year-old son, my father, or set his path towards a secure future? Charles was completely alone. Aunt Mary had swiftly married and headed back to Durban, away from the rough farmers. John Sanderson, her husband, was a Scot, an artist, a botanist and a newspaper editor who corresponded with the famous Hooker at Kew. She studies the classics in Greek, perfects her piano playing, and takes the evening air as the sun melts into the sea. Yes, the seeds of European culture survived like those beans denied light, with white tendril roots. We were not all bronzed and desiccated by the sun.

The ignoble merchant, Henry Joseph, loses no time and returns to Hull, replaces his feet on a fender and forgets a son, Africa, and a dead wife. He also remarries a widow with many children and sires a few more. In his genealogical record, there is no mention of South Africa or any previous children or earlier wife. We have been expunged. *'No known issue.'* is what the records state!

I don't exist, then? We'll see about that!

Was that the purpose of the expensive escape? To lose a son? Then, to deny he had ever existed? Oddly, my father's second name was Ashton. There were no other Ashtons before him, and in those days, people were not imaginative. Ashton was the name of Henry Joseph Barrett's business partner in Hull, perhaps my father Charles's real father? Perhaps the Ashton partner paid Henry handsomely to disappear with an illegitimate disgrace? Find me a better hypothesis for a rich merchant suddenly spending ten years in South Africa and then eradicating all evidence he ever had. Including returning without his son or his wife? I'm some evidence, and my father sending me to Shene, a finishing school in Holland Park, is another. I never knew who paid for that. My father had no money, and he kept it dark. Perhaps he didn't know, but some surreptitious Barrett, or perhaps an Ashton, must have forked out. Although I enjoyed three years of being 'finished' with painting, music and deportment with a fencing foil, something about the whole episode has a malodourous whiff!

I would omit my mother entirely, but she and the savage (although deserved) manner of her death will cast both a shadow and a summons in my granddaughter's story. As I am the last person alive whom my granddaughter can ask, I shall sketch her briefly and without the venom that rises when I think of her. How my abandoned father met and married has another strand to complete. The Boer and the Brit are matched by a similar history.

Six years later, another ship sailed, this one from Rotterdam. My mother, Eelkje Diederika van den Bosch—beat that for an unwieldy name— set sail with six siblings and her parents, leaving the Netherlands on the Agatha Maria in 1860. She was three years old and the fifth of seven. A brother, George, died on the voyage. Three further children, including a replacement George, were born in the Freestate after arrival. You would think enough already! Eeltje's father, Eelco Foppo van den Bosch, was the chief vet of the Netherlands, the only qualified vet to land in our Freestate world of cattle breeding and sheep rearing. Eelco's father, Petrus van den Bosch, had been the Surveyor General of the Netherlands. As surveyors go, no country could challenge expertise as much as that Canute country faced with the encroaching sea. Yes, we were Dutch aristocrats, if there are such specimens.

The parents of Petrus owned a considerable estate called De Roekebosch, and his mother, Popkje Nicolai, was allegedly a direct descendant of some Romanov Duke Nicolai. Since the duke was generally considered 'mad', it may have contributed a core of useful bloody-mindedness. Every member of my mother's family bore the name 'Nicolai' or, if female, Nicolina. Populating the world with identically named, vaguely Romanov children seemed to have been done as carelessly as lace-collared rabbits.

Like the Boers they came to marry they took on strong opponents. Fleeing cholera and the threat of war, they came well equipped to cope with a few impis. Fighting Zulus attracted quite a few chancers from Europe. That was the other side of my hybrid blood. The inbuilt war between them lasted after the shooting ceased. It still goes on, as our politics amply show: the British in the counting houses, the Boers on the farms, and the Blacks digging down the mines, all hoping to eliminate one another.

As a South African, it was pretty unique to be descended from a slave-owning British Colonial family and the Dutch, anxious to conscript new slaves or pick them off with a rifle. From early childhood, I was stretched between my silent and beloved father, Charles, and my mother, Eelkje Diederika, in black bombazine rattling with keys at her waist and a mouth drawn tight as a bowstring. She was a fiend, camouflaged in respectability.

I saw where respectability had grown gnarled when, after my happy spell in London, I was dispatched to Holland to pay respects to my Dutch family. I spent a week gazing out of a grand window on the Herengracht Canal at the passing trade because I was not permitted to wander unescorted. They had no concept of our freedom or my liberty from childhood to wander anywhere at large. The magical city remained unexplored. Then came an obligatory visit to Friesland, where an assortment of elderly women in kappies and lace collars inspected me as though I was a new species. To them, I was.

For my twenty-first birthday, I was toasted in very small glasses of advocaat, dressed in traditional black, and frog-marched off to a photographer in Leeuwarden to record my capture. That family had been pickled in tradition, and shrunken by the University of Leiden into puritanical diligent professions, many surveying the monotonous landscape with only the excitement of Sunday bible reading to interrupt. It explained my mother as nothing else had. She had never managed to shed the forbidding harsh judgements, or the tight disapproval—or the meanness! As a nation, the Dutch are very mercenary. All that will have some influence on my granddaughter. She will rebel, as I did. I do not doubt that.

So, I have dispatched the history of the woman who speared my gentle father as she might stretch for a delicacy with a sharp pickle fork. She was nineteen, he was twenty-eight, but no match for this harridan's intentions. Her family ruled the area around Harrismith. The nicest of them, my aunt Petronella— Aunt Polly— steered clear of marriage altogether and lived to a ripe age, which better makes my point.

∽

While I have the floor, I should add that I fear for the child. She seems to register how little she is welcomed. Her mother has been cruelly treated, certainly, but frigidity and shrinking are not an answer. I should know. Betrayal has been my kinswoman always; she brushes my hair and lays out my dress, but I disregard her gestures of apology. Ignoring betrayal is the only way to treat her until she repents.

I offered to care for the child while her mother trained in physio-therapy. Four years was possible, but not the seven she would need for medicine. Medicine was why she married Doctor Percy Raymond. I could see no other reason.

'We all have to trim our sails to the possible', I said. In all the lamentations, firmness was needed.

Now, I find myself well past child-caring, confined by an unloved toddler. It falls to me to love her! I admit she is very little trouble. It was good of my cousin to agree to house us both. I do believe that the first family memories shape all those that follow, and perhaps it is what bonds us, she and I. Both of us were born near this farm, both of us unwanted. It forges a strong bond. Maweni spreads a limitless kindness, and I hope its early sunshine will sustain her.

Philippa, for a young child, looks too early solemn.

Maweni Heights

Like early mist rising to meet the day, Maweni was where my memory emanated and solidified, slow fumes igniting sharp images. It captures short shots, some many times, some only once. The tungsten-lit farm, vivid in its shadows and light, creeps into every day as I wake on a glazed porch before there are sounds in the kitchen. The dawn fingers the veldt until the sun splashes like milk over the contours of the hills, lighting the bottom of the window glass before slowly rising like water for a bath. Once uniform, it suns itself to an even tan by noon. The sky can be tipped upside down from a tyre in a tree, and the seat of a rusty tractor rebounds and drives me over the fields. Doves in the dark oaks above soothe the day with their unceasing curoo, cuckcuroo contentment.

In the house, modest women with dirty bare feet pass above me carrying bowls or piles of laundry. They do not speak but clap their hands and lift aprons to hide their smiling white teeth. There is the smell of hot linen and spitting on flat irons clanged down and exchanged. I hear coals riddled in the kitchen and see steam rising from chattering pots. I wander through the golden grass that smells of dust and aromatic sap to paddle in the cold stream that roils from the pencil of silver falling forever over the great boulder cliff above the house. Behind that silver ribbon, there is a cave, and in the cave a python, so I am not to go near it.

Early, I registered water as miraculous. Other things slept; water never.

That was Maweni Heights, the family farm where squeezing spit-it-out sour grape skins shot bullets of sweetness into an open mouth and grew at a toddler's reach along the stoep railings. The slatted sun came green striped through the awnings. In the pocket, a stick of biltong and sour, eisch, so sour dried peaches, needing to be sucked before chewing without a full set of teeth. Always the smell of wood smoke and the night that dropped a black shroud to show up the kraal fires as I was tucked into bed, glimmering, flicking explosions of sparks into the dark. Fire at night; water all day.

To anchor that early breaking world comes Marna, my galleon grandmother who breasts the doorways, a spinnaker filled with wind; she moves across the day like an effortless schooner. Marna, I came to recognise from the hesitant deference of all who visited, was the Authority; of the scattered components called family, any incidental assembly, and every room she filled with Presence. Presence was not the imposing frontage I watched laced into place by a maid or the arches of her bony feet or the curse of hair as thin as mine which fell across her face.

After a breakfast of yellow corn porridge sitting on three cushions, Marna turned me out with a pocket of dried peaches and took to her desk from where she dispatched letters as though from high command to the field of action. Letters were Marna's serious art, slanted across thick cream paper in her perfected hand of an educated gentlewoman and the run-along-dear concentration that brooked no interruptions.

I would totter off to the baked earth kraal where women in layered rags plaited my silky hair into thin worms and offered orange segments, wiping my sticky mouth on their skirts, probably fascinated by this white umntwana at close quarters. Their sharp-ribbed dogs sniffed at me but refused the orange.

The farm, I later understood, was the modest baronetcy of the Van den Bosch, one spur of the Dutch half of the family that had strewn themselves on farms encircling Harrismith. They planted mielies, raised cattle, shot game, and repaired to the town for supplies once a week. Sometimes, they gathered for a braai and a game of polo across a dusty stretch of short grass. Tommy van den Bosch was Marna's cousin. He was seldom about.

After eating while standing, Tommy took a rifle from the rack inside the front door and mounted the saddled horse tethered at the back. I reached up, and he raised me onto the saddle pommel. That was when the arrow of first love pierced me. He turned the horse's head, and together, we three clopped off. Was there anything that would ever match those pointing ears, that dipping poll, that sweetest smell, those quivering nostrils, those nibbling lips? My Kingdom was newly horse.

Every day thereafter began with the riding between Tommy's knees and visits at intervals through the day to the field with carrots for love, in case the horse forgot. Tomorrow was an eternity to wait.

∾

"You must now be with Yourmother", Marna says. She is packing a small suitcase and brushing away tears, sniffing. "I shall see you both together whenever she can get away." She hugs me between folding things. She hugs me so often that I am not sure I will see her again.

"Yourmother has finished the studying part and now must train in hospitals, so she will have more time for you now." She adds a lunch box with an apple for the journey and loads me into a car of somebody driving to Johannesburg.

Through the window, she says, "Give Yourmother the little present in your suitcase, and tell her she has a beautiful daughter." I have no idea what she is talking about.

The man drives away from the farm as Marna waves from the lawn until we turn onto the road.

The memory of Maweni is distilled in some inaccessible part of longing, together with the smell of horses and the sound of doves, but they are soon obscured in the fumes of traffic and hard pavements. I will not return to Maweni.

CHAPTER 2

Yourmother

'Childhood has no forebodings; but then, it is soothed by no memories of outlived sorrow.'

I had turned three before I first met Yourmother. Delivered to a macadam driveway off a sticky brown seat, I held the small suitcase as the car sped off, lost in the roar of fast traffic that was so close it lifted my shirt over my face. I had never seen traffic, nor tarmac, nor known the noise of a city. Down the steep slope of a driveway, a thin woman with fair hair walked towards me. She looked as afraid as I was. She crouched down and reached for the bag. She nearly kissed me but changed her mind.

"I am Yourmother. This is where you are going to live now." She took my bag and then my hand, pulling me to follow. Ahead, there was a bank of winking windows in a building that was not really a house. I had seen houses in picture books: there were never as many windows as that. We climbed shining, polished red steps onto a veranda of wheelchairs and white legs, pointing at us. The fat white legs did not speak, but as we crossed the space in the middle some moved a newspaper to look at me. Some nodded and smiled, some glared. I sensed that I did not belong in this place of wheels and white legs. All of them belonged to men.

Yourmother opened glass doors into a hallway that smelled of polish and boiling cabbage. There was a black woman on her knees brushing a carpet, but she didn't look up; she just stopped while we passed by. They had done that on the farm, too.

"Don't be frightened. Those are all poor soldiers who come back from fighting in the war."

"Do I have to stay here?"

"Yes, for a while."

Yourmother led me along a corridor, up some stairs, past a row of closed doors before she opened a door into a bright room with windows to the front and the side and two beds with curved metal ends, with covers splashed red.

"That'll be your bed. Mine is this one by the window. That table is where I will work at night when you are asleep."

"I liked the farm better. Will I go back to Marna?"

"We'll go back when we can." Yourmother was going to be a fixture if she was so sure of that 'we'. I knew, at once, that she wanted that 'we' as little as I did. We both wished I was not there, but only she knew why I was.

∾

The not-really house was a nursing home for wounded servicemen. Yourmother was the only woman, and I was the only child. She left in a blue checked uniform after breakfast to go to the hospital for her medical training. I wandered through the house, looked at books and pictures on the walls and sometimes played draughts with a soldier in a wheelchair. One of them gave me reading lessons every day from books Yourmother brought from the hospital. Another showed me how to draw things smaller if they were further away. He drew lines to what he called a vanishing point so I could fit in bushes and stick-people between them. Once, he took me to the glass door and showed the same lines over what was there. I drew the bushes of the drive, the gates open at the bottom, and a small car going past.

The housekeeper who came for the daytime let me take round the biscuits and the milk for tea. I had sandwiches with the men on the veranda for lunch before I was taken to rest on my bed.

I cannot remember who took me upstairs, but I can recall the silence and the light moving behind the curtains as the afternoon tracked towards Yourmother's return. I never could decide whether I wanted her to come or not. She always looked so tired. Somehow, I knew that was my fault. On our own, we had supper in the big, empty dining room before all the men wheeled in to be given their plates.

On Saturdays, it was always marrow bones on toast. I used the bone in my bath to blow bubbles from soapy water. Then I was put to bed. Yourmother scrubbed harder than Marna had. Marna had a big sea sponge that dropped a cloudburst at a single squeeze. Yourmother had a washcloth.

I noticed that when she returned, they all sat up straighter and smiled more. One asked me

"What's your mother's name?"

"She's just called Yourmother" That made them all laugh. The one who asked took me on his knee.

"You are quite right, honey. She is ours too, in a way."

Maybe because, after supper, Yourmother would take them in turns to walk down the drive on crutches, massage their stiff necks, or give them exercises to strengthen their muscles after the plasters came off. She always looked happy when she was working with the men. But at night, in our room, she cried. Over the big book, her tears dripped and made blisters on the shiny pages, but if I looked, she turned away. I realised that crying was something she wanted to keep private, so I didn't ask, but I knew it had to do with me and the big book's drawings of legs without plaster. Muscles were striped red and blue and tied to bones with string. The blisters of tears lasted until I knew the title of the book, Grey's Anatomy, and until I understood the reason for them.

Once, when I went to stand next to her, I hoped she would tell me, but she just stroked my hair and took me back into bed.

While she cried and sniffed and turned pages and wrote notes in her scribbly handwriting, I thought of the farm and longed for the horses so much I could smell them. I could hear the wind in the oak trees and the doves that called all day until I fell asleep. I wanted Marna with her fat arms, her hugs and her wobbly cheeks, and the noise in the kitchen, with the maids laughing and the stars after dark so close that the butterfly net Tommy gave me could have brought them down.

∽

On my fourth birthday, the men gathered outside the dining room door. They made space for Yourmother to move through them to go to work, bowing a little and dipping their heads as they shunted back. After she had gone, one took my hand and clamped it under his on the crossbar of his crutch and swung us away down the veranda that showed white marks where his heels touched the floor. There were always white marks, but these were the first of that day, like the tracks of a heron Tommy had shown me in fresh mud near the stream on the farm. Those marks made the housekeeper angry and caused the black maids to click their tongues. All the other men followed like limping birds with broken wings. Some were already in wheelchairs down the drive, as though they were lining up for a race. The man led me to a large package of brown paper pushed below a bush at the top of the drive.

"Happy birthday, sunshine", he said. "Your present from all of us."

"What's it for?"

"It's for you. Open it." I didn't want to, not watched by all those eyes. I had never had a present, and I did not know what to do on something called a birthday. Yourmother was not there. She had disappeared on her sharp walk to work, going round behind the hedge with her fair hair dipping and reappearing up the road to the bus.

"Here, I'll start." The soldier made a rip in the paper. I joined in. Together, we pulled away the wrapping and exposed a small sort of wheelchair.

"It's a go-cart", he said. "We made it for you. Come, sit on the plank."

He pushed down my shoulders until I squatted sideways. "Now, lift up your legs." I obeyed, half excited but mostly shrinking from the small crowd watching. Why were all of them watching? He pulled me back between the high wheels and put my right hand on a long handle. "This is the brake. If you pull it toward you, the cart will stop. Like this…" He tilted me up to show the clatter and hiss of the brake pads against the running wheels of the one-time wheelchair. While he was telling me how it worked, several wheelchairs were making their way to the bottom of the drive.

"Now remember. When you want to stop or go slower, just yank on that handle. Never let go of it." He pushed me away, and the go-cart nosed gently toward the steep slope of the drive until, like milk over the lip of a jug, it gathered pace, careering down, lekker fast.

"Brake, brake!" he shouted. The go-cart slewed sideways and stopped so suddenly that I fell out in front of the others, blocking the drive's access to roaring traffic.

"Go again?"

"Yes!"

"Then use the rope and pull it back up."

My fourth birthday was spent with wounded soldiers pleasing a child. I can still see most of them. I got better at slower braking and a body balanced against the speed.

A few days later, the brake pads failed, and instead of the hiss, there was a stream of sparks and a flapping of rubber, shredded by too much enthusiasm. Two sentries flung themselves into my path towards certain death. We ended up tangled in metal, my foot caught in a spinning wheel, bleeding generously. No amount of dabbing stopped the welling red. It hurt quite a lot, but it was a proper war wound. Yourmother came and called a taxi to take me to the hospital.

I had a broken bone in my ankle and needed a plaster cast. Now, part of the gang with crutches, I could make white marks of my own.

ᘐ

Then the war was over, as though somebody had just clapped to make it stop. The soldiers were told they could pack. One by one, they came to say goodbye, while a car, a van, or a taxi waited with engines running, queuing up the driveway. They had homes waiting with mothers and brothers. Some said, sisters.

"Goodbye, sugar. Tell Yourmother goodbye and thanks."

"Her name is Louie."

"When did she tell you it was Louie?"

"No. She didn't. Her friend from the hospital called her that, so she must be."

"Okay. Tell Louie goodbye then, and tell her thanks from Ernie, and tell her thanks for you too. You entertained us, princess. Now you can read. Next, you will learn to write."

"I already can, a bit. Reggie showed me."

"I know."

By then, I knew my mother had a different name, but I was returning to Marna. I was not old enough for school and Louie was now nearly a qualified physiotherapist. First, she had to work across the military hospitals of Johannesburg, where men would await her daily visits in harnesses and slings. With the captives gone, there was no one to look after me.

It would not be to Maweni Heights but to Mafeking.

Louie's Story

This will be difficult. Yourmother was never given to disclosing anything, so to write as though she did would entirely misrepresent the person she was. As I have subpoenaed her for this story, and she was critical, I will cross-examine her as I sometimes did. She will have to answer. Before the talk, I will paint her portrait as I first remember her.

She was slim, her ash blonde hair mostly coiled, like an elaborate nest to conceal a fragile bird. There wasn't much of it, but with her sparse, thin hair, she made an effort. Her dresses were casual and simple, jewellery was minimal, perhaps a string of pearls, often earrings. Her eyes were large and a conspicuous blue, but more than that, they were always wounded like a child that had run towards protection only to be met with a lashing.

Before my birth, photographs showed such optimism, such steady, bright hope. As though life had held out a handful of promises together with a candle to light them: the promise of a man who might love and protect, the promise of dedication to medicine, and, in time, perhaps a family who esteemed her, for she intended to deserve esteem.

I was fourteen before I put the question directly, "You never wanted me, did you?" although I had known the answer since our first encounter. I was used to the guarded welcomes, used to the tension when bills demanded school fees, used to her turned back.

But I wanted her to admit it.

"No. You were the worst thing that could have happened at the time."

"What would have happened if I hadn't… happened?" She took some time to consider.

"Well, I suppose I would have been able to embark on medicine, and not the semi-drudgery of physiotherapy. I'd have had no distractions, and I think I would have succeeded…"

"And stayed married to my father? He would have helped?" She was cornered. By several struts, enough to box her in. I already knew most of them.

"No, Raymond made it clear. 'No wife of mine works for a living,' was what he said when I said I intended to go to medical school… You'd have thought an already qualified doctor might have approved!"

"So even without me, you would have divorced him?" She was skewered, and, as always, she lit a cigarette before trying to deflect me and pass the buck.

"Oh, I doubt I would have needed to. Raymond had already run off with his staff nurse, Valerie, before your arrival was obvious, even to me. He was getting ready to run…When back on leave, he stayed at the Officer's Mess endlessly drinking whisky and writing to her while I grew large in a dismal barracks…"

"Did he return for my birth?"

"No, I went to Maweni, and Marna. You took quick advantage and came well before time. I was rushed, panting and in agony, to the wrong clinic, a mission station where wimpled women in grey habits swaddled black babies and slid, as though on wheels, along the corridors. When I came to find you, you were conspicuous, with no hair and pale skin, like a caterpillar. You have never shown discretion, not even at the start!" She did not believe that it was my fault but made it so. I was not having that. I returned to the salient point.

"If Raymond cut off your physiotherapy support, he'd have done the same for medicine. So even without me, how would you have managed?" I had her cold, and she knew it. She tried blowing smoke rings but failed.

"I'd have found a way." Then she added, "Without my obligations to Marna, it would have taken longer, that's all. As it was, I could not impose you on her any longer."

That was a shock. She was suggesting that Marna's care of me had curtailed her ambition, but without either of us, she'd have 'found a way!'

I wanted to return to the long-avoided topic. She had never talked about my father. All I knew was that he was mean with money, the most heinous family crime. I also knew the thought of him was more than she could bear, as though entertaining any memory poisoned the very air.

"What made you marry him?" I dreaded the answer but needed to know.

She sighed heavily and took time to decide how much to tell. When she began, she took it at a gallop.

"You have to make allowances. Remember, I was still a schoolgirl, after being imprisoned for five years in England in a gymslip, with every hour prescribed, every book listed, and even our holidays in Wales were nothing but Chapel. Suddenly, Ursula and I were on a ship heading for life in Uganda. It was rather like the curtains opening in a theatre for a play we had not booked. No parents or teachers to tell us what to think or how to behave. We were both giddy with sudden liberty. What kind of play would it be? A farce, a musical, or a drama? I was unprepared for the opening act of Raymond. How could I recognise that suave ship's doctor in his fetching whites with their gold epaulettes as my nemesis in waiting? Someone looking so clean and perfect? He whirled me into waltzes and somehow, even at sea, found a corsage for my dresses. He blurred all sensible thought. His was the world I hoped to enter, and there he was, holding the door open. I just stepped through it. Mad. Mad through simply being naïve.

I was eighteen; he was thirty. He claimed to be smitten with me.

Smitten was the word. But I believed him."

"He never saw me? Never asked to?"

She could not look at me but lit another cigarette. Her shoulders were twitching as she gazed out of a window.

"The only time he saw you was the night I left him. He came back on leave and, after making himself comfortable at the Officer's Mess, arrived, unannounced, to hear you say your prayers. Prayers! You were hardly walking; you could hardly speak. To punish me, your father removed that small pillow you always needed, twirling a corner around your finger while you sucked yourself to sleep. You would not stop crying."

'Spoilt brat. This is intolerable.' was how he put it before he slammed out. I realised he was not only a bully but a sadist. So that finished it."

∞

After Raymond left, she packed a bag and took a train at nearly midnight. The last straw had toppled the marriage cart. It was over.

The baby on her shoulder slept, and my mother chose unmoving cramp, numb in the shoulder and in thought, as the clacketing wheels of an empty train bore her away. As the cloudy steam blew its farewell across the cinders of a dark halt and chugged off, my mother again heaved a sleeping weight over her shoulders and walked to a nearby road. A car stopped. She returned to Marna and Maweni Heights.

"Who chose my name?" This question silenced her. She did not seem to know.

"I can't remember. I just liked it. I suppose it was for Heli since a 'lover of horses' was what he was."

Heli was her father.

Perhaps somebody whispered in her ear. It was the one thing somebody got right. The love of horses would have to serve me before others were chosen for the same qualities. Both parts of the name would write my life. The Phil would have to find love where I might, the 'ippas would gallop in, and my mother would search for the life she had surrendered. We would live lives in parallel, both yearning, seldom touching.

~

Growing up, I knew nothing of that. I heard those details only when I asked for them. So began the sore thumb theme of being one of a kind, in the wrong place at the wrong time, conspicuous for things I could not help. It helps to see it established before I could be held responsible for it. This journey will show it richly embroidered. My father did not provide a penny for my care, and I did not meet him until I was sixteen. It laid the conditions for most of my life and the only prohibition. No other injunction was ever voiced, and nothing else forbidden. It was the great unspoken command that hung between me and my mother, the sword of Damocles.

'Thou shalt never betray a marriage. Or be the cause of anyone else doing so.' Infidelity was an utterly forbidden Pandora's Box. If ever it was opened, nothing would confine what tragedies, and what consequences would escape. Not even hope would survive since it had not for my mother.

The eternal punishment of my existence.

You can still surprise me! Why move ahead fourteen years to that conversation?

The bookends of my childhood? One opened, the other closed it. Perhaps because they both connected, together they wrapped up perspective and proportion. I learned about looking and how what you saw —or drew—had lines of confinement. Those were what people agreed upon. Yourmother was what other people saw, but my mother, Louie, only I saw.

Maybe Marna saw Louie, too.

Saw what?

Saw a young woman who had been defiled, I would say raped, by a man who took everything: her virginity, her ambition, her self-belief, and her hopes, and then punished her for leaving him, by denying her support.

So, I was a kind of superfluous afterbirth of all that? She could not even ditch or bury me. I was a millstone. Yet Marna had been through much the same 'use and discard'. It left an indelible mark on both of them and on me. I learned stoicism, but stoicism in Louie led to withdrawal. She became inaccessible. Marna became irreverent and contemptuous. I think I fashioned my version equally from both.

Anything else?

Yes. Gratitude. I had always believed I might have been the cause of a shotgun marriage. I was glad to discover that was not the case but that Louie had saved me from Raymond's brutality. She left him because of me; she did not marry him because of me. That was a great relief.

Forcing this conversation broke the silence between us, although Louie closed up again. What it did was enable me to see my birth as independent of either of my parents. I came for reasons of my own. That freed me to search for its meaning instead of dwelling on its misfortune. Louie wanted to love me, but my arrival had bruised her indelibly. A woman betrayed by her husband weeps, but a betrayed mother with a child turns numb and grits her teeth. She had to. So, her wanting to love had to be enough.

Was it? Really?

It led to mistakes in both of us, but for most of the time, yes.

Now I see that Louie had to adopt the position of 'brace-brace'. Not just the sacrifice of her longed-for medicine but because of the way I looked. Exactly like my father from the top of my head to the tips of my shoes that curled up, just as his did. I was a constant reminder of the man who so wronged and betrayed her. For as long as I lived, she could never escape!

We are getting somewhere now.

Did you know it all ahead of time?

No such thing as time. Memory is ever present and draws from both behind and ahead. That's where I lodge, seeing both ways, but for you, opus myopia, ahead is yet to be uncovered. A moment now to catch a train. *Your first ever train, to be followed by many others.*

Where are we going?

To a town called Mafeking where your forebears were besieged, and Marna will remember and tell you about it. It was the central division in your family, the Boers and the Brits. You straddle that divide, a gene fork and it will prove a life fork too. All is already scripted. As you know, the child is father to the man. Here is where the divide clashed swords and exchanged fire. Both sides drank brandy, but only one side called it 'Brandewyn'

CHAPTER 3

Heli and Mafeking

'If we had a keen vision and feeling of all ordinary human life, it would be like hearing the grass grow and the squirrel's heart beat, and we should die of that roar which lies on the other side of silence.'

The intersections between one life and another are where memory lodges as fresh mortar between the layers of an unbroken wall. Fear stays wet in the mind. The five-year-old I was, with limp hair cut in a sharp fringe, is handed through the door of a rail carriage occupied by a buttressed Tannie, who has secured her sole occupation by wedging her luggage along both seats. Seated next to the window, she is eating a boerewors sausage, dipping it into a mustard yellow sauce and watching pedestrians walk past.

"Room for a small child?" asks my hesitant mother from the passage. Louie seems nervous

"Ach Ja. Come, come." Tannie moves a holdall. Louie pushes me to sit down.

"Can you make sure she gets off at Ladysmith?"

Tannie wipes her mouth, leaving a smudge of yellow across her chin.

"Ja, of course. Must she travel alone?"

"She will be met by her grandfather. She'll be no trouble."

My mother kisses me and puts a book on my lap and a packet of food nearby. She checks the luggage label on my wrist.

"Make sure you keep that tied," she says before disappearing...

It is addressed to 'Jowitt, Director of Education, Government House, Mafeking'. I could be a packet of papers. Tannie is only interested in my sandwiches but not my seven sticks of celery. I loved celery.

On the Southern fringes of the Kalahari, Mafeking is a town without hope or purpose. A footnote siege in the Boer War, it is hardly a town, except defined by distance from anywhere else. So confident that they will expropriate the limitless and impoverished Bechuanaland Protectorate, the Nationalists in South Africa are content to let Mafeking remain as its administrative Capital for now. While Jan Smuts is in London, tidying up post-war, the Afrikaner Nationalists are speedily redrafting the maps to re-distribute their electorate so that apartheid Boers will capture the country to offset those liberal 'kaffir-boetie' Jews running the diamond fields and the mines. Bechuanaland could wait. Fortunately, its own diamonds that would enrich it, had not yet been found. In 1948, the Afrikaners will sweep to power in South Africa, and racist apartheid will become the official and entrenched policy within spitting distance across Bechuanaland's border.

All that fermenting brew lies behind Heli's intention to make haste and hope to equip its people with an education. Time is short. Heli has not only desert wastes to conquer but also his formidable wife. Marna will describe it as I heard her do to anyone captured long enough…

"Heaven help us! Let *me* tell you about that house! I had put up with make-do living in Uganda. I was never one for luxury provided one was among manners and gentle service, but this place? Well! My worthy husband was not a man with aesthetic sensibility. No one else would have darkened the door, let alone said yes. Heli's focus was always on the future; a camp bed, a tin cup, and a threadbare diet was his Methodist sufficiency. African education filled his days, filled his dreams. Not that he was still a Methodist; he'd been fished by those pernicious Jesuits in Uganda and was now a full-fledged Catholic. I must say it had not re-educated his tastes.

"Anyway…the house…Behind an ugly hedge, a straight cinder path between squares of dead grass led towards a deep, shady stoep, the only mercy in the heat. A pondok with all the imagination of the Afrikaners who built it, four-square, under tin; tin to make sure we would be not merely roasted but charred. Not even a cold shower alleviates the arid heat of the Kalahari. It burns. You would think they might have imitated the kind thatch used by the natives!

It was strung on a road of identical bead houses, but it did have a thirsty loquat tree behind the kitchen."

'Was this the best they could do?' I asked. I was still in my linen travelling coat and leaning on my stick. Heli's idea of furnishing was to place everything against the walls, as though even tables could not be relied upon to stand on four legs. There was nothing yet to sit upon except a bed. One cannot wield authority sitting on a bed.

He just stood there looking embarrassed, running his fingers through his sparse hair. That irritated me more than usual."

'Where are you going to work?' I asked since there was no space for all those minions standing about. The two miserable rooms on either side of a hallway would be ours, and the third was piled with boxes of files. They would be moved, of course.

'We were lucky to get it.' he said.

'The new Director of Education for the Kingdom of Bechuanaland was lucky to get this hovel?'

'We might have to move further into the territory later'. he added. As though that would comfort!"

I did not like the sound of 'territory.'

'You make it sound like Dr Livingstone, I presume, without any hope of rivers or a picnic in the shade.' I wanted him to grasp what he expected of me.

'Most of it is still like that. It's a wonderful challenge...'

'I'm sure of that, even toothache will be a challenge... it's just that I can't see the point of inviting malaria and dying of thirst if one doesn't have to...'

'It's too dry for malaria.' he said. Aren't men pedantic?

He then tried persuasion, saying he would work in Government House.

'Whose government? The one you work for? Or the one determined to stop you? They can easily close the border and then what will you do?'

"Heli was a clever academic but, like most of them, a fool. He never gave attention to realities that existed, only those he hoped to create, and where had that got us? They drummed us out of Rhodesia for saying openly that Africans needed a first-class education, not a preparation for serfdom. It was why we were there in this god-forsaken house, serfs ourselves; I would swelter, and he would be a saint. Too many saints in my life, and somehow, I always paid. I paid for the history of aviation; I paid for Catholicism; I was now to pay for universal education.

"I suppose a bath is not too much to ask? I admit he had thought of that, and the water was already hot."

༄

I could have been claimed by anybody, but that is how I first met my grandfather. He fetched me from a station in a hot suit.

First, I noticed how hot he looked. His face was red, his collar tight, his freckled hands gripped the wheel over the juddering corrugations as though he was controlling a bolting horse. He spoke very little but looked at me with kindness. We bowled along, creating a spume of rolling dust. If the road bent round a hill, you could see it for miles. That was the first time I registered travel as deliberate and chosen, home to Marna.

This was 1946. I was five. The rituals of the border crossings are branded in the memory. The South African border was manned by overweight men, who came reluctantly to do their duty from the shade of an acacia, smelling of beer and sweating in blue shirts circled with dark patches. Cars were few. They made the most of bored power in oppressing each one. At leisure, with their backs against a counter, they examined Heli's British passport suspiciously, discussing in Afrikaans whether he should have been there. What about there? Nee Man. All those visa stamps justified suspicion. Heli's irritation at the lengthy inspection of his car was barely contained. I encountered my kind but easily irritated grandfather in those first minutes of observation.

Eventually, they waved us through.

Four hundred yards further down the road was the Bechuanaland checkpoint, where a single pole was raised by a black man in a laundered khaki suit, knife-sharp creases, long green socks and polished boots. He wore a bush hat, its angled brim pinned with the state badge. Without checking any papers, he raised the pole and saluted. Heli had regained his home in African Africa and released a long breath.

Not many South African children had reason to register politics as early as I did. I encountered politics without knowing the name, as I encountered religion from its consequences, not its beliefs or convictions. I was lucky to pick up the raw and precious stone of Bechuanaland before its value was recognised, or it was polished. That was also true of Heli, who was my grandfather before he was a doctor of Education' or 'C.M.G'. Both came at me without handles, and both were arid and untamed.

If anyone had thrown a lazy lasso into the centre of Southern Africa, it might have fallen to encircle a Kingdom. At that time, Bechuanaland was a Kingdom without a King. The country, the size of France, lies like an indolent tortoise between South Africa and Rhodesia, reluctant to move but content to bask. Its unpromising dry shell is a bulwark between neighbours; dunes of Kalahari sand undulate only as a shoulder might to dislodge a horsefly. Elephants, here undisturbed, track miles for water, Baobab trees claw the uniform blue with twig branches above their corpulent trunks, small deer startle, spotted guinea fowl peck and run flustered. Its distances are hours of churning sand. Its delirious thirst must dig for water. An undeveloped country nobody wants except as a means for controlling others. Who would want this sand-swept place of beating sun and no vegetation? Even the flat profiles of distant acacia trees suggested that thrusting for the sky was too exhausting. Instead, they join canopies to cast shadows. Let's leave the sky undisturbed, as we are; duty to growth done.

Humans are hardly seen away from its embryonic, not-yet-capital Gaborone. In its arid centre, diminutive San track game, hunt insects and eat anything from snakes to locusts.

My grandparents were there because the King was not. Its patient Regent, Tshekedi Khama, is awaiting his nephew Seretse Khama, the hereditary Paramount Chief of the Bama-Ngwato to hand over its governance and enjoy his retirement with a flywhisk and his women kneeling to serve him beer at Serowe, the ancestral royal kraal.

Yes, Heli wanted this country, and when asked by Seretse Khama to establish education throughout its impoverished wastes said he would do his best in a place of no paved roads, little food, no money and no comforts. Seretse is studying Law in London while the British decide his fate and that of his country, a country they undertook to protect. Some undertakings by perfidious Albion prove unreliable. In a year, Seretse will seal his fate and unwisely choose his intended wife, English, white, and called Ruth. Most regrettable.

Britain, impoverished by the war, is dependent on South African gold and zinc and does not want to offend the new racist government, which has banned mixed-race marriage. Tshekedi and the Bama-Ngwato are not too happy about it either. Seretse will be a prisoner of his love for Ruth and shunned by both sides of the discussion. The usual marital mix: everybody waits. Nobody is sure how this will be resolved or how long resolution might take.

Heli's Story

I would love to give Heli the floor and hear his history, his hopes and dreams. It would flesh out the man I loved secretly because demonstrations of affection embarrassed him. We would hear his account of the transformation in his allegiance from an upright servant of the Empire to his saddened realisation that Britain was not sincere and had neither kindness nor integrity, but only the ceremonial appearances of both. It would conscript his energy to subject and impoverish innocent people who had been duped into trusting that sophisticated whites knew what was best for them. I could share in his disappointments or small satisfactions. But it cannot be. He never spoke of his private world nor any honours awarded. His story must be gleaned from fragments dropped by others, mostly Marna, or in books or reports I only discovered lately.

Heli, moving slimly through a world he sought to change but in which he was never recognised, had the constrained manner of a monk. I can assemble all the images of Heli flashing through many a holiday: in his academic gown on his way to teach, in the distance pacing and pointing out fencing to be laid, pausing to light a cigarette, or sitting typing endlessly while a minion awaited a letter to be dispatched to Whitehall. In all of them, he has the mien of a well-brushed badger, silent and wounded, in a world that knew only jackals and trotting hyenas.

Heli was born in 1893 in Yorkshire to Alfred Jowitt and his wife Louie —after whom my mother was named.

"They were a pair of minor saints," said Marna when she brought out a photograph of a family visit, all seated in a Yorkshire garden, with Heli and his sister Ethel—' everyone hold still'— in the rear. "Of course, people in Trade could never be full-blown saints, but they were the kindest, most honourable, virtuous couple one could ever meet. Look, you can see it shining, sweet-natured, generous, beyond reproach…"

"But?"

Marna hesitated,

"Well, they were Methodists…"

She seemed to expect me to grasp why that was a 'but'. In the face of my incomprehension, she elaborated. "Methodists positively sizzle with sanctity, but levity is beyond them."

"What's levity?"

"It's what makes bread rise, which reminds me… I have dough needing a prod." She bustled away.

It did shine out, the kindness in the older Louie, with a sweet and palpable benevolence. I doubt she had ever harboured an unkind thought or that the solid, honest Alfred in his braces had ever failed to rectify an error in supplies of timber. Their trade in Huddersfield was as builder's merchants for six days a week. Sundays were for Chapel. Obligations ruled in all directions.

Behind them stood Heli with his spinster sister Ethel, another gentle but disappointed saint who cared for her parents after Heli left for Africa. No wonder he was driven by evangelical zeal, to recompense, by aspiration and hard labour, his parents for his loss, and his sister for her loneliness. This noble family's legacy was to be reflected in his many echoes of it, for Heli also sought to build and provide the materials to do so: to build bridges between Africa and its colonial masters and to dove-tail education to foster tribal people if they were to escape their overlords.

He would offer them the means to do so.

After taking his first degree and a further year preparing to enter the Colonial Service, Heli set sail, never to return. He fell in love with Africa and its peoples, mastered Zulu easily, and wrote an early Zulu grammar. In a jacket and tie, Heli rode on horseback through Zululand, inspecting schools and training teachers. Someone from the foreign office, sent to observe him, wrote of his amazement that Heli's demonstrated lessons to his trainee teachers were in Zulu fluent enough to convey biology, geography, history and mathematics, whatever subject was on the timetable.

Soon made headmaster at Edendale African College, his youthful headship impressed a senior boy, a prefect who had turned a blind eye to some theft of food. It was not the theft that Heli rebuked as much as the breach of trust from a prefect with responsibility: That boy was Albert Luthuli, later the Nobel Peace Prize winner and founder and President of the ANC, whose mantle was to fall on Nelson Mandela later. Luthuli recalled this humiliating lesson in his memoir, 'Let My People Go', and the fact of his immediate forgiveness once absorbed. Who knows what influence a single man might have on the legacy he leaves in a later leader?

Heli always sought to make a school the centre of a community's life, in practical ways, even to a school's garden needing dung from the roving herds, brought by all in buckets. However, he did not agree with limiting education to merely practical subjects.

His idealistic allegiance to the needs of Africans did him no favours with the Whitehall mandarins. One of them, sent to review education in the colonies, described Heli thus: 'Jowitt is a man of vision, not only for the development of Africans but the country as a whole. He does not think Rhodesia can develop through the kinds of education which the colonial government wants them to receive.' Men of vision are usually blinded. Heli was persuaded to resign.

After Rhodesia, Heli was transferred as Director of Education to Uganda where daily life grew easier in Kampala with an open-topped car to venture into forests, with waterfalls, pools and picnic shade. Servants were speaking Swahili, clad in white, topped by a red fez. They bowed in deference to his status, second only to the Governor. Marna had a club for tea and talk, and Heli had university-level students, and the occasional company of visiting professors. Uganda was 'the pearl' in the Empire's crown, a quieter jewel, not required to sparkle but to glow.

Heli mastered Swahili with equal dispatch and made African Law and Administration his dominant interest, for he recognised that only an understanding of tribal structures would enable him to interpret the needs of Africans to the impervious assumptions of Europeans. His mastery of African languages was also a cloak of invisibility from uncomprehending whites who remained at one remove. He helped host a Royal Visit with the same attention as the mass rally of the Kabaka and his tribesmen to elect a successor.

None of the trappings of privilege held him. Methodism might have surrendered to Catholicism, but not its zeal for conversion. When Heli published a book, 'The Principles of Education for African Teachers in Training,' his frontispiece showed a photograph of an African child. Underneath it was the caption 'The Director of African Education.' In short, the pupil and his needs, interests and abilities must dictate what is taught and how it is taught. That has not been introduced anywhere, not even in Europe, to this day.

When I encountered Heli, I could know none of this. I did not know he had just been made a C.M.G, nor did I appreciate that its motto, 'Auspicium melioris'—Token of a Better Age—could have been written for him personally. Whether the 'better age' was left behind or yet to come, Heli's aspirations for Africans carved a narrow path between those he loved for their innocence and his future hopes for them and those he was shackled and controlled by. When I first met him, the better age of privilege in Kampala had been forfeited to take on the arid wastes of Bechuanaland.

In the end, the conflict between what he hoped to achieve and what was permitted him would wear him out and defeat him utterly. I would watch it happen, slowly and inexorably, as I grew to know the man called Heli (father), christened by the Baganda.

∞

For Marna, Bechuanaland offered nothing of any interest, no distractions, no library, no company, no radio, no music. After dispatching me to my mother, she faced an existence in torrid, unremitting heat and nothing to alleviate it. Heli could spread his idealistic wings on virgin territory from the back of a caboose; Marna would have to swelter among Afrikaner wives who spoke what she called 'kitchen Dutch'. Not that she spoke the other Hollandishe sort. I came to see that she was right: idealism is always paid for by someone. That was an early safeguard against utopian passion without a sense of its limits; its infection was always tempered by Marna's sardonic humour.

Marna was an inoculation against almost any system of belief, religious, racial, and political. She respected none of them. This was where that all began; my distrust of conformity through an awareness of tension, almost physical. It lay in the silences between them.

∞

That house I entered was the first marital home I knew. Days lingered, heat unswerving, and rain almost never. Marna let me run naked but for a pair of pants. I complained of the lack of the rolling stream of Maweni.

"I will get the gardener to dig you a hole in the shade," she said. So, she did. I sat making mud pies under a trickling hose all day. If I asked to eat up the loquat tree, the cook was dispatched to climb up to me with one hand and a tray on his head. There were a few tedious obligations to wear a dress and look like a granddaughter, but they seldom happened. She found them as oppressive as I did, although, by nature, she was always up for talk. Her audience in Mafeking was paltry and uncomprehending of her subtleties. Letters, as always, filled her days.

Heli asked me if I would like to go to school.

"Louie keeps saying I will soon, but she always cries when she talks about it, so it won't be nice, will it? Not if she cries."

"I meant while you were here? You could meet other children."

My ideas of children were all derived from Enid Blyton.

"The Famous Five are a gang. Would I be in a gang?"

The nuns were honoured to oblige, and I was admitted the following day. All the children spoke Afrikaans, which I didn't understand. I took to modelling plasticine saints, colouring in virgins and memorising short poems, which I recited to Marna's snorts of derision at 'all this Catholic blackmail'. It was nearing Christmas, so the crib, confused with Noah's ark, required duplicate animals and a roof of matchsticks. I was desperate to be a shepherd in the nativity play so I could carry a lamb, but I ended up as the feeble virgin who just had to wear a blue veil, sit still and look pleased for half an hour.

"I'm not pleased. Why must I be? It's not as good as a lamb. It's a doll. Nobody will think it's a baby."

My mother was joining us for Christmas and I was coached for a special recitation by being invited to choose my poem for the Christmas play. I had several lessons in the execution of this masterpiece.

For the final rehearsal, I drew the curtains of the living room and seated Marna and my mother for the grand performance. Heli excused himself. I entered with due solemnity in a pair of farmer's dungarees and searched for a missing calf (fingers up on either side of the brow) under the carpet, behind the bookcase. Horrified, I leapt back at the sight of a large hole (black paper). I gave the full rendition about disappearing rats with the rehearsed jerking of the thumb as taught by the 'dramatic nun'.

'You must make clear what you are talking about and where they are.' she'd said.

The tragedy in this performance was lost on Marna

I was mocking tears, but Marna's were real. She was in a paroxysm, shaking the sofa and dabbing her eyes. It went on for about ten minutes.

"You did it wonderfully, darling."

"Sinking ship?" said Louie, which started the paroxysm up again.

This is why Marna mattered so. She merely reacted to what she saw, life impromptu. When she took me with her to open a bank account, we were shown to the manager's office. He did not look up but went on writing, keeping her standing.

"Yes, thank you, I shall take this chair. Kind of you." She unpinned her hat and propped her stick against his desk. I stood beside her.

"Name?" he barked, still not looking up. There was a long pause before she answered.

"Mrs. Harold Jowitt."

He continued writing. "Never heard of you," he said, still writing.

Marna started to take off her grey silk gloves, pinching one slow finger at a time, easing each out. Even then, I knew that gloves off meant a proper fight.

"May I have the pleasure of knowing your name?" she asked.

"Eloff. Meneer Pieter Eloff" She inclined with her arch look.

"That is interesting", she said. "I have never heard of you either. Perhaps we can now begin."

☙

Marna elicited antipathy not only for her English accent but also for her confident carriage. There was more hostility between Afrikaners and the 'English'—those who spoke with (almost) received pronunciation—than between black and white. Black people were hardly noticed by the whites who employed them since they were merely servants, as was true for the servants of Victorians in England. But the Boer Wars lay within living memory; its humiliation and contempt well remembered by its survivors.

What they never realised was that Marna was one of them. She only revealed that to Afrikaners she liked and to the English she didn't. It worked well. She could sail imperturbably and unaffiliated between them, sometimes ingeniously. Our telephone was a 'party line' shared between some eight households. Each had its distinctive ring. Ours was three shorts. One of our co-sharers was a verbose Mevrou van Niekerk, who dominated the line with recipes shared at inordinate length. Marna, wanting to make a call, had tried several times. After the listing of endless ingredients, Marna interrupted

"Mevrou, I can smell your beans burning."

"Ooh God!" the woman dropped the phone and rushed for her kitchen. Marna made her call.

༄

Now enters a conflict not between but within; betrayal of a cruel kind. I only understood the reasons for it later. Its construction is laid bare in that house, though not to a child, its significance. Parents and the usual marital habits are unknown. Heli occupies a monk's cell, hung with a crucifix, a bedside table with slim volumes, theological commentaries, the Bible and prayer books. Marna's room across the hall is a little more comfortable, the bed is larger and there are photographs of her beloved Horace, an Airedale she had loved in Uganda. From his gaze at her, I'd say it was reciprocal. Then a desk, her Schaeffer pen and some casual clutter of a cologne spray, lipstick and recent correspondence. Neither of them enters the other's domain. They live entirely separate lives pinned together at meals and circumnavigating routines. She welcomes his colleagues, both black and white, and provides lavish food and humorous stories, although not until the ordained had removed their dog collars— 'I don't dine with dogs, they wait for scraps'— but unless they have company, they hardly speak. The wound is very deep but cannot be stitched by talk.

In Uganda, under the influence of the only men with whom he could exchange ideas, the Jesuits, Heli had become a Catholic convert. From Methodist to Catholic at a single vault.

Marna had no warmth for Catholicism.

"Of course, they fished for him. He had all those schools. As Director of Education, he was as good as a fat trout. He swallowed their bait, hook, line and sinker". Marna never tempered her talk.

Perhaps she thought it would wash over me or that I would not grasp the implications. Under the diktat of that Holy and Apostolic Church, Heli was forced to put Marna 'from him'. His marriage to her was annulled. She, being previously divorced, following the literal flight of her first husband, was persona non grata: conjugal rights were to be denied. Heli was exempted from the prohibited list of books and simultaneously exempted from his vows as a husband. He had rescued Marna from disappointed destitution, cemented his position with a dependable good marriage and promptly betrayed it.

Perhaps it was not prompt. His had been a lonely life devoid of glamour: the rituals of Catholicism, the habits of the high mass, and the censor swinging daily in the African dawn. All gave spiritual shape to a man of discipline, with little access to communion of other kinds. Marna was imperious. She had little reverence for Heli's dedication. He had his romantic hunger. He had fathered Ursula, my aunt and Louie first, which since I am here, was rather necessary to this tale.

Marna was abandoned by both husbands, passionate about other things, my mother by my father, and me by her thirst for medicine and Heli by Catholicism. He would, in the end, drink himself to death in disappointment at its empty promises. Those were the influences from each and all: the nobility of an unsatisfied longing.

All were fine, upstanding exemplars of principles, dedication, work, and austerity. I would, in turn, choose what had been already chosen. But there was liberty, too. I am awaiting my first safari but must first prepare for the family Christmas. I did not know I was part of any family until it happened. When it was over, the family was a tableau that I watched with interest but complete detachment. I belonged with none of them except my grandparents.

∽

Looking back, I feel that I was being turned on a lathe to face the 'no not this, no not here' lessons until what remained was solitude and perplexity. The doors not opened lead to the one remaining, and that leading past closed doors would be critical to the plunge into light—when it was offered. My relations were all doors closed to me. Yet they arrived as though on a catwalk, to be observed before they passed on.

Here comes a couple called Lynn and Vi, together with their offspring, Jonathan and Nicolette. They live in Salisbury, Rhodesia. Lynn, an architect, is Marna's firstborn and only son, whose father flew away in that b…y Bleriot. He is a quiet, thoughtful man whose head is held at an angle of permanent reflection, whose hand is always encumbered by a cigarette, whose mouth is mostly silent but mobile with a smile which raises an amused eyebrow. Lynn and Marna share a deep secret, so deep nobody knows what it is, beyond a bond that is unmatched by her daughters. He alone calls her 'Mother', and he attends to her slightest impulse. Lynn and Marna are so alike that they could be buds along a single branch. I register my mother's affection for Lynn, her half-brother, a tender, gentle man, ten years older.

His wife, it is tacitly agreed, was an unfortunate choice. Violet is as much like Wallis Simpson as it is possible to be: angular, in impeccably cut, slim, sculptured dresses and hats that resemble unbalanced birds feeding on a coconut. Hats in Africa are mostly of the solar toupee, or broad-brimmed straw variety, useful for the sun, not the preludes to the 'fascinator' some with feathers. Vi smiles a great deal, shows larger teeth than a yawning horse, and barks out a snorting laugh. For the sake of her beloved son, Marna tries not to notice Vi, but she does find this difficult; Vi has the same effect on Lynn's enthronement in Marna's mind as the Duchess of Windsor had on the King's. She is there, and that is all to be said out loud. Under Marna's breath, I catch the occasional 'ridiculous woman'.

Their son Jonathan, who never established himself as my cousin, is a trial. An awkward, silent boy of about ten, he will neither take himself off nor join the party. He drapes himself in doorways to overhear, and he appears to hold in contempt whatever is said. Nicolette, his younger sister, might have introduced me to friendship — she is only a little younger— but Nicolette is a girl-girl in socks and buttoned shoes with ribbons and sashes like Violet Elizabeth Bott with her 'lithp'. I am too steeped in William books to see her any other way. We have no point of contact, but the differences between us afford Vi much maternal pride. Those dirty bare feet and a girl in khaki shorts, how *could* her mother…?

Tom and Ursula Randall follow two days later, unwinding from a hot car with their daughter Karin who is three years younger than I am, still a baby. Tom and Marna have a different bond; no secrets to their mutual affection. The six-foot-two height of silent Tom, his thick lenses, his sprung thatch of hair, his natural affection is like living with a private hayrick, warm, light, sheltering. Tom is the personification of the beloved physician: gentle, quiet, and intelligent; everything Louie would seek in a husband. But Tom is firmly splinted to my mother's sister Ursula.

Ursula occupies a deck chair in the shade, shifts in the heat, and sighs. Tom wraps his arms around her, strokes her hair and protectively loves his 'poor darling.' Karin joins me in the making of mud pies in the hole under the loquat tree. This was the first gathering under one roof when I met all those whose names I had heard. It was also the only occasion I remember us all together.

༄

A family Christmas had high billing: It was heralded by a bag of walnuts, ordered from England, tipped from the leather post bag onto the polished tiles of the stoep, bouncing about like ping-pong balls. The post-boy was perplexed at the delivery of valueless rattling shells as he gathered them up.

"Ag missus, sorry. The blerrie paper broke, but most came with, so I left them to the last. Ah tried one, only the one, but by the time I smashed the shell, there was bugger all insahd. Whatjoo use them for?"

Mrs. Beeton's Christmas cake and its labour were introduced in Mafeking, and since the recipe is rounded out in neat pounds and one dozen eggs, I have it by heart; I am still chained to its annual obligation. In Mafeking, the raisins had to be de-pipped with incisor teeth, the sugared peel had long been dried but needed fine slicing, the cherries chopped, the walnuts shelled in fragments, and the stirring produced blisters. A bowl to lick before a kill-joy spatula was invented was the reward of raw cake with cinnamon and nutmeg. Before the arrival of my cousins, I had it to myself, a teaspoon at a time.

Marna's role as hostess was one she relished.

Cook was dispatched for cuts of lamb or a fresh tongue to be tied up with string and pressed, and the gardener ministered to mint below the garden tap. The stunted avenue of dusty trees outside Government House had been identified as Seville oranges, and Marna had purloined every last fruit for marmalade, much to the amusement of the local women.

"Ag, let her pick away. These Engelse know nothing. Wait till she tastes the bitter blerries...she'll have to make chutney..."

They were wrong. Fifty pounds of better-than-Oxford marmalade would last the year. Marna provisioned as though for another war; hers was personal, and it travelled with her.

∽

Karin and I have supper in the kitchen. I remember the first spectacular drama. The cook is drunk and keeps trying to kiss the maid like the rustics with Falstaff below stairs. Maid gives a giggling shriek. Heli rushes in like a dervish and, taking Cook by his collar and the seat of his trousers, throws him through the gauze door. It ricochets and keeps ricocheting, banging several times in the shocked silence, with the maid crouching down and covering her eyes with her apron. Heli has never shown any capacity for violence. Three days before Christmas, the cook is sacked. We have sausages instead and cold tongue for every meal thereafter.

That Christmas, I met more than relations. I met stories read aloud. 'A Christmas Carol' was first, and that was sad enough. Marna's voice quivered when Tiny Tim entered, but she ploughed on. Then, with all gathered on cushions on the floor, Marna read 'Jackanapes'. She never managed to finish it. Tears welled; her shoulders shook. She tried several times and gave up. I so much wanted the story to finish because the horse called Rollo—'the gypsy's Rollo'— was going to be ridden into the Battle of Waterloo, and I wanted to hear he had galloped through with a foamed mouth and been halted to survive. Instead, Marna mopped her eyes and accepted her annual cigarette, and someone whispered that her younger brother Victor had never come back from Belgium, and that was why she cried.

So that was what people call a family. Lynn and his ridiculous woman take their leave to relief all round, although I see Marna brushing away tears. Something deep and inexpressible lies there. Marna stores it in silence.

Sardonic disparagement to conceal what?

Blood ties that did not include me?

Or from which you recoiled? You were part of them whether you chose them or not.

I never felt approved of- except by Tom. And he was only family by marriage.

Perhaps that was the central lesson. Ties of blood mean little without ties of affection. You read that early. You also saw the effect of one affection upon another, confirming or destroying deeper ties.

Jackanapes stayed longer than any of them. A book could make Marna cry, so that introduced me to an understanding of a book's power.

Anything more?

Lots more. Being a boy, even a rebel Jackanapes was first seeded.

All the pictures in the book of Jane Austen's women, dimity, lawn, bonnets and pincushions meant nothing. The gypsy's Rollo and liberty was a boy's endowment, the freedom of it and the war of engagement, elsewhere, away from carefulness! Oh, I wanted that wherever it took me.

Wherever? Yes, it certainly did. Anything else?

I think, although it was embryonic and I could not have articulated it then, I realised that your friend's friend is not necessarily your friend, and the opposite, that your enemy's enemy is not necessarily your enemy. It was the beginning of discerning that each of us loves different things, and hates different things. Marna detested Vi's affectations but adored Lynn, who loved Vi. She had to leave that intact. It was my first lesson in careful communication.

One you have mastered?

Far from wholly, but I am more aware of the dangers. Once a marriage has happened, it is too late to express any opinion. Before then, an opinion can have value. I would have welcomed such honestly myself. My life might have been very different.

CHAPTER 4

Light: Love on Safari

'...some persons say the unsatisfied longing we feel in ourselves for something better than the greatest perfection to be found on earth is a proof that the true object of our desires lies beyond it.'

Christmas over, Heli was able to return with relief to work. He was girding up to make his initial survey of his territory without the roads or travel lodges. Not even a sleepy hotel. Horseback had to give way to a ten-ton 'caboose' to carry supplies for five weeks, depending on the rains. Fresh food would be shot and skinned, vegetables stowed in sand, ammunition and camping gear checked. A typewriter, spare ribbons and a collapsible table would provide a study under the baobab trees. The Director of Education was to venture forth with only rudimentary maps to find schools in his care. He had envisaged a solitary sojourn like many others in Zululand, only this time without complete mastery of language. His Zulu would suffice since all Africans are natural linguists. Marna had other ideas. Journeys were always her hope of renewal; the more and wilder, the better.

"Why not invite Louie and take the child? We need to throw them together. What an experience it would be for them after all their misery."

"I can't cope with Phil or the risk."

"I cope with the child every day. What risk?'"

"She could get ill. There are no doctors or hospitals."

"Well, add 'plus one doctor' to your list. Take Tom."

The expansion was a foregone conclusion; Marna usually won. If a five-year-old was to be his responsibility, with or without her mother, then a doctor was needed. Tom agreed with enthusiasm, and Ursula was safely indulged. Quantities of everything were quadrupled, including the staff. Feeding the five thousand would have to rely on more than miracles. One presented itself forthwith: Light, a Bushman tracker, by repute the best in the territory. He could not only track but shoot with a two-bore rifle and shotgun. Named for the colour of his skin, he was equally light on his feet and invisible in the bush. He could catch guinea fowl with his bare hands, or so it was said.

Light, with his oblique slanted eyes and high cheekbones, his prehensile toes and long twig fingers, was contracted but made it clear he did not cook, so Sixpence —rechristened Torka by Heli, who could not spend a name like sixpence—would come to do little else. Jacob would drive, and he knew both sides of a spanner. Three spare wheels and a full set of tools were added, along with an elephant gun, which caused Light to wrinkle his nose and promptly dismantle it. Water would be rationed to half a gallon a day, each, hung in canvas bags from the front bumper, to be cooled if we ever made any speed. Not much was speedy. The caboose was a ten-ton truck adapted for storage and as a travel home, part open-topped camp under tarpaulins, partly enclosed. It seated five abreast in the cabin. The servants travelled above on the tarpaulins. Below them, Heli organised storage for a touring office. Everything was designated its space.

Tom assembled surgical implements, malarial tablets, Tsetse fly unguents and imaginative solutions for the unforeseen, slings and the like. Marna's pleasure in an adventure kept adding luxurious necessities in awkwardly shaped baskets, which Heli stowed through gritted teeth. I was restricted to five books and a notepad and to Heli's sorrow, when I handed them over, they were all William books or Enid Blyton. Blyton blighted my reputation for many years.

Louie took two hats, face-creams and her textbooks. Ursula thanked God she was out of it. The bush was her idea of hell, and animals in the wild, well... seen one, seen them all. She would dab her forehead with cologne and sigh instead.

For most families, the annual holiday is a pleasant interruption of monotony, remembered mostly for its disasters. For me, holidays were the only contact with stability or family. Everything of importance in my childhood happened on holidays. I recognised that my mother's brittleness melted when she was with Tom, as though warmed by a brazier, the doctor she might have been who took the Hippocratic Oath as gospel. I came by slow degrees to sense that Louie was in love with Tom. Perhaps I was and assumed she must be? It never surfaced, but a bond kept its pregnant silence throughout their entire lives.

Ursula was one of those kitten-frau women who curled around a man's protective instincts and licked up its cream. Tom had no streak of steel that might have shaved her demands. There was no hope that it would ever change. It became a dictatorship of cloying calculation from this pretty petite woman in frills. In the early days, Ursula, with her mop of dark curls, laughed, and Tom hugged. Increasingly, her mouth hardened, and her voice grew shrill, though she always hummed below her breath like a bee.

Tom was the closest portrait of the father I would have ordered from a catalogue and accepted in damaged packaging. Like Louie, I adored Tom uncritically. We, Louie and I, both looked the other way. I did so because he was out of reach and she did because she might have been tempted to create wild havoc by biting the utterly forbidden fruit.

You understand all that now, but did you see it then?

I sensed it without understanding, atmospherically. Louie breathed deeper and Tom looked at both of us with surreptitious sympathy. Always. It never changed.

༄

I was woken by Marna, certain that I had not slept. It was bone marrow cold.

Departure was scheduled for four in the morning before the sun or the town was awake. The heavy truck laboured out of the sand like an elephant from a dust bath, and some apprehension quietened us four, abreast the driver. Bechuanaland would rely on enterprise and might reward it with limitless herds of galloping game, or spinning wheels and spades in a river bed. To me, being awake in the middle of the night was reward enough. Excitement gradually increased, along with the drama of the sunrise.

The low charcoal humps gradually gave way to sharp shadow, knives dissecting the muscles of sand, each grass defined, every contour floodlit by the miracle of the glowing sun. Nothing moved; the night melted; the engine toiled on. Up on the tarpaulin above, Light and Torka slept, covered in blankets, for it was desert cold before dawn. This was their country, and they had seen it before. Jacob, at the wheel, settled for the long distance with silent philosophy. Heli read and, with the help of a torch, made notes. Louie was transformed by the easy presence of Tom. This was as close to a family as I had encountered, warm, enclosed and safe. Christmas had been the appearance of it. This felt real.

In retrospect that pre-dawn departure into the unknown showed me something very clearly; I watched everything, every gesture, each half smile between Louie and Tom, and Heli absorbed. But I also saw they did not watch me. I fitted between my mother and Heli as an armrest. Perhaps all only children know this. There are no siblings to mediate, measure or comment; impressions are one's own. An only child must interpret the gaps between the pictures.

The best moments were the setting of camp. At last, after hours of arithmetical problems to distract me —if there are four fever trees to every mile, and we have travelled twenty-eight and a half miles, how many fever trees have we passed?' If it takes three minutes, thirty seconds to walk around an elephant, how long does it take if you short-cut halfway through its legs?'— the truck would pull off under a baobab or umbrella acacia. Liberty was jumping down into the sand and stretching. Light would disappear immediately. Torka had first to erect the loo because I was terrified of snakes and refused to squat until the hessian was around the posts and the ground beaten all about. This irritated Heli every time, but I wouldn't give way. Jacob and Torka would search for wood, which was usually plentifully strewn by elephants, and then the fire would be lit. Heli started work at his collapsible table, and his typewriter joined the percussion of rattling insects, clatter, clatter, ping... brrrrr...ping.

Tom, Louie and I would go for a walk with a gun over Tom's shoulder for reassurance. Since he was so short-sighted behind his thick lenses, he could not have hit the truck at twenty paces. I'd have had a better chance. Often, by the time we returned, there was a skinned buck hanging in a tree or at least a couple of guinea fowl plucked for the pot. Unlike school later, I don't remember ever being hungry.

In the beginning, we had potatoes and roots, pumpkins and squash. We picked occasional edible fruit like maroolas and Light dug up insects. He ate them raw with relish. We also had a straw oven to bake bread, rather unleavened but usually fresh. Torka heated the oven near the night fire and then buried it in the sand, raking coals over it to bake overnight. The servants regarded us as very extravagant with meat, not only for the quantities we ate but also for the fires they had to build to protect it from lions. We slept in a ring of fire in two tents. Tom and Heli shared one, and my mother and I shared the other. The servants slept wrapped in blankets in the open to make sure they fed the fires.

The Rogue Elephant was the only episode of real drama. We had just jumped down from the cab when Light buzzed an urgent alarm from the back. We scrambled back up without seeing any reason. Behind our intended baobab, an enormous bull elephant was flapping its ears aggressively. We drove off in haste. Not far down the road, a couple of huts had been flattened. A huddled group sheltering behind a wall said two men were dead. After voluble description and panicked gesticulations with a larger group gathering, Heli decided. The elephant had to be destroyed. He dispatched a runner from the group, with a note, to contact the nearest Government station. We waited, sleeping in the caboose. Two days later, they returned with elephant guns and five more men. The bull's rejection was to be compounded by its tragic and brutal end.

I identified with that angry elephant. Jacob drove Louie and me away until it was over. We left with its pitiful tusks lashed to the back and clattering against one another like outsize castanets. They could not be left with the carcass. The meat would provide food for kraals miles about. Tusks were not yet traded and it was not a habit to encourage, or so Heli explained.

"What will we do with them?"

"I don't know yet. I'll think of something."

My tears were dried by a sombre lesson in natural history and the cycles of renewal and death, sometimes being kindest. I did not want to be persuaded of that. Elephants were nearly divine, so I thought they should be exempt from 'cycles'.

We saw lions often, and once they came close enough at night to force us to sleep in the truck, but the only time they were a threat was after we had killed. Light was meticulous about leaving no blood anywhere. He was a fascinating sight, half stalking wild cat, with the ears and eyes of a deer, entirely at home in the bush, hardly noticeable. He slipped away silently and returned silently to sit and smoke a clay pipe when the hunt had been successful; his prehensile toes curled inwards, his bony knees and cadaverous long legs shielding his thin torso.

Once, he forgot himself. We had stopped because a herd of impala were leaping across our path. Light couldn't resist. From the back of the truck, he took a shot just as Tom descended to watch. The shot passed through Tom's hair, taking a clean path through his fortunately thick thatch. Light was forbidden to fire from the truck. Heli, shaken by the near tragedy, was incensed: He promptly deprived Light of his gun.

Although Tom could have been killed, he wasn't: were we all to starve?

Light waited only a day before the gun was restored. He touched his forehead for forgiveness and gratitude and resumed his duties.

Safaris were not common in Bechuanaland at that time. It had not yet been discovered as a game country. Nobody worked by safari. We were not there for the excitement of the game; they were incidental food. Water was a greater worry. From the dusty bags, allocated one each, rations were extracted. Pots were cleaned with sand and only rinsed with a teacup of water. We were inspecting schools, separated by great distances; the safari was a necessity, and with Heli, it was as rigorously disciplined as his daily routines in classrooms.

After hours of dusty journey, our arrivals were humbling; to arrive at a collection of remote huts and find we were always expected. The invisible bush telegraph was reliable. All the children in their best white dresses or boys in immaculate shirts, washed in a river somewhere and ironed, had work laid out and songs prepared. Teachers, palpably proud of their achievements, stood smiling, clapping to bring a child forward while the inspector asked questions of both.

Many decades later, I read Harold Nicolson's account of a similar round of inspection he had taken with Heli when Nicolson was in the Colonial Service. He refers to the 'eager' children and 'the forest of horrid pink palms' that shot up to answer any question. 'Horrid.' That was the word he used, a blow to the pit of my stomach. I could see those children with tightly plaited hair and ribbons, the boys in shining shirts in honour of the Big White Chief from London, who found their enthusiasm to show their learning 'horrid' and was contemptuous of the labour of their mothers in his honour.

In another letter to Sackville West, perched in her tower, that potentate from Whitehall wrote, 'You know how I hate niggers...' These were the kind of people let loose to comment on Africa. For Heli, the Nicolsons represented every degenerate value, devoid of compassion, moneyed, snobbish, deviant, and self-indulgent, yet he had to be polite to the man whose wife referred to the lower classes as 'bedints'. Perhaps that derives from Bediennung- service? Heli would have been their 'bedint'. No wonder he could never return to an England that esteemed such people as aristocrats. You have to ask what pot was calling what kettle black on apartheid later.

We visited probably twenty different rural schools, and although I can't remember each in detail, I do remember my awareness that for them, the chance of school was a daily gift, which the whole society celebrated. I loathed school later, its emphasis on unimportant things, its atmospheric constipation, its cruelty and competitiveness, but they walked miles to get there, and it was the proudest part of their impoverished lives. Our visits were all singing, clapping and gifts of food they could not afford to spare. Innocent joy. That's what I hunger to remember. That's what warmed Heli's dedication. He was truly loved for simply making it possible. Even his Zulu was his mark of respect for the equality they longed for and his belief in a future for which they would struggle to prepare. However long it took.

The end of the safari was Olympian. Heli decided to stretch the journey to see the Victoria Falls, about three days beyond the furthest outpost at Maun. To get there, we had to cross the Zambezi, which was in flood. The crossing was on a pont, paddled across the river by oarsmen, so we camped for three days until the river abated enough to drive the truck onto the raft. Coming out of the desert, we approached mosi-oa-tunya— 'the smoke that thunders'— to be enveloped in mist and rainbows, miracle enough, then a sight one never forgets. That shining power drawn to the brink of gravity was sliding towards fate. Once over, it tumbles in slow motion, with the volume that only a continent can produce, across nearly two miles of a single spine, falling forever.

It was celestial and remains daunting in the memory because no emotion is adequate, and no human expression is equal unless you are Beethoven. It falls and goes falling for eternity, spellbinding power, somehow silent despite the thunder, water as elemental creation. It unified the purpose of the whole safari, blockages followed by powerful certainty, inexorable... If anything persuaded me that man's origins lay in Africa, bones wouldn't; that water, those falls would.

We returned to Mafeking five weeks after we had left. I had probably increased in mental age by four years: all a school would notice was some facility for mental arithmetic. Heli was now the other tower to my bridge. Between them, my grandparents suspended my happiness.

And love for you was almost the only thing they shared.

CHAPTER 5

Three Wishes

'Here and there a cygnet is reared uneasily among the ducklings in a brown pond, and never finds the living stream in fellowship with its own oary-footed kind.'

I was to board. Whatever that was. It was a suitcase and a uniform and my mother's drawn face. Bills of any kind caused that face and had from the beginning. I occasioned the bills; I knew that.

Louie was tortured by the decision but had no choice; I knew she was unhappy and embittered. The second spat out sharp remarks. She braced herself to do to me what should never have been necessary; I inflicted the necessity. It was my fault.

This first school near Johannesburg sat in scrubland with a classroom block on a raised concrete apron and four rondavels for dormitories. Louie spoke to a rather severe woman. She called a black maid. The maid took me and my suitcase to a dormitory; she pointed to one of twelve beds in a clock face under an open thatch, spokes radiating, feet towards the centre—the room smelt of grass and floor polish. I stowed my suitcase under the bed and was left to sit on it. I saw my mother's car depart across the door. She did not look sideways to see me or my bed.

When other girls came in, they contemplated me from a circle as though I was an insect, pointing and whispering behind their fingers. They were twelve and looked tall, no doubt curious to find a solemn midget abandoned among them. They tried pinching my arm but drew only puzzlement. Kicking my shins caused a raised leg. They stuck out tongues; I did not know what tongues-out meant, though it was clearly unfriendly. Later at night, they put knobbly things in my bed. Enid Blyton had not covered apple pie beds. Perhaps they hoped I'd cry, but crying I had never tried, as there had been no acute causes and no one to hear if I had. I don't recall any practice in crying.

The latrines were in a separate tenement of corrugated iron that creaked in the wind; wooden seats over holes in the ground with a sand bucket and a solution of Jeyes fluid to the side of each. The smell made me sneeze. The buckets of sand were acrawl of fat maggots. Getting to the shack required a sprint across waste ground, which was guarded by a tall shamble-man. He mumbled and wiggled his head with a finger in one ear. He would rake up a guttural cough, hawk and spit loudly. With only one staring eye and a crippled dragging leg, he might have modelled for Arthur Rackham. That was the school caretaker. More terrified of him than the fat maggots, I held it in, waiting for daylight. The sabotage of sleep conquered me.

The fevered dream that followed would take me to a sparkling bathroom where it was safe to 'let go', comforted by warmth. Fatal. Every night, I wet the bed—the angry maid who came to make beds exhibited the wet patch to open contempt. Siestog! While the others went to breakfast, I washed the sheet.

I recall no lessons of any kind. The school was isolated in unoccupied small-holds of cabbages and fenced animals. I ran away. I found a stable with three mud-encrusted ponies and took refuge with them, comforted by their smell, their warm breath and their dirty straw. I suppose someone reported me missing. A search discovered me, and my mother came to fetch me, much displeased. I had been there for about a month.

Already beaten by my existence, Louie had little resilience. I was sent to another primary day school, more expensive and with lessons. I slept in a senior school with different twelve-year-olds who came to bed long after me. I walked alone between the two. Weekends I spent high up in the fork of a Jacaranda, my special place above the silent tennis courts. Because the others had gone home and the dining room was closed, my food was left outside the kitchen covered with a plate.

I got my games from books and companions of varied kinds, almost all literary animals. I don't recall being aware I was lonely. You need to have experienced friends to realise their lack. I had never had any, not then.

Sometimes, Louie fetched me for a Sunday out. It was not always a treat. She would find fault with something; my shoes had holes and should have been mended, or she questioned the bruises on my arms.

"Who did that?"

"Matron."

"What had you done? Had you been naughty?"

"She woke me up and said I'd been talking after lights out."

"Woke you up?"

"Yes."

"Then what happened?"

"She pulled me out of bed and shook me like a doll. Then she made me stand in the bathroom corner because I said I had not been talking. Nobody talks to me. She shouted I was 'answering back.' But I think she forgot me because I fell asleep on the floor, and Sister Janet found me in the morning when she came to wake us up."

"Good God."

God was not much good because after my mother asked Sister Janet, who admitted it had happened, 'most unfortunate' Matron just called me a miserable 'tattle' and put bruises on my arms almost every day. I learned two lessons for life: that institutions for the religious are not overly disturbed by injustice and that taking on a sadist just refines the sadism. After that, I did not tell my mother anything that would fire her to complain. It only made things worse. It also increased Louie's guilt, so it was worse for both of us. She could do nothing about it; staying silent was what I could do for her.

I learned that going slimly was safest. I never accepted offers of sweets or anything that would cost money. Once, Louie bought a whole pound of cherries and dumped the bag on my lap in the car on the way home.

"All yours, everyone," she said.

That remains a vivid red and shining present. Cherries were expensive. She did love me in spasms, and those spasms caused her to pinch my earlobe hard. Spontaneous pinches were Louie's impromptu hugs. She said ears had no nerves down there. I did not agree, but I pretended to because those moments were precious. A little painful affection was nothing when Louie caught a gust of loving.

Stoicism took a head start. I realise now that it was early training for what would come: a gnarled Bonsai, lopped and cut back to grow deeper roots and resistant bark. I said nothing when she suggested that a small boy in callipers called Peter-with-Polio needed my clockwork Hornby train set more than I did. Together, we wrapped it, and I gave it to him for Christmas as though it was my idea. They were even poorer than we were, and he couldn't walk. It took a little time, but later, I could see Louie was right. I did not miss it, and Peter had so little.

My sixth year would grant me the proverbial three wishes: For a mother's love, for a friend, and for a real family. The father remained unanswered but now was under threat.

First, to the unequalled mother: I was at school when Milly arrived. She was the same age as Louie, twenty-seven. I don't recall hearing about her before I was pressed against those large breasts on our first encounter, but immediately, I noticed the flooding sense of calm. The tenement flat smelled of beeswax, the surfaces gleamed, and there was a new order. Louie looked less haggard. Milly was like sunlight sterilising everything. While we made a bed, she told me some of what had gifted us with her miraculous arrival when I asked about her home.

Milly Thoko Ndaba's Story

"Can be difficult to splain, darling. You know nothing about Zululand. You never eva go there. It's my home, a place with many, many cows and some goats eva. Not so many people as here in Johannesburg. Ow, how can I tell you? My father is the Chief for many of the kraals, many miles between one and another one. Everybody must walk over many field. Such a long way, sometimes. My father is Zulu Chief, and he must say everything, like this, like that. 'You must pay so many cows for lobola; you must work for that man because you have been thief and must pay back with work.' Everyone must do what he says, like in a white-man court.

Sometimes there is a big umhlangano, like a big football, so many together. Then we kill a cow, and everybody drinks tshwala. We can all make it together, and then my father is talking with other headmans from other villages about how we must plant new fields, or together make a small road, or get together to ask for water. It can work together, when people talk first and everybody must understand why it must happen, and also for the school, we must together buy the books and give money to the teacher, and she must have food from everyone.

"Was that your school?"

"When I am very small, yes. Then later I go to another school in Paulpietersberg. I go every day until I get to Standard Three, so I can write, but darling, I am not so good with reading. I am very slow. Everybody can learn writing together, but reading is alone. Nobody has much time to teach me, but sometimes I take a newspaper and ask my mother. My father is not so good also. My mother is a Swazi, and she has a better school, I think. She has already passed away.

"How old were you when she passed?"

"I can be fifteen or sixteen, maybe. She got very sick for many weeks, and we have no doctors there. Eva can find one, so esspensives. I want to die also after she goes."

"What made you come to Johannesburg?"

"Ow, darling! It is through of my husband, Charlie. Charlie and I getting married when I am nearly twenty, in the Church just nearby my home—a small church but for anybody who can come. Charlie is Christian, like me, and also my father. I never completely know what happened, but when I come in many buses, take one, then wait, then take another, it takes me two days; I find Charlie is already dead. They say in a knife fight. I not believe what they say. No, never. Charlie is not such a fighter. He is a good man. Every month, without failing, he sends money and writes a letter, so when no money comes, I know something is happening. I come to find out. Now I think maybe someone killed him, but they never want to ask, so they say it is his fault with a knife. Then bury him, and everything is finish and all quiet. Police can never ask about a black man dead. I never eva can bury him near our home…

"Anyway, what can a person do with a husband passed and no money for the children? I have two children. They must go to school, and I must buy clothes and food for them. One is called Phyllis, and I have a son. He called Leonard, both still very small. So now is no money coming from Charlie; I must work and send money to my sister. My sister is not so easy, darling, sometimes she has very bad temper, but she can look after the children when I send money. Everybody in my village looks out for the children, not only my sister."

༄

Charlie had been the cheerful manager of the parking garage below the flat, so crammed with cars that getting one out needed the driving expertise of solving a Rubik's cube: the fewest manoeuvres for the quickest space.

Ours was the first door Milly Ndaba knocked at, looking for work.

On the point of leaving for work herself, Louie pulled Milly in and handed her the keys— to our lives.

What she became was the filter between me and my mother, gauze that softened us both. While Milly hummed under her breath on her knees, polishing the floor, making beds and ironing, a tenement became a home. Pots would be a-simmer, and the smell of chopped onions frying with meat cubed awaiting flour were all the signs of the authority of a young Zulu princess who simply had walked through the door like a divine gift for life. My very own Calpurnia had as sharp a mind but a more diplomatic tongue, and she was better upholstered.

She welcomed me home with homemade biscuits and lamb chops and chips for supper every night when I was at home. Laughter shook her shoulders at my indignations and demands for cutlets rather than loin-shaped chops.

"Ow, darling, can taste the same. You not eat the shape!"

Her cold block room on the roof of the flat was amongst those allocated to servants, devoid of warmth or colour and with only rudimentary cold showers to use before descending at six to make tea and begin the routines of perfection. Milly Ndaba mastered the telephone fairly quickly to order groceries. In her standard three copperplate handwriting, she wrote lists. Her entry had been tentative, her mastery of our lives rapid. In her early years, I saw Ndaba only during the holidays, the same fixture as Marna, always exactly as before; one smelling of 4711 cologne, the other of Nivea cream, and both laughing given any reason.

Ndaba sidled into our lives so quietly that it is difficult to convey her solidity in my happiness. She spread warmth, we chatted over the cooking, we collaborated over bed-making, she teased, and she admonished as I was her 'Chile'. Her views on right conduct were absolute, but she offered them with an arm around my shoulder. Misery over Louie's harshness was soothed with the balm of her kind judgements.

"Madam is very tired, Miss Phil. Work so hard, eva for us. Can forgive darling."

Louie's private practice increased to wealthy Jews in the Northern suburbs; their wealth harboured several servants and lavish kitchens. Louie would take Ndaba with her to spend time with their cooks, to master new dishes and to give her some entertainment with a mug of tea and gossip. Max, my step-father-to-be, had entered Louie's orbit, so Milly's repertoire was prepared for him, although neither of us knew it; borscht and chicken soup predated his invasion.

An interlude of Ndaba's absence underscored just how fundamental she was to our newly contented home. After a holiday with her family in Paulpietersberg, she was pregnant. She would not be allowed to keep a baby in the flats. Generous friends, once patients, built a room and bathroom in Bryanston, where Ndaba could have and wean her baby out of the control of the 'Group Areas Act' prohibitions. She was gone for about nine months. After delivering her infant daughter, Thandi, to her sister to care for, along with her other two, she returned. Nobody asked about Thandi's father, and Milly never mentioned him. We never saw her rural home, but such was the racial separation in South Africa; neither side suggested it.

∾

Sanie was gift number two. What I first noticed was how easily she took things. I used to watch her with longing, something between William's Ginger and Velvet Brown in National Velvet. Like me, more boy than girl, which was what mattered, Sanie attracted friends as a flower does bees, partly due to her irreverence, mostly her mimicry and easy disregard for opinion. Her popularity came from happiness, laughter as a natural sauce, sporty and energetic, short, thick, cropped hair, and brown arms. She was at home with anyone, expected to be liked, casually unafraid. Everyone was drawn to her; she was everything I wasn't. Nothing required seriousness; she swam through people as effortlessly as a fish through reeds.

I marvelled because I could not work out how she did it. She put no effort into pleasing. She brought lavish lunch boxes and shared them liberally. Every day, she gave me her apple cores and left flesh on them. I saved them tinged brown to relish in the fork of my tree after supper. I knew she felt sorry for me, her manner a little apologetic, but I did not understand why. I longed to get close to her, to be one of her friends, to learn how. I watched her handing out cards about a birthday party to everybody in our class but me. They had already been invited; the cards just confirmed where it was and when. Only I boarded at the senior school half a mile distant.

Desperation to get close drove me to a blatant transgression: even at six, I knew better than to invite myself anywhere. One brave impulse gave me the only diverse and happy family I was ever part of, more solid and predictable than my scattered and alienated one would ever be.

Sanie saw me standing and hoping.

"You can't come, can you?"

"No, I suppose I can't unless my mother will fetch me."

"Well, see if she will. It's tomorrow". She had no card. I watched her extract a card from someone else. She gave it to me.

"She knows where I live, doesn't need it. Come if you can."

I fought back tears of gratitude and apprehension, certain that I would not be able to go. But dressed in shame, I did, carrying a wrapped box of handkerchiefs my mother had never opened. There was no time to buy a present, and neither of us knew how people did children's parties.

Louie dropped me at the gate of a huge, rambling house to venture in alone. It had several doorways. I selected a kitchen entrance, sidling around pantries, crates of bottles and sacks of oranges, not sure what I was seeking except to remain invisible. I came upon Sanie searching a walk-in cold store, trying to carry Coca-Cola out for those I dreaded meeting. She handed me a couple and shut the great door with a lever handle. I thrust the present at her; she indicated I should tuck it under her elbow since all hands were full. I waited for the moment of unwrapping.

"I am so sorry. There wasn't time and…"

She put the handkerchiefs aside.

"My sister will like them, or my mother will." she said, "come for a swim."

That was my entry into family warmth. It was intoxicating, bathed in acceptance, teased by her brother and sister and given a whole estate as home. A swimming pool gargling, a grapevine dripping, a mutt of a rollicking boxer dog called Pluto—Mr. Pluts— an acre of lawn for croquet and people, endless new people coming and going, kissing and hugging, smoking and drinking. They came in zippy little convertible sports cars and played tennis in white clothes. In breaks between matches, they drank tea with scones and crumpets. Afterwards, they drank beer and laughed a lot.

Mac, the cook, would appear to count heads and lay for supper accordingly. A whole world of people that were kind to me, teased me too, fed me copiously. No household since has produced more than enough chips, gold crisp for any number of people. The Croziers rescued me and adopted me without hesitation. San and I were inseparable from then on.

Paddy, San's brother, was thirteen years older. He played boogie on a grand piano in the billiard room, which made him a demi-god. His room, a glass-enclosed porch with a huge bed and a sound system, was ours to use to jive and practise dance duos. His music was jazz and big bands, Sinatra, Fitzgerald, and Bing Crosby and it was always playing. Paddy had a contact who had a knack for getting the latest releases from the London musical stage. Later, when puberty knocked and romantic ideas ballooned, we mastered all the songs of West Side Story and My Fair Lady before they were released in South Africa. His voluptuous girlfriend Maryanne had a conspicuous cleavage and cataracts of blond curls. She wore a pungent perfume and a wide smile. She hugged me often. Of course he worshipped her. I did.

Paddy and Maryanne took us everywhere, often to the drive-in cinema. Always, whenever they went. They did a lot of kissing in the back seat. San and I sat in front with trays of chips hooked over the windows, steadfast eyes forward. It was heaven; to me, even then, it was miraculous that a courting couple took 'the kids'.

Being wanted was what it seemed.

Soon it became my home for weekends and many a holiday. Gradually, family secrets surfaced, sensed rather than spoken of. San's mother, a quiet, gentle woman, far from a beauty with sad eyes, seldom spoke. On her strong days, she came to sit in the sun and knitted. Mostly, she stayed abed with gin. San would remove the gin bottles from underneath her mother's pillows last thing at night. It was never mentioned but silently done by her children or Mac.

Sanie's father was seldom about. So seldom that some mentioned another household. He was a salesman, a sole agent for upmarket clothes, Stetson hats, Hawes and Curtis shirts and Paisley silk ties. Selling meant travelling to take repeat orders. He returned home only for a change of clothes when he emptied his pockets of loose change into two drawers, tiekies and sixpences for us for an ice cream and pound notes and half-crowns for Paddy and Marion. San would ration what was proper, no more than one or two a week.

That was an unspoken lesson for one as poor as we were. The poverty of us and the restraint in them meant wealth was never ostentatious, nor was money ever mentioned. Although nothing was withheld, I never took it for granted because San didn't. Each day was pinch-me-this-is-fun; this is how life is for some: enough of everything but never more than enough.

Marion her sister, was twelve years older with a boyfriend, James. James did the scolding. He was the son of a vicar and did not like us to swear. Once, I defied him.

'Bloody, bloody, bloody' I shouted. James caught me a sharp slap across the cheek in front of a party of his friends. I was outraged. I dragged San behind the shrubbery and made her hit me over and over until my cheek flamed red. James was unrepentant.

'My, you've caught the sun!' he said.

It would be easy to dismiss the ease and generosity as merely the overflow of wealth. It was much deeper than that. I learned later that the marriage had been a harrowing second choice for Sanie's father. I suspect a shotgun component. The gap of years between Sanie and her siblings created a second parentage; those cinemas that included us were the signals of a cheerful acceptance of responsibility. Ma was abed with a bottle, Pa was never home, and Mac was off duty; the kids must come with us. Paddy was my paragon pretend-brother, a perspective that sharpened the whittled stick of what I would never have known without him.

We had bicycles to roam further afield and throw unripe plums at passing cars from the botanical gardens. The concentric centre of our lives became the stables near Inanda. Paddy would drop us off every weekend to curry comb, muck out, and hang over railings to watch the show jumping. Intoxication was the world of horses. Gymkhanas, rosettes, saddle soap and the daily hack out in thundering groups that knew where the canters could begin. We would rush for the list pinned to the office door past the line of horses saddled, heads down, asleep, waiting under the line of shady tether trees.

"You lucky so-and-so! You've got Blaze! Swap?"

"With who?"

"Mole?"

"Not likely; Mole's a moke, hardly moves."

"Oh hell, I've got Snowy again."

The stable owner, Georgina, had a beau called Frank, a rat-faced, pock-marked, gnawed David Niven with a pencil moustache. A spectacular dare-devil, he took perilous jumps, lifting his animal with impeccable timing as though by a celestial cable. Front legs clear, he lifted the rear, the landings as precise as the take-off. Worshipped by our horse-mad bevvy of fans Frank swaggered in his skin-tight white jodhpurs, his flat tweed cap, and his highly polished boots, the only man in town. Bees-knees, dishy-duke, wow!

I scarcely ever thought of my mother and hardly went home. She was generous about consigning me to a richer world. If she was hurt, she never showed it. I knew that the riding stables cost more than she could afford. When she found a second-hand, black Savile Row hacking jacket, I felt equal to all the surrounding wealth. She never begrudged what she had no share in.

Her lonely Sundays stretched. Milly was at church, and I was oblivious.

By degrees, we advanced through dressage and show jumping to the drag hunt, which happened further afield. The Inanda hunt had a formidable Master. Mounts were expected to turn out immaculate, as though in Berkshire. Shaggy ponies were not welcome. Somebody lent me a mount painted by Stubbs, a thoroughbred called Pomeroy, a chestnut Arab with a racing neck. In truth a racehorse, but nobody thought to mention he had just come off the track. At the first bugle call, the field broke into a slow canter, the hounds gave voice, and Pomeroy was off to an instant gallop, streaking ahead of the Master and the Whips—utter disgrace. I struggled to bring him around and circled the field three times before he put his foot in a hole, fell, and threw me over his head. I managed to hold onto the reins with a broken arm, Pomeroy back on his feet and quivering to rejoin the race.

The Master swore as he passed. "Don't ever bring that animal here again," he shouted, coiling his long whip and cantering away, leaving me hanging helplessly onto the white-eyed animal, snorting and pawing the ground.

A rider dismounted and examined my useless arm. He was a doctor. With a large handkerchief, he devised a temporary sling. He gave me a leg-up onto Pomeroy and led us back to the meet by a shorter way, through a river so deep we had to lift our feet. What drama! I saw us as a book cover, an embryonic romance with my saviour and two heroic horses stumbling home. He had plaster of Paris in the boot of his car; he mixed it in a bucket and set the broken bone there and then. The delayed shock had me trembling and very cold, ashamed but elated. Summoned to dauntless courage, I would not wince; shame must be rescued.

The doctor offered to drive me home and accompanied me in the lift and along the grim walkway to our impoverished Hillbrow flat. Hunting people lived in mansions and hide-n-seek gardens. I quailed. Ndaba was Sunday best dressed and about to depart for church. Louie was out.

"Ow Darling! What can happen to you?!"

Satisfied I would be cared for, the doctor departed after giving me his card.

"Come to my consulting rooms on Tuesday. Rest tomorrow. I will X-ray to make sure I've set it straight."

Milly stayed home and put me to bed. When Louie returned, I was feverish, and she feared concussed. She was angry at me and herself for finding me taken care of. Sure that a bone set without an X-ray would need to be re-set, she was all for taking me to the hospital until I explained I already had an appointment for an X-ray on Tuesday.

"I'll be at work on Tuesday."

"I can go alone. It's quite close. I know where he works…"

The bone was straight—only a green-stick fracture.

"Do you do everything alone?" the doctor asked while he was covering the plaster with a thick bandage.

"Mostly. My mother has to work all the time."

"You are, how old?"

"I'm already nine." He frowned. "I'm fine. I have a friend."

"Yes. You must have. All done. Come back in three weeks, and I'll cut you out."

That was the first time I registered how other people saw me: tragic or neglected, simply because I did what others didn't. There was no tragedy in it, but children are supposed to need adults, and I don't remember that I ever did. Not really, not in that way.

Do you see now how much your inner strength was your outer weakness? The paradox declared itself early.

What do you mean?

Your certainty or self-sufficiency yielded no handles. Relationships usually grasp for some need to begin. It may be a small one, for a companion, or just to be liked, or a bigger one, like empathy, but you failed to ask for anything. Life would have been easier if you had.

But Louie was overwhelmed, and Ndaba and Sanie gave everything without being asked. I recognised the freedom in giving; I lacked the need to need! Was that your plan for my future?

We all make our own plans. You choose your family. Something in you needed them, melded with them, celebrated them. Why else are you writing this?

Because you dragooned me!

You agreed to come, and you are starting to enjoy it. But have it your way; realise the loneliness ahead rose upon every choice you made, including restraint and fierce independence.

I did not know that independence was 'fierce'; I thought it was considerate.

That depended on who was reading it.

CHAPTER 6

Brother Paul: Basutoland

'If youth is the season of hope, it is often so only in the sense that our elders are hopeful about us; for no age is so apt as youth to think its emotions, partings, and resolves are the last of their kind.'

With Sanie I swung through trees of abundance, easy affluence, making no demands. Time was for tennis, riding or spying. Pre-adolescence pays little heed to anything but the here and now — oh, come on, kissing's boring. Why do they do it? — a missile fight with the boys next door or another swim? Sanie's father left tickets on his table: tickets to shows, cinemas, musicals and the height of the year, the Rand Easter Show, for two weeks of swashbuckling in jodhpurs and yellow polo-necked sweaters, mooching down to the fairground to be sick on the rotor or ten goes—' bet you can't'— on the dodgems, then return with a coconut. Free tickets to everything. How many rosettes hung above the stable doors? Who cared? Another class, another round of show jumping and the practice jump in the paddock with the passing public watching through the chain link fencing, envious of all this effortless privilege.

All I had to offer was our bleak flat —another round of drafts? Or a radio play? 'Do you want another drink?' 'Can you bear to come on holiday with me to Basutoland?'

My home world was devoid of spontaneity; there was nothing to explore. Louie worked, Ndaba cooked, and time lingered. Basutoland was now to be my summer holidays and would mean Marna expecting manners at table and Heli looking holy. Horses were the only escape, up the long dusty hills and back.

It had happened as Marna had predicted.

Heli's dedication received a kick. Africans were being denied education beyond basic standards in literacy. Secondary schools were closing. The only tertiary college for Africans at Fort Hare was being wound down. The British were in the process of betraying Seretse Khama by questioning his suitability for Kingship. Already losing his battle, Heli abandoned the Colonial Service and took up an option at Pope Pius Xll's Catholic Mission in Basutoland. He judged the Catholic Church a more established refuge in which to plough the furrow of African education. He accepted the offer to lay the early foundations of an African tertiary college, which would later become part of the University of Botswana, Lesotho and Swaziland.

The three landlocked British Protectorates encircled by South Africa, all tribally different, are distinctive in landscape and atmosphere. Basutoland —now Lesotho— is the mountainous African Switzerland, where high bare peaks succeed one another as frozen waves against the pale sky. Maseru, its modest capital, was a collection of tin-capped houses, a small hotel, unpaved roads and Government House, where the Union Jack limply embraced its pole. Portraits of King George V1 hung alongside the bright Basuto blankets in every store, and strings of the conical grass hats worn by everyone shifted in the wind. Horses, the dominant transport throughout this land, were sleepily hitched outside any place of gathering, cars were few.

Basutoland is very different from the desert sands and the relaxed tribes of the Batswana. The Basotho, a smaller, darker nation, pinched by the repeated attempts to subdue them, are proud of their fierce resistance. The barren mountainous landscape of snow-covered peaks and small herds roaming at will, maintain consistent hardship, summer and winter. They are the Spartans of the African legions, learning the quick raids under Moshesh —King Moshoeshoe— retreating into mountain fastnesses to gnaw on bare-bone victory. Babies born in winter are often left exposed to die. Unlike the expansive Zulus or the soft-spoken, courteous Ugandans, the Basotho is unyielding. They ride rough horses with a distinctive tripling gait, between a canter and a trot, over stony ground, wrapped in bright coloured blankets and disappear with the efficiency of a posse. Suspicious, they seldom greet unless greeted first. Welcome is far from certain. It is not what Heli is used to. Their language, Sesotho, defeats him.

Roma Mission lay thirty miles southwest of Maseru, where portraits of the Pope replaced the King. Pope Pius XII College was built at the head of a broad valley, gazing at the naked Maluti Mountains, devoid of vegetation, combed by cold. On the rump of a rising slope, spread the arms of the Administration, a brutal building of uncompromising granite, crucifix glinting in the sun. The educational needs of the Catholic priesthood would be isolated from any distractions.

Below, half a mile distant, are temporary classrooms, a refectory, a chapel, and stables, surrounded by pecking hens, the odd goat, and scrawny cows. Deeper into the valley is the brick-fortress seminary, where young priests, many Irish, severed from their gentle rain-sodden landscape, are being lashed to the rigours of abstinence, facing a future barren of promise or surprise. At a fork in the road to the seminary lies a school surrounded by dirt; on a spur ahead, the convent and infirmary, and down a long hill, the general hospital with perhaps thirty beds. Within a few square miles, an entire mission village looks like the hurried leavings of a celestial picnic, half-chewed debris scattered by the wind.

Catholicism would have to offer large compensation for bringing their new recruit here, not to mention his imperious wife.

There was no house suitable even for an estranged marriage, adding insult to the injury already inflicted. Marna and I, during holidays, would lodge with the doctor; Heli would have a room at the convent while he supervised the building of a house. He would design it, but since he was neither in nor out of the cloth, it would be beyond all the enclosures on the furthest limit of Catholic influence. Surrounded by a panorama of mountains and in the same hewed granite that would have been suitable for El Escorial, it would withstand external weather but not the growing internal chill for both of them.

Our first Christmas with the Austrian doctor introduced me to an

African midnight mass. A compulsory afternoon nap preceded a small supper of savoury pastries, not a heinous breaking of the fast. Together we walked with lanterns to the convent church, lit by candles and smelling of blankets and sweat. Seated in front with Marna, I watched the unending shuffle of the celebrants receiving communion; in the silence, the muttering of the priest over each bowed head and supplicating hands. What mysterious drama was this? The silent returns from the altar completed, the genuflections and breast crossings over, then the extinguishing of the candles, one after another.

Profound quiet yielded, in utter dark, an African high summer night, the calling of distant owls outside.

Only the wimples of the nuns near the altar broke the black. Even Marna was quelled; that habitual sniff of disapproval stayed silent.

At the stroke of midnight, the high tinny bell outside creaked and tolled, and the congregation burst out with ululating halleluiahs that continued as the candles were re-lit. Never repeated, but never bone-shiveringly equalled.

Truly, Christ was born.

Christmas dinner followed, near one o'clock at night, the full complement of roast goose and additions, but I fell asleep at the table and was carried to bed. Christmas drama was magic!

The new house is christened 'Mountain Folds' and is now a house uncompromisingly divided; Heli folded in his study bedroom at the extremity, without any direct access to the rest. An external door admits students and message-bearing subordinates; Marna has the run of the remainder. It is not an abundant place to invite a friend, even an understanding one like Sanie.

Heli goes to Mass daily at six and appears for dinner at eight. In between, he passes windows in his academic gown on the way to and from lectures. To his main subject, Native Law and Administration are now added Philosophy and English Literature, another crack to be repaired between the two cultures. Reports to Whitehall, where the curriculum is still decided, are becoming increasingly irritable. Lying on his study floor, brass coin rubbing or constructing Meccano bridges, I hear the explosive epithets; 'insanity', 'bureaucratic blindness', and occasionally more damning. The gulf between elementary education in South Africa and tertiary aspirations in Basutoland would have to be bridged somehow and elsewhere.

As a sometimes quasi, surrogate Governor, with his understanding of Native Law, ritual murder cases fell within Heli's ambit; the collection of gruesome evidence, mostly of babies, followed by innocent explanations not susceptible to British jurisprudence. They were not frequent but more common among the Basotho than he had realised, and his need for interpreters irked him because he could never entirely trust the evidence or fully understand witnesses. The influence of the witch doctor underscored those things beyond the reach of the hospital clinic.

Heli became increasingly crucified by his loyalties to education, to governance, to marriage and the impossibility of reconciling or doing justice to all of them. The young priests who taught with him floundered; their catechism never matched by any secular subject. Teaching was never more than one step ahead of the next class. Heli's attempts at remedy were a continual strain. He would launch a lecture to get it underway and leave a young ordinand to complete it, making haste, late for his own lecture. Hopes, so fresh in Bechuanaland, wilted under the weight of his responsibilities and the absence of help. One or two lay teachers came from England. Not many stayed long.

I began to register the cooling temperature drifting between my grandparents; whisky was the Dutch courage of Heli's suppers with us. Catholicism appeared to need additional oiling. I could talk to neither about the other.

Marna's maids were all demure, convent-educated, with names like Benedicta or Annunciata; Catholic habits invaded even her pantry preserve. During their time off after lunch they would teach me the challenging clicks of Sesotho. I can still say, 'Tomorrow I am going to ride the strong horse' in Sesotho, about as useful as 'my Postillion was struck by lightning' in French.

The aimlessness changed on my second Christmas morning. It was not just what was gifted but the manner of the giving.

Before the sun was up, Heli woke me. He took me in pyjamas out to the garden fence, where a horse was saddled and tied in the gloaming of early light, with the cocks crowing and the mist against the distant mountains. It whinnied gently as we approached.

"Your Christmas present," Heli said. "Happy Christmas, Phil. Now you can choose his name."

"He will be Noel." Heli accepted the arms flung about his neck and unwound them gently. I think he had tears, but they might have been mine.

Noel was no child's pony but a mettlesome, strong, half-broken horse who would give hands and knees blisters. He stood nodding as though that was okay by him.

Inside, Heli gave me an enormous box.

"Since I could not wrap Noel, you have to have this." It did not rattle. It was not heavy. It must be a pillow. Or a horse blanket? Ten layers of packaging, box after box, paper after paper, until there, in the centre, in a matchbox, was a small horn-handled penknife with two sharp blades and a hoof pick! Between the layers of that wrapping lay Heli's undemonstrative but tireless affection.

I was never required to be a girl for Heli.

Together, Noel and I discovered the limits of one another. The early dawn of that morning has ever since penetrated Christmas. Noel was the blessing of independence and the freedom of the entire country. Horses had always been lonely Heli's companions; nowhere were they more essential than in the horse-dominated world of Lesotho. It was the equivalent of a teen's first car. I was just ten and had had no lessons in breaking in. Horses were the single means of access to the closest general store, most mountain peaks and the exploration of the deep dongas, which split the valleys to the foothills in frozen black lightning. I could ride invisible in their depths and shadow.

I could go anywhere and every day. I was never told when to be back or asked where I was headed. Nor did I need protection from the wild and remote mountains or those inscrutable people.

Marna packed me food and picked a quince stick from the convent orchard. Wherever Marna lived, there was somehow always a quince tree, always mint below a dripping tap and always Brompton stocks planted under windows for their scent.

It is difficult to convey the assumption of safety, but we were at home as much as the Basothos were; they might not have been forthcoming, but that was their nature, not because we were white. They were equally suspicious of other tribes. I only encountered threats passing the school, where precocious adolescent boys would try to grab the reins and pull me down. I got used to that and rode through them at a gallop on my way to the hospital with messages for the doctor.

I was slow to read those sexual intentions.

Of course I was. Abstinence was total in my family, although nudity was not. Both Marna and Louie stripped off with alacrity on beaches or beside a mountain pool.

Noel made Marna's errands less taxing. She could afford to be forgetful. I was now happy to be occupied with another five-mile ride to the store. Men, squatting between ploughs and cutters, were silently watchful as I climbed steps to the broad apron festooned by bright blankets. The dark interior smelt of maize meal, tobacco and cooking oil. Saddlebags, loaded with sugar or flour, the same silence observed my departure, not hostile, merely passively watchful.

Noel gave me physical escape, but on our long climbs up to the high peaks, circled by wheeling raptors, casting our plodding shadow ahead, he emphasised my solitude. He gave me knowledge of Heli and my mother, both dogged and alone, both stoical and disciplined. I longed for a friend to share the companionship of my patient horse. Sanie was behind, and how could I offer so lean a landscape after her largesse? How would she see my penitent family? How would she pass the day without pools, games, or music?

More urgently, I longed for a man for my mother. I saw her future of bitterness, following Heli, denying life by duty and, with it, growing blind to warmth. Warmth was still Marna, growing silent, writing endless letters, but always responsive to my return.

"There you are, darling, just in time for supper. Good ride?"

The mountains, barren and forbidding, became familiar through the travelling clinic. Martha Sigmund, the Austrian doctor, another earnest priest in all but name, single-handedly ran the hospital, raised funds, wielded a scalpel, extracted teeth, and once a month on a Thursday, she set off for the high peaks. Once, I went with her at Marna's suggestion. We took a pack-mule laden with drugs and visited the villagers who could not come down to us. They cleared a hut for us to sleep in. On the bleak hillsides, they waited, those silent conical figures wrapped in bright blankets, maybe fifty or more. Among the clean swept huts with the stunted peach trees, remembered as always in blossom, there would be, even in high summer, patches of stubborn snow between the rocks.

Martha set up a makeshift table. One by one, they came forward, producing wizened babies or small pot-bellied children from under the blankets. Martha vaccinated, provided drugs and advised on malnutrition until the last had disappeared into remote ramparts. On one of her clinic trips, Martha had almost ridden over a baby left exposed to die. She adopted him and called him 'Masapo'. It means 'skin and bone' in Sesotho.

Martha gave forty years of her life to those austere people; austere herself, she had an affinity with their restraint and poverty. Although I admired her, she never allowed me to get close. I suspect that she tolerated me as a favour to Heli.

After a few holidays alone, I had Brother Paul.

Marna fell for his lilting Irish voice and his mop of black hair, and he matched her teasing, giving her impromptu shoulder hugs. 'Go on with you, you Celtic princeling,' she'd say, coy and smiling. The femme he encountered was not formidable; he saw what I did. She was caramel-centred. Brother Paul seemed the answer to my prayer. His calling surely could be re-called, given an incentive? For a ten-year-old solitary, he was the perfect companion until he could marry my mother.

In the long summer afternoons, we rode together up to the mountain pools to swim, Paul singing 'The Londonderry Air' and 'The Mountains of Mourne' in a voice as relaxed and resonant as Bing Crosby, his cheeks often wet. I was simply content to listen and love him as the footfalls beat small drums on the hard-baked ground. His voice echoed off the jagged outcrops of rock and swept down into the valley behind.

> 'Oh Danny Boy, the pipes, the pipes are calling
> From glen to glen and down the mountainside
> The summer's gone, and all the roses falling...
> But come ye back when summer's in the meadow...
> ...the valley's hushed and white with snow...

We stripped off and changed behind separate bushes, and then, sunning on the rocks, he would talk about Ireland.

Brother Paul's Story

"...being one of eight for me poor mother, and no father to speak of, he dropped by only to leave me mother another belly before the able seaman set sail. I allays wondered what the 'able' referred to. The poor in Oireland had not too many options you see. Our village school in Cork was a scuff-boot, palm-lick sort of place, where all you learnt was how to use yer fists and stay out of sight. I used to sneak away to help on a farm, me mother was that grateful for fresh eggs; she pretended not to wonder how I came by them.

"Had one teacher though, grand he was at the reading. He gave us poems to learn by heart, not so much to train the mind, but he said it was the heart that could hear the music in them, sung aloud. It's the truth, you know; understanding the meaning is only the half of it. All the while, the Church was just bidin its time, waitin' to feed me and two of me brothers, and a few more besides. In Oireland, dere's a smooth-runnin rail from altar boy to the choir, den a small jump to seminary and den after a life in clodes too cold or too hot for de climate, we have the promise of a nun bringin in the bread and soup in an infirmary. A life laid out, start to end, see?

"So here we are, for the enduration as I call it, all of us here frozen, homesick, and no use in that state to spread faith, supposed to be good news. Sometimes, I wish I'd kept the singing quiet, fool that I was. Instead, I'm first to be called for the choir and leading the responses. I'd prefer to use the voice for something better, but dere y'are… I sometimes wonder why the Good Lord gave a man such a doirst for adventure and de glories of de world only to dress him in black to say no to all of it. Bit late to ask such questions now…"

"Marna thinks I am half Irish. She always sends me a green ribbon on St Patrick's Day.

"Nooo…never. Ged on wid'ya? Grand she is, your grandmother, and that's the truth, but she's never Oirish. I'd know if she was."

"Not her. It was my other grandmother. I've never met her."

"D'you know which part of Oirland she hails from?"

"Where there is a lot of racing. She keeps horses."

"Could be County Kildare…or maybe Killarney- dere tis a beautiful course, sittin jes below the McGuillycuddy Reeks, dat's a mountain range, but was dere ever a better word for the flyin clods of a soggy Irish race meetin? Gilly cuddy, gilly cuddy. See them go. Can't you just hear them now? Leavin specks of mud on the kiddies' faces …Ah well, we Oirish are good at three tings: words, whisky and wool, and allays de horses. But one thing, girl, I tink I must believe you. We would never have met in Oirland, but I recognised something familiar… Mebbe tis dose green eyes… Oh Lord, would you listen to me? Tis nearly time for evensong. God forgive me, getting carried away in praisin the place I chose to leave!"

∽

After stabling the horses, he would take me home on the back of his bicycle, my wet hair leaving a patch on his black cassock. He was always late, pedalling furiously and waving behind on departing: my tailor-made father-to-be.

Once, he was driven to an apocalyptic anger only shared by the bare-chested Christ cleansing the temple of Michelangelo's Last Judgement. I was changing out of my swimming costume and was jumped upon by a young Basotho. Two or three others were laughing. I just thought it excessive exuberance, until Paul loomed above the rocks, without a shirt, with his riding whip, laying about, lashing with real fury. The young Basothos fled. On the way home, Paul was tight-lipped, saying nothing. I was perplexed by a wild reaction so unlike him.

Nothing was quite as easy afterwards.

It was years before I understood his anger and his imprisonment. He could not protect me from that or admit how he knew I might need protection. Nor could he raise the issue, my intended father, who never met my mother. He was my first blind and easy male love after Tom and, in that, joined Sanie's brother Paddy.

Brother Paul and Heli shared fate in my mind. They were both victims of Catholicism, snared and entrapped; both too big-hearted to fit that collar and forbidding shoe. It has always seemed a form of abuse that love and allegiance so willingly given should have exacted so sharp a penalty. They felt called to something reputedly 'higher' that cared nothing for them. The cost to them and the Church was the pickling of their hearts; both reduced to misery. Decades later, I heard that Paul had left and married, fathering a Catholic brood. I hope that was so.

An echo of that brought about the same reaction in Heli. An elderly priest tried surreptitiously to unbutton my shorts while I sat beside him on a bench. I slipped away. I referred to it jokingly at supper. Heli threw down his napkin, stormed out to the car and drove off in fury. He called at the seminary. When he returned, he told me I was never to ride that way again or speak to the old priest. Sex, when it lifted its head later, had not had a good Advent calendar from the reactions of the two men who loved me.

I was heedless of that future, for I was still longing for my mother to find someone to help her laugh. Little did I realise that laughter was already in flight.

What you describe would be seen as willful innocence.

Do you mean 'not real' innocence?

Quite the contrary. I said 'seen as' because real innocence has almost disappeared. Children are innately unselfconscious. They absorb everything without imposing interpretations. Adults interpret for them, but you had few to indoctrinate you about religion, sex, or the urges of male adolescents. You simply report how it was. The sexualisation of children is an adult depravity. Why else do the Jesuits ask for children until they are seven? To hold them thereafter for life?

Because innocence is malleable?

Once usurped, lost forever.

CHAPTER 7

Max; and First Loneliness

'Every day's experience seems to deepen the voice of foreboding... The bliss of reciprocated affection is not allotted to you... possessing the fervent love of any human being would soon become your heaven; therefore, it would become your curse.'

On the horizon of Sanie's embrace and our heedless freedom, a lowering cloud loomed. Her sister Marion had been at school in Natal with her own singular best friend, Jocelyn Eagle, whose younger sister, Daryl, was already earmarked to be Sanie's best friend. It was never explicit, but I was made aware of it by Marion's slight reserve and occasional mentions of the future. I would do to be getting on with, but I was temporary. Sanie would leave me for St Anne's, a boarding school in Natal. It was hinted that I should prepare for that. Daryl and her nest of Eagles lived in Northern Rhodesia; boarding school would bring the younger sisters together.

For six years San and I had moved from childhood to teens, without parents present, never instructed when to brush teeth, go to bed, or change underwear. Like sibling puppies free to tumble, explore, and sleep, our transition had been heedless, free, abundant and unconscious.

When secondary school loomed, it came to pass, as foretold. My abundant world was shuttered, our freewheeling habits were shrouded with dust cloths, and the light of my life was switched off.

I was restored to solitude and loneliness, now as sharp as a stone in a shoe.

I was a full-fledged day girl at St Mary's Diocesan School, my erstwhile dormitory. and travelled by bus from the tenement flat, accompanied by Ndaba to and from the bus stops in the roaring commuter traffic of Hillbrow.

Without boogie, Paddy's laughter or the stables for company, my solitude had to invest in study. Lessons in French and Latin gave a glimpse of a wider, other world. Mrs Freeslick, a gaunt, tall classicist, fired me on Greece, and politics came closer too, with a rare chaplain, Trevor Huddleston, later lauded as a champion in the fight against apartheid. Marna met the famous during the Boer war, Smuts, Cecil Rhodes, Baden Powell, Sir Percy Fitzgerald, and his dog Jock: I met the famous and infamous in the race war fifty years later.

Maybe we all perceive those we know personally as diminutive against those who shine from the perspective of hearsay. Or the imprimatur of history when they stand on plinths, and we have to look up, blinded by the sun of their reputation?

Huddleston came from the Community of the Resurrection's St Peter's Church in Sophiatown to take our Sunday services. His Mother House, Mirfield in Yorkshire and that of our nuns, the Community of St Mary the Virgin in Wantage, were both the Anglican educational orders derived from the enlightened Oxford Movement, male and female, founded at almost the same time in England. It was a natural choice for him to be appointed chaplain. All were celibate, most Oxbridge educated.

Only later did Huddleston gain the reputation of a quasi-saint for his persistent and courageous opposition to apartheid. For us, he was simply our chaplain, who conducted the Sunday communion service. An arresting man, he would stride in, in a flowing cassock, with his determined chin elevated, his beak nose, and his prominent fly-away eyebrows in constant movement. His swift passage suggested he was already preoccupied with more important missions. His sermons were always about Christian obligations in the face of oppression. He left us in no doubt about who was being oppressed, and what it behoved us to do and to think about.

It was not usual to hear such explicit attacks on white privilege in the heart of white privilege. It was clear we were among the guilty. Huddleston was no Savonarola spewing brimstone, but rather like

Heli, only more explicit because he was working where the injustices were rife. I did not realise that his multi-racial parish in Sophiatown was facing the bulldozers, not then. Nor that his child protégé, the trumpeter Hugh Masekela, would invade my home and render valuable service later. Nor that the destruction of his school in Sophiatown would lead to a multiracial replacement in Swaziland —Heli's dream fulfilled— where both Seretse Khama's son and Mandela's son would be educated, and among them, Louie would end her days. The seeds of our future are threaded as though sequences were coloured beads along time.

The future is just as causative as the past or the unjust present.

South Africa is a large landscape but a small country for those alive to its tensions.

○○

Louie was always drawn to Jews. My recognition of their Judaism came many years later since, unlike Catholicism, it lacked any obvious hair shirts, no breast crossings, genuflexions, or sombre Sundays. Her best friend was a barking woman called Thelma Phillips. She barked out questions like a fox terrier that had seen a rat, but underneath, she was shrinking shy. Her mouth snapped out questions even while her shoulders hunched against her neck as though she was afraid of the answers. I liked her dry, sardonic teasing because she spoke to me just as she did to Louie. She never talked down. My answers disappointed her because I was never reading anything she approved. What I was reading was always her first question.

"It's another Famous Five."

"Oh, dear! No, really?"

"It's a good story."

"No, it's not. It is about silly girls in a dorm, thinking up japes."

"What's a jape?"

"The sort of word that the sort of writer, Enid Blyton, uses for unimaginative things that she thinks girls like you would like to do."

"Well, I would. I'd like to meet other girls and get up to japes. But

I'd rather ride Black Beauty or My Friend Flicka."

"There are other gangs you could join, like Arthur Ransom's gang, who go sailing?"

"I've tried Titty and her sisters. They're wet. They get excited about silly things like being out late. I mean! The dark happens every night. Not a big event, is it?"

"You have to learn to distinguish between writers who create something new and those who just churn out what is old."

"Japes are not old for me."

That wasn't true anymore. Sanie and I liked throwing rotten oranges at passing windscreens from the botanical garden and ducking behind its wall if we scored. We engineered fights with her neighbouring boys and plotted ways to trap sunbathing couples too distracted to watch their clothes. Japes were frequent, but we called them a dare-you hoot.

"No, I suppose not," said Thelma through the smoke of her cigarette, which she clamped in her teeth in a long black holder. Thelma wore slanted glasses on a red string that slipped down along her nose. She was constantly pushing them up like a praying mantis cleaning its eyeballs. Thelma taught English at the University and lived alone, close by, with her thin grey cat. She was like a character in a book: a Miss Marple, quietly clever. I don't know how her Jewishness arose; I just knew she was. Maybe Thelma was the reason I believed all Jews were clever, and later, when I knew about the Law, I found them liberal and courageous, except for one.

Thelma made fun of everything, not just me, so I never minded, because she thought me sharp enough to understand she only half meant it. She brought good things to eat and wine to celebrate my going to bed. Louie always laughed with Thelma, although she said she didn't know what Thelma saw in a 'bear with a small brain.' Louie meant herself. They had another friend from the hospital called Alison. I don't remember meeting Alison, but I heard how beautiful she was. She left physiotherapy and Johannesburg and went to England to marry a doctor. Louie thought she was mad to marry as she did not have a pressing reason like a me.

"Edgar has appeal, undoubtedly," said Louie. "But no man can be worth that sacrifice. Psychiatry is hardly Medicine, just certified quackery." I knew she was thinking of Tom, and after my father, Medicine guaranteed nothing; no marriage should come before a profession. I well knew why. 'Profession' was Marna speaking, who had never had one.

∾

Because Louie regarded Jews as naturally cultured, invariably politically liberal and generous, I was not prepared for Max. He defied all the values she believed were inherent in Judaism. Johannesburg's theatres, orchestras and galleries were almost entirely supported by wealthy Jews, as was the field of Medicine, on the fringes of which Louie's life moved. Many of her patients became her close friends, invariably sensitive to our relative poverty and quiet in their unobtrusive ways of augmenting it: a carton of her favourite menthol cigarettes on her bed if she was to stay, or a pretty dress they had 'outgrown' but which looked new to me. So, the first Jewish villain, clearly visible and casting a shadow, took some time to be fully seen.

Max, whom Marna called 'that delicate Jew', made a mountain out of being Jewish. None of the others had. Whether they were observant or not was never mentioned. Max was first introduced as another new patient, one with a slipped disc. His marriage had also slipped; it ended on 'Black Friday' when he lost all his money and was thrown out of his meringue mansion by his wife. The gleaming mansion, which I viewed on a drive-by, had columns, round windows, a tennis court, a swimming pool and what Louie called 'staff'. Max, now a decorated bankrupt, had moved into a single-roomed flat in Rosebank. A single room meant that I had to remain in the car with a book while Louie treated his back, so I heard a great deal about him before I met him.

Max's Story

In all the years I had to contend with Max, I never heard him speak of his past, his parents, his wife, or his children, so his story is like a pinboard mock-up of a chief suspect in an unsolved crime. There were fragments from witnesses, occasional facts, mostly the Max that Ndaba and I deciphered. He is better defined by the spaces unfilled. Not even straight lines connect them. I never saw him lost in a book, softened by an animal, or arrested by a view or new idea. His laugh was reluctant and tinged with contempt. Anecdotes always carried his victories, legal acumen and sporting triumphs against the odds.

I heard his father was Lithuanian, a brave immigrant fleeing from a pogrom, which sounded to me like a warthog breaking out of a wood. At ten, I was not yet familiar with Holocaust horrors, although they must have featured large in the papers. Our own horrors took immediate attention. Almost all the Johannesburg Jews had fled from something. I knew that much. I heard Max was a successful lawyer, so successful that he lost a lot of money, but Louie said losing money happened to everybody who had any. We didn't know any people with money, and now there was one more.

Louie seemed to admire Max. I realised he had been saved by losing money big time and being a victim of circumstances, as well as his greedy, heartless wife, who kept the mansion and their two children. When I met the children, I thought he was the lucky one. 'Poor Max.'

Poor Max gradually regained his feet and occasionally entertained Louie to dinner. She had to take me. Before dinner, we would walk around the closed shops of Rosebank Mall, looking into windows where he stopped to point out things he wanted. Max liked carpets and watches. Louie pretended to be interested, but I just took a skipping rope and jumped while they looked. I knew she had decided not to mind, and that was what made me fear. My straight-backed mother was melting into curvature.

When it grew dark, we went back to his flat and uncovered dishes someone had brought. I thought his Jewish food disgusting: gefiltre fish and roll mops that just tasted of vinegar. He would tuck a napkin in his collar and slurp Borscht and, between mouthfuls, nod at me as if to slurp up enthusiasm. I just ate his matzos with lots of butter. Louie would frown if I failed to return the nods and the smiles or disguise my silent dislike of this odious creature. What possessed her to like him? How was she so blind to his obvious intentions? When she could have had Brother Paul? Louie had always been curious to me, but her interest in Max made her a complete enigma. She was my mother? I remember, even then, beginning to wonder anew if she really was.

Max was a creature I had a lot of time to study while they talked. He had legs that belonged to a jockey, so bowed he could straddle a beer cask between them and still stand upright. That was from playing soccer, or so Louie said. An awful lot of soccer would be needed to do that. Even his trouser legs followed the bends and came back to kiss at his ankles. His back was stooped forward, so it matched the curvature between his legs at right angles. His thinning hair strands, heavily oiled to his freckled skull, were spaced, ideal for a game of noughts and crosses. But it was his nose that won every argument. As noses go, it would have merited a Nobel prize. I knew a high bridge was reputedly a mark of intellect and character; many clever men had one, but this spoke too loudly. Its shadow created a mirage of a moustache, leaving his lips struggling to compete, whether speaking or smiling.

Max's face would have made a mask hanging at the ready for a seasonal Punch behind a theatre in a canvas beach booth. I have not mentioned the hole. His nose had a hole above one nostril as though drilled for additional air, a deep black hole that might have served a buried chameleon during hibernation. His wide, thin-lipped mouth carried a leer, a static grin. His black eyes darted glances; flint struck, failed to ignite, and struck again. Being looked at by Max was like being peppered with grape-shot.

I decided Max must be a pretend Jew; he was such a masterpiece of ugly. I could hardly look and could not look away, mesmerised, like watching a slow-moving adder. My revulsion was physical, the clenching in my stomach, the automatic inability to meet his eyes, the shrivelling at any accidental touch. I wholeheartedly loathed Max, but

I also feared him. I feared his clear intentions, and I knew he hated me.

Meanwhile, on Sundays, it was Max plus his whining children, car journeys to places they wanted to go, endless ice-creams and lots of crying.

'Ag pleez Deddy won't you take us to the drive-in…Popcorn, chewing gum, peanuts and bubble gum, Ice cream, candy floss and Eskimo Pie'

Louie's penchant for Jews increased fivefold for Jews with suffering attached. Max made the most of both, adding a duodenal ulcer to the slipped disc and guilt for all his creditors he was determined to repay. He was a man too honourable to accept bankruptcy. With Louie now becoming financially independent and prepared to slave, Max would have the whisky-in-milk to soothe the ulcer and the means over time to honour his creditors. Louie would repay as she did for all the meals he 'treated her' to. All of us would pay.

I spent nights wondering how to counter his inexplicable magnetism for my mother. She could not, must not, marry him.

Yet, I always knew she would. Given her prime injunction I also knew that if she did, it would be forever.

Wag-n-bietjie! You cannot just slip off when the real villain enters. So much to unpack here. This was the first test in which what you had been taught (all Jews are noble, educated, discerning and persecuted- to name a few of their claims) was violently at war with instinctive revulsion.

So?

You never sought to argue instinct away? For the sake of your mother? Or peace?

No, because I recognised a leech who would destroy her, and so did Ndaba!

An early authority offered to instinct? Max saw it and knew his legal hair-splitting would get nowhere. You were at daggers drawn from the start!

I saw it as defending my mother even if she was blind and defenceless through that blindness.

You never wavered? He presented nothing to cause a softening. Few are entirely black.

Sorry, no. Max was entirely calculating, which meant all gestures were suspect. I look back from seventy years and still cannot remember a single act of redemption. In refusing to buckle, I marshalled what I hoped was a valour for Louie, Ndaba, and undoubtedly for myself.

It will not be approved! Jews are not criticised.

He was my stepfather. Stepparents are fair game; fairy stories are full of their malevolence. I think that cliché pre-dates the taboo on antisemitism! Marna said one did not count. It was Max I disliked, not the Jew. I liked all the others.

Fair point.

CHAPTER 8

Judith; Romantic Longing

'That child pilgrimage was a fit beginning. Theresa's passionate, ideal nature demanded an epic life; what were many-volumed romances of chivalry and the social conquests of a brilliant girl to her?'

How does a child shape a view of love or marriage or its place in human affairs when there are no signs of any of these in early life? Love I had known from Milly, Marna and Heli but one at a time, almost a secret from one another. I loved them separately. Marriage had left only misery and bitterness in its wake for my mother, a barren silence for my grandparents. There were no fond photographs of weddings, no laughing images of children tickled, naked and joyful. I had no siblings experimenting with spotty suitors and returning to redraft the criteria. Reciprocated love was defined by its absence, something embryonic but dead in the womb, although it fostered great literature. If there was a purpose for life, where did it lie? In the great silence to be trodden alone?

I felt I belonged nowhere. That sounds like ingratitude. It isn't. I knew I had one marvellous friend, and my grandparents could not have done more; few unhappy elderly co-habitants stripped of love and lacking any means of alleviation would have done as much. But nowhere could I see what a loving bond might look like. We were all alone. Apart from Sanie, who accepted me as readily as her Mr. Pluts but could dispense with me equally easily, I had no belief that I was worthy of being loved. Why else would this non-belonging be so consistently reinforced? Like Marna, I seemed to attract only conditional acceptance for an interval. What was wrong with me? That has been the central question throughout my life. I do realise it is the counter-side of the longing coin. Did I want it too much? Or were we all too austere, too puritanical to foster ease? Life had to be harnessed to some great purpose, nothing less rewarded life's endowment. I just did not know what my great purpose was.

Only through books did I begin to assemble the heroic elements of what love might mean—none of those that I fell upon by chance painted love as comforting, perfumed or beribboned.

After too long spent with Enid Blyton in dorms or camping, I encountered Katherine by Anya Seton and devoured the high romance of John of Gaunt—what a name for a romantic hero! It was his loyalty, his defiance of convention in a lifelong love for his mistress, that laid down the first essentials; the soil in which love would flourish would be a solitary allegiance to the single heart. Duty or obligation was not it. They could be upheld, indeed should be upheld, but love was so deep as to be untouched by lesser loyalties. Love was an inner state offered to the single recipient for whom it completed life. It would brook no opposition; it would die before it surrendered to opinion; it would forge steel to bind intimacy. Nothing would bruise it or deflect its shining certainty. It was indeed the sun, constant even behind clouds. Those reflected in its glow would recognise it.

It had nothing to do with marriage.

Gradually, through books and potted stories about great works, I came to understand that heroic self-denial is the crucifying measure of highborn creative love. Beatrice fuelled Dante's pilgrimage to Paradise through the hell of the Inferno and the long sojourn through Purgatorio. It gave, for Petrarch, just a foot, Laura's bel pié, to inspire a daily song. Abelard's castration was the price he paid before he was interred with Heloise. Love was never going to be a ride in the park, nor was it the lash of those flagellants in monasteries who thought persecution would attract the favour of God. Methinks, they mistook what is a gift as a reward, and tried to earn and secure it.

There are more immediate forms of adding gelignite to the pearly gates now, like Ayahuasca and tantric yoga. None succeed for long. Their promises dissolve in the descent.

Heli loved Africa, its people and their aspirations, and suffered for it; Ndaba loved me and sacrificed her children; Marna loved laughter and truth. Her truth was early stripped of illusions, and laughter dressed her wounds. Louie loved Tom and denied it.

Only love's denial could explain that sustained energy, that dedication and that intensity. I had the perfect family to point out the differences between love and marriage. The puzzle is how or why we, all of us, settled for loveless marriages.

My vision, that love was a perfect human intimacy, a state of being, was a pretty tall order born out of my disappointment; people never lived up to love. Tom and Brother Paul were both for my mother, but she had settled for Max. I had yet to shape any conception of anyone for me.

∞

My focal point, around which life had orbited, was Sanie, and she was gone. Bleak loneliness replaced her. Life hung suspended and drafted no plans. It was unendurable.

I would have to follow Sanie to St Anne's. I pleaded, I begged, I wept and beat my fists on my pillows. Louie could not find the fees, but surely… but surely…?

Heli intervened. A single war widow, which in a sense was true, with an only child who showed promise? He secured a bursary. It took a year.

I would go. Guilt would clothe me: guilt at the shopping, the identical six shirts, the six pairs of flannel knickers, the three gymslips of hideous box pleats in navy serge, the raincoat, the overcoat, the games skirts, the twelve pairs of white socks and the reinforced trunk to ship them. Then, the sewing of Cash's name tapes on every item, including the washcloth and the sponge bag, and Louie tight-lipped at my ingratitude. I was already at a much better day school, no longer a boarder but at home with Ndaba. Why was that not enough?

It should have been.

∞

The school train whistled its steamy intentions and we pulled away from my mother standing to wave. Looking wretched, looking resigned, and already looking lonely on the cross of my existence. I waved. She turned away.

On the other side of the guard's van, a solidly occupied barrier to ensure our virginity, were boys off to Michaelhouse and Hilton College. The journey through the night started with coloured 'bed-boys' unrolling soot-smelling linen rolls and then sitting on crumpled sheets, passing the hours playing cards or consequences, and swapping sandwiches. We left in the early evening and would puff and hiss through halts all night until noon the following day. Once or twice, the driver stopped to relieve himself or pick peaches that grew along the track, and the older girls welcomed boys daring enough to take the opportunity.

I could make little sense of that first exposure to bravura but watched the whispering and sniggering at all that kissing. Such surrender to spotty youths both intrigued and repelled. Would I ever want *that*?

We were disgorged the following day at a dusty halt called Hilton Road. The boys were bussed away, already talking cricket without looking back. We walked, trudging up the stony road under a baking noon sun, and reached the forbidding gates of the long drive. Trunks would follow.

Unpacking was immediately supervised.

A dormitory of white-sheeted, iron beds looked like every Victorian hospital in the Crimea, windows wide open, curtains for cubicles roped to iron poles, lockers to be inspected weekly with a ruler applied to align the corners of perfectly folded shirts. The three dresses permitted for 'mufti' in the evening were allocated three hangers in a communal cupboard. Sanie told me where, what, and how. Then she left me to it.

She did not need me. Almost at once, I realised that I had miscalculated, catastrophically misjudged. I had assumed that my desolation was reciprocal. It wasn't. She had many easy friends, and I was a weight as I had none. I reproached myself and watched her absorbed by others. As before, always the centre of popularity, always the focus of plotting or celebration, always sought and wanted. I would recover her in the holidays when the others had dispersed and her new 'best friend' disappeared to Northern Rhodesia. That would have happened anyway. I had sacrificed an education for a longing she could not assuage and lost both.

San was never cold or unkind; she did not blame me for coming; she hoped I would 'fit in' and, by ignoring me, tried to oil that hope. I felt mortified; Louie had been right. I had surrendered a good, diverse, dedicated education for an illusion. I could not complain to anyone. Somehow, I had to wrest and shape love from what remained.

St Anne's was utterly loveless. It stood on a knoll caught by chill winds. Endless fog, so thick in winter that on a hockey pitch, the ball would cannon at you without a trajectory, was its abiding legacy, both physical and educational. I believe it intended 'rounded' students, and the grit of gritted teeth did produce pearls of unremarkable but safe accomplishments—no remarkable irregularity or baroque misshapen. Uniform creatures with brushed hair would be threaded onto the needles of marriage or worthy pursuits, like teaching or social work, until our children replaced us with the next recruits for the production line.

Gaunt, symmetrical, red brick gables overlooked a circular drive, winking at a tall cedar tree across an apron of grass. Next to that, an ivy-covered chapel with its rounded apse adhered like a blister, clothed in inflamed red leaves in winter. From the main house, a cold cement walkway with unadorned pillars flanked the examination and assembly hall towards the classroom block, as quarantined as a leper colony. There, incarceration shifted feet, discarded shoes, initialled desks with protractor points and passed cartoon vulgarities, sniggering hidden by raising a lid. Caught at it, you waited outside until the Headmistress slid past and crooked a finger to summon the 'follow me'.

Headmistress Miss Dorothy McEune, M.A. Oxon, was quietly

terrifying in her Virginia Woolf buttoned shoes and long cardigans. Not even the cigarette to waft delicious vice. Here was the inflexible schoolmistress who spoke not in words but in se-pa-rate syllables with deadly emphasis. Her quiet voice held menace, always.

It was a mean world in which to declare love. Mine burst out like a single camellia: love for a young teacher of Theology, fairly fresh out of Cambridge. Miss N.J. O'Riordan, M.A. Cantab, had been lassoed by McEune after they both did time at Abbotts Bromley, the school my mother attended in Staffordshire. My mother's stories of school were carbon copies of my own and from the same stable. Miss O'Riordan, whose father had known W.B. Yeats in Dublin, still had the vestiges of longing and its poetry, which was the hook that snagged my devotion as much as her obvious loneliness. It matched and echoed my own.

She had a striking, finely whittled nose that carved a sharp profile in a thin face. Her short-cropped, prematurely grey, wiry hair framed large, clear blue eyes that widened at surprise. Since she had not yet lived, surprise was almost constant. It gave her the look of a startled horse. Perhaps that was the immediate affinity.

O'Riordan, arriving just as I did, introduced me to the very corner of England that had claimed my mother. Staffordshire was the county she remembered dusting her Panama hat with snow on the way to Easter Church, with the daffodils already bravely out. The one that, for Louie, made the Resurrection more important than Christmas? You need an English winter to understand the Resurrection.

But it was the Greek that nailed it.

Agape, Charis, Eros; the distinctions of love. Miss O'Riordan wrote all three in Greek in the lesson when I took the pulse of her loneliness. She was alluding to love under the covers of Theology and Eros she knew nothing about. I saw the courage in admitting the word, giving it the glamour of Greek lettering, and her vulnerability in the crude world of heartless sniggering. She was a palpitating snail undefended by any shell of pretence. That handwriting and the perfection of the Greek alphabet was the arrow of Eros for me. Oxford, Cambridge, Classics, she brought them all in her spinsterish long skirts, her beautiful hand, and it all ignited scholarship in me. The flames of love flickered around her,

All gave me the excuse to write to her in the holidays. I wrote essays; she returned them. It was something. It was more than something; it was aspiration and dreams of mastery, culture and dreaming spires, but mostly Miss N.J whose cardigan, left on the back of the library chair, was no longer there for me to put to my nose and breathe deeply; the scent of a particular soap I still remember. There would be weeks before I glimpsed her vertical posture, sitting up in bed, sipping her morning tea as I headed for hockey practice through the frost and fog.

When she returned from a holiday accident with a leg in plaster, I could carry her books as she hobbled on crutches. Her nickname had been 'Carry-one'—Dot and Carry One —but crippled, she was cruelly renamed Hop-a-long Chastity. She was my new crucifix. I was nailed to her with contempt. Nobody 'sucked up' to staff. I was a toady, a goody-two-shoes and despised. Despised but defiant, I was solid and proud of myself, for I loved her utterly. Whether she knew it or not did not matter; she was Katherine to my John of Gaunt.

Stoicism ladled daily, and academic industry was the only path remaining, the path to her attention. By becoming an assistant librarian to be near her, I followed by reading abstruse texts like the Proceedings of the Lambeth Conference to get a grip on the Ecumenical Movement which seemed important to her. I was abject in my devotion.

It introduced me to worship, both of her and with her. Christ became important, if for no other reasons than the 'he was despised, rejected…' identification. And I learnt to pray— rather urgently. Chapel and the liturgy, weep-worthy hymns and the romantic poets followed. Miss McEune did the poetry. In her crystal syllables, she dropped Keats like shards of glass. What she first chose seemed very odd: The Pot of Basil. In this long poem, love is betrayed by greed, and the hopeful lover is slain by the beloved's two brothers and buried in a shallow grave. His head is recovered by the desolate girl, planted in a pot to nourish a Basil plant with her endless loving tears of wretched grief, her life over.

Even at the time, I knew it described what I felt.

> 'And constant as her vespers would he watch
> because her face was turn'd to the same skies
> And with sick longing all the night outwear
> To hear her morning step upon the stair.'

I felt that for O'Riordan, the arid constrained schoolmistress, loved also by McEune. I suspect she chose the poem as a warning. Inappropriate love would wreak havoc, as the 'murthering' brothers showed. It was as close to Virginia Woolf and Sackville-West as I was going to get. It ushered in Boccaccio, took me to Florence, and acknowledged the undying nature of love; Katherine was newly laced with tragedy.

It was a very wide-ranging and clever choice, and I did, even then, detect the personal within it. McEune never forgave me for my competing love.

They would live together all their lives. I would encounter the threads of Africa's influences later in England when their bungalow near Winchester, smothered with roses, was decorated like a shrine, not to Africa but to their joint tatty tourism through craft markets in their holidays. While I longed for contact with O'Riordan and the world she knew about, she gathered artefacts from the bushveldt roadsides I knew only too well.

Although I assumed we would drift apart when school finished, a link had been forged. In time, she would seek me on another continent despite herself. In secret she would escape McEune to talk over tea of the life she would never live, of which I would live a surfeit. I became her book of revelations, wrapped with grease-proof paper and tucked into the side pocket of a leather hold-all when she drove away, with a false alibi as to where she had been.

So, Theology was the ground on which this love exploded, safely spiritual, applying to Brother Paul, Heli and now Judith M.A. Cantab, each wedded to a longing no marriage would complete—denied at its root? Have you ever wondered why it, and they, drew you?

Longing denied only grows?

And deepens. Precisely. I mean that literally, which was why books pricked it out, beginning with Jackanapes. The Soul flies to the bosom of shared longing and longing shared bends the knees to worship, beyond both.

So, denial secures the lovers to a greater purpose?

Strange. There is no answer.

CHAPTER 9

George Eliot and Raymond, my father

'There comes a terrible moment to many souls when the great movements of the world, the larger destinies of mankind, which have lain aloof in newspapers and other neglected reading, enter like an earthquake into their own lives.'

My first brush with George Eliot was almost accidental. We were not encouraged to read fiction. The library had little fiction, but once we had completed the prep set, we could choose a book from 'the book room', which was a walk-in larder stocking moral food, in which the diminutive teacher of Latin chose suitable evergreen classics. Dickens, Trollope and Walter Scott stood in forbidding dull uniformity, but an arbour nestled; a shiny green dust jacket led to Adam Bede. Here was another variation on love, humility, faithfulness, and quick and appropriate anger. It also painted the England of country manners, lichen trades and nettle-stinging politics. Its meandering lanes of cow-parsley, mud and gated fields called loudly in that barren schoolroom.

Adam's love for Dinah was embroidered; his helpless love softly entwined with her ardent upright Methodism. It climbed against the solid structure, as Marna's irreverence did against Heli's Catholicism. It was with Adam Bede that, at sixteen, I met what literature was for through what George Eliot brought to it. Fiction was her way to unwrap her sensitivity to inequality, injustice, and the inhumanity of the law, but above all, the creation of wondrous people, those I longed to believe existed in life. Once dreamt and clothed in words, they remained alive, for I was privy to their thoughts. Her people peopled my loneliness.

With a single book, my eyes were opened to stories, but much more than stories. Stories as the peel over succulent revelations or astringent criticism softened and made palatable. George Eliot rose in heroic stature, not only as a woman, although that was important when I discovered that he was, but for exposing institutions and practices through people suffering from them. She carved out lives that she turned into everlasting art. The art was in taking me into kitchens, walking summer fields, sharpening sickles and the authority of an evergreen antiquity. England entered with churchyards, traditional harvest festivals, calling rookeries, and careful manners. It is not easy to convey the impact that such solid self-assurance trod in the windswept sands and haphazard seasons of South Africa, but it called out some deep familiarity. Marna and Heli both referred to our English legacy in dry words, but George Eliot painted in colour and pumped blood through its emotions. It would be hard to overstate the impact of such a created world, more real than reality, more vivid than history.

All the other George Eliot novels followed to give me permission for a sharp eye on triviality and a disregard for pomp. Middlemarch, much later, dissected the illusions about noble callings and the betrayal of marriage. I was an embryo Dorothea and forewarned about any would-be, empty, studious Casaubon. I recognised the atrophied scholar, who so disappointed Dorothea's naïve idealism and, from him, believed myself forever inoculated. I took note of him through the asperity of Mrs. Cadwallader, for she was Marna, and her shafts aimed true.

'When you get me a good man made out of arguments, I will get you a good dinner with reading you the cookery book.'

I wanted to hug Mrs. Cadwallader for bringing my grandmother into the schoolroom. I had no idea that Marna would do the same for George Eliot, deliver her to participate in a family dinner, or that George Eliot would almost conduct my life and blast through my perceptions of those closest to me. That will come, but in my sixteenth year, she set down her marker early.

Other pursuits anchored England. I was reasonably good at art and chose History of Art as an optional extra subject, which introduced me to Gothic architecture. Scale drawings of Chartres and Salisbury Cathedrals introduced a comparison between English and French Gothic and the structural advantages of the flying buttress for the increase of light. A metaphor that stayed with me. Clear vision requires distance, as Reggie, the soldier, with his lines of perspective, had first shown. What greater contrast or more emphatic distinction could there be than in soaring buildings raised on faith that took longer to build than our ephemeral African history had spanned in total time?

The hunger to know England was planted alongside the hunger to know love. The belief that Europe held all the glory, all the valued literature and all the experiences worth having was seeded in the barren monotony of love denied and little hope of change. South Africa's intellectual crudity was daily evident in the contrasts between the anorexic Oxbridge pair, Dorothy McEune and Judith, scuttling like spiders along the walls of corridors, and the local recruits. Diminutive Tessie, who wore bee-striped sweaters and stood arms akimbo and legs athwart in the centre. Buzzing the staff-room door, shouting 'Walk don't run' and Jessie, the maths mistress, whose dismissal of wrong answers was a standard "Gaow an chew brick!'

∾

Shortly after George Eliot's entry came that of my father, Percy Raymond Gavin. Louie informed me in a letter that he had requested to see me. She also added that he had threatened that if she refused consent, I would suffer financially. Since he had never contributed a penny postcard, she met his threat with contempt.

'He does not deserve to meet you, but I shall not refuse, for that would please him. He likes punishing the wrong people.'

Miss D McEune summoned me to attend her. She informed me that I was to spend a weekend with a man whose name I shared.

"You will be collected on Friday after lunch and return on Sunday before evensong."

"Where am I going?" She raised her eyebrows and tilted her head.

"I am not privileged with that information. You may go."

On Friday, I stood in a corridor, newly shined, outside her study with the red light menacing above the door, an emphatic signal that she was busy with a man who called himself my father. At the far end of the corridor, odd staff would come out to view the spectacle of a sixteen-year-old meeting her father for the first time. They hoped to get a glimpse of the touching scene.

Red changed to green. I heard a chair move, and the door opened. McEune held it ajar. A bluff, portly man hastened out, looking as though he'd been quelled.

"Well, well."

He tried to kiss me. I drew back. McEune concealed herself and quietly closed the door behind him, leaving the specimen of daughter being examined.

"Let me take your bag."

I let him do that. He walked ahead. What had I expected? I was disappointed by this overweight man with thinning hair in a blazer. He could at least have looked like the villain he was. He held the car door for me, and I sat as close to the window as possible. Getting a weekend away was unheard of, but this was not going to be anybody's treat.

"I've booked us into a hotel in Maritzburg. Thought we could take in a film," he said, looking at me repeatedly. I could see how alike we were. I think that pleased him and displeased me in equal measure.

"Have a fruit drop?"

"No, thank you."

"Look, Philly dear, I know this must be difficult for you. Let's get to know one another. How's your mother?"

"Well, as far as I know."

"Don't suppose your grandmother is still alive?"

"Yes. She is still more or less as she has always been." What a dreadful, smug man this non-entity father is.

"Real battle-axe. Hmm? Your grandmother. What did you call her?"

"Marna."

"That's right, I remember hearing that."

We were winding down the long hill to Maritzburg, the town where he had abandoned us and from where Louie had boarded a train for Maweni. I wondered if he made the connection but doubted that he made many connections. He was anxious to make a good impression. I was reluctant to offer it.

"How did you hear? You were gone long before I knew her." I asked.

That rattled him, and he took a moment to compose his reply.

"Look Philly…" I have never been 'Philly'. How presumptuous! "I know I have been absent from your life but I have kept tabs on how you were doing."

"Oh? Really? You had spies watching? Pity they never told you my mother could have done with a little help…" This angered him and I saw the flush rising on his neck and his knuckles whiten.

"I think it best if we keep off subjects that are not your concern. I would have supported you. I would have brought you to England to live with us. You would have been educated at a good school. You'd have had my children…but…"

"But without my mother? Yes, I see." I added, "And without my grandmother, who is no battle-axe. Marna looked after me for all the early years…" I was not going to let him get away with any criticism without challenging it.

"More's the pity. Without her wicked influence, you would have grown up in England."

I remained silent. Raymond took out a handkerchief and wiped his neck.

"Always forget how hot it is in Maritzburg. Never a breath of air."

"You were stationed here during the war, weren't you?"

This rocked him and he grasped at its implication.

"Talked about me, did she? Your mother?"

"No, not much, nor very often. I just knew about the army. You were a Captain and then an army doctor in North Africa. That's about it."

He stayed silent. A weekend fencing around his blustering and fishing would be endless. Sitting in a hot cinema with this stranger would be hell. If we went on to Durban, I could at least get a swim in the sea. I was suddenly completely uncurious about him. I did not want to get to know him. Instantly, I wanted to avoid any disclosures about the people I loved.

"Where is your wife? Your children? Did you leave them in England?" He was surprised I asked but rather pleased.

"No, Val and the kids are in Durban. I thought you would rather meet me alone. Bit of an imposition, what? Would you like to meet them?"

"Yes. Why not? Get it over for all of us." Raymond was disconcerted.

"You are certainly your grandmother's daughter."

"Granddaughter. Stem of Jesse."

"Quite. We'll drive on to Durban. Must just collect my bag and cancel the hotel. If you're sure?"

"Quite sure."

The beachfront hotel in Durban was a distinct improvement. Val and the 'kids' were out. I asked if he minded me taking off for the beach. He seemed relieved.

"You won't go far?"

"I am sixteen. How far does that give me?"

"Righty ho. I'll wait for them here. And we'll come and join you."

And have time to forewarn Val that she was about to encounter my grandmother's battle-axe, Gorgon's offspring. I just hoped he would not expect me to share a room with his 'kids'.

Val was exactly as I had imagined. Red talon nails and a red gash mouth with grave-stone teeth, which explained why he called her 'camel'. It betrayed a hidden humour; she chewed exactly like a ruminant, giving thought to the wisdom of swallowing. Her hair was the appropriate cross between dun and chestnut, and there was a lot of it. Her laugh burst out in short barks, and her hands plucked at her children's shoulders, a camel snatching grass. Nicola, about seven, was a precocious show-off; small, frail Anthony, who was about four, looked permanently afraid.

We spent the two days on the beach or in sand-strewn cafés eating chips. I made the most of the sea and built sand castles with the children but made no emotional contact with this self-contained quartet that had no part for me. I verified that Louie had been right about Raymond's meanness; he counted the change and questioned every outlay. He examined menus with care and cut corners by dividing up dishes. Raymond looked at me when he thought I wouldn't notice, and Val looked at him looking. He was fascinated. Val disliked me and his fascination and showed it. As it was heartily mutual, this pleased me. It would ensure no repeat of this encounter.

On Sunday, he dropped me back at school, and I let him peck my cheek. There was no suggestion of further contact or letters. That was it.

I wondered why he had bothered. Thank God he had run off with Cruella de Val with talons to scratch out eyes. I newly rejoiced at my mother's proud stoicism and Marna's scathing contempt for this diminutive anaesthetist. Meanness was the worst crime of all.

I had met my father.

But you did not notice the synchrony?

Of what?

You encounter a book that lights for you a country, and pronto from that country comes your father, who tells you that country might have been where you grew up had things been different.

At the price of him and his dreadful wife? And the loss of my mother, Marna, Uncle Tom Cobley and all? Thanks, but no thanks.

The synchrony was there, all the same. From which to formulate what was important. The genetic roots you rejected, but the emotional roots of England called and will reach fruition anon. Seeds sown on fertile longing tend to sprout.

CHAPTER 10

Great Aunt Mary and a Cat

'Destiny stands by sarcastic with our dramatis personae folded in her hand.'

Idealism, like Marna's sea sponge, holds a lot of water but, squeezed by reality, eventually dries out. Catholicism was beginning to prove a thin diet for Heli, as repetitive physiotherapy in government hospitals was exhausting Louie's belief in the virtues of service. The orthopaedic surgeons in Johannesburg had recognised her professional dedication, and she was the preference for almost all of them, increasingly in private practice. Wealthy patients with slipped discs or intricate fractures from skiing or car accidents paid much better. It was far from the vocation she had envisaged.

While I was lost in bizarre academic interests, investing energy in a hopeless infatuation, Louie's life had begun to reward her with a professional standing and income she could trust. She had bought a house. Without reference or opinions from anyone, Louie had achieved a new peace with a garden. A place for spring bulbs and the pleasures of a washing line: a quiet room with a hot shower for Ndaba.

A peace short-lived, as Marna's blood pressure had reached explosive levels. She needed ready access to medical care that Basutoland lacked. Perhaps the pendulum of debt is always repaid by fortuitous necessity. Marna had banked a substantial obligation over a dozen years of my holidays.

"Marna is to live with us," Louie announced after collecting me from the school train.

"Marvelous." My reaction was sincere. Although my first thought was for Heli, abandoned at Roma, a question better left un-asked.

"I have a surprise," said Louie, driving in an unfamiliar direction.

"What?"

"Wait and see," said Louie, pleased at my curiosity, not so pleased by the penalty of her independence weighted by that imperious presence she could never ignore. Louie and the Matriarch had always been edgy together. Marna was already installed.

So, to a portrait of this house and its inhabitants: perhaps they have been there five weeks. I settle into a narrow room of my own, its door adjacent to that speedily vacated by Louie for Marna. Her sunlit room was exchanged for a darker one at the rear, and Marna has spread her sparse wardrobe on hangers that rattle in unfamiliar space.

The long summer holiday stretches ahead, limitless tedium.

House or no house, for two months, I must be without sight of the beloved. Miss N.J. O'Riordan is back in England, attending a conference and visiting her knitting mother, who supplies her annual cable-stitch cardigan. It seems strange that she has a mother, a mother who knits, and her imperious head-partner, who drags her off to game reserves, do not frame La Belle Dame Sans Merci, for one who saw herself 'alone and palely loitering'. Infatuation is writing the script. I am suffering for the cause. I have read enough to know that true love bleeds and expires—no la la la for me.

But while there's music and moonlight and love and romance… Let's face the music and dance—Cha cha cha.

After Sanie's rambling mansion of untidy ease, Louie's proud achievement, with its blue chintz covers and white woodwork, feels a conspicuous confinement.

Our sing-a-song-of-sixpence house nestles like a brooding chicken that has scratched out the dirt and, for the moment, settled itself in a standard plot on an ordinary suburban street in a northern suburb of Johannesburg. It is a pretty whitewashed house with elaborate thatch, which inspires Marna's name to newly grace the correspondence; 'Pie-thatch'.

I must now ferret out its feathered inhabitants.

The maid is not in the garden. The queen is not in the parlour. The maid, Ndaba, of royal blood, is in the kitchen chopping eternal onions and keeping watch on the simmering stock so we will not distract her with any need for courtesy. Courtesy always comes first for this saintly maid. In her flowered uniform and matching doek, her silent canvas shoes, and her smell of Nivea, Ndaba has centred my life for ten years, my ballast and my counterweight. I come home to her and now the substantial increase of Marna. I am so used to the dutiful but guarded welcome from my mother that I take that as read. It renders us both wretched; it is a wretchedness we are used to. When I think about Louie, I always want to weep, so I try not to think about her. Perhaps it is the same for her.

The nucleus of this new house has brought not only Marna but also Tom and Ursula within its orbit. For the first time, we approximate a family, rather like the frame of billiard balls before the unerring cue will scatter them. Tom has bought a smaller chalet on the bank of a rushing river just around the corner, from where he will keep watch on Marna's blood pressure. Ursula will keep watch on her three girls and train the rotation of domestic maids she can never retain. None will measure up to Ndaba. Ursula can never understand why that is. It is her growing inflammation because Ursula is bored. Even new recipes cannot fill the hours of the day.

Tom now works at Baragwaneth Hospital, the sprawling military hospital built for the war wounded but now entirely for Africans. As a chest physician, his department is for mine workers with lung damage, TB, cancer and emphysema; in his quiet way, he pushes through beds, all surrounded by women, who come to clean, bring food and keen at every death.

Baragwaneth lies on the ragged outskirts on the unfashionable side of the city, past the charcoal-coloured mine dumps, surrounded by spindly trees, dust and donkeys. From the air, with rust roofs and uniform walkways, it might still be an army barracks. It takes Tom two hours to get there. He returns, exhausted, to stroke Ursula's shoulder and ignore her tightening mouth.

After his dinner, Tom calls to place a stethoscope on Marna's back, and he stops to greet Ndaba who almost curtseys.

"Ow, Dr Randall! Such a good, good man, darling. Always he so kind."

Tom could have made a fortune in private practice, but money was never part of the Randall family's aspirations. Tom's father 'Pop', as bearded as an Old Testament prophet, when offered the Chair of Mathematics at the university, was interested, until they told him the salary.

"Gentlemen," he said, rising " I thank you for the offer, but no man is worth that." He replaced his chair, replaced his hat, bowed courteously and departed to his small holding to hoe cabbages and fish the river at Henley-on-Klip between writing mathematical proofs very few understood. Pop lived with his simple wife Munda in her flowered overalls, forever kneading bread. They had raised four sons, all intellectually outstanding: a Bletchley wartime code breaker, a Professor of Physics, Tom the Physician and one I can no longer remember. None made any money.

The disgrace of money was the one doctrine we all shared. Money was consistently ignored. Money ignored probably finds more welcoming pockets. It was not a virtue, this abstemiousness; money was just not the focus of any interest. Other things mattered more.

Ursula seldom calls; she hums ditties and sways her prominent hips. As she has no bottom, they have greater authority. Her excuse is always the same. 'I have small children to think of.' Marna is philosophical about Ursula, so philosophical that I suspect her affection for her daughter burns stronger in her absence. Marna has more fun with Ndaba on their afternoon walks with Windy, my mongrel terrier. Windy was found in a pound: A miserable, runt puppy that scrabbled at the wire mesh, licked my fingers and chose me as much as I did her. She was the only one I wanted.

"What about that pretty spaniel?"

"No."

'Or that…'

"No. This one or none."

"She may not survive. She's very thin."

"That's why I want her. To make sure she does survive."

Windy, formally Belinda, keeps Ndaba company while I am at school, and she goes berserk when I come home, running in a maniacal frenzy around and around the garden, yelping with joy. Marna loves her as much as I do. For Marna, all dogs are better than humans. She understands their uncritical devotion is not sycophancy but generosity; nobody is worthy of a dog.

The evening meal is almost upon us. Marna's solidity stands on those still-slim legs. 'Never took to those with beef-to-the-heel; always rather dim, I found,' and those legs now stand before a wardrobe in which five dresses hang inviting her choice for dinner.

"One always dresses for dinner, dear; it is a mark of civilisation that meals are respected by those that consume them." Her photo-familiar dresses, flower splashed, are now threadbare but perfectly ironed by Ndaba with a lace collar or gentle drapery over that décolletage which loses all arguments with gravity. Even her corsets yield and shed laces.

Now, to me, when I was called Spike. Spike was Tom's name for the 'awkward customer'; which was the name given to me by McEune in staff-room discussions and openly to my mother in a school report. I truly have no idea why I am an 'awkward customer' but I could start with the Lamentations of Jeremiah currently occupying my attention.

The 'Awkward's' appearance at sixteen is the embryonic future in transition. I still want to be a boy, so at home, I dress as much like a boy as circumstances tolerate: cropped hair, khaki shorts, bare feet, and right now, a tee shirt with a colourful logo in Union Jack stripes. Any reference to elsewhere is worth flaunting. We 'whites only' had the benches and the beaches but were beyond the pale for the rest of the Western world. I grasped any means of redeeming the pariah. I have passed beyond the influence of Huddleston, and adolescence is expressed in empty gestures. Even I know that.

Some gestures are emptier than others. Right now, I am doing the Lamentation Cakewalk to enter a rabbinical essay competition entitled 'Choose an Old Testament Prophet: Suggest his Relevance to Modern Life.' If I win the prize, I'll get a week in Israel. Israel would be the last destination of choice; in pictures, it looks like the Karoo, but I'd like to go anywhere but Johannesburg. I have two months to kill. I have never been out of Africa, and as that sort of money has never raised its head, anything is worth a shot.

"I suppose the second prize is two weeks in Israel?" said Marna, who seldom passes up an opportunity to be snide about things biblical.

I remember wishing I had chosen Hosea; done and dusted in half a day. Lamentations were tacked on to Jeremiah after the entry.

"You never knew he wrote them?' said the Beloved, "Well! That will count against you before you begin. Lamentations are crucial." Crucial certainly fits a tortuous, painful expiration in the setting sun.

Chap3 v 12 He hath bent his bow and set me as a mark for the arrow
v13 He has caused the arrows of his quiver to enter my reins

Reins? Surely veins? Too tooting relevant!

I have a horrid suspicion that the dragging in my back betokens THAT time of the month. It's been a year or more. I am no more used to it than when it first assaulted without warning. It ambushed me in Basutoland on holiday, luckily one of the very few with my mother.

He has filled me with bitterness; he hath made me drunken with wormwood.

And I said, my strength and my hope is perished from the Lord.

"What do you mean, years of THIS?" I yelled, "How MANY years?"

"Nearly forever. You'll have to get used to it," said Louie. She always became crisp at such moments. Physical complaints were never sympathetically welcomed. Perhaps a medical professional ekes out sympathy like a prescription: mini-dosage for menstruation: happens to everyone, even those who don't think they are a girl.

"I'll never, never never get used to it," I shouted, since not being a boy was now full frontal and could not be fudged with jodhpurs and a riding crop to slash at anything destructible. After the humiliation— Oh Jesus, Mary and all the Saints! —of sanitary belts and pads, I saddled Noel and galloped at full pelt through dongas and over the mountains, hoping to fall and break my neck, far from help. It was the only escape from being a girl, forever, irrevocably in your face, with dresses, make-up and all THAT. Being a girl was just ghastly.

I am now aware that the dress-for-dinner routine will soon be upon me. Since Marna moved in, it has been insisted upon. At any moment, Louie will nose her hump-backed, old, green Volvo down the drive, and the careful quadrille of dinner will commence. My mother will sniff at my choice of a that'll-do skirt and proceed down the corridor to remove her uniform and redo her hair that has learned to conceal a hairpiece to achieve a set of Greta Garbo snails on top. Then she'll pour the first glass of Vermouth, a nod to eventide.

After the starting gun, we will head for the straight furlong, Gin and Tonic rapidly overtaken by wine, white, Nederburg Late Harvest coming up on the left, at half a crown a bottle, shipped from the Cape. Louie's small indulgence, liquor, was the least she was owed for the life she led, working all hours in a profession she never wanted, to pay for the life I never asked for. Not as a girl, anyway.

Just as I refused to be a girl, my family refused other roles. Louie was never 'mum', Marna was never 'grandma'. Perhaps because we weren't a family in the way of relationships, they did not define us. I was a burden to Louie so I could hardly call her mum when she did not want to be. And Marna was far too three-dimensional to fit into two dimensions. Grandmother. A 'grandmother' sits in the corner knitting and stays quiet. Marna never did that. Even Milly was Ndaba to me. Ndaba means big discussion and big discussions were her prime function and consummate skill. Names are important. I am now Spike and happy to be so. It affords me an incisive power until I deserve the real thing.

Ndaba rushes into my room.

"Ow, darling! Come. You must come quick. Before, before. Quick, Old Madame mustn't see" Ndaba is rarely agitated but stands wringing a dishcloth around her wrist and flapping urgency.

"What on earth?"

"It's that cat. This time, big time. Ow!"

Ndaba grabs my arm and pulls me into the drawing room, pointing at the portrait that hangs above the dining table. Great Aunt Mary is now grossly disfigured. The serene woman with ringlets has always been there, perpetual wallpaper in every house of Marna's reign, looking sideways, eyes right, as though in decency to ignore the meals taken below her waist. Now, like a Royal Insignia, flown when the monarch is in residence, she honours us with her presence. But…

One eyeball hangs down. It hangs attached to a thread of canvas as though on a pulsing optic nerve. The remaining eye looks out, still serene, not even surprised at losing its lifelong companion, which hangs down the nose: a climber on a cliff with nothing to break the fall.

"What happened?"

"Ow, Miss Phil darling, you must take her away before Old Madam sees. Quick, we can do this together." Milly stands on one side of the frame and starts to raise it to lift it off its hook. I take the other side, and together we manoeuvre the heavy gilt frame through the hallway and into my room, leaving a square of discoloured paint and cobwebs. Milly rushes back with a brush for the cobwebs and resumes laying the table. I join her.

"How did that happen, Ndaba?" Milly stands back and puts down the cutlery to fully illustrate the evidence before the court.

"I already think you not going to believe. I am here, laying table, just like now. That cat is over there on the couch, nowhere near. Sudden, darling, that cat walk over, not run, not hurry, and then darling, she stand, look, then jump. She just jump for the picture, both hands in front, all claws together. She goes straight for the eyes and pull out that eye. She give one loud, so loud miaou, like she is pleased with herself, and walk away. She walk slowly, side-side, like she is saying 'job done.' I never see any cat jump like that. Stand, look, jump, walk off. Maybe she knows; cats they know…"

"Knows what Ndaba?"

"Ow, I never like that picture. She so…." Milly pulls her lugubrious face, the corners of her mouth pulled down, eyelids fluttering.

"You never said so."

"Not for me to say, darling. Old Madam, she loves that woman, she look at her every day. For me, that woman have evil eye. Cats they know about evil eye. Old Madame is going to be very upset."

"Perhaps she won't notice."

"For a clever person, darling, you can be sometimes so stupid. But before Old Madam sees, you must wait outside for Madam's car. You must tell her first. Then she must splain." Milly doubles up with sudden shaking laughter.

"What's so funny?"

"I never like that Max cat, but this time she do a good thing. Maybe Madam now must think about Max coming here. He will kill this family. That cat is just finding a way to tell Madam to think." Milly is delighted that Max's cat has disgraced him.

The pure white Persian with blue eyes was Max's 'Greeks bearing Gifts' present to me before Louie had decided about him. Tibby has not even earned herself a name because she spits and hisses and suffers no affection. Beautiful she certainly is, as queenly as a cold-eyed pre-Raphaelite model, standing statuesque to await Rossetti. Her plume of tail she holds aloft like a feather boa in the wake of her royal progression across the parquet floor. Not a cat but a sauntering envoy.

On that intention, which must be thwarted, Marna, Milly and I are in complete accord. It is not his Judaism Marna objects to but his 'delicacy'. Marna is usually pro-Jew, anything better than a Methodist or a Catholic, but Jew gives 'delicate' a pointed twist like some egregious Shtetl usurer on a bench outside a hut. Creaming pence from passing poverty. She could see Max, the insolvent with his duodenal ulcers, sipping whisky in milk for the rest of time while Louie worked to pay off his debts and finance the ulcer's whisky.

Marna will not live to see the half of it.

Aunt Mary, defrocked from the domestic pulpit, is concealed before Marna can see her savaged. Louie, having heard of Max's disgrace-by-proxy cat, contemplates Aunt Mary's now baleful single eye in silence. She stands, lips pursed and eyebrow raised, while I attempt to flatten its companion back in place. The pendulum eye rolls out to resume, thumbing its nose, waving from its sling of thread. It made Aunt Mary curiously and newly present.

Before now, she was some ancient 'relation' of no significance, without shoulders and certainly without breasts, but very well-combed hair.

"For heaven's sake, leave her alone."

"I wonder who she really was," I say. "She's been around forever, and now she's jumped forth injured, calling for an ophthalmologist or a plastic surgeon. Can she be fixed, do you think?"

"Quite dreadful," says Louie. "Turn it to the wall and cover it with something. Mother might catch sight of it." The disfigured Aunt Mary is hidden in a cupboard and we go through to dine.

"Why have you taken away my picture?" Marna asks, unfolding her napkin with methodical indifference. She is merely curious. Living with my mother and the philosophy of Ndaba has softened her vehemence.

"To be cleaned," says Louie.

"Not like you," says Marna, handing across potatoes. "What has she done to deserve a sudden scrub?"

"I thought it would please you, a refreshment…"

Louie has no idea whether the damage is reparable.

"You know she knew George Eliot?" says Marna, looking sideways in that birdlike way she had, challenging.

"Yes, Mother. You have mentioned it."

"I never knew her, you know. I wish I had."

Louie refills her glass and gestures with the bottle. Marna declines with a flat hand and sips.

"Hardly possible," says Louie, in that way wine always sharpened. "She lived in London."

"I don't mean George Eliot. Of course that would have been impossible." Marna pauses, eyes searching the ceiling of lost knowledge, "1880 it was. She died before I was born. Mind you, I was in London only twenty years later…no, I meant Great Aunt Mary. I never knew her, though I have always felt I did."

My mother ignores this. She ignores most things Marna says.

"Why didn't you? Know her?' I ask. Sometimes, Louie's quill cruelty to Marna demands smudging.

"She died when I was three. 1886. But she left my father her books, George Eliot's books. Have you ever seen the inscription? Fetch them, Phil, there's a dear."

I stagger back and place the pile on the table: four identical red volumes of Daniel Deronda. Like Aunt Mary's portrait, they have always been wherever Marna was, on her bedside table or shouldering out the rag-tag paperbacks. Louie shrugs and rotates her ring, pours more wine, then places her hand under her chin, waiting to call time. Marna settles her spectacles. Ndaba peers through the door.

"Are you ready for me to clear the table, Madam?"

"It would seem so, Milly. The stew was very good, but Old Madam did not eat all hers. She finds books more important than all your work…" How cold Louie could be; hoar frosted always, after two too many.

Milly begins to load her tray with empty plates.

"Can be heated up tomorrow, Madam, easily."

"No need, Milly, just leave my plate…" says Marna, "Milly, come and look at this…" She holds out the opened book. Milly eases her bulk around the table. Marna points to the inscription. "That says 'In gratitude for kindnesses shown to dear ones no longer living (1876)', and it is signed by a woman called George. George Eliot."

"Ow! George can be a man, Madame!" Marna laughs and places a hand on Milly's forearm, her thumb stroking the burn scar welts of many frying pan tongues.

"How right you are, Milly. That was the idea. She had to pretend to be a man to get this book published."

"Ow! Why, Madam?"

"Eighty years ago, Milly, women were not thought to be clever enough to write books. Her real name was Mary Anne Evans but she called herself George Eliot, and everybody thought her books were quite wonderful until they knew she was a woman. See, 1876, that is more than seventy years ago" Marna points and hands the book to me.

"But Madam, how you get this books? From the lady who write them? The lady George?".

I point to the inscription.

"Who was Mrs. Sanderson? It is inscribed to a Mrs. Sanderson?"

"At last. Penny drops. Great Aunt Mary Barrett became Mrs Sanderson. She who your mother has removed for cleaning. She married a Scot, John Sanderson, a botanist and a painter…" Marna's excursions into genealogy could get lengthy.

"Hang about. You had an aunt who received a signed book from George Eliot for kindnesses shown. What kindnesses? Shown to who?"

"Whom?" says Louie.

"Shown to whom?"

"I have no idea," says Marna. I received the books from my father, Charles Ashton Barrett, her nephew, to *whom* she had bequeathed them, almost a christening present for me without any information. She had no children. I suppose they might be quite valuable now. My father told me the little I know about her reading Josephus in the original Greek, on the Durban Esplanade. Can you credit? Perhaps there was some correspondence between them. George Eliot was keen on Josephus. Anyway, Phil, they will be yours one day, and Milly will look after them for you when I am gone."

Marna was issuing a public instruction.

"Ow! Madam. Don't say like that." Ndaba continues to clear the table, still shaking her head. I know what Marna means, and so does Ndaba. Louie goes across to the fireplace to light a cigarette. Ndaba leaves with the tray. I follow.

"Ow terrible, Old Madam. She knows, darling, that man is coming."

"George Eliot is a very famous writer, Ndaba. That Great Aunt Mary must have done something to deserve books sent from England by post on a sailing ship. In those days, it took months."

"Some things darling, you can never know, eva they send cats to say so." Milly nodded her Sophianic head and tucked in the tail of her doek.

I returned to Marna and my mother sitting in solid separate silence,

Marna still at the table, Louie a safe distance away.

Marna looks up, pushing the books towards me.

"I want you to have them when I go. Daniel Deronda is about anti-Semitism," she says pointedly.

"For me especially? You think I'm an anti-Semite?" I whisper.

"One doesn't count," Marna responds and winks. "I have a feeling you might write when you have garnered enough material. George Eliot was quite an advanced age before she ventured into fiction. Keep them safe. They've come a long way to find you."

I return the books to Marna's room. Louie says nothing.

I abandoned Jeremiah and put on 'See you later, Alligator" on my wind-up gramophone. Somehow, I want to dance and lug the gramophone into the back garden to jive on the back lawn, under the moon, curiously elated by something I cannot define. Something about a writer sending books twelve thousand miles to someone she had never met. Perhaps there might be hope for a bigger life, even one starting in South Africa.

Louie gestures from the bathroom window and calls me in. That gesture foreshadows the inevitability of disturbing Max, whose metaphorical luggage has already arrived.

While brushing my teeth, I hear Marna quietly singing, 'In a while, crocodile… Doncha know you cramp my style.' She is giggling as she prepares for bed. All three, Milly, Marna, and I, have been bonded by that hissing cat, which that night ventured onto the foot of my bed for the first time. It was a portent of this untold story, in which two women who never met were joined by a girl who preferred to be taken for a boy, as George Eliot did. At least theoretically.

෴

There was a postscript to the Episode of the Cat. Marna had tipped into reverie about her father.

"Charles Ashton was distantly related to Elizabeth Barrett Browning, you know? The poetess?"

"I didn't know. How related?"

"Not directly. She only had one son, and he had no children. I never did discover, not even from those formidable relations who inhabited an impressive edifice called the Methodist Theological College in Richmond, where I spent gloomy Sundays when I was in London— endless dreary chapel. The Founder of that pile was a Barrett, Alfred. He was called 'the Saint.' An interesting man, actually…" I had to head her off.

"Any others?" I asked.

"What do you mean, any others?"

"Any other famous relations?"

"Well, since you asked, you also have Romanov blood, the famous Archduke Nicolai…the mad Duke, but on my mother's side, and I'm not going into that…Let me show you something."

She opened her leather jewel box and took out a square copper cube.

"There!"

"What is it?"

"It is the Romanov seal. Look at the crest. The double-headed eagle?"

Romanov? Bugger off. I did not believe a word of it. But I forgave her. I dreamt big dreams, too, but mine were for the future. Marna's claims were flimsy thin, but they were all she had. Nobody half-decent would have stripped them from her, so I didn't.

Not long after the return to school, I received a letter from Louie.

Dear Phil,

This is not an easy letter to write and it will, no doubt, come as a shock and a sadness. I am writing to tell you that Marna has died. Although it could have happened at any time— her blood pressure— there were no immediate indications that it was threatening more than usual.

Last Thursday, I went in to say goodnight as usual, and she was propped up on her pillows with her lilac shawl about her shoulders, looking so serene and beautiful. I told her so.

'The last flicker of the candle, my dear,' was what she said. Those were her last words.

She truly looked younger than she had for many years. The change was very strange. In the morning, she was unconscious when Milly took in her tea. Tom came at once. He said she had had a fatal stroke, severe enough to give no hope of recovery. If she had regained consciousness, she would have been completely paralysed. It was merciful, really.

As you know, I am no believer that one should hang on to a half-life, so I am glad there was no need for any decisions of that kind. She lingered for nearly three days and then slipped away painlessly. Poor mother. Her last years have been a kind of lingering.

She will be cremated next Friday. I don't suppose there is any point in you coming. I doubt many will. I am not sure Heli will manage to come. I have not yet managed to hear from him.

I realise this will upset you, for you were very close. I suspect you possibly knew her better than I did, but take comfort that she died without pain or knowledge. Milly is distraught and weeping constantly. Windy will not leave her side and refuses to eat. Rather trying, but it will pass.

You will have the George Eliot books and a few small things when you come home. We will take care of them for you. I don't suppose you will want to attend her funeral.

As ever, Me. Your mother.

Louie had no idea what Marna meant to me. The loss of the centre of my life was compounded by Louie's inability to imagine it. That letter of cold information blew in the wind of what was to follow. Max.

Max would expunge everything Marna stood for. Before his invasion, I managed to be excused and took the train home for Marna's funeral.

The loss of Marna was where your own life began. She said you would write, and her funeral was where that began.

Yes, but decades later. I had to finger the mystery of her bond with Lynn and the unspoken trauma she held to herself. It threaded through my life in explosive episodes that were never fully revealed, leaving conjecture but no clarity.

Not as significant as the cat, the torn-out eye, and the vital warning about Max. Ndaba was right; she saw quite clearly the significance of that event.

But Louie did not. Nor did I. Not fully.

You have now and will have it reinforced inescapably. A murder and a miracle take you towards a deeper vision. Meanwhile, let's have that story.

CHAPTER 11

Red Hot Pokers

'But the end of Mr. Brooke's pen was a thinking organ, evolving sentences, especially of a benevolent kind, before the rest of his mind could overtake them.'

"Thirty-two stab wounds and not one too many."

That's what she said, my grandmother. To Louie. Honest. My mother thought she hadn't heard straight. They were standing to draw breath outside a shop window in Johannesburg, my mother ten, Marna already eternally old. The bald mannequins were draped with sheets, waiting for new fashion. In those days, white plastic manikins were never exposed naked for fear of giving the blacks ideas but modestly wrapped between changes. I suppose it reminded Marna of a shroud. She leant on her horn-handle stick and contemplated the wigless heads and bare shoulders, and the remark just bubbled up from nowhere.

'What do you mean? Who are you talking about?'

Marna eased her arthritic shoulder, flicked her stick, and then seemed to remember where she was. She leant on my mother's young shoulder, and together they walked on. She said no more and never mentioned it again.

The crematorium had done its best. Around four walls, in spaced brass jars, stood single red-hot pokers like sentries in attendance. Marna had loathed red hot pokers above all flowers. She had stopped journeys in transit to decapitate every one, slashing at them like a dervish. To the confusion of the priest, the whole family collapsed in giggles, and bladders being a family weakness, some dashed for the door. The dearly beloved were not gathered together but he battled on regardless.

That just brought Marna's shaking laughter into vivid focus, and now she was invisible, liberated us to let memory and loss enjoy hysteria.

"You do know why she hated them, don't you?" A prim voice from the back followed the coffin through the jerking curtains. Marna was trundling off. The priest packed up altogether, removing his stole, replacing his bookmark, snapping his prayer book and looking as sour as lemon for fish.

The speaker was Aunt Nell, a gaunt, distant cousin who had been the bane of occasionally required duty. Among other vulgar flowers like marigolds and dahlias, she had also cultivated red hot pokers, which was why Marna had not found duty over-pressing very often. 'I can't understand people without a sense of smell; marigolds reek of cat,' she had said of Nell. It was, however, to Nell and Uncle Eric we were bound for the wake.

I was fascinated by this prospect since Nell, with her face moles and her monosyllabic utterances, had managed to divorce and remarry Uncle Eric three times, although none of us had ever witnessed an exchange between them. Word had it that Nell was a visionary and read tea leaves without invitation. I was sixteen and I wanted to know what lay in store. Her personal record did not bode cast-iron accuracy.

"All nonsense, but it passes the time." Marna had said. I had sensed an edge about Nell that went beyond her indiscretions with plants.

We assembled under the single Jacaranda, where tables had been laid in a garden regimented by edgings and hard paths, prisoning a riot of purple, brass, crimson and salmon. Humour had evaporated. We stood sobered and uncertain while Eric was dispatched to fetch the tea, caraway cake and hard, teeth-cracking ginger biscuits. Marna had also loathed caraway. None of us offered to enter the unadorned rust brick house, which stood four-square, its jaw set against the garden and our invasion.

Tea was handed out in fine but unmatched china cups. Nobody spoke much. Nell and Eric, who seemed used to silence, ventured no openings beyond hot water or a lump of sugar. Marna was suddenly and hugely absent like a crater in our midst.

"Anybody ready for a reading?" asked Nell, as though the funeral had simply been a prelude to her planned séance. Nobody moved.

'Do you think it appropriate today?' asked my mother.

"Never more so," said Nell brusquely. "She's still passing across, within reach, you might say." Louie shot me a glance which was as clear as if she had spoken. We all knew that nothing would speed Marna into the ether quicker than being within reach of Aunt Nell. I had a brief vision of her assumption in her straw hat, her slim ankles dangling below the billowing clouds of concealment. She had been justifiably proud of her shapely legs. They were kicking her up to heaven. Into the silence, Nell threw her ultimate gauntlet.

"Well, I predicted the murder, you know. That should stand for something."

We stood upon a precipice. What murder? It seemed as though a fever had passed through, elongating Aunt Nell, dwarfing Eric, and turning the rest to smoke. Nobody was disposed to allow Nell to clarify, although she had lobbed an unexploded grenade that lay fizzing on the table. What murder?

"You don't want to know. None of you want to know. She would never speak of it either..."

Still, she failed to draw us.

"Well, I will. You can't all hide forever. You know Minnie's mother was murdered? Surely that cannot have escaped you...?" Aunt Nell was now determined to claim back the years of neglect. "I saw it all in the leaves. I told them... I see blood on the flowers, splashed all over the flowers..." She looked around for appropriate horror and faced stony withdrawal. Uncle Tom rose to clear the table, followed by Eric. They went off with a tray together, two of the wilting sex who could read a storm brewing.

"...and so it came to pass, five years later. Ouma Eeltjie was stabbed to death, and the child saw it all..."

My mother was suddenly compelled to speak. "What child?"

"Your half-brother, Lynn. He was only four, maybe five. Standing in his cot in the corner of the room, he watched a massacre. His testimony hanged them, you know...."

"Where was this?"

"In the Free State."

"There aren't any flowers in the Free State..." said my mother, leaping for the irrelevant.

"No, but she had flowered wallpaper in the bedroom, and it was splashed with blood...."

"But why?" asked someone called Alma. I had not heard her speak before nor ascertained how she fitted into this gathering.

"Nobody knows. Nobody was sure they hanged the right man. Nothing had been stolen. The child pleaded for his life at the trial..."

"A child of five?"

"He was nearly six by the time of the trial, and Zulu was his first language. He remembered everything they said. He was the youngest witness ever to send a man to the gallows for a capital crime."

Nell had lassoed attention. She had waited a long time for it. Her gaunt existence had tolerated Marna's galleon progress with a needle at the ready; she had punctured laughter forever.

"You're not suggesting...?" Alma's persistence was abrasive. Was she Uncle Eric's sister?

"Don't be ridiculous", said Louie. I had not yet conceived the ridiculous. What was ridiculous?

"...well, you have to admit Lynn never seemed to want any contact with his mother. Why was that? And why did he plead for their lives if they didn't do it?" I finally read Alma's pedantic poison: Was she a cheerleader for Nell's séance? I finally read her suspicion.

"If Lynn was imprisoned by his controlling wife in Rhodesia, it doesn't make Marna a murderer, not by you, not by anyone. How could you!"

I burst into tears. I snatched Louie's bag, extracted the car keys and stormed off down the dreadful drive. In the car, I sank into the back seat and contemplated that poisonous garden, that house with its smirk, those riotous vehement flowers. There was something insidious about that suggestive, leering woman and her obsequious husband who chewed at his cheek. It had contaminated us all. Red was for evil, and it had obliterated Marna's sardonic humour. She was no longer there to put her great disdain to purpose. I knew I would never stop searching for answers, but I wouldn't listen to another word.

On the way home, everyone was lost and silent. Suddenly, it occurred to me to ask, 'Why would Uncle Lynn have been with his grandmother? Where was Marna?'

"It must have been when her first husband abandoned her and went off to fly in America…His grandmother was probably just looking after him…" said Louie "…but it does explain something. Darling Lynn could never be woken without a warning. That's why, whenever he stayed, we had to keep a bell near his bedroom door. All the servants were told to ring it before taking in tea in the morning… otherwise, they'd find his hands around their throats. It was his instinctive reaction to being suddenly woken…"

"So, you think it's true?"

"I think it must be. Lynn never spoke of it, and nor did Marna except once, she mentioned it, outside a shop window in Johannesburg…" To think none of us knew the horror that lay at the heart of that disdain."

It probably accounted for it in some curious way. Having known the worst, the murder of her mother, nothing could ever threaten her again. For me, it explained that impulsively affectionate woman who knew her journey in the scheme of things and sailed imperiously through every wind and every storm and who made sure that we always knew we were wanted. It was why nightmares were smothered in her bed with chocolate and the smell of cologne.

That was where we had to leave it, the half-truth wrapping the anchor that moored our family. It was only half her story.

∽

That was Marna's dubious send-off. Unworthy of her, but there is much more to come. I now must return to school, having plumbed something of what bonded Marna and Lynn. No wonder they stayed silent, no wonder Louie and Ursula were afterthought children with nothing like the same claims upon her.

Yet why was Lynn, as a small boy, entrusted to the mother who was, even after being murdered, remembered with such venom? Why did Lynn take Heli's name? He became Driver-Jowitt. Marna never spoke of Evelyn Driver except about his abandonment and jumping a 'few hedges'.

Some injuries have no meaning that speech can homogenize, as Louie never spoke of my father, Raymond. Betrayal of a marriage is one, especially summary betrayal, without even the time for it to wear thin at the elbows. Evelyn Driver, the dashing, aeronautical pioneer with his moustache, and Raymond Gavin, the urbane, worldly doctor, were simply self-pleasing, easily tempted and devoid of loyalty. Both Louie and Marna had been young and deceived in their early choices. Both Lynn and I were the resultant baggage, abandoned on a whim.

Only destitution explained the entrusting of little Lynn to her hated mother, Eeltjie van den Bosch. Imagine the punishment Marna felt she had inflicted on Lynn, a small boy, not only caught up in a violent stabbing but also if what that woman said was true, the chief witness at the murderer's trial. The youngest witness ever to send a man to the gallows! How does a child live with that?

That savagery distilled something else. The saintliness of Heli before the Catholic Church ensnared him, adopting Lynn in every way and having the courage to father further children. What a complex mélange they all were, of nobility and utter blindness! With Marna dead, South Africa's claims upon us all became tungsten bright, fragments picked out by a torch in the dark.

But lacking any cohesion?

Hooked by George Eliot, pricked by a murder, snared by the white wag-n-bietjie thorns punctuating your safari, you stop briefly at a fire kindling curiosity. Did you ever see curiosity as the twine threading all events?

I do now, but threading that necklace has only just begun.

CHAPTER 12

Max, Milly and Mandela

'We may handle even extreme opinions with impunity while our furniture, our dinner giving, and preference for armorial bearings in our own case, link us indissolubly to the established order.'

When I look back on the receding tide of Marna's death, I see myself as a cuttlefish abandoned at neap tide, which no following tide would re-float. Life, like a frog prepared for dissection, had been pithed, the spine of its essence extracted, passively quiescent. Bereft of optimism, the loss of any home, and finally, the loss of the small hope that one day my mother would turn to embrace me. When Max entered centre stage, that hope fizzled and died. What remained was a vacuum. Louie's achievement, the pretty home for seasons, for candle-lit welcomes, might as well have been dust sheeted for the duration of a war.

In that bleak barracks, I wrestled with the Usurper, seethed with hatred for his smug satisfaction, and tried to make sense of… nearly everything. Those were my final years of school, but I was already imaginatively stepping into adulthood and into the reviled South African curse of being white, being 'English,' being poor and being powerless to change anything. Injustice on every front was all that I breathed.

My portraits from that period are coloured by frustrated impotence and fractured, if I am honest, by the temper of adolescence. Adolescence is universally known to be selfish and wayward, and I admit to both, but it is also clear-sighted in spasms. Nuance does not enter to spoil the clarity or argue away the insupportable. It was a bleak time, and I noticed things because there was very little to distract me.

Max is the cue that scatters that frame of interim family. Tom was now no longer needed. Heli struggled alone in Lesotho's thankless routines. I supposed that the nuns cooked his food while maids cleaned and morning Mass continued. Louie prepared for her liaison, who threatened from the sidelines. From the buying of our first house, life had been waiting for the death of our compelling nucleus. Her departure left a cauldron of simmering apprehension.

Both our home and the country held their breath. Heli had always anticipated that, at any moment, the political brew would boil over.

Few countries were as naked in the immediacy of politics. In 1948, hope was doused. The rabid, racist Nationalists swept to power under the diehard Malan. A single change in law had immediate repercussions. South Africans ate politics for breakfast, lunch and supper. Who they mixed with, what was safe to speak about, or whether their servants would turn up for work were constant uncertainties. Opening a paper would reveal the reasons why they had not.

Later, in England, I was bemused that a change of Government made no discernible difference to anyone or anything. It was indecent to ask what someone had voted, and there were no signs that might reveal it. In South Africa, your accent might betray you, but if not, how you treated a black man certainly would. Boers were paternal but, on the whole, kind to those they saw as dependent children; racists were abusive and belligerent; white British immigrants were superficially polite but stiffly uncomprehending of requests for a three-day funeral. So-called political liberals were generous but careful, never quite sure of where the opposition's clear lines lay. Few 'umlungu'—whites— could speak Zulu or Xhosa or understand the sly jokes and what caution and contempt lurked beneath that 'Ja Baas.'

As a training ground in which the inner and outer worlds reflected one another, it could not have been improved. In my family, the punctuation to that narrative was exact. Max would provide grounds for the over-use of the exclamation mark, for hypocrisy, disbelief, and incredulity. A Jew who had none of the tolerant humour of Judaism but all of its appearances. A self-professed liberal who was domineering, supercilious and a pretender to impartiality in the Law but who used the Law as a cover for patronising racism.

I had lived with Tom's dedication to black mineworkers' lungs, Heli's dedication to African education, and his mastery of African languages. My family was fairly unique in its encounters. Other liberal whites cared about injustice in theory but hardly ever encountered Africans socially. I only saw that fully later. One takes one's childhood for granted, and we knew few other families.

Initially, Max's Judaism argued in his favour. If there was a cohesive group of liberals, it was the Johannesburg Jews. Their bravery did not extend to their Capetonian brothers, Jews who seemed willing to go slimly to appease the brutal segregation. Their emotional betrayal was a common subject of conversation because the Cape Province had a large Malay and mixed-blood population, which might have given impetus to wider inclusion. Instead, comfort and luxury among the vineyards and serene Cape Dutch estates seemed to have dissolved Jewish outrage to bow heads, avert eyes, and keep silent.

The Jewish immigrants had more servants than most and the money to pay better than most. They also had the leisure to foster the arts and music, and many worked in Law. Mandela's defence teams in both his trials would almost exclusively be Jews, as would Helen Suzman be the single voice for the Progressive Party fighting for a universal franchise. Johannesburg was a political pot, always a simmer. There was every reason to believe Max might be among the liberals. He certainly made that claim.

∽

Marna had died, and without ado, Max moved in to occupy with my mother the bed she had vacated. Ndaba, still grieving for her fat laughing companion, had to take in tea to both of them as the day opened.

Max's Savile Row shirts were marshalled where Marna's dresses had breathed freely, his bespoke suits were covered with shoulder shields, his expensive shoes sported stretch trees, and his oily hair brushes kissed each other beneath her Victorian tilting mirror.

Ndaba crept and raised her chin when we passed; Windy clung to her skirt or stayed in my room. Tibby was no friendlier but seemed to wash more thoroughly.

Louie already looked defensive. She did not refer to Max but deferentially permitted his nine o'clock returns from his office, his two whiskies with their jug of milk set upon his chair-side tray. He seemed to revel in the paralysis his presence required. Milly, on her feet since six in the morning, was wilting with the wait to serve dinner. Dinner was now emphatically Jewish, although not kosher, as we had no space for separate fridges, nor was Max observant. He observed almost nothing. Every supper began with herring, chopped or in cream, requiring hours of deboning from the barrels ordered from Holland. Fortunately, both Louie and Max were out for the working day, so Milly and I could unbutton.

"What are we going to do, Ndaba?"

"Ow, darling, what is to do? This is Madame house. She must have who she likes."

"Our house, too, Ndaba."

"Madame pay for everything darling, eva my wage, eva my uniform. Eva his drink. Can say nothing."

"You could poison him? With rat poison."

"Ow, Miss Phil. Don't eva think. Can be the wrong person poisoned." She laughed.

༄

Political tensions were mounting outside as well, at an alarming pace. Max's presence brought them to a seat at the table straight from Marshall Square police headquarters, overlooked by his office. He saw the 'Black Marias' unloading collections of passbook offenders to be charged and beaten up, he met his legal colleagues with the latest cases, and he worked in the very hub of oppression. Seemingly unperturbed, immaculately well-dressed for his corporate clients, Max went deferential in his lines of legal duty: contract law for the rich.

Max professed politically liberal beliefs but spoke to Milly like a dog when Louie was absent.

"Milly! Tea," he would shout.

"Yes Sah. Come soon." No 'thank you' would follow the tray laid before him unless Louie was present; then it would be exaggerated.

"That's very kind of you, Milly. You know I love your biscuits."

I watched my mother's willful blindness with incomprehension.

He would place his shoes for polishing on the kitchen table without a sign or request. I tried to shame him by doing it for her. He would shrug and offer a sardonic grimace.

"*You'll* never reach professional standards."

At dinner, he would expound on political events and mention the names of prominent Jewish lawyers, many heroes I recognised later in the reports of the first Treason Trial when the crackdown and arrest of one hundred and fifty-six happened overnight, all charged with treason. Luthuli was among them. But those systematic night raids had not yet gathered pace. What did happen in 1957 was the bus boycott when thousands living in nearby Alexander Township refused to accept a penny increase in fares. For weeks, they walked, sometimes twenty miles a day, to and from work. Prolonged over three months, it caused great hardship. Some could not manage it. Louie took to leaving home earlier and gave as many as her car would hold a lift into town. Max's large Chevrolet could have taken six comfortably, but it was not so employed. He stayed home to perfect his toilette.

My detestation of this odious man and disbelief that Louie could submit to him and permit Milly to suffer reached volatile levels. I could scarcely remain in the same room. We lived in such political ferment that Max came to embody and bring home everything the world despised in the country. I saw Max as the axe that fell upon everything my family stood for. Louie's surrender to him betokened surrender to the overall oppression. Her actions contradicted that, but this rinkhals cobra was coiled in her bed!

The boycott triumphed when the bus company's survival was in jeopardy, and it was awarded a subsidy, so it abandoned the increase in fares. They had won! Full bus loads hanging on to strap handles resumed. That concession to black power was probably the beginning of the end that would take another thirty-four years when Mandela had served time and was released. That still lay ahead, but the tide was ominously building.

Another movement gaining increasing support—and oppression—was the fight against the Extension of the Pass Laws to African women, who would also be subject to summary arrest, curtailment of movement, or sent to the defined tribal areas, the Bantustans, dustbins for the unwanted. 'The Black Sash' women stood in silent protest where they would be seen. Most were black, but some white women joined them. Unmoving, a few stood for hours until dragged away by police, interned and questioned for standing quietly with a ribbon around their chests.

This reached right home. It would apply to Ndaba. Any holiday to see her children or a Sunday spent with a friend would run the risk of summary arrest. Louie would not countenance it. She started to plan and enquired into Milly's heritage.

"Ow, Madam. I am Zulu from my father, but I am also Swazi from my mother."

"Have you any papers to show your mother was a Swazi?"

"Maybe I can ask my family in Paulpietersberg when I go home?"

Before Milly left to gather the evidence of her genealogy, Max suggested the addition of a manservant to the house. I suspected Max was preparing for Milly's dismissal when Louie's plan, whatever she was hatching, would fail. He required a gentleman's gentleman. Louie would find his wages. Alfonse, a very tall, benign, but in Milly's view, rather a dim helpmeet, was appointed to occupy the spare servant's room and share her shower.

"Ow, darling! Men! What they for? Make babies, make work, useless!"

For all her chuntering, she welcomed his obliging help: washing up, reaching the top of cupboards, lifting weights, sweeping outside and having a confidant to talk to without any danger of being understood.

Alfonse was her private drain remedy for the swilling away of Max.

Louie sent Ndaba home to seek witnesses for her Swazi claims. She gave her money for a scribe and translator. She returned ten days later with a thin file of papers and was then dispatched to Swaziland to sit outside the Royal Kraal of King Sobhuza the Second. After a week, she was admitted to the Royal Presence in his black head feathers and skin skirt. She offered her evidence of Swazi blood and requested a piece of land to build a hut. He granted her a lifetime lease on a plot close to the South African border in a scattered kraal called Dwalili. It made her a Swazi National with the right to citizenship! Milly would never carry a pass or only over Louie's dead body. A capricious King could revoke a verbal grant at a stroke. That was a chance Ndaba took.

The moral victory came at a price. When women carrying passes became the Law in South Africa, Milly would have to ford a river with her shoes tied around her neck and her luggage on her head and walk some miles on either side of the border to escape the South African border guards, who would have refused a Swazi re-entry if they had recorded her leaving.

Slowly, she began to build a hut. Over the following few years, every Christmas holiday saw Ndaba disembarking from a bus and under cover of dark wading through that river. Then, heaving a bag of tools, she hitched a Swazi ten-seat 'Kumbi', the taxis that roamed the rural areas on the safe side of Swazi independence.

What neither Louie nor Max anticipated would be the reversal of the usual. Servants usually followed masters. In years to come, Louie would compel Max to follow Milly into Swaziland, the last of the Protectorates, to live out their lives where skin colour could not legislate, and however imperfectly, an African King ruled, and she and Ndaba could sit side by side in church.

∽

Max and I locked horns at supper when we were chained together. By the time we sat down I was simmering at his insensitivity to Ndaba's fatigue and Louie's refusal to ask of him what she would have demanded of anyone else. Max would tuck a napkin above his tie and commence to reach for dishes rather than requesting them. Then, he would begin fishing for my anger.

"This will interest you, Phil. Following the pass burning, what would you say was the correct way to deal with civil disobedience?"

"Breaking the law?"

"In a manner of speaking."

"An unjust law?"

"Law is never unjust, as such. It is just the law, and it could be said to be universal, applying to everyone without favour."

"Like separate doorways for blacks and whites?"

He would smirk. I had fallen into his trap.

"A good example. Blacks are prevented from using white entrances and vice versa. Where's the injustice?"

"The injustice is that blacks did not make, or contribute to the making of that law… Like Jews did not make the law on wearing yellow stars in Germany," I liked to use the Jews whenever possible, but so did he.

"Hardly comparable. Still, you are obviously in the mood for a row, so we'll leave it there. One day, you will understand the distinction between Statute and Legislative Functions…"

Men were bloody with beatings, strung up for want of a dompas, and Max spoke of Legislative Functions! Oh, Christ!

It worked every time. He wound me up daily like a clock and returned the key to his pocket, looking at Louie for approval while I left the table, incandescent and spinning with frustration at being unable to hit him over the head with her bottle. Oh, his smug, complacent grin, preening at his cleverness! It was always The Law. A child showing off would not have been so obvious. How could she not see what he was up to? When would she wake up?

In the kitchen, Milly would raise both hands and flutter them to calm me down.

"Ow, take it easy, darling. Take it easy. Don't give him cross; he likes to make you cross so Madame can think you to blame. Take no notice."

"If I take no notice, then my mother calls me rude Ndaba. I can't win here."

"Xactly darling. Nobody can win. So better not to start."

The real clouds of the coming bloodbath lay in the turbulence of the daily news, arrests, escapes, and fleeings. Looking back does not give the same view. Apart from the Sharpeville Massacre, there was no bloodbath, just daily blood-letting, but at the time, we did not doubt that a bloodbath was inevitable. It was only a matter of when. I once asked Ndaba whether, when it came, she would murder us in our beds. Or show someone else where we might be.

"Not me, darling, never, but the man who work next door? How can we be sure? Can be many very angry, and when the mens have a drink, who can say what they do?"

Max seemed almost to enjoy the racial tension, making light of it. He would disparage the indignation by shaving away its causes. To correct any impression of callousness, he would find a daily camouflage by mentioning the names of prominent Jewish, liberal legal counsel; Vernon Berrangé, Levy, Joffe, Bernstein, Goldreich, and Wolpe all appeared at our dinner table before they gave their services in Mandela's Defense. Max claimed to be intimate with all of them. He wore those claims as easily as donning a kippah at a bar mitzvah, not really a Jew but an exaggerated appearance of one, not a liberal but a false claimant, easily lost among the truly courageous who risked everything when called to it.

༺࿆༻

The other balls scattered by Max were the Randalls. Tom and Ursula moved away as soon as Max moved in. Later I wondered whether Tom left because he could not bear to watch Louie being bled dry by this leech. Tom was obviously no longer needed for Marna, and Ursula had found new 'political engagement' which found a natural home in a university commune called Frankenwald. She would not need to cook or clean, and her daughters could run wild with a group. Humming could take precedence, and exciting political gossip would be rich and immediate.

Their move did bring politics centre stage. Their immediate neighbour was Miriam Basner, whose husband, Bas, a prominent lawyer, was in prison under the Ninety-day Detention Act. Bas had been the first to employ the newly qualified Nelson Mandela. His crime was to offer Mandela professional work, which gave him the theatre of the court to exhibit his disdain for judges and policemen. Mandela was frequently threatened with contempt of court by judges unused to a black man telling them what was appropriate to a case or their judgments.

Miriam, raven-haired, beautiful, and wittily drole, had daily stories to tell. Her twice-monthly visits to the prison gave rich details, as did the prosaic telephone calls she received from Bas's distracted warder, Hans, who rang her frequently for advice on how to handle her irascible husband.

"What is it this time, Hans?"

"Yus Mevrou. It's the wors,"

"What wors?"

"Ah mean the salami. Meneer Basner won't eat it."

"He loves salami. Why won't he eat it?"

"Ag Mevrou. It's like this. He sends me to buy salami. Ah, come back, and he looks at it, turns it over and then throws it at me. Jus in ma face."

"Not good Hans. Tell him I said so. Did he say why?"

"He says it's not kosher. How th'ell am Ah to know wot's kosher an wot's not?"

"Tell you what Hans. Take it away, clean off any dirt, remove any label, wipe it over with vinegar, and give it back after two days. Tell him it's kosher."

"Really? That's all Ah must do to make it kosher?"

"Next time, just ask for kosher, but this time, just do what I suggest."

"Agh hell, you are a good woman, Mevrou. Thanks, eva so."

When Bas was finally released, after six months, he paid several visits to Hans, who invited him home for a 'beer or two'. That's how it was. Crazy. Both sides were caught in the vortex of insanity. The 'emergency' laws were punitive. No reporting of political prisoners was allowed, but many of the Afrikaner warders, faced with innocent prisoners, did what they could to be kind. Mandela befriended his jailers; after his release, he visited the Prosecutor who had called for the death penalty, as well as Betsie Verwoerd, the widow of the heinous Hendrik, who had enacted the most draconian repression.

What only South Africans understand is that however deep our differences, what binds us is deeper, it is what we share, the country itself. Perhaps that is why the Truth and Reconciliation Commission worked and why only a South African could have suggested it, a black bishop who understood that central bond of identity, which needed airing and to be faced mutually.

Miriam's situation put Ursula's in perspective. Without any income and dependent on the kindness of others, Miriam and her son Daniel could do nothing but wait upon the whims of arbitrary injustice. Tom worked longer hours and faced the results of occasional street rioting, people savagely beaten and filling the wards. Meanwhile, Ursula feasted on outrageous stories and hummed.

I was waiting to get my final matriculation results, to be free of Max, and I hung about Frankenwald, avoiding the overtures of a lusty bearded geography lecturer called Don.

༄

The final nail in Max's coffin was hammered on my eighteenth birthday. I was now at university, having entered to read Medicine. Scrub that. Tom questioned whether I could fully commit to seven years. I knew I couldn't. Perhaps Architecture? Fiendish mathematics; perhaps not. Classics? 'You have no Latin? What about Greek? No? Perhaps you'd better think again?' Theology? More Lamentations? Nah.

I finally settled for an arts degree majoring in Psychology, new, should be interesting, English, easy-peasy, and History of Art as a subsidiary. The choice of educational options was heady; political ferment added chilli pepper.

Almost immediately, the defiance of an all-black jazz opera, 'King Kong', staged in the University Great Hall, brought township vitality to shake its fists openly; the impeccable Miriam Makeba with her flawless confidence to triumph. Perhaps there was still hope?

A few weeks later, the central administrative building of The University was draped in a white shroud. Inscribed with a long statement that, summarised, simply meant 'closed to people of colour.' In 1959, hope died.

Somewhere in Lesotho, Heli wept.

~

For my eighteenth birthday party, I disgracefully arrived with the guests. Ndaba had been cooking and cleaning all day. Thanks to Frankenwald, my first new friends were young lecturers, not students. Louie was tight-lipped and cold. Ndaba was miserable but knew the justice of Louie's anger and avoided my eyes. One of the friends had brought a light-skinned, coloured man, whose name was Hugh Masekela. Handing out wine and introductions and trying to puncture the tension, I failed to register that Max was already home from work. He called Louie out and into their room.

She summoned me into the kitchen. "How dare you?" She was quivering.

"How dare I what?"

"Invite that…that man…" Louie could not sustain facing my incredulity or fury. She looked nervously over her shoulder, fearing Max might appear.

"WHAT?!"

"Max is an Officer of the Law. He could be struck off for this…" Ah, so that was it. "You must ask him to leave."

"I refuse. If Hugh must go, we will all go."

She tried to mollify.

"I'm sorry. It's not right; we both know that. But this is Max's profession at risk."

"His profession as a hypocrite? Then, tell Max to leave. If he leaves, he's not here. He can't be struck off if it's me and my friends drinking with a black man, can he?" Louie was unmanned. I knew Max would never agree, even if she dared to ask. By now, I knew she wouldn't, so much for her high principles. Her steel had melted.

Just as the stand-off reached explosive silence, Hugh joined us in the kitchen. He had overheard or sensed the difficulty.

"Look, it's easy," he said, "Let's party outside. Then nobody has to leave. My skin is invisible in the dark."

That's what we did. Everyone moved food and drinks, and under the weeping trees, Hugh Masekela played the blues on a solo trumpet—the same trumpet given by Trevor Huddlestone, my long-forgotten chaplain. Nobody spoke. We listened.

Hugh wasn't world-famous then. But King Kong had happened, as had the bus boycott. It was the night Max was toast, and I lost all hope in my mother.

> *Well, I never felt more like runnin' away*
> *But why should I go 'cause I couldn't stay*
> *Without you*
> *You got me singin' the blues*

CHAPTER 13

David: Marriage Knot

'Nor can I suppose that when Mrs Casaubon is discovered in a fit of weeping six weeks after her wedding, the situation will be regarded as tragic. Some discouragement, some faintness of heart at the new real future, which replaces the imaginary, is not unusual, and we do not expect people to be deeply moved by what is not unusual.'

The first clean fracture in my life, after several green stick alienations, was my mother's release from me when I went to university and headed heedless towards the marital tunnel of no escape. She had padded it well and installed electricity and emergency supplies. Her brief marriage to my father had coloured mine long before marriage had loomed into view. Her bond with Max ensured unthinking speed to all my impulses, and his presence fogged any clarity.

University, the sudden liberty of a life in which choice existed, was daily champagne. Having had no distractions, I had moderately excelled with a first-class matriculation.

Rewarded by the privilege of a single room in the women's residence, I was expected to reach new heights of scholarship. Single cells were for the hair-shirt studious. I shared a bathroom with Daryl Eagle, my nemesis as Sanie's best friend, who grew precociously vigorous orchids on a diet of cigarette ash and Coca-Cola, but I spent my days with a cousin to the Queen—a first encounter with the opposite sex, well... gender. Yes, the recently deceased Queen, then reigning Monarch. It surprised me to encounter this orchid between the paving stones of slummy Braamfontein — and I did not believe him— since South Africa is not known on the Royal Progress Calendar. He offered me the pillion on his flash-roaring bike, and we bombed about making exhilarating noise and getting attention. I dropped into the occasional lecture, but Everything was much more interesting than Something.

My co-rider's name was Christopher—no, he never went down with Alice. Christopher told improbable stories about the nursery at Balmoral and being bathed by nannies and ponied by grooms. He did not see much of his cousins, who were older and had Duties. As he was poor and hungry enough to eat Chinese pickled chicken legs at the local greasy spoon, I challenged this account.

"Why don't you ask Queenie for a modest allowance?"

"Can't do that," he said, "she already pays my fees."

Christopher was never going to be boyfriend material; he was too beautiful for every day. We were mates. Until, cast as a silent Paris in a production of Fry's 'Tiger at the Gates', his David Bowie profile took centre stage against a fluted Ionic column, and I lost him to a swarm of gays who ate him alive, leaving only his long gold laces. I saw him only once after that, when he grasped my hand and, with tears in his eyes, blurted out, "Why didn't you stay with me? Now I am alone and lost!"

He was the closest male friend I ever had. Friendship rarely survives romance; intuitively, we had avoided the dangers of sex: no kissing and much teasing. After 'Tiger', I turned away, leaving him to burn bright and took up with a mirthless psychology lecturer, a pseud called Peter. Christopher mistook this desultory associate for my new passion and was equally delicate in leaving me to my fate.

What he set in train was my approach to the Great Noose of marriage. I have swung from it ever since. After the exotic Christopher, I took a detour with the world-weary Peter, who had a friend, an architect fresh out of MIT. In the uniform dough of khaki pants and heavy treads, Julian Beinart was a slice of iced cucumber; he wore bright white socks, tasselled loafers, and thin knitted silk ties, American chic. He and his friends introduced unfamiliar food, and we sheltered a black journalist called Lewis Nkosi, who dropped by via the neighbour's compost heap for company, a meal and the occasional shower.

Lewis wrote dangerous exposés for Drum Magazine and was on the run. The frisson of Lewis's flashing foil wielded against the plodding clubs of Special Branch gave life exhilaration. Sometimes, when Julian was out, we would descend to township penny-whistle and jive on the grass. I learnt to play chess and listened to jazz, Miles Davis, Dizzy Gillespie and Thelonious Monk. I thought I was accelerating sophistication by pretending to understand and enjoy them.

My only real joy was beating Julian at chess. Once. He never forgave me.

A psychologist should have known better, but a man offered the opportunity is seldom caring enough to refuse. Peter occupied the top floor of a dismal high-rise building in what were previously servants' quarters like those once occupied by Ndaba. He called it a penthouse, a name appropriate to what I permitted to happen on his squalid bed with its dirty sheets. I was in a hurry to get to the other side of virginity. Being deflowered was like setting a mount at a jump. Once over, all would be a smooth gallop, so I approached it at pace, refusing to risk the pause that might have swerved around it.

The jump I had taken was painful, sordid, devoid of kindness; more the lancing of an unripe boil than an exhilarating clear round.

After he departed in the morning, I stood on the roof and watched, far below, the traffic crawling like lice over my revulsion. I had been chewed and spat out, fibrous sugar cane sucked dry of sap. I resolved then and there never to remember this pent-up night of horror. I took a shower hot enough to burn it away and to cauterise the memory. It had never happened.

Two months later, it found a way to remind me that it had. I was constantly and violently sick. I could not go home or tell Louie. Nor was there any legal way to get medical help. To get away and give myself time to think, I decided to attend the National Union of Student Conference in Cape Town. I missed all the pounding talk and the waving of banners to sample the amenities of the ladies' cloakroom. Emerging from it, I was accosted by a diminutive dental student waiting outside.

"You're pregnant, aren't you?"

"Yes, I think so."

He handed me a slip of paper. "Go and see this man when you get back."

The Greek doctor who bore the offered name made only two demands—sixty pounds in cash and an address with no other occupants for the next Sunday morning. The father of this unwanted baby had moved into Julian's small house behind a high hedge. Both compulsorily and happily absent, they left me in a backroom to face a needle and a countdown, 9,8,7,6…

I came round from the anaesthetic to see the doctor rolling up his stethoscope and clipping his Gladstone bag.

"Rest in bed today. Take these tablets for pain." A tall man with a prominent Greek nose, Stavros departed, covered with my gratitude.

I vowed I would not remember this either. A vow that I broke; I have never been able to forget it.

'The whirligig of time will bring in his revenge'?

Yes. With interest.

You will find that just?

In time, I will. I could not have done other than I did. I would have faced murder or rape, and either could have happened, rather than face Louie, but now it colours all my thinking.

About what exactly?

About murder, about responsibility, both personal and tribal, about society's indifference to the consequences of trivial sex, about women and men, about everything… Guilt roped everyone together: the psychologist for his exploitation, me for my heedless impulses, Louie for her frozen heart, Max for his usurpation of my home, even the Greek doctor whom another beneficiary would later betray, struck off and imprisoned. None of what I think now could have been thought then, so we should leave it for decades hence. Balance and maturity were not yet born at this point.

Very well. But you owe it to Christopher to clear his reputation

I do. In researching this book, I discovered Christopher was alive and well-married and still in South Africa. He told me he had never been gay nor eaten alive. But he had thought me committed to the weary psychologist and withdrawn. Quel dommage! How restraint conquers opportunities! The best friend I ever had who, nearing eighty, is still known as the 'beautiful one.' As he always was.

༜

Jumping over doing any studying into phony sophistication meant that I failed my first year. So, I settled for a David, whose Goliath I would become, by slow degrees and daily practice.

He started as the student next door. I hardly noticed when he moved into my small flat, to which the 'very disappointed' Dean had banished me. I was to manage without privilege someplace else. Someplace was a tenement up three floors of a depressing building with outside walkways. My mother's resentment was now well-rooted and watered with good reasons. She had, quite literally and imminently, other fish to fry.

Shortly after my departure, Max persuaded Louie to sell her hard-won home and abandon her profession for the sake of his health. With the proceeds, he bought a tea room and a shack with no electricity on the beach in Plettenberg Bay. The tea room, appropriately called the 'Why Not', was where Louie would strain her back leaning against a counter, waiting for rare custom in the winter or, in summer, the need to rise at five to meet the fishing boats and buy the entire catch. The deluge of holiday visitors would queue for a meal all day. In her first season, a large tattooed customer had waited for an hour before being seated to discover that only one dish remained on the menu.

"This place is not a blerrie Why-Not. It is a blerrie 'Have-not'. Yus, let me help.' He pushed into the kitchen, donned an apron and spent his fortnight frying fish.

Bed and breakfast guests doubled Milly's workload and added the cleaning of oil lamps, smoked black by guttering fumes. Evenings would find Max in the light of these polished glass chimneys, counting the day's proceeds, stacking piles of glinting copper coins in the gloom. Only Rembrandt could have captured Shylock in full chiaroscuro glory. He never darkened the door of the trade but banked the pitiful takings that remained after the waitresses had helped themselves from the till while Louie slaved in the kitchen.

Only my family could have failed to make a fortune with a monopoly on the most select beach in the country. The starving, coloured children dominated Louie's conscience as she ferried food to a hatch at the back where they clamoured for free 'kians', crumbs of batter skimmed from the fish fryer, which she scooped into cones of newspaper to augment their diets with vitamins.

Max's ulcer improved. Louie's independent professional life was over. When the café's lease expired, there was no source of income. Louie had to sell her potentially valuable clapboard shack on the beach, a beach lovingly embraced by the Outeniqua mountains and the hump-backed whale of the Robberg. It overlooked the rolling breakers, a five-minute stroll away, and Louie made a loss—my family's unerring skill.

∾

The trouble with marriage is that there are no dry runs and no testing of the harness for comfort. Does it chafe? Is it too loose? Too tight? No. The ring is suddenly through the nose and off you go, led away. I had never given marriage much thought. I just assumed the cheerful co-existence with the brother I had never had until now would continue. David's easy smile, and his fluency with bird calls had convinced me that he was a fellow at peace with his world, his world of the wild. I would scrub river stones to release caddis fly larvae. He would catch them in his net downstream, literally and metaphorically. There hadn't been time for much else: his Master's dissertation took the front pew from the off.

After the weary psychologist, David was a clean mountain stream. His thick dark hair curled into the narrow nape of his neck, his profile composed itself about a straight nose, his jaw was perfectly carved, and his manner was easy. He had started as my lab demonstrator and disappeared for a year's travel. Unexpectedly, I saw him watching a donkey race, standing on a wall, and we recovered one another as though retrieving a dropped coin. Straight away, he invited me to a faculty party in one of the university sheds where his jiving was confident, he twirled me like candy floss. Our bond developed pace and was much encouraged by my mother, who saw him as my rescuer from a liaison she had shuddered to contemplate. David, an only son of a widowed mother, was distinctly marriageable.

Margaret, his mother, a Scot, 'Stuart, not Stewart,' lived in the Eastern Transvaal in a small, pin-perfect, suburban house. Barberton was once a mining town where old prospectors lingered in the hills around, some still shuffling into the bank with small gold nuggets unscrewed from the corners of handkerchiefs to be weighed and paid for.

Margaret, a frightened, petite woman, was never seen outside without make-up, a bag over her arm and a hat, like the Queen. The trials of society, even a visit to the local cinema, were brave-faced with all proprieties in place, even the tip for the ice cream seller prepared, pocketed, at the ready. Our frequent trips to see her were clearly an imposition, but she adored her only child and did her best to accept me. I felt for her, so shrivelled by fear of public opinion, so lonely and so uncomplaining. Not someone I could talk to about anything.

His wealthy grandparents, her in-laws, treated her with peremptory rudeness and expected servitude. My outrage on her behalf forged a bond between us, for she had no outrage of her own.

Visits to her served a dual purpose. David had invested in an old Linhoff plate camera, which, mounted on a heavy tripod, enabled him to take high-definition shots for National Geographic. Colour negatives of studio size for covers had an advantage over most wildlife competitors, but they required hours of immobile silence under a black cloth to capture a rare, saddle-billed stork reflected in a river.

We were bounced into tying the sheepshank —it is not a knot to take much strain— by Louie, who would not hear of me accompanying him to a conference on locusts in Paris. Not in full view of Opinion. He was an invited UN delegate, and while he was listening to swarm statistics and viewing slides of decimated fields and swollen bellies, I would wander the boulevards and see it; see it all! Paris!

'Marry first, and it can be your honeymoon.' said Louie. She had already forgotten Marna's warning of her own imminent disaster. Perhaps the strain of balancing me against Max sought an easy relief in offloading one of us.

There was no pressing reason not to: David and I lived in unholy concupiscence already, and marriage was vaguely in sight. A photograph developing in a slow tank, not yet sharply defined nor really selected. Marriage happens to people, like puberty; we might as well. It would save Louie money, and Paris did not offer itself on a two for one basis often, not from South Africa, flight included.

Cavalier it undoubtedly was, but it's called adolescence: too grown up for dreams, too headlong to think. Besides, I had lost all hope of Louie. We hardly spoke at all. I had no longer a home of any welcome. Even Windy was hardly mine any longer, although I went back to see Ndaba when I could count on Louie and Max being out. They were gradually packing to leave for the glory of running a beach café.

The concupiscense was tepid and rare. I never understood why it gets the inflated press it does. The first time it happened, David was waiting for a black eagle to leave its nest so he could ring the chicks. It looked to be a long wait so we did something else with one eye out on the cliff face and the boots still on.

'Is that it?' I asked.

'Won't be long', he said, lowering himself over a sharp ledge as the great bird soared away down the valley below.

Maybe I should have paid attention to omens. The whole marriage launch was chaos, a succession of trip-wires: no champagne and no decisive trodden glass. Because the conference was in Lent and publishing church 'banns' was not permitted, we needed a Special Licence from the court. Max, who I assumed knew his way around courts, said I had to wear a hat. I dug out Marna's old church hat and we turned up in white lab coats, me in hat. Perhaps the magistrate was short sighted and hat-plus-white meant marriage. We were expecting a piece of paper stamped by an official and instead got, 'I now pronounce you man and wife.'

We thought it overzealous, perhaps a matter of form. After some secretaries were summoned to witness, we got the piece of paper we expected.

So, remove the hat and return to the dissection of a dogfish.

I had now switched to science, and David was paying his Master's fees as a supervisor. His profile continued to recommend him, and that was most often what I saw, as well as the occasional slow wink above other diligent heads.

When we presented the paper to the priest, he said, "But this is a Marriage Certificate? I can't marry you."

"But you must! Everybody's been invited."

"Young man, I need a serious and private conversation," said the priest who led him off.

"Cohabit?" No, of course we had not cohabited.

"Would he, although we were now legally married, undertake not to engage in intercourse until after the church ceremony?"

He would..

"Then I will perform the ceremony as usual, and no one will know. When we go into the Registry, it will simply be to restore this marriage certificate to you and wish you well in spite of this unfortunate irregularity. I do not want it known; I am taking a grave risk." Nothing as grave as the one I was diving into.

David did not say 'Gotcha, Vicar' but wanted to.

On the day itself, the sky mustered objections, too, hailing golf balls. We walked to the church under a beach umbrella. God had done his best to stop it, but I was not into God then. Going to Paris to share a honeymoon with locusts was the only thing in sight. I would go through any charade required.

On the subject of the honeymoon, I should mention that it was not only locusts we shared it with but a cheerful dipsomaniac. One of

David's university professors, an eminent geneticist when sober, was going too. David assured his anxious wife that we would do all we could as escorts.

"You know these events. People ply you with drink all the time. Please make it easy for him to say no." It was a plea.

"Of course. No problem." David assured her.

When the plane steadied, the stewardess came round for the drink orders. We abstained.

"Two orange juices? And for you, sir?"

"Since they're not drinking, I'll have a triple brandy."

∾

One alcoholic was sharply followed by another. On the nuptial flight to London, I had my last sight of beloved Heli.

The plane stopped for re-fueling at Entebbe and David and I were waiting, confined to the transit lounge with the already inebriated geneticist asleep across two chairs. An official approached and asked to see my passport. He checked it and asked me to follow him. Being singled out might jeopardise the onward flight. Why? He led me into the deserted restaurant. At a table, with his back to the door, I found Heli with the sad leaking eyes of a turtle, ruddy complexion, overweight and looking as hot in his suit as on our first encounter. I had not seen him for almost seven years when he was striding energetically about Roma in his gown. I had to bury my shock.

"How did you know?"

"Your mother cabled me."

"Oh God! I am only here for an hour if that…"

"Better than nothing, Phil. Let me look at you." He pushed me back to scrutinise.

"You haven't changed."

I could not echo that. He knew I saw him quite clearly, a disappointed old man who had stopped believing in anything, waiting to die. My heart ached and pined already for the loss. He looked destroyed. Hearing that I was to be within reach, he had prevailed upon some old friends to drive him the three hours from a remote convent where he lived, tended by nuns, to spend a precious last hour with me. He gave me a beautiful Springbok skin handbag as a present, but he had really come to say goodbye. We both knew it. He sat, spilling an occasional tear and stroking my hand. There was nothing worth saying that could matter. No news was worthy, no details were relevant. We sat mostly in silence, broken by his rueful smile. When the embarkation bell rang, he rose.

"At least I've seen you one more time. I hope you will be happy, happier than I could manage. Are you happy?"

"I'm doing my best."

"All any of us can do. You've already had more practice than most." He kissed me and ran a hand over my hair. He had not mentioned Marna or Louie or asked after anyone, not even my new husband.

I watched him shuffle to the exit. He did not turn round. I saw him stop to blow his nose before leaving to seek his lift home in an anonymous car park in the middle of the continent, over which we would continue to fly for hours while the rolling dust behind him covered his tracks. I could hardly bear to return to the man I had married who had no knowledge of Heli and would not understand the copious tears that flowed from a bottomless misery, not for Heli's loss but for his disappointed life of true valour.

Heli's life had been the tragic consequences of idealistic aspirations offered to the wrong institutions, on shoulders not broad enough to carry the burden of his solitude or the weight of what he opposed. He had done everything possible but knew it was not enough. It never could have been. He knew nobility but had never found joy beyond the joy in black children eager to learn and the response of a black man honoured by being spoken to in his own tongue. Africa had not disappointed him; it had been his deepest love; only its governance that he served had betrayed it, and through that, his promises to it: iAfrika!

"Old Master's Zulu, darling, better than is mine." Ndaba once said. Heli and she never spoke anything else. I remembered all those smiling local servants summoned by Milly into the kitchen to drink tea when Heli came to visit, to wait to hear them converse, just to hear his Zulu and prove her stories true. It was such a rarity.

His legacy to Ndaba, when he died a year later, was the royalties from all his books, little in value but great in symbolism. She understood him more deeply than any of us because they both began in Zululand, in the same arena of rolling hills, thatched kraals and the scent of grass and fires, where the school inspector did his first horseback rounds over what became his truly beloved country.

I couldn't tell David any of that. Instead, I showed him a handbag, and we manhandled a man in a stupor back to the plane.

༄

The geneticist had every kind of triple in every pub we passed. We were on a triple honeymoon in London and then in Paris, dragging him out of bars, knocking up the night porter to let him into several hotels where he stood, often in the rain, waiting with police. Putting *him* to bed was our nightly romp. It ended badly.

The UN put on a final dinner on the Seine in a spectacular barge, cruising slowly past buildings, especially floodlit. There were eight courses and a speech with each. When it came to the 'Mesdames et Messieurs' toasts, our companion staggered to his feet, held up his glass and said 'Ere's to the fockin locust' before collapsing, pulling the laden cloth with him and shattering the embossed porcelain.

We left on the first plane home without him.

So, a marriage hardly consummated and un-honeymooned, thanks to my mother's scruples. Considering that marriage had to be Forever, public opinion was a poor argument for a hasty decision in Lent. I saw a little of Paris alone, dogged by importuning men, before we undertook the first marital home and marriage unexpurgated began. It had declared its limits on the wedding night when the new husband heaved out of bed saying, 'I can't sleep with you. You're too restless.' and went out to sleep on the adjacent floor. I found it perplexing he had not mentioned this earlier—during the year we had co-habited— but timed it for the great transition between liberty and imprisonment.

The marriage bed was separate beds.

I went home the following day.

"What are you doing here?" Louie asked.

"It's a disaster…" I began. Louie shrugged and lit a cigarette.

'Well, my girl, you've made your bed and now must lie on it.'

I did not think I had made any beds at all.

∽

Now, I have to recount an episode that, for decency's sake, most would leave untouched. Yet it afforded an indelible new knowledge that changed the course of my life. Gory, yes, but also clean, clear and inescapable, it illuminated my willful blindness. It could not cure it at a stroke, but later exposures were quicker to trigger the alarms.

That Paris honeymoon was grey with the unbroken wash of knowing that the harness was a noose, steel clamped and throttling. Louie had failed to hear my appeal on the day following the wedding. I had nowhere to turn. Shackled and without any independent means of survival, there were no choices: no work, no refuge with family now scattered, merely the role of 'wife'. A wife that was not a wife in any sense at all.

While last-minute arrangements were being finalised for David's employment with the Mozambique Marine Department to undertake research on an island in the middle of the Indian Ocean, we stayed in a hotel in downtown Lorenzo Marques. A pay-and-go billet for travelling salesmen, it was bare-boarded, basic and soulless. It had no kitchen. Breakfast was left outside doors on trays by room service. Keys hung at a vacant reception. The creaking concertina-door lift worked.

Each day, I wandered the streets, mooched through a covered market's crates and ate alone at roadside cafés, leafing through old magazines. In unrelieved tedium, I faced full frontal the catastrophic mistake I had made. Not only did my husband not love me, he was entirely indifferent to anything I might want. His work would determine where and how we would live and whether there were any straws to be gleaned on the margins of his work for me to live upon.

Mentally and emotionally bereft, I was truly lost. I also took full responsibility.

Good God, surely I had seen enough in Louie's life and Marna and Heli's estrangement not to walk hastily into a facsimile loveless marriage? If my misery flicked towards blaming Louie, it was quenched by imagining her wilting over a beach café till and providing beds and food for the already affluent. I could not add to that by writing. Max had poisoned our well, as from the first I knew he would. My life had not yet begun, but hers was over.

Day after day, I faced the imprisonment of life with a man who hardly acknowledged I existed. He seldom spoke to me, never asked and never listened. That amiable brother who had smiled over riverbeds was now hell-bent on his career, but I could tag along. No, I *would* tag along.

David suddenly declared that he would be flying off for a week's conference on shrimp; far north in Beira.

Now was the chance of what had begun to grip me. It had been incubating since the wedding, a spore in the soggy petri dish of despair. After a taxi had called to take him to the airport, I went out to buy a bottle of gin, used the stairs to our room to increase my circulation and ran a bath: a very hot bath, very deep. The resolve brought a strange clarity. I looked out at the city and the high pink clouds and took a final farewell before drawing the curtains. I put the gin within reach on the floor near the taps. Then, extracting a new razorblade from his store, I placed it on the bath's edge, slowly lowering myself into the scalding water. I cut my left wrist with a clean single slash.

Too late, I discovered that with the tendons in one hand now useless I could not cut the other. Bugger! I would have to wait to bleed to death, so I sank beneath the waves of despair and swallowed gulps of gin. It amused me to realise that had I managed both wrists, I would not have managed the gin. Suicide is not as easy as people think. It needs careful step-wise planning. The pain was acute; it stung like an underwater burn, but it was a sharp, clean pain, not the bottomless ache I could never release. Gin seemed to have little influence on thought; my mind was as sharp as the razor cut. I realised that I did not care for gin. Brandy would have been better, but brandy is supposed to revive, and revival was not what I wanted. There was no counter impulse. I just hoped that I would be found lifeless before David returned.

I saw myself covered by a sheet in a morgue. I visualised the repose of a blue-white face. 'Can you identify…?' Then I wondered whether Louie would feel regret. Or perhaps, secretly, a little relief? Max would have more space to occupy and more money for his carpets. My contempt would no longer reproach her. Ndaba would weep and weep, and for that, I did feel wretched. Should I have written? What could I have said? Windy would weep with her. I did hope that Ndaba might find a way to escape Max. Clearly, Louie never would.

The bath was a bath of blood getting stronger coloured by the minute; with an indolent forefinger I made swirls of deep red in lesser red and watched them disappear. The painting of my end became diverting until no swirls survived.

Sinking into somnolence, I gave over and hoped losing consciousness would be quick.

"Oh, for Christ's sake!" Fury penetrated; I looked up to see David standing over me. He ballooned in and out of focus. For a moment, I wondered whether the oscillating liquid red man was a final hallucination.

"What the fuck have you done?" I sat up and watched him search the room. What was he looking for? He savagely swept back the curtains and, against a sharp sunset light, opened drawers, slamming them shut. I followed him as though through binoculars. He cleared the lamp and a book off the bedside locker, then used the locker to smash a window. Most of the glass disappeared down the six floors outside, but he carefully scattered some shards across the bed and onto the carpet. He replaced the locker, reset the lamp and re-positioned open the book he was reading. It was all meticulously done. Then he came to haul me from the bath, letting the blood-stained water escape before he tore an old shirt to tie a tourniquet near my armpit. With a severed sleeve, he bound the wound rather roughly.

"I liked this shirt. Don't move; don't want a bloody mess," he said, using the rest of the shirt to mop up pink splashes on the tiled floor.

Holding my slashed wrist above my head, he helped me into clothes, shirt first and pulling up my jeans with one hand and looking daggers, swearing.

"Fuck. Bloody stupid woman. Why the hell did you have to do that? I'll call a taxi. Don't move from the bathroom."

When reception called back, David threw his raincoat over me and shepherded me out, my injured arm clamped against his chest.

"My wife had an accident opening the window. Perhaps someone could help clear up the broken glass. Room 605?"

To the taxi he said in Anglo-Portuguese "To o hospital por favor. Rapido"

"Sim, senhor."

Although I had known he cared little for me, the man whose cool calculations had created an alibi before binding my wrist was someone I had never seen before. An embryonic James Bond whose instinct for self-preservation was total. His jaw was set; his look when he glanced at me was one of contempt. On the journey to the hospital, he offered not a word but gazed out of the window, entirely bloodless.

"Plane not take off?" I asked.

"Luckily not."

I did not bother to argue about the nature of luck.

"Can you wait to take us back?" David asked the taxi, who tapped at his meter. It would charge to wait.

The surgeon at the hospital gave me a local anaesthetic and waited until my arm was numb. Like a tailor finishing a buttonhole he calmly repaired the clean-cut tendons while David contrived a solicitous look of interest at his skill and concern for my misfortune.

"My wife had an accident," he said. The surgeon raised his eyebrows but did not respond. He kept glancing at David as he worked. I watched his eyes; David was watching his hands. He had read the truth but said nothing. After stitching the wound, he dressed it with gauze and a thick bandage and followed with an injection.

"What is the injection for?" David asked.

"Antitétano. Você cuide-se melhor? asked the surgeon.

"What does that mean?" David asked amiably, addressing his wife as though selecting a dish from a menu. I had had time for some study of Portuguese.

"Anti-tetanus. He also asked whether you'll take better care of me" David nodded emphatically and put an arm around my shoulders, brushing my hair from my eyes. He was getting rather good at this.

"Sim, sim, perfetto. Muito obrigado" David said.

The surgeon looked at me and shook his head sadly, rolling his stethoscope tube around his hand.

"Ask him what we owe him," David said. It needed no translation. The surgeon looked at me.

" Ele nunca poderia pagar-me bastante. Mas para você nada. Não faça isso de novo" he added to me. I understood. David could never pay him enough, but for me, no payment was necessary. I had found a friend sad enough to smile with liquid kindness. 'Don't try that again' was his final appeal.

"What was that?" David asked as he pushed me back to the taxi, his hand on the small of my back.

"Nothing important."

It wasn't important any more. I would not try it again. I would no longer care enough to die for the lack of love. Brutal truth would do instead. I'd live for that.

CHAPTER 14

Serpents: Handling the Natives

'N'atheless, I love words; they are the quoits, the bows, the staves that furnish the gymnasium of the mind. Without them...our intellectual strength would have no implements.'

The Mozambique Marine Science Institute had once been optimistic and built a rudimentary house on a cliff on an island in the Indian Ocean in the hope of persuading a Portuguese scientist to occupy it. None warmed to the idea. But David did. He would accept a research post that gave him his own laboratory, a house, and all the time in the world without interruptions.

I would have liked some interruptions.

The house offered the necessary two sleeping spaces — my husband added snoring to restlessness— a rudimentary kitchen with a gas cooker and a paraffin fridge, a primitive canvas shower bag fed from a borehole and an outside living room, screened by perforated concrete blocks from the unending glare of the sea. The sand blowing was nicely funnelled at eye level through perforations. The cliff had tried to shrug the house off its shoulder and succeeded in splintering terrazzo flooring, through which beetles foraged and cockroaches clambered. I tried softening the view by digging up a shady umbrella tree and planting it against the blocks, watering it after sundown. It died with speed and enthusiasm, leaving spiked branches that scratched the tin roof like nails across a blackboard. My lessons were all non-verbal: I dug it back up.

The island was called Inhaca, the island of snakes. Beyond the surrounding clearing of sand and the borehole was the bush, the singing, cicada-stultifying, intense, tropical bush, alive with snakes of every habit and venom. I was phobically terrified of snakes; not seeing a snake was worse than seeing one. David loved snakes and handled them with confidence. He also enjoyed my terror, inflating it by pushing a flickering-tongued head towards me with faux persuasion.

'Not really dangerous. Boomslang, back-fanged. They seldom bite, you see.' He pressed open a gaping pink maw to exhibit the small and lethal curved fangs before draping the bright green horror with its gimlet eyes like a scarf in a tree. From there, it might slide noiselessly anywhere.

Inhaca was my inescapable initiation: the marriage of the snake phobic to the snake handler. The first maid we had employed shrieked and fled when, first thing in the morning, she opened a fridge. A large comatose snake fell out. It was being chilled before posing for a camera. A chilled snake moves slowly. The maid moved quickly and without waiting for her wages.

David, now called 'O Professor' by the fishermen, departed with nets, bottles, binoculars and lunch just after sunrise to some distant mangrove, returning at sundown with scratched knees and samples. He deposited these in the lab below the cliff before ascending to the house. While waiting for me to juggle a supper, he drank a gin and tonic and read Time Magazine, twirling a lock of hair and offering an odd 'Hmm', should I be brave and speak. I had little to speak of.

One walk along the beach was much the same as another.

My week's only interruptions were the two walks to meet the fishing boats to receive his Time and hope for a letter. Letters were rare, the walks routine to slice the week into three equal measures. They took more than half a day, five miles and back. Depending on the tide, one way would be the beach, the other the bush, through sandy paths overhung with boomslangs or spattered with leaves to camouflage adders.

The jetty belonged to what called itself the 'otel, a square house with a veranda, where Mauricio, the manager, would manage 'una cerveja preta' and a bowl of 'langoustines peri-peri' at a table on the apron of short grass. There were no beds or overnight visitors. I would help Mauricio water his lemon and orange trees in wooden barrels and accept a lemon in payment. His 'otel' was never going to thrive; Rosina, his wife, came less often for the weekends. She cleaned another hotel on the mainland while Mauricio cleared coconuts and loaded boats.

"Não há nada para ela," he said, but what can a man with responsibilities do?

Letters that did arrive were uniformly envious: 'What a life you must lead on a tropical island! How much bliss could one person bear?' For a while, it was only good manners to agree.

Friends imagined the cover of a travel magazine, hand in hand, wearing a white kimono, leaving virgin footprints in sea-licked sand to the sound of plashing waves. Instead, the day was mosquito spray, dripping sweat and drilling cicadas. When the sun had sunk, after winking facetiously, the tree frogs took over, pouring out their treble ululation like tinnitus, only louder. David was always early abed. I sat outside to watch the haze of light expand over Lorenzo Marques as the clouds on the horizon reflected the invisible city. The glory of the night sky, the beam of moonlight across the sea and the singing frogs kept up persuasion but increasingly failed. Going to sleep merely sliced monotony: no books, no music, nobody. My shell collection grew unobserved and whitened as it aged.

Each day was an empty gourd filled with the rattling dry seed questions. How had this happened? How had I failed to see that marriage was scheduled, an addendum to a PhD? Marriage accomplished, next would follow the research to achieve tenure. He would decide on that, and *that* could be anywhere: Saskatchewan or Helsinki or a dismal villa in Des Moines. I won't be consulted about that either. The three years I spent sampling the educational options lay wasted. I met him traversing science over a tray of formaldehyde and got dropped into it to pickle; my life snipped clean, 'she'll do' and attached to his, a ribbon binding a file: marriage, now closed.

None of that could be written to anybody. Friends were determined to envy me, so where would I find the lyrical to please them? There was one abundance, and it was food. *That* could decently occupy pages.

The beach below fringed a tidal flat, a sea of productive mud when the tide was out. It retreated for over a mile. The fishermen's wives combed small pools and rocky outcrops in search of what the coral reef released lavishly. Every tide washed food to our feet. I would give them an hour's start and follow with a pocket of escudos, looking through their baskets to transfer lobster, crab, small fishes, octopus, mussels and squid to my own, a daily bouillabaisse. They could always replenish food, money for them was better. Since the mud flats had occasional stonefish in the pools, as lethal as snakes, both they and I were content.

Everything, large or small, rare or common, cost one escudo, about three pence; even a wild guinea fowl trapped in a snare and brought to the door. In the bush, cashew nuts hung for the gathering, and wild loquats added to the coconuts that fringed the shore. Natural food was five-star. We ordered gin, sugar, coffee, paraffin for the fridge and red meat from the mainland. These came on the fishing boats dispatched from a general dealer in Lorenzo Marques. Meat was simply meat, sometimes fillet steak, sometimes shinbone for stew, and both were the same price per kilo. It was a potluck life in every way.

Everything was abundant but uncertain, except the mistake of marriage, from which there was no variation. The marriage would be forever, and the mistake of it coloured every moment. 'Thou shalt never betray a marriage.'

I don't recall any reference to marriage doing the betraying.

∾

One evening, I discovered a window on the world. I was twiddling the knobs on David's transoceanic radio through crackling static and Portuguese shipping fragments when the glory of English broke through. It was a play and as clear as if I had bought tickets and been shown to a seat. The BBC World Service, London calling, and London received! A miraculous discovery. After that, every evening at five thirty, I sat waiting until the introduction and music began at six, gobbling up plays, news, commentary and weather reports with equal avid hunger. An hour of words, speakers and arguments fed the deepest deprivation, other people. The BBC was now saintly. I wondered how to express my worship and kiss the hem of its gown as it walked its six o'clock lamp through my life.

"Why don't you try writing something for them? Write a radio play. You've certainly got the time." David said.

"What would I write about? Plays need people, dialogue."

He read the barb. "Only inadequate people need other people; use your imagination."

Literature of a sort followed his suggestion. One night, he offered a morsel unprompted.

"I met some people today, a couple. Sailing to Durban on a catamaran."

"Why stop in here? What were they like?"

"Oh, you know, the usual."

"Did you talk to them? You must have!"

"Not really. He was rather standoffish, and his wife was covered in hideous scabs. God knows where they've been; they looked nasty, even daubed with chamomile. They had a couple of kids and a dogsbody cook, tall black guy."

"Where exactly are they moored?"

"Over on the open sea side. They'll probably be gone when you get there."

He knew I'd try since my inadequacy festered constantly.

The next day, I crossed through the perilous bush to the rolling breakers on the wild side, which tumbled, swept, and retreated to Australia. The crashing, thundering surf clawing the beach invited a suicide swim. There was no sign of a mast along the unbroken curve of the beach and none visible above the waves. Forlorn hope. Had people really been there?

A week later, I found their camp, not half a mile distant, on the lee side, our side. Two substantial framed tents, carefully screened by trees and invisible from all directions, were partially capsized. Around the site was a churn of footprints. A new fridge, door hanging open, was empty; a small cooker and gas cylinder were spattered with bird droppings. A washing line hung with pegs looped slack between the trees. Rubbish bags spilt torn papers, empty tins and discarded clothing. The pied crows had taken first pickings. Clearly, whoever they were, they had gone.

When I reached the 'otel, Mauricio was waiting. He came pumping out on his short legs, followed by a languorous, tall and very dark African.

"Um grande problema, o problema pior. Este homem precisa de ajuda" Mauricio's usual phlegmatic manner was whipped into a foam.

"What happened?" I asked. The African spoke.

"My employer, he just goes. In boat."

"Leaving you here?"

"Sim."

"Then he will come back to fetch you?"

The African shook his head.

"No, he mean to do it, he clever. He not paid me for two months. Two months! Food, no money. He say he just go short sail to test boat. I must stay to cook. He is not testing boat. He is going for good."

"Where do you come from?" I asked since the story explained the camp and the debris of a hasty flight.

"From Tanganyika", the cook shrugged. "Now, so far!"

Mauricio shrugged and went on wringing out disbelief.

"How will you get home?"

I knew what was coming.

"I have no money," he said "but you can help me take bus or train. Without ticket, Mozambique will arrest. English do this. Ow!"

I was the only thing with a passing resemblance to 'English' and would have to remedy it.

"Can he stay here for one or two days?" I asked.

Mauricio shrugged. He looked doubtful; 'English' tended to abscond. "We will pay you," I said. Mauricio was persuaded, not by the promise but by a lack of alternatives. "Falar com meu marido, O Professor." Better. He clapped the cook below the shoulder, and they turned towards the 'otel. I started for home.

As O Professor would not be back for hours, I took a detour back to the camp before the island fishermen stripped it. I had lost any scruples about privacy and wanted to get those torn-up letters and documents. All was as it had been. Roughly torn documents were crammed into one bag together with more diligently destroyed scraps of blue, private letters with a line, a few words apiece. A few had blown about and snagged on trees. I collected all I could see and lugged the bag home. I had not been allowed to meet them; in debris now, I would.

O Professor was unsurprised.

"I have to admit, I didn't like him. Arrogant British ponce with a cut glass accent, he was rather slippery. He definitely did not want to engage… probably planning this all along…"

"What can you do for the cook?" An appeal by a helpless woman might work. It did.

"Actually, that might be quite easy. The Institute is flying some glass equipment over in a couple of days. I could radio the pilot and get him to authorise a return rescue. He'll manage the onward flight to the border; these pilots all know one another…"

"And money?"

"I'll give him enough. Most of these small planes fly on errands; the return is covered. Anything at all is a bonus. Word in an ear is all that's needed."

The cook was ecstatic. A flight of any kind was ample redress. Two days later, Mauricio waved away the proffered notes. His small tractor was puttering and blowing smoke rings in anticipation of turning taxi to take his now-honoured guest to the landing strip. The small Cessna circled before descending.

"Então então, muito obrigado, você é um gênio" Mauricio called as he released the brake. The cook, who, with the hour upon him, was showing the whites of his eyes, clasped his hands and shook out the cocktail of his fear and thanks. From the short grass in the clearing of palms, I got a glimpse of a vibrating black hand as the plane headed away over the sea. That was the first moment the island felt like home.

I was no longer inadequate but a 'genius.'.

Literature had arrived on the wind. A sailboat followed by a flight now offered a new purpose: collecting paper. My floor became a scatter of jigsaw puzzles, and I kept an eye out for pieces missing, near the camp or blown further afield. They painted a compelling history. There were refusals from banks to loan any more money; there were threats from shops to instruct solicitors to recover debts in hot pursuit from Kenya down the coast of Mozambique: Chinde, Quelimane and Beira. Demands for credit payments on cookers and fridges, camp lighting and sleeping bags made clear that buying new everywhere and abandoning was their way to go. A parasitic life on the leisurely run, one step ahead and the sea put between.

My walks in search of missing pieces diminished my terror of snakes.

We had new animation at supper and even O Professor took to speculation. It was living literature, a rationed book which might never have an ending. The principal character was a daughter, Marisa, whose blue-lined notepaper made her the tragic heroine whose narrative was date stamped. First, she declared an intention to marry and was already making plans for a wedding. When might they arrive to be there?

Early letters began with pleading that they should arrive well before to get to know her fiancé. 'You'll love him, I promise'.

Then, she would be grateful for some financial help, if possible. Any contribution at all? Later, she was worried about the symptoms of a skin disease, and wouldn't it be better to go where treatment was available? It sounded serious; perhaps a fungal infection? Or worse? Were the small children likely to get infected? Boats were intimate places. Then, about her small siblings, were they ever going to start school? She was longing to see them again! Hadn't Douglas ever thought of that when he bought the boat for the trip of their lives? How long was his expedition planned to last? Did Douglas plan for anyone but himself?

David did not like to dwell on another selfish husband who cared little for his wife. He began to lose interest.

The three most recent were desperate. Why had she heard nothing for weeks? Where exactly were they? Were they still hoping to get to Durban before the wedding? Had they received her gifts, books for the children? Could her mother telephone, just to know she was alive? There was spluttering of anger; Douglas was pretty bloody selfish, wasn't he? What sort of man needed to be bailed out by other people? How could her mother even *ask* for money? No way. The last was tearful but resigned. If they were not going to 'make it,' she would still like to know. She would save a piece of cake for the children. A telegram when they were near a post office? Surely that was not asking too much? That was the last of the pages from Marisa to her mother.

It ended as it had begun, amputated, rather like sex, not much worth remembering, or why it had begun. I wondered whether to write to Marisa; her desperation had joined my own. The shame of her mother was hardly a wedding gift to wrap and send. Then I wondered; maybe the hasty departure was to reach the wedding. All might yet be healed, scabby skin included.

The lingering tragedy wafted away as smoke from a dying fire; wisps remained but could not reignite. Then, as it had begun, in a chance encounter, the story was concluded by a chance purchase. O Professor returned from his institute on a flight with a newspaper. On the front page was a brief report.

'*Unknown Sailors Feared Drowned.* It described the condition of the destroyed boat as '*lacking mast and sails .... washed up on the coast of Northern Natal after a severe storm...struck rocks before capsizing... boat registered in Zanzibar...registered owner said he sold the vessel and is still owned money for it...No bodies found...not possible to establish how many.... interior suggests there were more than one... survival feared unlikely. Anyone with any knowledge of a catamaran travelling down the coast should contact the coast guard in Durban.*'

"We ought to contact them, surely?" I suggested.

"And say what? That we have combed through their letters and discovered they were unscrupulous spongers?"

"I don't think she was…or the children."

"No. All the more reason not to. Give them a dignified sea burial on their way to a wedding. Marisa will grieve, believing her mother intended to be there. Everything has been lost; no point adding to it."

It made sense, really, if anything could.

This diversion had revealed my hunger for language, and lit an imagination about those I had never met. David's calculation in misdirecting my first search and his habit of diminishing me refreshed what I already knew. The pendulum returned to its still centre.

∾

One cook dispatched, another followed in a fortnight, no more voluntary than the first. Sam, head cook in a grand hotel on the beach in Lorenzo Marques, was caught syphoning off supplies for resale to remote areas and turning a tidy profit. After a short spell in prison, he accepted the option of exile for a shorter sentence. Inhaca would imprison him more cheaply. After three weeks, he asked to go back to prison.

Sam and I had much in common before we met.

One day, this imposing tall man in a beaded fez knocked politely at my open kitchen door. Would I be in need of a cook? His English was polished.

"Are *you* a cook by any chance?" I asked.

"No, not by chance. I am a cook by design. It's what I like to do."

"It's a lovely idea," I said "but we have no money to pay a cook-by-design."

"I am not asking to be paid. I would just like to eat. For that, I will cook interesting food for you. I have a hammock and can sleep outside if sometimes you will let me wash?"

Sam moved in and out of sight in the bush surrounding us. He showered when we were out. Supper was now three courses and merited candlelight and wine. Sam spent all day preparing a rotating spit over coals in the sand for slow-roasted guinea fowl marinated in juniper and chilli. He supervised the selection from the gleaner's baskets on the flats, negotiating more generous terms for crab and lobster but discarding the worthless, for which he would pay nothing. During the day, he wandered the island gathering edible salad, which he dressed with sharp sauces. He picked cashew nuts, roasted and salted them for pre-dinner drinks, usually gin marinated in coconut juice topped with lime and ladled, cold from a thick green calabash, scooped out with a scimitar knife to leave insulating fibre.

It began to feel like living, and letters were easier to write. Friends began to invite themselves. Sometime soon….?

When meat was due, Sam walked to the jetty, and after two empty-handed returns, he taught O Professor the right Portuguese words for orders to the dealer; less often shin or bone, more often filet-de-bœuf. If he did stew anything, it would take three days; the meat would fall from the bones like a layered cassoulet. For fillet, he set a bank of hot coals in the sand and flamed them, charred on the surface and pink perfect in the centre. There were always three sauces to choose from.

Crab he dressed with decorous edgings, and lobster served fork willing, claws cracked. Small langoustines he arranged like a dahlia facing the sun, their tails in peri-peri, draped over the edge of a bowl, ogling all comers. Terracotta finger bowls were ordered from a market trader, and the commission paid to the fishermen for delivery set up an easier arrangement. For a man who had run a hotel kitchen, this was a holiday. He knew everybody in the market over the sea and received screws of paper releasing seeds, leaves, powders and sneezes. Sam believed in finger food like every African but floated grapefruit slices on the surface of warm water to cut the oil between courses. Dessert was often coconut mixed with fruit salad or baklava-like pastries swimming in honey.

He had begged some old fish crates from the boats and made a bread oven, packing it into a hole in the ground, doubling insulation with a blanket and a lid of tin heated below the sand. It brought back the safari with Heli. Dough set in early morning rose, and when the sun was at its zenith, Sam flicked water to crisp the crust and baked it.

Sam made every day festive. The menu was never disclosed; his gratuity was our surprise and delight. O Professor came home earlier for his gin-and-Time. Occasionally there were flights to Lorenzo Marques as the research now needed the Institute's number cruncher. 'La Senhora' was offered a taxi to spend a day wandering through the market or swimming in a hotel pool before flying home, low over the evening sea, so low we could see the great rays basking near the surface and the scimitar sharks cutting the taffeta for a sumptuous iridescent gown.

To warn Sam about timing, we would circle the house in the small three-seater. He would emerge to wave a dishcloth as we headed to the landing strip. That would give him an hour and a half if the tide was out and two hours if it was in. Marriage was no warmer, but Sam made an invitation possible.

Rosie and Derek Langbridge had managed three sons in a hurry, one each year before the clock struck barren. The oldest was five. As parents, they were an odd and old couple; Rosie, a New Zealander, was tall, thin and athletic, who hoped to duplicate the cricket team numbers of her own family, where she was the only girl amidst a full batting side. She had only delivered a bowler, a batsman and a wicket-keeper. Derek did not participate in sport of any kind but minced his way like Noel Coward, tickling the ivories of any available piano, smoking cigars and making sardonic, disparaging remarks about everything. Rosie just laughed; she laughed with the joy of living with an absurd curmudgeon who had gifted her sons.

In honour of their arrival, the genius persuaded Mauricio to hitch a trailer to his tractor, and we met them at the landing strip with cane chairs and a calabash of gin and coconut milk. The three small boys were ecstatic, Derek almost prepared to be amused and Rosie took it enthusiastically, as always.

"Darling, simply wonderful. How clever of you." The journey overland was through the singing bush, lurching and spinning sand; Derek pulling faces, sitting on a chair peering down at the unreliable elephant he was riding.

They stayed a week, and Sam excelled, which mollified Derek for the extreme sacrifice he had made to risk his life amongst stonefish and serpents. Evenings were best after post-prandial languor had softened Derek and the exhausted little boys were abed. But nothing could hide the chasm in my marriage, which, in the full glare of Rosie's perception, deepened inescapably. It filled the silences as pungently as Derek's cigar smoke.

"Come for a walk?" Rosie offered. We walked down to the beach in the moonlight.

"What are you going to do?" she asked without preliminaries.

"I don't know. Have children to fill the void? Assuming I can persuade him?"

"Is there anything in that arena?" she asked.

"Virtually nothing. Never softened, neither before nor after the rare occasions. Those I dread. He pounces with the immediacy of a bowel movement and flushes it from any further reference. Not even an arm about a shoulder or the sharing of a smile."

"We knew this was going to happen; it never looked good."

"Why the hell did you not say so? You never thought to warn me?"

"Would you have heeded if we had? Besides, everyone has to make their way. Now, you have defined your need to love and be loved. Some never do. But don't have children. You have nothing to stand on, and children can deepen the void. They will never fill it. You'd be mad."

That was another caution I ignored. It was mad, but I went ahead anyway. Betraying a marriage was never an option. If I couldn't find anything to love, I had to create it.

So, you were honed or whittled? Words on paper were the puzzles to understanding.

That's obvious.

I meant of yourself and your hunger, not the sad details of a boat in a storm—but the creation of an interior world, both imaginative and observed. Yet you were determined to detour through children? Have you ever wondered whether they wanted to detour through you?

That hurts.

It will do. Not just hurt but nearly destroy.

How could I know? I had no experience of children except the lack of them. Literature paints the joys of children persuasively.

Some propaganda betrays. This life is all about lack. Children are the rewards of an abundant life; they do not fill an empty one.

Emptiness was all that there was!

To enrich everything that follows. Context is all.

CHAPTER 15

Cassirer: A Perceptive Philosopher

'Providence, in its kindness, had supplied him with the wife he needed. A wife, a modest young lady, with the purely appreciative, unambitious abilities of her sex.... Society never made the preposterous demand that a man should think as much about his own qualifications for making a charming girl happy.'

At the very feet of Eros, I was collared by a vision that took hold of my lapels and said, 'Look. See what is there is to be seen.'

I had flipped through London on that fateful honeymoon, airport to airport via three depressing hotels near Russell Square. Now, while David is supervised for his PhD by a Professor at Queen Mary College, London is to be home for a year or more. We need a home; I need a job —imagine a job! A place to stand. Colleagues to greet.

Right now, on our first day, we are standing against white tiles under Piccadilly Circus, trying to fathom how the underground works. People in bowlers or flat caps tip over the lip of escalators like a synchronous shoal heading towards the dark. Others are swimming upwards towards the light, and nobody is looking at anybody else. Delaying anyone with a question is out of the question. The geometric map behind us might assist if we knew where we wanted to go.

A sudden cascade of commuters flows down a staircase; the swirl fills the hall, stirred by an invisible spoon. Above them, a shock of white hair makes its steady way, leaving a clearing behind him as though parting the Red Sea. Suddenly, the progress of this distinguished profile, with its high bridged nose and a halo of silver, stops. Looking straight at us, he changes course, manoeuvring through the crowd, an arrow seeking its target. Behind him the clearing also changes, a ripple behind a duck.

"Young man," he says, looming over us. "Why don't you love your wife?"

David recoils.

"Look," says the stranger, taking me by an ear and turning my face away. "Her ears? Have you ever looked at her ears?"

"I think I've seen them before." says the Husband.

The interrogator draws up his full height before speaking with indulgent severity, "Young man, if you would like to know what will give you a long and happy life, meet me outside Swan and Edgar's at two o'clock."

With that, he turns and walks away, followed by two dachshunds. They explain the clearance in his wake. Not once does he look at me, nor at his dogs that keep their noses on his heels. The parting of people follows him up the stairs and out into the light. It was an electric shock that travelled out of sight, leaving me craning after him.

Husband is furious. I am bewitched, and I am resolved.

"Where is Swan and Edgar's?" I ask a passerby.

"Just up those stairs overlooking the Circus."

"Forget it, we're not going." David is now pulling me towards the down escalator. "Who the hell does he think he is?"

"I don't think he *thinks*, he knows who he is." I do not add he also seems to know who my husband is.

"There's no way we're going."

"You may not, but I certainly shall." I head for the stairs up and out. David follows.

I was riveted by the disappearance of that tall stranger. Husband had shrunk to almost irrelevance, newly pitiful. There were two hours to kill in Piccadilly. We spent them arguing over a sandwich, throughout a twice-round-the-block walk and over three tables heaped with books at Hatchards. This venerable bookshop also offered a spectacular cloakroom, which I fully enjoyed, preparing to meet my new mentor.

"We are supposed to be flat hunting," David said when I emerged.

"Why not play the caveman and go seek? I'll wait for you to come back with some keys."

At five to two the stranger is waiting, the dogs curled together, taking a chance of a quick nap at his feet. He is reading a paper, leaning against a window. With a better view, he no longer gives the impression of a homeless tramp with a distinguished past. He has the mien of an academic, delaying the start of a lecture on Emmanuel Kant. His tweed jacket has shaped itself to those broad but sloping shoulders, its pockets stretched by a pipe and pouch. The long legs leave trousers hanging loose to ripple in any wind.

"I thought you'd come." he says, "Follow me."

He walks rapidly down the street, his dogs' noses still attached to his heels. We trail behind, David bristling. At a café with outside tables, he sits down, and pulls out two chairs, immediately occupied by his dogs. He moves one dog to a shared chair and signals to a waitress inside. David sits opposite him; I am to his right.

First, the dogs get served ice cream, which they delicately lick from bowls on the table. He orders coffee for three. The waitress winks at the old man; he is clearly familiar. When coffee is unloaded, he indicates I can do the necessary while he turns his shoulder and engages Husband, who is fidgeting and feigning a great interest in the passing show. David is determined to give no ground. His rudeness to this old man acts like a telescope on my re-miniaturised husband.

"You are an academic, I see?" The old man glances at David's briefcase. "Books? What do you hope to get from books?" David scoffs with a derisive, curled lip. I realise he has hardly registered who this interlocutor is or questioned who he might be.

"They pass the time. Anything wrong with that?" The old man shrugs and gestures towards me with a thumb. I am still pouring coffee.

"And this wife of yours? How does she fit into this oh-so-heavy passing of time?"

"I don't think that's any of your business." The sudden Galahad preserving the privacy of his consort is beneath notice.

"That's where you are wrong. The death of love is everybody's business. Love is all there is, and you won't find love in a book. Not even a very good book. What you will find there is the end of love, or the hope for love, or the joy of it, but not love itself." Husband gives this contemptuous dismissal.

"You'd know? Would you?"

"I should. I have read a few." The old man abruptly changes tack. "Tell me, where are you from?"

"South Africa."

"I thought so. And you mean to return there?"

"Of course. It's my country."

"Is it? Who would claim to belong to South Africa as it is now? You are even blinder than I thought. Blind to everything. I have cousins in South Africa, and they are just as stupid. Let me show you something." He reaches into an inside pocket and brings out his wallet. Leafing through it, he withdraws what resembles a savings book, much tattered.

"Do you know what that is?" He offers it to David who ignores him, shrugging and looking away. "That is my monthly compensation from the German government for the blindness of all my family. They did not listen either. We were so important, you see. It would not happen to us. So, they ended up in Sobibor or Auschwitz, and I get paid for idle time to talk to more of the blind, like you, on the streets of London."

He hands the pocket-book to me. I read the name, Professor Heinz Cassirer, and hand it back. "Come," he says, taking my arm and rising to his feet. He drops a handful of coins onto the table. "Since there is no point wasting my time with you, and therefore I cannot help your wife, I am going to buy her a present. Not so valuable, but something, nevertheless."

He tucks my arm beneath his and walks us both back towards Piccadilly and left into Bond Street. Husband follows, a sulky cur behind a wagon. The overhead bell of a small haberdasher announces our penetration into a cluttered shop of ribbons, lace, and stands of thread.

"A nice pair of silk stockings, Christian Dior," he says.

"Certainly, sir. Colour?"

"What would you like?" his enquiry is intimately kind, I hesitate.

"Grey?"

"Ah yes, grey is very sexy. But now you will disappoint me. You will ask for seamless?"

"Afraid so."

He nods at the assistant. "I knew it. The modern young woman has no idea of that ladder to heaven. Still, we must please her preferences with the sacrifice of pleasure. Please wrap a pair of grey, seamless silk stockings."

∾

On the street outside, I kissed him.

"I shall not forget you," he said. "but now I have an engagement with a young priest, tortured by his homosexuality, and I must go. Ridiculous, isn't it, in this era of real torture to fret about such nonsense." He turned to David "You will lose your wife. Not immediately, perhaps in a few years; you will have cause to remember me." He bowed slightly before walking swiftly away. David reclaimed me, or so he thought.

"I want to go back to that bookshop," I said.

"Why on earth, after that?" David was still pretending to dismiss the madman.

"Just to seek and maybe show you something."

I found two books of Heinz Cassirer's in Hatchards. In the flyleaf of one was a photograph of 'Professor Cassirer, Professor of Philosophy, Glasgow University. I handed it to David, who did, for the first time, look abashed.

"Not love, perhaps, but sometimes you can learn something from a book." David stuck out a tongue. He was trying to melt his rude contempt. It failed. His petty resistance was crayoned more vividly when his respect was given to a photograph and prestige rather than the generous old man I had kissed. There were other books by Heinz's father, Ernst Cassirer, also a Professor of Philosophy at Oxford.

The future at work when important synchronies manifest was new, then. A grainy picture of Heinz's father, who looked exactly like him, united past and future. Heinz, a Jew who converted to Christianity as a result of studying St Paul, would go on to publish 'God's New Covenant', a new translation of the Gospels from the Greek. Certainly, a book about love: I had no ideas of that sort then, but life itself did. They would become almost constant, but this was the occasion when it took me by a collar.

Christianity and Greek combined were always powerful since I first loved a teacher of both.

Cassirer's momentous clarity did not filter down immediately because I had not yet learned the practical implications of what he had said. It remained in the realms of philosophy, a belief rather than a practical truth. Synchronicity needs a few repetitions before you see the connections between thought and event. A bombshell had detonated at a critical moment; I had done nothing to deserve it.

Its repercussions would set off small explosions ever after: about the importance of books, the unimportance of books and above all, the search for love and the preservation of love, wherever encountered.

∽

We found a flat, a single room, grass carpeted, overlooking the Regent's Canal through gothic arched windows. The coal barges delivered Dickens, Austen, Trollope and Woolf, unloading soot and logs and parping for attention. Men in coal hoods stood proud, navigating the ancient waters painted by Turner. The Thames ran softly along our small tributary at the bottom of the garden.

It was, at a stroke, deliverance. David disappeared to the East End to don a lab coat and foster his future. I went in search of work, intoxicated by the challenge of independence and a new realisation that all of literature was there for the breathing, for the wandering, the mastery of the number nine bus route. I was head over heels in love with wonderful, autonomous London. I could not breathe deep enough or walk long enough past all those landmarks familiar from books, and all were still there! Those street names, modestly uniform, made me laugh. Who could just walk past Threadneedle or Fleet Street without stopping to remember how long they were in the mind before being encountered? I knew many names from Monopoly and visited the blue ones early, marvelling at those porticos flanked by columns along the broad, quiet streets of Mayfair or Kensington.

The impervious self-sufficiency of London rendered me anonymous but, in that anonymity, utterly free. I would make no scratch upon its solidity nor melt its history with any questions. I walked for several days just to revel in its glory, crossing great squares into high-sided lanes. The black pinpoint of the Angel tube station would get me home from wherever I meandered. The marvel of London was its size and great population, all finding their way home as I now could. Both purposeful and impervious was this city of the mind, a mind that was cast in stone but breathed through the green of its lush parks.

Cheyne Walk near the river bared a blue plaque; 'GEORGE ELIOT 1819-1880 lived here.' So, it was from here that my books were dispatched? Affluent with its four stories: noble outlook over the river. I imagined a quiet library and three maids with quiet shoes. How different from her beneficiary, Aunt Mary, facing the sea and the rickshaws, sweating over her Josephus as the Indian Ocean salted her breath.

I was now re-reading Middlemarch in short sections because the portrait of disappointed love was still potently acute. I was not ready for resignation or simple duty, and Cassirer had newly ignited hope for something else. I was not sure what it was or where I might find it, but that lovely, kind man's hope remained. He had seen me as a woman, the first man who ever had.

The cabs I could never afford were liberal with directions as they waited for those who could. It was the courtesy of London that hugged, an extra coat in the cold, a polite averted privacy that a small request could always interrupt. 'Let me walk you part of the way.' Nobody noticed how raw I was, or they were too polite to notice.

London was pure magic. I could hardly believe it. It did exist. Just as imagined, but harbouring those never imagined; Cassirer and his fellows, who had found its refuge and its kindness.

∽

Gabbitas and Thring sounded like solicitors until you climbed the narrow stairs to their grimy offices near Piccadilly Circus. I had no teaching certificate, only a shiny and inexperienced degree in Psychology and Zoology. This estimable, long-established gateway, Agents to the Independent Schools, was my only hope of teaching. It was a non-existent hope but worth a try.

"Come," said a voice when I knocked. There was no receptionist or outer office.

An elderly man behind a cluttered desk was stirring tea.

"Sit. Do," he said, pushing out a chair with a foot through the arch of his desk. "Have a biscuit?" It seemed friendly to accept. A crumbling digestive was probably not wise for a first interview.

"How can I help?" He leaned forward eagerly and smiled encouragingly, a gentle Mr. Chips in a tweed jacket and with very long legs.

"I am not sure you can…"

"Well, tell me what you've got?"

"Not much. Only a first degree in Zoology- as a teaching subject."

"Oh dear." he said, "You've come to challenge me…no Botany at all? Not even a smidgeon?"

"Sorry. Not a seed nor a shoot. Afraid not."

He rose and went to a filing cabinet, pulled out a file, perused it, replaced it.

"No, no good. Where did you graduate?"

"In South Africa," I said apologetically, thinking that would terminate the interview.

"Ah, lovely country. Now that gives me an idea." He reached for a phone, looked up a number and dialled.

"The High Mistress, please." He winked at me. "Long shot, but you never know."

"High Mistress? G and T here. I have a young applicant who might just suit that maternity leave… comes from your neck of the woods… which university?" He signalled for me to provide the answer.'

"Witwatersrand," I said.

"I can't possibly pronounce that?"

"Witz", I offered.

"She says something like wits, seems to have some too. Tell her to come. Tomorrow at ten? Righty Ho… no, glad to. What we're here for." He hung up and turned to me. "Connections, you see. If you hadn't mentioned South Africa, I wouldn't have thought of it. The High Mistress is South African. I'd heard she was an unlikely appointment for St Paul's, so she might just take you, a fellow at Court, perhaps. It is almost the only school in the country that offers separate A levels in Zoology and Botany. They need maternity cover, and you never know; people don't always return, it may be longer. One of those strokes of luck."

I had had a biscuit and now an interview at the top girl's school in the country. Only I did not know that. I wasn't quite sure how to thank him or what was required.

"Do I owe you anything?" He put a hand on my shoulder and took me to the door.

"Just do a good job if you get it. The school pays our fees. A pleasure to meet you. Be sure to be on time tomorrow."

I wanted to hug him, too.

Improbabilities began long before I looked for them. I was launched upon a crash course in academia's assimilation and regurgitation. I was twenty-two, and my pupils, the pick of the intelligent crop, would be eighteen.

∾

On all those days spent on my tummy in Heli's study in Basutoland, brass rubbing coins, or making Meccano models, I had heard about education. It was almost his only topic of irritation. His explosive frustrations with Whitehall were salted with explanations that Africans were in a hurry.

"What is the point of Latin until they study English?" he would cry out. "What connects them to Rome from here, for heaven's sake? Without linkage, there is no meaning. These mandarins understand nothing!" He would type furious letters for which a patient minion would wait outside before cycling away up the dusty Roma hill with an envelope heading for Whitehall.

Throughout my childhood, Heli had told me that Britain meant education first and foremost; superior, cultured, and so self-assured it spread through literature, music and drama as naturally as ink dropped in water. First, it needed a grasp of history and literature, and since Basutoland was part of the British Empire, it was their history, too, and should also be their literature. Heli slammed down another file of correspondence.

" Idiots! I am not running Eton. Yet."

"What's Eton?"

"A very famous school near London: Probably the most civilised school anywhere."

Throughout my raw exposure to South African ersatz approximation, I had always picked out the pearls that foreshadowed a little of that Oxbridge lustre. McEune and O'Riordan, in their cardigans and buttoned shoes, their precise syllables, and their fluent scripts, had given me a taste of what to expect. I had lusted after that refinement, that self-assured cultivated taste, that ease of citation. They had soaked up literature with mother's milk. I had painted its dripping blisters over a dusty surface with haphazard reading.

Armed with a map and a copy of the Times, which I hoped would convey a mature gravitas, I found my way to St Paul's Girls' School, its impressive gates and gabled portico flanking a triangle of grass and tennis courts. The High Mistress's secretary gave me the tour on the first day of the new term. I took in the oak panels, the broad arched corridors, the wide staircases and the light-filled rooms in my stride. Of course, there would be concert halls, theatres, and, in the music department, individual, sound-proof practice rooms with pianos. All schools in England must obviously be like this, and all Heli had said proved true. I simply walked into the school he had sketched for me, leisured, gracious and sure of itself. Entrusted to its reputation, I would acquit myself as expected.

If I was awed, it was not by its grandeur but by my sense of being completely inadequate to swim in such company. I had no idea that I had landed in the most academically prestigious girl's school in the country, the equivalent of Eton for the second sex. Heli's indoctrination had been so all-encompassing that it blinded me to the extraordinary privilege of being there for a first employment.

The teachers, mostly Oxbridge graduates, and most of them spinsters, whose devotion to education as the highest calling echoed all Heli had instilled. I was shown to the upper staff room and introduced; they welcomed me with restrained smiles. Just what I imagined a novice in the drawing rooms of Bloomsbury would have encountered, as Virginia Woolf signalled with raised eyebrows to E.M. Forster, "What *have* we here?'

The austere 'faculty' had levels; the two-tier staffroom upstairs might have been a country house drawing room with large couches on which slim women sat in silence, marking papers or researching through sources. I would discover other such rooms later, only in the upper common rooms of Oxbridge colleges. Downstairs, a buttery was where we smoked and took tea or coffee and where fresh, warm scones on silver chafing dishes came, wheeled in on trolleys during break. Fragments of conversation happened downstairs; upstairs held a sepulchral library silence.

The challenge was unspoken. I was initially appointed to teach elementary Zoology to the lower forms, but on my first day, the High Mistress told me that the senior zoologist had taken her maternity leave early, so I would teach A-level Zoology as well. My pupils were the daughters of Ministers in the government, including the Minister for Education, along with a clutch of Bishops, Captains of Industry, successful architects and consultants. I was as exposed as if I had mounted a packing case at Speaker's Corner. With little to conceal my rough-hewn background, my naked naïveté was exposed in front of sophisticated and lethally perceptive students.

I took the tube from the Angel and walked the few blocks from Hammersmith to Brook Green, partly intoxicated by the sense of being suddenly at home in London, partly terrified of every day that stretched ahead. Nights I spent trying to stay one step ahead, cramming up topics I knew little of and marking. I learnt the disgrace of television.

"Oh, Miss! said a pert pigtail. "Do *you* watch television? It is SO boring!"

Television had never reached South Africa. Banned by the nationalist government, it was a forbidden fruit, the fount of dangerous knowledge. The political atmosphere was febrile enough without introducing the wider world, with its disturbing facts and interviews requesting the views of black people as if they mattered. I relished Dr Finlay's Casebook with its portrait of kind idiosyncratic rural Britain, and Dixon of Dock Green with human coppers that joked, Bentleys and constables that removed helmets, so utterly unlike the thugs with their flat hats and batons I had known at home. Everything confirmed the confident superiority of a country I had read about and which had welcomed me but I did not deserve. Yet it had, from the beginning, felt like another home, one for which I needed to grow larger and breathe deeper.

On the bitterly cold day of January 30th 1965, I wept at Churchill's funeral as those stork-like cranes slowly lowered their beaks over the Thames while his catafalque chugged past on its barge towards his funeral at St Paul's Cathedral. He was born on the same day as Louie, November 30th. That struck me as important. When his coffin lowered onto the gun carriage after the service, I remembered with a shivering, vivid gust the other funeral of a coffin on a gun carriage when I was nine. Louie and I had stood on a street in Johannesburg for the funeral of General Smuts as his horse, with its empty saddle, clopped slowly past. A slow, muffled drum kept pace with hooves. Louie, who almost never cried, openly wept. Her tears streamed down as Marna's had to 'Jackanapes'.

Only fifteen years separated these two funerals of the two men who had served together in both War Cabinets and together signed both peace treaties of the two World Wars. My divided heritage of loyalty to both stretched even to the Boer War when they first fought one another: like my own tribe, by loss enlarged and stretched across the globe.

London introduced the steaming vapours of the war I had missed but lived with, and which united my divided family. I had never experienced the Blitz nor rationing, but growing into London life needed a recollection of what it had endured. My dues could never be fully paid. Those cranes told me that.

∞

I am glad you captured your naïveté before the recent disillusion about the culling of humanity by bank-orchestrated wars. Or learnt of Churchill's less-than-noble stratagems.

Why?

Because that naïveté is shared with your generation and anybody who might need to forgive themselves, all called to self-sacrifice and nobility and values that remain precious. The deepest part of being human. Worth remembering. Worth celebrating.

Even if deceived and betrayed?

Yes. Even then. Doubly valuable for the betrayal.

∞

One of my duties was to stay late on Thursdays to supervise the orchestra and, after rehearsal, to make sure they all left the building before locking up. I began my musical education by listening to performances and coaching by the Director of the Royal Academy, whose post there required his duty at St Paul's for a number of sessions. Gustav Holst had been the first, and his St. Paul's Suite was written for that very same Thursday evening orchestra I was to supervise!

I could scarcely comprehend a school so in the hub of creative life that even schoolgirls were privileged by creative London beyond, swinging in through the gates with a score as wet as Mozart's delivered from a carriage. I tried some reciprocal gifting by suggesting that David might give a talk to the Natural History Society on African wildlife.

He illustrated it with slides of fiddler crabs on Inhaca, herds of buffalo in the Bushveldt, and side-winding adders in the Namib Desert. He talked about the speeds of cheetahs, the family habits of elephants, and the migration routes through Okavango. In front of twenty adoring and attractive girls, David came alive. It was as foreign a world to them as London was to me. They made the most of questions during the tea that followed. I watched my husband and saw him through the eyes of others, a revelation of what did not exist for me.

"He looks just like Alan Bates. What a dish!" said one.

"Dirk Bogarde, here I come." said another on their way out.

"More interesting than the Zoo Quest fellow, too."

"You've fallen on your feet here," said David, clearly impressed.

"Perhaps I walked in?" I ventured.

I recognised all the tributes as being faintly just. David had a schoolboy charm, just not for or with me. It helped, though, in making my way towards acceptance that I had a 'dish' in the domestic. One that already sounded better than David Attenborough, who in those days spoke only on the radio.

I got pregnant in my third term. I cannot remember whether I was pleased. I felt I should be, but London was still exciting, and my independent life had only just begun.

∞

During the spring holiday, I received an invitation from Miss N.J O'Riordan to spend a night. Louie had told her that I was now teaching in London. Teaching lit up a passport to her reinspection of the 'awkward customer' who had shown scant promise four years earlier.

It came as a surprise to hear from your mother that you are now embarking on education as a career. Your mother mentioned a post at

St. Pauls Girl's School but I suspect she must have misunderstood. No new graduate would be admitted to its prestigious reputation, but if you were to accept this invitation to visit us, you could make all plain. Any school in London will certainly test you! Who knows, one day, you might aspire to St Paul's.

Miss McEune and I have returned to England. She has retired, and we are now living just outside Winchester in a village called Twyford. Unfortunately, I still must earn my crust, and I also teach at a girls' school, St Swithuns. We wondered whether you might like to spend a night with us. I could meet you at the station on Friday, and we will have an evening to share our respective developments. Four years will have changed you. Are you still reading theological discourses? I suspect it's unlikely, although I confess you were my only pupil with a real interest. The new bishop of Winchester has some unorthodox but adventurous ideas! I met him at a conference quite recently.

We would be interested to know your first impressions of the home country. Quite a culture shock, I imagine....'

It was not an invitation to warm cockles. Her disbelief that I could be at St. Paul's was one definite attraction, but I also wanted David to meet the Bloomsbury-in-aspic pair I had spoken so much about. He assumed I had exaggerated.

'Can you manage a husband as well?' I wrote back. I could see and hear Lady Bracknell McEune saying over the steaming oatmeal, 'A HUSBAND?' Not fortissimo but served with startled eyes and a gulp.

Yes, they could manage a Husband. So, we took a train without warning them about a conspicuous bump that was the visible disgrace of said husband. The chance to blow marriage and all its messy consequences through their retirement home was too good to pass up. Besides, it would offer a chance to see more of the country. We had hardly left London.

"We'll probably be assigned separate rooms," I said to the husband, whose reluctance was tempered by a touch of fascination.

"That'll do nicely,' he said without irony.

Judith awaited us, as she had said she would, in her 'small grey car' at the station entrance. 'It will save the need to pay and park. One does conserve where one can.' She was chewing. Suddenly, it all came back, all those school meals when I had calculated how to be seated next to her. The staff rotated at the head of each table, and we, the pupils, rotated as well. It took some counting to predict how many meals before the glory of conversation with Miss N.J. It did not command much competition. I had lived for it.

"She eats counting. Fifty chews on each side before she swallows," said someone. Seeing her emphatic, rolling chewing, I remembered. I waved to give her time to swallow. She got out. The only thing altered was the long skirt. It was now stretchy trousers and soft-laced shoes—holiday gear.

She took David's hand and seemed reassured by the thick, trimmed hair and good looks. It was what most people noticed. If she registered the bump, she did not show it. We drove through what still did not qualify as 'country' in my book. England was just a very large garden. She turned into a sloping driveway and pulled up the brake with some force. I could tell this was going to be an ordeal. Husbands are difficult to ignore.

We entered the nestling bungalow beneath a rose arch. The front door opened onto a hallway with a flattened buck skin and a collection of horn and bone-handled walking sticks; a crane in Kruger Game Park might have lifted it, swung it across the Atlantic and dropped it in Twyford. The curtains were sprinkled with springbok; the cushions slashed with zebra, a shrine to the game and their joint journeys through the Bushveldt. David's smile was hard to read; that my refined purveyors of poetry and Greek should kit out their home as a safari ranch was deliciously incongruous. Even the loo roll was impaled on an antler.

The food was not much fun: no braai to match the décor, but something white with potatoes boiled. McEune managed to make us feel that the trial of hosting a 'couple' was not one she looked forward to repeating. They did emphasise that 'delicate constitutions' necessitated 'plain food'. There was water or apple juice to drink.

The knotty question of St Paul's was much alleviated when they discovered I was only appointed 'temporarily'.

"Oh, *that* explains it," said McEune, reclining back against her chair and fingering a bread roll, "Maternity leave is such a trial to a Head. One never knows how long it must continue. Still, a privileged experience, even temporary, is not to be sneezed at." Contented, they turned to ask about my mother and then David's research project: "How very interesting, but a strain on the eyes working on such small creatures through a microscope. Wouldn't you have preferred something larger?" Finally, they switched to a recent holiday in Sienna. "Would you like to see our photographs?"

We would love to look at anything that took us faster to bed.

Judith showed us to our room with its continued array of bushveldt mementoes. Here, bedspreads were of elephants. Twin beds. A glass of water next to each with two biscuits in a waterhole saucer for the night. A duiker sipped from its edge.

Breakfast was tea and a choice of muesli or All Bran.

"See what you mean," said David after Judith had deposited us back to the station. "You will never include the husband again. Punish yourself if you must. Next time, count me out."

"Judith is much better on her own," I offered rather weakly.

"If you say so, I do not intend to find out."

That was the first of the running stitches Judith would prick through my adult life.

∽

The pregnancy offered my first trial as a teacher. Part of my responsibility with the third form was to cover sex education. I knew that few thirteen-year-olds needed the mechanics, yet how else did one begin? Preliminary questions elicited the expected sniggers, and many raised desk lids or hiding behind files. I lost all patience.

"Please, all of you, stand up." They sighed, shuffling to their feet. I put down the chalk, came out in front of my desk, and stood sideways to make the most of what was still a modest bump.

"Now tell me what you notice about me?" There was pin-drop silence.

"Go on. You are supposed to be bright and observant. Now, let's see if you are as brave as I am?" Finally, somebody ventured a whisper.

"Are you pregnant, Miss?"

"Well done, Julia. I am pregnant. And do you know how I got that way?"

Averted eyes, pursed mouths and tossed manes followed.

"Now you may all sit. We are going to talk not about sex but about love. Is that all right with you?"

"Yes, Miss"

"Yes, Miss"

"Of course, Miss."

We had an animated discussion about when sex was all right, too. When the bell rang, they rose reluctantly and filed out.

"Sorry, Miss"

"Really sorry, Miss."

"Thank you, Miss."

In the following break, one of the spinsterish old-guard who had taught for an eternity asked rather loudly.

"What *have* you done to the Upper Third? Something has hit them hard."

"Just talking about sex, and… and love and how to distinguish, and when you can."

"Marvellous," she said "well done you. One question. Why bring John of Gaunt into it?"

"Loyalty to a wife and to love as well? Not always co-existent, but where sex belongs? Where devoted loyalty lies?"

"Never thought of him like that. Hmm. Well, if they stay like this, we'll all be grateful to you. Moral Biology. Certainly different. Brave woman!"

It was a very good moment. I had given a good lesson even though I knew nothing about love. I had read enough to imagine what it might be like.

Defining something by its absence was another beginning.

Writing this has made me realise how dovetailed it all was.

The spinster teacher of theology who dissected out an Eros she knew little of, the Professor who noticed ears he did not care about and a lovelorn teacher, accidentally expecting a precipitate child, who gave a lesson on love she knew nothing about? Faking until making.

༄

The perfected clichés of England sometimes overplayed their hand. The scales did fall on occasion.

We received an invitation to spend Christmas with a couple alerted to two unattached South Africans stranded in London. Sanie's sister, Marion, had appealed to her brother-in-law, Anthony. We arrived by train on Christmas Eve after dark. A first Christmas in winter, that took time to get used to.

We were collected from Bishop's Stortford station and driven to a picture-perfect, thatched cottage facing a village green.

So far, so clichéd. Country Life was completed with a gaggle of geese and lit windows, each with a lit tree. Christmas was standing to attention, pyramids in uniform. There was sherry, there were exposed beams, a crackling open fire and a hostess groomed for the Tatler. The guest room was chintz with a dormer window overlooking a churchyard. It was every Christmas card in three dimensions.

So remote from this stood the African Christmas, in searing heat, too hot for roasting and Marna without the heart to cull the long-fattened turkey, so it survived to scratch the dirt and gobble its defiance. Pictures of a Victorian Christmas were the annual fiction that arrived on cards. Only reading Dickens aloud had linked us to it. But this was the real thing. So cold in that pretty cottage that we slept in socks and put coats over the beds, waking frequently to shiver. In the fretful night, God wrapped the world. It snowed and kept up the silent obliteration behind drawn curtains.

In the morning, I drew those curtains back. Blinded by the churchyard pillowed in white wool, with sentry gravestones sending blue shadows across the pallid sunlight. Not a footstep had fallen. The present was decorated, as a parcel might be, with a small holly tree on which a red-breasted robin sat, for you. Open it. Happy Christmas. Ludicrous, too perfect, unbelievable. Then, the bells began. I could only laugh. I had never seen deep snow close up, never seen holly, never seen a robin.

Things went downhill after that. We went to church where paltry, quavering voices apologised for carols by singing them half-heartedly. Everybody said 'Happy Christmas' as though it was an escape clause before hastening away. David, with the other husband, repaired to the village pub while our hostess and I cooked lunch. We finished the meal with chocolates and the Queen's Speech. Then, two intoxicated men fell asleep while the two women washed up and scraped encrusted pans. That was Christmas enacted to tradition.

They returned us to the station for the last train. It had all gone perfectly.

I remembered Marna and her weeping to an unfinished story, consoled by an un-inhaled, wicked cigarette. Time to weep myself for my brave, beloved country and those ululating halleluiahs. ¡Africa!

∾

Life with David had not changed. He still ignored me, but I had begun to accept that and seek outside that lovely room, with the barges gliding past and the beginning of friendships elsewhere. London was growing comfortable and welcoming.

Ingerland swings like a pendulum do
Bobbies on bicycles two by two…
Westminster Abbey, the Tower of Big Ben
The rosy red cheeks of the little children

Carnaby Street's pizzazz had put a spring in the walk, and music celebrated a renewed life in the sixties for everyone, so a Mary Quant coat in fine grey wool with its signature, petal scalloped collar was my delicious gift to myself. I was well on the way to becoming almost invisible. David's deprecation no longer chalked my measure of myself. I had succeeded in teaching at the top of the tree and nobody was laughing. Instead, those sophisticated girls covered me in flowers as I left.

'Good luck, Miss.'

Well then. Spell it out.

The moderation of illusion? England was a touch too complacent, too certain of its superiority. What had been greener grass viewed from South Africa was a touch arid when matched by Judith and Dorothy, living on nostalgia for the Bushveldt. They were me in reverse, all of us with opaque dreams. I had envisioned George Eliot's sun-flecked pastorale but discovered a manicured landscape with invisible 'do not walk' signs written in tut-tut, clicking tongues.

More important than that, but yes, certainly signalled by such indications. What about the brisk wind of self-sufficiency? The success of bravery? The rawness you believed limited you had worked better than any safe strategy. The beginning of adult flight emerging from the chrysalis of inferiority?

Let's walk on.

CHAPTER 16

Jessica, Rosalind and Etiquette

'I tell you there isn't a thing under the sun that needs to be done at all, but what a man can do better than a woman, unless it's bearing children, and they do that in a poor make-shift way; it had better ha' been left to the men.... I tell you, a woman 'ull bake you a pie every week of her life and never come to see that the hotter th' oven, the shorter the time.'

I always knew, for want of a partner, that motherhood would be solitary. What I did not expect was that it would also produce immediate opposition, the domination of the medical profession, and the assumptions of other people, nor that my now familiar, comfortable solitude would be invaded. As soon as I became a parent, I became 'subject' to a collective that I had not foreseen.

Perhaps because a child belongs to a future? To a world you may not live to be part of?

Being a mother was going to fill my emptiness. The only hope left.

I was referred to the Middlesex Hospital. I went believing, as I had in British education, that it would be professional, expert and sensitive. I knew that it was a teaching hospital and students would be present. Naturally, of course. Medicine needed a future of recruits, and in Tom's and Louie's hospitals as a child, I had seen students-in-trailing behind every consultant.

Shown to a curtained cubicle in a large ward, I undressed for this most intimate procedure. Naked, but for a shift, I sat on a bed and awaited the group beyond the curtains to surround me. The consultant was late.

I could hear the students discussing other patients.

"Did you notice the old bat's varicose veins? She's gonna have problems..."

"Nothing like those of the anorexic in bed five!"

"You think she's anorexic? I reckon drugs, heroin most likely."

"I quite fancy the redhead, though a man would have to wait for the damages of a breech birth."

"Breech? Is that certain?"

"Looks likely. She's eight months gone."

"You valiant hero, you! The squalling brat would make for interruptus…:"

It was insupportable. These crass adolescents with access to women facing harrowing exposure had no respect, no sensitivity. I snatched up my clothes and, in tears of anger and humiliation, dressed and left. Nothing would induce me to give birth in London. I would go home to crooning Ndaba, whose broad back would welcome the weight of a baby. And to Tom.

David was happy to discharge me to South African Airways. I had to fly before seven months were up, which gave him two full months for an affair with a girl who worked in the British Museum. She would occupy my bed and cook in our kitchen, and he would only tell me about her after a second child was born. He would fly out for my confinement— such a decent and respectful word— almost at the first indecent gasp of labour.

∽

A first-time mother without an early memory of a mother or a mature sister is thrown into motherhood without a rubber ring to keep afloat. Instead, she has assumptions to manage a dog paddle through waters of panic. Being pregnant alone floats promises: a creature to love will be born, and tucked somewhere is a list of things not to do. No absences, no boarding schools, no concealing how she feels; she will express even anger. Louie's pursed lip and averted tears had been the deepest misery of my childhood, like the chief injunction on being a writer, loving meant showing. I hope for a daughter because I know nothing about boys, real boys. That was about it.

In short, I stirred into my recipe for motherhood everything that had made me miserable. Things not to do.

Before the confinement, and let's face it, confinement is what motherhood is for life: strapped down with duties, smothered with anxiety, tethered to routines and padlocked by hope.

I suppose most babies gather security on a lap or a shoulder, hearing a lullaby and rocking through wind and tears. There must be small routines that, being repeated, make for a sense of place. Arms and faces get distinguished as 'family'. Sunlight and moving leaves, laundry with the scent of air, and deep, dark, too loud awake must distil a growing introduction to the existence of a self, a self that finds its toes at will and the certainty of a thumb. That learns a cry summons and lifts, and a smile is always mirrored.

It was not until my mother died that I had glimpses of my own babyhood. A pair of albums showing me mostly asleep on a rug gazed at by Louie sitting at a respectful distance. They were rather contrived for the photographer; perhaps it was Heli: none in her or anyone's arms and one grasping a playpen, standing and smiling without teeth.

On to motherhood with no memory and no experience.

Hope is for more than just a perfect, healthy body and a responsive, intelligent mind. Hope is also for good looks, good fortune and, above all, being equal as a mother to foster confidence and impart joy. I would do this with flair, no mandates, no presumptions; motherhood would be instinctive. There was nothing else more worthy of investment than the hope of love and something to give my life for.

Just do it.

I went to stay with Tom and Ursula. Louie's gift was to dispatch Milly to attend the due date. She did not come herself. When labour began, Milly sat alone in prayer and fasted.

"It is our way. Each woman having a baby has to die. At that moment, you must also die. We sit with her together to make sure she wants to live after."

Signs of the future were declared early. Jessica's birth followed labour too early induced, perhaps two weeks early, and she was not ready. Tom sat by my bed in the ward through twelve hours of second-stage contractions coming at three-minute intervals. Later, he said he had never seen a labour so punitive or relentless. It was as though the child fought against birth, held me in a vice continually tightened, as though to pit her reluctance against my life.

David, in a mask, was called in only for the final delivery at the voyeur's end of the bed to get a good view of what he had never seen before. The disapproving obstetrician thought fathers had no business in a maternity wing; he also thought it was bad form for another consultant to 'muscle in' on his patient. The best possible father, Tom, was dismissed when most needed. David took the bundle and bore it away while I was stitched.

For the first few weeks, Jessica was hungry, with little milk, and much crying. For hours, Tom walked up and down a passage, reading the Lancet, with a loping, staccato thumping, the bundle against his chest soothed and quieted. Ursula heard that Guinness would promote milk. She ordered a case and drank a great deal of it. Ndaba knew the answer and strapped another baby against her back while she washed nappies and sang Zulu lullabies. That worked without fail.

David continued to read Time Magazine and then departed to find a house in Miami. His next post was in Miami University's Marine Department. Freed from any need for delicacy to the husband and father, Tom persuaded me there was no disgrace in being unable to breastfeed. Formula bottles brought quiet. The sleep of both parties. At last.

Six weeks later, an exhausted mother and an incessantly crying infant boarded a two-day flight to Miami. We spent much of it in the lavatory to spare the suave Spanish architect in the adjacent seat.

Miami Airport's corridors were an unending marathon maze. After two sleepless nights, my arrival with a finally inert baby, a Moses basket and two suitcases was like entering a Star Wars dream on another planet. The temperature delivered a body blow, a body instantly soaked, under neon lights but no view, on and on, up ramps, round elbows, and on again. Another parallel labour: push a trolley some more, then a final heave to meet the waiting father.

☙

The house David had rented in Coconut Grove was a lack-a-daisical, wooden-fronted bungalow set well back behind oaks and a spread of grass from the unfenced street. The light, quelled by rampant vegetation, left the dark undisturbed inside. The dark looked cool but was a sombre entrapped heat, as though the house, its eyes closed, was gently expiring. The sprinkling of such houses in the oldest part of Miami was casually atypical; the canopy of oak, the occasional Banyan and palm obscured its suburban proximities. The house had one air conditioner, which spat its breezy relief across the bed in the bedroom, where the last of the summer played itself out. Alone again to grab a little sleep and rock.

Rosie Langbridge was right. Children can never fill the void but make its existence more apparent. I was yoked and I had accepted that. Of all the injunctions to myself, having an only child was the prime taboo. Another child was imperative. I would, in time, invite a repetition so that the two would always have one another. It was not an intention to comfort me at this juncture of supreme loneliness in the punitive heat.

Jessica, named after Shylock's vehement daughter, was blessed with ruthless courage. To me, she looked perfect even without fingernails. Her life would be spent weighing up whether I passed muster. She never did decide. Whether I did or not hardly mattered in her headlong rush to master life, precocious in every physical accomplishment.

I had nothing by which to compare her. I failed to notice that her confident walking at nine months always solidly walked away. Refusing to sit on my lap or suffer a hug was a measure of her fierce independence. I respected that. Before she could talk, she wandered off and I rejoiced that she felt secure without me. As a besotted mother, and I admit to that, I celebrated that her self-sufficiency meant I was there to remove obstacles. She did not need me emotionally; she did not arrive to love or be loved. She came to be victorious: to conquer life, to succeed and to win. She conquered me in every sense.

Against her cheerful indifference, other small children seemed endlessly whining, always needy, mostly indulged, receptacles into which their parents poured coercion or persuasion. In comparison, Jessica and I enjoyed a kind of tolerant coexistence. She grinned a lop-sided smile, refused with an implacable, unbending certainty and flung herself into deep water without hesitation. David taught her to swim, at which he had been a record-holding champion. He moved through water like scissors through silk, unsplashing as a seal.

She could swim before she was eighteen months old and ride a bicycle with stabilisers like a fierce, racing hornet at two. Not a comfortable toddler but a midget adolescent. Not heeding what she lacked, I believed we were both doing motherhood quite well. I enjoyed the few ministrations permitted, like the evening bath and the hair brushing, the lovely clean smell I was not allowed to kiss, her head always jerked away.

Beyond the garden, America was the strangest country to decipher.

I cannot put a finger on the great abyss of non-comprehension between Europe and America as it first struck me. It is as though the familiar language, whose meaning is clear, i.e., it is English, stems from an entirely different, literal, pragmatic world. What is said is both simple and self-evident, but courtesy demands more words than necessary. It is my habit to rely on shorthand and irony, which produced incomprehension and suspicion that what lay beneath might be a mockery. The manners of America are not easily abbreviated without seeming rudeness. I felt hobbled, not intending to offend yet desirous of something straighter, more incisive. Have a nice day! Must I? What would it look like?

A nice day was always Wednesday when a barrowman, with his brazier and barbecued spare ribs, wheeled in to save the need to plan supper. Those spare ribs stay in the memory as clearly as the langoustines of Mozambique smothered in peri-peri, alongside black beer and chewy bread. Street food is remembered forever. Those spare ribs have never been equalled.

The use of prolix language contrasted the smooth efficiency of service and a world which anticipated every need. An automated society, where everything had its place, posed questions for someone who had never had a place nor knew what to shave away or hide. A supermarket was a new adventure into piled and polished fruit that tasted of nothing. I had never seen a supermarket. London had street markets or food halls for the wealthy, Johannesburg had separate shops, butcher, baker, and candle-stick-maker, and Lorenzo Marques had a vast dispatch market with crates of things to dig through.

The Stepford Wives is not entirely a parody, perhaps simplistic, but something of its polite conformity disoriented. Manners were unmodulated, the same for a passing shopper as an intimate introduction. I felt I walked upon three feet and spoke a rude, unfamiliar tongue. I hardly met a soul. People from elsewhere dominantly inhabited Coconut Grove, some foreign, many from northern states; not many wealthy, comfortable but not rich. The Grove was perhaps as free as suburban America gets, but as I never lived anywhere else in the States, I should not generalise from this unique, tropical quasi-paradise. Later, it assumed the fame of Greenwich Village of the South, but in the sixties, it was preparing for Bohemia by wearing its sandals and sarongs and practising its nonchalance. Negro maids still came to iron and clean, and cars continued to be washed on Saturdays.

The weekly delivery of clean diapers—and the obliging removal of the soiled in their perfectly disinfected pail— was miraculous. Where else would an entire industry revolve around routine birth and remind you a year later? The still-working washing machines and cookers, awaiting disposal along our quiet, unfenced street, were perplexing. Nobody minded us lugging them away, as they were good enough for us. But they did object if we failed to mow the grass and found polite ways to tell us.

"Honey, we all do like the neighbourhood to look tidy. Y'all can borrow our mower any day...'

Next door lived another kind of mother, appropriately Martha.

She had a son the same age as Jess. Euan had the proportions of an elongated, frescoed putto foreshortened on an Italian ceiling, with tousled, tight, fair curls and a dummy in his small mouth. He held a stuffed toy in one hand and his penis in the other, always. His bottom half was never clothed but permitted simply to pee wherever he was, followed by Martha's 'Oh Ewe-ann!'. Visits left a trail of puddles without even the signal of a cocked leg that might have hastened a puppy outside. Euan's solid, blue-eyed gaze of incomprehension did not salve the irritation. Martha believed in liberty.

The sixties in Coconut Grove sported many flower children, and Martha was very flowered in loose smocks and patterned, chiffon hair scarves. She was deeply kind, a gentle presence, a baker of brownies, and a willing childminder, but reciprocity came with a warning. I grew a touch crisper to avoid it.

Jessica and I spent time on the swings in the nearby Peacock Park under the Banyans and sometimes at a nearby arts shed where, for a modest contribution, you could paint or throw pots on the kick-wheels and leave them to await the next firing. Jess would fashion small animals on a rug at my feet. There, I drank juice with people my age and situation, young mothers of modest means, enlarged bellies and joyful expectations. The world was on the cusp of change; bras were for burning, music festivals were heavy with the smell of marijuana, and Florida was the perfect climate for near nudity.

People still seemed to breed in the old way. That surprised me. It contradicted the conviction that all *that* was already past. Pregnancy seemed so old-fashioned a way of doing the wonderful, never-look-back future about to break, the day after tomorrow, of which there was no doubt whatsoever.

Rosalind was born two years and forty-eight days later. Again, I returned home to Tom for her delivery. With almost black eyes and a retroussé nose, she could not have been more different from Jessica, a nuzzling puppy, a laughing fawn. As soon as she could haul herself erect, she jumped and smiled. Life was going to be abundant. Jessica gathered all her toys together and spent hours sitting on them rather than let Rosalind near her Lego or her Fisher-Price telephone, happily denying herself rather than surrendering and sharing. Every mother of a two-year-old expects this, but it will never change.

Rosalind seemed not to notice or to mind. Neither would alter in any substantial way. Jessica would machete and slice through the jungle; Rosalind would accept and bend through her own forest of Arden, a flexible Ganymede, chewing on any green shoot without too much thought. Nothing has convinced me that we come fully formed as personalities more than the difference between offspring, raised together yet alien to one another, not even similar in appearance or tastes.

Names to me are so much the essence of a person that I now wonder whether the naming of a child plucks that name's history from all those that bore it and stamps some composite for the name's reprise, like a familiar song in a new key. They were David's daughters, but I never foresaw that his hostility to me would, in time, infect them lethally.

Perhaps that was inevitable. Both joined Marna's 'tribe of strong women' and loaded their own heads to weave their paths away from me. Every child does that to its mother. It will be encouraged by motives not yet fully-fledged and bitterness not yet thickened or distilled. But their propensity for alienation was already apparent: in Jess, perhaps innate, and in Ros, in her easy yielding to any influence.

~

David, in the heat, was becoming restless with the routines of research on marine invertebrates. He was reading a book by Konrad Lorenz, impressed by the man's open-hearted, almost spiritual interpretations of animal behaviour.

"Why not go and work with him?" I suggested.

"Fat chance of that!"

"Well, perhaps the National Geographic will sponsor you?"

David had maintained his contributions to its photography, achieving an occasional cover. A letter I drafted received a simple yes.

A wife has occasional uses. They would sponsor him for a year.

The start of observations that imply a growing detachment from early assumptions?

You mean believing my children would cleave to my skirts and wrap arms about one another?

Children are not your children but come with their own longing to ensure their independence. Children were a door that opened onto a pathless barren field, beyond which no sunlit uplands called, merely the weight of new responsibilities. You also learnt that a language understood is not enough to be 'seen'. Appearances belied casual hippy tolerance; 'polished apples tasted of nothing' was a metaphor for it all. But now, no longer quite so defined, or so black and white?

You recoiled from America's brashness without valuing its liberty.

True. I had, without realising it, soaked up complacency from British facile judgement. I am ashamed of myself now. But another encounter with America will destroy much of that criticism.

It's called relativity. You were still young with rough edges. Much heart sanding is needed.

CHAPTER 17

Frau Fick: Bavaria

'What a pity that ... doctrines infinitely important to man are buried in a charnel heap of bones over which nothing is heard but the barks and growls of contention.'

I don't remember what I expected of Bavaria twenty years after the end of the war. Perhaps the excited anticipation of Europe in general obscured Bavaria in particular. I had been enthralled by London, bemused by its familiarity from all the books I'd read, entirely new yet already known. Despite the superficial freedoms of flower power, I had been lonely in Miami; its soggy heat, its mosquitoes and its insularity about neighbourhood mores, probably because it had no place for me to stand. The United States was the most foreign country I had visited. I spoke its language, but no one spoke mine.

Bavaria, I knew, would be Foreign and have no expectations of me nor me of myself. I could explore without preconceptions. Little did I anticipate heading for a personal Anschluss, the passive imprisonment of Frau-mit-Kinder meeting the legacy of war with all its horrors seated by my fire.

I imagined a sophisticated, self-assured Munich, for which appearances would be important. I would conquer it with couture. Breastfeeding does anchor the day. Having delivered Rosalind, I spent her sleeping hours with Ursula in Port Elizabeth mastering Vogue couturier patterns and making two suits: a long three-piece Pierre Cardin suit in olive twill and another, short and sharp in wool; olive and cream checks from Courreges; waistcoats would ring the changes. I would attempt sophistication for the first time. Ursula's habitual boredom found a new challenge in teaching me the refinements of tailoring, at which she was adept.

'If you can manage couturier Vogue, you will manage anything.'
So, no simple Butterick with patch pockets.
Fine. I was in a hurry to cut mustard.

∽

We landed at Munich early, where one babe in arms, and another able to walk undid all my intentions of striking the right notes. I smelt of milk and vomit and carried blankets, bottles and stuffed toys. David did better with a leather briefcase and strode ahead.

Hermann was the name of the man awaiting us, a one-armed man with a loose empty sleeve, the other holding a placard against his chest. He had a kind, studious face behind his spectacles. Once loaded into his comfortingly modest car, we hit an empty autobahn. His knees steered when his good hand changed gear. David smiled; I heaved and shushed in the back. So soon after the war, a man without an arm limited the safety of questions.

The country was spic-span clean; that was its first impact. It conveyed a domestic kind of routine as though attentive maids were now below stairs, having ironed the newspaper of the day. The sky had been hung out for airing, the water of the lake swept and polished, the road raked, the trees dusted. Since nothing moved, it awaited our critical inspection.

Herrsching-am-Ammersee, a picture postcard taken in a lucky light, had tile-hung turrets topped by black breasts, hipped roofs, volkische wooden chalets and cream walls nestling like cygnets along the fringe of a lapping lake. A narrow, unpaved lane clung to timber palings as Hermann cast the car towards the big fish of Die Alte Mühle, which turned the shoulders of its gables towards the water and scrutinised our approach.

A weathered shield stamped its authority between the regimental windows, observing, through their lorgnette, our navigation through an outer gate. Once disgorged and untidy, we stood beneath a great tree that defended an arched doorway into an inner court. The bell pull of a bracketed iron rod echoed with the empty sound of a Trappist convent. The clattering of heavy keys preceded the formidable presence of our landlady. She acknowledged only our chauffeur but gave us scant glance.

"Guten Morgen Professor. Kommen Sie doch bitte herein." She stood aside at the wide, white door, surmounted by a well-disciplined, red rose which offered a single rationed bloom. Pushing past, she led the way up a staircase to the right of a wide hallway, admitting no glimpse of what lay behind its bulwark door to the interior. We were heading for the servants' attics. Her feet, at eye level, were encased in the sort of shoes called 'stout', black buttoned, heavy, half heels. Above them, a grey stretched hair skirt moved independently of any reference to what it enclosed, like a lampshade. Above that, a dark black bun was crucified with pins; no stray hair would dare.

Unlocking the door to what was to be our apartment, she stood back and indicated we might enter. Having admitted us to the privilege of occupying the top floor of Die Alte Mühle, she departed without a word, back downstairs.

"Your home. Ich hoffe es tut?" Professor Schöne was anxious for reassurance. He was not wholly comfortable.

"Wonderful." It was, in its way, for what it looked out on, a skyline of a foreign village and a lake.

The apartment was a narrow alley running the length of the roof. Professor Schöne looked disturbed, perhaps slightly apologetic for his countrywoman's imperious rudeness. He led us to the windows, leaning on the empty left sleeve of his missing arm. Later, we learned that our Russian allies were responsible for that amputation, but by then we were very good friends and forgiven.

The rooms, though small, were filled with light. The front one, cantilevered over the Ammersee, was a small boudoir, reflecting glimmering water on its white stone walls, its foundations slapped by the wakes of ferry boats doing their time-lapse scuffle from the tourist trade across the water. The gulls glided close, dropping to scrap for scraps below, emitting that mewing plaint, which turns all water to sea coast and evokes childhood in their dismissive liberty of held wings and sharp eyes. Gulls always seem disdainful of humanity. Their world we invade, they do not cede it.

"It is, even now, a functioning mill," said Hermann, taking us to the other end of our alley-flat and pointing to a pond elevated above the inner courtyard. His right arm tracked the cantilevered, narrow mill race from the pond to the creaking wheel, which we could feel but not see. Opening the heavily glazed window, he admitted a rhythmic, grating sound that arose in the bowels of the building, giving a sense of sailing through time, suspended in some aspic purpose. A splashing sound was the churning wake of this stationary ship, like the bilge of high-sided steamers in port, preparing to sail.

"Behind here is a boat builder using the water power for his saw. Es folgt einer sehr alten Tradition, nicht wahr? Welcome zum echten Bayern." Hermann's sardonic smile was apologetic.

After unloading our baggage Hermann departed, saying he would call for David until we had achieved a car.

The light on the village roofs with their bulbous towers, two hungry infants, and this solid, antique Mühle held on a line cast from the village were the unconnected elements of a dream. I found sheets, made beds, and managed food, not yet aware this was the beginning of the end.

It was also a new beginning. Now would begin the distinguishing of the outer from the inner worlds. I had been floating in one; in Bavaria, I began to incubate the other. My solitude had now to encounter the world I had largely escaped. Munich was where Hitler had begun. Frau Fick was his legacy, a personal encounter with the aftermath of fascism. I had missed the war. I had some catching up to do, to disengage from the comfortable affluence of sun-ripened fruit, sea-splashed, waited-on-hand-and-foot South Africa. I had no idea and no ideas yet. Harshness I had met, but not the indomitable assumption of superiority that would never yield the field.

I sensed the dimensions of my ignorance but in the post-war flux, merely attributed the landlady's stiff-necked formality to resentment at military defeat. I had half expected it; I had come expecting to offer compassion. I would soon realise that there was nothing defeated about Frau Fick.

It was very different for Professor Schöne, whose military service and a conspicuous missing arm was a punishment wrapped in regret. David and I were sailing towards the end of our marriage, briefly docked and delayed by this excursion into the cauldron of Nazi Germany. The Third Reich was not entirely over; its low flames still flickered.

~

A knock at the door. Frau Fick stood with a willowy, tall girl of about sixteen. With long, black hair loosely tied and serene grey eyes, she stood resolved to fulfil her role in the stiffened presence of her mother. She bowed slightly.

"I am Fräulein Frederika Fick," she said in separate and correct syllables. "My mother wishes to speak with you. I am here to translate." Frau Fick gestured that she wished to enter. It was not a request. She laid out her bullet points in German as though from a Luger pistol, using a forefinger on the palm of her hand. Frederika led us to the window of the bedroom, where a half-poster bed was in indecent disarray. She pointed down to an enclosure of scrubby grass near a boathouse with a fringe of water and pebbles.

"That beach is private. My mother says you must use it, but only if we are not using it. We do not often go there.

"The children must not run in the courtyard. They must not go near the pool in the courtyard because it is *zu tief*", she caught herself, "I mean, it is too deep."

"The large boathouse at the back is *verboten*. Nobody is to enter it or disturb the working man."

"If you like music, you must like it quietly and not after ten o'clock in the evening."

To each injunction, Frau Fick nodded. She clearly understood the language she would not utter. She interrupted with an afterthought. Frederika's eyes betrayed the rehearsal of something unforeseen.

"My mother asks if you have a washing machine?"

"No, not yet." A flood of German followed.

"My mother invites you to go with her to Munich, where you will buy such a washing machine. She will pay the half, and when you go, you will leave it here."

That seemed fair.

"You will hang the washing only in the courtyard, never on the windows." The prospect of a trip with our forbidding landlady did not light enthusiasm.

"Perhaps we might go to Munich when my husband can stay at home for the children. Tomorrow, he goes to the Max Planck."

Frau Fick did not need this translated. Max Planck warmed her visibly. She nodded with emphatic approval. In the salad of shrugs and sober gestures of respect and mentions of the Herr Professor Schöne, I gleaned that it was only the Max Planck Institute which had secured our quantum shell, in which we were to trace a disciplined orbit around the nucleus of Frau Fick.

They turned to depart, delayed by a further instruction to Frederika.

"Tomorrow, my mother will accompany you to the village and introduce you. You will buy at good shopping and because you are living here, they will give good prices. She will take you in the afternoon at two o'clock when the children are sleeping. I will have ears for them when you are gone. Is it understood? Thank you."

David, Herr Doktor, held the door and merited a brief nod. They departed.

David clicked his heels. "Well, aren't we lucky? Achtung. The children will now be sleeping to order. You will be trading to order. Jawöhl."

"And you will fuck off to Max Planck and leave me with a gorgon who will eat the children?"

"Oh, don't get hysterical. It is just the way they are."

It certainly was. Frau Fick's chauffeur stood to attention in the grey-blue uniform of the Luftwaffe with its Loden touch of a velvet collar. She was seated in the rear of a convertible Mercedes while I wondered whether to ride shotgun in front. She indicated that I might be seated beside her with a slight gesture. Once released in the town, her unbending progress through Herrsching was a royal procession through removed hats, deep curtseys, and deferential steppings-back. Every shop she deigned to enter made the honour palpable in the wringing of hands and spry attention, which she acknowledged with the merest assent.

"Ich möchte meine Untermieterin Frau Doktor Hughes vorstellen. Sie wird hier einige Zeit verbringen, und ich erwarte von Ihnen, ihr gute Aufmerksamkeit zu geben."

"Natürlich, Gnädige Frau."

I got the 'Frau Doctor' who needed their close attention, as my unearned title and guessed the rest. The 'Frau Doktor' felt more dishevelled and less deserving with each encounter. We sailed back to Die Alte Mühle; she left me at the door without a glance. Clearly, the first necessity was to learn German and break the bonds of all this unwanted privilege.

That privilege came from Frau Fick's acquaintance with Der Fuhrer, a chum of Hitler's. Her husband, Roderick Fick, had been Hitler's principal architect who began the building of the Berghof at Berchtesgaden. He was replaced later by Albert Speer. Fick also built the Adolf Hitler Bridge—renamed Nibulungen Bridge—in Regensburg and Martin Bormann's house and, after the war, continued as a dominant architect for Nazi bigwigs like Hermann Goering. Frau Fick, an architect herself, was in charge of the preservation of Regensburg. She had every intention of keeping the Nazi flame alive, which was not difficult. Dachau concentration camp was but a stone's throw away. We had landed among the crème de la Nazi crème!

༜

David was going to escape the trials of paternity. I had only known of the Max Planck Institute as a research outpost studying animal behaviour and bird migration centred on Konrad Lorenz. I had no idea of its prolific areas of research or its unique support for anybody to receive funding for almost any pure science. The Max Planck at Seewiesen was one of fifty specialist institutes; which scattered its languorous laboratories across an almost meadow. Poly-lingual young academics, almost heady with the new world of post-war euphoria, all spoke English or Dutch but not often German.

They lay on the grass in shorts and sandals and wandered into seminars with doors open to the sunlight. In winter many of the girls wore tartan kilts and Arran sweaters. The reasons became clearer when I got to know them better. Night enclosures for ducks and geese lay along the perimeter where flaxen-haired children wandered, followed by the resolute waddling of goslings. Some families of senior staff lived permanently on the site and their pre-school children provided informal research assistants. Lorenz conscripted children for his study of imprinting; all they had to do was be present for the hatching; after that, each became a Mother Goose with a clutch.

It all had a charming improbability. David had a spacious laboratory in which to contrive a legitimate field of study of interest to Lorenz, whose magnetic reputation had drawn him there. Lorenz was a burly large man with a goatee white beard, spotted occasionally in the distance, like a rare kudu in the veldt, best left undisturbed.

We had arrived in a glass bright, autumnal, late September. Less than a week later, October struck. Nobody had prepared us for the Oktoberfest in Bavaria. It began with a knock on our door. Frederika had come to invite us to their 'Faschingsfest, a celebration, a party'. It was a fancy-dress party downstairs,

"The evening of tomorrow at exactly eight hours."

Setting aside the babe at the breast and no transport in a foreign country without the language required, the fancy dress would have to be my Laura Ashley, with a lace collar and a bustle. I would speedily let out the zip, since baby weight still lingered.

I suggested David could learn to yodel, go as a German-Swiss and find himself an Alpenhorn. Lederhosen were readily available everywhere.

"You could wear one of those feathered hats as well as the

embroidered braces?"

"With my legs? Anyway, hardly diplomatic." He settled for his only suit, which I thought dull.

∾

Children in bed, we descended. A portly, wax-mustachioed man opened the door. In a top hat, striped trousers and spats over patent leather shoes, he had taken 'fancy' soberly but meticulously. He bowed low, clicked his heels and offered me his arm for the progress into the great hall, leading me to a chair like an invalid seated by Trollope. One that lacked an elegant coiffure or a lace fan. David hovered. The floor of polished tile was cleared of rugs, a piano, centre stage, was draped in a fringed shawl. A few guests were compacted at the far end, standing uncertainly, as though the honour of their invitations had failed to clarify what was expected. None seemed to have taken a fancy to fancy dress. Perhaps we were the victims of mistranslation? Men stood about diffidently in lederhosen and ruffled shirts. Two portly women conversed animatedly, showing a great deal of bosom but curiously in children's dresses that looked far too small. My Victorian primness was clearly wrong for the intended mood, although the mood had not yet had enough drink to swing.

There was no sign of Frau Fick. A desultory half-dozen stood and shifted; one or two guests inclined their heads in acknowledgement if eyes should meet.

I sat.

David stood.

A maid in a short white apron and black fishnet stockings brought round a tray with glasses. On her second circuit, I recognised Frederika, in seriously frivolous mode, the hostess had sunk to serving maid. Everything was serious; even the bowls of snacks came with linen napkins. I sipped what was probably schnapps and contemplated the great horn of his-master's-voice turntable that sat upon the piano, inscribed with curlicues in gold leaf. Without the fox terrier, it was going to be a long night. Not even a little Schubert?

Mein escort had temporarily disappeared. When he re-entered, it was to adopt a pose in a doorway, strike a hanging triangle for attention and clap his hands. The dim talk fell silent. He slid his way across to the gramophone and lowered the needle. A Strauss waltz it was. Well, it was a party. I had resigned myself to being an invalid when I looked up at the shadow that fell. The man in spats was asking me to dance! He took my hand, raised me from the chair and swept me into a violent waltz, one of those waltzes that changed direction frequently, with much emphasis on the lowered arms and the abruptly raised profile. I was being pumped like an obstinate, deep well, yielding only splashes.

The schnapps and the waltz combined faded the room to a blur. When the music stopped, the room did not. I was lowered into the chair, reeling. as my dance champion withdrew. Finally, the room quivered into focus. David, still vertical, did not look at me, unable to quell the independence of his mouth.

"It wasn't *that* funny," I hissed.

I thought it was my spectacular performance propelled by a stout man who looked like the advertisement for just one cornetto. David managed to whisper, "He's Frau Fick."

The information turned my blood stone-cold. My blood believed him before I did.

There were four more dances after that, all waltzes, and each reached deeper into a kind of horror that the dancing belied. I was exhibited like a rabbit before being skinned.

Finally, I said, "I must go and check on the children." Frau Fick assented with a triumphant Hammer Horror smile. She took off her top hat to expose the bun and bowed. Deutschland über alles. I fled.

That was the start of my education.

Somewhere deep down, I knew of the cross-dressing proclivities of the Nazis, hence the horror, at skin-prickling speed.

༄

The trip to Munich in the chauffeured limousine had me anchored.

Frau Fick was now in a floral blouse and a loden hat, and the bun nestled loosely in her nape. She held a capacious bag on her firm knees. The disposition of her body, her grip on her bag and her gaze out of her window signalled I was neither of interest nor to be trusted.

"Sie sind glücklich. Deutschland macht die besten Waschmaschinen in der Welt," she said, underscoring the best washing machines in the world with her personal stamp.

We drove to a large electrical store where she deliberated, inspecting AEG, Siemens and finally Miele. She ordered the Miele, the most expensive. She did not consult me. It would be delivered and we would pay her later. The washing machine had been a pretext; I was irrelevant to the decision. The real reason for a trip to Munich was to tour the bombed sites as a captive.

She tapped the chauffeur's shoulder when she wished me to survey the worst damage: Die Alte Pinakothek Museum, where bomb damage was stabilised in perpetuity. Its jagged, arrested collapse was entirely my doing. I had many minutes to take in the full reprehensible destruction.

"Schrecklich, fürchterlich, unglaubliches…" the words were spat out. We drove on to the next bombed building. After four, I had had enough.

"Frau Fick. The war is over."

"It is *never* over," she said, "*never!*" The first use of English.

"Well, perhaps you should come and look at London?"

She sniffed and looked out of the window, muttering about the obscenities visited upon Köln and the Ruhr and then went on to Dresden. I picked up the names.

"I have seen pictures," she said, still using the foul language that contaminated, "and we spared your Cathedral, Saint Paulus,"

"Not spared, just missed."

She tapped the chauffeur and turned us in a new direction. We drove into a leafy, broad boulevard in the residential area of Schwabing, very affluent housing thoughtfully spared. We entered a semicircular drive before a column-flanked entrance.

"Das Haus der Familie Beck, ich habe hier Geschäft," she said as she got out. "Sie wartet im Auto." The 'Frau Doktor' was ditched at a stroke.

I watched the door opened by a maid, and after deferential exchanges, she entered. Half an hour later, she emerged with a large envelope and the bowed courtesies of a man showing her out. She looked restored, poise recovered, gracious almost. She climbed into the seat, tucking the envelope on the side away from me.

"Meine guten Freund. Herr Beck, Verlag since two hundred years! Here in Die Sommer, we hold private concerts in the garden. The... wie sagt man? Dirigent, Herbert von Karajan comes to..." She beat a bar with her wrist...

"Conduct?" I offered.

"Schön. Wunderbar."

The contrasts were pointed: my nation's barbarity against hers of ancient culture and tradition.

After the war, the family Beck had little else to do but call for Wagner. They had lost their publishing licence. Their collaboration with the Nazis made them prime targets for American punishment during the occupation. They had done very well mopping up the businesses of Jewish publishers, forced out in Berlin and elsewhere. For this bruised period, they lie low, as does von Karajan, equally accused of collaboration. Musical soirees under leafy canopies will keep the flag fluttering while they hatch new plans. Nazism in Bavaria was deep-rooted; its privileges continued underground.

Perhaps you might amend that?
Underground in Antarctica? Will that do?
And overground in Los Alamos and on the ski slopes of Argentina?
And protected by changes of identity by the CIA?
That'll do.

∽

In the aftermath of the war, the atmosphere of the Max Planck struck me as dreamlike, a quasi-kibbutz where residents, students and children lay on the grass, poured beer, had barbecues and dipped in and out of languages that made me ashamed to be limited to one. Apart from the scattered, low buildings, there was a small planetarium where studies of bird migration involved measuring the smallest indications of orientation in birds chained to a perch as the night sky revolved around them. It was not unlike playing God with many days allocated to the seventh day of rest. Creation could take as long as you liked.

David received Frau Fick's approval in his purchase of a second-hand Mercedes, which was allocated its own space under the large tree. He departed early, leaving me with heavily accented German to decipher and no transport. Lugging was my lot. I lugged children to the village and children plus food back home. A bar of Lindt chocolate was a weekly treat that made me long for Cadbury's; so perverse is food when nostalgia taints it.

In the snow, a weighted sledge dug deep furrows along the lane. When spring lit the candles of green, the 'private beach' was where I sat while Jessica built pebble castles and Rosalind had no nappies on a rug. I wondered what my life was for while the shrugging wavelets refused to answer. From the great bulwark of the house behind came the sounds of Frederika's flute practising, starting on the hour and ending on the hour, from nine to ten every day. After that, it was an hour of Goethe and Schiller. That was during the holidays. Her schooling for her Abitur involved the chauffeur to the gymnasium before we were up. She was not encouraged to improve her English with us.

Twice a week I took German lessons from an elderly couple, Herr und Frau Schlachter, who were patient with my slaughter of their language. Although mastery of grammar came slowly, invention with words tacked together in ever-increasing length caused much hilarity but seemed to be understood. After two lessons together, David decided he did not need German, and I persisted alone.

To please his new young friends, David was generous with my availability as a sedentary babysitter. Since I had infants of my own and a beach available, there was no reason why I should not have theirs as well. One was a regular, a just walking toddler who came on Thursdays from eight a.m. to eight p.m. Her mother was an ambitious Hungarian pianist and needed to practise. They all slept on a mattress under a Steinway grand in a single-roomed apartment, so a beach…well, why not?

Whatever they fed the child came out in pure glutinous, thick evil-smelling liquid, in such profuse quantities that she needed to be changed in the bath. It was like changing a cow. Then the bathroom needed hosing down with the windows wide open. It was a service David rendered to his appreciative colleagues, filling the diary of his confined lesser half.

Before this became all there was to life, I asked for one day off a week. Jessica could attend the Max Planck crèche, and Rosalind could gurgle and kick in a playpen in his laboratory. On Fridays, I boarded a train in my changes of suit and went to explore Munich and master formal German. That was seldom necessary because the polished English I encountered in bookshops and restaurants made any attempts at German embarrassing. Frau Fick informed me that Koln, where she was born, spoke the perfect 'Hoch' Deutsch. I had no choice but to settle for Bayerisches Deutsch, guttural and approximate. I limited what I chose to learn from Frau Fick. Even her name had the last laugh.

One day, she appeared with Frederika to ask for a favour, or that's how it sold itself. They were both needed in Regensburg for her monthly meeting, so would I oblige and open the outer gate for the postman when he called?

"Natürlich, mit Freude" said I — Of course with pleasure. The real 'freude' was yet to come.

The imperious bell sounded. I hastened down with the ring of keys to open the heavy gate. The postman thrust a bundle into my hand, unable to look at me, and cycled swiftly away, wobbling on his bike. I turned back to the gate and saw a note appended.

"Für Fick, bitte Frau Hughes lauten." written in a loud, looped hand.

It was not until I showed the note to the father of the Thursday penance and he fell about that all became plain.

"Okay, okay…what's the joke?"

"Perhaps I'll take up the offer," he said

"What offer?"

'It says that anyone wanting a fuck can ring for you."

Names and nouns are both capitalised in German; I am sure the insult was deliberate.

That managed to diminish my terror of Frau Fick. Instead, the absorption of what had marinated her implacable power took a deeper hold. I began to understand the fathomless gulf that separated the war generations. Many of the students had no contact with their parents, shunning even widowed mothers and choosing to speak English. The prevailing taste for Scottish clothing was in every shop window and the bookshops exhibited piles of works in English. Taste, culture, and clothes all conspired to deny the recent past, which only crayoned the elephant more vividly. The elephant lay wounded, sprawled in Dachau, which in 1967 had only been 'opened', if that is the word for a memorial to inhumanity, for just over a year.

What can I recall of it before I read anything? The name was less familiar than the others, Auschwitz-Birkenau, Buchenwald, Sachsenhausen, yet I now know Dachau was the refined and experimental daddy of them all, where suitably trained camp commandants learnt how to enforce the pattern elsewhere. I recall a journey of about an hour from Herrsching; most of the small shopkeepers I dealt with daily must have known of its existence. Nobody admitted ever knowing anything, but I wondered why there was such collective silence if that were so. Its opening to the public was recent. Surely, shocked horror would have followed ignorance?

Logically I must have gone with David; I only recall a fathomless aloneness on entering that barren stretch of clinker, overlooked by watchtowers. Words found no voice. Nothing prepared me for that death camp, the death of understanding, the death of imagination. Entering it was akin to a moon landing without moonlight or the sight of stars. There was no transit to connect it to the rest of life. There it lay. The unbroken view over demolished barrack huts, carefully aligned like ribs from the central spine, stretched to its perimeter, which was almost invisible. That made its psychological enclosure more pressing. It enclosed not memories, not people, but a belief system, now mostly denied, but for me underscored by Frau Fick's unrepentant hatred that still burned, felt no remorse, would do it again. *The war is never over.*

Walking down the avenue between the demolished huts, delimited by low walls and paired in number, brought home the anonymity of its victims – all numbered, numberless. No birds sang. No one else was there. My footsteps cracked and found no echoes. I walked down to the gas chamber, a ghostly relic.

Imagination could not stretch to envisage it. Numb, I wandered. I took in the watchtowers, the double wall and ditch, the barbed wire. On the far-left corner were the gas chambers, the disrobing room, the shower heads' persuasion, and behind them, four incinerators, like rusty caskets, aligned, with gaping maws that gobbled on bodies, assisted by clanking shuttles to feed them furious. The mind took it in; the imagination refused to. They sat in a thin wood of birch trees that must have carried smoke away from the high chimney.

It was my first visit to the capacity for living hell. Not fiery, but cold and indifferent, ruthless and efficient. That is the fascination with fascism, its efficiency and its deep blood, solid chill.

How could anyone call that building through which prisoners entered from rail wagons, with its record of medical 'experiments' that lined the walls, a 'museum'? Shaven heads in striped pyjamas, dead-eyed in their cavernous cheek-claw skulls, were exhibited, page after page, in tattered pictures like some demented nursery school where all would get the prize of being recorded. Recorded, then dumped in rows or piled in mass graves as the Allies advanced. *Unglaublich? That* was unbelievable, compared to which rubble-brick art galleries held a kind of cleanliness.

I could not react to Dachau, except in contrast to the town of Dachau, where daily life gossiped on the street and took home cakes beautifully wrapped. The camp lay like a rotting corpse and nobody seemed to notice its existence permeating the atmosphere. Every politely raised hat and smile turned to something else from the population that had been frog-marched by the Americans to look at what they had ignored. There was no way to fully absorb either except to suspect that comprehension lay in the wordless gulf between them.

The rawness of Africa and its black-white, Boer-British divides were still in formation. They had not had time to solidify but were the abrasive consequences of the rough-hewn, the ignorant, the fear of the black man's smile. From early childhood, I had absorbed a belief that Europe was old enough to know better. Those established cultures, with their imposing buildings, boulevards, and literature, could not conceivably produce jackboots and Frau Fick, let alone that bleak barracks of systematic torture and efficient murder. An hour with Goethe and another with a flute was an inexplicable sham, a cloth of culture laid over festering decay and denial. Why was it necessary to put that on my menu?

Because you had never encountered it, evil to you was ignorance, the failures of compassion; this was evil actively sought, embraced, heralded. It is difficult to imagine evil as chosen and perpetuated unless you encounter those who actively celebrate it. They exist.

Perhaps it was to strip out those comfortable illusions, my sense of raw inferiority? To anchor value below appearances, below my inflated over-regard for what Africa had never offered. Instead, to value what it had: the liberty to try and to fail. To begin the ascent of the foothills of independence, to evaluate without preconceptions and then, in the Gothic arched crypts of culture, to confront horror?

Independence from marriage was the most obvious achievement, though I did not see it at the time. David and I were like ships passing in darkness, only the deep swell beneath lifted or dipped. I had the days with my daughters, so different from one another that they might have been from different parents entirely.

In that milieu of stark hypocrisy, I was beginning to see clearly for the first time, without apology. There was always a bloom of apology in we South Africans for our country's harsh inhumanity, but also for our cultural youth and its crudity. Bavaria and Frau Fick forced me to reassess everything. I began to confront my absence of self-love; so insecure had I been to seek it outside and from others.

I knew that there was a door closing on any hope of my own. I would never betray the marriage, so I made the most of what there was—the challenge of mastering not fluency but the sense of its language's shape and its music. I tried to ski, rather tentatively and visited the mad castles of Ludwig II: Neuschwanstein and the rather gentler Herrenchiemsee. We attended Figaro in the glitter and baroque perfection of the Residenz Teater courtyard. Rain came down like an unexpected drum-roll. Black umbrellas went up with military precision, and Suzanna continued to sing, drenched, without a second's pause in her coloratura arabesques. The ice cream and hot raspberry sauce were what I remembered most about a concert in Schloss Nymphenberg, not the performance. It was all so confected. Life was carved in meringue; all those gold filigreed domes, applied with a spatula above their patient, plastic virgins on the point of weeping and choking back tears.

As the year drew to its end, I waited for Germany to swing its baroque bucket and throw us back to Miami, where exploration and hope would die. David would have tenure at the university; we would buy a house. I would wait for school, sports days and barbecues. I was almost resigned.

But a letter arrived.

Now for the great reveal? You wrote all that before you knew better? Before Frau Fick was proved right?

She was right about the war not being over. She was probably justified in her bitter contempt. I knew nothing of the needless carpet-bombing of the German cities, nothing of Eisenhower's death camps, starving German POWs to death by the thousands. The war crimes of Churchill and Roosevelt were kept well hidden. Do I know better? I admit I know different. I know that much of what I observed was accurate, but also that I was looking through the lens of what I had been programmed to see. Frau Fick was unrepentant, and perhaps she also only knew what she was programmed to see.

What do you think now, now that you have read more deeply?

I have read Hitler's letters suing for peace before the war began, several of them. Also, the Soviet Marxists invented the atrocities of gas chambers, intent on maximising and sustaining the vilification of Germany and planting the future of Jewish reparation for the Holocaust. Instead of death camps, they were labour camps and 'gas chambers' were not for extermination but to de-louse workers to control the spread of typhus. Naked piles of corpses were largely the victims of typhus and, in the end, starvation. The incinerators, rusting under the birches, were incapable of disposing of the bodies in the numbers claimed but placed there deliberately to support the myth of extermination. It does not diminish the hell of the suffering, but suffering was universal, not exclusively Jewish.

If that is persuasive, what about the local population genuinely not knowing? Did your local shopkeepers in Somerset know about the POW camp in Wells for Italians and then Germans? Half an hour from where you now live?

They knew about the miles of dry-stone walls built by the Italians, mostly for the estates of the local gentry. Free slave labour. Here as there!

Not very different, then? But did anyone enquire where they slept at night? Or in what conditions? No army in any war is wholly honourable, but the German soldiers did not generally rape or loot as the British, Americans, and Soviets did. As someone said, history is written by the victors, wrongly attributed to Churchill, who did much of such writing.

When I think about it, the bombing of civilian Dresden was indeed an atrocity, as was the carpet bombing of Hamburg and Berlin. Churchill was far from the heroic saviour I had believed him to be. I did always wonder why he did not bomb the death camps and put an end to them.

Perhaps he had intelligence and did not see any evidence for gas chambers, or perhaps he did not care one way or another. So?

I saw what I expected to see. I cannot now claim to know anything.

Very good. A necessary prelude for what lies ahead.

But I did not know what lay ahead!

No, but we did. Bavaria was a preparation for eliminating any certainty. Future proves past, as future guides present. New knowledge changes the picture, sometimes unrecognisably. It was as well that you recorded your first naive impressions. They were all contrived to foster hatred on both sides. You will find many reasons to amend your understanding. Just as facts are not truth, the past is not over. The palimpsest is continually overwritten.

CHAPTER 18

Terry: a Man Who Came to Dinner

'Most of us who turn to any subject with love remember some morning or evening hour when we got on a high stool to reach down an untried volume or sat with parted lips to listen to a new talker, or for very lack of books began to listen to the voices within, as the first traceable beginnings of our love.'

"Good to meet you, bright eyes. Have fun." That was all I remembered from the tall stranger standing below the steps to his house, the house he had offered us while he went on a sabbatical break with his wife and daughter. We were back to search for a house of our own. The 'bright eyes' lingered: something truly intimate about being noticed for any reason. I had forgotten how that felt. Mind you, his eyes were conspicuously shiny. He threw me the keys to their house and their car and departed in a taxi.

A postman, cycling through smatter snow in Bavaria, had delivered a letter from a total stranger.

'I hear you are returning to Miami and are intending to buy somewhere. You would be welcome to use our house while you look around. Feel free to use the car too.'

The fake Spanish villa close to the beach basked unclothed in the heat, all doors open to the sea, all beds white sheeted. The children could run naked while we perused glossy photographs and went a-viewing. The formality of life with Frau Fick burnt off quickly like an unreal nightmare torched by sun and liberty.

Right next to the house we had previously rented, we found a modest chalet concealed by immodest bamboo and oaks, celebrated by energetic, glossy blue jays that had squatted without invitation, using the empty tank for puddle washing. The tank was exalted as a 'pool' by the realtor, as it had steps up and steps down; swimming in circles was on offer once we had mended the leak and filled it.

A Florida shack in Coconut Grove, built of board and metal with aluminium-louvre windows, was a contrast after an eleventh-century mill in Bavaria. Since it lacked the unrepentant nazi landlady, it was a goodish paradise. I could walk about almost nude with nothing much on except mosquito repellent. Escaping the fires of fascism gave another perspective to this return to sixties euphoria, rather like an extra drafted into an episode of Baywatch, all fun and frivolity.

We moved in before the host strangers returned and the respectable grey Mercedes soon followed. At this midlife snapshot, we looked like any other Kellogg's cornflake family: car out in front, washing in the back, settling down for a predictable life of trivial routines. Desolation had bedded down and mostly looked like acceptance, even to me. I hardly remembered hope and had scratched at disappointment until it bled and was wiped away.

We occupied their house, used their car and departed after stripping, washing and filling. We had no idea who they were or how they had heard of us.

We invited them to supper to thank them and find out.

First impressions across a patio: Carol was buxom; to me, any woman with a generous cleavage was buxom, and her dress made the most of it. I had only once sported such a dress, post-partum, feeling delighted to get a taste of 'womanliness' and the power of it. It was deliciously unfamiliar, a new identity altogether. Sitting behind breasts was like having a rampart from which to fire or simply observe, moving behind it unobserved.

David had been outraged; 'no wife of mine dresses like a tart.' He had returned it to the shop after one viewing.

Carol was clutching the bottle of wine, and my husband was not such a prude when he relieved her of it. She had a wide face, broad cheekbones, and a habit of dipping her head when she smiled, as though smiling was a substitute for conversation.

David hastened inside to pour gin and tonics and led the tour of the jungle garden to the tank, now bubbling with water, followed by the children in pyjamas on tricycles, soon due for bed. I was laying out snacks and last-minute touches to the meal and waved intentions from the galley kitchen.

Normally a dinner is with friends or some inkling of purpose, some connections, celebration or news. This one would be an adventure: strangers and dragonflies in a Florida garden. We did have one thing in common: we all spoke English with almost British accents.

I glimpsed Terry, the tomahawk husband, above shrubbery with his luxurious long hair, a nose fit for Sitting Bull, and a mouth wide enough to swallow a whole egg. Later, I got to see his eyes again, liquid brown loquat stones that melted anything he looked at. His was not a physical attraction as much as an empowered presence, a panther in a tree, wild with the sense of imminent prey, but no agitation, simply there and certain.

Once seated, preliminaries included their recent visit home to Somerset and a swift tour through their married past. Her bitter, sardonic summary revealed that I was not alone in disappointment. Terry had trained and worked as a plumber; Carol as an assistant in a chemist in Bristol, ladling cough medicine into bottles and sticking prices. Tired of the English weather and plumbing in bathrooms for the County Council, he had hitched a ride to Spain, found a crumbling mansion on a beach, and after a little more plumbing, been invited to manage a hotel for an obliging widow. Between the lines of Carol's terse mouth and conspicuous disinterest, I had the impression that obliging widows had been an oft-repeated theme.

In Spain, they specialised in snorkelling and diving holidays for package-holiday companies in landlocked Manchester, unlikely to read the small print. Between seasons, they played backgammon, and Carol became pregnant.

Allocated to a quota of Spanish immigrants to the United States, they found a new resurrection in a tenement in Brooklyn, where plumbing paid double for the night trade to a string of brothels. Carol was on a double lock-and-chain with a baby buggy, and knife crime was the neighbourly norm. I read Carol's editing gestures; with his wife under lock and key, the midnight cowboy's affairs were easily achieved and easily concealed.

The next stop was, predictably, Florida for the sun, clean, dry laundry on a line, and Terry turned fisherman, leasing a boat in Tampa and following other boats to the fishing grounds. He made an adequate living, but his one-night stands fell away as fishing takes hours and leaves a smell.

It is but a short jump to our quadrille in a Miami garden.

Terry is now nearly respectable as a laboratory assistant in the Marine Department of the University, and his off-piste girlfriends have better hair and cleaner nails. They have managed a mortgage on the Spanish villa with its pink grapefruit tree and its easy stroll to the beach. Like my own, their marriage had crumbled into a monotony of acceptance, but it was more comfortable to be bored in the heat when distractions wilt and sipping iced tea consoles. All this I gleaned from between the lines of slightly sardonic past life reconnoitre, narrated by Sitting Bull but punctuated by Carol's waspish commentary.

Of the meal, I remember little except David's surprising coquetry, entertaining the cleavage and replenishing its glass. I seldom saw him truly animated unless behind a camera when something worth a front cover loomed into view. Again, I observed my husband through another's eyes, the schoolboy tousle, the wry remarks, and her reciprocal seduction, which played with him as she twirled her glass. Sitting Bull was not impassive but talkative, hunched forward, with expansive gestures to illustrate his newfound conviction that he had solved the riddle of the universe. Voila! It did not exist.

Carol was obviously familiar with this enthusiasm for non-existence, and increasingly, Terry directed it at me. The night fell, the candles spread their glow over the table, the children stayed asleep, the moon sailed impervious to its non-existence and the tree frogs ululated.

I was captured, not by the truth of his claims, since the nature of the universe had never held my attention, but by the conviction; those loquat eyes shone, the voracious teeth gleamed, but mostly it was the tribute he paid to a belief in my intelligence. He spoke to me as though I would follow his dissection of matter into his stacked Chinese boxes, which sub-atomic physicists were busy constructing.

"They are conceiving and thereby creating what they believe they are finding? Is that what you think?" I asked

"Pretty much."

"Don't flatter him. This is six months of weed talking. Mr. Oddjob truly thinks he has solved the riddle of the universe," said Carol with real venom. "Oh, Terry, wrap it up."

"Think I will," he said, rising to his feet. He threw the car keys at her. "I'm leaving, you drive home. I'll walk." She shrugged and gave me a look. Men, what are they like?

He bowed to me.

"Thanks for supper and for listening." He turned and made his way through the bushes, disappearing in the moonlight.

With that, he walked out of his marriage.

Carol stayed, drank coffee, and persisted with the half-hearted flirtation. I did not notice her leave. David cleared the table.

Something had changed irrevocably.

I had no idea what it was, but it was hug-myself precious, the idea that the universe was made by thinking, and what you saw was what you sought to see. That was as far as it went, but from where I had been standing, that meant there was hope, hope of an alternative. Too precious to surrender to sleep, I held it on my lap all night, remaining under the stars. I knew that this was the beginning of seduction. I also knew it was very far from the usual. It was seduction, if not rape, by an idea. Unwinding it as the night deepened was accompanied by a Joni Mitchell song I played over and over, 'Michael from Mountains.'

'There's oil in the puddles in taffeta patterns that run down the drains
In coloured arrangements
That Michael will change with a stick that he found
Michael from Mountains
Go where you will go to

Know that I will know you
Someday, I will know you very well.

Yes, he had changed the patterns. Creation was thought-engendered. That was what gripped me. One day, I, too, would know it very well. Terry had re-ignited a lamp of faith that had been blown out. It was the small embryo of myself I had found under the stars. ….

I went to bed only as the sun rose. Excitement spread and warmed the sheets but I could not define what it was for, only that for the first time since I married, I felt alive. I was grateful to Terry for his voracious appetite for non-existence, as it had ignited my very real sense of joyful existence. That Florida night spiralled a new Universe, and I caught a wisp of its tail. That's as far as I'd go in defining it, then.

The remainder of my long life would validate and embroider upon the light that a conversation with an incidental plumber had lit.

∾

David woke me. It was disreputably late morning.

"Carol is here. She wants to talk to you."

"Good God, why?"

"No idea."

I went out in a dressing gown to find last night's seductress sitting on the patio step, swollen from crying, mopping the flood. She dabbed ineffectually at her eyes; her face turned away. She gasped out an opening punctuated by convulsive, gasping tears.

"I don't know why I am doing this. It should be the happiest day of my life."

"What's happened?"

She paused, refolded the sodden handkerchief and turned to look at me for the first time. "He's left. My husband has finally gone, the fucking bastard. Why the fuck am I crying?" With her shoulder towards me, I was near to a bare arm. I stroked it. She flicked off my attempt at comfort.

"He's done this before?"

"Many times."

"Well then, he'll be back…" She shook her head and looked at the ground before recovering my face, which was, I admit, struggling to adopt an appropriate expression for the happiest day of her life that was causing so much distress. I hardly knew the woman. Why was she telling me? Didn't she have other friends?

"No, this time, it is different. I know that. This time, it's forever."

"How do you know it's different?"

She turned a frank, solid gaze and held my eyes. Hers had stopped welling. There was accusation in them: accusation but also curiosity.

"Because he hasn't slept with you. He says he's in love with you. He's never been in love with anyone else." The absurdity made me laugh a little, but decency doused it.

"When did he say that? We only met last night, and I am not sure even that is true, he talked to me. I hardly talked to him." She drew out a scribbled note from a pocket. "This is what the fucking bastard left. I got home, and yes, okay, a little the worse for… and found this." She tossed it at me.

'I'm leaving. It's all yours. I am in love and have everything I need. Try and live. Bye.'

"It does not say it's me. Why do you think? …" She tossed an impatient head.

"For fuck's sake, it's obvious. You have not slept with him; you would not sleep with him even if he asked, so it's you. Fucking he knows about, my God the man can fuck, but loving he has never tried."

Anger had rescued her.

"Can I get you something? Coffee?"

She snorted and offered a mocking smile. "I'd say you've got me pretty well everything I didn't know I needed, wouldn't you?"

"Carol. This has nothing to do with me. You do know that?"

She put a hand on my shoulder. "Yes. I do. But I wanted you to know before Terry fucks over your life. There is nothing my husband can't do except play straight. Watch out if he comes for you. Once you've slept with him, he won't hang about."

"I have no intention of it."

She began to gather herself for departure. "Don't ever depend on him. You'd be building on sand, and sand blows away pretty damn quick. Another thing you need to know is he has no time for kids..." She appeared to be constructing what I had never, would never, conceive of doing. I shrugged.

She kissed me, surprisingly, and tripped back to her car without looking back. David appeared and motioned a silent query. I shook off any explanation.

Her husband would repent and be back.

I needed some serious coffee.

&

Whatever had been unleashed that night under the stars gathered pace and aimed with precision as though throwing darts to attract attention. I gave the evening and its extraordinary aftermath little direct thought but felt curiously light-footed in the early settlement of what I had begun to feel was a new home. Something had loosened the pin of my despair. I realised I would be alone forever, but the liberty of sunlight, a garden, and the freedom to walk out began to forge a small determination to find meaning. I now knew where not to look. Marriage would be management, children, like plants, would need support and nourishment, but between times, I might read and try to write.

Our end of Coconut Grove was where we had begun, the throw of latticed streets with tall oaks and unfenced houses set back behind shrubbery, some affluent, some unremarkable, but all overhung with greenery, the hum of insects, the flash of blue jay. After the rigidity of Bavarian society with curtseying and locked gates, our return spread a kind ease of warmth, privacy and smiling as I pushed a buggy or mowed the grass—the conformity I had previously resented now invited celebration. Prolific birds, leaping squirrels and visiting black maids all celebrated with me. A smile on a black face somehow shines wider.

I rediscovered the accessible, small shops, a supermarket, a drive-in bank and the familiar park on the edge of the water where Banyan trees clawed the bare ground and small sailing boats clustered. It was a place to spread a rug in the sun while the children used swings and a push roundabout. With friendly younger women and other children, I watched the football in the early evenings and shared a cigarette. David drove the car to work, and I walked to whatever was within reach. Occasionally I dropped him at work and kept the car to explore further away.

A few days after the supper party, I drove to a distant beach, and there Sitting Bull was; lounging against a whitened log.

"I knew you'd come," he said.

"I didn't know I would until half an hour ago."

"Well, there you are, bright eyes. I told you time does not exist."

"Perhaps you did. I can't remember most of what you said."

"Does it matter?"

It did not matter. We sat and talked while the children paddled and built sand castles. It was good to have adult company. His eyes shone; his smile bestowed his pleasure at being with me. He was living in a hammock on another beach but had taken the day off work. He just felt like it. Living rough, happy to be so, especially since Carol had now 'shacked up' with another man called Bill.

"That was quick?"

"I suppose so, but he seems nice enough. It helps that he has money. Carol likes money. She tells me he is a millionaire and currently between wives. His last was his third so I guess he's a fast mover and needed my roof and a fourth."

"You don't mind?" I asked, still not really believing that anybody just ups and offs without second thoughts.

"Why should I? I've not given her much of a life. I am glad to release her properly this time. Did anybody ever tell you how beautiful you are?" He said this as though he was stating a fact, not asking a question. It carried no intention, so there was no requirement to be bashful or dismissive. I? Beautiful? No, nobody had ever said that.

"No. I've been called lots of things, but never beautiful."

"Well, you are. All the way through. Like clean water, completely transparent. Perfect. Someone should tell you every day. I'm glad I'm the first."

He changed the subject, and we talked of other things until the sun dropped lower and the children were tired. As we made our way back towards my car, he carried Rosalind against his shoulder, putting his other arm around mine. It reminded me of Tom, his height, his ease, his protection. It was as companionable as a brother or the father I never had. Nice. Yes, really nice. A new kind of easy affection, but no more than that.

He loaded us into my car and followed us with his dark hair fluttering in the wind above the steering wheel of his battered old Triumph. He waved farewell as I turned off towards home.

Over supper, I mentioned to David that Carol had a new millionaire, so reconciliation was probably unlikely.

"I thought her a lady of easy virtue; I'm not really surprised."

"You seemed quite taken with that easy virtue. Or gave a good impression of being susceptible?"

"How did you hear that?"

"What? The millionaire? If indeed he is?"

So, I told David about the encounter but left out being beautiful. As he had never noticed it, quoting would have misrepresented the manner in which it was said. He was unconcerned, appropriate, since there was nothing to be concerned about.

After that first one, unplanned meetings happened almost every day. If I went to the park, Terry was there; he was in the next aisle at the supermarket; in the queue at the spare rib barrow. Once I decided to escape and drove to Key Largo, and there he was sitting, waiting on another, more distant, more deserted beach. Every encounter was more improbable than the previous. We did not communicate. He lived in a hammock somewhere; I knew not where. No phone and no obvious woo-woo of clairvoyance, we simply synchronised until it became habitual. We began to assume it would and failed to register that communication was without a known medium. Meetings fell like dealt cards, one for you, one for me. We picked up the hands and played.

The cynic would call it planned seduction. The cynic would say, 'Here is a compulsive womaniser hanging about in hope and getting lucky often.' But I knew that something else was happening; something else was taking control of our respective lives. Our impulses were in synchrony. His abandoned wife was immediately taken care of and treated to new everything: new cookers, new fridges, new holidays, abundant clothes, limitless wine. She needed nothing from him.

"She says she's having a ball," he said. "She looks pretty good on it."

I needed nothing from him, nor did he ask for anything. Had there been a glimmer of seduction, I would have turned and run. Not only because marriage was absolute, however arid, but because with me he was liberated. He was impotent. Sex and sexual desire had evaporated.

"Who was it said, Lord, make me chaste but not yet?" He was stretched out on the grass of the park, gazing at the clouds.

"St Augustine, I think. He of Hippo,"

He sat up. "Hippo or elephant, he knew nothing. My chastity has not come a moment too soon. Bloody marvellous! Have you any idea what liberation feels like?"

"I'd like to, but no. Never been my thing, really."

"Sex?"

"I've never tried it."

He rolled over.

"Really? "But you have children?"

"That's called impregnation. Not the same thing."

"How do you know it's not if you've never tried the other?"

"Literature is full of how it should feel, and none of that applied."

"So, you're a virgin, really?"

"Pretty much. I've had two virgin births but no annunciation presenting a stem of budding lilies."

He rolled back to watch the clouds and frame his description of being free of sex.

"It must be what an ox feels like when you remove its yoke after a hard day's ploughing. Shake, rub, and roll in the hay with hoofs in the air. Yes! I don't ever want to want it again."

"Rolling in the hay?"

"Exactly. None of that. I do love you, but I don't want you. I want absolutely nothing. I have everything right here, whether I see you or not. Though it's great when we do."

I felt the same. It was all so easy. We wanted nothing at all, and nobody would get hurt. I could be Beatrice to his Dante without harming a fly.

I went home to a husband who saw that I was happy and had remembered how to laugh. To begin with, he laughed as well. I sewed myself some new clothes, a long, black, wool winter skirt with horn buttons down the front and a simple black and red, fine woven blouse, and I knew I looked good. I cut my thin hair in a bob, and it shone. I was loved, and I was free to be loved and to love not only Terry but David as well. Life was abundant. Glorious. And I wanted nothing more. Yes, I, too, knew how that felt.

Not being loved by my husband was no longer important—poor man. Love was out of his reach, but I had enough to spread around. There were no plans, no plots, no intentions; it was not even for or about me. From the outset, I knew it was a state of mind that found it good. Life was perfect, but not for me alone. I told David about all the conversations and encounters. I never concealed them, for there was nothing he could not share.

David tasted the sample and, initially, also saw that it was good. He was determined to love me, but sex was not love. He did not press it, but there were other means of geligniting the pearly gates to Paradise. He took mescaline with a group of friends at the university.

"You should try it," he said.

"I don't need to."

"I felt sick as a dog afterwards, but it was interesting while it lasted."

I became alarmed at the atmosphere of growing desperation.

"Interesting? In what way?" I knew he was determined to reach me or something I now embodied. I also knew that drugs were not the way. It was not finding but losing that held the key. If he could let go of hope, there might be a chance, but whatever mescaline had opened, he wedged ajar with plans and stratagems. I had found love by accepting love without suspicion or questions, but it was all-encompassing; it was not personal. Each day was perfumed, and every small tribute to living, whether it was cooking, walking or reading to the children, spread that perfume. I needed no confirmations or encounters with Terry. When we met, we simply shared the celebration, smiled a lot and kissed tenderly only to greet and bid farewell.

At one, now obsolete, level of evaluation, I recognised that Terry and I had little in common. His name, for a start! I have always been fastidious about names. Fastidious had to go. There was a rough, unsubtle quality that I attributed to a lack of education, little reading and little discourse. His lack of fear was the most noticeable quality; he made no effort to be liked. He was naturally expansive. He judged nothing and no one. I never heard him criticise, although, occasionally, I saw him shrug. I also saw his magnetism for women; his American Indian profile, with its beaked nose and long hair plait, had a primitive at ease with his surroundings, whether at a dinner party or in the wilds. It was a natural self-confidence which promised protection. That was, as I would discover, mistaken. He made no promises to anyone.

Somewhere in the Everglades, Terry had planted a small stand of marijuana. He would return from his visits there with carrier bags full of weed. He never sold it but enjoyed handing out bagfuls to whoever happened by. Whoever happened by would always take all his attention. He lived in the Now, long before Now became a well-publicised destination.

Later, when people asked how he had infected me and why him, I could only say that he was a big man, big in frame, big in acceptance, big in generosity, big in simply riding the high surf of catastrophe and emerging still breathing. He did not duck. He took blows. He took poverty and grinned his voracious, wide smile before deciding how best to deal with whatever needed attention, from broken-down cars to the fare for a passage on a ship. He stood at the tiller of his life and steered through calm and rough seas with equal composure.

I see this now, although, at the time, I would have qualified the question by saying we were infected together and shared the disease of unsought joy.

To begin with, David accepted that he was invited to the table of grace and was desperate to deserve it. He had started to love me or was trying to. Starting to see me as distinct and perhaps beautiful, spread the new infection. I also sensed that if he could settle into the nest of loving, he hoped I would choose to fold my wings with him. I also knew that choosing was no longer an option. I had been chosen and took the veil of acceptance as if called to attend upon the Oracle at Delphi, a chaste service to some flaring, smoky, spiralling purpose from a golden lamp; I knew not what. No one deserved what I had received without being asked for servitude, a joyful servitude, free from desires; I had found myself and with myself the perfect world.

I know from this distance it all sounds a bit sixties, somewhat spirito flaky.

But I would not have defined anything as divine. Divine implies revelation, some awareness of the extraordinary, but the celestial was everyday ordinary, life newly lit up, benign, peaceful, fulfilled. It was as though my journey had reached its destination; the becalmed waters of marriage simply turned into a harbour. Now I see it was only the beginning, not a harbour, but the weighing of the anchor, the first anticipation of a flapping sail towards an open sea.

∾

David asked me to accompany him to an evening with his laboratory friends. I knew none of them.

"Please come." He was beginning to offer me opportunities to refuse, which gave me opportunities to give.

"Sure."

On the way in the car, he looked across at me several times.

"You look so beautiful. You've never looked like this before. You never looked like this for me."

"Because you never loved me."

"No, I never have. I've never seen you before. Is it too late?"

"I honestly don't know."

I did not know because I sensed the residue of hope in a personal and exclusive bond that was now impossible. Yet, for the first time, we were talking to one another as equals, honestly, both talking and hearing. I saw him anew, too, as clearly as a bud broken free from the ground, searching for light. He was still so very young. Instinctively, I saw his soul's youth, a nexus of fear and insecurity, as small again as when we met Cassirer. I realised now how that old Professor had recognised it.

The house was a brick and glass garden studio with a broad overhanging roof, deep patios close to the water. The night's silence enveloped us as we triggered the bell; an outside light came on. Several guests had arrived and were drinking around a table where buffet food waited. David greeted one or two colleagues and introduced me. I realised, from their curiosity at my presence, that they had met before, probably several times. My existence was a surprise. From the expectant atmosphere, I sensed that something was planned. I accepted a glass and a plate; the conversation was superficial, and I wandered out onto the patio. David followed.

He was anxious. "You'll be all right?"

"Of course. Why wouldn't I be?"

As supper was finishing, several wandered deeper into the room against a fireplace where scattered cushions awaited in a rough circle. One by one, they adopted the approved, cross-legged postures around lit candles. The virtuosi took up the lotus position, closed their eyes and did the Om in low humming, like a group of bees. Oh God, I thought, an evening of humming and omming. Two large joints were doing the rounds. It was not looking like fizzing entertainment. I passed the joint without taking a drag, but nobody noticed. Perhaps fifteen minutes passed before my sobriety irritated.

"Oh, for God's sake, woman! Just lie back and look at the candles," one said. Since David was already far gone into the realms of dope, whatever those were, and there was no way of getting home without him, I had little choice. I eased forward, stretched horizontally and decided to try to sleep.

A mild vertigo had my head swimming. I must have drunk more wine than I realised and wanted to sit up, but after the admonishment didn't dare. Vertigo accelerated as though I were riding a fairground rotor, faster and faster, so I hung on, seeking a still place in the spinning. Was this what they called 'tripping out'? All at once, I felt a burning in my chest as though my heart was on fire, a blazing coal to char my ribs. The heat intensified until, explosively, I burst out of that rib cage, rising upwards, trailing a sheen umbilicus, glutinous silver, shot with violet and blue streaks, that linked my escaping occiput to the plexus of that body. I felt the strong pull in the back of my neck, an inverse, larger, magnetic adhesive of that maternal bond, severed at birth. I rose towards the ceiling and then through the roof, feeling a change of pressure, like a meniscus between water and air, as I floated out into the night. The umbilicus became a thin thread, hardly visible.

The liberty from gravitation found me wafting suspended above that circle of seekers. I could see them through the transparent roof, foreshortened, their knees illuminated by the candles, their heads in shadow. I also saw my own prostrate body and realised that I was now truly free. I was out of my body! Above me, the dome of stars; below, the black hydra fronds of the palms, and spread sideways the lights of Miami, the curve of the sand beach, the silent creeping of the waves, shrugging small rollers into suds, retreating into lace. The rhythmical pump and suck of the wide ocean against the lips of the earth. How perfect was this aerial view of creation!

I could travel anywhere!

Thinking would take me.

I would visit my mothers in Swaziland.

All at once, the lights snapped out, and a rushing wind enveloped me. I saw myself as a picture painted by Blake, a streamlined body of grey, torpedo light, hair streaming behind. The silver umbilicus disappeared. The speed and force changed the thought.

How will I come back? What about the children? One thought, one fleeting fear, dropped me from a high cliff into that prostrate shell which reclaimed me by drumming heels on the floor and shaking as though shocked by an electric bolt. It lasted for several seconds. A voice beyond the candles said

"Wherever have you been?"

I could hardly grasp where I had been. Instantly I knew that fear is all that connects us to our bodies, and fear is visceral. A thought containing a whiff of fear is felt in the very cells, and, gripped by fear, they are more powerful than thought. My renewed, triumphant entrapment made me understand the power of the body's life and why it is so difficult to escape the magnetism of the body's own will and its vital authority. From my brief escape, I also knew that matter is not solid but can be penetrated by higher-level vibrations. Thought travels faster than light and is not blocked by the material. Transparency is not merely visual but relative, through mediums transparent to one another. Escaping the body had illustrated Terry's thought-creation. I now *knew*.

I had sensed the truth of what he claimed because I already knew it in my cells; now, I had confirmation in my mind.

The meniscus of the roof was an interface between densities, which finer consciousness could penetrate. I wondered at the almighty rushing wind. Was it a warning about the viable distance between a body and its subtle soul? I was about to exceed it? Or simply that the traverse of space-time has a small dimension of delay? One that the wind signals? From the moment of the thought, I was instantly no longer above Miami but already over the Atlantic.

I have never been out with a full waking consciousness since, so those first puzzles remain unanswered. That fall from a cliff into my reverberating frame, which drummed its heels in triumph, has stayed with me. In dreams, I have been 'out' with some measure of control to fly at will, land in trees, and cruise over the congregation in a Cathedral, but never fully autonomous. In those flying dreams I have a fledgling remembrance of what conscious and willed free-flight requires. I practise taking off and landing and notice how the quality of thought, like helium, affects elevation.

The return to the prison of my body was a shock, like plummeting from a height onto solid rock. It was quite a fall! It instilled a fear I had not had before, now a cellular fear. I often lament this tether and long to repeat the escape, for it was a taste of true liberty, hovering over a city to observe a static group, a man running with a light on his hat, the sweeping of the palms, the shooting star, all inter-meshed. What was indubitable was that everything connected. The matrix of space-time wraps around each disturbance to extend it and accommodate it throughout, like a wind across a lake. Nothing, absolutely nothing, happens for itself or by itself. 'Not one sparrow falls to the ground without the Father's consent' and 'the hairs on your head have been counted'. The universe of consciousness registers the smallest dislocation and perhaps the largest windswept longing.

That foray into space-time left its hallmark, although its stamp faded, obscured by daily doings. There is no forgetting. There is sometimes not remembering. They are not the same.

There's not much to add to that.
 Did I get out of my body too early? Before I was ready to control it?
 Yes and no. Being shot from the barrel of your body gun instilled a certainty that material reality is not solid, nor is it the only 'real'. That illusion was forever shattered. You understood reality as relative to a state of consciousness. You had sensed its truth; you received the confirmation of that. That is your no.
 The fear left by the fall was unfortunate, but omelettes need eggs broken, nicht? We needed you to be more protective of your body. You tend towards carelessness in its care, so there is your yes. You learnt what was important for what was to come, but we needed your renewed tether to your body as well. Without it, you would have sailed away long before the work yet to be completed.
 Yes is usually also no. Nothing excludes its opposite.

CHAPTER 19

Opening Pandora's Box

'...a young bride, who, instead of observing his pen scratches and amplitude of paper with the uncritical awe of an elegant minded canary bird, seemed to present herself as a spy watching everything with a malign power of inference.'

The euphoria did not last. It could not withstand David's slow slide into misery. He began to watch me, not to look at me, to watch with a careful imitation of carelessness. My outings were questioned and reasons to obstruct them were contrived. I knew he was taking various drugs to work a last-minute magic but in growing desperation.

He would wait until the children were abed and disappear, keeping me trapped at home. After eight years of being utterly indifferent to me, he turned insidious Thin Controller. One night, while I was brushing my teeth, he quietly came behind me, and when I straightened, put an arm around my shoulder, stilling me to look at the two faces in the mirror.

"We're a good-looking pair, don't you think?"

Gruesome. We were no longer a pair. We had never been a pair. I slipped under his arm and away. He looked part angry, part wretched. I felt for him, but it was only the fear of loss, a small loss of what he had never valued, that drove his desperation. My choice was to deny him or to reoccupy the barren box of magnolia pretence. I knew he had not relinquished possession, merely pretended to.

He became a shadow in my sunlit world and darker with each passing day. The life of spontaneity grew calculating. I joined a university writing course on a Tuesday evening and enjoyed the talk of books. Participants would meet in their houses in rotation, but when it came to hosting it, David was out. The children interrupted, and he was rude when he came in, which was not like him in public. He was losing self-control in the exercise of controlling me. Shame was added to sympathy. Although he had never loved me, he was turning curmudgeon to the world; his boyish charm turned sulky. Indifference gave way to passive aggression. I knew that what imprisoned him was fear. There was only one way to sever this bondage.

I would have him face what he feared. For as long as he believed I had not betrayed him sexually, this control to prevent it would continue. Although our marriage was virtually abstinent, it was, ironically, the only thing he now cared about. I would spend a night away and openly cut the bond of fear. With a swift blade and resolved in cold blood, this decision was to release the weeks of strangling tension: the silence at meals, the children plaintive, the trapped nights alone, and the peremptory contempt in front of witnesses that grew increasingly brutal.

Once he had faced what he was sure I would never contemplate, he would be free of fear. I had no plans to leave him. Nor any expectation of sex as Terry was impotent. That I depended upon, as it ensured the purity of what I intended. I would fake infidelity and have him believe it.

Few will believe me, but I know it to be true. A sorry little tumble would solve nothing and cheapen what I still hoped to preserve. Terry, even sexless, was no security for the children and had nothing to offer any of us. How could an exchange of one man for another have helped? We did not share many interests. I loved his essential spontaneous core but not his dope-dependent friends or his irresponsible, freewheeling life. He was fun, but he was feckless. It was because I was so sure of this that I decided to do it. Paradoxically this was for David and the hope of restoring the marriage to a free alliance between equals, for the sake of our girls above all. I was already on that rock-ledge; he needed a hand up.

So, I cook and freeze, wait for his Friday return and depart, after kissing children, with a bag slung into the back of the blue Triumph that belches black smoke and sputters before settling to speed. Heading for the end of the continent, the wind in the hair, over the long bridges, past the Keys below, with shacks and fishing nets. Where the land runs out, there are white verandas and shuttered windows on the wide streets of Key West. A gracious mansion with generous walkways, lemon trees, and bougainvillaea offers 'Rooms $30.00.'

It wasn't meant to happen that way, but in an arbitrary room at the toe-tip of the continent, I lost my virginity. On white sheets behind white, blowing gauze curtains, and with the last of the day, I discovered what all the fuss was about. So did an impotent man. Coming or going, we came simultaneously and lay back to marvel. No word was spoken afterwards. My initiation was total and would never be repeated. We slept curled like spoons against the curve of his seawall back that smelt of salt and sunlight.

༄

As dawn breaks the egg of the day, we go down to see its yolk rise over the deep, sending its shafts over the pan of the undulating sea. It spreads its silken white to the ripples bubbling near our feet, rising up our calves to turn skin rosy. No one is about. The light turns from white to golden. I look at the man beside me, and he turns to face me.

As I look, his face cracks like the shell of the egg and moves sideways, taking the landscape, the sea, the beach and the palms with it; a laser broom smoothly sweeps the painted shards of the world to the periphery of vision. Everything disappears, leaving only a solid luminescence. It seems solid because it is not blinding nor fluctuating but a pellucid, alabaster orb into which, from a far distance, an eye slowly moves forward to hang between us or between where we had been sitting.

One all-seeing eye.

Motionless, unblinking, a single eye.

It hangs, gazing simultaneously forward and backward; all-seeing, all-knowing, wise, compassionate.

"Can you see it too?" Terry's voice asks. Whether through air or direct to my mind, I cannot say as he is invisible.

"The eye?"

"Yes"

"Describe it to me."

So, I detail this whole of Creation's eye: its green-gold iris flecked with brown, its cornea of light, its lashes still, its look of total clarity and limitless love.

When we have verified the identical eye that has removed the natural world, it begins to retreat, slowly fading away into the middle ground of the faience light. It extinguishes like a bulb switched off.

After a moment, the fragments of shell on which the world is painted slowly reassemble, sliding from the periphery to reconnect his stricken face, the beach, the sky, our hands, the sand and its perfection in this new dawn. The no-longer solid world slotted back, recovering solidity as we remained, struck dumb.

Whatever had bonded us had loosened the bonds of everything else. In a state of union, the separate world did not exist. It had taken care to contrive two witnesses to one single certainty. God was all there was, and God was love, not a sentimental love, but a dispassionate acceptance of everything, turning all to beauty.

The natural world was two-dimensional, and deeper below it was One. Memory fashioned its apparent solidity and memory was mistaken for time. Terry had been right. Everything was God, and everything was conscious. There is no separation of past and future and no time. All are eternally present. The net of the Fisher King ensnares the Creation.

∽

I realised, and increasingly the more I thought about it, that each step had prepared this revelation. From the first pricked encounter in Piccadilly when Cassirer had said, 'There is only love' to the letter delivered in the Bavarian snow, all had followed, synchronous and dove-tailed.

For a few hours, the luminescence remained as a cellular infusion, and other people saw it.

"What has happened to you?"

"Whatever have you found?" people asked, "You glow."

Shopkeepers and the boat hire man refused any money. I had never considered God as knowably present; his abstract comfort had visited me in moments of deep loneliness, but a constant companion, seen and aglow, was scarcely believable, wondrous if it could be!

When I returned home to David, there was no need to speak. One look was enough and he wept but not in anger: in acceptance and clarity.

"I've lost you. I know that. I deserve to lose you. I know I do."

"Nothing is lost. Everything is still possible."

"But not what I wanted?"

"Perhaps not what you grew to want. Nobody can have that now. Not even me."

At that moment, we were clean. Marriage would be different; it could be warm friendship, collaboration, and affection. But it was not to be.

That inner light dimmed, and in its loss, wretchedness and anger took its place. David had seen what we might have been.

CHAPTER 20

Snakes and Ladders

'But something she yearned for by which her life might be filled with action at once rational and ardent; and since the time had gone by for guiding visions and spiritual directors, since prayer heightened the yearning but not instruction, what lamp was there but knowledge?'

A spider in its woven web will catch all flies that fail to see it. A husband weaving a web is versatile; the web moves to fashion a cat's cradle that adapts to the time of day, the one he formed earlier, and other demands. It starts with loud music and verbal silence. No use of a car is convenient; no meals are shared, and no children are comforted. It moves to never coming home, so a wife who might wander out for an evening stroll is pinioned. Colleagues are loudly entertained without introductions and offered innuendos about the unidentified woman, who might be the babysitter. She refuses to rise to provocation and 'I'm only joking' and disappears, lingering where the company are not.

Loud gusts of laughter reach her wherever she is.

After weeks of such games and refusal to rise to them, the wife departs to cohabit with her lover on a beach with miserable children, sharing their second hammock. They all get dangerously sunburned and divide meals out of Styrofoam. Still, the husband refuses to discuss anything. Mescaline and LSD have faded as solutions, and now he relies upon the marriage knot. He refuses to visit his children or care for them at night.

"But they are wretched."

"You should have thought of that. Your problem."

After five days, she crawls back with her keys to give two miserable waifs, with white strap marks across vermilion shoulders, a long, hot bath with their floating ducks, wash their hair, cook a meal and read them stories until they fall asleep comforted with a thumb in the mouth. Home again, blissful, curled like puppies and smelling sweet.

Husband, contented, also returns. Wife is back where she belongs.

He has made the opening moves. She's in check.

Now, they will share a bed. They never have before. They will now. So, Wife castles, sits up and sleeps very little. In response, he does not come home until three in the morning, night after night. Days she is home, nights she is home, weekends she is home. With a man who is rarely present but, when he drops by, is silent or sarcastic. One who married without love and who will continue to live without loving but exercising control, absolute control. He has the home, the money and the car keys. He had always accepted not loving and rather enjoyed the demonstrations of indifference, but she had been introduced to joy and could no longer accept it.

It was like watching an insect: his small rituals of pouring his gin and tonic, his compulsive reading of Time magazine, his rifling through my post. Nothing was different; it simply revealed what I should have noticed earlier. I was married to a man who not only had never loved me, which I had forgiven, but who I had mistakenly loved, for he was calculating and mean-spirited. Nevertheless, he had to face the necessity of putting our children first. He would play games until I forced him to see that honesty was not a game, even when joy had vanished.

> *I can't go back there anymore,*
> *You know my keys don't fit the door*
> *You know my thoughts don't fit the man*
> *They never can, they never can...*

Tearing my heart out by the roots, I left the girls. I put them to bed and wrote a letter.

'I am going away. Not sure for how long. I have no money to give the girls what they need: a roof and a routine. You know that. They are now your responsibility. I hope you will come to see what they need.

They need us both to be adult and, whatever we might feel, to put them first. I am going to Bermuda with Terry, who has work for the Marine Department on a research vessel that sails out of St George. You may contact me through his department. I have no idea how long his work will last or when we will return.'

I packed a bag and stowed it under an oleander. When David's car lights swung into the driveway, I recovered it and walked away, disbelieving and desolate. Leaving him for one night had inflamed his possessiveness. Leaving him with sole responsibility for the girls must surely shock him into facing that game playing was not going to work. If he could not let me go emotionally, it would inevitably mean leaving him physically and tearing them apart. Being fully responsible must concentrate his mind and shake him into accepting that there had never been anything worth holding on to. Not in the way he was now avid to achieve.

I crawled out blind, numb and weeping deeper tears than I understood but still believing that he would come to his senses. How could he not? The terror in the pit of my stomach precluded feeling anything or allowing any fear to stop me. It was my last throw to shake him into caring more for his daughters than for himself. For that, I had to risk them too.

∽

The shack on a wooded hill outside St George was as empty of comfort as my heart. An outpost for the accommodation of visiting marine researchers, it lay on the tip of a narrow island and was used for temporary visitors to the laboratory. Its windswept desolation reminded me of Inhaca. Terry departed for his research vessel to take ocean-floor core samples with a blond assistant I knew would share his bunk pronto. I did not mind. In some ways, I was glad of it, for I had never seen him as more than an agent who introduced me to love and loss. His preoccupation with his speedy new seduction was something I could watch with regretful detachment, regretful that he was in thrall to something so compulsively habitual and that his Augustinian freedom was scrapped at the first opportunity.

The fate of my children blocked out everything else.

Terry and the blond were soon gone, relieved to be free of my silence.

I was an experienced stoic, but yes, I admit I felt hurt that I meant so little. I knew showing it would only irritate him. Terry's attention was always on the immediate present. The next sex was now full frontal, and the urgency of it for both of them made my presence puritanical Dettol. Or maybe just spring water. Abstinence no longer quenched his thirst. They departed arm in arm to cast off the ropes and leave me behind.

Detachment was profound because my entire life was under the microscope. Sacrificing the children completed the abandonment that had begun the night of the dinner party. I had given up caution by simply listening to a stranger, given up questioning all those synchronised meetings, and finally defied, obviously and publicly, the single great injunction about infidelity. Axing each rope in turn: fidelity, marriage, sobriety, routines and finally, my children, I had unwittingly become an anchorite in a cave, remembering an evaporating vision. Lest I mistook its importance or doubted its reality, Terry was peeled away, appointed the consigliere of no-turn-back, a bulwark against retreat through the door that had opened into a new future, a new world—one without any boundaries.

Wherever I was heading, whatever was in control, I had first to safeguard my children.

I cast them upon the fragile, floating belief that David would recover some kindness and see that they needed me, perhaps without our joint, constant presence, but both of us available and crucial to their growth. Until he did, we would find no way to talk. I believed the demands of their vulnerability would be all he needed to forge a path of co-existence with their mother. Immediately, in my absence, their needs and their loss would turn uppermost, surely? What shape our future would take, I had not formulated, beyond imposing on him a critical acceptance that although, for their sakes, we might stay married, I could never be his wife, nor anybody's wife in that spliced-as-one sense.

I could see this clearly, for I wanted nothing for myself.

I had no idea what dangerous wild sea that severance had now cast me into. Terry and his new lover had a new direction, a deux; I had cut loose from my past and all my ties without even a shoreline future. Pandora's Box had been thrown wide open to let loose all calamities. They took no time before manifesting.

The layered palimpsest of time rose and retreated; winged and beaked creatures escaped the confines of rationality. Visions opened domains hitherto suggested only in dreams where gushing rivers spilt, great lizards heaved, and forests and deserts replaced one another, spreading landscapes of ethereal beauty and hells of serpents. I knew that the Eye was what I was looking through: the Eye of Creation, the Eye of all time and no time. All life and its memories were simultaneously present.

Being timeless, it had no clear beginning, any more than drowning does—one moment, you are breathing, in the next, gasping and overwhelmed.

Others would call it the start of madness. Unlike those whose drug-induced forays into visions were brief, returning to ordinary life with neat adventures and summaries to recount, I lived in this revelation as an interlocked tapestry, the water table underlying the leaves on the surface. Normal life was so superficial when deeper life rose up. Without any domestic or practical constraints needing attention, I dived again and again into the fascinating field of thought that could move mountains. Overwhelming it was, but swimming in it was intoxicating. I never wanted to haul myself out of its richness. I had no reason to. Madness was kinder than the life I had abandoned. Its focus was not upon me, but I was drunk upon it.

Hallucinations were constant but I knew them as emerging from within myself. I had unleashed the furies into free-floating layers of experience. The currents of time broke over one another, bringing memories up from their strata, like shells cast on the smooth sands of observation: an experiential geology through layers of past living. It was an internal complement to what Terry was doing out at sea, drilling down to take core samples from the rock strata of past aeons. I was sampling the inner experience of what others call time, drilling through memory, not merely my memory, but all memory. The Akashic Record was available, and I dived below its turbulent tides.

Bermuda was, in miniature, a kernel store of my current life and its conscious memories. The 'setting' was the present, the place where I was. The small town of St George evoked the colonial architecture of Durban and Key West with verandas, shutters and cobbled squares; its vegetation of palms, ferns, cedars, and mangroves washed Inhaca and Mozambique back to my door, and the rocky beaches recalled childhood holidays with buckets and spades on the Natal coast. It was my pocket life, rolled like tobacco, to smoke and re-encounter so that I would emerge from the depths back onto a rock from where I had departed. Tumultuous was this impressionistic sea, but it summoned me, and I chose to dive into it.

I wondered about Atlantis and the Bermuda Triangle, where disappearances of aircraft without a trace had happened and several UFOs were reported seen. Had I been stripped of my children and deposited free to explore where the veils of illusions about history had already been thinned or punctured? Was Terry similarly selected? Not only a deflowerer, an available joint—in both senses—witness, but also a man with access to a boat in the Bermuda Triangle? His past as carefully employed and now as focused as my own?

Describing these days of madness, its currents, tides and rocks, its menacing tentacled creatures, shattering the small craft of logical tidy connections, reduces it all to a seeming stroll through unfamiliar parkland. That is the difficulty with linear language, time-bound and sequenced. It cannot manage the simultaneous or multi-dimensional. Words have a chronology; the timeless does not. In the re-telling, a somersaulting tumult is reduced to a pedestrian stroll through a parkland, momentarily diverted by a folly or unexpected grotto.

Instinctively, I knew that if I were to comprehend it, I had to allow it free-rein to tumble me, teach me to swim and hand me out. Or else I would over-edit and doubt its truth.

Through that speeding, turbulent madness, I travelled on impulse, rocked by wonder, shivering in fear until slowly, slowly, I learned to control the oscillations between them. I was alone in the mid-Atlantic, with no routines or observers, so I could give over and explore the interface between inner vision and outer events. Gradually the integration between them unwound and the ordinary world began to be visited by figures not fleshly; some benign, some malevolent, ghostly forms that watched and guided. Often, there were snakes, my most potent, embodied terror, snakes and fire. I knew that by cutting free of every tie of family, wife, daughter, and most recently, motherhood itself, I had opened a rusty gate into the rose garden, the garden of Creation. With all its perfumes and all its thorns.

～

Bermuda is almost entirely free of snakes, but I did not know that. Such tropical areas of wooded slopes would harbour many in Africa. Those I saw were logically, by force of number, hallucinations, but there was no distinguishing them from the real. When I had read of hallucination, I imagined such visions would be fleeting, vaporous, and suggestive, not these threatening, three-dimensional tongue-flickering asps, adders and hooded cobras. It was a barrier I knew I had to overcome, this terror that conjured them, but my involuntary recoil rendered me paralysed, scarcely able to breathe. One day, while I was carrying a bundle of washing to the line, a tessellated adder lay coiled in my path. It rose to strike, with iridescent jewels along its back. I froze.

Suddenly, I was looking through the snake's eyes at myself, equally terrified of the woman standing above me with a basket of washing. The creature was braced to strike by its terror of me. A split-second later, I was back in myself to watch it explode in a shower of sparks, a bubble bursting, pierced by the needle of a moment's compassionate love. After that, I never saw another, and even those I now encounter in dreams do not wake me as they once did. After blasting through my most confining terror, the landscapes grew broader, more multi-dimensional, with inter-penetrating layers, like the gradations in the visible spectrum. But these were emotional layers, from dark terror to the most pellucid joy.

By registering these gradations, I came to see that access to memory is bounded and curtailed by fear. Fear and love are the coordinates that form the matrix. I had faced all my fears of loss. I had sacrificed each love for a greater love until the loving Creation had embraced and absorbed me. I was free to explore it, although I was a novice, helpless in its power. Helpless was not passivity, I chose to allow the maelstrom to take me, but some autonomy remained. Taming its terrors could be navigated by calling up natural images: geese in formation, a mackerel sky at sunset, frogs slim and palpitating, a bird feeding its young, a sweep of sand brushed by the lace of surf, dolphins leaping, the dawn rising, and the arms of the ocean soothing the fretful earth. I could visualise myself out of fear through the ladder of ascending love, the inherent beauty of the natural palette.

Emotions are what anchor memory; memory calls out events that evoke emotion. It is emotions that filter and refine our sensibility, not the intricate arguments of the intellect. When we recover memories in dreams, the moments that wake us are when strong emotions prevail: surprise, perplexity, joy and fear, for it is those that pin memories to the corkboard for further attention.

I travelled for many days, in and out of the 'normal' world and that more seductive vast adventure, becoming more familiar with controlling where and for how long. It was always available. I found I could enter it simply by letting go of ordinary preoccupations, not thinking of plans or the future or the next meal. But I realised that ordinary time was running out. Terry's work would come to an end and, with it, a roof. He would return to the university, and I had nowhere to go unless David had come to his senses and we could reach an understanding. Whatever it entailed would have to curb all options for the sake of our daughters.

Before the disciplines of ordinary, temporal life took hold, I knew I had to write an account of my travels and something of the laws prevailing in terra interiora, the space-time universe of history. I was afraid of losing the clarity that uninterrupted immersion had afforded, where I could recall setting forth, taking steps, traversing time, and using imagery for orientation. The realms I visited co-existed; they were both past and future, layered between the tissue of ordinary linear time. Losing the connection between them would be truly losing my new, coherent mind.

I hired a motorised bicycle and rode to Hamilton every day to work in the main library. I went to seek the continuous cord on which science had threaded an edited intermittent history. Science, with its narrow focus on linear time, this-before-that, this-causing that, relegated change and progress to the accidental. It had lost the integrated layering of dimensions in the division between thought and the seemingly 'external'. I went to catalogue the history of consciousness, annotated by others, for everything was part of the whole space-time field I had fallen into.

I had to choose a language and a discipline by which to trace this severance. Since my last academic studies had been in the field of animal behaviour, it would have to do. Choice of language was arbitrary, but what better field was there from which to trace the expansion of consciousness? I had to, somehow, frog march the overlapping veils into a macadam tramp along the narrow footpath of chronological time.

In the reference library, I took up my daily table between shelves of biology, embryology, evolutionary theory, and the history of science. The standard texts were there, and again synchronicity took hold. Whatever book I reached for opened at a critical page, furnishing my argument with illustrative facts, surprising anomalies, contradictory experiments, and critical authorities whose names I remembered from ten years earlier: Huxley, Alister Hardy, Jung, Kohler, Pavlov, Tinbergen and Konrad Lorenz again, but now in his writings.

The bridging between what I had 'learnt' and what I had 'experienced' forced a new emphasis on the pre-eminent role of the individual life. I now understood the discernment of the life that had prepared me; my solitude, my necessary stoicism, Marna's contempt for received opinion, Heli's defiance of authority, Louie's distracted discipline, each had prepared me for this sharpened lance and this windmill revelation. My indecision about academic interests, veering from medicine to philosophy, fine art, zoology and psychology, had also offered a broad vocabulary. Emotionally and through languages, I had been prepared, turned on a lathe and whittled under a sharp blade.

How would such a perpetual record be safely stored and handed down.? At the time, in 1968, only four per cent of DNA was considered 'used' for protein synthesis. The rest was called 'junk'. Junk implies that earlier drafts had never been relegated or consigned to the bin. Nowhere else in nature is such wastage evident. I was sure that 'junk' was really a jewelled necklace, with the beads of experience threaded along the spine of DNA. A newly arriving life wore that necklace, perhaps arranged according to similar traumas, like my multitude of snakes or one great Cathar conflagration, which spews flames and ashes into the lives that follow.

The drafting of the Theory of Involution took about ten days, and it caused giddy nausea throughout. The incubation pregnancy of this idea demanded the abandonment of control, and the body could scarcely contain it. The mastery of an entire field of theoretical knowledge in such a short span now looks superhuman, but I was not sifting or evaluating but seeking corroboration that aligned with the truth I already knew, pegging out a portrait of an alternative to the much too slow, much too inflexible Darwinian hypothesis. After what I had learnt, the theory of Evolution simply seemed absurd, as did the slavish adherence of scientists to it. The experienced Cathedral stood brightly illuminated behind any scaffold theory bolted together with words.

When I had finally finished writing, I was exhausted, lay down in a hammock, hung outside the shack, almost delirious, and fell asleep.

I was shaken gently by an elderly man, rocking my shoulder.

"I am sorry to disturb you. I wondered whether this might be of use to you?" He handed me a leaflet advertising a conference, 'On Nature, Man and God', due to be held at Culham College, Oxford. I did not remember seeing the man before. He had the kind, lined face of a thoughtful academic. Such professors were becoming familiars.

"Why did you think…?"

"Well, I cannot make use of it, so I thought you might. Anyway, I'll leave it with you." He turned and made his way back down the slope between the trees, stopping to call out his name. "Tell them I recommended you."

How curious? He seemed certain I would go. I wondered whether I had encountered him in the library. Or had he taken a glance at my scribbled notes?

I was becoming alert to the signals offered. I could see no way I could pay for a passage to England or attend this conference, nor had I any thoughts of presenting the paper as it was, crudely assembled and in need of polishing. I had written it for myself to secure the heights before the depths re-claimed me.

༄

The depths lost no time. A phone call from David immediately followed. A maid called me to the research office.

"Just rang to ask two questions," David said, "First, and I want you to think carefully before you answer, is there any hope that you will come home to me?"

"What do you mean by home?"

"Come back as my wife with all that implies…"

"In that case, no. Why are you asking me now?"

"Well, I've met someone. You might as well know. It's Carol."

"Terry's Carol?"

"Yes."

"I thought she had a fellow called Bill?"

"Never mind that. The thing is, I don't want to start anything with her if there is any chance you'll come back."

"Not in the way that you have defined, no."

"Well, in that case, can you have the kids for a week, including little Terri, their daughter? We want to go to Atlanta to the music festival. Jimi Hendrix is playing."

"I suppose so. But can't I return to look after them at home?"

"Carol's moved in."

"So, you have *already* started? That was quick."

"I needed help with the kids…"

"Well, presumably, since she is occupying my house, she won't mind me looking after them in hers? Hers and Terry's, to be exact…"

"She's rented it to Bill, for a while anyway."

This took some absorption. My belief that David would have to see the children's need for their mother had magnificently back-fired. He had replaced me without a second's thought or delay.

I had spectacularly miscalculated.

Another door was resolutely closing; David had another woman, one with her millionaire tenant. Terry had a new sleeping partner, and I had no way back to ordinary existence, no home, no country, no children. My head reeled. I stood silent, clammy and cold all over. What did this mean? Should I have them briefly to foster David's new affair with Terry's wife? Was that also part of the plan?

"I suppose so, but I doubt we can stay here beyond a week. Terry's core sampling is almost finished."

"A week will do. I'll let you know what plane to meet. So long." David hung up.

It was at that point of abrupt termination that I fully comprehended what I had done. Instead of bringing him to his senses, I had merely made it easier to dispose of me completely. In leaving the children, I had given a controlling, bitter man the reins of my heart. He knew I had nowhere to go; he knew I could provide nothing without his help. It was then that I remembered his ruthlessness and an episode where an alibi took priority over an ambulance. They both knew they held all the cards. Carol had no doubt apprised him of Terry's compulsive womanising and indifference to children.

Yet I wondered. Was this some kind of solution? Could the design for me have conceived of a benign worldly outcome? Was offering David Terry's discarded wife a matching solution to the new order? What order was there? The thought of my lovely daughters cared for by that bitter, angry woman and her vulgarity was hard to stomach. One thing was now certain: David had no care for them or for me as their mother. Somehow, I would have to forge a life in which I could provide for them. I had put us both to the test, believing he would care. Instead, he whistled up a convenient bystander and offloaded the problem of his children. My children.

Terry returned that same evening, leaner, browner and without his pigtail, to find me dissolved in tears of wretchedness. His lab assistant departed without delay.

I told him of the paper I had written, and he glanced through it.

"Looks impressive. Jeez, too many words. It's no good; nobody will take any notice of it…" I showed him the leaflet about the conference. That interested him.

"Oxford might?"

As always, he jumped both feet together,

"Okay, let's go."

"How can you? You are due back at the lab next week."

"I'll resign and take you to present the paper. Got nothing better to do. I'd quite like a spell on the old home turf… I can't let you go alone. Where would you go?"

I then told him about David and Carol getting together, and wanting to go to Atlanta. He was less upset than I was, except about the renting of his house.

"That's my Carol, always an eye to the lucre. I don't suppose she'll send any of the rent in our direction…"

"Have you any money at all?"

"Only my salary and an insurance policy on my life. I could cash it in. It would get us to England."

The children, all three, came for a week of beaches and swimming. When I put them on the plane, I saw them cross the runway and mount the stairs, feeling that I might never see them again. They turned to wave, uncomprehending.

Terry's insurance got us two one-way tickets to the conference and as far as Southampton on a Fyffe's banana boat. In a mahogany stateroom with its en-suite shower and a place at the captain's table, with a fruit bowl replenished daily by a steward, I had the voyage to polish the thesis. It was my new lifeline, the hope that if well received, my theory would earn me the hope of an income. The Purser lent me an old typewriter and I worked all the days while Terry smoked good Jamaican weed, lolling on the deck with the crew.

We landed with ten pounds and a manuscript and hitch-hiked to Somerset to meet his mother.

Do you realise that very few people have the referencing knowledge to make sense of your deep dive into the Akasha? Most will call it schizophrenia and assume you are clothing it in rational disguise. Few will understand that either.

They could read Jung's Red Book. It's a good preliminary guide.

Well, not many understand schizophrenia or that Akasha is always ready to penetrate any open portal. Most people are dislocated and confused by it, often permanently. I also know that it never overwhelmed you. You were always, sometimes only just, in control. But you secured a knotted string and from it fashioned a hypothesis, a good one.

It was richer than anything I had read or experienced, and it fascinated me after I had made peace with the serpents guarding its gate. Besides, you had laid out the pathway first. It drew, no, it compelled me.

You see that now, but it was both foolhardy and brave.

It furnished a lifetime of work; the Delphic assistant was what I wanted to be. It gave me my own lamp to light and polish.

Ours, as well. You stretched the risks almost to their limits and

caused great anxiety.
   In you?
   In everybody.

CHAPTER 21

Promised Land

'I wish to be among the ranks of that glorious crusade that is seeking to set Truth's Holy Sepulchre free from a usurped dominion. We shall then see her resurrection.'

Mother, a determined, dumpty woman in a headscarf and apron, is not welcoming. She stands, arms folded, at the door of her council house in a straggling village called Norton Malreward, near Bristol. Never were signs less propitious.

"Who's this?" she asks.

"She's a friend. Can we come in?" Terry is leaning on his arm along the door jamb.

"Where's Carol? Where's little Terri?" mother barks.

"At home, mum, where else?"

"Where you should be too-an-all. I am not having 'er in my house, and there's an end to it." She closes the door. We hear the key turned.

"Where next?" I ask.

The abandoned farm hovel has had a number of uses. It leans; even in sunlight, it weeps, lamenting better days. In the long grass of a derelict orchard, its tin roof is red with rust, its stone walls patched, its door hanging dislocated on a single hinge, like a drunk propped on one arm taking a swig. Its most recent use was as a pigsty with a barricade to keep a tusked boar from its grunting sows. Further ago, it must have been occupied by a farm hand, as it sports a single plug a-dangle on an old, black flex and an up-ended, zinc tub spotted black, rime-encrusted, seemingly sound. A Victorian grate sulks half-burnt paper. A tattered curtain droops against the single window. We contemplate this gloomy sanctuary from the sunlit doorway.

"Could you manage here?" Terry's brother Jeff had secured it in haste since his mother had made a phone call to make clear she wanted the disgrace of her older son and 'that woman he's got hold of' removed forthwith.

"Take them away and out of the village; I don't want them here," had been our send-off from the head a-bristle with pins. Terry's mother required our speedy banishment.

"Of course, we can. Two on a shovel for half a day…" said Terry

"Brought a slurry shovel brutha, and a kettle and a basket of kitchen wotsits."

"Your wife knows?"

"Course. She packed it. She also says come for a bath when you start to smell."

Jeff unloads a tandem bicycle from his mud-encrusted Landrover and departs.

So home is a pigsty with ten years of dried manure to shift. Outside, the late Somerset summer spills blackberries over the hedgerow, and old apple trees yield pockmarked fruit. A neglected vegetable bed suggests potatoes might be found among the desiccated fronds of carrots. The stone building leans into the hill as though edging its insecure way down a slope it fears might slip, but the valley below spreads in small fields, orchards, hayricks and distant drifting mists. Small clusters of sheep and an occasional puttering tractor are the only sounds apart from the contented wasps gorging on fallen fruit. Here, we will wait for a little over a week until the conference, and from here we will embark on our separate futures after that.

We both pretend not to know it will be separate. The flare of our beginning had been doused, a match into a rain-filled ashtray. Terry hides his guilt, and I hide my recognition of it. The celestial awakening had taken everything from us but not yet offered any future. All hope was pinned on the conference. After all that careful orchestration, surely there must be something destined to continue?

Foraging and scrumping better apples than our own and exploring his childhood haunts occupied the days in the unfamiliar country that was as remote from London as Miami.

"This was the farm I helped harvest in the summer term… this was the old-age home I provided twelve bathrooms for and never got paid… this was my local school… this was where…."

My calves ache, his broad back obscures the view and I couldn't care less about any of it. The zinc tub, heated by dangling the kettle on its electric cord, like submerging a rat by its tail, took time but was dangerous enough to make a wash in warmth a small triumph of invention. We go to sleep hungry on spread blankets in blackness. I rise stiff and more desolate every day. Ladybird, ladybird, fly away home. Your house is on fire. Your children are gone. They are all I think about; he never mentions them. I don't risk it either. Tears would scarcely help.

We reckon that hitch-hiking to Oxford might take two days, so allow three. Instead, we are deposited on the ring road within five hours with two nights and two days to kill, sleeping rough. Luckily, the sun shines, and my Indian cotton dress stays dry. We hitch on towards Abingdon and then walk perhaps three more to take a chance on the Theological College, where a kindly porter might admit us early.

It is locked and silent but stands in grounds that are better and more private than anywhere else. Behind a broad cedar, a backpack will suffice. A day later, staff arrive with trucks of catering supplies, and carry in lecterns and urns. The day after that, the delegates we are destined to join arrive. We watch sleek cars directed to a nearby field to park. In a discreet interval, we make a quick visit to a pub in the nearby village. While Terry distracts the barmaid, his most practised skill gives me time for a complete wash, sitting on the basin behind a locked door and emptying the paper towel dispenser to dry off.

∾

We return and enter the grand-panelled lobby. Behind a table where name tags await in serried rows, an elderly organiser is checking lists. He glances up. We are also glancing up at the elaborate plaster ceiling.

Hastening out, he waves his hands in modest panic.

"No, no, no. You can't come in here. We are not open to the public. Please leave at once." He claps his hands as though we are uncomprehending goats.

Terry towers over him, scrutinising his list. "There's a conference due, isn't there?"

"Quite, quite. A conference. It is an important conference, so you will oblige by not lingering. I must attend our guests…"

"Can anyone attend?"

The man glares through his glittering spectacles.

"Of course not. Only delegates attend. Esteemed academics and clerics are coming from all around the country. Even from abroad. Now, Madam, please let me show you out."

He waves an arm back and forth behind my back, chuntering and gesturing for me to hasten before it. We both realise it is my gender that engages him. Terry takes the chance to approach the table and secure our name tags. He follows the fallen woman and her escort to the porch.

"Excuse me," Terry said. The man spins round, apoplectic at delay. "We *are* delegates. See, here we are. Esteemed and expected delegates on your list."

The man snatches the name tags. "P. Hughes and T Thomas? These are you?"

"They are indeed."

"But, but," he consults his room allocation. "Your booking never mentioned your… your…"

"Sex?" I offered.

"Exactly!"

"The question was not asked."

He glowers and returns to his clipboard, flicking over pages.

"But I don't have another room. You are down to share. It won't do."

"It'll do fine," says Terry. This nonchalance fuels a roseate glow rising up the aged man's neck.

"I won't have it! This is a Theological College. We are expecting ordinands not..." he searches for a suitable description and settles for, "...the likes of you. I insist you leave immediately." Terry perches across the corner of the table.

"You want us to go?"

The retainer flips the corner of his clipboard at Terry's stomach. He bats it away. "I don't *want*. It is not a choice. You *will* go!"

Terry extracts the leaflet from his breast pocket and finds the name he needs.

"Could I speak to Canon T.R. Milford? He is due to Chair this Conference is he not?"

"No, you can't. He's not yet here."

"Then we'll wait." Terry folds his arms. I sit some distance away on the fender before the cold hearth. In the silence that follows, the receptionist shuffles cards around the table and re-examines his list, hoping for a sudden vacancy to spring forth.

Terry begins again very simply.

"You do realise that you will need to refund our fees. We booked in good faith that our booking would be honoured..."

The receptionist quails a little but rallies, "Well... well, perhaps a proportion might..."

"No, not a portion; we'll have the full English," says Terry, standing up to tower over the flustered diminutive. "Let me clarify: We have travelled from Bermuda by boat and by train and then waited for ten days for this conference, and this conference alone. It is why we are in England, the *only* reason we are in England. Your refund will be for the total cost of our journey and our accommodation since it is you who is deciding to cancel our pre-booked and confirmed attendance..."

At this, the man throws down his clipboard, goes into an adjacent lobby, finds a key and throws it at him. "Oh, very well..." The key catches the edge of the table and bounces across the floor. Terry picks it up with slow deliberation. He looks at the number.

"Would you be kind and indicate the direction of our room?"

The man jerks a thumb without looking up as a new delegate enters through the portcullis of privilege.

"Thanks a million. We'll go and find those who came for God." Terry calls over his shoulder as he holds a door open for me.

∞

A room overlooking a courtyard with two beds, clean linen, an en-suite bathroom with white towels and a tray for making tea. The tea and the biscuits first! Wow. Three days of quiet luxury and all meals provided, hard-fought, hard-won but finally worth it. Right now, all aspirations to conquer academia theologica have evaporated. Getting clean is all that matters, and a warm, comfortable night's sleep to come.

'Nature Man and God's' delegates were all male, suited or dog-collared, some in full cassock regalia. One or two sported bishop purple. They stood about with sherry or orange juice, thoughtfully inclined to give attention to moderate talk, nodding or unobtrusively moving away. Waitresses in black offered trays of finger food. This corps-de-ballet was a slow tableau choreographed by Noel Coward before the flying entry of the principals. As we entered, heads turned and remained turned longer than I thought necessary. I searched in vain for another woman. We accepted sherry and food.

"Do return soon, we're starving," said I. The waitress winked.

"We are not exactly inconspicuous," I said, watching the stolen glances of curious incredulity that rose up my dress. Finally, a tall priest approached and held out a hand that took my fingers with a limp pinch.

"I'm Dr Llewellyn. You are?"

"We're nobodies," said Terry, "and we're clearly not welcome for that reason."

Frankness brought recoil. Llewellyn recovered. "You have names?"

"I am a Mr. Thomas, and this is a Mrs. Hughes. That's all we have to offer. Nothing fore or aft. How do you do?"

Llewellyn struck out for distraction, looking about the room as though to embrace us on behalf of everyone present. He waved generally.

"Well, isn't this nice?" We remained unconvinced. "Tell me, what is your interest here? Why have you come?"

I decided to assist and match Terry's achievement.

"Well, I came to present a paper, and he came out of interest in its reception."

"A *paper?*" Incredulity was blatant. "On what topic?"

"On Nature Man and God."

"Well, of course, obviously. But specifically?"

"Specifically? Specifically, that they are all different names for the same thing" This caused a pause while he endeavoured to decide whether I was serious or an idiot. He chanced it.

"Can you expand a little?"

"I can and came hoping to. Specifically, consciousness creates Nature, and consciousness is what Nature really is, the outer manifestation of consciousness, embodied in complex forms throughout time…" At this, he stepped back. The idiot was in the ascendant.

"Ah! A bit Buddhistic, if I may say so. That won't be well received here. We're all evangelical Christians. The Trinity is fundamental. Where do you fit Man in this hypothesis? That is to say, if you fit Man in at all?"

"I fit Man as the species that created the divided world that this conference is seeking to bridge. Animals don't make that mistake."

Llewellyn looked around seeking a rescuer and failing.

"Teilhard de Chardin?" I offered, "Christogenesis?"

Llewellyn grasped for the handhold of a respected name. He shook his head regretfully.

"I always *meant* to read de Chardin, Tried once or twice. Very mystical he is. Not easy to grasp, have you? Mind you, there is one person 'ere will match you, and that's the Chairman, Canon Milford. Very keen on de Chardin ee is…" The Welsh was showing as clearly as an untucked shirt tail. I liked him better for it.

"That's who I hoped to talk to."

Llewellyn patted my shoulder.

"I'll make it my business to introduce you. Very fine mind ee 'as."

"While you are smoothing my rough road, could you point out Sir

Alister Hardy?" Llewellyn laughed.

"Y'ave me ther! I'm no scientist." He whispered, "I'll make enquiries and let you know when I identify the specimen." Smiling, he moved off. Terry raised an eyebrow.

"Well done. Made a small conquest with him."

"It was probably the name Hughes. We Welsh stick together."

"Since when were you Welsh?"

"Since ten minutes ago. Come to that, Thomas is Welsh, too."

"Count me out, look you. I'm not having any truck with being Welsh."

Somebody struck a small bell, and we all moved towards the refectory for the first meal in a fortnight.

I confess I expected a little respect simply for the effort and expense needed to be there. We might look as unwelcome as a rat at the bishop's tea party, but England had sampled an empire and encountered many in turbans or half naked in a skin skirt or of the wrong colour. I assumed mere youth and perhaps self-evident poverty would not be too much of a stretch.

~

I never did present the paper. I did identify the cavernous gulf between those who held the accepted credentials of the cloth or academia and those too young to be permitted to hold an idea, let alone expect it to receive attention. More significantly, I sniffed the winds of ostracism, the gentle winds that gusted constantly in the subtle dismissal of a voice, an averted head, the chilly glance. These all took their cues from our relative youth and the audacity to penetrate their bastion of membership, their peer reviews and their habits of referring to things by acronyms. Granted, we lacked the long servitude to academic apprenticeships, but if we had so served, we would not have been there. It was Terry's embryonic, regrown pigtail and jeans that outraged the conference and my modest décolletage without a cleavage.

But there were three wise men we had been 'sent' to meet. Each was more improbable than the last.

Llewellyn was as good as his word. He found an opportunity to conduct me to the side of Canon Milford as he unfolded a napkin at lunch and suggested I might be seated beside him. The old man smiled with warmth and assented. We spent close to an hour together, and I outlined the Theory of Involution between mouthfuls. I had observed him with interest at every presentation earlier because, despite holding the chair, he appeared entirely relaxed.

Dick Milford was cloaked in modesty, not an ostentatious self-effacement, but one devoid of any sense of importance. A thin man, a little stooped in posture even when seated, he resembled an aristocratic racehorse put out to grass, with a long, thin face and prominent, broken veins over an almost visible skull. His pronounced cheekbones flanked a finely shaped long nose. His blue-mottled hands moved gently to articulate a point, crumbled bread as he thought, and dabbled at the air when hesitation sought words. Unlike the ecclesiastical vestments of the others, he wore an old tweed jacket over his narrow dog collar, which might have been an apologetic vest.

I had noticed his mild irritation when questions were asked in Latin, and his courteous translations, 'For those of us here who lack a classical training' were a mild rebuke to the pretentious priests as much as a courtesy to us; perhaps we were the only ones? Some tried it in Greek, equally effortlessly translated.

Dick Milford was the quintessential, eternal scholar, drafted by Evelyn Waugh or E.M Forster, seated in a book-lined rectory study, open to ideas, from whomsoever they came, thoughtful in approaching them, and genuinely intrigued by anything new. He weighed the new against his great store of the familiar. His deep reflections on de Chardin bonded us. His response to Involution was close to excitement, and he ended the meal with an invitation.

"You must visit me. I can't give your ideas serious attention here—far too much nonsense to attend to. I'm in Dorset. Where are you?"

"Somerset."

"That's easy then. No more than an hour apart. Good, good. You promise?"

"I promise."

"Send me your dissertation first. Here…" He wrote down an address.

"I've only got a single copy with me. The truth is, I have only one altogether."

"Most unwise. Look, go to the secretary and tell her to run off some copies for you while you're here. Tell her I authorised it."

I don't know whether he ever heard he had authorised fifty copies: collated, paper-clipped and offered in a binder.

∽

The next was a small, almost bald man, who approached with a teacup and small bustling footsteps. Conservatively besuited, he looked very uneasy, his eyes flicking sideways, but he bore down with clear intent. His fussy movements suggested suppressed irritation, as though landing near us was the obligation of a scouting wasp to sip, sample and leave.

"You are wasting your time here. These people haven't begun to wake up."

"You mean…?"

"I mean, the Church is not a place to offer a welcome. It's stuck in its own importance. Added to that, you are ten years too early. Go back home to America. They are more likely to understand you. That's all I came to say."

"Would you care for a copy of the paper we hoped to present?"

"Certainly, I shall read it. Certainly." I extracted a copy and handed it to him. He added, "England is no place for visionaries and even less for new ideas. I should know."

He exchanged it for his teacup and scuttled away on his little duck-splayed feet.

I had no idea who he was or how he knew we had come to be 'understood' or were visionaries.

The waddling man's abruptness suggested an emissary briefed with a message, but his assumption that our home was America implied an inexact briefing. It was perplexing, but in the sea of ostracism, he came like a floating plank to hold on to. Discrete enquiry of Llewellyn yielded his name.

"That's Dr. Martin Israel. He's a medical man—Royal College of Surgeons' hallowed halls. Fellows in white coats and some teaching, only when moved to it, mind you. Mostly research into nasty diseases. I have no idea what he'd be seeking here! Jewish, too, by the name. Talked to you, did he?"

"A little."

"That's more than I got! He's not one for talking, look you. Honoured you are."

The third of this Trinity was Zoology Professor Alister Hardy, about to retire from Oxford. I had dipped into his books in the Hamilton library and word had it that he was embarking on research on cows' milk yields and the growth of cabbages when offered a rich diet of Mozart. It suggested that he was dipping a toe into consciousness and might be receptive. I began by suggesting that his books implied a possible interest in my paper. He dismissed that.

"I'm a busy man with more students than I can attend to, but by all means, leave me a copy before you go. I'll see what I can do."

"Thank you."

"No promises."

We departed to hitch hike back to Somerset, cleaner and better fed than when we arrived. Hope lay betrayed. We had no place there.

August days stretched with blistered feet from walking, chafed thighs from cycling, and the disappearance of hope that any of the copies of the monograph would provoke interest. Terry rummaged through supermarket rubbish bins for outdated food and worked occasionally in a local pub washing up to bring back whatever he found on plates.

Dick Milford was the last remaining hope. I realised that Terry was a worthy street fighter when needed, but philosophical discussion was not aided by his tendency to blunt summary or crude analogy. If I called on Milford, it would be alone, at least for the first occasion.

How clichéd are assumptions! After meeting Dick Milford, Chancellor of Lincoln, Master of the Temple, chess champion of Dorset and Chairman at the conference in his tweed, patched jacket I had envisaged his abode. It would be a gracious, gabled rectory near an ancient church flanked by twisted yews. His study would be oak-panelled with a view of clipped lawns, a ha-ha with sheep safely grazing beyond. His wife would be a formidable granddame in cashmere and the family pearls. She would direct the serving of tea by an elderly retainer and tolerate the invasion by a young woman whose claim to call had not been clarified. She would escape any need for more than a cursory welcome and repair to her conservatory to pot cuttings. It would not be a house with a doorbell but an ancient pile that would expect the preliminary courtesy of a warning.

On Jessica's birthday, with an ache I could not salve, I hitch-hiked from Bristol to Dorset in the hope of that welcome. It took over four hours, and when I was in the vicinity of that imagined gabled elevation, I counted out coins and entered a phone booth.

I gave my name and asked to speak to Canon Milford. A voice I took for a domestic just said. "Wait a moment, will you?" The time he took imperilled the coinage, which I lined up, praying it would hold out.

"So glad you called," he said at once. "We must meet. Unfortunately, I can't arrange a time right now, because we're taking the grandchildren to see the lions. In fact, we are just off, but do call again."

The coins survived. I hitch-hiked back. The birthday was over. It was dark when I limped into our midden.

"Did you meet him?" asked Terry.

"No, he was going to see the lions."

"I would not have imagined him a rugby fan. How strange!"

"Probably to entertain grandsons."

∽

We would have to be proactive. The response from Martin Israel had been encouraging.

16 Cranley Place
25th August 1970

Dear Philippa and Terry
  Thank you for letting me read your excellent paper. I have only the highest praise for it, and I hope it is published soon. Your thesis is bold and important: it puts inner experience in an objective light, which is very important. While I realise that Maher Baba is your particular guru, I think it would be wise to quote from some other mystics about the unitary state. Do not appear to be chelas of one particular master; it creates a bad impression, and you will be seen merely as missionaries of Meher Baba instead of emissaries of a larger truth. Have you read 'Mysticism and Philosophy by W.T. Stace (Macmillan)? It helped me a lot, and it could be valuable to you also.
  But these are just little helpful criticisms in praise of an excellent production. Yours sincerely

  Martin Israel.
P.S. I could meet for half an hour in Lincoln's Inn Fields if you would like that. It would have to be at one o'clock. Let me know.

~

Lincoln's Inn Fields had spectacular, spacious Victorian conveniences behind a heavily corbelled frontage and an almost pagoda-tilted roof. Large enough to wash with warm water and emerge superficially restored. The Royal College of Surgeons stretched along the south side, impenetrable. Martin Israel had not suggested we entered, so we sat conspicuously on the bench nearest to its portico and waited for his eminence to patter through its colonnaded porch and across the street. I was too nervous to watch the nearby tennis, but Terry stretched out and almost fell asleep. I saw the little man bustling over and nudged Terry.

"Good. You found it," Dr Israel said.

"Thank you for seeing us," I offered. Israel twitched his trousers and sat down between us.

"I thought it might help to meet. I must clarify that I can't offer anything practical…" he pronounced 'practical' with some emphasis, rotating to us each in turn and nodding regret. "I'm not in any position…"

"No, we didn't expect…"

"Where are you living at present?" he asked.

Terry laughed. "Not sure it would be called living, but we occupy a farm pigsty near Bristol. We only came for the conference to present…"

Martin interrupted.

"I know. A fine paper, as I said." He turned to me. "It needs expansion, much too concentrated; although I can follow it, others won't. They won't want to, so don't make it too easy for them to reject it. Perennial truth in scientific new clothes. Well done." Terry was anxious to clarify that he had had little to do with the writing.

"She'll do that. I can't write, or not in that way."

"I thought that might be the case. No matter. Why is your name appended?" He shot the question like a bullet. Terry smiled easily.

"Her idea. She thought it might help us both into some sort of academic environment…."

"Not in England, it won't—quite the opposite. No academic here would support it. Much too hazardous." Martin's voice held an edge of anger.

I interjected. "Well, Canon Milford said he might try once he had absorbed it."

Martin rocked back a little. "You know the Milfords, do you?"

"No, but he invited us to call on them."

Martin looked surprised and pulled back a thoughtful chin. "Well, now he's retired perhaps he might risk it. It won't impress the C of E if he starts dabbling in the mystical. Perhaps he no longer minds. It's more his wife's cup of tea, I'd say. She's an impossible woman though…" he scratched his toe against the gravel path while deciding how to define why the woman was impossible. "Don't suppose the

Canon could satisfy her." Martin gave a hollow laugh. I recoiled from that brazen double entendre. It was savage, as we knew neither the Canon nor his impossible wife. From a man of spiritual claims, it clanged like a Tibetan gong. He quickly followed it. "Not that I know her. I avoid that sort of woman, but the Canon seems a lonely man, not even very well fed!" Suddenly, he stood up. The meeting was at an end. Martin concluded it with a formal leave, dipping slightly.

"I am glad we met. Keep in touch." He turned abruptly and bustled away. We watched him return the way he had come, up the steps one foot first. The same foot first. Terry shrugged, a little disappointed. I just felt the amputation of hope. Terry was quizzical

"What d'you reckon? Why did he propose a meeting?"

"Perhaps just to clarify that he could offer nothing?" was my lame suggestion.

"Nah. He could have done that by ignoring us. He was after something. Not sure what, though. Strange."

It was both strange and a little bleak. To suggest an encounter in order to say he could offer nothing? I looked at that dark doorway behind the columns and thought of the white rabbit. Follow me? Was that what he wanted to convey? I could not imagine that diminutive busy in that great mausoleum. Perhaps he hid behind his microscope or filed himself between glass slides in a silent drawer of specimens? It was very odd. Now that Terry had mentioned it, I also felt Martin wanted something from us and hoped we might divine it. Or follow a trail of crumbs?

∽

We arrived back at our hovel to find a man sitting in the sun on the doorstep. He looked to be dozing while he flicked away over-familiar wasps. As we limped through the gate to the orchard, he rose. Terry recognised him.

"Bill! What are you doing here?"

I had never met Bill, Carol's reputed millionaire. His two-tone brogues, his chequered sweater tied across his shoulders, and his button-down collar all declared his Sears Roebuck habits. Discomforted, he rose to his feet.

"How did you find us?" asked Terry. Bill ran a hand through sparse hair and brushed off his pants.

"Your brother told me where you were."

"Jeff? And how did you find him?"

Bill shifted and gestured to be invited in. Terry blocked the doorway.

"No. Not yet, and maybe not at all. What d'you want?"

"I came to tell you…" he broke off "…no, I came to tell *her* that your respective partners are heading out to Africa, South Africa. Thought you might wanna know."

"And why might we want to know?" Terry was seldom menacing, but his threat was undisguised. Bill tried wheedling.

"I came as a favour to you, doncha see, and it's cost me a few bucks…" Terry grabbed Bill's collar and half lifted him off his feet.

What Bill had said was beginning to percolate. David was taking the children with Carol to South Africa! Beyond recovery, beyond contact forever!

I spun with the thought.

"Terry, stop, stop!"

Bill nodded at me. "Thanks, honey. Thought you'd see…"

"See what?" Terry tightened his grip. "See a miserable self-seeking old has-been who wants my wife back, huh? You thought you'd come and terrify her with the loss of her kids to get what you want? My wife, my house? What else, Bill?"

Bill started pulling wads of money out of his wallet; hundred-dollar bills were fluttering to the ground. Terry picked them up and shoved them down Bill's shirt front.

"Take your fucking money. We don't want it. Why would we even believe you? It's clear what you want and what you'll sink to, to get it…" Bill extracted the notes and tucked them into the wallet.

"Well, thanks a bunch. I came to warn you. That's all."

"No, you didn't. Just go, and if you can get Carol back, the best of

British luck to you. You're welcome to her." Terry gave Bill's rapid exit some forward thrust and I dissolved in silent and breathless weeping.

We heard a car start up down the lane.

∾

For a long time, Bill's naked audacity and the terror of losing my girls obscured the recognition of another synchronous improbability, the equal of all the others. This puck, with his cloven two-tone shoes, came to give me the money to return home as soon as the conference with its introductions was over. Terry's assumptions about Bill's motive— wanting Carol back— were obviously correct. Bill and his money had afforded comfort to Carol, keeping her nest warm until she thought David a better bet, and the lady of 'easy virtue' jumped ship with added rental income to oil persuasion. The moment that occurred, Bill turned the use of his money to me.

Terry's violent reaction was largely guilt, for he was not usually reactive in that way. He wanted to get rid of me, the wretched woman pining for her children. Being offered that chance by Bill thrusting hundred-dollar bills at him was too blatant. It was early in my initiation to the flawless use of natural talent and available resources. I still selected the gentle, benign and unexpected as serendipitous and failed to see that greed and selfishness were just as advantageous. A millionaire at a loose end was perfect for the process that included all of us.

Bill? What better name for one with the wads to pay all the bills? His swift visit achieved what he had come to do: persuade me to go home to my children and accelerate the end of what had run its course. *My guy Bill!* I also saw Terry quite clearly. He had been a generator and a joint witness of what compelled me, and he came for the ride, but for worldly life, he was a roué on whom I could not afford to put any weight. Much as I might love what he could be at his generous core, his core would never be reliable.

The supercilious hostility of the conference had been equally economical. I would never pass muster in England, nor would my idea gain any foothold. It was time to attend to the claims of my children and shoulder my responsibilities, for David clearly cared nothing for their need for their mother.

∞

Two days later, I landed in Miami and took a taxi home. Jeff had lent us the money, and I now knew that I had to fight to keep children that David did not care about. I was now sure of that.

"Mummy, mummy! You're back!" They jumped up and down like puppies at the door, hugging and pumping little round fists, pressing faces into my belly. It was like the long-dead sun rising out of the sea of cold. The warmth had not yet reached me, but I could feel the light breaking inside.

"Oh, it's you," said Carol, shrugging and sashaying back towards the kitchen." Far from pleased.

"Yes, I'm home. Only for my children. You are welcome to my husband."

∞

The home was rather crowded, with both Carol and her daughter added to a two-bedroom bungalow. I shared one with Ros, Jess shared with Little Terri, who was ten, and David and Carol spread their large bed in the living room, where a lot of noisy sex went on both day and night. David had found his libido and was making up for lost time.

Autumn was mild, and the park offered a welcoming escape after I collected the girls from nursery school before taking them home to bed.

Bill continued his occupation of Terry and Carol's house and paid her rent. It had been on the market to finance South Africa, but that was now in limbo. David no longer talked about divorce. We all waited.

I was waiting for David to accept that our marriage was over. Bill was waiting for Carol's return. Carol was waiting for her next marriage to begin, and David was waiting for deliverance from any decisions at all.

Then came the car crash. Wallop and bang, symbolic and providential.

༄

I had just delivered the children to school when a car jumped a stop sign and cannoned into my newly rented car at high speed, hitting the passenger door with such force that I ricocheted into a protruding gate post on the opposite side. I ended up skewered on the brake with a broken nose pouring blood, unable to open either door to get out. It was a trailer for a bad film. Just crash, bounce, a spinning hubcap and silence.

The woman who had hit me sat behind a buckled fender, powdering her nose very deliberately. Looking into the rear-view mirror, she was powdering from a compact. Dab, dab, look, dab, dab. She replaced this in her handbag and drew out a lipstick. Pulling her lips taut, she applied that with equal care. She might have been a sales rep in the powder room of a grand hotel.

Such disconnect held a fascination: I was mopping at the pouring blood while the unharmed woman was preparing for the police ball. They duly arrived and were unable to release me but sent for a wrecking crane while listening to my brief account through the window. I had not seen her coming. The police examined the road, but there were no tyre tracks, no skid marks: My car, a neat ball, was holed-in-one by a skilful club. The club was that calm woman with her powder; she knew her way around insurance claims.

Finally, a crane pulled off the left door, and a policeman helped me out until I tried to put my foot on the ground and shouted in pain. My lower leg was broken. The police carried me to their car and delivered me to a hospital.

I returned home in a taxi on crutches, the leg in plaster to my knee. Then the jokes began and grew wearisome; the wait became unendurable. Carol fashioned cornbread and swanned about in a negligee and face packs while David was at work. In the evening, she cooked delicacies for two. I took my shift in the kitchen for the children and ate later, alone in the garden.

They were smoking me out.

After six weeks, I was rescued by a man in the park. A gentle father of a small boy was sympathetic. I unburdened in spasms while pushing a swing, leaning on a crutch. It came in gobbets as the swing swept away and was silenced as it returned. We swung our respective charges in unison as I told my sorry tale.

"I have a friend in the law. Go and see Clifford Alloway. He teaches law at the university: main campus."

CHAPTER 22

Clifford Alloway: A 'Mafioso' Godfather

'Signs are small measurable things, but interpretations are illimitable, and in girls of sweet nature, every sign is apt to conjure up wonder, hope, belief, wide as the sky....'

With one leg in plaster and a crutch, the two flights of stairs take time.

Clifford Alloway LLM's office door is ajar. Visible from the passage is the occupant taking a nap with a pair of wrap-around shades and feet on the desk. The light from behind casts his face in shadow. I hesitate.

"Yeah? What can I do for you?" He removes the feet and sits up but leaves the shades shading. What I can see suggests a fiftyish man, slim, without a tie, whose hair is thinning; with the light behind it looks reddish. The resolute shades are disconcerting.

"I was advised that you sometimes take private work. I came hoping you could help me."

"I am an academic. Not a social worker. I teach law, if you can believe that. Can anyone teach law? Helping is problematic. Depends on what, with whom, how long and how interesting? So, shoot. I'm listening." He replaces the feet on the desk and lies back to resume his repose.

"I think I need a divorce." He sits up again and leans forward.

"Think? Die-vorce is kinda final, like death. You ought to be sure before you ask. So, tell me why you *think* you need a die-vorce."

Telling him takes close to an hour. I don't leave out much, not even the adultery. When I fade into an ending, Alloway takes off the shades. His eyes are humorous, but his mouth is severe.

"Lady, if ever I heard a woman who needs a die-vorce, *you* need a die-vorce. In fact, you need a brain align or maybe a good butt whack.

So, where are you living right now?"

"With my husband and his new woman in my-stroke-our house."

"The woman still married to your lover? The one you called Carol?"

"Yes. She rented out their house to her millionaire boyfriend…"

"The dude called Bill?"

"… and moved in with my husband together with her daughter. She must have thought he, David, was a better bet. I have nowhere else to go."

"And this disposable husband of hers? Where does he go?"

"He goes with a hammock on any beach until he's moved on."

Alloway rearranges a number of pens on his desk, looks at them thoughtfully and then tries triangles. After a pause, he looks at me.

"Let me understand this. So, your better half and his mistress are living in your house, collecting the rent from her husband's house; they have your two kids plus hers, and you are lodging with them?"

"Pretty much, yes." He jerks his head towards my plaster leg.

"He did that?"

"No. An obliging woman jumped a stop sign and rammed my car, broke my tibia. But I'm grateful to her because they gave me a visa extension of time to wait for a court case. She denied guilt, but since she rammed me on the side, she was clearly guilty. Police said so. But it gives some time to sort out the separation."

Alloway scratches his head.

"Got a date for this hearing?"

I took out the court summons, but he waved an impatient hand.

"The court is in two months."

Alloway takes out a calendar diary and runs a pen along the edge.

"Two months is thin. Might manage. You realise die-vorce is a one-way ticket, if I do? No visa back here, only a one-way ticket out?"

"That's why I have to get custody of the children. I know they need their father, but he does not see a need for their mother. Given that, I need to make the decisions. Right now, I can't drive or get out, and I'm getting tired of the white elephant, wounded-in-combat jokes. It's been over six weeks. David is refusing to talk about any kind of settlement."

"What's his game d'ya think?"

"I think two things. Carol wants him, and he wants money. They are planning to sell both houses and move back to South Africa. He figures that if I have nothing, I will return to my mother. He will have me and the girls where he wants us, just around the corner in African terms. Getting all the money will let him start afresh."

"Could you do that? Go to your mother?"

"No. There is nothing for me there. She has almost nothing except my stepfather, who bleeds her dry." Alloway slams his hands together on the desk and his collection of pens scatter.

"Goddamn it. Your husband sure plays the circus manager. He has the money, he has the mistress, and he has the wife imprisoned as a nearby, full-time nanny. Yeah, I see. That's why he isn't talking. Talkin' leads to loss. That I know about." He switches tack.

"How did you find out about this? It seems in the nick of time. You were in England in a coal cellar?"

"Pigsty, but that's academic."

I tell him about Bill's visit to England, finding him on the doorstep when we came back from trying to foster a future. I tell him that Bill said David was suing me for divorce on the grounds of desertion and insanity.

"Yes, that figures, a court might believe that. I kind of believe that. The insanity, I mean. The desertion, not so much."

I tell him about Terry taking Bill by the collar and throwing him out and his shiny briefcase after him.

"I'd have liked to be there," says Alloway. "So, how did you raise the airfare to get back?"

"Terry borrowed it from his brother."

"Does your husband still want a divorce? Seems a bit reluctant if you've been home for six weeks."

I then had to explain about the phone call before leaving Bermuda, and David asking if I were sure I would never return to him because if I might, he would not go ahead with Carol.

"Jeez. Cool dude. You are his wife, the mother of his children, and he's offering you the decision after living with her for what, three weeks? Kind of like, look, come soon if you're coming. Otherwise, I got plans for your replacement? We can conclude that you are the pick of the crop, but if you're not available, he'll settle for her. It's a pity he never worked that out earlier. Now I know what I'm dealing with, it gets easier. If he can't have you, he will have her and all her money instead? He works it out, sure does. You have to admire such self-interest." Alloway was looking a little flushed, not quite angry, but as close as he probably allowed. He scribbled a few notes before looking up, smiling. That smile with the shades had a wolverine cast. He looked pleased with whatever he had conceived.

"So, here's the deal… It seems we need two divorces here, and your husband is not getting your kids or all her money. Half of that belongs to your lover boy whether he wants it or not. So, here's what we do.

In Florida, it is your husband who pays my fee, so I'm not gonna charge you. That way, he knows I'm in for the long haul, and his lawyer will get agitated because if I'm in for the long haul, so is he, and there isn't gonna be much at the end. So, he'll pressure him to settle. Now, you say you don't want any money? With kids to support, only a mad woman doesn't want money; even in Florida, mad women don't get custody of their kids. We cannot go to court because no judge will give you custody without money. We have to handle this real gentle and get it done first. Go to court when we need the stamp.

Your husband wants money, and it seems to me he wants money more than his kids because if he didn't, he'd be talking to you about them and what they might need. So, by taking no money, you're really buying your kids off him. I shouldn't let you do this, but something tells me you'll take good care of them."

"Well, by leaving them with him, I hoped he would realise they needed both of us. I never expected Carol to be such a swift mover. She was planning to marry millionaire Bill when I left." I am rather tearful at this, and he looks at me sharply.

"Well, he didn't care about his kids, did he? Honey, d'ya know this man at all?"

"I don't recognise this one, I admit." I had long forgotten that window smashed in Mozambique and all the other indications of this man.

Alloway opens his desk drawer, takes out a chequebook and writes a cheque with a swift hand. He pushes it across his desk.

"Here's what you will do. This is to get you away and out of the country. Not far, someplace I can call you back when I'm sure I've got this sewn up. Is your fellow around to help?"

"I think so."

"He'd better be after what he's done" He flicked his fingers to indicate that I should leave. I rose to go. He pushed his legal pad towards me.

"I will be suing for two divorces—one for you and one for your fella. Write full names, addresses, and contact numbers for your husband and his new woman. I'd better have that address for millionaire Bill, in case. Then, when you get to where you are heading, you contact me, telling me how I reach you." He handed me his card and the cheque.

Five hundred dollars would cover a flight out.

"Mr. Alloway, I don't know how to thank you…" He stood up and accompanied me to his door with an arm around my shoulders.

"Honey, I have to say this one is interesting! I never got two decrees nisi for not even the price of one simultaneous; I never turned everything inside out before. I never had to balance on a thin argument for nothing. This sure is different from the usual."

He was still watching me from his window as I limped, swinging out of the building. When I looked up, he waved a pensive hand, then stretched and yawned. I loved him to bits, that gruff philanthropist. He had accepted me as I was, my story as I told it. Very few would have managed to.

Terry was not my fella, and I knew he never would be, but he would have to stand proxy.

Three days later, after the plaster was removed, I took a bruised blue leg and the children from an afternoon walk to the park with only the clothes they were wearing. I had searched for Jess's security blanket and realised that David had hidden it. Just like my own father, Raymond, he would punish the child to punish me; he assumed I would not leave without it. All I packed were underclothes in a carrier bag. It would have to be close, cheap and hot. Terry parked the Triumph where he could reclaim it, near the airport.

We flew to Merida on the Yucatan peninsula to sit out a wait for a divorce, entrusted to a lawyer who had simply believed me. I would stay there with the children; Terry would return.

∽

It was almost winter, but Merida was hot, baking its caramel squares between the arches of overhanging shade. White walls, white light, white clothes on the women who sat behind embroidered huipils they hoped to sell. Fanning themselves and chewing betel, they watched us as we looked to each of them for someone capable of communication. Perhaps we clung to the outskirts, where the hope of a room was more realistic than in the broad boulevards. I recall none of the Spanish grandeur now evident from photographs, which, in itself, takes a photograph of my state of mind: suspended, desolate, and with little hope of rescue or a future. I hardly noticed anything; I had no interest in looking. There was no way back and no future foreseen. I just had to cut loose from a man who had never loved me, not even at the beginning. Then, I would discover if I still existed or ever had. All the glory had spiralled away like dust devils after a cyclone.

In the Mercado, tired carts took noon in the shade while the broad-cheeked women making flatbread, roasted by the sun, slapped tortillas between their sweating palms. I bought huipils for the children for pennies and some string hammocks in case a palm would have to serve. For how long?

A uniform, something between a policeman and a municipal official, suggested that we try at a local resort where wealthy Meridans had vacant summer houses on a beach. An asthmatic bus, billowing fumes, took us to a necklace of modest, wind-blown shacks encircling a beach in a place with an ironic name— El Progreso. We decamped to survey.

The children, exhausted, had ceased crying and fallen asleep, dead weights on our shoulders. Another smaller market, with bowls of chillies, guacamole and small piles of lemons, harboured an interpreter who managed Terry's rusty Spanish. He led us to a breeze-block carapace cast off by a giant crab aeons ago. Little more than a shell; bare rooms, sand-piled floors and holes without glass, but there was a roof and a clapboard door, hooks for hammocks and upstairs, one bed. It exuded slaughter, an abandoned abattoir. A terrazzo surface at waist height defined the kitchen. A cooker without gas, no fridge. The narrow beach outside the door gave a clear view of two sharks, slicing past with halberd blades, patrolling ten yards away. Swimming would be splashing under supervision.

There was nothing to unpack and nothing to cook. The sun blazed, the terrazzo sweated, the children whined; the place was godforsaken. Only flies celebrated with enthusiasm.

Terry disappeared and returned with a basket of food. He had secured a cylinder of gas and a wizened, old woman. Consuelo would buy cheaper than I could and bargain with the fishermen in Yucatec Maya. In short order, she would also introduce us to liquid, bitter chocolate and tamales. Like Sam before her, Consuelo would be content with a share and the interruption from picking her teeth while waiting for summer employment. Having connected the cylinder and provided an intermediary for us, Terry departed.

It was an impoverished echo of Inhaca, sharks not snakes, and a cook lacking Sam's versatility. Bereft of company and again without books, society was a bus to collect post in Merida's Poste Restante. Again, I would walk a beach, make shell patterns and sand castles with the girls, and rely on the word of a once-met, distant lawyer to be rescued. The end of my marriage was a reprise of its beginning.

The ancient, local habits of human sacrifice, the sacrificial altars of Chichen Itza's pyramids, the fathomless black cenotes merely underscored our possible destiny, and I longed to leap into those pools of oblivion. Instead, I drank rough wine after dark under moon or cloud and tried to hang on to hope. I was a tattered rope moving against a moored boat.

To increase the menace, the Tonton Macoute arrived from Haiti, and terror took over. Consuelo shivered and hastened away home whenever she caught sight of these blue-shirted men in Raybans wandering the beach. When I queried her fear, she put a finger to her lips.

"Los hombres muy malos, bad Voodoo," I knew nothing about the Macoutes or their habits of spontaneous murder or their reputed abductions and alleged cannibalism of children. Their casual confidence, clicking fingers and almost military habits conveyed the sinister; I noticed none of the locals approached them. Doors were quickly closed, washing snatched off lines, and the streets they walked were instantly desolate. I was very afraid because the locals were. I had no idea why.

I secured the holes of the windows at night with wood slat shutters and placed trip wires from stacks of Consuelo's cooking pots to the door handle. I gathered driftwood to lay across the floor to impede and give warning. My weapon was a wine bottle with a candle by the bed. All night, I lay awake, hearing the rattling of the slatted shutters and calculating at what point I would shatter the bottle against the wall. Bare feet up solid terrazzo stairs would be silent, a shadow? How close? Too early, it would be my own feet cut as I leapt to defend myself, but too late, I would be garrotted before I could. I fell asleep only as the dawn broke. Every morning there were black handprints in pitch on the shutters. Sometimes, the slats lay strewn across the floor.

The sudden arrival of a family of Americans on the beach went someway to alleviate the terror. They also pitched; they pitched tents within calling distance, a couple with three small children and a nanny. The nanny and I became friends and would occasionally share a bottle after her charges and mine were asleep. Another Rosie, hers was a tragic story, and like me, she was escaping from the inescapable. We bonded instantly.

The first Rosie had warned me against having children; this second had just surrendered a child but was burdened with others instead. Such patterns were becoming commonplace. The shadows of the past were relentless in keeping tabs.

On one of my habitual trips to the Poste in Merida, she accompanied me, relieved by a day away. Consuelo was willing to look after my girls and take them fishing. Liberated from her own demanding, spoilt charges, Rosie became increasingly ebullient, giddy and light-headed. In the turmoil of people, hooting taxis, panting dogs and heat, I had difficulty holding on to her feverish, wild state. She talked of flying back to California, she talked of jumping off a roof, she soaked herself in a fountain, and laughing and crying simultaneously, hung about my neck. I knew enough about her recent past and the forced adoption of her illegitimate baby to realise that my friendship had sanctioned her indulgence in wild grief. She was dangerously unstable. I needed to re-anchor her.

I took her to an expensive hotel neither of us could afford just to use their facilities for the price of tea, to clean her up and metaphorically hose her down amidst the potted palms under a lazy fan. In her state of resumed sobriety, we managed to catch the last bus and return her to the family on the beach. Afterwards, exhausted, I lay down on the bed and drifted into a febrile somnolence.

A gaunt woman appeared at the foot of my bed. She had the countenance of a disapproving headmistress very like McEune. She spoke.

"I have come to tell you that you are endangering your life."

There was nothing celestial about her; she was simply concerned and quietly authoritative. An apparition with a halo would have been more plausible than an Oxbridge spinster in Yucatan. I did not register her as non-corporeal; an aura did not surround her; she did not glimmer; she was simply and shockingly unlikely. She spoke punctilious English.

"What do you mean?" I asked.

"You must protect yourself. That girl was drawn to you by the light that you cannot perceive. She has debilitated you. You are physically very weak. Pay heed to what I am telling you. Protect yourself."

She turned to go but paused, "Oh, and by the way, I don't think they are going to let you lead the life you imagine for yourself." She disappeared through the bedroom door; already open. I heard no footsteps retreat, no lower main door close.

I sat up, electrified.

What was going on?

～

What *was* it all about? After the shock abated and I was able to still her at a distance to consider, I reviewed the improbability of each event in turn. Taken singly, each could have just been fortuitous: the letter to Bavaria from a stranger, the constant meetings without pre-arrangement, the invitation to a conference from another stranger, Bill's interventions, the suggestion of Alloway, his cheque going in the wrong direction, and the neat parcelling up of my husband and Terry's wife, a deux? But this gaunt visitor was of a piece with that eye on the rim of the continent. I did not understand any of it, but all of it, taken together, suggested it was time I did. The eye had revealed a world that could be splintered, disappear and move with a thought. If I was merely a moving piece in a greater thought, what had it in mind for me? Clearly there was a kind of programme that had a concern for my survival and safety. Why?

There was only one human authority who seemed to 'know' things. One who had encouraged the validity of my thesis. I had begun to register the balancing of mirror events, but this phantom guide suggested direct interventions. The significance of this made me a cog in something I did not understand and did not like, however superficially benign it appeared to be.

I wrote to Martin Israel.

February 11th 1971

Dear Dr. Israel,

I am sorry to impose upon you. Since meeting you at Culham, there have been inexplicable (? improbable) events that are now beginning to disturb me.

I am currently living on a beach, awaiting a divorce from my husband, who is understandably perplexed by the change in me, but that is to be expected and is not the reason for this letter.

There is a young family of Americans camping nearby with a mature nanny for their three children. Yesterday, she accompanied me to the local town to collect my post and became very unstable and euphoric. It took all my energy to keep her 'tethered' and to persuade her to return to her employers.

Afterwards, I lay down exhausted. I was not asleep. An extraordinary woman appeared at the foot of my bed and warned me about my fragile state and said I was endangering my life!

That did not worry me, but when she turned to depart, she added, 'By the way, I don't think they are going to let you live the life you imagine for yourself!!

I did not imagine her. I was not dreaming.

What does this mean? Who is in control here?

I would be grateful to have some advice, and I sense that you might be the person to provide it.

I apologise again for this imposition, but I have no one else to ask.

Yours sincerely

I addressed it to the Royal College of Surgeons, London, without any address as I had no way of discovering one. The Royal Mail was renowned for its enterprise. I provided Terry's Miami address for any response, as well as the Poste Restante Merida. None came.

Instead, Terry appeared without warning to say he had come to fetch me. Alloway had achieved an agreement and we were to meet at his downtown offices. Consuelo wept and hugged the children. They jumped for joy. We bequeathed Consuelo the hammocks, the gas and a small collection of towels and stood outside the market for the first bus, sucking oranges surrounded by dark-eyed children, silently observing from their haunches in bright, plastic sandals. Leaving Yucatan was a curious wrench. Desolation melted in the kindness of benign curiosity and goodwill. These impoverished people with so little had made space for us, and I had no way to thank them. They stood in the clouds of dust, waving. I registered them fully only as we left.

Do you and yours often adopt masks?

What else are people but our masks? Some know it, very few, but yes. You accepted the gaunt's authority precisely because she resembled your headmistress. In such guise, she convinced you. Another mask or a discarnate soul would have occasioned doubt. You were in a dangerously fragile state. We had to intervene. You needed to understand that our mission in you needed care of both your body and your soul. It worked. You wrote a letter.

And I sealed my future fate! Was the old academic in Bermuda who sent us to Oxfordshire of the same stripe? Another of your timely minions?

Of course. You will soon understand his necessity, but through him, the receiver of your letter had been introduced. They were linked. Everything is linked.

So, you know the future?

There is no such thing for us, only for those who separate the mind from its mirror events and believe that time is unidirectional and that the material with its events is divorced from consciousness. They only see a cause as emerging from the past, whereas, in the present, past and future intersect. Some read from left to right, some from right to left, but we read in both directions.

CHAPTER 23

Cutting the Knot: Exile

'...she saw the long avenue of limes lifting their trunks from a white earth, and spreading white branches against a dun and motionless sky.... The very furniture seemed to have shrunk...: the stag in the tapestry looked more like a ghost...the volumes of polite literature in the bookcase looked more like immovable imitations of books.'

"Your visa has expired." The tired passport official tossed it back. "Sorry, you cannot be admitted."

I took out the Court summons, now dog eared.

"Will this change your mind?"

He perused it indifferently. "Why should it?"

"I am due in Court next week. Look at the date."

"What are you charged with?"

"Nothing. I was smashed up in an accident, and there is an insurance claim. I am summoned as the claimant, the victim." He demanded the return of my passport and disappeared. Might it all have been worthless? Would I be repatriated back to Yucatan? After an eternity of apprehension, the officer returned.

"We have taken a copy of the court date and extended your visa only for a week beyond that. You will leave before it expires. If you don't, you will be arrested." We thanked him and withdrew, pushing the children in a barrow down the endless corridors.

"Perhaps they'll repatriate you for us, send you to England? It would be cheap." There were times when Terry's pragmatism, however logical, stuck in the gullet. Yet I realised I had got off lightly or through impeccable foresight in timing.

Terry had mastered his instructions.

"Alloway was very insistent. You and David first at two-thirty, me and Carol separately at three, on the dot. We are not to meet each other before we meet him. You are to take a taxi; I'll follow later. Once it's over, we can do as we please."

I arrived early. Alloway dispensed with any pleasantries, just eyed me up and down and leant on his desk.

"I am glad you had the sense to come early because I want a serious word. You talk good. You got the words. You got far too many words, but today, your talent stays under wraps. Not a word, not a single word from you. You don't even ask for the bathroom, which is down the corridor second on the left. Deaf mute and some, yeah?" I opened my mouth to reply, and Alloway shook his forefinger. "Not even to me. We don't really know each other. Got that?" I nodded, and he gestured to a chair. I sat down, and he returned behind his desk.

David was late. Alloway looked at his watch and pulled a face, raising his eyebrows. The room was dark from drawn blinds. I sat.

Finally, the door opened, and the boy I married pushed in, dishevelled. He looked lost but attempted bravura. Alloway gestured to another chair.

"Please sit down. I won't be a moment."

David affected a posture of contrived indifference, legs splayed, arm behind his head. Alloway glanced at him sharply, then returned to his document. David rose and scrabbled through a stack of magazines, selected one and sat down, flicking over pages with aggression. He was sore, as the locals would say. He stopped and perused a page before turning the magazine around and pushing it towards me. I took it. The centre spread was a vivid photograph of a Mozambique beach: away beyond the aquamarine, translucent sea, silhouetted palms stood sharp against a deserted beach. Above the photo, a title: 'Inhaca- an Island Paradise for the Adventurous Getaway.' Spoof? Mockery? Thumb on a celestial nose? David was urging a response. Alloway frowned. I handed it back without one. I ached for David; he looked lost. It was a bleak, wretched end. He was reconstructing what had never existed, and from it filled an empty amphora that this procedure was coldly emptying.

Alloway rose and gestured for us to follow him into an adjacent, brightly lit back room. He handed us each a copy of the divorce agreement and said,

"Just read it through and sign on the second page. I've marked where."

I read and signed quickly. David took his time.

I was surrendering any claim to a share of the marital home. He was surrendering any custody of the named children. He stopped to question a clause.

"It says here I am to pay a monthly allowance. I thought she had agreed to ask for nothing, no child support?" Alloway did not answer but tapped the fingers of his hands together. It was a minute before he spoke.

"You're quite right. She, your wife, did agree to that. But we have a little problem. I have to place this agreement before a judge. No judge will accept a mother with two children to support without any income. Your wife has to leave the US in a little over a fortnight. I don't know how she plans to finance that, for she is destitute, but to get this die-vorce, you have to agree to support your children. Whether you do or not is up to you. If you don't, nobody can make you, and no jurisdiction will reach her. So, sign." He tapped David's copy with contempt.

David signed with a flourish and rose to leave. Alloway gestured for him to sit down.

"Not so fast. You leave when I say and not until then, understood?" He indicated I should also sit down. Abruptly, he left us alone. There was a knock at the outer door. I heard Terry and Carol enter together. I could not hear the low instructions given, but after a moment, Alloway returned.

"You can go now." He placed himself between the intervening doorway, holding the door to block all vision of them and spread his arms to shepherd us out with dispatch. He winked at me.

David went to seek a loo or a lift. I used the stairs. I did not feel he was waiting for Carol. Once outside and behind an oleander, I watched my husband of eight years slump forward over the wheel of the Mercedes with his forehead in his palms. It was over for me. It looked equally terminal for him.

Terry emerged with a house free of any claim by Carol, and he had signed away custody of his daughter. He had a new tenant called Bill and the income to support his hammock. I still had to leave the country after the court hearing, this time with the girls.

∞

The Court awarded me $1000 for medical damage. Before they would release it, the insurance company needed the medical report. The doctor would not release the report until we had paid him. Three attempts to explain that I had no money to pay him until the insurance was paid out were brushed away. These were the occasions when Terry's past life imbued him with flexible responses. Deadlocks were there to be picked.

He lingered outside the doctor's rooms.

After the doctor's departure, Terry slipped in and leaned over his secretary. Young, pretty and tired at the end of a working day, she was at her most susceptible. Clearly, she was familiar with her employer's cosy relationship with the insurance company, who would pay his $120 fees once I had left the country. Doctor and insurance would share the spoils due to me. Those liquid eyes were, undoubtedly, fed into the persuasion. She agreed to give him a copy of the report but could not risk the original. She ran off the copy in exchange for a glowing smile. I suspect Terry kissed her and promised to see her again. He emerged with the copy and later initialled it in an illegible scrawl.

The next morning, we visited the insurance company, whose minion blocked any application to release the funds. He called the manager, who demanded to know how we had achieved the medical report from the doctor.

"We paid him. How d'you think?"

The manager reached for the telephone. Terry grabbed it before he could lift the receiver.

"If you don't immediately release the funds demanded by the court, I shall go to the police", he said. "You and Dr J...... will be charged with fraud, collusion and the subversion of justice." The manager leapt about as though stung.

"I'll, I'll, I'll"

"No, *I'll* accompany you while you go and write a cheque. You have a copy of the report. It is all you need."

Terry pushed him into the lobby outside.

"I'll need a receipt." I heard the manager say as they retreated.

"You'll get one."

Terry returned, pocketing a cheque for $1000. We drove to the bank, where Terry deposited it and asked for $120 in five-cent pieces and a bag in which to put them. On the bag, he wrote 'Swag' and a dollar sign.

The last part he did alone.

He returned to the doctor's and flashed out the bag for the secretary who admitted him to the august presence, trying to hide her smile.

"I have come for the medical report for Mrs Hughes, as previously requested," he said.

The doctor smirked. "As I said, I need my fee to release it."

"I have come to pay it", said Terry, emptying the bag over his desk where the stream of coins shimmered, clattered, bounced and fell on the floor.

'I'll leave you to count it," he said 'I don't need a receipt. The bank has provided one." He threw the swag bag on the desk. "You might find this useful. But first, I need the medical report." The doctor was close to apoplexy. He rang an overlong bell for his secretary, who entered, report already in hand.

"How very intuitive you are," said Terry. I hope your employer values your excellent services." She surrendered the report to Terry. He held out the report and a pen, standing close. The doctor signed. Terry folded the report slowly.

"All done," he said. "So nice to do business with you."

Afterwards, in the glow of my admiration he confessed that the only part that he had feared was exposing the secretary's initial help.

"She took a helluva chance for us. Thank God that never happened."

"You cannot be sure of that."

"Yes, I think I can. In case she gets sacked, I gave her Alloway's number and told her to go to the police. She would too. She said she was really pleased someone had stood up to him. That nice little arrangement has bitten the dust.

The compulsive roué always had a rough, rudimentary sense of honour.

༄

My departure for England required a detour. I was pregnant. This delayed, out-of-nowhere, immaculate conception was as much a mystery as everything else, as unexpected as the car crash. I was limping along with a blue leg, and then impossible fertility remembered and put me in a time-lapse spinning lock. Fertility had always triumphed: through an indifferent deflowering and throughout a contemptuous and almost abstinent marriage. Every time a coconut. Perhaps I was just a virgin vehicle for intentions that did not consult me with presentations or advice—only forbidding ghouls to keep me on somebody's track. I was also destitute and as frail as dry grass. This blessing was my final kick through the door.

But even I had limits. Be it unto me according.… was not an option—time to say no way, Jose.

Terry accompanied me to New York, where abortion was legal. While he entertained the children at the airport, I took a taxi to a suburb, where I alighted outside a clinic that looked like a postal depot for unclaimed mail. Seven others, middle-aged women, awaited my arrival for the start of a black mass. They were encouraging. It won't hurt, they said. They were clearly familiars of this down-at-heel club. I was the only novice. At the time, I was almost unconscious, but the injury, added to the previous one with the Greek doctor, would find its revenge much later, and its revenge would last forever.

Right now, for the sake of my children, I had simply to survive.

I flew on to London, bleeding copiously, to nowhere and nothing. Nowhere to go, no one to know. It was not a marriage ended; it was a whole life ended and no clear start to another. I had committed the only heinous and unforgivable crime. Not even my mother wanted to know me. It would take three years before she enquired whether I was alive.

Terry returned to a new girlfriend. This one was called Victoria. She hailed from Oregon. Bill lingered awhile and then returned to his last wife. Terry put his house on the market. He will give Victoria all the proceeds: Two hundred thousand dollars for the girl at his elbow. It will buy her a house in her home state. With Terry, the sail of life caught the nearest wind until it subsided.

Celibacy had died, and he never did promise me a rose garden.

∽

Before I boarded, Terry had handed me a letter courtesy of Bill to whose address it was delivered. It was a delayed reply from Dr Martin Israel. I read it over the Atlantic.

> 16 Cranley Place,
> London SW7
> 3rd March, 1971

Dear Philippa,

Thank you for your letter. I am replying a month after you sent it because of a long postal strike which ended only a little while ago. I received your letter 2 days ago.

No, when one is an instrument for spiritual work, one's freedom of choice is severely limited, but what is unlimited is one's ability to react, respond, learn and consummate what lies before one. Like Francis Thompson's "Hound of Heaven" we are led on by God, but much suffering is in store for us.

Your relationship with Terry is a beautiful thing. I shall always treasure meeting you both. You are indeed catalysts—

as I am—in a greater scheme, but you are expected to use your faculties (intelligence or wisdom as well as emotion and intuition or love) wisely. If you or Terry were ever to die now, look what a tragedy it would be for those you are helping. Of course, there is a time when we may have to sacrifice our lives in order to know eternal life, but that is the last resort, not the first.

Stability should be actively sought because one can act more efficiently from a fixed base, but stability is a servant, not a master, and one must always be prepared to move on—a paradox, but I hope you see what I mean. Likewise, you must protect yourself from psychic depletion by the numerous unfortunate people you encounter. This is done by careful discrimination; otherwise, you will have a breakdown that will damage your work, perhaps irrevocably.

Love needs separation as well as togetherness, restraint as well as commitment. Never feel guilty that you have not done your best; only be aware of the other at all times. Remember, God works through us and loves us, and all others also. He does not want us to destroy ourselves but to reach full humanity.

The figure you saw in your vision is a part of your true self, a friend. But do not be afraid. Go on in intense commitment with Terry. You and he will never be separated in eternity. While in the world, the work for the coming of the kingdom takes first priority.

You will never make others happy until you radiate happiness yourself, and this means taking care of yourself "that thou shalt love thy neighbour as thyself". Therefore, while regarding yourself as freely expendable in the great quest, also take care of your body and mind in order to be a more profitable servant.

With all blessings.
Martin Israel

He was wrong about almost everything and pompous with it, but I held on to the hope of a 'quest' since I had no hope of anything else. I had been guided, chivvied, injured, and constantly rescued. All did what they intended, persuading me to let go and trust. Trust in whatever lay beyond any pitiful plans I might manage.

The 'quest' is life's quest in you, not yours for yourself.

I had a British passport, but not a friend nor a contact. I would land with two small children and no destination. My past was signed off, bound in a file and consigned to a vault.

Life on the run would become life as tumbleweed, blown by circumstance.

End of Book One

BOOK TWO

Voetstoots*

* An Afrikaans legal term, meaning all included; taken as found. That abandoned Victorian dresser is yours, and so are the blocked drains and leaking gutters

Caveat Lector

'It would be a poor result of all our anguish and our wrestling if we won nothing but our old selves at the end of it.'

This adventure into an unknown country will not be according to expectations, for the unknown will never conform to the known. How could it? She does not realise that the way of purgation has its own temper and tempo. It appears to be an arduous climb on a steepening slope, upwards towards the sun, but it is also a vortex, drilling into the depths. Both are simultaneous, for this journey is to reconcile all opposites; the Self is an inextricable weave from both; both make a new all.

An 'awl' that penetrates what is called memory, which is a word for the familiar imaging of past experience as much as the imaging of the desired and the possible future. Both are equally available, for both coexist. Always. Memory floats words in fragments in which to capture emotions in poetry, and the poetry of movement to keep fear at bay. Movement quiets the mind. Where they intersect lies meaning. From the outside, you will not perceive the meaning, for the intersection lies in the weaver's mind, which will discard the fixed lines of logic or causation. Spontaneity looks wild but has a logic of its own and a deeper impulse.

Our protagonist —a word most appropriate for the battle ahead— is exploring a country new to her. One, since early childhood, she has absorbed through reading. Its testimonies of poets and novelists are all confirmed with every step, and she finds its familiarity intoxicating. Yet her preparation, being stripped of each claim of identity, was not to create an accidental tourist. She has been flayed to prepare for the systematic travel through an inner landscape, one not yet read about but already known to other mystics. She has read nothing of mysticism, which is just as well since any preconception clouds judgment. The Eye revealed the illusory nature of material reality. She has now to explore the nature and structure of illusion itself and master navigation through its inter-penetrating layers.

We are heading for what some call madness, yet she has chosen its freedom deliberately. That is still to come, but I warn you of it, so you will not mistake its nature or call it 'a mental health issue'. It is a mental health issue but not in the usual sense; not an aberration of confusion but a climb to glory, the recalibration of the meaning of the Eye, that Eye of deeper vision. Sometimes, it will look like Bernini's 'St Teresa' offered up to ecstasy, and sometimes like Goya's Black Paintings of Bedlam. Géricault's Raft of the Medusa describes it better: cast adrift from a solid deck, she will scan the horizon while tumbling in the wild spume of heaving waves.

Take my hand and step upon the journey; it will set out on a calm sea and will ultimately prove a prosperous voyage.

CHAPTER 24

Margaret and Dick Milford: Hoeing in a Cabbage Patch

'I set a bad example- married a poor clergyman, and made myself a pitiable object among the de Bracys- obliged to get my coals by stratagem and pray to heaven for my salad oil...'

The envisioned, gabled rectory, with its yews and a stroll to an ancient church, turns out to be a modest bungalow at the point of a sharp elbow on 'Spring Lane.' Above it rises the buttress of a steep hill. Away in the hazy distance stretch the hills and fields of Dorset's winding expiration to the coast. I am sure this address must be an error, but 'Spring Lane' holds a small spurt of promise. I knock at a glazed door. It is opened by a diminutive old woman, not four feet in height, in bright pink trainers, a crocheted tabard of purple wool and thick spectacles. She peers at me like a bright robin at a large crust.

"Oh dear, you're early. Dick is off playing chess, and I'm sure you know chess cannot be hurried," She glances at the pair, one holding each hand. "What are these?" She peers at Jessica and then inspects Rosalind as though I was offering pawpaws.

"I have heard them called children...I am terribly sorry, but..."

"No need for all that. Your children?"

"Fraid so."

"Dick never mentioned children. I thought you were an academic. Should never put the studious into a mother's yoke; something will ail. I should know. He's been studying your paper. He's quite taken with it. You'd better come in. I'm Margaret, Dick's wife. Now, what would they like?" She relieves me of both children and leads us into her kitchen. "Plums? I've got some plums. I was planning to make jam with them but happy to have an excuse not to. What about some orange juice?"

She dispenses the juice and gives Jessica a bowl of plums.

"Why not take them into the garden? We need to talk, your mother and me."

The girls oblige, and Margaret watches them weave careful steps down the rough stone path flanked by rows of carrots and cabbages.

"Still so tiny, aren't they? I have almost forgotten that stage. I had four once." She breaks off. "Now let's make some coffee, and you can tell me why you're here. Dick said you were American. You don't sound American?"

"I was visiting from the States when we met at the Churchman's Conference."

"Ghastly those conferences. Or I think so. Self-important men being clever about God. As if God cared a fig about cleverness." She sets a tray and carries it through to a small sunroom overlooking the vegetable patch. "Let's sit here and you can tell me why you've come?"

∾

That was my introduction to the wife of Dick Milford, the long-faced aristocrat, who had said, "You really must call." That was months ago, and I doubted he would even remember suggesting it. The 'call' was to discuss my paper, not the visit of a destitute pinning hope on an unlikelihood.

I was reluctant to confess that I had come because I knew nobody else in the whole of England but her husband, with whom I had once shared a communal meal. Nor that I hoped he might have rich connections that needed a maid, a housekeeper, a secretary, or a librarian, with a cottage thrown in. Nor that I had seriously miscast them by an over-clichéd imagination. Fluent Greek and Latin do that to a colonial; summon up Oxbridge and hallowed halls with Virginia Woolf's affluent connections needing a domestic. I did tell her I was hoping for work and needed to find somewhere to live, and wondered perhaps… whether…if…

"My dear, say no more. I understand. Well, we haven't much to offer, but you see that caravan," She pointed to a green shape obscured behind climbing bean canes. "You are welcome to that until we find something better. It will be damp, but nothing a good airing won't solve. Hmm?"

"Margaret, I can't impose."

"No, you can't. I'm offering it. Let's go and see." She marched out and ahead. I followed, and the girls disposed of the plums in an empty bird bath before falling in behind. Margaret yanked on the swollen door and fell backwards when it suddenly yielded. There were two narrow bunks, a rolled-up mattress, and, yes, a patterning of mould affording a ripe smell of forgotten Stilton.

"Oh dear," she said, "Worse than I feared. We never have guests in winter, and we make sure that they don't linger, even in summer. Still, any good?"

~

So began my welcome to my new life. I had to return the car to the farm in Norton Malreward. Terry's brother, Jeff, and his kindly wife, Christine, had lent it for this pin-in-a-map excursion.

'Please help her if you can—she's on her tod,' was what Terry had written in dispatching us to fate. Christine had accepted all this without any questions, which gave some insight into the liability of Terry as an occasional relation. Most families have a feckless skeleton that rises to rattle somewhere.

When I parked back at their farm, Christine hurried out, looking hopeful.

"Any luck?" she asked. I explained that I had the offer of a caravan designed for a single shepherd between shearing.

"Why not leave your girls with me? Mine are the same age, nearly. Jessica can go to school with my Andy, and your younger one can keep my three-year-old company. It'll make finding somewhere easier, won't it?"

"For me certainly, but not for you."

I hitch-hiked back to the caravan in the bean flowers, leaving my daughters in a farmyard with calves and dogs and a familiar swinging tyre in a tree. They were already happily climbing.

☙

Living with Margaret and Dick was a revisiting of Marna and Heli—two very different people living separate lives and mine oscillating between them, independently. Margaret was my day and Dick my evening. With her, I shopped, cooked, sewed and took excursions, as she called them, in search of employment that came with housing. She crocheted in the car with a thermos of tea while I tried my luck at any house large enough to sport a cottage. With Dick, I washed the evening dishes and talked about Teilhard de Chardin, Sri Aurobindo and Meister Eckhart and told him of the Eye. He asked a great many questions. Dick loved to be teased, and Margaret loved to be listened to. I finished his limericks with my arms in the suds. He dried.

He began

"There was a young man so naïf

He ventured to ask 'What is Li-eef?'"

I followed with,

"Having despaired of solution

He took his own in conclusion

And found that, whatever it was, he was sa-eef."

"I shouldn't let that go. Disgraceful!" I could tell he approved.

"Scansion c minus, meaning a plus? Comes of reading Schrödinger, it befuddles the finer instincts."

Dick paused and looked hard at me. Then resumed drying before he asked, "Were you always so certain?"

"I'm not certain of anything. What makes you think I am?"

"You don't seem to care. You never try to persuade me. That smells like certainty to me. D'you know, I have spent a whole life in contemplation, trying to find what you tip out and ignore. How did you do it?"

"I did nothing. It just happened."

"That's what Margaret says when she wants to poke me with her stick of told-you-so. You are a very bad influence on her."

"And what about you? A bad influence?"

"Having you here is more fun than we have known for years…well, maybe forever. Are we done?"

∞

I doubt that any married pair could have had less in common. Margaret's passion was sport: tennis and cricket heroes occupied her mantelpiece, and Wednesday's Match of the Day's football was an immovable fixture. When Wimbledon dominated their small living room from dawn to dusk with the sounds of pounded balls, she sat in a peaked cap with the curtains drawn. Dick packed up the car with a pup tent, a small gas ring and a billy-can for tea and took off for Dartmoor with a book of chess problems. He did not return until tennis was safely over.

Margaret's religious observances were T'ai chi in loose trousers on the small lawn in the early morning and reading the tracts of wilder fringe groups like the Sufis and Subud. Her bedroom was lined with books on esoteric alternatives: Madame Blavatsky, Theosophy, Annie Besant, Cathars, any fringe breakaway sect or pre-Christian mythology, and anything spiritual with a tongue out at established institutions. She had no truck with the C of E that had occupied Dick's life. Much like Marna, she had paid the price of his dedication and had a similar contempt for what had promised so much and betrayed his heart. I told her it had also betrayed my expectations of an ancient rectory hard by a church.

"Oh, you would have been right twenty years ago!" she was dismissive. "Not a mere church but Lincoln's great cathedral just outside our door. Lincoln's Chancellery was a wonderful pile of stone, with things like wainscots, stained glass, bosses and brass fenders. It was quite spectacular, but the pittance they paid him meant polishing for yours truly. Not a free house but unpaid drudgery. That's the thing with the Church, very good at pomp, not so good at circumstance."

I learned that Margaret was Dick's second wife. The first, Nancy, had been a very beautiful distant cousin, a great-granddaughter of Charles Dickens. She had died very young, leaving him with two daughters the same age as mine were now.

"In our time, one did the right thing. Not that Dick would ever love me as he loved her; I accepted that, though I hoped love might grow. I was just a surrogate housekeeper for two small children. They never accepted me. I just kept a conspiracy of three against me fed. Then we had our own two, and I managed two families always a mile apart, his daughters and my replica after-thoughts."

It had never been a happy marriage, but for my visit, unhappiness was kept at bay by cheerfully talking about it.

"One day, I shall leave Margaret a very merry widow," Dick said.

The reprise of my grandparents' alienated existence made me feel at home. As a result, they both came to seem more comfortable about being rudely honest which drew the sting from silence. Margaret became almost girlish, wearing pretty floral dresses and colourful hair bands. They returned from a concert, and after Dick had retired, she filled two glasses with his home-brewed elderflower champagne and said, "Let's celebrate. Dick actually held my hand. All the way through! He's never ever done that. Imagine starting a romance in your eighties!"

We were a tacit trio suspended in mutual support. Both believed in me, and I loved both equally, Dick wrestling with the Laocoon of faith, her irreverent dismissal of any need for it. Margaret just believed.

"You are a catalyst. I am sure of it," Margaret said. "It's why I think you know something, and I don't need to know what it is."

"I don't know what it is either…"

"Good. Then you won't try to explain it."

∾

I went further afield to explain it. Not all my imaginative suppositions about Dick were wrong. Both he and Margaret had grown up in Oxford. His family were all notable academics, dons of Oxford Colleges, or founders of Cambridge Scientific Instruments. Margaret's branch of the family was sporty and sweatier. Dick was reputed to be the Church of England's prime intellectual, which explained his appointments; as Master of the Temple and Chancellor of Lincoln. He told me the story of his indecision.

Dick Milford's Story

"I was always drawn to the Church, but I rather doubted the depth of my faith. It's never been wholly secure. I wondered whether I was just taking the easy option to get an appointment as a chaplain to an Oxford College.' So, when the First World War was imminent, I was rather relieved to be able to enlist. It would give me time to examine my calling. It was rather a whisper, truth be told. I was in my regiment's signals division because I played the flute— near enough a signal for the Army. I spent the war in Mesopotamia and then in the desert near Cairo, making a piano out of surplus signal wire and drinking warm beer.

"No calling shouted, so I thought it was time to stop being so fey. I would read Greats for fun, and if theological training summoned, I'd let God decide. When I graduated, and after a few jolly years teaching in India, I thought I'd query God again and train for the ministry in Cambridge. God said thank you very much and gave me my first posting as rector of St Mary the Virgin, Oxford: rather better than a college chaplain. My role was overseeing all the colleges, but subject to none. Instead, I followed Wesley, Newman and Keble into its historic pulpit. I suppose that was my answer! If it was good enough for the heretics, Latimer and Cranmer, it would do for a vacillating doubter like me."

I discovered that Dick's first Church, St Mary's, had spawned the Oxford Movement, from where were launched my first teachers at St Mary's Johannesburg and also Mirfield, which launched Trevor Huddleston to fight against apartheid. Links hold hands across time.

Dick's connections would not run to vacuuming a stately home. Instead, they yielded an invitation to present Involution to a group in Cambridge, calling themselves The Epiphany Philosophers. He had sent them a copy.

"Very rarefied, high-brow evangelicals, philosophy to physics, and a couple of Divines who know me. They publish an esoteric journal called 'Theoria to Theory', so inspiration might catch fire. We must get your paper published. They might kindle. You'll have to be on your toes if they bowl a googly." said Dick.

"I bet they're a rum lot," said Margaret. "Don't give them any quarter; stand your ground."

"Not sure where that is exactly. A quarter of rum? "

"… and a yo ho ho." She stepped a flippant, quick jig.

☙

I had never been to Cambridge. The flat fens spread out like a cloth as the train hooked out a warp across watery ditches and ice-blue sky. Out of sight were the well-studied elevations of King's and the 'backs' of daffodils, where gowns took the air in measured paces. They couldn't eat me, could they? No, I would be courteously shown into an oak-panelled room lined with books. The light would spray across old shoulders from a high mullion, and the air would be hazy with pipe smoke. A tentative elderly voice would invite me to summarise Involution so that they could unpick it gently, exchange observations, and introduce caveats. These would be dons well acquainted with incoherent undergraduates, nodding encouragement, affirming progress, raising thoughtful brows…if I stumbled, they would catch me.

The station was cleared of disembarking passengers, hastening away. I had no idea where I would locate the Epiphany Philosophers. An elderly man in a green corduroy jacket approached, and when he was close, I got a glimpse of the dog collar.

"You are come to beard the dragon? Brave woman. I am sent to deliver you, but don't worry; I'll stay and bring you back." We shook hands and exchanged names. He led me to his car and held the door.

"Is it a dragon?" I asked. He looked at me sympathetically, with kind, sloping eyes buried in wrinkles. He glanced at me several times as though to register something he was unsure about.

"You're very young..." he said, steering away from the station.

"Too young to be here?"

"Yes and no. Just not what we're used to. You fall between the younger undergraduates and the dons, who are much older. Still, you can't help that." We were navigating bumps in a suburban street through chalet bungalows that blinked myopic windows. It looked like a retirement village for the marginally independent.

"Nearly there," he said. We pulled up against a large garden with bricked beds and gravel paths and made our way towards a village hall of brick with plate glass.

"Our meeting house for the torture of ideas." He took out a bunch of keys and opened up. The large room was already laid for the meal to be made of me. On an endless stretch of pine, expectant chairs sat in an ovoid. At one focal point, a single chair might have been set for Mastermind. 'You have ten questions starting.... NOW!'

"Would you like some tea?" He moved towards a small kitchen and switched on a large urn.

"Have we time?" It would take half an hour for that great urn to heat.

"Lord, yes. Some are always late. Are you going to give me a sneaky preview, or rather an audio précis?"

"Haven't you read my paper?"

He was laying out cups on saucers and glanced across.

"No, I have not had that honour. I'm just on for janitorial duties, taxi and tea boy. It must have impressed someone for you to be invited."

"I suspect it impressed Dick Milford, he sent it." He swung round.

"*The* Dick Milford? Canon?"

"I suppose so. I only know one."

"Well, then you come with credentials! That explains it." This jousting was making me increasingly nervous. I decided to dismount.

"You're obviously surprised by something but don't want to be rude. Why not just tell me what it is?"

He contemplated me for a moment and accepted the invitation to be rude. He walked across with a dishcloth over a shoulder, pulled up a kitchen chair and straddled it.

"It's not you I must be rude about, or shall we just call it candid? I overlapped with Milford at Oxford. I never knew him personally, but I knew of him parcelling up in the tower, all those packages heading for Greece. You know he started Oxfam?"

"No, I didn't know that."

"Well, he did. St Mary's Tower was a depot for parcels for his starving Greek children. Anyway. Cambridge is not Oxford. This tribe is ruthless. It will happily savage anyone with the pretension of an idea. Why I was puzzled is because I have never heard of you. Should I have?"

"No. I haven't heard of me. No reason why you should."

"Well, most who are deigned an audience here have published widely and been bloodied elsewhere. Most are well-known, so their work speaks for them. Your youth suggests that may not be the case. The unknowns are unknown here."

"You are right. Nothing much speaks for me."

He shrugged. "Well, if Milford put it forward, he must believe in it, so just take the fences as they come. It's all anyone can do. Don't let them intimidate you. Mostly old, well-tempered philosophers, but there's one who will try, called Ted Bastin, very brainy physicist, rather pleased with himself."

He rose to fill a pot as the first of the huntsmen entered. I decided to linger in the kitchen rather than exhibit my nakedness to one at a time. The hall gradually filled. Two women with grey hair and shawls came in, talking animatedly. A professorial giant took what I knew to be his accustomed chair from the way he secured it and sat down. A rotund priest with gold-capped teeth smiled and dipped like a Japanese butler. A rather belligerent younger man in a windcheater removed it and hung it on his chair. That must be bombastic Bastin. He looked more than ready for a fight, rolling up his shirt sleeves and stretching back, running his fingers through his curly blond hair; a Cassius lean and hungry look.

One or two took tea and placed it on the floor. I hovered, aware that almost no one had noticed my presence. Perhaps they thought I was the cleaner with a mop to stow? My taxi rescued me, took me to the centre chair and introduced me. Should I sit or stand? I sat.

"Right, let's begin," said one of the women, flipping over the pages of my paper. "Interesting or not interesting? What do we think?"

"Well," said belligerent Bastin, "Do we still find Berkeley interesting?"

There was muttering but no definitive opinion about Berkeley.

"Tell you what," he continued pugnaciously, "why don't you, in three short sentences, give us reasons to be interested? Just the gist because I find this incoherent. You use the word Involution for two entirely different processes, the interiorisation— was there *ever* a clumsier word? — of experience, and then for the recovery of that same interiorised encoded…" He was not there to listen to me. He was the youngest, brightest thing. The women were rapt in admiration of this young warrior and smiled and nodded at each other.

I did my best in three short sentences.

"So, you are saying the Universe does not exist? I manage to bark my shin against non-existence?" Bastin pulled up a trouser leg and mock rueful sought its injury. The women tittered.

"No," I began, "I am suggesting it is a consensual construct, imagined over time and encoded throughout. Relativity describes differential relationships in consciousness."

"Imagined! What does an earthworm imagine?"

"It imagines it's an earthworm. It consents. Since it's been imagined over time and absorbed that as its existence."

"I suppose it consents to the bird that eats it too?"

"Yes, that too."

So it went on. Had I read? Does this relate to? Was I aware of…? What about? Each served an opening and watched me fail to return a stinging riposte. Instead, they batted each other's serve, and I was merely the wall against which balls bounced back. It was a good game for exhibiting contempt in an abundant variety of strokes.

"All right," Bastin's bombast was now a trickle. "Supposing we, for the moment, accept your hypothesis that the Universe is an integrated and collective field of imagination, with which we all concur. How does it help? What can we do with it?"

"Collectively change it? Science is floundering, searching for missing matter. It's only missing from the paradigm that has been consented to and thereby persists. Accepting *that* might start an alternative of perceiving it differently?" It was my plea for indulgence. It failed.

Bastin returned to the fray.

"So, what you're saying is that evolution, as we all know and love it, is deluded about the material?"

"No."

"No!?'

"What I am hoping to convey is that what you call the material, following your implacable laws, is the product of intellectual division between the field of consciousness and the understanding of it. In its own enclosure, the brain, matter exists and it obeys all of Newton's laws. From a unitary perspective of matter-mind, only consciousness exists, and matter is not distinct from it."

The older woman interposed a little more gently, patting her bun.

"Can you elucidate why on earth you spent time, and I'd say quite a deal of time, to write this conceptual hypothesis? What did you hope to gain?"

From the question, I realised I had not even levelled the ground across which to drive persuasion.

"Nothing. I hoped to gain nothing. I hoped to give an alternative to bleak science that is chasing its tail, looking for insufficient matter to balance its books. I just thought…" The aggressor rose in some fury, lifting himself off his seat before sinking back.

"Let me get this right. You are suggesting that consciousness creates matter?"

"Yes, creates it and can change it. Over time"

Bastin snorted. "So, we could all sit here, close our eyes, and create a different reality?" He smirked, waiting for me to fall into his elephant trap.

"With due respect, the company of your society is no match for the ballast of what has already been imagined and created. Trees might have other opinions; fields of wheat might join forces…all is consciousness. I am not talking about intellect limited to a very small biological sample…"

I had roused him to insult. "Okay, Madame Defarge, tell us how you see quantum theory in your guillotine decapitation of Darwin. In quantum theory, things exist or fail to manifest according to the measurements to which they are subject. How, if at all, do you explain that?"

"I would guess that at microscopic, ephemeral levels, imagination might create instantly and destroy simultaneously, but I don't know enough about quantum theory to argue the guess. I suspect Murray Gell Mann's omega minus particle appeared to exist because it filled an imaginative gap without displacing what already had been sanctioned by many like you. I don't really claim to know. We could talk about Renaissance painting and the emergence of three-dimensional representations, after which the Enlightenment and Newton solidified…".

"Oh, for God's sake, woman! Is this Tuesday or Leicester Square?" He rose, snatched up his anorak and made for the door." It slammed upon my reply, offered to the embarrassed shifting group.

"Probably both. Leicester Square has seen a fair number of Tuesdays. The hairs that cross on both have their own history. Didn't Einstein talk of space-time? Thought moves faster than light…" There was a long silence as the door reverberated. Nobody moved. One woman closed the file straddling her lap. Someone coughed, and a teacup clattered. My taxi looked rueful, massaging one hand against the other. He had shifted back out of the circle.

I sensed the ordeal was over.

The other woman addressed the general assembly with a high-pitched falsetto of benevolence.

"Shall we invite Philippa to join us for evensong?"

My knight, my simpatico taxi, saved me. He stood up.

"No. What Philippa needs is a strong drink, and I'm taking her to the pub."

We left the hall together.

Over his beer and my wine, he asked me to explain Involution, and I drew diagrams on the beer mats. I told him about the Eye. We were there a long while.

While we were waiting for the train, he said, "Take this to Oxford. Cambridge has never been a kind place for a new idea, and something tells me you are on to something. You seem so very sure. None could really unseat you."

"That's the problem when you come face to face with God."

"Perhaps you should have told them of that encounter."

"I was prepared to let them demolish my hypothesis, but not my experience. Pearls are precious, best not thrown to swine."

"Oh, dear. I fear you may be right. But thanks for offering it to me."

He kissed me before handing me onto the train.

∾

That was my baptism by fire in the world of academia. It had shattered the illusion that science, philosophy, and those engaged in it were in pursuit of truth. What I encountered was a dogged determination to reject not merely a too-young, too-optimistic thinker but any idea that did not belong in their approved journals or which failed to support their sanctioned positions of elevated vision.

I had expected rigorous examination or the winkling out of weak connections and fallacies in logic, but their contempt came first, and their pleasure in expressing it was a gladiatorial contest for the applause of one another, like adolescents stoning a lame cat.

I wished I had just managed a glimpse of Kings College's new Adoration painting, the famous 'backs,' and the Cavendish Laboratory, where Rutherford had walked and worked. Perhaps it was better not to cross-contaminate those pioneers sinking a contemplative fork in new ground with the heartless, who believed they alone held the lease. I feared Dick would be disappointed. Where would I go next?

∾

In case I was insufficiently subdued, two letters awaited my return. Margaret had propped the envelopes against a vase of daisies in the caravan together with her note. 'In London for daughter's birthday, back by Friday. The key under the mat if you want a bath.'

The first I opened was from Alister Hardy. Three closely typewritten pages revelled in demolition; a wrecking ball on a swinging chain...

'It may be a work of genius just as many people consider Teilhard de Chardin's The Phenomenon of Man to be...I do not share that view. I regard Teilhard to be a great saint, and his book is more of an epic poem...in no way scientific. I feel much the same about your thesis. Your reference is too glib...I dislike your statement... far too glib, quite unacceptable...completely the wrong way round. Your whole approach I find quite unscientific. What might be good journalism in a Sunday paper is quite out of place...I strongly object.... this is biological gibberish...I cannot say I like your argument concerning the evolution of consciousness...I particularly dislike your diagrammatic representation...I have no sympathy...just seems to me to be ludicrous.'

After two such pages, he continued, 'I have not time to go into the points which I find myself at variance with your views'...then he added, 'I don't find meaningful your comparisons of convergence and divergence...I am sorry this is not at all my cup of tea. You ask my advice about publication. I am bound to say don't. I would strongly advise you to wait at least ten years and master some biology before you attempt to go into print.

'When you have done much more reading and studying, you may yet produce something worthwhile. You are young. You have plenty of time before you. My advice is to return to your work as a physicist, return to that and read all you can of biology for a better foundation. Yours sincerely, Alister Hardy.'

I cannot pretend I managed composure. I felt capsized by contempt but also the desolation of any hope that I could find a way to support the girls. I walked down Spring Lane in the closing light of day and the extinguishing of prospects like a penitent in a book by the other Hardy. Thomas Hardy's Tess walked these same Wessex hills, weeping, betrayed, reviled. In England, literature visited barefooted on every street, in cold comfort. I was also angry at God and my naïveté.

Alister Hardy had written similar conjectures in his book, The Living Stream. His current work was embarking on collecting stories of religious experience, which would furnish his next work, The Divine Flame. I did already know that my thesis needed expansion and polishing. All I hoped for was the chance to do it. Was it that he wanted ten years to give him time to publish similar ideas first? I was face to face with the jealousy of academia. It wasn't pretty, and I had no credentials to challenge it.

From the other envelope, the scrawl of Terry's hand released a cheque. Enough to pay rent! Somewhere modest for a few months to house the girls.

I could go to find a cottage, cheque in hot hand.

The left brain ruled academia. A too-young woman with a hypothesis that transgressed every accepted rule? Why were you surprised?

Because you and Dick had led me there, was I in need of more humiliation?

No. You were in need of help in closing the wrong doors. You still expected some respect, if only for courageous originality...

True.

Originality is the greatest threat to Academics. They have mastered certainty, and originality upsets their apple cart. It turns them violent. Martin Israel had warned you, remember? Ten years too early?

I do now. It turns out it was fifty years! The memory of that annihilation alone prompts this different work that camouflages its 'theory'; I offer life instead and a few threads from which to weave anyone else's theory.

You learnt a lot from contempt and rejection, no? Especially when you knew you were right.

I learned why obsessive geniuses who believed what they had 'seen' were often locked up!

CHAPTER 25

Georgina and Combe Cottage

'It was that moment in summer when the sound of the scythe being whetted makes us cast more lingering looks at the flower-sprinkled tresses of the meadows.'

I had alighted from a small van, consulted a map and set upon a quiet road in the drowsy Sunday afternoon. The long walk up sun-baked hills was relieved by descents into steeply wooded valleys, where water and shade cooled, and startled birds erupted in flapping alarm, matching their indignation to my solitude. The advertisement for a cottage to rent simply said 'Provis. Batcombe.' Would Provis provide for my own Great Expectations— God's plan for my life? I trudged on and, after dipping my feet in a stream, mounted the final steep push towards a tower on the crest of a hill. At a crossroads, I stalled. Left, or right? The pub, visible below the tower and called 'The Three Horseshoes', might fit this lame duck a fourth.

The pub door rang a lazy bell but appeared deserted of publican or custom. I swung the door three times.

"Sorry, we're closed. Open at six." The publican had the look of a man drawn from a doze, shirt escaping the braces.

"Sorry to disturb you. I'm looking for something called Provis?"

He shuffled in slippers to the door, pointed back to the intersection and said, "Go right till the lane bends sharp right. Last before that corner."

The lane, flanked by a farm with clipped grass and a large yard with geese and a chained dog asleep in the shade, took me to smaller stone cottages, shouldering one another like orderly children awaiting a parade. 'Provis' was charming but bizarre, an austere but elegant mistress in charge, with white shutters to scarf her windows, a surrounding veranda of elegant proportions, surmounted by a glazed roof confining a vine that dripped quantities of unripe grapes. She might have been moved from some Caribbean plantation and unloaded on a village street for reconsideration while men wiped brows and straightened their backs.

It was a confined setting for an aristocrat, but she was deposited anyway. Her wicker chairs on the veranda had cushions but no occupants. I rang. The rudely imperious sound pierced the bee-somnolent afternoon. The woman who came to the door was both startled and forbidding. The long case clock in the hall ticked through my explanation, wagging its disapproving finger.

"The cottage? Oh, the cottage. I can't show you now. You need to make an appointment. It's around the back, a separate entrance. We won't take children in case you have any. Too dangerous on the corner." She accompanied me to the corner. "You see. There's no garden, and…" The cottage, once a coach-house, rose with a steep outside stairway behind a fig tree; an eyrie to salve, to save, to promise, in the lee of the Caribbean with figs, grapes and shutters.

"You really won't consider children?"

"Sorry. Afraid not."

"And you know of no other?" She gave the question a moment's thought.

"Well, back down the lane, I had heard Combe Cottage might be to rent. No idea how you find out. It's unoccupied. Sorry, I can't help."

I retraced the lane. Combe Cottage had its toes against the street behind a low wall. Like a miniature Haworth vicarage, it stood four-square symmetrical with small windows on either side of a door, the name scratched above. I peered and approached. In the corner of a window, a card read. 'To Rent,' and added a telephone number. I wrote that on the palm of my hand. Through the windows, I could see a flagged kitchen with an Aga and a stable door leading to a garden flooded with light. An Aga! The other window revealed a small sitting room with a fireplace, a couch, and a lamp, also drenched in the light from the garden.

I had to have this Bronte refuge! I, too, could wear a mob cap, find a desk, think, walk, write, and drink coffee on the grass. There must be grass behind. I could not wait a day or a night, uncertain of this perfection.

From a call box near the church, I rang the number.

"I want to rent Combe Cottage in Batcombe."

"You can't. I'm the agent, but we're closed on Sundays."

"But you answered?"

"I shouldn't have. I just popped into the office to…"

"How much is the rent?"

"Twenty-five pounds a month."

"I can pay for six months."

"But you haven't seen it!"

"And you haven't seen me. Shall we both just take a chance?"

"Well…"

"I've been walking all day."

"Walking!?"

"And hitchhiking…"

"Oh, all right. The key is under a flowerpot on the left of the front door. Go in, have a look and ring to confirm. I'll come out if you're sure."

"I am already sure."

"Then I'll come. Be about an hour."

The door scraped across the flagstone floor below a ramrod staircase to a window above a small landing. Before moving further, I stood to measure its welcome, for it did not feel uninhabited, merely waiting for a return, familiar, swept and curtseying. The kitchen on the right had the pallor of a dairy awaiting the milking, as though a wet cloth was wrung out and laid over to keep moist and protect: smooth stone floor, whitewashed walls, a scrubbed oak table, and the stable door to the garden opened onto a stone terrace baking like bread in the afternoon sun.

Combe Cottage was a home enfolded by the pillows of the smooth hills that cushioned on either side. Hills smoothed by aeons of grazing sheep but ribbed as if secured by subterranean fingers under the short grass. Below the terrace, the garden stepped down to its disappearance beyond a hedge, punctuated by a bright willow flashing sun against the dark ravine below. It was an opening in cloud, with its shafted focus concentrated to kindle a fire to warm a new life. Far more perfect than Provis's gaunt elevation, this benign cottage was all sunlight, all peace, as simple and unaffected as a day's new-sprung daisy.

I ventured up the staircase to a low-ceilinged bedroom, quite large and covered in apricot carpet. Apricot velvet curtains soaked up light from a window on both sides: one overlooking the silent street, the other the floodlit rear garden. Here, I could ripen out like any fruit tended and protected. In that room I recognised the tightness in my shoulders, the shallowness of my breath, and how wretchedly held were my hopes, bound by fear, wrapped in an aspic that excluded the danger of expectations.

I had not examined the wounds of courage, the savagery of David's indifference, or the dangers I had ignored in setting out. I lay on the bed, and for the first time since leaving America, I stroked my own brow and comforted my agony of being completely alone between a life that was lost and another not yet begun. Combe Cottage would hospice me, teach of seasons and sunrise, candles and fires, a convalescence to find my unknown self—a place to be newly born.

Across the corner of this room, a ledge-and-brace door suggested a clothes cupboard. Instead, a spiral of wooden steps led up to the attic, the span of the whole roof, where a roof-light gave the sky; not a glimpse but the whole uninterrupted blue span like having a private observatory where the night stars would rotate above the mattress spread beneath.

Descending and retracing back across the landing, the second room for the girls was also large enough for two beds, toys, and chests—nothing lacking, nothing superfluous, nothing ugly.

So 'Provis' and my 'Great Expectations' was a chance for fate to play an anonymous Magwitch for another Pip? That chilly doyenne placed an advertisement, and this was offered instead? Heavenly.

I returned to the Milfords with a lease signed and reassurance that Somerset County would permit a four-year-old to start school, via a school bus that stopped outside the door.

∞

Margaret found me a car, a sit-up-and-beg black Hillman minx that resembled an apologetic, now retired London taxi, very old and discovered under a tarp on a farm where she went for fresh eggs. She took me to rouse an elderly man with rheumy eyes, half asleep in a wicker chair. He followed her to the back of his shed.

"What do I ask fer 'it? I ask twenty foive pahnds and no' a penny less. T'was me muthers as she were aloive. Needs a tune-up. She'll drive sweet'n stately, you'll see."

Together, Margaret and I shopped for a few essentials: an enormous and beautiful bowl for the kitchen table, which she thought essential for decorative reasons, and a bag of useful clean rags essential for prosaic ones. She delved into the backs of her kitchen cupboards to find un-matching plates and camping cutlery, and a heavy old kettle to steam sweetly on the Aga.

"I do envy you an Aga. We had one in Lincoln, and I miss it. No idea how you'll pay for fuel, disgustingly greedy…"

I would fetch the girls as soon as their term concluded. Until the car was tuned and taxed, I walked to explore the surroundings. A pin stabbed in the map of Britain could have found no more magical place to fold feathers and nestle quiet. The village threaded on the winding lane draped itself across the crests of two hills. Now much 'sought after', Batcombe was then a tumble of farms and workers' cottages, as well as the odd circumspect grandeur behind high walls for wealthy London's weekends.

The lane was often gifted with the manure dropped by a herd, scripted by Thomas Grey, as they wended their way to a distant field. From the village to the nearest small town of Bruton, steep ravines were wooded with oak and beech so that Batcombe, storing the last of the daylight, seemed a forgotten legacy of another age: A place for once wealthy wool merchants whose fine church stabbed its claim at its highest point with a perpendicular tower of Somerset tracery above the now deserted nave, hung with tattered banners of arms. In heavy snow, the village sometimes required helicopter drops of provisions when it was inaccessible by road. It was a vantage village for a prolonged siege.

I walked the lanes in a kind of suspended ecstasy. The remembered rural literature was newly painted: Hardy, Brontes, Jane Austen and George Eliot were all seated in parlours with dressers or shelled peas on a garden bench. Mrs Poyser knitted her stockings at the open door of the farm, Mr Craig clipped the yew hedge at the vicarage, and children raked the hedges for over-spill blackberries. All delight to discover a hug-yourself perfection after the hard edges of concrete, steel, glass and automobile America. Time stopped in those first days of celebration. I woke and lay down with the sun: the natural order re-ordered me.

Which was how I came to be in search of milk before a shop was open. I had walked the five miles into Bruton and had an hour to kill until nine. The street was free of movement or traffic, so I mooched along, looking into windows at antiques, silver, jewellery, vegetables and the drawn blinds of a small supermarket, postcards in a post office, cat baskets at a vet, books in a library with tattered notices stuck to its door. Opposite the library, I crossed to sample another. On that door hung 'Open', so I pushed and went in.

Vaguely antique tables were littered with bright pottery, wooden implements, old shoe trees, a black dressmaker's dummy stabbed with hat pins and draped with beads, folded chenille cloths, and a rail of clothing. While I shifted hangers along, a voice said, "What are you doing? I'm not open yet." A woman stood half obscured by the inner door, hiding her dressing gown below a crown of wayward short curls. Her eyes were kind, her hands anxious, fiddling to secure the cord.

"I'm sorry. It said 'open', so I believed it. On the door."

"Oh God! Does it?" She hastened across to the street entrance. Closed and locked it. "My fault. I forgot to lock after fetching in milk for the cats." The dressing gown embarrassed this purveyor of small items of good taste. "Can you come back later? I don't open until noon or thereabouts."

"So, I can't buy this nightgown?" I had spotted a Victorian night dress of pin-tucked Broderie Anglaise, a ridiculous extravagance at twelve pounds, a confection to ice the glory of my virginal nights and grace the terrace for the sunlit coffee. It was my gown for my marriage to myself: reciprocated, happy solitude.

"Buy?" she said. "You want to buy?"

"Isn't that what shops hope for? People that buy?"

"Well, yes, but I've only just opened. Today, in fact. You are my first customer."

"You'd rather have a different one?" I asked. She giggled.

"Of course not. Are you sure? Really sure?" I looked at her, suppressing both embarrassment and disbelief.

"What is it with the English? They never believe you when you say you're sure; they are all closed when they're not. Does anyone here know what they mean?" She cocked he head to one side.

"It's a good question. I'm not really sure. You're not English, are you?" She was hunting for wrapping paper for the night dress and shrugged. "Fuck. I forgot tissue. D'you mind if I use newspaper?"

"I am truly trying to learn to be English. Fish comes in newspaper, why not lingerie?" I exaggerated the American pronunciation. She giggled again. Her giggle was a delicious pleasure. She contemplated ribbons and lace on newsprint and pulled a face. "Don't worry. It's fine." She took the note and disappeared to get change. She reappeared with my fish and escorted me to unlock the door. I felt our meeting prematurely amputated, so I paused.

"Would you like to come to supper?"

A broad smile was followed by more disbelief. "You really mean it? When?"

"What about this evening?" She affected a finger checking through a diary.

"No, nothing on. I can fit you in." She added, "I have not had anything on for six months. But I'm not desperate!"

"Me neither. It'll be simple. Supper. Want of the readies…"
"Mashed potato will do. I mean it. It's Georgina, by the way."
"Maybe Philippa will manage a sausage."
"Never before met a Philippa but a sausage! A sausage is persuasive!"

I told her about Combe Cottage and how to find it. We had both arrived at the same time; she to open a shop, me to close one, from similar circumstances and opposite ends of the earth.

※

Supper at my new table, warmed by the marvellous Aga, stretched until three in the morning, and when Georgina departed, there was not much we did not know of one another's crazy histories. Both of us had been blinded by hope and scarred by its betrayal. Bonded by foolish marriages and delighted to feel less alone.

※

Georgina's Journal.

March 19th. 1970

Finally, my day of opening! Shop presentable. The Shopkeeper was far from spry when first invaded. A waif appears at the first crack in hippy camouflage, barefoot, long floral Laura Ashley. My first thought, God, an escapee from Glasto here to read Tarot and persuade me to mend my ways! Not so fast, Georgina. Quite the opposite. Turns out she's sharp as the proverbial. Pronto, the waif buys a filigree nightgown and doesn't mind anything, not even the newspaper wrapping, appropriate for plaice-n-chips!

She invites me to supper! Not sure, but obviously must accept. No point in being choosy. Yet.

No other custom, all day. One or two browse and leave embarrassed.

**Must remember that repro table on offer.

※

Not only had Georgina blest my home as a friend, she followed through with a letter. Two days later, a blue envelope on my doormat christened my address. Her handwriting sat with its curved, wide bottoms comfortable upon a perfect baseline, one of those removable templates that ensured perfection. Basildon Bond. Even the tails and towers were perfectly aligned, worthy of a professional sign-writer. Georgina must have attended a good school for the impeccable graces required by her once-upon-a-time Holland Park address. Much too elegant for a dealer in bric-a-brac in a hick town. How had the mighty fallen, thank goodness.

Georgina's Story

Dearest P.

I am still dizzy with our night together, so please make allowances for an excess of affection. It meant SO MUCH! You cannot imagine. You have arrived to comfort me and to rebuke me for all my self-pity. You made me see how spoilt I am/have been—not that I intend to give up the whisky. A girl must have some pleasures—or the cigarettes or the long baths.

Well, what a night it was! I do not do that ever; I mean weep and confess all or raid my hostess's supply of tissues on a first dinner date. It's those eyes of yours; they pull out a confession like a dentist pulls bad teeth. I did not intend to burden you with my marriage to Bertie-the-bastard. I feel rather ashamed of myself whinging about losing my grandeur, my cellar and all my handbags when you sit contented with almost nothing. I have to say you have made me see how very indulgent I am and always have been. Surrey does that to its golf club denizens. I will do better. I will take myself in hand and sit at your feet and learn something about stiff upper lips. Perhaps you may need fewer of them if I can manage more. Shift the load, loosen the corsets?

All that talk of the Eye did fascinate but it was more your acceptance of Terry. (He could use a better name! Was that all he was given? Or is it really Terence?) and the determination not to rely on him. I will follow suit. Fuck it, I have managed without a man before. I can't remember whether I told you about being an editor for Vogue or training as a stewardess for Pan Am. I was convincing in both capacities and I can do it again. We can be sisters in determination.

I have already made a start. I have bought something that will rely on me, a sheepdog with a gammy leg and a dodgy hip (so I got him cheap), and together, we will walk the hills around Batcombe, and you may replenish me with top-ups of resolve. If I bring a bunch of primroses? I have called him Mr. Boots, since he will demand I slide daily into my new Wellingtons- green with a flashy buckle! Even country life can have style. I'm already seeing myself on an inside double spread! Vogue moves out of Holland Park to conquer the provinces?

When your girls join you, perhaps you can introduce me to a new species— children. I have no idea about how they think or how to talk to them. Perhaps I am frightened of them? Children are so uncompromising! Can I make the most of you until they join you? You have so much to teach me. I wonder what I can give in return.

I am already fantasising about introducing you to the parents, but that will take courage. I suspect you would despise them for all their routines: sherry before lunch and drinky poos at six, as well as the standards needed to become members of Lloyds of London- that is their bottom line! My mother would not understand a word you say, and my father would harrumph and prefer that you stay quiet. (I love the old duffer, but he is a bit of a xenophobe, if not a racist and misogynist. Women should be decorative and not opinionated!) I have a suspicion that you would never moderate your words to his audience. No. Much as I want you to know all about me, I doubt I would want you to meet one another; since the honesty of your talk (perfectly acceptable in the cow byres of Somerset) would act like paint remover in Surrey! You have no idea of the different worlds we occupy that change within fifty miles.

When you have been here longer, you will understand. Perhaps I have things to teach, too?

I just had to tell you how much the evening meant. I know you will make my new life of duty (which I was finding hard to swallow) something more heroic and something I might end up being proud of. The funny thing is, I suspect, after all your descriptions of Terry, you would probably rather like bastard-ex Bertie! So, you definitely will never meet him. I could not bear you to like one another. Hating Bertie keeps me going. Feeling wronged keeps me warm at night! You should feel wronged. Why don't you? You don't even hate David. You should.

You can, however, meet Mr. Boots.

With much love, Georgina

P.S. I am still on cloud nine. Don't really understand your magic, but it works.'

∾

Dick's evangelism in promoting Involution continued. He now suggested I should disseminate my ideas to what he called the 'laity'. He invited me to give a talk to his small group studying Teilhard de Chardin. Driving to this meeting in Shaftesbury, I considered the reactions to the paper so far, from physicists to the theologically educated. If they grasped none of it, what hope would I have with earnest matrons filling in the idle hours of their retirements? I threw the copy of the paper out of the window and decided to fly by the seat of my experiences instead. No Theory. I would not take refuge in intellectual safety.

About eight elderly women had already been seated. I began.

"I realise that you are here because de Chardin interests you. I cannot compete with him. So instead of talking about my theory, which is merely an echo of his more beautiful Christogenesis, I have decided to talk to you about love instead…" There was a sharp intake of disbelieving breath but nothing else until I had finished when a chastened silence descended, and fiddling with handbags began. The youngest woman present approached and put a hand on my knee.

"My dear, you are a brave creature. If ever you need employment, come and visit me." She handed me her card. 'Barbara Warley. Principal, Croft House School, Shillingstone, Dorset.' She took a swift departure. Luckily, I kept that small flag for the future.

∽

Unknown to me, Terry had been corresponding with Martin Israel from Miami. A letter from Martin to Terry was forwarded as though Martin stood proxy for Terry's absence of care. I read its intention: this Prospero in London must become my solitary and only beacon. Like the earlier letters to me, his spider scrawl of a wild script filled the page diagonally to its extremities, with words jammed against one another at the edges. It was emphatic, a gospel thumper of a letter which the actual words belied,

> *Dear Terry,*
>
> *Thank you for your two letters and the little book of Philippa's lovely poems, which I shall return to you when I see you again- soon, I hope.*
>
> *Your second letter was a special joy to me, for it shows you are coming through the emotion of loving to the "beingness" of true love. When you know this love, you will be in a state of inner rest, experiencing the peace of God that passes understanding that the world can neither give nor take away. While love is identified with emotion, it cannot endure, for emotions fluctuate, even within seconds. Love never fails, on the other hand, as St. Paul writes in 1 Corinthians 13.*

You and Philippa are meant for each other- despite your difficulties, there is a pre-ordained harmony between you. Whether you are destined to come permanently together in this life or not is beside the point- though I pray that this union is to take place- but what matters is your inner awareness of this treasured union in eternity.

Do not trouble yourself that Philippa is the stronger partner. This is, to put it mildly, the usual situation. The woman should normally be the stronger partner in a relationship based on emotion and spiritual love. She is indeed a most radiant soul, highly gifted and a beacon of light. I am privileged to know her- and you. I am honoured that I should be found worthy to share in her love; this is my joy, but it in no way intrudes upon your relationship, which is of a different order altogether.

May God bless you in all your works in the Spirit of Truth, Love and Light

Martin

The letter was disquieting, as though I had been written out of life. Martin talked about me as if my star had already waned and yet wanted to share my love 'of a different order altogether.' Did he already know what lay in store? Something about him had, from the start, implied a blueprint to which he was privy.

So, George Eliot's eloquent summons to set sail for England was entirely rewarded?

Yes. For quite a long time. Her descriptions were both accurate and after two hundred years, still there in the idyll of Batcombe and Somerset. Did you plant Adam Bede with that purpose when I was still a jejune sixteen? It drew me here, of that there is no doubt.

Perhaps we did, or perhaps your own longing found her? Or she found you via the mediacy of a cat!

What plants longing?

Affection. Past happiness. Nostalgia. Remembered love.

Why was Martin Israel so purposefully introduced?

He shared and understood longing. It was almost all he was! You were drawn to him for that reason.

Not initially. I just thought he knew what I needed to understand. Then, later, his longing was a magnet. He seemed so bereft of warmth, so palpitatingly inadequate socially, that I felt empathy, perhaps even pity.

Dangerous. Investing in someone you hardly knew.

You brought him to my party!

In that case, we also brought Margaret and Dick Milford! You chose where to place yourself!

CHAPTER 26

Martin Israel: Storm

'I should never ha ' come to know that her love 'ud be the greatest o ' blessings to me, if what I counted a blessing hadn't been wrenched and torn away from me, and left me with a greater need, so as I could crave and hunger for a greater and a better comfort.'

For the first few weeks it was as I have painted, idyllic, a teak-oil buffed perfection. The girls were on holiday and took to the woods to make a camp. I baked bread, made soup, and planted nasturtiums to spill across the terrace. Georgina and I had long evenings of mutual exchanges, although her shop absorbed most of her time. In truth, I was expecting the return of Terry; even hoping for it, but equally dreading it. We had unfinished business; the shooting incandescent star had fizzed up on its rocket trajectory but had not yet fallen to earth. The messiness of my divorce had obscured the garden of the future like smoke from an autumn bonfire; mere survival and a future for my girls took precedence, but our relationship waited for some kind of settling. The whirlwind of destruction it had wrought needed to 'bed down'. The head told me we had no future; the heart still wondered whether he could outgrow his sexual adolescence and let the confident man emerge to hew wood and draw water.

I have to admit that he attracted and repelled in equal measure; opportunism worked in all directions. He was my first Adam Bede, the forthright solver of problems: the simple man who saw, did, and moved on. He detected the misery of my unloving marriage, extracted me from it, and cycled away. He signed no contracts of longevity.

Unlike Adam Bede, whose nature accepted dogged obligation and undying faithfulness, Terry's contract was only with himself. In the army, as the top cadet awarded the Sam Browne belt, he was assigned to teach the King of Jordan to shoot, did so efficiently, then bought out his remaining commission and left. Success frightened him; it would imprison and write a future he was not yet willing to sign.

Terry always bailed out. In the Tour de France, within sight of victory and in the lead, he dismounted and walked across the finishing line! I should have seen that from the start. A life with him was incubated but never destined to hatch. At that first dinner, he told all, and it was of a pattern, always the same. A plumber became a Spanish hotelier, and as soon as a hotel was dependable, he transhipped to New York to keep the brothel trade running. When that became predictable, he decided on a fishing boat, then fancied life half-yoked to academia. Always at the cusp of success, he abdicated. With me, he had done it again.

So, what was he searching for?

A perfect love of the troubadour stamp, dulcet sweet and wholly giving, an untarnished Rossetti paragon, combing her hair, reflected in still water. He had created a glimpse of something like it but found it cost too much. Ecstasy is very demanding; it cleans out obfuscation, half-life, or indolent excuses. Constancy was as difficult for him as licentious was for me. Martin Israel tried to diminish his guilt by sanctioning an ultimate destiny of union and blessed his journey towards it via carnal detours if necessary. Martin's letters made clear that he would outgrow promiscuity in time.

Terry truly wanted to be equal, strove to help, and sent money when he could, but he hoped to outwear sex by having it in excess with a variety of partners whose names were like 'dish of the day': Louise, Amy, Shelley, and Victoria. We were suspended across the Atlantic, dangled from the past, but not yet reconciled to the end. The beginning had not been matched by a fitting end, nor had Pandora's Box clicked shut. Synchronies continued but they were smaller and muted, as though I lived behind gauze to recover necessary contact with solid earth to reunite with the demands of motherhood.

After months of silence, Terry remembered Christmas. He turned up and simply walked through the front door to the back terrace, where I was clearing leaves.

"Good God!" was all I could manage. I should have known it would happen, but I had forgotten his impromptu habits. Impulse gives no warning, so he probably shared the surprise of finding himself strolling into Combe Cottage.

"Pleased to see me?" He grinned in his challenging way and offered a hug, brushing my hair back from my face and looking hard. "You've lost weight. I shall plump you up while I'm here." That made his temporary intentions clear.

I felt up-ended, as though a lever was applied to my pivot, which had begun to stabilise into loneliness and was beginning to get comfortable. I decided to take him to meet Georgina. It would give the appearance of a welcome and give me time to decide whether I was pleased. Terry had the unnerving ability to be immediately at home without introductions or even looking as though travel had intervened. It made any reservations somehow petty. I was aswarm with misgivings.

"All right, if you like," he said to the suggestion of a visit. "Would the girls like bicycles for Christmas? I am moderately flush. I could teach them to ride."

"They would be ecstatic."

"Right. Your friend first, then bicycles, and time to hide them. Got a shed?"

"Coal cellar."

We found Georgina making chicken paprika for guests due down from London. Paprika betokened people of importance.

"You should have told me he was here, and you could have joined the meal," she said quietly but with reproach. "Now I don't have enough."

"He's just arrived. A quick coffee will be fine."

I watched Terry's magnetism work as it always did. Georgina melted. He gave her intense attention, his long legs stretched beneath her marble table as though he already knew everything worth knowing about her. He took a bowl of potatoes out of her hand and began peeling them with his expressive, long fingers and unerring skilful economy. It was that easy familiarity again, keeping well clear of presumption. The man moved like oxygen into a bell jar, and everybody breathed deeper and smiled without a reason.

When he excused himself to find the loo, she gave vent. "Bloody hell. I was expecting Rhett Butler, from all you said, a disreputable Lothario I was ready to dismiss. Instead, you invade with Black Elk, who knows the secrets of the fucking Universe. And now I must ask you to leave so I can prepare for an evening of pureed tedium."

"Sorry. We can come again."

"You'd better. Next time, with due warning! I want to enjoy it."

He kissed her when we left. Well, of course he did. He was that kind of naturally physical man.

For Christmas, I unwrapped a sexy dress, deep décolletage for the rude exposure of my non-existent cleavage, in a silky floral fabric, tactile and explicit: pretty, but not for me. I hoped he would grow up; he hoped I would grow down. That was the declaration of the battle ahead.

Deflowered in Key West but never since wanted to 'make love'? Nobody makes love. To screw? To 'get laid?' English, determined to debase it, is vulgar in all its words for sex. I now knew that making love, if I had to settle for one, was truly and only appropriate for worship, candour, and trust. With worship, there is no place for desire, a goal, or an appetite. The driving force of sex was abhorrent, the culmination of imaginative worship glorious, applause for a pas-de-deux. I could never again confuse them. If that is prudish, I am a prude. I know that most people enjoy sex as they do a shared meal. If well-cooked and nourishing, they light a post-prandial cigarette and blow smoke rings.

Literature offers abundant examples of casual sex, familles-a-trois, or serial adultery. Since the roaring twenties we are expected to be cool about its unimportance. For me, it is more important than that and less important. Perhaps it is not prudishness but fastidiousness. I would claim a different word for no inclination. A voracious, undiscerning greed consumes without celebration. If I am to offer my most intimate truffle self, I'd prefer it to be valued. If any passing Tracey can replace me, I would rather read.

It was why I could not surrender to this charming but different Terry; no longer impotent but compulsive, and for that, increasingly repellent physically, although I loved so much else about him. His sexuality was like eczema, an itch that demanded and disfigured. We were locked together on either side of a barrier neither could change. He truly strove to change by scratching. After the girls were back at school, I tried to escape, spending long days enfolded by the roots of a favourite copper beech tree, consoled and asked for nothing. Terry wanted so much; we were paralysed, unable to come together or break apart, and no future visible. I wanted him to leave me and to break the Gordian knot. He wanted to leave my antisepsis equally urgently, but he felt tethered by my near destitution and his guilt. Finally, desperate about this stasis, he wrote to Martin Israel. I read the reply.

16 Cranley Place
London SW7
February 27th 1971

Dear Terry,

Thank you for your letter. You must paddle your own canoe and be independent.

As regards the meaning of love, it is so deep that no one can define it. In its highest, it means helping the beloved to freedom in God, in whom alone is true liberty. I should not worry too much about concepts of fidelity at present. Try to move to beneficent detachment, Buddha-like. This may provide a clue to future relationships.

Of course, we are all one in God, and we are our neighbour. There is a deep relationship between you and Philippa, but it will take time to stabilise. Persist in honesty and seek your own salvation in fear and trembling. Only then can you be of help to others.

With blessings, Martin Israel

Martin, after his impromptu recognition, had become our lifeline. With neither family nor employment in an unfamiliar world, he alone held the key to our self-belief. We had been thrown together, witnessed the Eye, and been assisted at every turn to move forward, however bleak the future looked. We waited on a hill in spring-ripening Somerset as though for an embarkation on an arid coast. Terry lingered, unable to leave but not fully staying. Martin's lonely, accepting life called across the compulsive, restless one I tried to escape by writing in my beech where I stored a rug in its hollow roots. I wrote poems for a lonely man treading the inhospitable London streets, and one, after a blustering wind, I bravely sent.

Letter to a Celibate

Dear Catalyst (you call yourself)
How does your city edit and keep the template trim?
Amputate each impulse, damp down or mute the string....
One moment, sir, excuse me ...
Was it your vibrating wing...

Let fly this day of hawk-high quills,
Which looped the light, split staves, lit spills?
While oblivious clouds soaped destinies;
Insouciant slaves to the boiling brass...
Till they dropped the bowl and splattered the trees,
Bubbled the hills, splintered rivers with glass.

Was it you told those blousy and billowing girls
To pepper the pot with tossing birds?
To fly the gull kite, by the headwind tethered,
To throw up sparrows in fists of feathers,
To mop and tickle the nostrils of trees
Chasing the notes, the drawn bow sneezed.

No? Pardonnez. Have I caught you just in time
to offer you my chariot in lieu of railway line?
Suppose I walk you to work? You'll lose nothing thereby,
neither handkerchief from pocket nor love from loving eye.
Today, God did the laundry. Can Love's servant accept
pianissimo, bel canto, this Monday minuet?

Occasionally, Martin telephoned as though to take a meteorological reading on the weather of our future. These calls were brief and peppered with enigmatic aphorisms. He usually spoke to Terry. He would content himself with brief codes to me. We called him 'The Voice' since that was all we knew of him.

"Not long now."

"Darkness is darker before dawn."

"Addiction reaches satiation. Be patient."

"For Terry, it will be touch-and-go."

Terry was having vivid nightmares in which his mother came armed with shameful chamber pots and prohibitions. He chewed upon his misfortunes, the poverty of his upbringing and his lack of education as though he alone had been singled out for punishment. No rational counter-arguments prevailed. Suggesting that the strength of his abilities and creative versatility had been fostered thereby, cut no ice. I wondered whether this new obsession, revisiting every aspect of his rough childhood, was the equivalent of my deeper delving into the childhood of mankind. He, too, had cut ties to employment, marriage and country, and perhaps that had unleashed shallow lying memories, the scum on the surface of his present obsessive life?

His resentment was as corrosive of faith as rust upon iron. I had little enough on which to stand, but the splintering platform of our relationship would topple us all. I knew his ingenuity would survive without me and that, without his restlessness, I might limp with my children into some kind of purposeful future. Together, with his weighty self-pity, I knew we would all sink. Yet he stayed on and on, railing at injustice, lamenting his compulsion, and masturbating his path to transcendence.

He seemed to believe that a sudden vision would release him, and he would jump clear of his past. When bathing the girls, I found Jessica's bottom bruised blue from a beating he had given her. I saw it not as sadism or cruel violence, for neither was true of him, but the loss of control that desperation had unleashed in a fundamentally easy-going man. It was a symptom of pent-up frustration— which Jess had the unerring skill to inflate; provocation in her was a calculated craft. It was still a livid shock to see it.

I began to wonder whether my writing of Involution had held up a mirror to his rude, unlettered life and created what he had never before known: envy and inadequacy and a challenge he feared to fail. He was emptying bilge from a ship in dry-dock in the hope of lightening the load of his compulsion before sails were unfurled. I shared his belief that what we had experienced could not have been simply to deliver this vacant, poor, purposeless existence. But Terry was sure the delay was the wait necessary for him to prove morally sea-worthy. To that end, he rowed like a maniac.

Much as he admired Martin, he began to talk of him as a rival; nothing I said dented the patent absurdity of this.

"For God's sake, Martin is a hymn to celibacy, a semi-priest, a doctor, a counsellor. Not after every skirt from sixteen to sixty! Get real. This is not about sex, although for you, that seems to obscure any other focus."

Obsessions are not susceptible to logic. Terry was essentially a simple man with simple explanations and simple solutions. In the world of practicality, they fostered economy and dispatch. The intuitive, more complex knitting of causes and consequences eluded that straightforward mind, for he dismissed them as spurious fallacy.

It was David swallowing mescaline all over again.

I longed to release him, to release us from one another.

∽

"I am going to London," I announced it at tea time.

"To see Martin?"

"Naturally."

"Good. Let's launch a change. It's bound to. I'll help and stay with the kids…"

I dislike the word 'kids.'

The car refused to start.

"I'll jump start. Use the choke," Terry said. He wanted this impulse to succeed. Finally, it fired and I backed out. "Take as long as you like," he shouted. The petrol tank was empty, but having launched, I refused to notice that.

I drove to Gillingham station on an empty tank, parked amidst a rough patch of daisies and left the key in the ignition. I felt I had to give fate the reins and, deep down, I knew this was almost suicidal. I had no intention of seeing Martin, but the pretence of an encounter would give Terry the excuse to cut loose. Cutting ties had always initiated adventures out of control, but seeking to ordain them had been worse. Leaving David to work out what to me was obvious had merely sanctioned his brutality and allowed him the freedom to express it. This time, I gave God the keys to my coming life and cast off.

I was indecisive about the ticket.

"Single to Waterloo, no perhaps…make it a return." At this point, a return was uncertain. I felt that I was stepping off the world into a swirling vortex.

∾

The carriage was occupied by a man reading a newspaper and another large woman eating. Fat women eating on trains was a pattern; there was always one.

I sank into my fear and tried to pray. Terror held me. Would he get stoned and forget the girls? Would he realise if they went off on a dark escapade? Remember their supper? When, or if I returned, what would remain?

As the train slowed for a station, I felt a blow on the back of my neck, which sent me sprawling to the floor.

"Andover. This is Andover," came over on the Tannoy. Hand over?

Sure. It sure was a handover.

"Here, let us 'help. Was you asleep? Like you was hit, it looked. One minute closing yer eyes, next…Oi'll help yer up."

Oh God, the girls. No, please not. I have to go back.

"Where are we?"

"Next stop, Basingstoke." The train lurched. Base. Stoke. Stoke Base. Hellfire, feed the fire…

"Tickets, please. All tickets from Andover?" The guard stood rocking in the doorway.

"Is there a train back to Gillingham?" I asked. Slit the gills, prick the ham.

"No trains till the morning now. To go back, you should have got off at Salisbury." Salt in the wound; bury your head.

"Tickets, all tickets, please," He moved off without asking for my ticket.

She's got a ticket to ri-hi-hide, but she don't care? I had no ticket to ride this journey. No petrol, no ticket; I am on a train to hell. My children are possibly dead. Yet I recognised it as the start to a Calvary, the blow, the fall, and this wash of words dissolving and carrying my mind away with it, flotsam on an ebb tide.

To an outside observer—and for this linear narrative— I am perfectly safe on a train to London, and all these allusions are self-created through terror and apprehension for my children and any future at all. But I now see this was the dissolution between the outer and inner worlds. The Eye initiation was now to be a manifest Golgotha, the sacrifice of my life and my children to save that vision. The first blow to make me fall and then the chanting of a train: Basing-stoke, Basing-stoke, Woe-king Woe is me, Waterloo, down the loo, Blackfriars, Friar her, fry her, pyre, pyre, Mont Segur, Inquisition, Cathars, Heretics, dungeons of darkness, the rack of confusion. All signalled a vortex descent into hell, signposted by reference to the great myth of supreme sacrifice, the first blow and fall.

There it all was: the leering hissing contempt, the warts and tridents of Breughel, the details of Cranach, da Vinci's grotesques, Velasquez's dwarfs. People were suddenly diminished to caricatures, and as I had seen the threading of memory on the emotional, I was a sponge to raw feelings: deep repressed anger, avariciousness, greed, envy, all served neat, undiluted. I was swimming towards the gaping maw of hell. The dog-eat-dog world of lust, fear, hatred. Consciousness coded in emotion: as I had sampled and now again remembered.

My reminder was now rooted in the infernal ordinary.

It was a writhing, satanic darkness, smoke and abandonment. My impulse had unleashed some yellow, mustard gas of pure evil, and I reeled against marching indifference, storm-trooping commuters. Then came a second blow, and again I fell. A bell tolled. Do not ask for whom the bell tolls. It tolls for thee. Dead, dead, my children are dead.

Where was the Voice? What had he said? Dark greater before the dawn? Was this what he meant? Could I find my way to Kensington? I would call out. He must answer. Into the blood-red booth, I go to dial.

It rings. It rings and rings, and then the third blow knocks me to the kiosk floor while the phone swings, the censor of a black mass, a rope of execution. Again, a bell tolls. Above me, felled at the knees, the muted ringing Brr Brr…Brr Brr…Brr Brr… D'ya ken the way to Kensington, where no birds sing? I'll go anyway.

Ten bells to choose from, one to toll me back. Please answer. Please. Please, God, please.

No answer. Martin had said it would be 'Touch-and-Go?'

So, I touch, and I go. Then I run. I run and run through inferno's smoke, syringes and vomit, and leering, pinching people, cackling, cawing with skeletal, plucking fingers, and expletives, 'Wanna fuck?' 'Over here dearie' 'Ooh nice butt', and somehow, I run to Waterloo, over spread legs and tripping, until I find the dark snake of a train with its scaly doors open like the gills of Leviathan expelling steam. I crouch in a corner of an empty coach. Doors slam; whistle blows, and slowly, slowly, it pulls out, away from diabolical into rhythm. Chukka chukka… chukka chukka… I give over and fall asleep.

Georgina's Journal

April 29th

This takes the biscuit! Terry is on the doorstep close to midnight! On my way to bed nursing last nightcap. 'She's off her head,' he says, 'can't cope,' I know who he means. Invite him in. Hand him a glass and hope for a coherent explanation. He is muttering that he was the one supposed to be 'fucked over'.

Start at the beginning, I suggest. He tells me P went to London to see Martin Israel. Why? To release me, he says. Why would her going 'release him'? She released David by being unfaithful; she reckoned it would work again. Do you mean she went to be unfaithful? In cold blood and with a conspicuous celibate, a man almost penitential in a cassock? Hardly. He's too distraught to argue with, so I ask when did she leave. 'Last evening', says he. And when did she return? First thing this morning!!

So best beloved did not have time for a tossed salad, let alone a quick fuck! I let that go. How was she on return? Bloody ecstatic. She cooked breakfast, saw the girls off to school and went to bed!

How's that called being off her head?

He's too tired to explain but suggests we go to bed instead. Attractive offer! Lie watching the car lights passing behind Black Elk's profile. He fancies a fuck himself. I was easily persuaded. So we do, in a gentle way. It had been a very long time, and after all, it was clear he was leaving. Why not?

Over coffee in the morning, he says he will continue to do what he can but the relationship had 'run its course'.

Just like that?

Martin will take care of her; they have an 'understanding', and that makes it okay. Aren't men good at justification? Like a knackered old nag to the bottom field, but someone will give her occasional hay?

He swings a duffle bag on his back, kisses me and departs for *the station.*

Should I feel guilty? I'll give myself time to find out, but he looked one happy man!

I wonder what I do if P really has gone loop-the-loop? I should visit but rather dread it. I must erase the night with Terry first. A vision of man as a passing friend? New thought! No socks under the bed or screwdrivers left out? I wish P and I were lesbians. It would solve a lot!

Can you identify how you knew that cutting free from Terry would unleash the ongoing journey?

I am not sure I fully did or even that I wanted it to. What I knew was that I had to undo his stranglehold on me and guilt's stranglehold on him. It was suffocating us both. It was simply an instinct to release a brake.

And the free association of words and images? How did you interpret them then?

I suddenly saw the power of words and their associations, both in meaning and sound, as new arising mantras and signals. Like internal billboards, advertising directions, and warnings of danger. Economical and ever-changing… As indications of the power of memory to signal the evil of the world, the prevalence of greed, hatred, lust…

The seven deadly? Newly naked? And now?

Now, I recognise the dissolution or the new dimension. I had crossed some kind of portal between the limits and solidity of the time-bound, linear world and the deeper, fluid one of memory's associations. I know that the guardians of that portal were all the fears, both my own and the collective fears of others. They manifested both to warn and curtail me.

Did they succeed?

They tempered the speed at significant moments of the plunge into that new sea of fluid immersion but not the determination to explore and comprehend it.

CHAPTER 27

Torpedo: Love: Finally

'It was this which made Dorothea so childlike, and according to some judges so stupid, with all her reputed cleverness of throwing herself, metaphorically speaking, at Mr. Casaubon's feet, and kissing his unfashionable shoe-ties, as if he were a Protestant Pope.'

Georgina did venture up to Combe, but I am not sure how long after Terry departed. I was not living with any sense of time by then. The rituals of the nights remained: the sacrifices, the thrown eggs, the putrid smells and the cold. So cold. Not weather cold, evil cold. At first, I attempted rituals of my own; the dried palm crosses pierced into mouldy bread, the bread of life mocked by an atrophied, empty religion. Even darling Dick lost his faith in it.

Where are you now? All you who claim the certainty of prayer? You who ask for processions and chanting? Silence. Mockery seemed appropriate. I sometimes spat; I mimicked those ghouls with chin-out gestures and a flounce. If you cannot beat them… but I refused to fear.

I drew the mystical triangles in chalk and a mandala around a plate. I danced and spun to mock their terrorising. But I grew tired, so tired. The ghouls remained, getting closer, and their breath on my neck. Black cowls watched me. The Aga exploded when I tried to light it. I wanted warmth, but fire mocked me. Boom! Smoke without fire! No fire. It knew how deeply I feared it. I left the lids down and the fire door open. I know you. If you ignite, you will be short-lived. Boom. Whoosh, billowing, thick grey dust. Again.

The mausoleum of my once immaculate dairy kitchen drips with water, tuk… tuk… tuk over the door, like a tapping finger waiting for my surrender. Against the window, shredded rope moves against the light, the residues of the hangman's art. The bells ring in the distant belfry— a ticket, a tocket, a hangman's pocket, and here comes a chopper to chop off your head. Excrement smeared in handprints slide down the garden door. Did I do that, or was that them? They intend to drive me out, to drive me mad with fear, so I dance to shut them out. In my mind, I create music to dance to. You will not succeed. I will dance until I die. Or you give up and slide away, grinning malevolent grins of triumph, if you must.

So, this was what going to Martin unleashed? Just the appearance of betrayal enough to unleash the hellish opposition?

But I did not even see him.

You half-intended to, but what if he had answered?

He didn't. You did not let him.

Dare I go upstairs? Will they follow to throw me from a window? I might see the sky? Dare I go into the garden? Some 'kind' neighbours will call for assistance. What do you want of me? You want me to abandon this travel? They smile with green teeth into their sleeves.

Get out, get out.

I must go through this. I know that. I must conquer all fear, even fear of dying and of fire. Was I a witch once or a Cathar in the Languedoc, dripping fat onto a pyre in agony? Probably. Your snivelling scarifiers can have another egg, and it comes with an Easter bonnet. See! All flowers and innocence. White dresses and singing, girls with sashes. Bastards. I shall show you beauty, and you will quail as I do at your black horror, do your very damndest… I do not, will not, surrender to fear. What you want, I will deny. I can still defy you. Ha ha? Yeah.

I shall go in search of the limpid sky, and for the sky, I shall dance until I drop. I'd better take water with me, for perhaps I shall never descend. Perhaps they will fire the house, as they do in horror films? I will miraculously douse a pyre with a glass of water? A benediction from a glass tumbler.

A cackling laugh follows me, but not a ghoul, not a hooded presence. In the attic, I am alone. Alone, alone. Oh, for a draught of vintage that hath been Cool'd a long age in the deep-delved earth… that I might drink and leave the world unseen. And with thee fade into the forest dim. Where is the blushful Hippocrene? More dull opiate for the swilling, gurgling drain? My tree, my beech, are you still standing, or have you fallen to the axe of these prowling troops of Midian? What I'd give for the arms of my tree! I would curl in my blood-coloured rug and see the stars turn, the deer trip silently, and the slinking fox going lairward. I could see the sunrise. Will I ever again see the sunrise?

"Oh Love!" she says. I did not see Georgina enter. She comes in on a gust of fear that blows hard and strong, almost solid—a matron of concern.

"My God, what's happened? You look like a starved tree sprite!"

"I have unleashed evil; I have dug so deep that the earth gave up its ghouls."

"What d'you mean? Dug?"

"By abandoning all safety and defying all prohibitions, I sampled the pits of evil, and they followed me home."

"Why are you moving like that?"

"To keep them at a distance."

"What's 'them'?"

"Embodied terrors. Many. These are not only my terrors. They hold their haunts too firmly just to be mine."

My movements disturb her.

"Can't you stop that?" She cannot see what they describe: intricate nests, birds in flight, all images of natural beauty, the rolling surf and its lace cast across hard sand, that fizz of surf's broad satisfaction. Pictures translated into movement keep fear at bay. I remain in control, and she thinks I have lost my mind! She cannot help that. I look raving. Unwashed. Cadaverous. Mad. Of course, mad.

"No, I dare not."

"Why can't you?"

"Fears take root, and I seize up, paralysed. You can feel it, too. You are afraid."

Her fear simply increases the cold. I see she does not understand.

She is shivering and cannot meet my eyes.

Then she says, "Terry's gone. You know that?"

"Of course. He had to go. Some of this filth is his legacy. Not all of it." I try to present her with an olive branch of peace. I shape it and hand it to her. She does not recognise it. I know Terry had gone to her. I also know what happened. I also see she hopes I don't know that. How small a habit for me to mind!

"I brought some coffee. When did you last eat?" Georgina's kindness always begins with coffee.

"Not sure. Maybe days. But I can't eat. Coffee would be wonderful, but the kitchen is pretty sordid. The kettle may still work."

I'm not sure it will, but I have to warn her. "Don't worry about all the signs. I was just trying everything to ward them off, even throwing eggs. I'll clear them up when I'm strong enough to face the kitchen." I want her to see that I am still thinking. Her face struggles to control her recoil. I know she longs to run.

It seems hours before she returns.

Time now is compressed, a world in a grain of sand. Space and time are space-time here. I can put a girdle round the earth before the next breath.

When she comes back, it is with a tray, a clean cloth and a sprig of jasmine. She has found Margaret's special cups with saucers. Don't blame her. The mugs are submerged in brown water.

The first hot mouthful is nectar, but I cannot swallow it. I spit it into the saucer. My palate cannot take its strength.

"I'm so sorry. I can't swallow that, divine though it is. I'm truly sorry for all your trouble. I only sip milk. Can't manage anything else."

"Love, what *is* going on?"

I have to try to explain if only to sanction her departure.

"I am learning to navigate in a new medium, the field of thought, or rather solid feelings like thought frozen in ice-cubes of envy, hatred, vile, vile, you can't imagine! Right now, I am surrounded by evil and trying to swim through, beyond and above it. Using my body helps me concentrate and shut out the fear. It was easier when I could fully dance on the grass outside but I got exhausted and thought it unwise, neighbour-wise. Now I make pictures in my mind, and these arms describe them, emotional dancing to…." I am really trying, but all I see is Georgina's incomprehension.

"Is there anything I can do?"

"No. There is nothing anyone else can do. I have to get through this alone, but even if you thought you could, you are afraid. That only attracts more evil because evil feasts on fear. Gobble, gobble. You can't help judging me because you cannot see anything except its debris, but bless you for coming…" I stop weaving for a moment and look at her quite still, and I hope reassuringly. "I will get through it; I just need more time and greater courage."

"What are you 'getting through'?"

"Fear"

"Your fear?"

"Mine is part of it, but no, the deeper dimension of all fear. Mine is just a link to universal embodied fear. It manifests and buggers about in an atomic realm, with things like lighting fires and electricity. How long has it been?" I ask as she draws away.

"How long has what been?"

"Since I went to London?"

"Four days."

"Really? Is that all? It seems weeks."

"I'll come back—promise," she says.

I hear the front door pulled shut then her car starts up. I wonder whether I will ever see her again.

༄

I have to learn to die, to offer no resistance. I cleaned the cottage, cleaned Vim bright, lemon yellow clean, scrubbed the walls, dettolled the floor, bleached the sink, and shined the table. The bastards have taken leave. All the crucifixes seem to keep them out now. Remember Palm Sunday and the Stations of the Cross; all that incense wafted at faded pictures of Calvary. It is amazing what comes to hand when needed. The fire is alight, and those people who came for the girls will take care of them until I touch down. Will I? Ever? It was best to let them go. I am not a fit mother floating six feet above ground. They thought I would resist, how they do like a fight! Probably to justify what they intend to do.

The Unsocial Services seemed very cross when I said we would wait until the girls came home from school so that I could pack their favourite things and explain where and why they were going. They would have preferred me to rail or weep but had to sit stirring tea until the school bus delivered their intended captives.

Ros looked pinched and frightened, but Jess just said, "Good, I want to ride on Ginny again. Can I take some carrots?" My pragmatic daughter!

I am glad I remembered Terry's brother and his wife, Jeff and Christine, and suggested they might return to the farm. Apparently, the social services will pay for it. Wonderful what being 'off one's rocker' brings forth! I am a victim of stress, poverty and neglect, a single mother like so many unable to cope. That's what they think. How little they know. I chose this and went after it like a hound after a rabbit.

Anyway, my darlings will go back to Norton Malreward. I should have registered that name, where Terry's childhood marinated in that mother! What a name at this time, for what was described as a 'spell' by that lavender cream puff with her bouffant and her lipstick. 'Spell' it certainly will be if she has anything to do with it. Now I mustn't get shrewish.

My girls will find Ginny the donkey, the calves and the dogs and let me pay full attention to navigating a solid return. What I can't explain to anyone is why I have to go on in order to come back intact. I know there is a destination, and I know I will recognise it when I get there.

I wonder who called them? The Priddles next door? Probably. She's a motherly sort. My new shiny kitchen surprised the unsocial services; they hoped for squalor so that they could be saviours. I switched on the rational, the clear, and the logical, and from that, they concluded I could just 'pull myself together.'

'Can't you just calm down?' he asked, that Adolf Eichmann in his glinting glasses with his breastplate pens; playing the uncivil servant.

That's exactly what I'm doing, pulling all of myself together. All of the expanded me, the bulbous, overflowing me forever, back together in a narrow tube called this life, its propriety called sanity, called conformity. It isn't over yet. Sometimes, I think it is; oh, how I wish it were! Then something happens to remind me to go on.

∾

Now, heave-ho, to run the nightly bath. Not hot, tepid. Hot exhausts me. By the time tepid is cold, I am oblivious. I have come to dread it, but I know it's working. I lower myself into marvellous water. We should worship its resilience and its instinctual love affair with gravity. I shall approach the cliff edge of drowning to think clearly. Where the bee sucks, there suck I, in a cowslip's bell I lie, there I couch while owls do fly. The curfew tolls the knell of parting day, The lowing herd winds slowly o'er the lea, The ploughman homeward plods his weary way, and leaves the world to darkness and to me. Peace. Poetry is so soothing, like sipping sweet dew.

Drip, drip, the lute of the dripping tap plucks out my filmed eyes and amplifies the drum of my beating heart, dum, dumdum, dum, dumdum. From here, I can revisit the setting scenes of childhood, hear the convent bell in the valleys of Basutoland and ride the long hot trails into the mountains, smelling the sweat of Noel to wash clean the debris of confusion, the wrack of jealousy, the bitterness of love affairs and unloving affairs. I can see a man crippled by lust and watch him go. Another, more bitter, bites his own arm. Dum, dumdum. The water is the temperature of blood and oozes its way down my nostrils, heading for the sponge of my lungs. I don't swallow. I cannot feel the meniscus between air and water. The water of my body dissolves in its own medium. I roll over like a beer barrel and sink.

Arms lift me and carry me wet to bed.

I sink into unbroken peace, no cold, no wet, no sensations—just the tolling bell. Now I feel a pressure fill my head and balloon downwards. I have testicles lying like snails without a shell. It must be odd living with that. It is a man with a club foot, and he struggles to possess me or escape me. I point my eyes towards the dying light and find the wild geese flying. He marvels and relaxes and goes out as the convent bell rings. Here is another, crabbed and angry, whose presence is like gall, spitting. I take him to a shining lake and cast a line; with him, I watch the line taken and rhythmically oscillate until it springs free, and he is gone, like smoke from my navel. The bell tolls again, briefly.

∾

There were many such initiation nights, floating like a Japanese lantern on windless water, paper thin. On that last night, fifteen souls passed through me, from pain to poetry. Exhausted, I lay with the afflictions they bequeathed; the residue of a club foot twisted my ankle, so I was obliged to limp and drag my limb, and a port-wine stain coloured my neck. I learned that deformity is the result of mental torment, and we bring it with us into this life. Only love and love of beauty alleviates it. Healing is showing. Poetry hands anguish over to acceptance. Was I training to be a viaduct through which the morphology of pain would be sluiced away, a spiritual Cloaca Maxima? A drain to wash away agony? Only something like that would need this veritable scrubbing, balanced on the needle of sacrifice, self-eradicating. Am I a panpipe blown clean to release free-floating cures, dancing like bubbles from a line of white wind-blown washing?

I can happily do that if it would grant me sleep. A night of velvet sleep. Just one. What I would give for unfettered, dreamless sleep!

On the rough stone wall opposite my bed, a man takes shape, crouched and rubbing hands together, abject, self-abasing, a Uriah Heep wheedling, diminutive. He emerges as smoke and solidifies as plaster; then his features sharpen, and he smiles as Max used to. A 'got you' grin, malevolent. It is Martin Israel!

I recoil, disbelief, horror and pity all battle for dominance. Is this his true nature? It could not be! No, this is the effect of evil distortion.

I cannot; I will not admit its poisonous deformity. Like the jewelled snake, I see myself through his eyes. I, crouching back against the pillows, a Pre-Raphaelite Magdalene, is shrivelled by her accusers. I won't look at it.

I bid it be gone. Still wheedling, it withdraws, fading back into the nobbled, rough stone, a priapic satyr, a rough goat. No, not Martin. It is the temptation of St. Anthony, a tormenting mockery. Was I being tested? Is this the trial of my commitment, the test of loyalty and love? To prove I can retain my own deeper image of a lonely, tortured man? Something takes me deep into sleep.

Finally, a sleep of fathomless unconsciousness.

∾

'Slept sweetly, love?' At the moment of waking, I hear Martin's voice.

Martin?

'*I am always with you.*' His voice is clear, unmistakable. In my head, but he might as well be sitting on the bed.

Whenever I call?

'*You have only to think. We are one. You are my delight.*'

I? I delight you?

'*You have always been my joy and my consolation.*'

Have we both been always searching?'

Was he the love I had hoped for? His loneliness to find completion in mine?

'*Time has no significance.*'

Time held me green and dying…

'*Though it sang in my chains like the sea…*'

Not a thought is hidden from you?

'*Not even the impulse to think.*'

How can I speak to you? You are me and not me?

'*A paradox. You are no less you for being one with me.*'

Can I come and see you? Today? Now?

'*In the flesh?*'

If flesh it is. Of course. I long to see you, to grasp this, to confirm it.

'Your longing is mine also. I have, admittedly, some apprehension…'
Martin!
'Of course, you must come. Forgive me. I shall wait patiently.'
Can you see me?
'No. that may come later.'

That's how it began. Saved from drowning in a bath, lifted and plucked from despair by a divine pincer, and elevated to spin giddily. This time. Yes, yes. This time, I was going to London to see my reciprocal lover, the one drawn out of a dull conference in a suit and tight shoes. No leprechaun offering three wishes: perhaps the ugliest man alive, with papery dry skin and a restless tongue flickering over his lip. I did love him. Yes, that's what I said. Love bade me welcome. My soul did not draw back. It surprised me as much as the telling of it will surprise you. Or it would have if I'd questioned it. Strange to be assaulted by the recognition of a love that rose with the dawn and came in the shape of an unhappy, imprisoned, pedantic doctor-priest.

Yes. Let's go.

I had no expectations of this. None. Terry had envisioned this sort of union, but only in his delineation of love as sex. A projection of his obsession or his need for an excuse? Perhaps as a way to reduce us both to his dimensions? Martin had enrolled and lodged himself from the first moment we met him at Culham and then perched between us at Lincoln's Inn, an unlikely Cupid, breathing encouragement down several phone calls. Now, he lay easy in my mind. I found no reason to question it. That pernicious, crabbed vision from the stone wall I had unequivocally shunned. Instead, that gnomic pedant entered in, and 'I did sit and eat'. Nothing that had happened since the Eye was explicable in rational terms. I had accepted the role of some servitude to a process that had familiar stages— my personal Golgotha— but assumed these were trials and assimilations to prepare me for some service, as yet undefined. Healer? Interpreter? Lamp-lighter? Companion? Lowly servitor? Any. I had no desires but service to enraptured dissolution.

The scissor Eye had cut the bonds. Now, I stepped free of them entirely. Leave all and follow me?

Each loss was followed by inexplicable, synchronous events, adultery, divorce, the accident and exile, the Milfords' kind husbandry, Combe Cottage's healing, and each secured my independence and still wrapped my wellbeing. Casting off from Terry by faking a trip to see Martin had finally thrown open a second Pandora's box, releasing every plague of terror, mockery, glittering calculation, all trust and all restraint, but what did remain was hope. Hope alone persuaded me to follow whatever the gods had in store.

I was blind. I could not yet see, so runes and signals were all that I had.

I believed Martin would convey what next, and why, and why me. We would coil around a companionship that would not question but follow where such acceptance led. A companion who knew what and where I'd been would be an ultimate richness. Better still, a lonely pathologist who understood disease since I was a novice introduced to its causes and cures. Perhaps that would be it? He would diagnose, and I would rescue with ropes of poetry, hauling the afflicted back from the abyss of pain. I knew nothing about Martin beyond Dick's reluctant admiration, 'Behind that sonorous voice, do you see a sausage frying? Would such certainty admit of appetite, d'you think?'

'Oh, you pompous priests!' Margaret had responded. 'When does sonorous sermonising add to anything? I'd be impressed by a child on his knee or a dog at his heels. His books are impenetrably smug. I know, and I'll make sure you know I know!' Margaret and Martin had no time for one another yet had never met! I should have questioned that more deeply.

∾

Waterloo! Again. I'm meeting my Waterloo without even a Wellington boot or waterproof cape. I needed no protection except from joy.

'Are you dancing?'

Imperceptibly. Just a little. The city now doth like a garment wear…
'…the beauty of the morning. Don't.'
Don't dance?
'Don't dance. You'll gather a crowd to follow. They will mistake your reason.'
And you? Shall we meet outside? On the bench of our first encounter?
'I'll be down when I can.'
You sound apprehensive? Are you?
'A little, I have my reputation to consider…'
Your reputation! Here I dance like a discalced Carmelite novice longing to see you, to confirm what you helped set in train, and all you think about is your reputation? Martin!
'I *am* always with you.'
With? Or in?
'Can you stay quiet?'
Not think? Do you mean not think?
'If you must speak, soliloquise. I have to concentrate.'
Sorry. I thought you could just turn me off.
'Not if you beam at me. We'll meet, say, in about an hour?'
He sounds rather tense. Perhaps even he did not expect to find himself joined at the hip… well, not the hip, heaven forfend. Joined by the invisible worm that flies in the night, and does thy life destroy? Last time it was Keats, alone and palely loitering and now Blake, who found my bed of crimson joy. I wonder whether these infections of words simply float past and lodge in the crevasses of thought, bees thick-dusted with the pollen of a special encounter? I begin to look like consumptive Keats and sweat Blake from pores of joy. Mad. I am mad with joy and must tolerate the small man's fear of the female. He fears I might make demands or pounce? Shall I dispel that by saying, 'Just look in a mirror, and then ask me again?' Perhaps effective, but a little cruel? I must adopt the demeanour of a nun, eyes downcast, muted voice, and paint myself in the modesty of a van Eyck virgin reading a psalter while, behind her, the river cascades to the sea.

Well, here we are, Martin and me. I shall hie me to the establishment Ladies and behind that tip-tilted pagoda drink water and brush my hair. I'm glad I wore this skirt. I love its rich tapestry of opulent colours, crimson joy, thick pile, and shiny chenille that carries a bloom like a plum! And this silken, wide-sleeved chemise. I like that too, an'all. Can I wonder where he is, this new love of mine? Without alerting him? Suddenly feel very tired.

'Why not lie on the grass?'

Terry!? That voice, the laughter behind it, was just as distinctive. I am possessed and hung between the nails of two men. Pealing in my bell-like head.

'Yup. Nigger in the woodpile, what's that word? Metaphorically speakeasy? In the way, am I?' Terry's irreverent presence is curiously comforting.

You could say that. I am waiting for Martin.

'Where are you waiting?' Terry-in-the-head asks.

Near that bench in Lincoln's Inn Fields, where we sat with him, remember?

'Philippa! Is Terry with you?' Martin sounds agitated. Who's beaming now?

With? Not exactly. Not in the flesh.

'Never say no to a bit of flesh.' I can see Terry's wolverine grin. I bet he's barefoot at the marina, watching a line and smoking a joint. Terry does love a wind-up.

Terry. Can you just stay quiet? Or better still, bugger off? There is silence on the inner telephonist's line. Then he plugs back in.

'He won't come, you know.' Terry means Martin won't come. He can't know that. *'Oh yes, I can. I can see a frightened rabbit in a white lab coat.'*

Odd that Terry also sees a white rabbit. I never shared that.

'Philippa, has Terry gone? You must refuse him.' Martin's voice is single malt vinegar.

Martin. If I am open to you, I am open to him. I did not determine your capture or his interruption.

'In that case, I must withdraw. I certainly cannot run the risk of being seen with you in the flesh.' Martin is all aquake with righteous anger.

'Told you. He's chicken.' Terry's voice holds contempt.

Terry, you know, sometimes you lack all charity. Just because you can live as a bum, you think he should. He does have his reputation to consider.

'Yeah. Reputations! We've seen too many of those. No, actually I don't. I think he could live up to all those words of spiritual charity and come and buy you a cup of weak tea and be gentle unto you.'

My! You've changed. That was both true and not true. Terry was occasionally gentle and often solicitous.

'Hope so. Maybe. Anyway, he's buggered off. He snuck out the back and took a taxi home.'

Could that be so?

Martin? No answer. Like from that phone booth the last time. I am just an ambulatory phone booth and one getting very tired. Am I losing my mind?

'You do need his help. He's all you have. You know where he lives. Go to Kensington. Beard him in his bachelor pad. Let him cower behind his curtains. Leave his public image un-besmirched.'

Big word for you? Where did you pick that up?

'Amazing the words you find on a beach when you are linked to Divine reproach. I can pick them up like pebbles from his trite disapproval.'

Now you sound like me!

'Why honey, thank you kindly. Now you jes git yosel on a bus, and I'll be riding close by yo side.'

Terry, this isn't funny!

'I think it's hilarious. I'm a-comin whether you like it or not. I wanna see you knock at his door. I wanna see that rabbit in the headlights of yo shinin' face and yo big shinin eyes...'

Christ! Just shut up.

I'm exhausted. Suddenly, I feel Terry's arms enfold me and his hand stroking my hair. He whispers, 'I know you are. Just dance a *little, concentrate on the sky and cleanse the confusion. You are getting frightened.'*

I was. In the face of Martin's vinegar, Terry was a sponge of clean spring water.

'I'll stay quiet, but I'll be with you. You have to find out what Martin knows and what he wants.'

What makes you think he wants anything?

'Just do. I think he always did. You are the key to something. I don't know what.

∽

I got off the number ten bus and walked the broad pavements of Salubria back along the tracks of that dreadful night, now flooded in sunlight. On the street where you live, Fair Lady, and say hi to the blood box of that axe and swinging receiver, unreceived. Judging by that woman's sharp disapproval, I should be wearing shoes. Are bare feet indecent in Ken-singalong-ton? Right here we are. Cranley Place. We're hardly crammed in Cranley, columns to raise the umbrella above the door and a regiment of windows to gaze down. Which bell will raise the rabbit? Here comes a man with a key.

"Just going in. Can I help?" That's efficiency at the portal! Knock, and it will be opened unto you?

"I'm looking for Dr. Israel?"

"First floor, door on the right."

Man-with-key leads. I follow. He indicates the door, and he goes on up. Another rabbit from a hat?

Martin's is a solid-panelled, glossy portal, giving nothing away. Oh God, perhaps he'll be cross and forbidding. He'll be embarrassed with a biscuit and caught indecent in a silk dressing gown. What do I do?

'You knock him up, then knock him out.'

Terry shut up. I wasn't asking you.

'Not much point asking yourself when you know you don't know.'

I'm too tired to think.

'Just knock. Loudly.'

I knock loudly. What a brave girl I am. Nothing. Try again. Is he hoping I'll just go? Is there one of those camera surveillance things? I can't see one. I put my ear against the door. Is that a ticking clock, or is it just my heart ticking? Not a sound. Perhaps I'll just wait. He's bound to appear sometime.

'Why not just sit down? There's no one to see, and if the front door opens, you'll be up before they will.' Terry's syllables are gentle and caring. Why shouldn't I sit down?

Bliss, just to sit down. London is an unfriendly city. You sit on benches, not marble steps in an empty stairwell. Pretty flush this place with its balusters and polished rail. Here, this man I love ekes out his days coming and going, and nobody knows who he is or what he thinks. Not even me, who loves him!

I suppose I drifted off. I am woken by a woman a-prickle with hair pins under a netting, a stinging wasp of a woman in overalls—another in hairpins, all hostile like porcupines.

"Whasa you a doing 'ere. How are you coming inside? Who is you want?" she bends over me, arms on hips, silhouetted against the light.

"What?"

"Thees is private 'ouse. Why you lie on floor? How you get in?"

"A man with a key let me in…"

"I do not see man. Where is man? Who is key? Who you want?"

"I have come to see Dr Israel."

"Dr Issyrail, he is never taking visitors. Thees is not 'is room. That 'is room. Do you have an appointment? He expecta you?"

"He's a friend."

"You don't look like friend. You go. Now straight." She yanks me up savagely, pulls me down the stairs, opens the entrance and throws me out, slamming the door behind me.

It is now spitting rain through the sun—a fox's wedding, which seems prophetic. I need milk. I see some dregs in an unwashed bottle two doors down. Shall I dare? I sit in a doorway and ponder. Terry says one thing, Martin another, man shows me in, landlady throws me out. I am so tired I could lie down and die….'

But I am always with you.

You keep saying that, and always my heart leaps…

It is not with Martin, nor with Terry…' This penetration is by a deeper Familiar.

You are not either!

I am all, each and all. Forgive me the deception.

But it was mine. Of myself?

I'd say we collaborated in your deception.

The tail end of hope? Wasn't it?

You needed creature comfort or belief in its possibility. The depth of aloneness is profound. I conspired to lead you here with audible masks. At last, we are together, and…

I am always with you! To You, at last to you. What a fool I've been…

A new dawn of understanding; the spectres of camouflage now fled. In the moment's silence, the spectres covering identity evaporate like mist under the blaze of the sun.

No. Neither courage nor faith was foolish. Forgive the deception. It was necessary to free your understanding. You have only yourself in a world wholly hostile. You need to rely only upon yourself. I had to betray you for your own good. Now you need food. There's a pint in that doorway; take it.

I stole the milk and met my true love, my deepest Self.

༄

It was raining. Together, we sat in a doorway over a pint of stolen milk as the odd pedestrian walked past. Nobody noticed us. Happiness was simply sitting there, alone with My Love.

Had you never recognised me earlier?

Yes and no. As an agent, you left clues, people, and turns of phrase, but of a 'fancy that' variety. No, I lie. When you lifted me out of the bath, I knew and surrendered to you. When Cassirer walked over to accost David, I saw you in that shock of accusatory hair, inclined and bent to a purpose. Inescapable.

Only improbability made me inescapable? That's not much of a welcome mat! I have walked beside you for thirty years, and those were the only occasions…?

Forgive me?

No need. That doorway was our altar, that milk our blessed libation. Ah, it was sublime that nymph in a chenille skirt embracing our union. Are you going to invite the reader to continue, or shall we end it here?

If this was a romance, I could expand on glory and wave in a sunset to close over the sea in which we drown, as I once drowned with the white stallion, my crin blanc. I'd like to rest a little longer.

Come. Closer. Close your eyes. You are now safe with me.

CHAPTER 28

Judas: Galloping Through Fire

'It is the favourite stratagem of our passions to sham a retreat, and to turn sharp round upon us at the moment we have made up our minds that the day is our own'.

I am, yet again, en route to London. Something persisted in pushing me to confront the undeserved and sudden rejection from a man who had, all along, pressed me to continue. I had to understand it. Only he could tell me what had changed and why. This time, I dress in Marks and Spencer's reassuringly dull, mid-calf conformity. I have been to the bank and extracted ten new one-pound notes. I remembered my passport, just in case of the unforeseen. I am driving with perfect coordination between gears and accelerator and I am a vision of sobriety. No dancing permitted; no falling necessary.

Total control, yes?

With your help.

Do as much as you can without me. Turn your eyes to the world, remember time, heed peripheral vision and plot your own course. I am…

…always with you/me?

Quite so.

Margaret persuaded Dick to lend me their efficient blue mini because my old black taxi is becoming asthmatic and, above everything, I must avoid any surprises. No opportunities will arise for uninvited come-ons from chancy mechanics. She understood that. I heard Dick mutter about being dependent on their car and Margaret hissing that 'somebody has to believe in her and show it.' Dick surrendered because he still believes Martin would make sense of it all if I appear with the demeanour of a spinsterish ex-nun.

Martin will calm down and take me through an eloquent analysis of his letters and how accurately he read my instability as deserving of his severity. I shall be contrite, duly thank him, come away sobered, ready to reclaim my darling daughters and give them a mother wholly whole, perhaps a part-time teacher. Surely, with all his talk of compassion, he must? Until he does, I hang, perplexed by so many signposts directing me nowhere except into orbit.

Right. That's the B roads safely navigated, and I venture onto the A303. No decisions for a while; just keep to a selected lane and a constant sixty mph. This is easy. Why was I so nervous about it?

God, this traffic is travelling fast! Mid-morning on a Thursday? Where did they all come from?

Keep to the slow lane. Just control the car. Voice no questions.

Ask me no questions, and I'll tell you no lies.

Concentrate.

Right. Now, we merge onto the M3? Three lanes belting over a slope and each faster than the previous? Jesus.

Stick to the middle merge lane and keep some latitude on both sides. Well done.

I'm doing seventy-five! But they all are.

Yes, this is very dangerous. Stay steady in this lane.

Why is he flashing lights at me? Okay, okay. I can't move to the left. He's overtaking. You are not supposed to do that on the left. All right! He flashes again as he goes past. What's on my tail? A bloody blunderbuss lorry like that menacing film with blacked-out windows. Stay back, won't you? No, you won't. He misses me by a foot. Fair-Trade Logistics? Yeah right. Up yours, an'all.

And now? What's this? A concrete mixer, doing over seventy and with the drum rolling? Ta-dah. For our next act, total solidification. He cut right across me! Shit. Sorry.

This is getting out of control. We are going to have to get you off this road.

There's only one way to do that. Supersonic thrust, so I rise over them all like a spitfire Pegasus?

Shut your eyes.

What do you mean, shut my eyes!? This traffic…

We will take over the car. Just trust completely and let us take control.

I suppose that's not entirely new. What have I been doing all along? Never before on a motorway at suicidal speed…

Relax. Sit back. Let go. Now close your eyes…

There. You are safe.

That's ridiculous! How did they do that? I'm halfway up an embankment separating the motorway's two directions. At rather a rakish angle, it must be said. Ta ra! They all flash past, and nobody seems to notice. Perhaps I am invisible?

Put it in gear and use the handbrake. Pull tight. Slide across and get out through the lower door. It's safer. Now drop down and shimmy to the edge of the road. Don't stand up. You will need to cross it. Wait. Not yet. Now! Good. Into the field.

So much for control! What happened?

You attracted attention.

I did no such thing! Unless my intentions can be read like a vapour trail?

Exactly. Thought creates. You already know that, but you keep forgetting. There are forces able to manipulate time and matter. You have met them. Now, we must conceal you.

I submit. Clearly, the dimensions of this are beyond my comprehension. I could be crushed as easily as an ant by a boot.

You fail to understand because you cling to false modesty.

I am unequal to the responsibility!

Now she tells us! You do not know your responsibility yet. It depends upon this journey and what transpires.

So, be it unto me, according to thy word?

Your scepticism is the result of too much book knowledge. Nothing is identical. With a part of yourself, you imagine you are deluded because you draw false parallels.

Is that surprising? I obey every cliché in the well-thumbed manual.

The insane are perhaps closer to me than you realise. To complete this journey, you must be cleared of doubt. Otherwise, you will be sure to

lose us. Remove your raiment.
Raiment?
Clothes to you; just to light the difference.
So, somewhere off the M3, I'm lying naked as a babe in bulrushes. The sharp, scythed wheat gently lashes back and thighs, hiding from sight the dragon coiling and uncoiling across the sweet-smelling earth, crawling with lice that screech and snarl. That contemporary dragon belches fire and smoke like any other. It must be perplexed; its prey nicked from its metal jaws… But here, the skylarks sip and stitch, hastening before the tumultuous clouds which gather and ferment. The tractors in the distance hurry to defeat the rain, a triad of tractors nosing home. Here it comes. To stone my back in single pellets while the sun remains to square its fists. I lie on my clothes. They and I both benefit. The knives of this shafted rain will make another Saint Sebastian—more like Gulliver, trussed by little things. I am not big or small enough for martyrdom. Am I cold, or is this shivering the trembling of the wind? What is cold but withdrawal? It is time to sink and melt…The rain recedes and stops, but still, I feel the sprinkling of water. Is that you?'
That is we.
Me?
We
You said 'we', but I heard 'me'.
You and we are one.
I heard 'me' again.
You heard both at once, or you would not have asked.
Are you narrowing the gap, closing the gulf between us?
The gulf preserves your independence. You may dress. For the moment, we have el-u-ded cap-ture.
Now you speak in my hand!
I inhabit the temple of your body; fall again. Now, you hear more distinctly.
But you speak in my words?
In your mind, in words and images meaningful to you. We only have

what you bring to us.

They would say I was projecting my own thoughts…

He/They slow to maestoso.

And-what-would-you-answer?

I would not answer, but thanks for maestoso me; it helps.

How will you continue your pilgrimage?

Swallow the pill and grim and bearage? I'll hitch.

Solitary woman as flag, spattered by tyres hurling grit; in the distance, the sun snared in a basket woven by a single field. Bugger, I've dropped my bag, so no money, only a field caught on camera. Damn. So well prepared, so easily distracted! A car screeches to a halt in a spray of gravel.

"Get in."

"What?"

"I said, 'Get in'. How angry he is, a red-faced man with a paunch in a checked shirt. Mister Mercedes Benz. Livid, fury incarnate.

"Bloody fool."

"What?"

"Stop saying what; get yourself killed, that's what…"

"You'll get us both killed if a hundred miles an hour is your minimum."

"Shut up."

"You're in a jolly mood."

"You know perfectly well it's illegal."

"What is illegal?"

"Hitchhiking on the motorway."

"I forgot, but I had an accident…"

"I saw no car…"

"You probably passed it in a blur."

"My driving is my business. You keep quiet."

"Okay. Can I just ask where we're going?"

"I'm going to London."

"So am I…"

"Not with me, you're not. I'm dropping you off at the first service station just to get you off the road. Silly idiot."

He puts his foot down harder. We sit in silence. He drives in the fast lane until he sees a 'Services' sign and then swings to the left.

"Here you are."

Little Chef. Serves up abuse with fries on the side.

"Thank you."

"Don't thank me. I'd be happy to see you written off. It's others I'm thinking of…"

Off he goes in a squeal of contempt.

He was quite right. You were a perfect fool.

Well, thanks…

We went to considerable trouble to get you off that motorway, and the moment you are offered a choice, you head straight back onto it…

Of course. Of course! I didn't think.

It would help a little if you did.

Why didn't you warn me?

You are in control. We do not dictate. We aid; no more.

I give you leave to bang me on the nose whenever I need it.

Dear love. We are only as strong as the strongest link…

And as weak as the weakest, c'est moi.

You cannot know which is which.

Because Your strength is made perfect in weakness? Does Martin know I am coming?

We endeavour to prepare. We are doing all we can.

So, it's possible?

Anything is possible. Always

∞

Can I dance?

Discreetly. This London world is dangerous.

No, stop. Stop! Police.

One takes out a notebook. The other signals a car parked. It turns and rolls towards us. Damn.

"Right you are, madam. Name?"

What shall I say?
Give it. He will check.
"Address?"
I give that, too.
"Somerset? You're a long way from home?" The shorter policeman looks sympathetic. They have no idea just how far I am from anywhere.
"In you get." One holds open the rear door. He gets in with the driver—the other nods and stays.
Comply. Antagonism will not aid us.
I manage an amiable smile of acceptance. "Where are you taking me? I have done nothing."
"There is a warrant to apprehend you."
"Why?" They offer only silence.
We drive to the Richmond Police Station. I am left in an outer waiting area while they make a phone call. It is getting dark. Then they reload me and drive for several miles before sweeping into the entrance of a Kafa-esque, red brick building with limitless, unblinking windows lit like searchlights.
Where are we?
Just concentrate.

∾

A trussed nurse stands steely; arms folded over a stretched blue uniform.
"Got her bag?"
"She has no bag. No nuthin, no shoes, no comb, no willingness to talk…"
"Right. We'll see about that. Take her other arm. No good struggling, my girl. Pull her hair, Wilson. If she…"
Bugger it, bugger it. What do we do now?
We get sensible. We watch where we're going and take note of the passages.
Where are we? This does not look good.
This is Long Grove Hospital in Epsom, a notorious, high-security

psychiatric hospital. The most dangerous place of all."

" Oh, when the saints go marching in. Oh, when the saints…"

"You be quiet." She clipped me!

"Arms behind her, Wilson, and hold the hair."

"…go marching in. Oh, I wanna be in that number…"

"Be quiet. You'll wake the other patients."

"Out of their comatose nightmares? They'll thank me for it…"

Control the defiance. You merely justify what she enjoys.

This is Martin's idea? Why did they contact him?

Watch where we're going. Since your visit to him, you are on a police file. When they picked you up, they linked the name and called him.

And he's committed me here?

"Patients on a Police Order are always returned, so no point thinking of running… Twist her arm, Wilson—this one's trouble. We have experience with trouble. Tell her how we…"

We will run when we're ready.

"Right. Up the stairs."

Round to the right and right again. "There we are, Trouble. Private accommodation with en-suite facilities. And don't you make any noise to disturb the other patients? They are all asleep." She slams and locks a door that looks like steel, about five inches thick.

My God! It's a cell and a bucket. A bucket! Luckily, I don't need that except as a weapon. At least it's empty.

Subtlety, my dearest love. You are no match for these people physically. You must use wit to outwit. Think.

Right. Let's think. The cell is what? Seven feet wide, perhaps one, two, three, four paces…twelve feet long. A single dim light bulb, too high to smash. This is one of those Victorian loony bins with cells tucked into stairwells for the raving. No window except a small pane in the door, but covered with something outside—one of those inspection grills you see in police procedurals. I see you…hoo! Squint and slam. Sod you too!

The door opens outwards. Why? To stop the crazy hiding behind it? So three stalwart dragons can block any hope of surprise?

That bed is disgusting. No room service here. Bare springs with a thin mattress rolled against the iron head. Rather like the beds my mother and I were allocated in that rehabilitation home for soldiers. Those were white. This is black. Naturally. Am I just being reminded of things I should remember? Ernie and my go-cart. Adaptation? Re-purposed memory? Naturally.

Those spots? Blood? Probably rust. Two thin, grey blankets like army issue, and a pillow. Hang about, hang about. If I unroll the mattress and tuck the pillow and the bucket under one blanket, and scrump up the other to give me a pair of legs… how does that look?

You might take the view from the door.

Shoulders, but not much of a torso. Hump up the pillow?

Better.

Not bad. The insane sleep restless? Right. I crouch against the door below the pane. Invisible. Like not being able to view one's upper lip, the nose of steel prevents it. Good. It helps having thought of it. It shows I still function. I shall get stiff. It could be all night.

Exercise. Stretch and bend. Keep flexible. You will hear any approach.

So here I am, pinioned by a frightened man. A ruthless man. Why did he choose this place?

Very few ever leave it.

He wants me destroyed?

Yes. Completely.

There is the sound of footsteps going towards the outer door of this locked ward.

Get ready. Crouch. Stay still.

Sounds of clinking keys. The outer lock clicks loudly. Macbeth's watchers on the battlements? Voices whisper. The outer door swings because I feel the air on my toes. Someone's coming. One person? Two? They stop outside. The grill slides up. A torch beam catches the wall above the bed; the beam slowly sprays downwards along the bed, from head to foot. Back up to the head, then it clicks off. The patient is asleep. Decapitation and no one to know? I hear a key in the lock turn quietly. The handle lowers slowly.

NOW!

That door sent them sprawling. The outer door was left open!

Run. Down. Left. Straight ahead. Across this yard. Keep to the shadows.

There is a sound of pounding after.

Go left.

It's the outer lodge!

Run, faster, run.

"Stop her!" There are three ready for me! They must have been warned.

"Got you! Now, we'll just take you all the way back."

"You are all sadists."

"Been called worse. Roger, put on a hobble."

They tie around my knees. Two march me back to Wilson, who waits at the foot of the stairs—the one with the fob-watch peers down from above.

Valiant attempt. You will succeed.

Back to the cell. They have cleared away the disgrace, the bucket restored to its lowly place.

"Wilson, bring the wrist chains."

They shackle me to the bedframe.

CHAPTER 29

Cuckoo's Nest

'He had not actively assisted in creating any illusions about himself.... the large vistas and wide fresh air which she had dreamed of finding...were replaced by anterooms and winding passages that led nowhither.'...' And by a sad contradiction, Dorothea's ideas and resolves seemed like melting ice floating and lost in the warm flood of which they had been but another form.'

After three days chained in the cooler, they released me to the fuller light of society. Up to now, I have been mad in the world of so-called sane; now, I shall be sane in my very own Bedlam. I did not see this Victorian pile from outside because I was dumped here under cover of dark. I am now in a ward for the terminally deranged, to which Martin Israel has committed me, to spend final days among inmates who will live here until their existence is a record in a ledger.

They lead me out from Cell No. 3 along the line of other cells, some padded with stained fabric. My chains are removed. They rub chafed wrists with alcohol. It stings. There is almost blinding light from the windows. Straight ahead is a dormitory, one of two. This ward is for women only, where green-covered iron bedsteads lie undisturbed; patients spend the day compulsorily in the day room. Keeps things tidy.

Here is the day room for those who were once human. Isn't this nice?

A large television is always on, flickering bluish light over the insensible and indifferent; nobody glances at it, but it serves to mask the grunts and odd emitted cries that happen for no reason. Never mind that.

See the dribbling catatonics slumped on chairs in a circle. They are made comfortable on water-proof cushions. Catatonics do not move or register themselves or others. I never liked dolls for the same reason. They have the same glass eyes staring at the ground, and they stay as they are positioned. No fun. They cause no problems beyond needing feeding, toileting and leading away to bed and back. There are some, called the 'ambulants', that move. They shamble about, peering into faces and shuffling on. The active schizophrenics mutter the same repeated noises or jerk repeated movements, on and on and on. Fairground automata. Anybody vertical must be watched with an eagle eye. The maniacs might do anything, ha ha ha.

"You will get used to it. This will be your bed at night time. For now, Twiggy, you must join the others."

"I'm not Twiggy."

"You are now. Later, you will take your medication and learn to be cooperative. We prefer cooperative patients."

What did I get used to? In my regulation hospital dress— a white shift, waistless, collarless, much too large— I slowly learn to live in Goya's animated black paintings lit by flood-lamp windows behind the impervious backs of those with eyes on the floor. They are less frightening than the movers and shakers. Here are leering projected teeth, lolling tongues and grinning, lascivious, plucking fingers tickling a neck, lunging at a groin. Words of brave crudity cause self-hugging delight. It is clear that any movement is instantly suppressed with an injection; sedation is universal. Catatonia and mutism, if not coming naturally, are the preferred conditions. The nurses are all Chinese. Slapping comes easily; they are untroubled by violence, the inmates impervious to it: some squeal, some whimper.

One woman, so black she is almost indigo, with close-plaited hair and glitter eye-shadow, plays her variety of basketball, aiming at any elevated tray carried high to provoke her expertise. She has the accurate kick of a mule and long, skittle-solid, muscular legs below the flashy hot pants and halter-top bra. A crashing of dishes splashing a sea of glass is a regular event, followed by shrieking delight as she slaps her own cheeks and caws, a laughing jackass. Three nurses are needed to get her thrashing to a bed. She and I have one thing in common: resistance.

Thievery of food is constant and triumphant. Meals served from a communal table bring out raw violence: grabbings, spittings and hastenings away with a bowl under an arm, guarded by a neck-less chimpanzee lolloping off with hugging fingers. Lip licking, lip smacking; food brings out the only enthusiasm. Getting more, getting better, getting. Food is primal.

∾

'Twiggy', as I am thornily addressed, defies the dayroom edict and lies on the cool floor in the ward beneath her bed, whose green cotton covers filter the light and brings back my copper beech in the green woods. I fill it with my girls on a swing, their voices and laughter.

There, I could block out the hideous noise, the suddenly emitted cries and the churning yatter-yatter of the television. I thought only to plot an escape. It infuriated the ward sister, who dragged me into the day room, where I shut out the horror by doing yoga postures and movement meditations. That had the rest of them screaming or imitating with thespian mockery, auditioning for pantomime. She let me leave and feigned not to notice.

I swallowed none of the pills tipped into my hand but pretended to; now an expert at the braced cave of the tongue offered to the watching dispenser: look? Gone, see? Then, spat them out. My tongue was raw beneath but clean above. I still ate nothing solid but took a helping under supervision, which was easily disposed of into any gobbling inmate's loaded plate. They began to queue close, plucking their claims on the prison dress's sleeves. I usually managed some milk at tea time.

Nights were worse: from stabbing cries streaking the dark to the low moaning of nightmares, the inner torments of twisted souls, all casualties of human combat in its rich variety. Collective wretchedness scored for abrasive instruments played out the symphony of human suffering; every night, the dark took up its baton. I was reminded of the string quartet that played the orderly file into the gas chamber. This was a concentration camp, a camp without the symmetry of Dachau and devoid of its unequivocal methods of dispatch, but a camp all the same—a holding pen for the lost and living dead.

An old, rather aristocratic face with ginger hair, crisped in waves, and a mouth obliquely gashed with vermilion lipstick developed an attachment and would stand silently by my bed whimpering as though she knew me. If I registered her presence, she would run her fingers over my face in a desperate, avid search until I led her to the loo and back to her bed, a little comforted by attention.

One night, I managed to run a blissful bath in the empty communal washroom and was found in the morning, floating peacefully below the silent water. I had practised that often enough, but a day sister, coming on duty, panicked and shouted at the leaving night staff. I might have drowned! I found that rather comical in a bitter way. Peaceful death was a matter of reproach while we were all kept prisoner at public expense to live no life at all. No one was treated; they were all sedated zombies except me. Defiance kept me alive and told me I still was. No doctors came, and no interviews happened. Days turned without variety. Only the Chinese nurses' simple names changed; otherwise, they were indistinguishable.

Nobody in the living world knew I was there except the man who had consigned me. He threw away the key; the one who had described me as luminous, radiant? Was this the end? My interlocutor kept reassuring me. We talked beneath the bed, but I could see no hope.

The ward was double-locked. Every entrant gained access under pass-keys. High wire fencing surrounded the building, which I scrutinised from every window. Under my bed, I hid. I could see any approach from the door and, if necessary, put a bed between me and the stout white shoes bent upon subordination.

"Twiggy. There's a call for you in the staff room. Keep it short…We don't…"

It was a trick. I knew it. To get me out and grab me.

For all our sakes, answer it!

Bound out and disarm with an Excalibur flash of a smile. A call! From Margaret.

"Ah, at last, my dear! It's taken days to find you. How are you?"

"Wonderful instantly for hearing your voice. How did you find me?"

Somebody knew! A bridge to the world. Margaret and her dogged persistence.

"Believe it or not, we're now rather pally with the police. After I failed at every London hospital, Dick asked them to trace you. I hoped you were in a Trappist monastery doing whatever Trappists do. What's it like?"

"If I said, you wouldn't believe me. Forced feeding, forced confinement, and amongst the terminally hopeless…I'm so sorry about the car…"

"Never mind about that. We must get you out. Now listen. Don't try to escape because Dick would have to turn you in, it's the law. No good asking Dick to break the law. We have to extract you legally. We've made an appointment with the psychiatrist…"

"When?"

"Not for six weeks, and we had to press…"

"Six weeks! I am to stay for six weeks? I won't last."

"I'll send you some of your nice dresses and some good inspiring books. Why do they call you 'Twiggy'?"

"New name, new identity. It's how they strip you down. Margaret, this isn't therapy; this is punishment. No grapes by a bed, no newspaper round. Not what you know about. It's not a hospital."

"My dear, I'm sure you're exaggerating. Why not go for a walk?"

"I am not allowed out."

"What!? No fresh air? That settles it. We'll try for an earlier. Meantime, now I know where you are, I will send some of your nice things to cheer you up. Better ring off, or else I'll never get through again. Be cooperative, and don't run away. Goodbye, goodbye."

Darling Margaret with her uplifting cadences of belief. Thank God! *Better?*

A thousand times. Thank you.

The sister looks livid. She moves the offensive receiver closer to her large buttoned chest.

"You won't get out in six weeks. Nobody leaves this ward." She spits it out.

"I shall. With help."

"You are as sick as the rest. They don't lie under a bed. Once you've had the operation, nobody will be able to help."

"What operation?"

I suddenly feel faint.

"Routine. Since medication isn't working, you are down for a lobotomy. In a fortnight. Now, you *will* have an injection."

She grabs my arm and gestures to Nurse Cheung and Nurse King to assist. It was a trick!

No, opportunism. She saw her chance.

They hustle me to my bed. One holds my arms, the other my legs. Sister holds up a syringe, expels air and tries to lift my shift. I wriggle and turn at the precise moment. She misses.

"Now, look what you've done. That was a perfectly good needle… Oh, doctor, I didn't see you."

She reaches for another needle while he approaches the bed. I've never seen a doctor before.

"How are we doing?" he says. He's addressing me. Sister steps back.

"Doctor, can I go for a walk?" I seized my chance.

"Don't see why not," he says. "Sister will provide the supervision, won't you, sister?"

∞

Cheung, King and Twiggy head out for the walk, and Sister keeps her syringe.

Your timing is impeccable.

Luckily, timing is obedient to necessity. Now, keep alert. We're out and must stay out.

Is it true about an operation? Am I to be turned into a vegetable without a memory? Who authorised that?

The same. The one you worshipped enough to write poems to.

There is an open gate! I spot it between the rhododendrons and appear to amble easily, stroking Cheung's arm with gratitude and smiling at King. When we are close enough, I trip and start to fall. They let go. In a flash, I am out and running down the edge of a fast road as cars flash by. The nurses are not permitted to follow. I see them run along the fence on the other side. A car stops, and a door opens. As I get in, I see the nurses clinging to the fence, a pair of agitated Macaques.

"Where can I drop you?" the driver asks, "Epsom Station? Will that do?"

"Perfect," I say. Since I am still in hospital garb and shoeless, he knows I have escaped. As I get out, he hands me a note and smiles.

"Good luck." He drives away.

I love you. I love you.

Mutual. We know. Now it's back to Kensington.

Not again! Why?

Martin has to release you. Only he can. We hope that this escape will persuade him to see you differently and realise what he's done.

If he doesn't?

We make no predictions. We offer choices.

⁂

There he is! Dr Martin Israel ignominiously waiting at the exit of South Kensington Tube Station, craning over heads, scrutinising faces. Good, they must have phoned him. He spots me and approaches, looking not unfriendly..

"Poor Philippa!" he says. "Would you like to come back to my place?"

At last! Would I ever! He sets off, and I follow at his shoulder along the broad boulevard, the doctor in his tight shoes and dark suit leading the degenerate waif, shoeless in a prison shift. He glances at me. Several times, he looks me up and down. He tries to smile but smiling was never his forte. We reach his outer portal.

"Could you wait here a moment?" he asks.

"Of course," He must have the moment to clear crumbs, hide slippers, and brief the Spanish dragon. Within a minute, there is a policeman on each arm.

"You'd like us to take her back?"

"Yes. At once."

"Right, sir."

I look at Martin, and he really does smile now, the hammer-horror smile of triumphant victory. It stays fixed in place while he closes the door. I shall never forget that smile.

∽

Now you really do know.

Yes. I really do.

As do we. From here on, you are utterly alone. Finally, you accept that?

I must.

It will make you both creative and versatile.

It began at once, that creativity. I was handed over by the police to the porter's lodge, clearly expected. I thanked the police. I was being taken back to the locked ward when I spotted the doctor walking with another.

"Doctor, can I speak to you?" I had to shout. They both approached, looking dubious. "Doctor, I didn't run away. I went to see the man who committed me. I hoped he would reverse the Police Order. Instead, he's just sent me back under police escort." They nodded. "Doctor, I don't need to be locked up." He shrugged but looked persuadable. "If I promise faithfully not to run away, can you transfer me to another ward?"

"You really do promise, faithfully promise?" I spat on my hand and held it against my chest." Cross my heart and hope to die…" His doctor friend nodded.

"Now I know there's no point running away; I won't."

He walked back with me and my escort to the ward. The other

doctor waited. We climbed the stairs rather companionably, I thought.

"Sister, can you get me…what's your name?"

"Philippa, but here I'm known as Twiggy."

"Philippa's notes and belongings?" Sister looked thunderous.

"She has no belongings," she said, as though that was my diagnosis.

He took the notes and both doctors provided my escort to the open ward.

CHAPTER 30

Adrian: Released

'Like enough,' said Mrs. Poyser, 'for the men are mostly so slow, their thoughts overrun 'em, an' they can only catch 'em by the tail. I can count a stocking - top while a man's getting's tongue ready an' when he outs wi' his speech at last, there's little broth to be made on't.'

Open it was, this careless extension of the fortress: it had the atmosphere of a transit lounge for flights grounded or waiting to be re-routed. A rag-tag citizenry of all ages wandered about, aimless but not impatient nor obviously unhappy. Nobody was looking to leave, and none committed to stay. Between the men's and women's dormitories was a small pool table in a communal space, where the dust blew in and where coffee and tea appeared. A stand of blue gums and worn grass secluded us from the passing cars.

There was no enforced segregation; affiliations determined who talked to whom. Patients helped with serving meals and washing dishes in a casual, voluntary way. It was a laboratory with specimens free to reveal kindness, mild antipathy, or bored indifference. One woman occupied a bed in the centre of the dormitory, beached like a whale, a weeping mock turtle. Unable to disembark or turn over, she was attended by a red-haired youth covered in scabs and plasters. He breezed in and out, helped her dress and wiped her constant tears. They would sit and hug one another all day.

She interrupted the weeping, and he stopped self-harming.

The staff appeared oblivious to the intuitive awareness that ran like a draft across the slightest emotional disturbance, as though animals in a cage simply moved over for one another, co-existence in easy tolerance. Their unquestioning lack of condemnation was new. I could read it as from a book: antipathy had been bled, hostility siphoned out, misery of an accepting kind made space for other's miseries. The nurses were brisk but the inmates had time— time to tease, to gently mock or to share a cigarette outside on a bench. Nobody was going anywhere. Here, the habitually maladjusted, the alcoholics, the addicted, the enclosed autistics wandered vacantly, all those ill-fitted for life, for the most part gentle and simply lost.

After the locked ward, it was a kind of haven. Yet, given my promise, I still had no hope of ever being released. We saw no doctors who might reassess. Was this to be my fading end?

Margaret had sent me some of my clothes and enclosed a warm letter.

> *My dear Philippa*
>
> *I have chosen the dresses you most often wear, but the underclothes I simply plucked from your untidy drawer. Given where you are, I trust they will serve. Now, before I tell you of our good fortune, I must assure you that I won't stop until we get you released. It has to be official since you are on a Police Order, and that's the law. So be good and don't try to escape, or Dick will take a dim view, which won't help.*
>
> *I have put in a couple of books of poetry. Rumi and St John of the Cross should be good companions and can be consumed in short bites. I have also added a packet of dates and some raisins and prunes.*
>
> *Now to our news! Thanks to you, we have a new car. Not just any car but the very car I have always wanted, a Morris Traveler. A half-wooden car is exactly what old fogeys need, and it has room for Dick's folding bicycle so he can go camping without even the need to fold the tent!*
>
> *A brief history of how the Tiggywinkles achieved their new charabanc:*
>
> *When you failed to return the mini, we were visited by a portly policeman with one of those noisy radios on his shoulder. When I saw him, I feared the worst and assumed*

you had had an accident and been killed. He collared Dick digging up potatoes and waited for him to remove his boots before enquiring whether a blue mini abandoned on the M3 was ours. He already knew that, or he would not have found his way to our door! When he said it was not in the least damaged, I confess the relief made me rather heady.

He was rather severe until we told him we had lent it to you (and my dear, we were forced to identify you and tell him where you were.) Then he became quite sympathetic about your ingenuity at managing to abandon it on the 'central reservation' of the motorway and 'at a perilous angle'. They had to wait until nightfall to close the motorway and recover and identify it. He demanded we fetched its papers to identify ourselves!

After that, he drove us to the garage in a very fast, white car with an orange belt around its waist, a fit for Mr. Toad. He was rather a spoil-sport. I suggested he could turn on the siren (I always fancied being worth a siren!), but he said, 'This is not an emergency, Madame!' There on the forecourt (you will see I am mastering police speak) stood the mini, looking like a stray dog that had caused some trouble. I have always disliked that car.

The garage man wanted to know if we would like to sell because he had an interested buyer. Yes, forthwith, says I. Then Dick asked how we were going to get home if we sold it. The garage owner jumped straight in. He had a car that might suit us better. He took us round the back, and there stood a Morris Traveler, just as this doctor ordered! Dick kicked the tyres, as men do, and then popped the question, 'How much?' 'Nothing.' said the man. He would do a straight swap because nobody wants to bother maintaining the woodwork, and it had done more miles than ours.

So, thanks to you, we drove home in the perfect free replacement! Dick is beginning to admit that you always pull *it off and restore harmony. I am thrilled, and he is warming to it. Dick likes woodwork and practical things to interrupt his study. He can now sail off for his chess in style.*

Of course, I couldn't tell you all that on the phone call, but I wanted to reassure you that there was nothing to feel guilty about. I'm delighted,

Much love, Margaret.

༄

I was free to roam the garden or visit the art studio, a low tenement where a heap of over-squeezed tubes of acrylic, a tub of clay, and large sheets of cheap paper gave limited options in solitude. Until a man with clear and unpleasant intent followed me in. I never felt safe to forget him or others like him. There were a few like that. I still danced, and still needed to fall, but less often. Yet I was in limbo, unable to return, severed from my girls. I thought of them constantly and wondered how they were doing. Did they miss me? Or were the immediate claims of farm animals enough? I longed for them, yet now felt insecure about the wisdom of their recovery, erased from the life I had thought to live.

'You will not be allowed to live the life you have imagined for yourself.' Was this to be the life I was permitted? Was this what she had predicted? That headmistress ghoul in Yucatan?

We don't predict. We offer choices.

And occasionally warn?

"And where are you going, my pretty maid?" The voice came from the foot of a tree where a leprechaun in a feathered trilby with crossed legs sat, looking as though he had lost his flute, impish and impudent—another chancer, Irish. I'll ignore him.

"Why do you wear such prissy dresses? What are you afraid of? Ah, no need for the haste, you scurry. I can hardly harm you out here in view of those windows. Let me fetch you a cup of tea, why don't you?"

No harm intended.

"Okay, but no tea, just a cup of milk."

"A milkmaid we have, then? You'll not be minding if I bring you both, so I'll be having the extra?"

You need to learn to talk to people.

Even a chancer in knickerbockers, dark green corduroys with the buckles hanging loose?

"There we go. And a biscuit?" He has a humorous face. "No, I notice you don't eat so shall I be having that for my pains? I saw yer dancin. You move well, but tell me, those trees y'talkin to, do they answer?"

"They comfort without talk."

"Course they do. Reliable indeed, trees. The sky, as well, I find that too stays quiet. Why do you? Dance, you know? D'yer feel you must? Or is it something else, deeper?"

"I do it to clear fear and confusion. Sometimes to let out my joy."

He considers that and nods. "We all need that. And the fallin too? Why's that? You just let go, and then you get up like fallin is…?

"Falling is the body's deepest fear, face that and you find it sweeps away all the smaller ones along with it, a sort of broom. You've been watching me?"

"I have an'all. There's not a lot else to take the mind. My very own ballet, you are. What I want to know is how you got here. You are not the usual…"

"How do you know?" I ask.

He scratches his chin and shrugs.

"What the hell. None of us is perfect. I almost live here. T'is me fourth time, me annual spell of temperance for indulgin in what me priest still calls de demon drink. We Oirish are almost as good at de demon as de Scots you know, only our whisky is better. So, this is me 'oliday 'ome. I like it well enough. What's your story?"

"I was committed. On a police order."

He startles. "Serious stuff, begorrah! What had you done?"

"Danced and fell but perhaps in the wrong places…and made a nuisance of myself."

"Get on wit yer. Nobody gets a police order fordat. A nuisance, you say. For who or what were you being a nuisance?"

"Never mind."

"Oh, but I do mind because dat's no reason to commit anybody on a police order." Suddenly, he seems too interested. What does he want?"

Ask him.

"What's your name?"

He smiles. "I taut t'ask yer the very same. Then I taut, mind your own business, Adrian, a name is offered, not demanded."

"Adrian?"

"I've a few names and some I don't care for, so that'll be the best to use."

"Philippa", I held out a hand.

"Well! Tat's a pretty name…"

"You want something, Adrian, don't you?" He laughs. Then he looks long and hard.

"Well, I do an'all. I was wonderin whether you might be prepared to lend me dat dress you're wearing? Not for me, you understand. I'm not that way inclined, and it t'wouldn't fit, even if I were. No, it's for dat poor, wee girl…"

"The one you pay great attention to. The long fair hair? The one who came in three days ago? You hardly leave her side." I had noticed them solidly together, although not entirely mutual. He talked, and she was silent, twisting her hair around a forefinger.

"It's not what you tink, y'know. Though given a chance, I wouldn't say no. No, I do my bit on de suicide watch. They all need watchin' at the start. She was brought in after discharge straight from de hospital. So, we all keep an eye out, make sure she's not on'er own. Ting is, they picked her up almost gone across, so I suppose they didn't stop for her what-d'you-ma-calls-its? Accessories. Now, she says she needs her contact lenses. Blind as a beggar, she is widout'em. Now see, I am allowed out, so I said I would go and fetch them if she'd just let me have the keys to her flat, but somehow, she taut she might still need her flat and t'would be better to go herself. You can hardly blame her. We've only just got acquainted. That's a good sign, y'know. It looks like she might have changed her mind about checkin out from this carnival called Life. But she can't go out on er'own.

"Now, if you were to lend her dat dress, I could get her out, and nobody would notice. I could sneak her past the lodge and have her back afore we were missed." He seemed satisfied with the logic. There was only one flaw.

"So, you take her out and get wasted, she commits suicide, and my dress is responsible?"

Adrian was shocked. "I rather liked you before," he said. "I don't fetch tea for just anyone."

"I'll think about it, but I'm not saying yes or even maybe."

"Tink quickly then, because today is Tursday and Saturday, the staff won't know or care. If we're going to go, and I'm to get her back safe, then it must be Saturday."

"Thanks for the tea." I got up. His look was reproachful.

"You could trust me, you know? Tis one ting to betray meself. I am very forgiving; I forgive myself right readily. I've had a lot of practice at it, but other people, you, for example, may not be so forgiving. Wid dose dresses keeping de world at arm's length, I doubt me you'd ever need to forgive anything…"

He had no idea how much practice I had had.

"Tell you tomorrow when I've had a chance to talk to her."

"Taut I could count on you!"

"Haven't said yes." He watched me go. I could not help liking him, but I had spent my honeymoon with a man I liked who was unable to pass a pub.

It was a big ask, being an accessory to suicide.

∞

That same night, I woke from a dream of Ndaba and my mother. What was it? We were back in the miserable tenement flat in Hillbrow, and something scuttled away. Why had it woken me? I could not track it, but I knew it was important. I went back to sleep, pleading for the dream to return. I don't think it did, but I woke holding the scuttle of a rat by its tail. It was a name: Edgar Udwin, the name of the man who married my mother's friend Alison. I remembered my mother saying, 'Psychiatry is hardly medicine; just licenced quackery.' when she told me her friend had married. Edgar Udwin was a psychiatrist! Maybe he might get me out? He's probably in Canada or Australia? Perhaps not; I remembered my mother writing to Alison in England. I had to find him!

I went in search of Adrian and we struck a bargain. I would lend the dress if he would get an address? He would have two reasons to bring the suicide back safely. She listened alongside and nodded.

"Sure, it'll be a piece o'cake," Adrian said, tucking the name into his shirt pocket. "If he's a consultant, he'll be listed on a medical register, and from there, Oi'll track him to a hospital or an electoral role. You know the fella, do you?"

"Never met him. Just heard the name."

He pulled a face.

"Oi'll give it me best." He put a solicitous arm round my shoulder. "Don't put too much weight on hope, see. He doesn't know you. No reason to care, really."

"Someone with the right credentials has to get me out."

"You know, we'all tink dat. We talk to someone. For me, it is usually the AA. We get out, but den we'all come back for the annual reunion dinner."

They departed early. Adrian returned alone. The suicide had done a runner, so I lost the dress, but he brought back an address; Broadmoor Mental Hospital, Crowthorne, Berks. where Dr Edgar Udwin was a senior consultant! On hospital-headed note paper, I wrote to him, reminded him of Louie and Alison's friendship and asked for help.

After the criminally insane murderers they had captive at the highest security mental hospital in the country, I would scarcely rank for incarceration! Surely?

If he answered at all?

༶

I saw them through a glass door of the private consulting room. Edgar

Udwin was facing the Milfords with their backs to me. Udwin used an index finger to emphasize his points. Dick's back drooped wearily. Margaret nodded a great deal, standing waist high to Udwin's six foot four.

Dr Edgar Udwin, a kind face with a prominent nose and a very wide mouth, had come at once. The day before, we had taken a walk through the hospital grounds. I consulted the higher consultant first.

Don't mention me.

Don't talk about the Eye.

Don't dance. Don't fall.

Don't enjoy your new philosophy of consciousness. In fact, don't use the word.

So, deception is the new stratagem?

Masks are sometimes needed. You needed incremental persuasion to believe in me. Work with natural inclination. No psychiatrist talks of consciousness, so don't push it. We need your help; leave it there.

How do I explain being sent here?

He will know about Martin Israel's referral.

Will he have called him?

Unlikely. Consultants tend to rely on their own opinions.

So? What do I say?

I am not telling you. This achievement is your doing, so own it.

I managed deception by sliding out facts. Through a long narration, we walked through the rhododendrons, up a small knoll, along the gravelled paths, Udwin listening with his hands behind his back, me in my most respectable long dress and mostly an earnest, straight face. I told him about the breakup of my marriage. I told him about visa expulsion from the United States. I talked of poverty and my children in care. I mentioned the strain of no support from my mother, which clearly shocked him. All embroidered the victim.

He asked whether anyone might assist in my recovery from such deep misfortune. I gave him the Milford's number; he telephoned them, and here they are to meet him and take instructions about me.

Dr. Udwin comes to the door and calls the unfortunate in.

"You have very kind friends who have agreed to supervise your recovery and administer the drugs I have prescribed. You are very malnourished. I can, therefore, discharge you to their care and wish you the very best, and the best to Louie when…."

Margaret interrupts, holds out the car keys to me and says, "My dear, we are very tired. Would you be so kind as to drive us home?"

Was there ever a friendship of deeper faith?

Another set of car keys! An open call of belief like the first. One to launch a new vision; this one to return from it.

A small signature, initialling our congratulations. It was well done.

As I drive out in their new half-timbered car, along the drive, I see Adrian waiting. His hands, held together against his chest, open wide, outwards and upwards to let fly the bird we both wished he was holding. I waved. In the rear-view mirror, I saw him doff his hat and take a deep bow.

My own Feste for my own Twelfth Night Saturnalia.

Revels now were ended.

INTERLUDE.

Distillation: Setting Sail for Integration

If this were a novel, our fragile heroine escaping from a high-security prison to which she was unjustly condemned without a trial would be followed by bunting and jubilation. Bubbly would be poured. The press would flash evocative photographs, and the villain would go into hiding with others in pursuit. You, as the reader, would breathe deeper and believe you always felt it would end well. No novelist would ask you to follow the intricacies of clues and connections without rewarding your faithful companionship with a sigh of relief.

The trouble is that this is a real life. That easy it isn't.

Incarceration and escape have left her exhausted, not jubilant but perplexed, far from triumphant. She is empty of life or purpose, stripped of belief, and now devoid of all those words to explain herself. Wretchedness is silent; perplexity is mute. We, the double shuttle, have woven her life through people and places, holding the threads in gritted teeth, so complex is the pattern, so inclusive of all. Now they hang loose. The pattern makes no meaning of its complexity, and until it does, we must simply tie off the fringe. She hoped for and knew she needed time to integrate, and that dream of a monastic cell must now find alternatives. This Icarus flew too close to the sun and returned not sobered but melted, shot down by a man she did truly love. For what she took to be his solitary courage and spiritual longing: the hope for a companion in stoicism, with all those she had loved before him for the same qualities.

Longing is almost as indestructible as hope.

She is but thirty-two and already has lived a cat's nine lives, each wrapped and sugared in conflicting loyalties, each demanding more courage, the courage to believe in love, however punishing a love it might be. She can no longer believe. Without belief, she finds no impetus to continue. But she has children who need her to live; they need to be recovered by a mother strong enough to reinvest energy in their futures. There is no energy. There is nothing left of that shooting star that fell, burnt out. Resurrection will need others and a programme that will strengthen. She still has a rudimentary pride, and that is all we have to work with. Her stoicism is well-honed: neither to ask nor to expect. It has taken all this elimination of false hope to bring her to the depth of her aloneness and have her finally accept it—the necessary pre-condition for her purpose.

The life she had not imagined has begun.

We are only halfway through this life of a writer who has not yet written. The book of her future has uncut pages. We have assembled the material— its colours, contents, ideas. We are, by now, aware that it is the future for which that assembly is needed. Awaiting us is a new cast, a new act that might bring this life to a truly satisfying, rounded conclusion, perhaps accepting a peaceful death on the final page. We have travelled the 'port out'; we must now traverse the 'starboard home'. No enchantments reach others until captured in logical ideas, shapely phrases, in sonorous sounds. The interior must be turned, like the glove that fits its hand, inside out.

First, let her rest a little to begin to remember what delivered that white-among-black infant and why she felt compelled to remain distinct and driven by an undefined purpose. She believes her Quest is over. It has only packed its capacious carpet bag. There is enough material to furnish a lifetime of books. First, she needs languages and her feet in clay.

CHAPTER 31

Loose Ends

'All existence seemed to beat with a lower pulse than her own, and her religious faith was a solitary cry, the struggle out of a nightmare in which every object was shrinking from her. Each remembered thing was disenchanted, was deadened as an unlit transparency.'

The journey back to the world happened in silence. Dick folded himself like a half-open deck chair across the back seat and soon fell asleep. Margaret perched on her cushions in front, keeping her eyes on the road. Occasionally, she glanced at me and put a hand over mine on the steering wheel. My relief at being rescued was replaced by a growing realisation that, far from their shared joy, I was now a carbuncle in their lives. The tension between them was my fault. I had pitched them into the necessity of Christian kindness, which gave them little choice but to do this onerous duty. As I pulled up in their driveway and switched off the engine, Dick sat up and put a firm hand on my shoulder.

"Now I want this understood. You *will* take your medications. Is that clear?"

Margaret winked.

"Yes, Dick," I said, knowing that I would not. Drugs would merely impair the delicate balance of this tentative return to time. I knew I needed acute memory of each and every step that I, not under any drug, would log and determine. Instead, I would control any signs of mania, cease dancing and relieve them of my sober self as soon as Dick felt assured that I had 'recovered'. Margaret looked miserable and apologetic. I hugged her before making my way to the caravan. She had prepared the bunk with fresh linen and placed a bowl of fruit and a posy of sweet peas on the small table.

After a short while, she knocked. "I need to talk to you."

"Of course you do. I promise to go as soon…"

"No, that's not what I want. Take no notice of Dick. He is confused. I think you'd better read this to understand why." She handed me an envelope with Martin Israel's unmistakable handwriting. She perched on the bunk, and before I drew out the letter, she added, "I'm very angry with Dick for writing to him."

"Why did he?" I asked.

"Oh, you know. Men are so gutless. Dick wanted to know the prognosis and whether we should undertake to get you released."

"But you didn't. I got myself released."

Margaret snorted. "Exactly. That's the point he fails to see. You'd better read it. I have never seen a more cracked hand. The man is clearly unbalanced. Look at those crumpled letters, every word crammed into a space too small. He might as well have locked you up himself; each word is a key in a lock. I studied graphology; I know whereof I speak. You'd better keep it; it is pretty savage." She settled back with a small bunch of grapes while I read the letter.

16 Cranley Place,
London SW7 3AE
July 18th 1971

Dear Canon Milford,

Thank you for your letter. Your understanding of poor Philippa's condition is truly Christian, and she and the children will be indebted to you for the remainder of their lives.

P absconded from Long Grove. She rang my doorbell on Monday morning and was very ill indeed. With police help, I got her back to the hospital. As a Section 25 patient, she can, indeed must be brought back if she absconds from a mental hospital. However, I am glad to say she is sufficiently improved to be transferred to a more open ward called Hubert Broad Ward.

> *Nevertheless, I regard her state as very serious still, and I do not look for a speedy return to normal. I say this to you lest you are deluded into a state of false hope. This means that you will have to see that the children are all right for some time to come.*
>
> *As regards P, she is a law to herself. When she comes fully to herself, she is unlikely to brook much interference—or advice—from you or anyone else. Nevertheless, you must <u>love her sternly</u> - not sentimentally and try and get her to devote her enormous psychic reserve to helping other people. We cannot evade our worldly responsibilities, no matter what mystical transports we may have experienced.*
>
> *I shall never wash my hands of P. Such an action would be a betrayal of all I stand for. But again, <u>I shall be stern</u>, not only to protect myself but also to lead her into real freedom.*
>
> *With kind regards*
> *Yours sincerely, Martin Israel.*

Margaret stood and waited for my response. I was numbed by the letter and could hardly formulate one. She had had longer to digest it and burst out.

"Mystical transports! Sentimental! Since when were we 'sentimental?' The presumption! He hardly knows us. I was furious with Dick for writing in the first place. I told him that if you'd been charged with murder, you would have had, at the very least, the advice of a solicitor and been held for no more than a few hours. Instead, you were locked up without a second opinion, and I still don't know how that happened?"

"It was Martin who authorised it."

"You mean he condemned you himself? On what grounds?"

"Calling on him unannounced deserved a Police Order in a locked ward."

She looked dubious. "It can't just have been that. What did you do?"

"I went hoping he might refer me to one of his monastic retreats where I could come down in safety. He did not ask me in or even ask for an explanation as to why I was there. But immediately, he just called the cops, and they were equally perplexed. So, I did return, more than once, to question why. I felt it must be a question of crossed wires…I probably looked pretty distraught…"

"Right now, I am exceedingly distraught myself." She flushed with anger.

I needed to calm her down. "Look. Here he says I knocked at his door on Monday. I did not need to. He was waiting for me at South Kensington tube station. The hospital had warned him I had escaped. He does not admit that because Dick would realise that it was Martin himself who had committed me. So, he lied." This exposition failed to calm her—quite the opposite.

She took a deep breath before speaking. "You escape a high-security mental hospital unaided, find your way to South Kensington unaided, and on return get transferred to an open ward unaided, and Martin Israel still says you need to be incarcerated and stern love is what we must marshal because you are a law unto yourself? Just as well you were! It stinks. The man is not only dishonest but evil. And my husband trusts him!"

"Margaret, Dick believes in authority. He can't help it."

"I shall see to that. I can do authority. Give me the letter." She snatched it from me and marched away up the path between the cabbages. Watching her stop to demist her glasses, I resolved to relieve them of my company as soon as I could convince Dick that his responsibility for me was not needed. I was being aided, but this semi-believer in God would be unlikely to believe the nature of such aid.

At supper, an uneasy truce reigned.

I left after five days of Margaret feeding me with extravagant fruit and muesli and Dick looking doubtful. He regretted his doubt but could not hide it. I kissed them both and promised a daily report. Margaret gave me the infamous letter as I started my car.

"You'd better take this. You may need it," she said.

Combe Cottage brooded. No longer the sanctuary of benevolence, or echoes of literature; it admitted me with cold austerity, void of sunlight. Although it was almost high summer, the kitchen was cold. The aftermath of ghouls and explosions had left behind a swept chill, clean but arid. It reflected my despair, which I had had to suppress with the Milfords. Their misgivings and generosity required me to make a calm and carefully contrived serenity my outer demeanour. Now, I could admit to desolation. It was over. I had failed.

On the doormat was a letter from Louie. I could not face it. How right she had been. Outwardly. The inward remained to explore after numbness was over. Somewhere, behind some twisted root, in an undiscovered cave, I must find a still pulsing revelation. It could not all have been for nothing.

The journey of high belief deposited me on this shingle of grey emptiness, sharp as flint fragments on the tentative treads with which I stepped through the opening day of solitude. What had it intended for me? Why was I led to scale such peaks of understanding? Why such joy and ecstasy? Was I as 'ill' as Martin had claimed and deluded by expectations of high endeavour?

I regarded myself in a mirror. Who was I? What did the owner of that face tell me about the woman behind it? Very little. It proclaimed a harrowing that had carved great incisions about its mouth and left the faded green eyes empty of lustre. It was a mask that had lived through hell, a hell that bruised the flesh purple around the eyes and proclaimed a return from a boxing bout. It needed a blood transfusion. It needed the warmth of a fire and the comfort of a blanket to wrap it for a long, undisturbed sleep. It was the face of a spectre haunted by an unanswered question. Why was I chosen to be wrung out like a towel and shrivelled for no purpose? What was it all for?

No answer came.

I read Louie's brief note. My father had requested my address. Louie had sought Carol's help. *'I spent last Christmas at their lovely house amongst the game. Quite special! It was good of them to invite this dreary old woman and entertain her with talk. Carol said that her ex-husband Terry knows where you are—somewhere in Somerset, she said. I now have it. I have sent the address to Raymond, who no doubt will be in touch with you. I hope the girls thrive in spite of being deprived of their father. I am sure David would wish to see them; in fact, he said as much. You will come to your senses in time. Yours Louie.'*

P.S. If Raymond should offer any financial assistance, I hope you will not be too proud to accept it. He has replied and said he intends to visit you. Does not say when.'

So much for my first contact with my mother, as stiff-necked as only she could be. Would she ever find it possible to forgive me? Being proved right was not enough?

I would take up my bed of emptiness and walk without asking any questions.

I managed to load coal and clear the Aga. I found small splinters of kindling between the wheels of the two small bicycles in the coal shed. My babies, where were they? How far away they seemed across the aeons of a separation longer than time. The whole adventure had taken not quite three months. I had traversed outer Mongolia on foot and returned to a life that had familiarity but no warmth, an outworn dream milked of meaning. Would they even recognise me as I now am? Would I want them to see me like this?

The Aga ignited at the first attempt. The small flames flickered and settled into reassuring crackling—an order of a minimal sort.

"God love! What's happened to you?"

Georgina did not attempt to conceal her horror. Bending down against the firebox, I had not heard her enter. I watched her hope of pleasure evaporate, water down a drain. Enthusiasm was beyond me. "You look leeched of life. What did this to you?"

How would I even begin? I hardly understood it myself.

"Not sure I could begin to tell you."

She bristled a little. "Well, please try. I have been calling almost daily in the hope you were back. I have to say those friends of yours, the Milfords, are not the easiest; they were not forthcoming either. Seemed to think a pot of marmalade and some leeks would see you right…"

"Pot of marmalade?"

"They descended on my emporium demanding to know where you were. I must say it was pleasing that they did not know either! Anyway, I ate the very excellent marmalade and threw the leeks away. It was almost a month ago. So come on. I want to know everything."

I did my best at a factual account. When I told her about Martin's referral to a locked ward for a lobotomy, she dismissed it."

"No. He could not have done that. You must have misunderstood. We all get people wrong at times."

"I didn't get him wrong. He got me wrong and was determined to destroy me, but let's leave it."

"Tell you what. Let's go out to lunch. I fancy a nice salad with a glass of sauvignon. My treat?"

I was not up to anything called a treat and said so.

She went to the kitchen door and opened it to the terrace. Then she put on a kettle and tapped a foot, waiting for it to deliver. "So, have you contacted the Milfords?"

"They rescued me from the loony bin. I have been with them for the past week."

Georgina shivered and distracted herself, rinsing mugs needlessly. "And? What say they about the near lobotomy? Do they believe you?"

"Margaret does because she knows it's true. Martin told them to give up on me. I would be unlikely ever to recover."

"Well, I don't think anyone recovers from a lobotomy," Georgina said comfortably and finally ready to dispense coffee. "Last time…"

"I remember. I couldn't drink it." She gave a sharp look.

"What else do you remember?"

"Everything. You hoped I didn't know you had slept with Terry, or if I did, I would not mind."

"You don't?"

"Course not. Terry slept with everyone available. I was used to it. Martin's letter also referred to mystical 'transports' as though I was on a self-aggrandising ego trip. It's what you think, too. Isn't it? That I'm an inflated egotist on some bogus mission and finding the evidence to fit?"

She was speared on the hook of its truth, enough to stop pretending. She looked at me really for the first time. "Well, to tell the truth, love, it does look a bit like that. You seem to be central to some efficient conspiracy, one that ropes in assistance with car crashes and invokes obliging Irish drunks. Things just don't work like that. If they did, the powers that be would have taken better care of you. You look like a praying mantis, with little left but eyes and stick arms, almost transparent. What you need is tender care. They might provide that."

"I'd say they have already begun. They got me out and saved my life."

I then told her about a visit from social services to the Milfords, who had tried to secure a small income to help me get the children home. "Apparently, I should have been paid child support for the past two years. I had no idea that an immigrant could simply put out paws for a handout. Social services will manage a back payment for six months. That's the legal limit. But those you call 'they' have managed seven hundred quid that I never even asked for."

Georgina managed a deprecating nod. "Well, it's a start. Better than my glass of wine."

"That's not all. You won't believe this either…"

"I'm listening, only just. No more miracles. Meat and two veg will do."

I told her about the letter from my mother and that my father was due to call.

She looked palpably relieved. "Well! That's got to be good, hasn't it?"

She desperately wanted to reduce my self-importance to prosaic happenstance. Something in me rallied.

"Guess how my mother, who said she would never speak to me again, found me? Apparently, she's now pretty pally with David and Carol, pally enough to spend Christmas with them in their new game reserve. Somehow, both of them being divorced does not worry her as much as the same disgrace for me. Anyway, Carol got my address from

Terry but guess the reason my mother wanted it? Not for herself. Not for the reunion with her only disgraceful child, but, wait for it, because my father does! My father! Can you believe that? This so-called father who has never sent so much as a card now descends? At this juncture?

Now, just tell me that a man I first met at sixteen, and never since, turning up at this juncture isn't a sign?"

"Of what?" Georgina could be slow. "A sign of what?"

"I'll try and make it easy. I am now thirty-two, so the planet of Raymond, consultant anaesthetist, re-orbits the sun of his daughter's existence every sixteen years. This time, just at the point when her plum ordinary, feet of clay, meal-to-meal existence is going to begin. Madness has run its course, and creature comforts are being rolled in from all corners of the bloody earth."

We got there in the end.

It was clearly a relief. Georgina wanted me firmly re-rooted. "Perhaps you'll get on?"

"Perhaps we will. He must be used to people out cold. Or putting out a willing vein to be rendered insensible. I'm already insensible…"

∽

Raymond gave me half an hour's warning. Enough time to light his path with directions and put on make-up. He had not changed much. His hair was greyer, girth was larger, and he adopted the bluff manner with the flair of a handkerchief in a music hall.

"Well, well," Again. Not really very well, and even he, a doctor, had to notice.

"You don't look good. Been ill?" He did not really want an answer with detail. I remained silent. "In hospital?"

"Sort of."

He did not pursue what sort of sort of. Instead, he removed his jacket and invited himself to sit down. I stood as he looked me up and down. Then he fished in his inside pocket and removed a notebook. "Which hospital?"

"I don't think you really need to know since I am now thirty-two, and you have not needed to know anything about me before. My misfortunes, illnesses, and accidents have all passed without my father knowing about any. I'd rather leave it that way."

He did not react. "Anyway, it's clear you need looking after. You look starved for one thing. Someone needs to feed you up. What d'you say to going home to your mother?"

Par for the course. Dumping me on my mother was how it was always played. Rather that, than being housed with Cruella de Val with her talons. He tried persuasion. "Look, I'll send you home; pay for the flight?"

I told him it would be for more than one, for me and the children.

"You've got children! Why didn't you say? How many? Girls? Boys?"

"Chameleons. You didn't ask. Two. Girls."

"Names?"

"Jessica and Rosalind."

He quailed a little. "Tell you what. Why don't you go by ship, get some sea air together. Do you all good. I'll pay for steerage for the three of you. Can you go right away? As soon as I get a cabin?" I admitted that there was nothing to keep me. He replaced the jacket, pecked my cadaverous cheek and departed, complimenting me on my 'snug little cottage.'

Three days later, the tickets arrived with a note. 'Windsor Castle. August twenty-seventh, Southampton to Durban. The same ship on which I met your mother, wouldn't you know! Small world. Take a taxi and bon voyage' He enclosed fifty pounds 'for the taxi and incidentals.'

༄

I collected the children from the farm. They looked apprehensive. Ros clutched a stuffed donkey.

Georgina drove us to Southampton, dripping tears. We waved from the rails, with the wind whipping hair across our faces, before going below, far below.

When the ship was nearing Cape Town, I cabled to ask her to retain Combe Cottage and continue to pay rent. By then, I was sure I would have to return, but to explain, I followed with a letter, one I had had all of sixteen days to write and little else to occupy me, being superlatively cared for. I tried to make her smile.

> Dearest Georgina
>
> Well! It's another story not to believe. Our 'holiday'. Postcards from a packet steamer. After letting the sun go down on deck, we descended many iron stairs to our stateroom, aka broom cupboard. Not exaggerating. My father was skilful; he secured the smallest space possible—a clapboard berth, three bunks roughly two feet wide, like an ossuary for slim skeletons. Luckily, we are all slim. Only one lay like a corpse, two restless wriggled, which shook all three: no port hole, no natural light, a fluorescent strip which flickered. Space on the floor for one at a time to slither into slacks- they are slacks when on a ship, nicht? 'Slacks' conveys the casual white linen elegance that drapes against the rails and strolls about a deck. Trousers or jeans are utilitarian. I forgot to pack slacks.
>
> Pretty average food in 'sittings'. Ours was the third since our cabin was in the bowels; the usual gammon with pineapple, something unidentifiable with custard, blancmange perhaps? Anyway, the children ate. I drank. In my state, it was unwise. They are semi-excited. The 'semi' is probably the cupboard cabin and a mother who isn't in the mood for quoits. So, whoopee, I look forward to a fortnight roaming the decks to make sure Jessica does not see how far she can lean over the rails with only her feet hooked under. The sort of thing she thinks up, as you know.
>
> Rest? Wot rest? It will be the rest of the scoutmaster on the annual camp. I had visions of a cabin on the port side with a private view of the waves and at least a shower. Our allocated ablutions facility is down a passage with a queue. Ah well! What did I expect from a man renowned for meanness? And so to bed. One at a time. I wait outside

while they undress, then slip under a shelf too low to read. C'est ne pas going to be much of la vie! That is the view before the real glory begins.

In the morning (we've hardly cleared the channel), I feel rather rotten; my eyes are watering, my nose blocked, dicky on my feet; I weave my way to the loo, and when I get back, Jess says, 'Mummy, you've got lipstick, everywhere. Why did you do that? All those spots?' I take a look in the mirror, and guess what? I am a perfect illustration from some medical text; you know those livid skin eruptions that illustrate what the tropics might have in store? We are not yet at the latitude of Northern France. I look highly contagious. Okay, this is sent to polish me off. I have survived starvation, insanity, exhaustion, and some sneaky bacterium has come for me? Okay, right. Do your damnedest.

I send Jess to find the ship's doctor. (If there is one) 'Don't tell him what I look like. Just say I need to talk to him. Otherwise, he might not come.' I sit crouched on my bunk, shivering and febrile, wondering what the hell happens to the children if it's fatal. It looks fatal, it looks angry, and it itches. I am hardly robust. He comes, this other ship's doctor. This one's for me, but I feel too ill to register much, except he looks smaller than a doctor should and too young to expect any experience brought to bear on diagnosis. He takes one look at me and says, 'Stay where you are.'

"I am not wearing a bloody balaclava or wielding a gun!"

'You have measles,' he says. 'You will be highly infectious. I don't want anyone to see you or cause a major panic amongst the dowagers or parents.' (See, a sardonic promise from the off!) Oh great! How can a respectable adult, or even an un-respectable one, get measles? He pulls out a thermometer and takes my temperature. It's 104! 'Okay,' he says. 'I'm taking the children, and let's hope they're not yet infected. You stay here until I come for you. It'll be a while.'

I lie on the bunk with my nose and eyes running and feeling sure I am going to die of a child's disease. Anyway, you must admit between us (you and me), we've been efficient because here the children are, corralled on a ship due to be met by my mother. They won't need rounding up or transporting by anyone. I probably drift off. I feel dire, probably delirious. Sometime later, he returns. He helps me to stand and wraps me in a dressing gown and a mask. I look like I am heading for surgery or the black and white minstrel show, with those black eye holes and a slit mouth.

We go on a circumnavigation along, around, upstairs, downstairs, in my lady's chamber, his hand on my shoulder.

'Here we are,' he says. 'Sorry it took so long. I have never had to use this. It's the isolation hospital. It needed a lot of clearing.'

Come with me and let me show you my new stateroom. Huge and filled with flowers, vases everywhere, smells of lilies. Against the only flat wall, a state 'lit magnifique', almost a double with crisp white sheets, a posy on the pillow. He pulls back curtains against a semi-circular wall of window where the wake churns like milk and gulls weave their zigzag watch, beady-eyed, wings immobile held by thermals and the hope of kitchen slops. This is the stern, all of it.

'This is all for you, this deck. It's been roped off, so when you're better, you'll have it to yourself. Hope you like it?' He might have been a proud bell-hop on his first assignment and very anxious to record my delight. He had gone to enormous trouble.

'Spectacular. Where did you get the flowers?'

'Lucky that. Last night's welcome for first-class passengers meeting the captain. I pinched what they will only ditch tomorrow. It smelt rather musty from all the boxes and life belts that are usually stored here. Best bit...' he led me to a steel door and opened it, 'your private bathroom, and the water's fresh, not saline.' Huge claw-footed slipper bath with handles and fluffy towels, yeah!

So here I have been since day one. Luxurious bed, long baths, and private deck around the stern, meals from first class on trays and my very own different angel of light, this ship's rather different doctor. He comes at night and reads to me since I can't read; in fact, he forbids it. Most of the day, I sleep while the crew supervise the children. They swim; they produce paintings and get, he tells me, 'as brown as hazelnuts.' They also get bedtime stories after the teeth brushing and are even kitted out in fancy dress for crossing the line. No, they have not asked after me! They are having a tailored cruise, and I need the rest earned by two years of frenzy. Doctor's orders. Witchdoctor?

Gulls and porpoises keep me company, and I saw the spout from a whale, lying among pillows, kittiwakes, smaller gentler gulls sometimes and then when we got past the bulge of the west coast, the distant speck of an albatross that flew itself like a motionless kite attached by a thread. I should be in an E.M. Forster novel, were it not for the skin, which would beggar his capacity for graphic description. It goes from bad to worse, but I shall not dwell on that except to make a greater hero of Robert, the doctor.

He is Welsh, and I have to admit (when I recovered an ability to take things in), he is perfectly formed. I can't describe his features save to say they fit together to compose the kind and laughing face of an almost boy, flushed, high bones, slim neck—a mid-sized man with a straight nose and thick brownish hair. I can tell you more about his hands, as once he has removed his shoes, he climbs onto my bed; we interlace fingers, and then he opens a book and reads. He chooses the menu. I can lie back, close my eyes, and together, we plough the sea with words.

He is not too conspicuously Welsh (none of those look yous) except when the cadences of poetry call it out. He comes only to inject me with Dylan Thomas and Yeats. Then he administers those I've never heard of, such as R.S. Thomas, who writes of the 'untenanted cross' and the contradictions inherent in faith. Have you ever dreamt of a man who seduces with the reading of poetry? You should try it! Somehow, Robert knew that the untenanted cross might dress the deeper wounds of betrayal.

And in the foreground/The tall Cross/Sombre, untenanted, /Aches for the Body/That is back in the cradle of a maid's arms.

Magically profound; it cuts my misery down to size!

I know you are in danger of switching off, so listen to a lovely man read these marvellous lines thrown out to catch glistening fish spindling in our wake. I have never felt so comfortable with anybody, ever. He really is the beloved brother I never had. We share the same sinews.

'Now as I was young and easy under the apple boughs/ About the lilting house and happy as the grass was green, / The night above the dingle starry/ Time let me hail and climb/ Golden in the heydays of his eyes, /And honoured among wagons I was prince of the apple towns/And once below a time I lordly had the trees and leaves/ Trail with daisies and barley.... Down the rivers of the windfall light....

I have always loved Fern Hill, but that lilting, gentle voice re-awakened my truest love, words and those that shape them. I could stir and drink such lines to sink me in a swoon of pure worship. Imagine writing that!

After Robert had gone, I realised that the call of the Sceptred Isle—I can't call it Great Britain, too prosaic, nor is it just England after recent saviours in three Celts! — was just that: literature and the finest poetic landscape anywhere. I must return because I know that love, the bond between words and landscape, is the deepest and most trustworthy one for me and always has been. I had to put to sea to remember it, and to meet a doctor to heal the wound of that other doctor who seeded and abandoned me to my mother and now sends me into kinder arms. Strange? Perhaps not strange at all. And you think my faith in an orchestrated life fanciful?!

We dock in five days, and my mother will be there. She called to tell me to disembark at Cape Town. She will take me, tight-lipped, to Swaziland, the last of the Protectorates where I have never been and co-habitation with Max! Home is no longer home, yet it aches. I am now riven, divided from Africa as from her. Neither knows what they mean to me. Only the pain of absence defines that. 'We can never really leave', my grandmother once said. I understand my grandmother now.

God knows what happens next. But this interlude was God sent, for sure.

Love P

Believe it now?

Georgina replied by ship's cable. BLOODY HELL! Stop. I BELIEVE, stop. LUGUBRIOUS HIPPY ATTENDS YOUR NASTURTIUMS, stop. NO IDEA WHO OR WHY stop I MAY END UP HATING YOU! Stop. COMBE SECURED.

I had failed to offer her an address, but the cable was delivered by a man on a bicycle in a country I did not know—Swaziland, to a house where I had never been via the ship's Bursar. Nothing ever gets lost.

END OF BOOK TWO

BOOK THREE
VERSAMEL*

* Afrikaans: Gathering Together

Disembarkation

'Every limit is a beginning as well as an ending.'

When you have been labelled as mad, or in the sneaky and allegedly kinder phrase, 'mentally ill,' there is no way back. It is the ultimate tar and feathers and nothing peels it away. Kind friends will appear to forget or overlook it, praise your 'recovery' or your 'courage', but the stain sticks, and so too the nervousness that 'it' will return. 'It' is believed to have autonomy; its victim is powerless. The idea that its 'victim' might have determined the travel and found ways to navigate gains no traction. Such a suggestion is dismissed as spurious justification to escape the stigma.

The preparation for this travel you, reader, have witnessed. The savage consequences you now know. My 'aberration' of being in need of incarceration had lasted a little over three months, and the knowledge of it was due to disclosing my need for help. Not for my condition. I was never confused or out of control, never took drugs to get there or to get back. 'There' was a realm in which time was condensed and thought was powerfully causative. Instantaneity and orientation to it took time to learn, elevation and descent took time to master, and the control of thought required anticipation and censorship of the unthought thought before it broke into the surface of the mind. Any thought had instant consequences and attracted interference, both benign and vicious, sometimes almost lethal. There was no interpreter or map. To learn the ways of this realm and its language of creative thought, like any other new world, one needed to immerse oneself entirely.

To do that, I had to leave the world of my children and their time-bound needs, routines, and schooling. Not to travel to a foreign country but to absorb the presence of that country, one I had believed lay 'below' but increasingly saw as intermeshed with and underpinning the one they and all others shared: the beautiful mirror world of time, seasons, continents, seas and the love that permeated it. I knew that all I needed was solitude and the protection of that solitude until the orientation and integration were secure. Not for a moment did I ever doubt that I would return, able to live in both worlds. But I also knew I had to return the way I had left, by slow degrees, taking steps home, each step secure and available. To lose any rung would be to sever one from the other and truly lose my mind.

Many, like Christopher Bache, the author of 'Dark Night, Early Dawn', have ventured into this world with the help of LSD. He took controlled forays with controlled dosages, his wife as a guide and emergency nurse for the violence of vomiting, giddiness, and sometimes terror. Isolated from any demands, he set aside days to venture forth, and to recover from. Each of his sessions took him deeper and more expansively once he had learnt how to control the orientation. When Bache read of my travels, alone and while still navigating the world of time, he said it was a miracle I had survived.

It was the instinctive strategies of survival, dancing and falling, that enabled me to shut out the confusion of answering to two masters: time and eternity. Movement to internally played music and, when threatened by confusion, surrendering to falling, tempered the nausea and giddiness and shut out the world's clamour. But they afforded all the excuses others needed to label me mad. Nobody stopped to ask why I fell voluntarily onto concrete, like a child into a swimming pool, and rose unbruised.

Martin Israel had encouraged me to believe he knew where I was travelling. He was the only person I could ask, believing he knew what was needed and that he had the influence to mediate for a sanctuary. Through his enigmatic and abbreviated references, as well as his letters, he encouraged me to persist and to trust.

His betrayal stripped me naked.

I was lost, alone, endangered, and believed to be mad. The removal of my brain, or the sentient part, was in his gift, and he had exercised that power unilaterally and without exchanging a word with me or anyone else. In doing so, he broke every medical injunction.

When I escaped, in the nick of time, his response was not to question his judgement but pettily to wreak revenge by writing to everyone he knew to strip me further.

He and what he did was a looming mountain that has cast its shadow ever since.

The life I returned to was a garden denied the sun for most of the day. What could be planted and grown, fostered and supported, had to bear that shadow in mind. The perplexity rendered whole areas unfertile, even reading books that echoed what I had learnt. Or any temptations to return to the insights first pricked out by Terry's Chinese boxes. All had to be packed away. What might life have been like in fullest sunlight? I shall never know.

The abrupt change in Martin, the 'spiritual mentor,' whose encouragement had underpinned my willingness to trust the unfamiliar and often terrifying journey, was inexplicable. I cast about for every insight that might help me understand him. A friend of Margaret's, a doctor who had met Martin Israel a few times, believed that he was a damaged and repressed homosexual, terrified by a woman to whom he found himself susceptible. His sacrosanct celibacy was suddenly punctured. Rather than examine the puncture in himself, he saw her as a veritable Jezebel, tempting all to sin. This made sense in many ways; it explained his refusal even to talk to me; it explained his desire to withdraw and shun. What it did not explain were all the letters to others, letters which made his own fear sufficient to sever any friendship and destroy any hope of help. If he believed me a Jezebel, I could understand his personal rejection, but not the wider destruction, let alone the call for the lobotomy. The world is full of Jezebels. Why would one more matter? As an explanation it held water, but not enough.

A gardener must make do with the available acres. The legacy of that betrayal and its darkness left, forever, a question. Did that punitive strike and bewilderment corrode my intended future? Or was my survival alone enough? In any event, what was left to me proved rich in earthly ways: a new family and new skills required, new interests pursued, and seemingly the consistent help from my interlocutor. Daimon is …

…always with you.

I was not abandoned. Comfort came through children, animals, trees, music and miracles of timing. But, after the glory, the light was muted. The question remained, but survival took the top tier, standing room only.

Bare survival was inventive with the chances that remained. It returned me, force majeure, to the 'meat and two veg' existence Georgina had asked for, and perhaps my reader may welcome it as a respite. I had to re-learn how to live at time's pedantic pace.

CHAPTER 32

John: Toil and Spin

'The remote worship of a woman throned out of their reach plays a great part in men's lives, but in most cases, the worshipper longs for some queenly recognition, some approving sign by which his soul's sovereign may cheer him without descending from her high place.'

Louie's fatigued welcome on the docks in Cape Town was half-expected. Her first view of her grandchildren elicited little more than a mild interest in how different they were from one another. Together, we all boarded a train and chugged across the Karoo in a compartment we did not need to share.

I suppose I have to, have to, have to. I told you so, told you so, told you so. I knew it, knew it, knew it, went on clackety clack for hours. The train bearing us away from the Cape mountains and its sumptuous surf chanted Louie's vindication. The dusty scrub of the arid Karoo gained speed past the window as she sat motionless, her sharp nose framed against the light. The girls, quelled by her chill, sat miserable, unable to ask for anything, sidling apprehensively to the loo and edging apologetically back to their seats. Not even a new country could dent their recognition that we were unwelcome. How could it have been otherwise? My condition made me a supplicant. The measles spots had faded but were still there, my body still a transparent mantis. My mother felt obliged.

I ventured no openings and said very little. Disdain was her variation of a QED. She had known it would happen. How many times had she proclaimed ruination? What had I expected!? Now, I was including her in my rightful punishment by landing, yet again, courtesy of my father!

Ndaba's joyful welcome is a flaring warmth. "Ow. Isn't they already grown, darling? What beautiful children. Miss Jessica looks just like…. but Miss Ros is too thin, darling. She must eat. I can make her eat." She rattles on, pouring welcome from the jug of her limitless affection for me and, therefore, mine, burying Louie's reserve like prunes under cream. Natural to Ndaba, that halleluiah is fully conscious of the atmosphere of duty but no warmth. Ndaba and I regain one another within a split second. Together, we will silently navigate around my mother, as we always had. Ndaba has baked a cake, and cinnamon biscuits are cooling. She has remembered the child she crooned to sleep five empty years earlier. It is Ros's birthday.

~

The silence between me and Louie had become almost solid, but hers was now extended to Ndaba, liberally peppered with my guilt. Louie's house was a modest clapboard shack in a stand of trees, with walls that permitted overhearing her rebukes to Max and explanations to Ndaba. I watched Max before any journey, polishing his glasses with an ironed handkerchief and then returning for something else, just to keep Louie waiting. I watched her conceal her irritation because I was watching. I had no financial means to relieve her of my dependence and the imposition of children she had hardly met. I realised that Louie was never easy with children; it was not just my childhood that asked more of her than she was able to give. I was burdening her with two more. She did not deserve any of it.

I was still physically weak and slept too long. I had returned without joy to offer or energy to contribute. Without either, I had no place in a country that simmered understandable resentment; whites were not really welcome; it showed in every gesture.

Louie, oppressed by Max, who has stripped her of self-respect, who feeds off her small income and who still expects Ndaba to iron his shirts and still shouts for tea, has burdens enough. She does not need my clear eyes observing what she can only just bear without them. Her long days she spends reading at the Casino's spa waiting for wealthy

Johannesburg women to appear for a massage while their husbands are golfing or gambling, a world she had always despised. No medical employment was available, so Louie serviced the already spoilt while Max played at conveyance law and sometimes joined the punters at the Casino in the valley. He seemed to be enjoying the privilege of being white in an impoverished black country, but her boredom and misery were palpable.

Only Ndaba had grown easier. It was her world of large women laughing on their way to church and mielie porridge under the blue gums with friends. Louie's instinct to secure Ndaba's future had been right.

It was time for me to take up my bed and walk. Where to? How?

No sooner was it thought than the means arrived to do.

As always, Terry's arrival in Swaziland was unannounced. He rang from the airport.

"I haven't come to stay. I just came to see you were all right and bring you the last of the house money to get you back to England. Georgina told me where you were, and some of what has happened. You asked her to hold on to Combe?"

He brought nougat and crystallised fruit from Georgina and a letter.

"I paid the bills, but this looked private. Who's it from?" Terry asked.

"Nobody you know." Judith's precise script no longer held its magic, but I breathed a faint echo of my idealistic passion, all in that meticulous hand I had once so longed to receive.

He shrugged and went off to hang a swing for the children. I had bought rope and a seat. Terry did have the knack of appearing when needed. I opened the letter.

'Well, Philippa! What have you done!?' it began. 'I confess I am at a loss and have been ever since our last encounter, which gave me three days of dyspepsia, but nothing prepared me for what I have now received from Martin Israel. I thought you said he believed in you; no, not believed, but positively encouraged! Personally, I did find your experiences worrying, so I did write to him. (Did I tell you I attended *one of his retreats at Ammerdown just to get some sense of the man you esteemed so highly? You did, didn't you? I found him a strange, tight creature but in public an impressive orator; an odd contrast)*

Now, he tells me to steer clear of you. In no uncertain terms! You will be a 'malign influence'! You are seriously deluded. You suffer from an acute form of schizophrenia, and you will be unlikely to recover! What am I to think? I don't know what to think, although Dorothy certainly knows what she thinks. Wildness is not D's cup of tea. How has this happened?

I briefly wondered whether a calm spell on a farm with friends of ours would help, but in view of Israel's warning, I cannot take the responsibility of inflicting you on anyone. I regret that because I think you and Alison would have got on. I was less sure about her husband Wray, but that is now by the bye. Setting 'malign' aside, you are strong meat on a good day. This does not ring out as a 'good day'!

I thought you should know about this and perhaps you will reflect and benefit from doing so. You were always our 'awkward customer' but 'malign' I never anticipated. Nor do I believe it!

I am hopeful this will not be a final farewell.

Yours, Judith.

Was there any limit to Martin's determination to close off all doors to kindness or help? Would any crutch be kicked away as soon as he spotted it? What had I done to deserve such publicly broadcast slander? Was this a 'spiritual' man's response to what he called illness? That smile rose to answer. That unspeakable triumphant smile as he closed the door on hope and summoned a brain surgeon.

I showed the letter to Terry who whistled. "Jeez. What the hell caused that?"

"I hardly spoke to him long enough to be judged incoherent, let alone operated on. Now I am out; he has turned vicious."

"I always thought he was after something, and it stays with me. You—or both of us—were the bearers of whatever it was."

I had thought that, too. I did not say so. Terry was easing out, and I did not want to apply any adhesive 'we' to anything.

He stayed two days. Louie's forbearance had reached its limits. She had loathed him on sight. His easy confidence and long pigtail screamed for her outrage, this Lothario who had broken my marriage. She could take no more. She was brusque when she spoke to me and ignored him, never so much as glancing in his direction. But I had a way back! Terry had sold his house; Victoria had bought hers, and I had the fare for a ticket. We knew our liaison was over, but his coming was both timely and generous. Nothing about Swaziland appealed to him; he couldn't wait to depart.

Half-heartedly, Louie talked of me staying and teaching. It was not what she or I wanted.

~

I left the girls with Louie and Ndaba to wear green checked gingham and go to school in Mbabane on a bus. When I had managed employment and a roof I could finance, they would join me. Meanwhile, they had the gift of my childhood, Ndaba. She would make lamb chops and chips for them as she had for me and laugh that merry laugh. "Ow, darling! You can never taste the shape!"

~

Although Combe Cottage awaited me high on Batcombe Hill it was to Georgina's cluttered shop that I returned. The horrors of that time of drowning, visions, and evil were fading, but Uriah Heep still rubbed his hands in the whitewashed stone, and my dreams lay desiccated on the sunlit terrace. I could not bear to remember how much faith I once had in myself or how much belief in a purpose now dissolved. Its poignant promises had fled. Their loss was like chewing dry bread.

Chin up.

I accepted an offer to be Georgina's minion, polishing brass and sewing chenille smocks to earn my keep. She was brisk and determined to set me on fruitful endeavour. She strengthened me with sharp instructions and beef tea, preparing me to face the world. I took lessons in makeup and appropriate clothes; she played the maiden aunt, unsuccessful herself but fully aware of what the world looked for. 'Transports' and 'conjectures' had to be brought to heel if I was to prove work worthy. Who was I to argue with an ex-editor of Vogue?

∽

A diffident young man was sitting at Georgina's kitchen table when I returned after shopping, choring and posting cheques.

"P, this is Pete. It's due to him that your garden blooms and your terrace is clear. He's been maintaining your cottage at Combe." Georgina pulled an 'I should have told you, and please look appreciative' face. I was. I did. To prove that I had forgotten the word 'lugubrious', I drove him home to a nearby village.

"Will you come in and meet my parents?" he asked. It was ungracious to decline.

Perhaps I will be as bold and bald as the powers-that-be were— as they lost no time in taking me by the circumstantial scruff of my neck— and say, 'Reader, I married him.' Not the constant gardener, but his father, called John, in a V-neck sweater and highly polished shoes. An ex-marine always buffs his shoes, even when his cavalry twill pants are too loose. After Georgina's coaching I am developing the sartorial eye.

I never intended to. In fact, I never asked Pete to undertake my garden, which obliged me to drive him home. He had bridged the divide between the old and new life; by turning my sod. That fits, a bed ready for new planting. It was through Pete's prompt borrowing of Georgina's garden fork that I met this future husband of my new life, and rather sooner than decency will approve.

Pete's mother, Audrey, was an anxious woman who kept a tidy cottage and a tidy garden that needed a dustpan and brush for wayward leaves blown in by an inconsiderate wind. She laid out the best china and was welcoming in a pinched, anxious way. I perched, she hovered. I had a sense that unexpected guests were rare. His father was smiley and interested. He asked what I did for a living. When I said I was looking for a teaching post in Biology, he rose and said, "I'll just make a phone call. You never know."

When he returned, I had a job.

"You can start after the Easter holidays."

"No interview? No references?" I asked, amazed, and yet not. Serendipity was now a handmaiden to my narrow path.

"Mother Superior took my recommendations for you on trust. That, and talk of a teaching alumna of St Paul's."

"But you don't know me!"

"I am sure we'll have time to remedy that," he said.

Just enough time to bone up some basic biology, start nibbling on botany and find a home near the school before the term began. It had so quickly snapped into place. I felt like a rat that had sniffed and not even nibbled before the trap sprang. My tranquil re-entry to time's world was as amplified as it was to madness.

ࠔ

The wooden bungalow in the spacious garden was a prefabricated eco house with large windows overlooking fields, a wooden apron terrace, and two bedrooms. Utilitarian after the charm of Combe, but simple, affordable and bathed in light. The landlord, a retired naval commander with a regulation-trimmed beard, was nervous when I said I had children.

"Not sure I want that," he said, "children can be noisy and uncontrolled."

"Not if you control them and tell them what you find difficult to live with…?"

"You wouldn't mind?"

"Your ship, your standards. More likely to obey the captain than me."

"What a sensible creature you are. Very well. Never thought of it like that."

His name was Gooden, and he was a good'un. So, I moved in.

ࠔ

Before the term began, I received a visitor, a policeman. He removed his helmet, took out a notebook and asked my name. I gave it. He asked for my previous residence. I gave that, too. Then he held out the mouldy remains of a rust-coloured cloth, ripped in places.

"Is, or was, this your bag?"

"Good God! Where was it found?"

"In a field by a farmer. It got snagged in his harrow. He found your passport and handed it in."

I remembered the field and the clothes I removed just off the M3. It seemed years ago already.

"I lost it about… months, many months ago."

"Where did you lose it?"

I told him where but not why. I also told him there was money in it.

"There is. A pound."

"No. It was ten pounds."

He handed me a flattened, cracked purse from which I drew out a note. I suggested he came in. With a thin blade, I separated ten notes.

"Well, I'll be damned!"

"No. I'd say you'll be blest. You and an honest farmer. Want some tea?"

"Why not?"

We had tea. He told me the exact route he had travelled to find the owner of a mouldy bag, a passport and a pound: via Combe Cottage, its neighbours, Georgina and finally to an eco-house in a distant field. Not a tassel left unbound on the fringes of a new life.

∽

The first term commenced. I taught polite girls of moderate ambition and supervised hockey practice. John—Director of Studies and History— and I remedied our lack of knowledge over sandwiches and the gear stick of his car during lunch hours. There was a distant Italian belvedere with stone benches overlooking fields of sheep where we explored one another's lives, his of longing to stretch and mine needing to shrink. He was easy company and his pleasure in stories rewarded their telling.

Audrey joined us twice a week, the days she manned the school bookshop when her trite disapproval and censorious summaries clogged free-flowing exchanges, which halted and then fell silent. There was no need for him to trot out the 'my wife and I don't see eye to eye' line. Their eyes never met. It was a marriage dipped in oblique and tentative suggestion met with bitten tongues. The contrast in John when she was present was like seeing a snail shrivel in brine, a hare freeze below a raptor. Alone with me, his enthusiasm for ideas flowed, for places, for the travel she would never consider; his longing for a wider, spontaneous life stood out like a thirsty dog's tongue. He was hungry for a life already slipping out of reach, heading fast towards its 'best before' date. He was fifty.

His nascent hope reminded me of what it looked like. I could feed it with ideas, stories and laughter. I never meant to offer marriage. It was Audrey who pushed him out the door. The light in him she was determined to douse. I knew all about it. I had surrendered to just such a marriage, which laid itself naked before us both, inescapably. How could we not be bonded by such an unspoken revelation? I did try not to see it. I certainly tried not to show that I had.

Warmed by his enthusiasm, affirmed by his attention, I was inspired to tell good tales of Africa, which he had always longed to visit, but I was not in the market for a husband or a lover. John became a warm friend, for we were both alone; then he became a desperate friend in need of a refuge. Having, like David, rejected any physical affection for decades, Audrey now hammered at his door all night, just as David had. Sleep was rationed and increasingly denied to a man whose day began at six and seldom closed before ten. The contrast between his arid, tight cottage with its perfected rituals and my hut in a field was food and wine for a starving, exhausted man. Such starvation always hooked me. What else had drawn me to Martin Israel but his narrow, imprisoning existence?

Your evangelism in relationships was always your undoing. Who were you to correct the narrow choices of others?

I have a sneaky suspicion it was not me but you, doing the correcting!

☙

In the depths of a dark, windless night, there was a hammering at *my* door. It must have been about two, and I was deep asleep. I opened it to Pete, who did not step in but blew in, his duffle coat billowing behind his frenzy. He had walked ten miles. He slammed the door behind him.

"I want to know. Is it true? You have to tell me the truth." He paced back and forth, wiping the back of his hand across his mouth and stealing glances at me.

"Is what true?"

"You and my father?"

"What about your father?" He stood behind a chair, holding it as a support and a shield, nodding emphatically.

"You are in a relationship with my father? How dare you?" There were two parts to that accusation. I took them separately.

"Not sure how you define relationship? Yes, we're friends, I'd say close friends. But I have no intention of running off with him if that's what a relationship spells to you. As to how I dare? That's really none of your business. I am not answerable to anyone for my friends." Something in his assumption that I owed him this explanation in the middle of the night outraged me. He was nineteen and more than inconsiderate. I expected a howl on behalf of his mother. Instead, he slumped down on the chair, his shoulders twitching, gazing at the floor.

"You have no idea what you've done. I have loved you for years… well, two, maybe longer. Why do you think I looked out for your garden? Just to be near you. How did I know about Georgina? Because I watched you. I have watched you everywhere, and now I don't know where to turn…" A little in me wanted to laugh. Another to protest. A better part refrained from either.

"Pete. How could I have known? If I had, what could I have done about it? But I am so sorry, so very, very sorry," He glanced at me from below a lowered brow and half smiled.

"Yeah, ridiculous. That's what you think?"

"No. I don't think that. I think it is deeply sad, and I am honoured and should be. I feel miserable for you and believe me, I know what it feels like to love the wrong person without hope."

"Really? You? Why would you? You could have anybody?"

I was not going to pursue either my history or my condition.

"How did you hear? About John and me, since we're not in what you call a relationship?" He shifted uneasily and took time to answer.

"Not my most honourable act, but I read a letter that Georgina wrote to the guy I am doing a painting job for. A bloke called Clive. She seemed to think you and my dad were an item. There must be a reason she said that. I came to find out if it was true."

"You never thought to ask your father?" He looked away and shrugged.

"My father is not always candid. It would have embarrassed him if it was true and made him angry if it wasn't. Then my mother would have got involved, and all hell broken out."

I made him some tea. He became more cheerful, almost as though amusement was gaining an upper hand. I was feeling less amused by Georgina writing about me to a 'bloke called Clive.' I kept that to myself.

"Classic," Pete said. "I make a prat out of myself and now have to tell my dad I've gone all oedipal on him. Fucking classic."

I thought John would be appalled.

"Well, luckily, you don't have to kill him."

"Dunno," he said, "I'm tempted."

I had to get rid of him. I had a day's teaching ahead.

"He's still paying your fees? In that case, I'd wait."

I led him to the door, and the young pretender to my heart walked away in the dark. I felt for him. I could still remember being nineteen, with its swelling agonies of unrealistic dreams. Poor boy. Poor John. How would he take it? Audrey, his mother, had not been mentioned.

On course to be a diligent breadwinner, I then found myself upended: I was pregnant. It was the best of news; it was the worst of news. Squeamish about liberty, I decided John did not need to know. I wanted nothing to impel any decisions he might make. But I was determined to have this baby, alone if it turned out that way. The first of my children conceived in love. I began to plan a return to Ndaba, my port in every childbirth storm.

When John did decide, after many consultations with a Franciscan friar —he mentioned a brother Jonathan— that loving was better than duty and that a leap of faith had simply to leap, my swelling belly and he were aligned in a 'no way back'. He slipped into the wild adventure of opprobrium, rejection and poverty and submerged under the wash of events; holding his breath. Before the girls returned, I took him to Florence, his first 'abroad', where he was too numb to enjoy it. We would never have another chance.

The girls returned, reclaimed their bicycles, and changed schools, beds, uniforms, home and country.

Six months later, a child was born at noon on a cloudless midsummer Sunday. The shared hilarity with the obstetrician stitching me and the midwife who had delivered a new perfection was as though we had all had laughing gas. Georgina and John shared champagne in a pub opposite the hospital. So began the resurrection to a new life.

It would prove a life played on 'repeat' that drew in all the cast, some to celebrate, some to scream oaths and beat breasts. She was named Juliet for her right to dream; even the doctor who checked on us a day later said, 'I have examined your baby, and I find…. her… perfect.' I think it was the calm, the clear open eyes, the look of contented familiarity that checked the world against the other she clearly remembered. In case Juliet would condemn her to inevitable tragedy, she was also called Emma, after that pragmatic Austen heroine whose management of affairs left no time for tragedy. Both names were soon contracted to Jem, for, after the depth of despair, she was that above all.

Commander Gooden accepted three rather than two children

and tolerated the bicycles flashing past his windows on the way to a village schoolroom, an ancient golden-stone building with a ringing bell and free milk. Outwardly, we looked like any production line family. Inwardly, John struggled with the financial need to provide for Audrey's new flat, and his worry about her caused him intermittent gloom. I, in blinkers, refused to look down, determined to juggle many balls in the air on virtually no money since I was again unemployed and temporarily unemployable. But I was truly joyful.

I had regained both purpose and the world.

Mother Superior was grieved, but she was civilised. She and John agreed he would have to resign. Their beloved and esteemed Director of Studies—almost an honorary nun— would leave in disgrace after a lifetime of safe, tweed respectability. In the twilight of a career steadily marching towards an assured pension, he now found himself responsible for a new family and unemployed. He was delighted, equally overjoyed, and terrified.

At this juncture of impending destitution, David arrived.

Realising that poverty would not drive his ex-wife back to her mother, he suddenly appeared chequebook in hand to support his daughters. The impulse was impromptu, or perhaps he had spies? He never clarified his timing.

His timing answered the call of necessity. It always does.

What he had baulked at was now freely offered. He wanted access to those he now might lose to another father. I had never wanted him to lose the girls or to deprive them of him, so I accepted his offer. and reciprocated by asking whether he might be godfather to this new serene infant: a time to heal wounds and unify the new with the older family.

I truly believed that had to happen. If David could be included and the injury of that wretched divorce erased, it would enrich us all. The three girls would have two families, one in South Africa and one in England and move between them. David could continue to live under canvas with Carol, and John and I would offer the stability of schooling and dull routines. It would meet the needs of everyone.

∽

The christening happened at Hillfield, a small Franciscan friary high on a Dorset hill, a home for a few brothers but also for the itinerant tramps that wandered in for a modest meal.

Brother Jonathan in his brown habit, with its rope belt, had been the detached counsellor for John, racked by the conflict of leaving Audrey. After several penetrating cross-examinations, Jonathan expressed the view that John's marriage had died almost at its birth and survived as a husk of habit. "If not now, when?" he'd asked.

He offered to be the child's other godfather. After the simple ceremony in the chapel, we took tea with the tramps with their winter scarves about their faces. A couple waved to greet John, who had a habit of occasional whisky-with-tramp that passed his door, a small defiance of Audrey. Juliet was handed from one to another; her cheeks stroked by rough hands and speculative forecasting.

"Oi'd say she'll be a killer. Whaddya say? Look at them blue eyes. Looks roight through yous, doesn' they?"

'Tis the gift to be simple, Tis a gift to be free, 'Tis the gift to come down where you ought to be, and when we find ourselves in the place just right, We'll be in the valley of love and delight.'

Georgina, in her pert straw hat and pale linen suit, was Juliet's godmother, sitting like a heron over a pond, watching fat, brightly coloured fish swim past. Surrey had never stretched to monks or tramps, let alone at the same table. David was disposed to welcome John. He joked about the woman being passed, 'Long on memory, short on logic' was David's wrapping of me, his gift to John. He offered me quite convincingly.

The christening was of a wider inclusion than just the child to worlds none of them had met before.

∽

John's mother was the next frightening challenge to face. 'This will kill your mother,' Audrey had said with certain delight. 'Just wait until Ida hears…' So trembling was John at the prospect of killing his mother that he took a train to Bristol and a bus to her flat in Clifton rather than trust himself behind the wheel. He let himself into his childhood home to find his mother already in bed. Perching beside the old woman, he told her that he had left Audrey and not only that; he had just fathered another child with someone fifteen years younger. Ida looked at him with a gentle smile and then snuggled down preparing for sleep.

"Now I can die happy," she said. "Just fill my hot water bottle and leave me to enjoy being happy. Pity you left it so late, but happy, oh so happy…"

We had not yet met.

When John returned, he told me of a curious peace that had descended as he rode the bus up to her flat from the station.

"A man got on, and I don't know what it was about him, but suddenly, I knew it would be all right. He was very tall, I can't describe him, but he seemed somehow other-worldly. He just stood, strap hanging. We didn't speak, but before he got off, he smiled the loveliest smile as though to reassure me. I just knew my mother would be okay about it."

"That was Terry," I said. I knew it was.

Years later, Terry called on us. Yes, it had been. He had left Florida for a snatch visit back to England. To bless with a smile a man trembling with apprehension and pass his old parcel with easy affection. He rode that bus for a reason.

☙

There was a notice, and I noticed it. Martin Israel, newly priested, was due to conduct the Good Friday service at Sherborne Abbey. I would go. John would stay home with the children, and I would be conspicuously sober near the front. Martin Israel would see a perfectly controlled sanity that belied everything he had done to destroy me. I wanted him to face it. I needed to face him, so I arrived early.

There were a few on their knees while he was preparing in the vestry. I sat. The stained glass threw colour across the flags and gradually crept up the columns as people filed in. I did not look around. The soaring vault concentrated my impulse to confront him as though to enclose the great crevasse that remained from Martin's destruction. I was shaking at the thought of seeing him but determined to beard him in his new sheltering lair.

I knew something significant would have to happen. It had been a long time since I had darkened any church. Round me flickered the flames of school chapels, Huddleston's exhortations, the nuns of St Mary's, Heli's early hastenings to Mass and all the gaunt hanging Christs of the convents. Marna was there too, tilting her chin, sardonic eyebrow raised. Marna always came when I was tempted to be solemn.

The Christian presence throughout my life breathed, both repellent and comforting. The conflict both pushed and pulled. So much of loving— Heli, Judith, Brother Paul, Louie weeping at Easter always— yet that same summons had destroyed most of them. I had never quieted its call. It was still there but muted, yet I questioned. Was it an arrogance in me that found it impossible to embrace it fully? I sat wrestling with memories and glancing at the Stations of the Cross candle-lit along the aisles. Those, too, I remembered rather differently now, as the badly painted portraits of searing events that should burn holes in stone. Not hang as tokens on its surface. The route to Golgotha was internal; how superficial were the Church's rituals! No wonder Dick floundered; its promises of love substituted with words and gestures; oft-repeated and emptier each time; year in, year out.

When Martin entered, a cold wind swept past as he bowed to the altar. How small he was! His fussy gestures resurrected a chilling fear. Resolve barred its entry. I knew he had registered my presence. Solidly, he avoided looking towards the right.

"Let us pray," he began. There was a shuffling onto kneelers, but I continued to sit. My prayer was an internal one. Let him at least acknowledge me. I still live. I exist.

The service lasted for six hours, and not once did he glance in my direction. I began to enjoy his angry bondage and hoped for a crick in his neck. A fatted calf of a restored woman banked against the obedient parish was enough to slice an Abbey in half. How could I have endowed him with authority and written poems to this tightly bound, waddling midget?

As the congregation filed out slowly through the west door, I joined the queue, waiting to take his hand.

"Hello, Martin," I said, holding out my hand. He had anticipated me. He smoothly refused my hand, stretching his for the next in line. His eyes slid past me; his tongue flickered across his lips; he permitted not the slightest twitch of recognition. I was invisible, a large vacuum that had sucked out the air.

"He didn't even recognise you," a voice behind me said. I turned to see Judith and McEune leaning eagerly together. They had been directly behind to view the encounter. I had not noticed them. McEune's hauteur was mixed with triumph. Judith was perplexed and quelled. She tried to speak, but McEune put out a cautionary hand.

"He certainly *did* recognise me," I said with some spirit. McEune sniffed and turned to acknowledge someone else.

"We sat right behind you," Judith added as if bestowing a gift.

"Well, then you got a good view of a priest unable to repent or make his peace. So much for your Easter message." I felt a sprouting contempt for all three of them, bonded by their pleasure. They had sat, knelt, and stood for six hours to get their ringside seat for the momentary joust. God worked a miracle of clarity for each of us. From which I was still numb but growing angry. Religion as it had ever been! Marna, where is thy sniff, and hell thy victory?

McEune firmly led Judith away, hand on her shoulder.

As they descended the steps from the Abbey terrace, Judith glanced back. I offered a token wave. She looked mortified as she hastened after her tall keeper, sliding towards Cheap Street on ball bearings. McEune had not changed, not one iota.

I had not seen Judith for five years. Not since the stormy seas had tossed me against the rock of Martin Israel. Yet they had risen like ghouls from the crypt to witness a clean rejection, nod and evaporate.

I returned home to my new life. The previous one was now signed off. Today was my thirty-fifth, my half-mast birthday. I had a new baby waiting with her frank and open eyes, and we would have cake for tea.

∞

Audrey's new flat's rent and her allowance had first claim on John's modest income. Employment was beneath her, and she had no intention of seeking any. Our unmarried state's disgrace meant John accepting any employment. From the Oxford graduate Director of Studies, Head of History, he took a demeaning post teaching remedial mathematics and supervising sport in a school that had no academic standards, an institution for excluded and uneducable young thugs expelled from other schools. They were wealthy, louche, spoilt youths, resistant to remedy, and arrogant about their deficiencies. He was also made a Housemaster in a confined, modern villa, which required us to share a small living room with twelve pairs of trainers and beer cans aimed to clatter into a cold hearth. After a few weeks of breastfeeding in a chill boxroom, I decided it could not continue.

John surrendered the honour of being an unpaid janitor, although not the teaching. Our family of five was suddenly homeless. I remembered that card slipped across at the end of a talk. 'If you ever need work…" and drove to Dorset.

Barbara Warley, Headmistress, as good as her impulsive word, appointed me as a Housemistress, together with three children. "Just don't let the Bursar see you all together. He has a fit spinster in mind. He doesn't need to know how many we're housing. If he finds out, I'll be in trouble." She accepted Jess as a pupil, and Ros would go to the local primary school. I would escort a crocodile of uniforms down to breakfast and back after supper, my days filled with sorting laundry, pairing socks, and reading bedtime stories before lights out. Jem, just walking, toddled between groups of girls and climbed stairs in a great Edwardian house, rather like the nursing home for the wounded that had provided for me at the same age.

The future had written our present. I was now in Dorset; John was in Hampshire, living as a lodger on the farm called Nutley that belonged to the Alison, whom Judith had considered might house me and with whom I might have 'got on.' After Martin's warning about my malign influence and the Easter spectacle of a symbolic 'stoning', Judith had stayed away, and all contact ceased. Now, she found herself seated opposite me at Alison's tea table.

Judith had never known about John, another liaison, nor a new illegitimate child. Like a teacher called, without warning, to summarise an essay she had not read, she was severely disconcerted.

"I can't understand what it is about you. Everything gets laid before you. You do seem to attract special privileges, sneaking into my friend's farm without me even knowing! Clearly, 'malign' does not seem to worry providence!" She peered through those large blue eyes as if to take a second reading on what should not have happened in a just world.

"It was John who sneaked, if that's the right word, for being introduced by Alison's son Mark. Nothing to do with me."

"I find that hard to believe."

"Well, ask Alison."

Alison nodded her agreement but seemed happy to let Judith's indignation have the floor. I decided to throw kindling in its path.

"I would have once, but you should be getting used to a perfect orchestration that needs a piccolo on occasions. It happens to be true. You saw this place as a possible refuge for me. I didn't deserve it. You said as much. So, instead, it was offered to John. Alison and I never met until John had been here for weeks."

Judith sniffed and gazed out of the window towards the sunlit downs, where a group of walkers justified her gaze. Alison gave a look that suggested I might throw the floundering Judith a raft. I did my best.

"If anyone introduced me to divine possibilities, it was you, Judith..." She turned her large eyes upon me and waited. "Just look at the whole arc. My mother goes from Uganda to a school in Staffordshire. Later, you get a first post at that same pin-prick school to teach religious studies. Then you and Dorothy head for the penance of St Anne's in Natal at precisely the same moment as I do. I get ignited by religious studies. You admitted no one else did. Then you head for Winchester, where you teach Alison's daughter, so you end up here, at Nutley, as John does. But not through any direct interventions by you. Or me. Isn't that what bothers you? The unlikelihood of all those linked events? Why *do* they bother you?"

Judith raised a defiant chin. "Perhaps what bothers me is your reading of them. There is always chance. Improbable things happen."

"Call it chance, if you like. Not sure the name matters. The resolute improbability is more interesting, and it never gave up. Chance was pretty persistent. Clearly meeting Alison was intended, despite you not co-operating in God's plan. Still, you were right about one thing: Alison and I do get on. She seems to like strong meat."

Alison laughed first, and Judith managed to smile. I could see it still troubled her, but she had no idea why. Those who cite God are often troubled by the thought of His creative presence, perhaps because He refuses to be confined by their expectations. A mad woman locked up one minute has no business being forgiven and fostered the next. Not a long enough penance has been served. Vengeance is His, they all say, but penance they do like to hang on to, and apportion selectively.

Judith and Dorothy kept to a diet for their delicate constitutions and took dramas in small doses. Reassured by her friend Alison's sanction, Judith now began to call on me, bringing her own sandwiches, to hear the latest instalments of wicked disgrace, which I offered as though they were drafts for her perusal. She drove away contented. Dorothy was never disturbed by knowing of them.

I was learning to navigate through other people's cautions and their fear of those they claimed to love. The great cataclysm of my life, the one that had promised me a 'speaking part' in the great play, had gradually become merely a diverting travelogue. I was learning that my adventures only appealed to others when offered in light-hearted anecdotes of self-ridicule. No pairer of socks or folder of laundry could hope to join the mystics or offer raptures. Yet there were cattle prods occasionally to remind me that I did not have to settle for appearances.

This play has a small cast plucked across the globe. All have deep reasons to meet and re-meet one another. Some appear fortuitous to signal the future; the itch of a perplexing past drives others. One of the latter was Dick Milford, who drove over to see me without warning, alone and without Margaret. I was reading in the large rear garden when I heard the echoing bell amplified through the silent house. I found him on the doorstep, very distraught, clutching papers in one hand.

"I came to say sorry. I am so very sorry." Tears were coursing down his cheeks. I took his arm and pulled him through the house and onto a bench in the sun. He kept wiping his eyes and attempting speech, so hesitantly I imagined that some dire news had choked it.

"Dick, what is it? What has happened?" He did not answer but took my hand, tapping it on his bony thigh as though to force speech and comfort with it. Three or four minutes elapsed before he turned to look at me, with desperate eyes searching mine. I had no idea what he needed from me.

"I betrayed you when you needed me most! I had to tell you that I now know you were never mad. Can you forgive me?" His plea was heartrending, although the betrayal— if caution is betrayal—was long gone and forgotten.

"Oh, that! Dick, I always knew that Martin Israel had got at…"

"No. Martin Israel was not the only reason, although I heeded him far too readily. It was that essay you gave me and the blow-by-blow notes of your experiences. I had not really read it until the other day. I brought it to show you. I was checking through my diary and all the facts fitted, dove-tailed my own. You knew exactly where you were and when. Nobody mad could do that. I misjudged everything and endangered the very sanity I doubted…when I think of how close you came to destruction, I grow cold. I am so very sorry." Dick's shoulders slumped; remorse sat bleak and abject.

My swelling love replaced the relief that it was nothing more. I laced my fingers through his; he looked at me, managing a regretful half-smile.

"You once spoke of the atrophy of the heart by the intellect. I'm an old tortoise, aren't I?"

"Dick, there is nothing to forgive. I always knew you could only see one side. I could see that because I had access to both." He nodded.

"That's exactly it! I see that very clearly now. You were very kind to me, all things considered. The Epiphany Philosophers' massacre was my doing. I suppose I wanted them to see the side I couldn't…"

"The fact that you wanted to was enough."

He squeezed my hand. "Margaret knew, didn't she?"

"Knew? Perhaps, but she just believed. She'd read of others, Cathars, Theosophists, Sufis, so she took it on the wing. She had been softened up to believe." Dick rose slowly to his feet and put an arm around my shoulders.

"I'm glad I came in time. More importantly, I'm glad you loosened all my laces. I am better prepared now."

We both knew what he meant. I walked him back to the car my not-madness had gifted them. He fluttered his fingers as he drove away. How lucky we had been to be seated together at a table for that first supper.

Luck had nothing to do with it. Recognition is a better word.

☙

John and I met up during the school holidays.

Audrey remarried after three years and released John from her financial dependence. She moved into a solid four-square house as an efficient housekeeper to a wooden husband. When a stroke fells her, it will be John sitting at her bedside until her end, her second husband never opening the curtains.

Jem was two when John's mother, Ida, died. We had found a warm friendship that took tea together in Bristol and swapped reminiscences of very different lives. She rejoiced to dandle a new child and played Scrabble with the older two. Ida had never owned a house but squirrelled away a small nest egg. She bequeathed us all her savings: fifteen hundred pounds. It provided a deposit on a Victorian terraced cottage that lay on a railway midway between Dorset and Hampshire, which made meeting easier and somewhere to be together in the holidays.

∽

Tisbury was a scruffy small town with the kindness of pavement talk, a popping in or passing wave. Another child was now on the way. It was not good news, but I owed life some surrenders, and this ill-timed child was the dues I owed to two others who were, by me, denied life. That was in the past, but she came for the future. What was due to happen hence, would need a duplicate family. The future knows best.

No sooner had we moved into this very basic, bare-boarded home opposite an ugly garage when the bell rang.

"Delivery for you, mam." The driver was using his weight to prop against a great and clearly heavy box, unbalanced on the step.

"Must be a mistake. I have ordered nothing." He pulled out an envelope.

"Asked to give you this," he said waving to a companion parking up the road.

'Nappies need an Aga, but since you have no space for that, this is a good alternative. Love Margaret.' It was a solid cast iron Rayburn cooker which would dry nappies and simmer soup. Brand new, very expensive, and Margaret and Dick could not afford their christening present to heedless poverty and a new child.

The new child, another daughter, Olivia, was born exactly to the day, the same age difference from Juliet as Rosalind was from Jessica. Life reprised; shall we do this better this time? Olivia was to commemorate my twelfth night and was named to be beautiful and self-sufficient, although she was always called Kate. Beautiful would have to wait; she was covered with eczema.

"A baby born with eczema will have beautiful skin later," said the midwife. She was right about that. I was right about the self-sufficient. Kate always lands bottom in butter, as Marna would say. She sails through life and a following wind finds her.

Our chaos of too many children in a narrow house was outdone by a similar family living opposite. Jini was a biblical Martha, an effortless mother managing seven, so many children that I never did master either their names or their ages. Her kitchen was a steam of simmering soup, breadcrumbs on boards, discarded shoes, large mugs of strong tea and talk was of books and ingenious ways to make stretched ends meet. Mark, her husband, quietly passed through with cameras a dangle; boys dipped in to snatch food or ask for something while she juggled her painting, her abundant bread making, and told me fascinating stories about rural Ireland, from where they had recently returned. They had tried survival and homeschooling near the seashore of Cork before, like me, taking refuge on a railway line that would relieve the pressure by getting them all within striking distance of schools.

Jini was abundant in every way, in generosity, irreverence, and laughter. She smiled all the time at everything and, like me, was struggling to find time to write. Daughters with heads in books drifted past; the oldest son thought he might join the army. 'Of course, if that's what you'd like', she said imperturbably before mouthing 'ain't never gonna happen' at his retreat.

It was reassuring to meet another woman, casual about motherhood and mad enough not to care where the next meal might come from. From her carelessness arose the brilliance of all her artistic children, but the theatrical talents of Ralph and Joseph Fiennes had not yet manifested or the romantic aspirations of my much younger two.

"You mean we lived right opposite the dishiest boys in the world, and you never told us!" said Jess after seeing Ralph in The English Patient.

"Ralph, I recall as being rather a taciturn fifteen, profound in silence. Joseph was about seven. You were eleven. Their and your potential was not yet obvious or pressing."

"Still. Jesus! What a chance missed!"

What we did inherit from the Fiennes family was Anita, their temporary home help, a sharp-featured, angular young woman who moved in for Kate's arrival. I went into labour almost as soon as she appeared, so I had no time to evaluate the wisdom of Jini's kind donation of her domestic angel. Anita drove me to the hospital, returning home to look after my tribe and call John at Nutley. He drove straight to the hospital, so he was entirely unprepared for this legacy to our ménage.

After the excitement of birth and the anxiety of a further extension to feed and educate, John drove home exhausted. The house was quiet when he returned but for tinny, quasi-Eastern music behind a closed bedroom door. He knocked. The music continued. He knocked louder, and the door opened a crack to offer a woman stark naked, draped in chiffon scarf ribbons. The dance of the seven veils was underway. She peered at him while attempting decency with inadequate means.

"I'm John," he said, looking away.

"Oh, you're the husband. Howdy do," she offered a proffered hand, clawed through the crack. "Sorry, you just caught me. I'm practising for my audition. If you give me a moment, I'll get dressed."

Anita had clearly caught the virus of theatrical ambitions and was auditioning to join a strip club. Nannying was not her forte. Nor her intention.

Instead, I assigned to her our catering department where her efforts were so successful that they kept the children anywhere else to scavenge or go hungry. I knew when Ros was back from school by the thump of a bag thrown through the door; then the door slammed as she scarpered before being dragooned to help with the unleavened bread, as tough as a dry corn husk, which was Anita's speciality for the school lunch boxes.

"Not even the ducks eat it", said Ros. "That's cos it sinks."

Ros, in those days of sleepless nights, was the true helpmeet. She wheeled Jem in a pushchair to the laundromat, loaded the machine, and waited in the churchyard for the wash to cycle, pulling back the toddler piled high with folded laundry. There were few outings and no treats, so for the Queen's Jubilee, I made an effort. The two older girls would go as mediaeval pages to a tiny Queen Victoria. Two days before the event, Ros was stung between her eyes by a bee, and her face swelled alarmingly, her eyes reduced to slits.

"I can't go looking like this!" she wailed at supper. "I have to have a mask or something."

"You'll be the star, Ros," said John.

"Yeah, course I will. Shining all twinkly… What d'you mean?"

"You can now be Miss Juby Lee. You'll get first prize."

We all fell about. Ros slammed out.

☙

It took four years to establish separate survival before we sought to manage co-habitation. We needed work that would keep us all in one place and under one roof. An interview at a school which sought both a mathematician and house-parents seemed possible? Invited to a joint interview, we were questioned separately, John by Headmistress Pandora, who disconcerted him by slowly unbuttoning her blouse as their talk proceeded: Opening her box, a button at a time.

"I am sure she was unaware she was doing it." John said, "It's quite difficult being persuasive to a bra."

Professor Barraclough, a philosopher from Oxford, dallied by talking to me—they file in, this camel train of thoughtful philosophers—he assisted Pandora's distracted headship. His questions ranged widely; his interest hooked out Involution, a morsel long neglected. It was good to remember I once did more than pair socks and unwisely, I expanded. He listened. He asked many questions. Finally, he said

"It's been very interesting, but a word of warning. If you talk like that one of these days, you'll get locked up."

"I've already been locked up."

"Well then, be sensible. Keep quiet and get married. Just make life a little easier for yourselves."

To foster our future, we bit through reluctance and got married to make life easier for everyone else.

The magistrate concluded the ceremony as if by rote: "I now pronounce you man and wife, and I hope you'll both be very happy…" as he turned to face the assemblage of children ranged from two to fourteen and added, 'as you obviously already are.'

Then he hastened away, his gown lifting behind.

What value do you place on this humdrum period?

Challenging but never humdrum in the living. Looking back, I suppose it occasioned a large dose of modesty! I encountered a world of bare subsistence without the inflation of grand designs. The proximity of the Fiennes family, equally impoverished, showed me that grand designs had a life of their own and were not halted unless you let poverty conquer them.

You joined the world driven by necessity, certainly. Anything else?

I encountered the kindness of the future that had anticipated everything needed, from employment to lodgings and schools, as well as the affirmations from friends loving enough to encourage.

And in the present?

Perhaps more empathy, more fellow feeling. I met people occupied in simple routines: the man who ran the allotments, who had travelled no further than Shaftesbury and who disapproved of green peppers. 'Never seen'm before! Better plantin leeks,' and the shoemaker who could copy a Victorian picture of velvet boots after a lifetime of stitching soles. 'Passing fair? Yes?'

Yes, I did need the ordinary saints.

There is no other kind.

That's what I learned. Indelibly. A necessary lesson for one who had lived in her head, in dreaming spires, and over-estimating the importance of culture and intellect. There are no ordinary people.

CHAPTER 33

Incubation of a Writer

'It would be a poor result of all our anguish and our wrestling if we won nothing but our old selves at the end of it.'

Life had chivvied and turned its pages, revised and repeated. At intervals, it paused for reflection. One such pause was after the birth of Kate; with calm, confinement and a new baby came the prompt to remember: to weave life into words, to make art of small episodes as I was bidden to attempt again here. That time in Yucatan with the grief-crazed Rosie who had lost her baby now haunted me, undeservedly content with my snuffling child in her Moses basket. The contrast demanded expression. The depth of misery that would never leave, guilt never assuaged, now pressed its face against the breast of a mother renewed. I could not imagine it. How would one live with that pain? It was an imperative; to imagine it and to dedicate that imagining to the girl who had wept on my shoulder in Merida, drained dry under that lazy fan. I wrote it for her.

A Shadow in Yucatan, written as a poetic narrative at breakneck speed, was dedicated to 'the nameless girl, a troubadour of sorts and for others that remember the eclipse of joy' as a gift from a mother who now knew just how deep that pain was. That Rosie might never read it, but I cast it upon the waters in the hope that she might stumble upon it and know her tragic tale had been transformed into my first stab at art.

The work wrote itself. Poetry finds its own expression, and its cadences musically shape themselves. I found my first call not so much to write but to open myself to words that would bind emotional sympathy and give it permanence.

It was the bridge we and George Eliot had laboured to build. George Eliot once said: 'Writing is just opening a vein to let empathy run.'

Philosophic realism made life the source of wisdom, not study. Professor Cassirer had tried to tell David that, and sixteen years later, you came to grasp what he had meant.

'You won't find love in a book?' Cassirer said. No, what you find is the love to write one.

The work was not long, but it flowed as fresh as spring water that threw sparkles of light and fluid undulating depths and, once completed, detached itself, like a placenta, with no memory of how it came into being. The writing about birth happened as it does in giving birth. The amnesia of both joy and pain washed its creation away. The story of Rosie's loss winds back to itself in a harrowing yet also comforting way when the grieving mother, a hair-dresser, gains her first view of her son and discovers his fate while cutting his adopting mother's hair.

Rosie's baby, never before seen because he is hidden beneath a sheet and borne away from the delivery room, is placed into her arms for the first time. The unaware adopting mother pays her bill and confirms his identity by reading aloud from a letter Rosie had herself sent to a nameless mother for her son. After that, Rosie carries her beloved baby to a pram outside the beauty parlour and watches him wheeled away.

It was after this that she fled to Yucatan; this unbearable encounter was what brought us together on a beach.

'I could not trust myself not to haunt the house where he now is and that I now know where to find.' Rosie had said.

The Wisdom of Solomon was quietly re-enacted, the rending of a mother's heart for her child's sake.

That was the first story that found a kind of completion. The other story, one that began at Marna's funeral, revisited me for a second instalment, as John and I walked home after hoeing vegetables as the sun was setting.

Stories demand shapely endings. Here is what happened next.

Red Hot Pokers continues….

On an early summer's evening in a Wiltshire village, John and I are trudging home through unseasonable heat. We have been working our allotment high on the hill, and the cool dark of the village pub proves irresistible. We prop fork and spade at the door and go in for the pint, the Ice-Cold-in-Alex pint, and bear away the brew to a far table in the gloom.

The glory of a cold drink and a dark seat is all that occupies us. Exhaustion precludes all talk.

Gradually, a voice penetrates. A tall man in a hat, turned obliquely, is talking to the publican.

"No, well...That's why Ah'm yere. To give talks. Ah tell you, you English haven't a clue. Apartheid isn' what you think, but Ah can unnerstan that. Y'ave to know the country..."

"What part exactly?" the publican is all for deflecting the sermon with facts. He is busy polishing glasses.

"You wouldn't have heard from where Ah come; a small place called Harrismith in the Vrystaat."

'Harrismith' electrifies—a name from my deepest dream. The family farm was near Harrismith, a dusty tin-lidded dorp of unpaved roads, remembered for sherbet twists with liquorice straws brought back to Maweni by Tommy and produced from his pocket as he unloaded on the kitchen table.

After that, my ears strain for every word. I have become too English to interrupt, but that voice and that place summon a yearning as though water is being poured into sand. Ignoring the publican's indifference, he goes on to elaborate that he is on a mission.

"Honest, I can talk, an Ah'll go wherever... Enny school, enny church, enny social club, maybe even the Universities. Ah have to make you buggers unnerstan. It's not as simple as you seem to think..."

His innocent belief that he would be heard, understood, and given the respect of an honest question had fuelled his mission. This simple farmer was travelling unescorted through England to communicate his belief that 'seppret development for 'Blecks' was in their best interest. He was earnestly sincere.

"Ah mean look. Ah'm a Boer, an Afrikaner Boer, but do Ah look lark a man who would hurt a person? Does a sjambok come to mind when you see me? D'you think Ah could deny my bleck farm boys anything they needed? Or their three wives each? Or their kids? We unnerstand each other, but they are not used to our ways. Tribal people need to obey; they obey their chief, and if he says kill, they kill. They need time, time to grow up. In their own homelands, they will do that; away from their chiefs, they will develop. There will come a time for voting an all that, but it's not yet. Ah just thought if Ah could make you British unnerstand...."

I want to weep. I had been that man once. My family had never shared his politics, but I know his soul. I also know that it will be invisible to his audiences. I can bear it no longer, and we rise to leave. As we pass him, I say

"I was born in Harrismith."

He spins around and looks at me with eyes that Afrikaner farmers have, a shrewd, penetrating blue created by looking for rain, sizing up a salesman or searching for beasts.

"I ony wish I could b'lieve you, meisie," he says and turns away.

It was a stab to the heart, and I trailed home, swallowing salt.

∞

Every sound of Africa crowds my mean house with its contrivances of England, its poverty of carefulness, its crazed jugs of wildflowers. Deep in my kitchen, a servant on her knees hums below breath to the baby on her back; cocks crow as they do all day and a rusty windmill turns. In the distance, women with loaded heads call to one another on their way to their kraals to light fires. That guttural accent has resurrected a world of smoke, of sun, of laughter. He has transported me home, and I am sick with longing.

I also see in his disbelief that his rejection is already absorbed, already forgiven and his courage to continue to confront it. He cannot afford to believe that I should prove his countryman. He needed implacable stoicism to continue. In that pub with its Toby jugs and its horse brasses and that indifferent publican, I might have toppled his resolve.

The following morning there is a knock at the door. He stands there, his hat in his hand.

"Lady, forgive me. Ah'm really sorry. Were you really born in Harrismith?"

"Yes"

"Then can Ah come in? My name is Kirk... Kirk Bezuidenhout."

He steps through the front room to the kitchen, places his hat on the back of a chair, and sits down. He is in no hurry to speak but examines me and the room as though inspecting a new cow stall. Its bare boards suggest little else.

"Since you're from the Vrystaat, you'll know it's a koffee for me. Ah take it strong, bleck."

"And where's my peach brandy? Any biltong?"

"Ah'd have brought you some if Ah'd known. So, what family?"

"Van den Bosch."

"No! Serious? Which branch?"

"I heard about two boys close in age, maybe twins, played polo..."

"The Mandy twins, the same family, would be older than you. How old are you?"

I was glad he asked.

"Their younger cousins are now jus as bad, wild as assegais...straight into town on Saturdays to blow their pocket money and send up the dust... riding always bareback even though they've got good saddles. Never train a Van den Bosch, but they all know horses. Which farm?"

"I don't remember the name, but I do remember that it had a waterfall over a great high rock and a huge cave behind the fall. I only remember yellow porridge with butter and brown sugar... I left when I was very young."

"Maweni. Maweni Heights. Beautiful place. You cawn't remember ennything? You don't remember the stroompie where your family tried to cultivate fish, and all they got was otters instead. You don't remember the oaks they planted? They did well, but my God the water they wasted on trees... nee, but water they had plenty.

I had a sudden imperative question.

"Kirk. There is something I want to know. Did you ever hear of a murder on the farm?"

He sat back. He looked at me reflectively, obliquely, immobile. He took out a handkerchief, rubbed his nose, and placed it slowly back in his pocket.

"Meisie...Missus. Ah wouldn't have brought it up if you hadn't. You mean the murder of your...?"

"Great grandmother."

"Himmel God! What can I tell you? What did your grandmother tell you?"

"Nothing. She never mentioned it." He sits back and meshes his fingers behind his head. Then he reaches into his pocket and hesitates.

"Ah should ask. Do you mind if I smoke?" I shake my head. He draws out a curled meerschaum and slowly fills it from a leather pouch. I push a matchbox towards him. He puffs in silence until the draw satisfies and replaces everything in his pocket.

"Well, it's not surprising she never mentioned it. You know her little boy saw it all, a child, maybe he was three or four, standing in his cot in the middle of the night. He must be your uncle, ja? He was the chief witness."

"Yes, that I did hear. They hanged them, didn't they?"

"Yes, poor bastards."

"Were they thieves?"

"Are you mad? Thieves didn't kill in those days. They might soon if things get any worse. In those days, thieves just took. No, they volunteered..."

"What do you mean?"

"They drew lots, and the two with the short straws had to do it. Kill her. For the sake of everyone."

"They thought she was a witch?"

"She was, but not the kind you mean. She was the cruellest woman anybody ever heard of. She tortured her little girl, your grandmother. She ties her with cotton thread to a riempie chair every morning after breakfast, and after two hours, if a thread is broken, she ties her up again. If she cries, she's beaten, but not with a stick, with a rotten fish, or a thorn branch on the soles of her feet, so she can't walk. She never leaves evidence. It was the same with all the farm workers; she tortured them all... Her husband was not like that; he was a kind gentleman but weak and mos frightened of her. If anybody tried to stop her, she just got worse and more devilish. He spent all his days walking the farm and crying to keep away from the sight of what she was doing, especially to his little girl. She would never let him take her wuth. After he died, the Hex had no protection, and that's when they got rid of her.

When your grandmother came to fetch her child, it took three people to uncurl his little fingers from the bars of the cot...He was so petrified he couldn't let go. You must want to know why I know all this?"

"Tell me."

"Because Ah was the newspaper boy. Ah was eight. Ah'd never sold so many papers or taken so long to get around the district. It was a terrible thing, but the poor buggers were only doing a public service. They buried her on the farm next to her husband, and you know, nothing would grow on her grave except aloes and red-hot pokers, but on his, until she joined him, there was sweet grass and mimosa. You should visit sometime. Anyway, thanks for the koffie."

He rose and took both my hands in his.

"You know, that murder probably saved you. You should be grateful. Even your uncle pleaded for the murderers at the trial. After the killing, they turned around and saw the klein kerel watching them, sitting up. One says to the other, 'Now we must kill him.' The other says, 'Nee, I cannot kill an innocent child.' So he takes up a blanket and lays the kerel down. 'Sleep well, little Master' he says and covers him with the blanket. Your uncle told all that at the trial. Makes you think, doesn't it?"

Kirk shrugs and looks deeply into my eyes. Then gathers up his pipe, checks his pocket, and holds out his hand.

"Now Ah'm off to talk to something called the Chapter. It's near Salisbury Cathedral. Sounds like part of a bible, doesn't it? They won't know what's hit them, a Nederlandse Kerk Elder with a hat! I won't be back this way, but it was good to meet. It's a long journey...Totsiens."

I watched after him, sloping back up the hill with long strides, still puffing.

Ja, Kirk, it's a fact. You have to know the country.

∾

That was the first story that began at Marna's wake and now lassoed an itinerant missionary to rope me back. That was before I fully appreciated that we are all created by stories to be their characters. We live so that they might find some endings and begin anew. My renewed life was just beginning; this was a reminder that nothing is left behind. The wisp of old smoke ignites a new fire. I met my deeper longing and my loyalty. It made me shed tears for Marna and all of us scattered by divided loyalty and severed lives. Her hated mother was stabbed for understandable reasons, but her son was traumatized forever by that liberation from a sadist. Her secret fuelled her emphatic refusals to be cowed by anything. I met her afresh and admired her even more.

The future pulls up the past to create the present.

Am I a quill being shaved to write? Or is writing the only thing remaining that will harness the discipline my wilder travels abandoned? If so, it was never a choice.

Only a choice you had already made, one lit by the candle of George Eliot that gutters in an alcove. Not even this story has ended; it merely asked you to turn pages and place a marker in the future-past. A new tense is being born. Linear time is a Mobius strip: in is out, and the past curls back to become the future. There is only time present.

Is the rest all an illusion?

Memory would be a better word.

Of the future?

The parallel alternative. Imagination creates and marks pages for re-use. With a higher perspective, you can see both equally causing choices.

Was the murder of Eeltjie Diederika as tidy as he claimed? The swift dispatch of a sadist?

Story crumbs for pecking at! Wait for the full loaf and see.

CHAPTER 34

Hedley Haynes: Skips and Reclamation

'...if everybody tried to do without house and home, and with poor eating and drinking, and was allays talking as we must despise the things o' the world as you say, I should like to know where the pick o' the stock, and the corn, and the best new-milk cheeses 'ud have to go. Everybody 'ud be wanting bread made o' tail ends, and everybody 'ud be running after everybody else to preach 'em...'

"Wouldn't you rather live in my barns?" said a silhouette in the doorway. The shadow was stooped, tentative and it wore a flat cap. He was framed against a white self-hire van steadily disgorging the contents of one house into a much smaller farm cottage with two bedrooms for the six of us. Marriage had helped. John now had a new post as Head of Mathematics at an academically ambitious school, and we had to move. We had sold a solid house with an ugly view and bought an ugly cottage with a beautiful view of rising hills and punctuating elms. I was wedged against a door jamb since the couch refused to budge. He removed his cap before speaking in an educated, quavering voice.

I did admit an interest in his barns. "Your barns were the reason we settled on this cottage, just so the children could get out of the rain."

"How many children?"

"Four at the last count."

"Lord, that's brave. Well, you should have my barns. Plenty of room."

"We could never afford them," I said, mezzo forte across a divide of yards, unable to move to see his eyes.

"I'll make it possible," he said. He named an absurdly low figure for four derelict barns, prime development cuts on the corners of a concrete farmyard. Ripe for plucking by a developer with limitless funds to carve up and make more.

"We'd first have to sell this, even to find that, generous though it is…"

"I'll wait," he said. "Hedley Haynes. Take my card. Get in touch." He wedged the card in the door frame. I had not admitted that the hope of his barns had already made enquiries of the adjacent landowner.

"Oh, the world and his wife have been after those barns. The owners are not interested in selling" she had said. She had been right; the owner preferred to give them away and chose us.

He waited for eighteen months. No contract had changed hands; nothing had been signed. He refused three offers of almost triple his requested price.

Hedley held an auction to dispose of vintage car parts presently stored. Bidders for bits of metal came from all over the country, and since we had the only nearby telephone, Jess ferried bids from afar for rare gems like copper headlights and Morris Oxford wipers, sixty old rare bicycles, five petrol pumps and a Delage chassis. After bidders had borne away their precious metal, all that was left was a pile of lumber tossed in a corner.

"What am I bid for the wood?" asked the auctioneer.

"A pound?" I called.

"A pound it is, to the lady at the back."

We moved in with a wheelbarrow, a pickaxe and a sledgehammer. That pound bought oak panelling, handsome lintels, a Maple kitchen, and a pine floor. So began the decade of construction. With the gift of a home for which to scavenge, to rise early and by which to keep a waist trim and muscles toned. Now, construction would learn new laws of gravity: levels, plumb lines and mortar mixes. Matter will shake its fists in vehement protestations about its non-existence!

ಎ

First, the Vernacular Records Society asked to be permitted to visit, measure, and photograph before conversion desecrated this historic dereliction. I watched as they tramped about with a camera on a tripod and examined the dry-stone wall, which was its only beauty, covered with yellow stonecrop and moss.

"Good God!" shouted one and leapt back.

"Watch out. It's an adder! Stay clear..." The malevolent head was coiled back to strike; the diamond markings looked livid, and its black tongue flickered rapidly. Adders are repellently muscular. We backed away. I hoped it was no omen.

"In all my days surveying waste ground, I've never seen one." said one man. "Find them in Cornwall but pretty rare in lush Somerset. It's very odd."

The creature was making its winding way back below the wall, leaving a sense of menace—I shall be back. Would I ever feel comfortable about a serpent? No longer frozen with terror, my recoil was as clear as the adder's. Would I always be conscious of the snake in my Eden?

∾

A barn dance in October kicks off the celebration of space in the light of flares and the loan of straw bales. An accordion, two violins and a caller come in the owl-dark night. 'Swing yer partner, now dozy doe, and once again and around you go'... People arrive, obscured by the black, and beer is spilt as Ros cooks pitta bread pizzas on a charcoal grill and melted butter greases chins. Jess joins the guests to compete in the Gay Gordon with loud whooping after a jar too many of rough cider. She rather fancies that builder's boy with his floppy lock of dark hair watching her. A sudden influx from the Dorset Opera Company —who invited them? —spatters German protests from a formidable Brünehilde at the use of a field for essential relief. 'Ich? Nein. Nie kann ich ein Feld verwenden. Danke schön, gehe auf.' (I can't ever go in a field. Thank you. I'm off)

A pit and a portaloo would be the first excavation. The torches pick their ways away down the lane as the instruments fall silent and the stars reappear. This will be home and matter will assert that whatever I believe about its existence, it would begin to matter in the narrow shafts I now would plough through the solid resistance of clay. This home-to-be already wrapped a shawl against the shiver, and the moon smoothed out concrete milk churn stands and a collapsed roof, our family seat-in-potentia.

During the giving of the first gift, I was immobilised by a heavy Chesterfield. The second began when I was asleep and visited by a detailed dream. In it, I listened, in a bare-boarded room, as a solo cello played a romantic sonata next door. I could not see the player. It might have been Schumann or Brahms, but one never heard. All three sonorous movements played before its closing cadence when I awoke. As I was no musician, there was no way to capture this coursing composition. It lingered for days in fragments of melody. I had never known a string player nor could I read music, but the Bach cello suites had always been favourites. The dream concentrated the call of the cello. I mentioned it to John's landlady, Alison.

"I have a cello. It used to be my daughter's. Would you like to borrow it?"

Between mixing concrete and laying bricks, I began to learn to play the cello with cement-shrivelled fingers. Five-year-old Jem asks for a violin for Christmas. We manage a Chinese quarter size complete with a bow and a case. In four days, she is picking out carols pizzicato and then with the bow. The cellist merely bridged the silence until the real musician's entry, scored 'improviso con moto.'

The tribe of strong women marches on.

Perhaps this clarifies the early imposition of Marna's genealogy. Our tribe was forged in the steel of determination on the anvil of impossible. Nothing is irrelevant, as life kept repeating. Alison, the First, had provided a husband psychiatrist who saved me from a lobotomy. Alison the Second provided a home for John and then a cello to ensure a future for a yet-to-be-violinist.

Pregnancy, conflict and poverty had launched us into marriage; this time of expansion stretched it like a taut sinew between building, catering, cooking, children, cello and then an amateur orchestra, which I joined to hasten mastery. Since I could not yet play with much confidence, I made myself indispensable by arriving early, setting up chairs and bagging the back. The orchestra would provide the ensemble and the sightreading for Jem, the six-year-old, within a year. She would spend Monday evenings sitting with aged adults and fall asleep in the car going home. It was a substitute for the lessons we could not afford.

Perhaps the refuge for John at Nutley was to prepare for a child to play the violin and a woman whose marriage had atrophied to rediscover, through another friendship, her love for her husband before her end. Both John and Alison were starved of company and enjoyed walking and talking, and occasional picnic trips to historic homes. John and I were both only children. We had had no practice in jealousy. We married to make things easier in the eyes of the world, not to narrow possibilities. I already knew that. He discovered it with Alison. Wray, relieved by his wife's new happiness, was freed to potter about the farm and welcome them back, and I could consign John's anxiety to her gentle teasing care. John renewed Wray and Alison's marriage. I understood. Alison understood. Wray understood. It was easy all round.

ᖴ

In the film 'Witness', there is the building of a communal barn for the Amish community by all the men. Together, hale young bloods erect, balance, drill and peg a noble structure for the common good. It takes a few days. Our derelict barns take longer but have something similar in intent. The vivid assembly that files in, one at a time, to assist are far from young bloods, and it takes years, not days, but some of the valiant are worth capturing. They consolidated friendships across a wider landscape that I would never have known without them. Trading estates and the bonhomie and wisdom of tradesmen became my frequent beat at first light. They were liberal with free advice.

The year 1981 was, for the Chinese, that of the confident,

hard-working Rooster, but in Britain, it was declared the 'Year of the Disabled'. I am not sure they were grateful to be publicly celebrated for the quality they would have preferred to be without. To a man they were more Rooster than impaired; these generous saints with hands holding hammers.

First up comes Derek, the carpenter, a swarthy wild man, lean as a mountain goat, with a tin leg that gives him the rolling walk of an old sailor. It emits a satisfying clang! when he hits it with a hammer, which he does quite often in frustration; it has as many dents as a rally car. Derek is asked to create a mediaeval roof truss out of large oak beams recovered from the collapsing roof, which he will lay out on the floor to tongue and groove with tongues as large as a camel's. He has never done this before, nor has he much confidence in this way of supporting a hipped roof, but he'll give it a go. He indemnifies himself first. "Oi'll leave it in your 'ands when it fails. Interestin' mind."

The designer of this traditional truss is Mick Gill, a short prophet with a jutting black beard, a swagger gait, thick lenses and a tendency to dictate. He knows a lot about building, so stand aside everyone and listen up…We all stand very aside. When the time comes to elevate this five-ton truss into position, Mick assembles a scaffold tower to stand on, from which vantage point he barks instructions as the two legs of a triangle's plane get levered onto opposite walls. It is now upside down. A rope around the scaffold tower, with Mick on one end and the other end around the apex of the triangle, is hauled upon, to inch-by-inch —'steady, steady, right side now…more left'— the truss to the horizontal and onwards to the vertical to span the breadth of the room. When it is vertical, held stable the right way up, Derek's third mortised leg will be slotted in to anchor the triangle on the three walls. Simple.

"All understood?"

"Si Senor"

"Good. Here we go. Pull, pull, watch out, heave… all together… once more… heave. No! Not like that. Everybody stop! STOP!" A lot of that.

The scaffold tower is tipping, and Mick is imperilled, swaying back and forth. His weight is no match for the skewed truss, nor is his strength. Everyone underneath is in danger of death. I am in the team of heave. John hovers at the entrance; he can't watch but can't not. We are about to be sued for limitless damage and several fatalities. Mick continues to shout and sway. Nothing else moves. The truss leans drunkenly, threatening to collapse the walls. All wait for Mick's changing and peppery instructions.

"Jest 'and me over that piece of batten, will 'ya, John?" says Derek, ignoring Mick. John does as asked. Derek places the flimsy batten on a short off-cut of wood, creating a see-saw over a metal tube. The other end of this slim strut he wedges under the immovable leg of the massive oak truss. With his tin leg, Derek steps on the lever, raising the batten under the weighty oak, which rises three inches to clear the wall. Derek swings it into perfect alignment with the toe of the tin leg, lowering it peaceably onto the top. He does the same with the other side. Then, he climbs up a ladder to slot in the third leg of the triangular structure. Bravo!

We have a medieval truss to support the entire roof on three walls. Derek disregards Mick, whose arrogance he has suffered for days.

"Principle o'moments see Jahn," says Derek, "elementary mathematics innit Jahn? You'd know about that, bein mathematical?" He rolls away, dusting his hands against his pants. "Oi'll be buggered. It worked. Oi leaned summat."

Nothing separates the men from the boys as clearly as building. Derek was a mensch who saved another roof. It was six o'clock on a Sunday morning when he heard the weather forecast and realised the jeopardy of a half-enclosed roof, a tunnel closed on three sides but open to the West. The wind would have no exit. In his van, he raced to save it. In lashing rain, he unrolled roofing felt, putting the bags of its plastic packaging over his head until he had hammered it safe, perilously balancing on that tin leg in a force nine gale, six metres from the riverine ground.

Then came Andy, the drain expert, who loved laying drains better than Christmas; he rolled up on Christmas day. Andy was both man and boy; a minor criminal about paying bills or completing work but only when he'd had a better offer. If the offer was persuasive the electric tools might get discarded in pouring rain and the work abandoned. Although digging and levelling drains was his favourite thing, he was also a welder, a driller of steel beams, a driver of a digger and good with explosives. Sinking a septic tank hit solid rock.

"I'll sort it."

We could never have managed without him, but managing the boy took bitten tongues, averted eyes, and lashings of flattery.

Then there was Hugo, who came on the first day he was cleared to resume work after being laid off. He was a gentle giant with red hair. Hugo came to help me batten another roof. He was working on one side; I was on the other. I saw the top of his ladder keel sideways and disappear. By the time I climbed down, round the building and into the field, he was thrashing in the mud, in the throes of a grande-mal epileptic seizure. The straw bag to cushion the ladder had fallen with him, so I tried to put it under his rocking head. He grabbed me with both hands round my throat and began to squeeze and throttle. I pushed him forcibly back. Luckily, he let go. He could easily have killed me while wholly unconscious of anything. Then there was the suicidal glazier… On the third of his days, he failed to appear. His life was over.

These assistants were both rare and widely spaced between John's digging of foundations and trenches and my detours via the cul-de-sacs of material collection. People were the rare entertainment in a life without electricity, water, or any release from hard and very cold graft on roofs or digging trenches by hand. No books, no music yet, and no television. Nor any time for such pleasures. Nobody wants to know how I got stone —whistled at by passing traffic, demolition by a woman without a hard hat— nor do they want to sit with me and the butterflies digging up bricks from under hummocks of grass which concealed a long-ago burnt-out brickwork, to stack in a pile for John to load fifty at a time on his way back from school.

I did what I alone could manage. I managed first-fix carpentry, brickwork, lintels, windows, flooring and rough plastering and came to enjoy the three-dimensional jig-saw that was stonewalling. 'You never search for a stone; you use the one you pick up' was my first instruction. That honed discernment in the 'picking up'.

John mastered the use of a scythe and was good at digging down, although his anxiety doubled the depth necessary and doubled the concrete required to fill it; I built up. Others to help were for the things impatient Heath Robinson could not risk doing, like electrics, plumbing and joinery.

Margaret's beautiful bowl for Combe Cottage was our only bath; a kettle of hot water, stand, soap all over, and throw the water over the head. The younger two children slept in a space small enough to heat with paraffin; the older girls had a soggy caravan a piece, as two collapsing caravans on the site were included. John and I slept with the swallows dive-bombing and dropping lime over our beds. At Christmas we had more snow inside than out. That was the moment David and Carol bestowed their first residential visit to spend time with his children. They never took off their coats, complained of the cold, and found warmth in local emporia shopping for luxuries. I built during the day. In the evening, I cooked supper for eight. I think they washed up once.

Unity means different things to different people.

∞

The home I dreamt of came slowly into being, built as Involution had been, with reclamation from other people's skips. The first gathered chronological ideas to clothe a skeletal theory; the second accumulated anything useful for a home: arched Gothic widows from a Methodist chapel, a staircase in two parts, and brass door furniture. It was the perfect complement to the life of the mind, the down-and-dirty discipline of children and the practical. The Countess of Suffolk's Manor, just up our road, was being converted into 'managed luxury for the elderly', and its skips were a weekly Friday bonanza after the builders had departed for the weekend: Victorian panelled doors, a wicker throne loo, a marble basin. To these were added the donations of saplings her newly redundant gardener hoped to save from the retirees.

All those Dornford Yates novels of Edwardian houses unwrapped for summer were in the mind while the concrete mixer turned and the back ached: where future holidays would bring children and grandchildren, divorces would be healed, perambulators would park infants under leaves, and dogs would have their own cemetery. I had never really had a home. Ndaba and Windy had been 'home' a moving target between institutions, but my children would have the one I had longed for, one flexible enough for all harmony and any discord. Come Armageddon; we would have the ground for artichokes, rows of asparagus and cloches forcing rhubarb— the kinds of vegetables that need patience. I was building the dream of my childhood, a place of permanence, a store for memories.

Jess did not see it quite like that. Rather than submit to a cold caravan to watch passing labour heaving timber, she demanded to board. David, after a few uncomfortable stays to see his daughters, understood. Jess departed to complete A levels in a dormitory that was heated.

David was filming for National Geographic or the BBC, so Etosha, Costa Rica, Galapagos, and Namibia were the holiday destinations for half our family; great times on beaches or game parks. They returned home brown-skinned, with a store of brown jokes to offend their prudish mother and photographs of Carol smiling. She had the perfect life to smile about. Her daughter boarded and spent holidays with a friend, and David's daughters were cared for elsewhere. No worries. Our remaining two had to be content with John's cricket and a prickly Yucca for a wicket.

John educated David's children by getting them into schools, helping with their homework, driving them to extra lessons and tolerating their sulking and slammed doors. John's daughters, Jem and Kate, were never invited on any holiday. Not once. Nor was there money for an equal education; they would have to manage scholarships. Music would assist those.

We used to refer to how the 'other half' lived, meaning half of ourselves, with money in a Swiss bank and cavalier camping in luxury lodges in exotic places. Free to make money since we did the caring and the school run, year in, year out. So much for my unified family, another dream that relied upon collaboration

John, the historian, was now a mathematician wrestling with calculus in his car while he waited for violin lessons and rewarded them with a doughnut and a walk along the beach. Since neither of us had siblings, parents or cousins, we had not a single day off from childcare in nearly twenty years. In compensation, there was never any need for a dustpan and brush.

∽

There were other occupants, constantly loyal, unspeaking but critically important.

The first dog, which began as the runt of a litter of small black pigs, turned into Bella, a long-coated cross between a collie and a German Shepherd. She was so beautiful that people assumed she was a rare breed and stopped to ask its name. With melting brown eyes and an affectionate nature, she was also an inveterate thief. Bella was really an honorary horse and constantly set a course of jumps in the garden with a pink lamb strapped to her back and a pocket of biscuits to ensure the clear-round rosettes. Her thievery had been well-trained by bribery. Jem was as horse crazy as I had been. After a broken collarbone in a gymkhana, her acid choice was horses or violin. Bella was the first occupant of the cemetery but was seventeen before she was.

I think I first loved George Eliot for her portraits of dogs, her vivid dog characters, Adam's faithful trotting Gyp and Bartle Massey's Vixen, his 'woman' he should'ha drowned ...true feminine folly, though looking all the while as wise as a dwarf with a large old-fashioned head and body on the most abbreviated legs.' Every household in Adam Bede holds its silent dog, 'calm matronly' Juno, and Pug, 'the maiden lady' on her cushion; each reflects something of its master, as mongrel Windy did for me. Ordinary life has spanned a four-dog succession, with graves now silent over three.

∽

Money ran out since there was very little to begin with. It became clear we would never run to water that ran, loos that flushed, heating oil we could pipe, or lights that worked by switches rather than fading torch batteries. We would have to sell one of the buildings. To do that, we would have to delimit its boundaries and install basics. We needed money to make money. Up until now we had managed on selective robbery of rubbish tips and demolition.

The bank manager might consider a loan but would need to inspect progress so far. His secretary made an appointment for a few weeks ahead. So far ahead, I forgot it.

I had taken Jem to her violin lesson, which meant the disapproving company of her teacher's Mexican wife. Pilar was a petite and impeccably groomed woman with glossy hair, moisturised skin, and perfect lacquered nails. Sensitive to her aesthetics, I climbed out of building overalls and managed a dress.

"You know," she said, "you could look not bad. The hair is the problem. There's nothing you can do. I have a suggestion." Our family hair, or lack thereof, has no Rapunzel options.

Her suggestion was a wig. From a collection nestled in a hat-box, she drew forth a veritable explosion of short, bright, red curls. Standing behind me and in front of a mirror, she put it on my head. Marvellous. I looked a convincing Glasgow streetwalker; it certainly transformed! A new Boadicea was I!

I thought I would use it to frighten John so I borrowed it and drove home in a wig partly concealed, for casual realism, under a tartan beret.

Sitting in our concrete yard, between blocks and heaped sand, a Mercedes awaited. An impeccable man in a tailored overcoat got out. No bells rang. He's probably from the Council I thought. Then I remembered *the* Bank Manager. Our future was in jeopardy for being late, for forgetting the critical power of the Bank, and now for looking like a prostitute. I tried to fudge it.

"Terribly sorry to be late… traffic… am I late? Have you waited long?"

"I was early. Bramwich," he held out a hand. I shook it and began the tour of the site. He kept looking sideways at me.

"Who have you contracted for the build?" he asked.

"Oh, I do all the work…" I began and knew it couldn't continue. I peeled off the beret together with the wig, offering him the unfortunate in chemotherapy. He leapt back in horror. "I'm sorry, Mr Bramwich, I can't keep this up. The wig was meant to scare my husband; I completely forgot you were coming…" He recovered and laughed.

"Well, thank God for that. That's much better," He was graciously unfazed. As he was peering through a window into the gloom of the barn to be sold, a swallow flew out, narrowly missing his eye. "Another shot in the eye," he said. "This is a dangerous place. I think I've seen enough."

I was sure he would refuse the loan. Not only had I given every impression of frivolity, but until the barn to be sold was legally severed from what we would keep, he could not even ask for any security.

"I'll do some figures and let you know. If I get going, you can put the wig back on and scare your husband. It certainly scared me." He smiled and drove away.

He approved the loan. Perhaps it was the shot in the eye—tromp l'oeil was becoming a familiar— or merely a corker of a story.

The loan launched yet another detour, building a house with all trimmings, taps, and dimmer switches for Other People. The Great Wall of stone, six feet high, between who they might be and what remained to us, took three months. Parting with that barn would prove worse than sweet sorrow. The people who bought it would destroy part of our wall to embark on a programme of boundary litigation to get what remained. That stone wall—oh sweet and lovely wall—did protect us from the fate of Pyramus and Thisbe. Ovid's lovers ended up dead for the sake of a breached wall. We survived, but only just. I added nine years of mastering the legal history of adverse possession to building and the cello. Who can afford a lawyer?

I had to absorb British case law over a few centuries of boundary disputes. Case law judgements in British Law have a perfection of subtlety, humanity and common sense, which is quite inspiring to discover.

Parading as a thrusting solicitor in a borrowed sharp suit and carrying a briefcase, I gained illicit admittance to the London Law Library. There, I found cases and precedents that no lawyer would have shared without a fat fee.

After nine years of letters from the neighbour's legal Rottweilers, they withdrew their bogus claim at the door of the court. I had not buckled, and costs would backfire. They sold up and departed. We had lost the best part of John's future pension but were still in possession of the gift. Envy is a most dogged and persistent energy.

It taught me that nothing is more important than boundaries, physical and metaphorical, a lesson I came to take very seriously in ordinary life. The sharp contrast between extraordinary life without boundaries of any kind and the cut-and-thrust life I was re-entering was carved at every turn. The transition from one to the other took me time. I have not mastered it fully, not even now, but I can spot a green eye at twenty paces. The gladiatorial legal fight offered me mastery of evidence but also an instinct for reading jealousy and predicting its devilish stratagems. It spreads beyond envy of possessions to envy of boldness, even of laughter.

~

Jem, at five, armed with a quarter-sized instrument, was called out in front of her first Suzuki class and given a public dressing down. She had no right to 'play pieces ahead of the others. Who has been teaching you?'

"My mother helps a bit, but nobody. I just work it out from the book."

"Well, don't. And don't listen to your mother. A cellist knows nothing about violin fingering."

After six months, she could sightread and play folk music by ear. She had perfect pitch. Three teachers took her on but refused her requests for technical training.

"At this age, music must be fun, not scales and studies," they said, talking to the six-year-old but directed at her mother.

"But I find studies fun. I want to play properly, not just have fun."

She was hard work to teach because she devoured everything and clamoured for more. They assumed I was pushing; 'ambitious parents are all the same.' She soon joined the orchestra, where I struggled, but she didn't. We played duos, simple parts for the cello and more complex for the violin, but I could not keep up. The orchestra was mostly elderly amateurs or rusty ex-players. It attempted works far beyond its technical ability, like early Beethoven symphonies. On one journey, we were singing the themes of the second, and I realised Jem was flicking from right to left.

"Why are you doing that?" I asked

"I'm turning the pages," she said. She had a photograph of the violin part in her head. I believe the cello for me was merely to offer a violinist an entrance into the world she would make her own. Most musicians have musical parents or those familiar with the world of music. I was just an emissary to ensure she would play and given a two-year start.

Passion usually invites crucifixion. I knew it. She didn't. She entered the world wide-eyed and expecting a welcome. In that, we were twinned. I had long assumed that something about me and my disposition had invited rejection. It had been there from the beginning for me. But Jem was utterly unlike me with an aureole of fair hair and eyes wide open; sunny, natural and easy in her passion. For her, the violin carried no kudos since she had never encountered its world. She knew nothing about prestige or competition; she just loved to play. On a brief holiday in Portugal, an ocarina seller recognised a fascinated musician and gave her the best of the wares hung about his neck.

Within half an hour she had managed to reproduce the tune he played to attract custom and gave it back to him. He joined her in a duo and added a hug.

What followed was watching her destroyed, battered by jealousy, from jealous teachers, competitive players and her sisters. Her sisters were the hardest, for they turned her easy passion into gritted, dogged determination. The natural joy of music fled. It was a different crucifixion seen from the base of the cross. About which one can do almost nothing except lament and moisten a sponge with vinegar.

So, a perfect example of the future guiding the past? You have a dream about playing the cello, which lays the foundation.

It's a pity it never included any mastery of the cello, merely its aspiration!

We, and you, had other plans for you. There was no point diverting an aged cellist to aspire against the odds when there was something you would make your own, far more important to us. The child would need your understanding of her passion. That you gained, no more was needed. Your passion lay elsewhere.

Okay. Have it your way.

Our way.

A very long and arduous detour through illusion?

What illusion?

The illusion of domestic unity for one; through the belief in the stability of home, for another, in the glory of music and its call to discipline and maybe even the virtues of motherhood! They were all shot down.

Ah, but what did you learn?

Sorry I couldn't hear you. Speak up.

Okay, I learnt that I was mistaken in all of them.

Were you mistaken? Or were their requirements beyond your control?

Okay. Both. Unity needs collaboration and shared values. They were absent, so the home did not call out what I hoped it was for. Music does demand collaboration, but it fights endless competitive envy. As for motherhood, it may have its virtues, but they are mostly resented!

So, where does that leave you now?

Alone.

Were you ever not alone? You learned the skills of construction and the modesty of those engaged in it, the perfection of common law but distorted to serve the rich, and the languages of music that lie often above the reach of its practitioners—also, the limits of motherhood. In essence, every dream in each arena gives you both its potential and the limitations in its practice. It closed doors to the fruitless without destroying the fruit. I'd call that a period of great acquisition. You also acquired a home you love, gifted for a long life ahead. Gratitude would be in order?

Yes. I hoped for too much! For dreams to remain untarnished. I am sorry.

No need. You mastered the necessary skills. Sanding back to bare metal precedes a new and flawless finish.

CHAPTER 35

Scrapbook: Limits on Loyalty

'Then comes another Jesus- another but the same- the same highest and best, only chastened- crucified instead of triumphant- and the soul learns that this is the true way to conquest and glory. And then there is the burning of the Heart....'

I have never fully understood what it is about me that has so consistently invited rejection. I admit to being verbally direct; I admit to being no good at concealing disbelief at the flutter-past of a half-truth. I value liberty, especially the liberty to reject. I sometimes like people who dislike me. People find that strange, but I respect an honest dislike. I know about direct speech acting like paint stripper, as Georgina defined mine, on certain denizens who protect themselves under climbing subordinate clauses. I have asked, but nobody could explain or could bring themselves to tell me. I truly wanted to understand.

Alison had a stab at it. She said, "Well, sometimes I feel like a fish you have filleted on a plate. Nothing is left hidden."

"You're saying I am intrusive?"

"No, not you. You stand well back. It's your perception that feels intrusive…Even before you speak…"

"How can you read my perception before I speak?"

"I can't answer that. It's just there. You can't help seeing, and we can't help seeing what you see. That's perhaps why people withdraw. Your eyes give you away. And then your pithy way with words just confirms it."

It explained but did not really clarify. By rejection, I don't mean a shrug-of-shoulder indifference but the application of the lump hammer to the nail of my existence.

When it reached my own daughters, perplexity lay like silt below the waters of misery and disbelief. Perplexity is not an adequate word. It carries a whiff of remedy, a morning mist that will burn off. Instead, I would use nonplussed—nonplus, no more possible, no longer bearable.

Others were free to choose, and did not matter; my own children were different.

Each took it in turn. To begin with, I ascribed it to the necessary growth of adolescence. Without siblings or family of my own, I was an ingenue; books told me of the need to shrug off the claims of mothers. I had never done that myself since Louie did it first. I endorsed their liberty, which sought to take root in independence. I celebrated their differences. I waited for adults to seek a friendship. Instead, the friendships they sought were with partners who assisted the calculated destruction with flamboyant rejection. It was as though they believed enough misery would bring me to heel. I would beg for contact; I would yearn for grandchildren. They would bestow gestures for birthdays or Christmas, but delivering duty through a pipette is no substitute for natural affection.

I have delayed the writing of this chapter and wondered whether I could omit it altogether. In this chronology of my life, I have sprinkled my children with brown sugar and left them covered with a plate in a dim pantry, hoping to find perfectly formed crèmes brulées. The pale bruises of their rejection would fade with understanding. But nothing has caramelised. Now, I see the clearing of all remaining claims as part of the consistent pattern: another cul-de-sac closed and boarded. 'No Through Road, no descendants.' I would not be a Marna immortalised in the memory of anyone.

I am tender and still hurting. I will make errors in talking about any of it.

My reluctance to write about this, against the legitimate expectations of my reader, who, having been entangled by my children and my friends and asked to care about them, might question why they evaporate halfway through. I have tossed through nights of conflict.

Last night I had a dream in which I was trying to bury an ugly galvanised spade. I pushed it into a pile of rocks, but it sprang up, handle visible. I tried to bury it in a bed of clay, but the clay refused to yield. Then, the spade became a great empty milk churn lying on its side.

I read the wisdom from an ugly, rust-resisting churn. The foundations dug by an everlasting spade were, in reality, my milk of motherhood. The limitless supply of care now spilt and empty? All my energy was marshalled for their lives to come. Unlike Louie, being a mother was central to everything I did; it is a cliché to be as unlike one's mother as possible. I had two families and had set out to unite them, to provide a home of welcome, a refuge against disasters, enough independent space for creativity or divorce, and, in the event of a cataclysm, a garden to grow food. For the child I had been, that would have been rich; for my children, it was richly unappreciated!

You failed to master the one skill most critical to motherhood: restraint. You went at motherhood as you did the cello, assaulting Bach suites like a scythe to green wheat before it is ready to fall. You anticipated every need before it happened. Restraint waits for the season.

I had two families of identical composition: two girls apiece, exactly the same ages apart: one blonde, one dark. My mistake lay in trying to weld them as one. I even imposed David's name upon the younger two, along with John's solid Welsh handle belied by his nature; 'fiery warrior' he was not. I failed—as Margaret's similar family of two pairs of daughters failed to unite. Our cut-clean fracture was the birth of Jem and her shining, effortless embrace of life itself. Music drove her as a way to celebrate it. Music for her came as naturally as walking, but jealousy towed in its wake, seaweed round her ankles. Without the kind of money music demands, I had to find strategies, planned and time-consuming, rich compost in which jealousy thrived. I think that was the start of the tipping imbalance, which easily levered into simmering resentment, not of her, per se, but of my dedication to the demands of her music.

I was late to realise that my imperatives, discipline, work, and managing without money were probably forbidding. Evaluate? How does one sift through all the things a mother is, and apart from 'is,' how she affects her daughters without knowing?

Spike? Awkward customer? Strong meat? Too clever by half? Are you also Numbskull? What about Magnet?

What about it?

Two poles, equally strong to attract and to repel. You have attracted a few who instantly adhere and want you to themselves and many others who seek to destroy you utterly.

Why not just skitter away? Like obedient iron filings?

Both John and I, only children, had never known jealousy, rivalry or competitive resentment. We failed to notice its incubation in the years of dogged survival. But there were happy routines, scones on the lawn, summer barbecues, camps in the woods and summers to the beach, much mimicry and laughter. Looking back, I could find nothing heinous to explain such emphatic forsaking or such growing hostility.

It was nothing that you did. It was what you were. Exhausting. Optimism was un-ending: a musical monastery, nine years of legal battle, more years of musical battle, and a home to create from selected rubbish. Each impediment circumnavigated, and survival against all the odds was a perpetual mirror to others who lacked that indomitable resolve. You took on the demands of a Goliath and had no right to succeed.

Do you call it resolve? It was only a refusal to be defeated: 'Indomitable' was simply dogged treads and climbing over or around the blockages.

The pebbles from David's sling rained down and I failed to see any of them, and they were kept from me. My older daughters were gone without farewell, and in all the years following, clarity and understanding never dawned. The chasm lay cold and dark, never filled for those who remained.

When survival meant that we might have to rent out our house,

Jem and I began to clear out cupboards in preparation. It was then that we found three shoe boxes of letters and cards tucked behind the skirting of Ros's room. In them, years of David and Carol's injected propaganda and pointed smutty innuendos were still in their perfectly slit envelopes. In another box were the cards and letters John and I had sent. The contrast between them could not have been starker. Ours were celebratory and chosen to evoke memories; theirs were vulgar and chosen to offend; to offend me.

Those boxes were found too late to save me from incomprehension and wretchedness. Since I had given David no cause for hostility, with an open welcome to stay and free access to his children whenever he asked, I did not anticipate the depth of his bitterness. After all, the tedium and demands of growth and education had fallen to us. I had asked for nothing and denied him nothing. What had sustained such bitter gall?

His revenge was served very cold indeed.

∾

As soon as Jess left school, David spirited her to university in South Africa. Which one? It was never discussed with us. John had secured her entry to schools, the dull routines of transport, extra lessons, and we were now surplus to requirements. We did not know for over a year. When Ros left school, she was speedily dispatched to Vevey, Switzerland, to train in hotel management. Why? She had expressed no interest in it. Both girls were summarily plucked from what had been their home in England.

Ros came back for a few virago holidays, during which the embryo hotel manager inspected her once home and found the head honcho neglectful. She covered the kitchen with newspaper, and every object was spit and polished under a hail of heavy sighs. Objects were marshalled in height but not purpose; sell-by dates were inspected, and offenders were binned. De-cluttering was ruthless. John and the dog took refuge elsewhere and I attempted points of contact; impressions of Europe? Have you tried skiing? Or learning any languages? Is there perhaps a boyfriend? Only a turned back and a frenzy of Brasso and iron wool.

Of my daughter, I saw little. I saw a tightened mouth, hunched shoulders growing thinner, and a nervous look that darted black glances like a vulture at a road-kill.

Ros's insecurity had been fed incrementally. Jess was very obviously David's favourite, sharing his contentment in the wild, indifferent to other people's traumas, and temperamentally detached. She deserved cameras and camping kit. David would make sardonic references to Ros's academic difficulties with a show of false sympathy, poor dear Ros. She was left in no doubt that she was a cuckoo in a nest of pure-bred warblers.

David had never witnessed her contribution to cooking or child care or her consistent mothering, pleasing others with food, cycling home from domestic science with 'Rushin Fish Pie' on her handlebars. Ros had been my most reliable helpmeet during years of domestic struggle. I doubt I would have managed it without her, which was why she deserved the first finished Laura Ashley papered and carpeted room. Other people were her centre. She makes and keeps loyal friends. These were not things her father valued. 'Only inadequate people need other people!' But David would ensure her financial future by ushering her into expensive training for a career in which she had expressed no interest, Swiss Hotel Management, deliberately far from us.

Bristling anger replaced her enjoyment of her home. What at? It was never declared. I could not get near her. Each visit left an admonishing finger of surgical rebuke.

I accepted this as transitory, although the depth of anger was hard to fathom. The changes in both my older daughters were as though I had never known them. I took comfort in the belief that they would surely seek renewal after liberty and time. Without sharing her decision with us, Ros joined a cruise company, first as a tour guide and then as ship's purser and was gone forever.

We wrote occasionally, and I went on hoping.

The shoe boxes were still hidden in the dark.

∽

Inevitably, boyfriends who ended as partners followed. Two, in rapid succession, came to be called 'two cricketing Rs'. The body-line bowler was Jess's offensive R. (OffR) The first view of him was on a postcard sent with him in profile, stark naked, silhouetted against a mountain. There was no mistaking the middle finger. He had been introduced in the manner which satisfied Jess's compulsion: to throw a grenade on any white linen—the more brazen the offence in polite company, the better. Jess had an addiction to the paralysing silence of shock.

Ros's wicket-keeper, defensive R (DefR), was a quietly-spoken Indian who first visited without her. He looked like Omar Sharif, with impeccable skin and manners, courteous and visually spectacular. He brought a friend to stay the night. At first, he said he intended to study medicine, which soon changed to aviation. He came and went a few times before Ros returned from cruising. They were almost engaged when he invited John and me to his sister's wedding in a large hall in North London. We were charmed that he asked us. I truly celebrated that Ros would have her world enlarged with the vitality of an unfamiliar cosmopolitan culture.

We were the only non-Indians present in a hall of seated suits and saris. The ceremony was happening on a raised dais with hennaed hands, slow rotating movements, and some chanting but nobody appeared to be attending much to it. Grey-haired women with buns shared animated interests between mouthfuls of samosa, rising to kiss and namaste and moving to others. John and I met DefR's father briefly when he gestured to a buffet, saying, "Help yourselves to food." before abandoning us to make our way. We sat in an aviary of birds with extravagant plumage alone at a white table. When the ceremony began to subside, the band struck up.

"Will you give me the honour of the first dance?" asked Omar Sharif, bowing slightly and holding out his hand.

"Delighted to," said I.

DefR led me to the centre of the dance floor, where we managed a kind of untouching jive, to which I gave more enthusiasm than was perhaps wise. He circled me around the perimeter of the floor before turning to a younger, beautiful girl and ditching the embarrassment of the old woman.

Through the turning heads, falling silent, I made my way back to John alone.

It recalled my dance with Frau Fick. I had been exhibited to all the Indian aunts as DefR's intended mother-in-law, amputating all designs and cancelling any orders for red saris. A public exhibition was economical; DefR had broadcast his intentions on the billboard of my presence, and all those gossiping hopes and rolling eyes could be crossed off at a stroke.

As we rose to leave, DefR brought his mother in a green sari and introduced her. We smiled. She dipped her head. We left. The purpose of our invitation had been accomplished with the dispatch of removing and pocketing the bails. Game over.

∾

The first face-to-face encounter with Jess's OffR was a continuation of the earlier written introduction. After a delayed audition, Jem and I arrived a little late for a meal with David and Carol in their grand rented Hampstead flat. We were due to collect Jess and her unmet partner to spend a few days in Somerset. The lighting of a short fuse kicked off this carnival.

"I was lucky today", said David, passing a plate, "we were given tickets to the Ring Cycle." The fizzing rope snaked, and I walked straight into it.

"Rather you than me," I said, unthinking.

"You don't like opera?" said Off R like a bullfighter sweeping a cloak; I failed to hear the drumming, steel-tipped heels.

"Some. I don't really enjoy Wagner."

"Perhaps you will when you grow up," said the blue-chinned fighter to his future mother-in-law. He looked around for the applause, which duly came in nodding and smiling from David and Carol. That's the way to handle her. It had all been orchestrated and, after that, lunch passed almost in silence.

As we were leaving, David said loudly to OffR, "Make sure you mind your p's and q's." I had been billed as a dreary Mary Whitehouse, and this first meeting had been scored for solo snare drum. When we reached my car, OffR held out a hand for the keys.

"I'll drive," he said.

I rallied. "Do you know the country? The way? The car? No? Then, as it's my car and my country, and I know the way, I'll drive."

He sulked for the two-hour journey and, when we reached home, kept to their room while Jess ferried trays for three days. John returned them to the airport.

The visit was never repeated.

∽

After the birth of Sebastian, Jessica's first baby, she proposed a visit to Cape Town. She had many air miles she could not use, which paid for my ticket. I could come, not for the birth, which I had suggested, but after David and Carol had had first joy and departed.

I was allocated an outside room with a separate entrance, a modest kitchen and bathroom and told on arrival that it would be 'best' if I did not enter their part of the house if OffR was at home.

As it was an opportunity to seek a retirement option for Louie, I suggested she and Ndaba should join me and I found, close by, a room that would take two old women of different colours. We three spent a fortnight visiting gated communities and retirement homes, with Louie increasingly tense and Ndaba trudging bent backed in her wake.

OffR's opening salvo to Ndaba was as offensive as his to me.

"How many wives does your husband have? Are you number-one wife?" he asked, showing off his familiarity with African polygamy. Ndaba hit that for a confident four.

"I am only one wife, sir. My husband has passed away, but we are both Christians," she answered with her courteous dignity. Howzat!

Louie found and immediately bought a flat in Fishhook, as much like hers in Mbabane as possible, and immediately instructed an agent to let it.

"I hope she's not coming here expecting me to visit her," said Jess, who had spent countless visits to Swaziland imposing on Louie. There was no expression of pleasure and Louie read the lack immediately.

"Jess does not want me here, does she?"

∽

The sharp pain lessened as the years went by, but it left hollow disbelief. Grandchildren, two apiece, were born. I had known of Jess's first, but none of the others that followed. Ros's children were born without our knowing of them at all. A visit when they were almost teens happened.

"What do we call you? The young maiden asked in a watchful silence. It was a good question.

I replied "Philippa is my name, and is usually enough." There was silence from the parents of the innocent. It was the wrong answer.

An echo of a visit from my father, Raymond, when he stopped by to check on me and my new family in the farm cottage before the barns began. I offered him tea. Ros had gone to make it, leaving us on the rough grass outside. She was about twelve and staggered out with a tray. As she poured and handed out mugs, Raymond looked at me and said,

"It must be nice to have grandchildren to make you tea."

I looked at him. "Yes. You have, and she did."

It took fully two minutes before he registered. Those two minutes were eloquent. We had nothing to do with him, and, in turn, I had nothing to do with my grandchildren. Patterns, as Marna would have said: patterns of abandonment and cruel severance and all irrevocable.

∽

How well watered they had been was only clarified with the finding of the three shoe boxes, and the horror of their discovery. Jem and I sat with our backs against a bed and passed choice morsels across. Such letters began when Jess and Ros were about twelve and ten and lasted until Ros had left home to work away, carefully preserved. They were not open attacks but the slow drip of eradication. We did not exist. We were never mentioned; the appropriation of my older daughters was incremental by the constant vulgarity to offend me, the tight-lipped prude, a shared joke. All were letters to Ros, carefully saved, carefully hidden.

From Carol: *'You're a big girl now, chicken; you can come to us. We don't have to go there anymore.'* 'There' was the home that had welcomed Carol and David to stay from its inception. 'There' was also a home built for everyone. That was the axe that had split the log of home hearth before Ros was thirteen. My family seat had termites in its foundations, carrying away fragments in every letter before it was built. There had been small signals of this: when I offered to survey a house Ros and DefR were considering buying, his curt answer was, "I would rather employ a professional." He was, from his introduction, firmly on the 'other side'; the side I never knew existed, the many signals of which I failed to see.

'If you think your mother will be hurt that we were so close and did not visit, just don't tell her.' Carol openly invited disloyalty.

(on a card) *'Happy Birthday/ You're young, you're healthy and in the prime of life. You little shit. Added: P.S. Thought we'd forgotten, didn't ya! Love Carol, Love you, Dad.'*

Yes, she did think they had forgotten because they almost always did. Every occasion had brought misery that David was so uncaring. Years of David's indifference and John's tact, never encroaching on the role of father, had been a frequent source of tears. My suggestion that Ros should challenge David always brought the same answer: "Oh, you know me, Miss Peace-at-any-Price". Her peace did not ever include me, as these letters of intrigue made clear.

A few samples will suffice: From Ros's DefR early in their 'romance' before she returned from cruising.

'I tried to call Phillipa (sic) today, but nobody answered. THANK GOD!! .... Naturally, I'll do the honourable thing and offer my liver for the Sunday roast.... '

'Just got off the phone with Phillipa. Sanj and I are planning to go

down for the night tomorrow. I had a long, fruitful chat with the woman, and I think we both get along rather well. PHEW!' He and Ros are not yet engaged, but he has invited himself and a friend, and I am already 'the woman.'

(about the sister's wedding)

'Maybe I've just had my fill of eager aunts and uncles…sizing me up for whatever reason. But I would never begrudge you the statement… that I silently knew what I was doing by inviting P and J to the wedding.'

Clear as daylight, that billboard invitation openly declared. And openly sanctioned by my daughter!

(On first meeting with Carol)

'I met Carol. She's smashing. She said if I wasn't going in for aviation, I could be a film star!'

∽

The shock of this compendious discovery was lessened by now fully understanding how it had come to be, over how many years all colluded in deprecation and contempt. How blind I had been! Carol had seduced both the respective Rs and extended it to my mother, invited for Christmas. Louie was low-hanging fruit, easily plucked.

Ndaba was the sole pinion that never fell, sturdy in her loyal, unwavering affection.

If I had nursed any residual hope in restoration, that collection definitively doused it. Jem and I sat contemplating the debris of paper scattered across the carpet, unable to grasp just how long-lived and comprehensive the demolition had been. Now, I knew I had not been wrong in reading runes. Now, they had been made explicit, a personal Rosetta stone, sharp-carved and inescapable.

Just as Martin Israel had tried to sever me from the Milfords and Judith, Jess had corralled my entire extended family behind her slander, including the distant cousin Jonathan and even my totally absent father, Raymond.

"What are you going to do?" Jem asked, "It's all so unjust."

"There is nothing to be done. They clearly detested me; it seems they all enjoyed expressing it."

"No, I think they feared."

" Feared what? Fear tends to avoid. This is not fear; it is consensus, almost a conspiracy, on concerted destruction. Why?"

∽

Has that 'why?' been answered in the thirty years since?

I struggle with it. Had two abortions merited this return to exact revenge? It seems likely karmic reparation. I deserved it. It makes more sense than anything else.

Do you think that?

Nothing has alleviated or ever softened the rejection—no letters, no requests for conversation and never any regret. I once invited Ros to meet me at a halfway house to see if there was any level ground on which to walk towards one another. I asked, 'Do you have no happy memories of your childhood?' Without a moment's thought, she answered, 'I had a very disrupted education.' That was true; survival had been perilous and frequently on the move, but was that all? Neither daughter seeks to repair the relationship or rebuke their partner's savage attacks. They were people who knew nothing of me before I was 'the woman' or, as OffR so kindly put it, 'the great undiscovered thinker of the universe!' My humiliation roped in every steer or old knacker-out-to-grass, parent, partner, sibling or friend. That's some karmic bile!

Or something else?

Such as?

Karma from the future? To undermine any belief in yourself? To prevent what we hoped to achieve?

It did the opposite. It cleared all desks of alternatives, no grandchildren or dates to celebrate, no emerging needs to find ways to finance. If anything, it concentrated attention on what remained. My need to make sense of all that had happened. Including the harrowing loss and the writing of this record.

Ex-act-ly

After the prolonged traumas of flamboyant rejection, I have looked hard at the influences that switch close friends or even children into deadly enemies. I now realise that people can only influence others if the accord is already in embryo. What already exists can be hooked and moulded but, in the absence of any heinous crime, not injected.

Dick and Judith had doubts about my sanity and were fearful of encouraging me, so it was easy for Martin Israel to weave doubt into a durable basket of wise and total withdrawal. '*I do not look for a recovery. Her children will need care for years to come.*' That basket called itself responsibility and reasonable caution, so not only did it weave together many virtues, but virtue is light to carry away.

My complete recovery without recurrent 'episodes' was an objective truth that did not cause any swerve in certainty. Objective truth does not address or alter emotions of guilt or suspicion. They were afraid of encouraging what they already feared: their inability to evaluate. No early reader of this book believes I had no 'recurrent episodes.' My refusal to admit to ever taking drugs means I must be lying. Pre-conceived barriers limit any grasp of the entirely new. Those who leap into new revelation are shunned by those left behind it. I had seen all that forever.

Strangely, it prepared me for what we all have faced with the pandemic hoax. False belief either binds or gets discarded. Those bound by it come to hate those who discard it, and there is no bridging the gulf between.

My older daughters were jealous of the dependable education that my second family enjoyed and the time given to music. No amount of luxurious travel compensated; jealousy wove itself into rampant insanity, favouritism, and failures of love. David lived with a new wife, unsure of his total dedication, so he was deft in eradicating any need for communication or contact. 'You are better off without such a mother'. Yet that was not enacted until parental duties were over and they were old enough not to impose routines on him or Carol; it was a carefully controlled demolition, falling neatly into its own footprint!

I have lost most of my friends through the influence of others.

Georgina and Margaret also moved away.

Georgina married the 'bloke called Clive', an occasional decorator, an undemanding wastrel who chain-smoked his Hamlet cigars, while Georgina inherited wealth from a succession of elderly aunts. Together, they moved into increasingly opulent houses, which secured him occasional paper-hanging while she hosted therapy groups of various persuasions. The last of these jewels in the Lake District, an ancient farm with a view of Derwentwater and the music of distant sheep, was profitably carved up to provide Clive's work-free retirement in what was once a Linen Bank, an imposing mausoleum in a town on the Scottish borders.

"You and Clive diminished one another, so I had to choose between you. I chose Clive." was what Georgina said. Distance grew into years of silence. I missed her, but she admitted that children did not interest her. Mine had centred too many initiatives and absorbed too many hours. Only after Clive died, rather predictably of lung cancer, did she resume occasional phone calls, but a friendship obedient to another's curtailment never quite recovers its elan. Warmth returned near her end when smoking, whisky and phone calls were all she had. Rather like Louie with Max, Clive had managed to strip hope and limit plans until her life's routines were wholly his.

She died in a lonely, hired, adjustable bed constructed in Clive's 'library' with only her loyal factotum, Jill, present. Jill and I received generous codicil bequests penned at her last gasp. We became good friends. It fell to Jill to dispose of Georgina's obsessive collecting: rooms stacked with still-boxed bric-a-brac, sewing samplers, vintage clothing, and rusty typewriters. Never unpacked but never forsaken, a life always on hold.

Through driving rain, Jem and I drove to Scotland for her funeral. In the faint drizzle, we stood; a few friends whose names I had heard years earlier but never met, on one side of Clive's grave and his now suddenly wealthier young nieces on the other—a shafted break in the cloud floodlit the closing scene of a film. The credits rolled over a stumbling reading by a humanist, someone licensed to inter, as Georgina's coffin was lowered on top of Clive's. It seemed curiously indecent and unwise to share such a prickly bed in perpetuity.

As the hearse slowly drove away from the cemetery of undulating grass, enclosed by low hills, the rows of modest headstones were newly punctuated with an exclamation mark: a pointed, Gothic slate gravestone standing emphatically tall, an obelisk of dominion.

∽

For Margaret, the stake in the heart of friendship was music, followed by jealousy.

Margaret believed all my pursuit of music was a detour. She wanted the destruction of the Church's certainties, and she hoped I would manage that with a well-aimed Howitzer. All the Milford's were musical and nobody should start the cello at forty and succeed at it. She made that explicitly clear.

"There is something more important to be doing, and nothing should obstruct it. You won't ever play well enough, and many others can do it better. Nobody else can write your thesis. Devote yourself to that."

She was right; I would never play well enough, but I remembered Marna's inversion. "If a thing is worth doing, it is worth doing badly." So I continued playing but never referred to it.

After Dick died, Margaret was indeed a merry widow. I made her annual Christmas cake, called in on most Mondays without admitting being en route to a 'rehearsal', and John joined her for Match of the Day on Wednesday evenings, taking bottles of his home-brewed beer. Once, I arrived to find her in a long evening gown of blue glitter, with a shining necklace and a home-sewn tiara in her hair. She was looking ten years younger.

"You're on your way out?"

"No, my dear. I am very much at home to celebrate. When I'm alone, I dress for dinner every night. I light candles, I pour the last of Dick's elderflower champagne, and I toast myself several times. Can't you understand why?"

Nobody could understand better. The moonlight over Inhaca's sea swept back in memory, and I recalled the nights watching the sailing moon calling to a lonely woman on a cliff.

Many months after Dick died, a memorial service at his first parish, St Mary's Oxford, necessitated a trip to Salisbury to buy something appropriate for Margaret to wear. She fell upon a wool suit in episcopal purple.

"Just the thing. Now, at last, I'm bishop of my own diocese."

I had to alter the suit for a diminutive prelate.

The service was attended by people normally only seen on television, the great, the good and the familiar, for forgotten reasons. Afterwards, the reception moved to Milford House, the Oxfam Headquarters where tables ranked glasses of orange juice and small starvation rations, sardines on limp lettuce. I spotted Margaret dwarfed by the Archbishop of Canterbury leaning and nodding. She winked over his shoulder. After he moved away, she came closer.

"Calls itself a broad church, but I can't even risk a broad smile. Just think! I shall never have to do this sort of thing again."

No sooner shorn of clerical propriety than Margaret's daughters descended and decided she would toast herself alone in a sheltered flat in Oxford, where they could keep an eye on her. They would sell her small house and move her out. When plans were underway, I dropped in. Dick's second daughter was firmly seated. Margaret looked wretched but pleased to see me. She made gestures warning that her life was no longer her own, the contents of her modest home were being re-assigned.

"I'd like you to have something. What about Dick's birdbath? Would you like that?" It was a charming shape Dick had made to resemble a conch shell.

"You can't give her that. One of us will want it." was the daughter's rapid interjection. Margaret raised her brow but did not argue.

Once she was in Oxford, I was forbidden to visit. When I called in, Margaret opened the door and panicked, her shoulders hunched in fear.

"I can't invite you in. My daughters are due any minute and must not find you here. Please, please, you must go…" She was quivering in apprehension.

"Margaret! Not even for a minute? Why?"

"Don't ask. No, no. I am not to see you. I now depend on them. Please go."

It was pitiful. My dearest friend, the courageous, determined little warrior, was crumpled under the weight of influence.

I never saw her again, my bravest ever friend, who had saved my life.

Many years of silence later, David died after a short spell of rapidly spreading cancer, which began as melanoma and spread to his liver. His ashes were handed over from a doorway in a trading estate in Cape Town. There was no gathering, no service of remembrance, nothing to record his life or passing. Ros grew close to David in his final months. After his death, she re-construed her father as a saint, and the memory of all the tearful years of his indifference evaporated. Just as little Terri, abandoned by Terry, was the one to finance his return home to England from America to die. It merits thought that the two girls most injured by their respective fathers were the most generously attentive at their ends.

David bequeathed me the exact sum of money he had never paid for those four initial years when it was most needed, carefully invested. To authorise the receipt, I had to ring Carol to discover his date of death.

"You can find that out yourself," she said. She was very tight-lipped but added, "It's a funny old world." before hanging up. Over the intervening forty years she had clearly known nothing of David's belated honour to a divorce decree he had once been forced to sign. That response told me everything I needed to know about her jealousy and the destruction it had wrought. Their relationship required my elimination, even by my children.

I think my forgiveness and John's open welcome denied David

power over me. He had hoped and initially planned that my poverty would have to plead. Instead, poverty drove determination. His bitterness denied Carol the belief that she had fully replaced me and, as the ancient Greeks well knew, the choleric disposition lodges in the gall bladder. My eldest daughters had spurned us, and there was no loyalty to me at all. Just deserts? How deep do the threads stretch from the past to snag or twitch the future?

My united family had been a chimaera all along.

∞

A few months after David's death, in the depths of the night, I returned to bed after going to the loo. I was aware of a presence in the room as I re-entered. David was in my bed. He took me in his arms and said, "I came to tell you how very sorry I am. I am truly deeply sorry. I had to tell you. I need you to forgive me." He held me, and it was as though we were within concentric rings of injury that flowed out in succession, becoming less intense as each replaced the other. The layers of long-endured loss of my daughters were free of content, just bitter pain endured. Sharing them, held close, made his contrition as agonising to him as my loss had been to me. After the last encircling ring left us, he slowly withdrew.

The peace that passeth understanding. Was the home a hollow victory entirely?

There are no more children. The desire for revenge did as it was bidden; 'first, dig two graves'. Revenge bound us all equally like the cotton thread that tied Marna to a riempie chair.

We have almost come full circle. Your desk has been cleared of children and friends. All that remains is the recovery of your origins and the call of your deepest affection.

I have lost sight of myself.

There is finally work waiting, work for which all this has been an overture.

The overture has introduced the themes. The themes now merit harmonic composition.

CHAPTER 36

The Miracle Worker

'One must be poor to know the luxury of giving.'

On the eve of Louie's eightieth birthday, 30th November 2000, we had our first ever real conversation. Winter had already closed the curtains on the year; the ordeal of Christmas would march in lock-step until I dragged the withered tree to the bonfire. I rang her with the usual tightness in my stomach.

How desolate our sinewy bond had proved, how resigned we were to what was absent, yet always held together by a hope of warmth, or better, the recapture of those rare bursts of laughter she had forgotten, but I remembered with fading anguish. The photograph that hung on my bathroom wall reminded me nightly of her bright and wide optimism that once leapt naked into a rock pool and the gasp of shock that followed. In those days, her mantra was always 'You never regret the things you do, only the things you don't." Long lost, that kind of living, destroyed by Max bleeding her dry. A brittle shell remained, dutiful, dogged, closed to the palpitations of pain, and filled with sand.

"Thought I'd get in first," I said to explain why I had not waited for the day proper.

"Oh, my dear! There will hardly be a stampede. How lovely to hear you."

There was sunlight in her voice and none of the usual 'You shouldn't have…' or talk of expense that was customary.

"What news?" I asked.

This caused a hesitation. "It was inevitable, of course. As you know, I've been expecting it, but they could have trusted me to understand. Quite a shock seeing it in the paper."

"What did you see?"

"They have advertised my job. The Clinic is seeking a new physio. I just wish they had warned me."

"Oh, mum!" Across twelve thousand miles we embraced over a silence of perhaps a minute. Her work was her entire life, and it was to be stripped at a stroke. Nothing rational would ease the loss or the heartlessness of her dedication made instantly superfluous. Not many work until they drop. We had discussed it often, her refusal to anticipate it always pushed to the back of the cupboard, like some rare culinary choice for which she was never quite ready. Inspected and replaced, after articulating, 'I could never live without the colour in my life', which meant her patients, their starving children, their accidents and recovery, and the singing from distant women on their way to church. Her intended annexe in our garden, which I had built for this moment, had long been occupied by tenants. No comfort in England could replace her single and central role in Swaziland's modest needs. Her England was of a person she once was but was no longer.

"Enough of that", she said. "Let me hear about your girls and their doings. Before you tell me of the others, I must tell you that Jess asked to come and stay and for the first time, I refused."

"She's never an easy guest."

"I can't cope with her anymore. I worry. She keeps to her room all day on that machine and then goes out at night. She never talks to me. I pace the floor until about one o'clock when she returns. It really is not safe. Rape here is frequent. I can't cope with the worry or the sleeplessness, so I said no."

We talked for almost an hour, not the confessional I had once longed for, but the sharing of small triumphs, large disappointments, and new hopes for both the girls at home and the two forever departed. I had never had such acute attention, or close questions or such ready identifications. It was as though her shoulders had sunk into relaxed ease; the years of brittle hostility fell away. This sudden communion was both new and yet familiar, as though compounded of those moments of laughter, of shared embarrassments over Marna's delicious irreverence, of Max's oblivious humbug, and those rare holidays with

Milly in Plet, walking with Windy chasing waves along the beach in the early dawn. I met the mother I always knew was there.

I did find tears with the joy of it, quiet tears distilled from much longing, the longing born when I first realised how much she wanted to love me and how blocked that was by misery. We both found it difficult to break off.

"This has been….so lovely…such a birthday treat…oh, why am I crying?"

I cannot really remember how we ended. I do remember being unable to move from the hall chair, pinned by the weight of finding her, and the thirsting denied part of myself filling up, a fountain revived after a long drought as though a rock had been moved from its throat. What might we both do with such a flow of honesty to drink?

A week later, she was gone.

∽

Did I leave South Africa because my mother could not express the love buried by my arrival? Because being with her was a running-sore reminder of that? I think it is possible.

You left for love certainly, both its promise as much as its absence. It was a larger life that called, not simply a damaged one that repelled.

True. I had, in fits and starts, become a hesitant, unsuccessful writer, mostly to secure what it was about Africa that explained me and, yes, to give something of that to those who know nothing of it. Mostly short stories, drawn from memories of lost friends, and stories mostly true, diary entries for the work that lay ahead. Yet the distance and the years spent away had veiled its sharp light and dark shadows, and my mother's untimely death forced me to see how much I had neglected, how much I had betrayed. I went to bury her, not to praise her, in a country I did not know among those I had never met.

∽

I flew to Johannesburg expecting a three-hour delay before boarding the small connecting flight to Matzapha International Airport. From there, I would find a way to get to Mbabane, rent a car or take a taxi. Instead, after landing and finding the transit lounge, I was greeted by a young woman in a doek.

"Are you Philippa? Louie's daughter? I'm Lizzie."

Dimly, I remembered references to Lizzie in Louie's letters. Lizzie had escaped an attempted rape by banging on Louie's door in the middle of the night. Louie had taken her in, and she had stayed. Lizzie, 'my other daughter,' had filled Louie's life; they became very close over the years when Lizzie trained in social work before her charity sent her to Malawi.

"We've come to drive you to Mbabane," she said. She indicated a hesitant man standing back. "This is my brother. We will drive you."

Lizzie had been visiting her brother from Malawi when she heard of Louie's death. They had a single day planned together. They would spend it driving four hours to Mbabane and turn round immediately for Lizzie to catch another plane that evening. The dimensions of Africa lie in the hearts of such impulses and the distances such hearts will undertake. The contrast announced itself before I had even registered my return. Africa has slow rhythms but certain impulse. Lizzie and her brother delivered me to the door of Louie's flat after a journey spent being explicit to ensure I knew what Ndaba would need without my mother. Whites can never be relied upon. In all the years of my absence, she, understandably, could take nothing for granted. After hugging Ndaba and a quick mug of tea, they drove straight back to Johannesburg.

What follows is my story of this return by a prodigal who deserved no welcome. I wrote it after I had absorbed its pitiless portrait of my mother's life and my neglect. It was a blinding exposure. I can never salve its savage portrait—of me. I stand back to see it without flinching.

The Miracle Worker

It was the wrong driver. That was the first indication. The old Gogo's blue Toyota, which looked as though you could open it with your teeth, had developed new manners. It stopped at traffic lights and found its way into the right lanes. To begin with, that confused everyone. The whole town had so long hesitated before deferring to its imperious passage, immune to signals of any kind, that its new sobriety brought the traffic to a halt, and crossroads became a game of dare. How much trust could be placed in unlikely sanity? The driver seemed unaware of the stares that followed her but signalled turns, braked without skidding and parked with economy, even in reverse. What hesitations she exhibited had nothing to do with driving.

Then, they all agreed it was long overdue. Old Gogo Kavnat had obviously found herself a driver, and everybody started to relax. The deference she had required, which began as the instinctive respect for age, had developed into simple self-preservation. They took comfort that not only might they live a little longer, but Gogo would be secured to their service, for a while anyway.

Nobody really knew her to speak of, but throughout the country, she was recognised: the white Gogo from the Clinic, as scrawny as an old cockerel, in the company of the fat black Gogo, trudging bent-back in her wake; the two arguing incessantly through the market, the Mall and over the boot and bonnet of their blue tin stall. The two Gogos together were the daily Punch and Judy show, delivered by the Toyota to set up and bicker over how many lemons they might need and whether mushrooms were too 'esspensives', and proving masters at forgetting. No sooner loaded up and waved out of the parking lot to the accompaniment of shaking heads and concealed laughter, they were back for the shoe repairs, the tin of floor polish, or for the white Gogo to shake her finger at someone who had failed to attend an appointment. The Gogos were an institution, as certain as the drink deliveries; they may be late, but they would always appear.

Thoko Ndaba, the black Gogo, with her stooped back and her flat-footed gait, shrank vertically as the years went by. Old Mrs

Kavnat, the white Gogo, shrank horizontally, and the thinner she got, the more steel-like her grip. Her grip was what most of them had experienced; as the only physiotherapist, she had seen their babies into the world through the ante and post-natal clinics; she had urged all the accident casualties to greater effort on crutches and had massaged the paraplegic stroke victims in places no woman had the business to be. The Clinic on the hill was the staging post, and the austere, formal old woman, a female boatman to the transfers in and out of life and back and forth from the surgeries in Johannesburg and Nelspruit.

But nobody really knew her.

The black Gogo they knew only too well. Milly Thoko Ndaba was another kind of keeper. The daughter of a Zulu chief, she had the mastery of morals, manners and the uselessness of men. She supervised whatever needed supervision, the wards in the Clinic, the rubbish collection from the block of flats, the appropriate funds to give delivery boys on Boxing Day (depending on the year's conduct), the meticulous ironing of lace altar cloths, and any affair of the heart, any heart. She advised parents about the unruliness of their offspring; unmarried mothers, kept captive with bread and tea, were left in no doubt about their stupidity, and quite a few orphans were collared and sent to school. Together, the Gogos seemed to quietly supervise the town despite the incredulous head-shaking and the daily thigh-slapping anecdotes.

One thing was agreed; those sisters of the heart were both better on their own since that selfish Max Kavnat had been buried ten years earlier with scant ceremony. The sudden cessation of his taxi rides to the casino to spend their meagre earnings had robbed only Sibande, the taxi driver. Neither of the Gogos had stopped long enough to order a headstone. Good riddance, waste of space.

The whites of the town only knew Mrs Kavnat and that she was fortunate to have such a reliable and capable maid. They did not know her either. She visited the library, she donated to the SOS Children's Village, and she appeared in church with her obstinate habit of sitting with her maid, near the back. One or two invited her to lunch out of kindness and weathered the sense that their fine wines and rich food meant less than they merited. She was courteous, even gracious; she always brought a present, a bottle, a cake, or flowers but departed early without a backward glance, juddering down their paved driveways only just avoiding the guard dogs. You had to admire her; so selfless, really, but not exactly companionable. Not an easy guest.

They could not imagine how she filled her solitudes in that poky flat without even a television. She was never seen to buckle or admit any lack. Her fine hair, carefully coiled with tortoiseshell combs, her simple clothes invariably blue; only her penetrating eyes in their folds of misery and her puckered mouth told the story nobody ever heard, a private person who could never unbutton. They knew of an uncaring daughter somewhere. They could do so much more if she would let them. They would have liked to do more.

It was the boy at the checkout who heard first. The white Gogo's bread was accumulating so he followed the driver of her car at some distance, picking his nose with ten loaves banging in a bag at his heels.

"Gogo forgot the bread. You can give it to her."

"What bread?"

"The yesterday bread. The bread she take for the villages. You can take it now."

"What villages?"

"How can I know? She drives to the villages every week, and she takes the bread. We keep it for her."

"I'm sorry. I can't give it to her. My mother has died." The boy seemed not to believe what he had heard. He wiped his mouth on the back of his hand and ran a tongue across his teeth.

"You are Gogo's chile?"

"Yes."

"You have brother or sister?"

"No"

"You Ony Chile? And now she passed away? When she pass away?"

"Last Sunday."

"You from UK?"

"Yes."

"You been here before? You know this place?"

"Once. For a short time."

He turned away to take the knowledge with the bread and then turned back.

"Other Gogo can pass away very soon now. You can wait for that."

Ony Chile watched him retreat until a gathering of faces at the window of the small supermarket identified her; now, all the town would know. The White Gogo was dead.

~

Milly Ndaba, bleached with grief and bewilderment, kept returning to the hole in the window as though it held the key to understanding: a single hole in the glass of the bedroom window, high up, as though aimed from the mango tree outside.

"It wasn't here before. How can I not know if it was here? Ow Nkosiam!" said Ndaba, picking off small shavings of glass and testing the clean hole with the dimensions of her forefinger, prodding back and forth. OnyChile watched the old woman distracting herself; the hole did seem impossible to explain; a clean shot might have caused it, but surely the glass would have shattered? She led her into the kitchen.

"You are going to have to tell me, Ndaba. What happened?"

Milly wiped her eyes with her apron and then reminded by the affectionate use of her surname of all the accumulated but forgotten intimacy of OnyChile's childhood and all the unspoken things that had bonded them, made tea in the best bone china, and set out biscuits. Almost forty years had severed any certainties, but routines of service came as naturally as breathing.

"Ow, darling. How must I eva start? I think Madam she knew. Why else did she send me home?"

"Knew what?"

"That she is ready to die; maybe she can eva be killed. A person can know sometimes. You can see for yourself. Everything finish. She pay everything: rent, electricity, and telephone. She leaves everything just so, and then she sends me home. Why for she send me home? It's nearly Christmas darling, and you know every Christmas I go home for two weeks anyway, but Madam say I must take all the food for the children and see about my telephone. Still, I am waiting for my telephone for five years, eva, so why she think this year I get it at Christmas? Ow Nkosiam! Makes me no sense."

"Who found her, Ndaba?" The question was like turning a knife. Milly winced upright and looked at OnyChile as though deciding whether the woman near sixty was old enough yet.

"Madam, she say I can come back on Monday. I stand at the bus station, and no Madam to fetch me. I think maybe she can forget, so I walk darling, and the hill is steep and I am not so young anymore... Then I come just by the garage, round the corner. Everybody is standing by the door, and then they bring Madam out under a blanket. They never eva let me see her face..." The water poured down the stone-grey cheeks as unimpeded as the memory. The mug of Rooibos tea, placed between her feet, sat untouched. "...they take her away darling, and I never eva see her."

"Who called them? How did they know to come?"

"It was Old Evie, that woman with the legs all bent, like chicken wish-bone. Every day Madam is giving her a lift to the Clinic. And like me, on Monday she wait and no Madam. She nearly crawl all the way, darling, and then they come because of Evie, she tells them. Also, they find the bathroom window closed. We never close the bathroom window because bathroom must always stay fresh, so they call Mr Robertson, and he breaks the window, and they find my Madam on the bed. They say she is dead since Friday. It is through of the Clinic. Yes, darling. They pretend they are very upset, but Madame die through of them." A vestige of anger caused Milly to sniff and sip some tea.

"What do you mean, Ndaba? How can it be their fault? If it was anybody's, it was mine." OnyChile looked around the flat for the first time, the threadbare chairs, the old Turkey carpet, the familiar paintings, and somewhere, in the spaces between polish and light, read the prison of her stoic mother and Ndaba's small gestures of comfort in bowls of hedge hibiscus and gleaming copper. The room itself was the clock of two women's co-existence, with the Clinic both financing and commanding its currents, its purpose, its routines of early tea, laundered uniforms, and time at midday for gossip under the blue gums beyond the washing lines, interrupted by mouthfuls of stew and mielie-rice.

"I asked her over and over again. You know I built a flat in the garden for her. She would never have come to England. She couldn't leave you…"

"I know, darling, but she left me for sure now. I think it was through of work. Once she sees her work is finished, with an advertisement for her job in the paper, she just gives up…"

"She was upset, but mainly because they hadn't told her. She expected it, Ndaba. Every year she has said they would not renew her contract…it was bound to happen. She was eighty, Ndaba. It couldn't go on forever…"

"My Madam wasn't old in her heart. I am also eighty, and I still work. But how must she pay me? How can we eat? That's the reason. She tells God to take her…"

"And the hole in the glass?"

"Maybe with the bathroom closed, her soul must find a way out. I think so, eva. That hole is clean, can be angel make it so." Ndaba drained her mug and stood up. "Anyway, they say heart attack, and she die very quick. Thank God. Nkosi Ow!" Ndaba sniffed, lifted the tray and put it down again. "Darling, you must fix everything very soon. Here with everything of Madam, especially silver and now people know, can be thiefs. I must stand day and night until Madam's funeral, then you pack and take it…"

"But it's all yours now." Ndaba shook her head dismissively. "In my house, everything can be steal in two days, but I can take that table. Nobody can carry that. Ow, I like that table; for nearly fifty years, I polish my friend, and that table can smile. We can remember together." She padded out with the tray.

∞

Whether her mother had secured a neat arrangement with God was debatable, but OnyChile found that Mammon had secured his percentage. It was all as Ndaba had said; every bill was paid and laid out on the desk in the bedroom, and the neat list of investments looked far healthier than ever imagined. They would secure a pension for Ndaba, not lavish, in no way proportionate for a lifetime's devotion, but equivalent to her wages. OnyChile remembered the conversation only a week past and her mother's dismissal of sympathy.

"Of course, they don't want an old duck like me. Who can blame them? Why should they employ a pair of arthritic hands when there are all these clever new machines I can't work? Oh no, my dear. My time is up, and I've had a very good innings. It would have been nice to be told, that's all. Now let me hear your news…"

In hindsight, there had been something new, a certainty, a freedom and an unaccustomed interest in OnyChile's daughters and their doings. Perhaps the conversation had prompted the informal codicil to her will, scribbled on notepaper by her bed, leaving each a small legacy. Had it also prompted the Living Will stuck in the pages of the bedside bible? OnyChile examined it. Signed ten years ago and witnessed by Mr Robertson, solicitor aforesaid.

'No resuscitation, no maintenance of life by Artificial Lung or other means….'

༄

"Your mother was quite a friend, you know, and she did so expressly want me to conduct her funeral service." The women seemed very certain that OnyChile would accept the instruction. "We often had lunch after Eucharist…"

"She anticipated her funeral then?" Something frozen had crept into OnyChile's voice. The woman fished in a pocket and produced a scrap of paper.

"I wouldn't say anticipated, perhaps a premonition. Anyway, this is what she wanted read. So suitable, I think. I never imagined it would be needed so soon." The poem meant nothing to OnyChile.

Perhaps her aversion to the bossy priest robbed her concentration, but it rang no bells. Clearly the woman had something of a stake in the proceedings, helping herself to Ndaba's cake and pouring more tea.

"Tea for you?" She waved the pot.

"No, thank you."

OnyChile realised that the woman's command of her mother's ménage and her death was probably the punishment she deserved. Ndaba would permit none of it. She came as close to sweeping in as arthritic ankles allowed and swiftly cleared the tea. She turned her back on the priest and addressed OnyChile.

"Darling, you can talk to the Jews. Madam, she has a burial place in the Jewish cemetery. That nice Dr Hubbert did buy it for her. She must lie there." The priest replaced her cup with a clatter. Ndaba took that with her and departed behind the kitchen door.

"Am I to understand your mother was Jewish?"

"By proxy and inclination only. My stepfather was Jewish and all her lovers before him, but if she converted, she did not tell me." OnyChile felt herself on a roll, although lovers-plural was a stretch, except perhaps for the mysterious and latter-day Dr Hubbert, of whom OnyChile had had intermittent reports, but mostly of his virtues, his deceased wife and his inconsolable grief.

"Anyway, I must obviously talk to the Jews. Is there a Synagogue?"

The priest conceded there was one, but she had never visited it and wasn't entirely sure where exactly... If OnyChile needed her services she had only to ring, but as far as she had been led to understand...

She departed with Ndaba courteously holding the door and shutting it firmly behind her.

"I don't know why; I cannot like that woman, eva she is a priest."

"How long has she been here?"

"Ow, it can be nearly three years, darling. She smile, but she have no feeling inside."

☙

The Jews were not happy. Yes, Mrs Kavnat did have a burial site, and yes, it had been paid for by Dr Hubbert, who was himself interred in the adjacent bed. As Mrs Kavnat was not herself Jewish, it would make for difficulties were they to permit... in consecrated ground...They would, however, undertake to maintain any alternative in perpetuity if OnyChile would concede the claim. Dr Hubbert and Mrs Kavnat had no business lying together in death. OnyChile found herself hoping that they had managed it in life.

The Clinic was not happy either. The police had requested an autopsy. Would OnyChile, as the sole next of kin, consent? OnyChile would not consent. The Clinic receptionist expressed her thanks and support.

"Very wise. Totally unnecessary. Your mother had a history of high blood pressure. The Superintendent has told them that an infarction was both likely and merciful. Few of us will have such an end."

OnyChile needed the anonymous Mr Robertson. He had found her mother, he had witnessed her living will, and the question could not be asked of Ndaba. But once the question was asked and answered, any funeral in any sanctuary would be blighted or refused. OnyChile would keep her suspicions to herself and swing the funeral like a censor over the heads of the card players. Nobody wanted to know. Nobody would have to know.

Marjorie-priest was riding high.

"I knew you would come round. Your mother was a devout Christian. I shall be delighted to conduct the service. I was thinking..."

"I'd like to say there will be music..."

"Music? Oh music. How lovely. I'm sure the choir will..."

"My daughters will come from England. They are both violinists, and they will play."

"What a treat for your mother's funeral. She was so proud of them..."

"She never heard them."

༄

It seemed as though God, if ever He had had a hand in this, was changing His collective mind. Once the Jews had been appeased with the choice of a burial site just outside the City of David's wall (but within reach of its hose) and the police were mollified by a signature (exempting them from any responsibility), and the priest had been sat upon, the day of the funeral would be the coming Friday. The newspaper carried an obituary, publicised the time and requested all donations to the SOS Children's village down in Kamhlaba valley. The next spoke in the wheel was Ncwala. Ncwala sounded like a home-brewed drink. Ndaba was needed to interpret.

"Ow, darling! Ncwala is very big here. The King is everywhere, finding he a new wife. Nothing, not eva a fly, can move on Ncwala. Maybe can be no grave diggers. I think can be no grave eva. After Ncwala on Thursday, everybody can be drunk on Friday. Maybe nobody can eva come. Ow! Maybe you must choose another day..."

"But Ndaba, why did you not say so before?"

"Ow! How can I remember everything? I forget all about Ncwala!"

OnyChile decided that nothing could grease the axle of this wagon mired in refusal. Her mother had always been philosophical about African time. The flights for her daughters were booked at such short notice they were via Dubai; the United Arab Emirates could not change or refund. Marjorie priest had cyclostyled the funeral programme; the press notices from white friends had been published. Ncwala was a public holiday, that's all. Besides, who was going to come anyway? Her Bank Manager and a few medical colleagues?

Marjorie-priest was succinct.

"Take no notice. These people love to make a fuss and wallow over death. It'll be lovely with the music and all. One bit of advice... They do all tend to traipse up to the cemetery, and we have a teensy problem with time management because there is another funeral immediately afterwards, so we do need the church hall cleared before four, and the tea should take precedence, don't you think? Could I make a suggestion? I could announce that attendance at the grave is for family and close friends only?"

"There probably won't be a grave dug if Ncwala is sleeping it off, and we'll find ourselves back at the mortuary."

"Splendid. That settles it then."

That settled it.

~

At dawn, OnyChile crept out, leaving the jet-lagged daughters unconscious. Even in sleep, they were so different; Jem coiled around her pillow, and Kate spread-eagled, almost naked on the floor. Ndaba was quietly humming in the kitchen as though to lullaby her grief. The little car started without protest and seemed to know its destination, climbing smoothly through the wood-smoke of early fires and the shafted light that flashed through smudged hills and ignited the golden grass up to the cemetery. The dead had the best view, spilling their tumbled headstones below the blue gums and straddling the crest of the hill above the town. The myopic stones kept watch on the long, slow road approaching from the low veldt, unattended by movement. Nothing stirred except lizards.

OnyChile got out, any hope of a grave evaporating.

The chosen site was marked out by small stones, at an angle to the regimented Jews, clothed in bamboo and Euphorbia, shoulder to shoulder under granite. Her mother lying there would forever be challenging their whitened sepulchres. OnyChile contemplated the headstone she had dragged from under the tap, a smooth shoulder of rock, worn by tears and water from the filled vases, somehow symbolic of her stoic mother, who had allowed herself no tears but been worn smooth nevertheless; a Swazi rock, not a polished granite anchor to warn off moss and insects. It would take a simple inscription, name and dates on bronze, affixed, as her life had been, to the surface of the country she had loved.

Two men appeared from beyond a distant hedge, and hope billowed. They urinated side by side and, zipping up their flies, walked off. OnyChile walked back to the car.

"Don't worry. It'll be done in time, somehow." that impossibly young woman undertaker had said. OnyChile thought, not for the first time, that she had no right to worry. This was her mother's country, and however it was done, it would be their way, not hers. It was for Ndaba she wanted dignity and in lieu of all the things she should have done before.

☙

At home, Ndaba seemed anxious; she had company, and she presented them.

"Darling, these are my daughters, you never see. This is Thandi; she is my youngest, and this is my oldest chile, Phyllis. They came last night from Johannesburg." Ndaba stood back so that OnyChile could face them alone. Both dipped slightly. These were the children abandoned by Ndaba; farmed out to relatives, denied a mother so that OnyChile could become her sole beloved charge.

"Did you know my mother? Have you come all that way just for her funeral?"

Ndaba rose to the rescue.

"Ow! How can a person not come for Madam's funeral? Of course, they come. Thandi did see Madam one time when she came for holiday…"

"We came for our mother, rather more than yours," said Thandi, throwing salt accurately at the gaping wound of guilt. Ndaba dragged her off, followed by Phyllis, stopping only to instruct.

"Darling, you can take us early to the church because there is no room in the car for everybody and the tea cups we can lay together. We ready now, and you with girls come later."

OnyChile waited in the car, thankful for the distant sounds of violin practice from the bowels of the flat.

The three women were silent on the journey, each nursing a cake on a lap. The church stood on a bank above the bungalows behind Frangipane trees and suburban plantings, watered early. It looked deserted. As the bulk of Ndaba was reversing out of the passenger door, a diminutive young man in a gleaming white shirt appeared from behind a tree and stood until she straightened to face him, breaking into a stream of welcoming Zulu. He was hugged and pushed towards OnyChile, who got out to meet Ndaba's "adopting son, he is Samson."

Samson bowed and took OnyChile's hand in both of his. Clearly, he was familiar with all that had concerned Ndaba. She was patently proud even in grief. "Isn't he look grand, darling? Ow! Such a beautiful son I have. Now we can take care of everything, and you go and get dress." Samson bowed again to release her and followed his bustling mother as she shepherded her brood towards the church hall, momentarily eased of grief. OnyChile drove away.

Her mother's world, past and present, had been a book she had never really opened, so preoccupied with the small and immediate concerns of motherhood, she had failed the large hearts beating and being beaten in the country of poverty and relentless sun.

When she and the girls returned, it was to a mass rally. There were queues slowly edging at every doorway, seemingly unable to enter, shuffling forwards by inches. The silence of so many sombre people was a dream. There was no sign of a hearse. OnyChile and her uncertain daughters encumbered by absurd violins felt, with the eyes upon them, like thieves after the church plate. They were saved by Samson, who led them through the vestry to places in the front pew.

There were perhaps thirty white faces seated near the front. Behind them, the pews, the aisles, the side aisles, and across the back were filled with black faces, standing and still edging forwards. Ndaba was on her knees. Now the moment of formal farewell had come, her face was buried in her hands; Samson steadying her twitching shoulder. The two girls slipped out and found a small space in the apse of the side aisle, where they set up stands in readiness and sat down upon a step, accompanied by an almost uniform turning of heads.

People were still finding space. The silent shuffling, the absence of any evidence of pallbearers, hearse, or priest, seemed to demand someone to take charge. OnyChile wanted the sea of Jericho to swallow her, or an organ to sound out, a choir to stand, something, anything… Where was the wretched Marjorie, who'd been so keen?

Suddenly, the west doors opened, nudging against the crowd, and— praise be— a hearse was visible. Moments later, the coffin entered, swaying perilously through the crowd at an angle, with the sheaf of mimosa, white roses, and eucalyptus slipping hazardously but lit by luminous relief.

The coffin was set on a bier, already scattered with flowers. Where had all these extravagant bowls of flowers come from, at the end of the pews, on every altar? OnyChile suddenly knew that she was superfluous to this gathering. She would have to scrap the carefully prepared speech. There was also a disturbing doubt: had the two funerals become confused, amalgamated?

That would have been too simple.

OnyChile ascended the chancel step and began by asking their pardon for presuming to talk to them about her mother, whom she had come to realise they knew better than she did. Instead, she would talk about her black mother, Milly Ndaba, and the gift given to an only child by a lifetime's devoted service, one that had liberated her from anxiety and gifted certainty instead, about the care of a lonely and widowed mother. She told them of her memories of Ndaba's laughter, her earliest music, and of strong criticism behind closed doors, that were her earliest lessons, and that what she knew of generosity had come from Ndaba's unbending sense of right and wrong and most of all her forgiveness. She hoped they would find it possible to forgive her and to realise that Ndaba's devotion had made possible her mother's dedicated service to all of them. Her mother's work was her life, and her work had been with and for them. They had blessed her work and been her life's sole enrichment, what she had described as 'the colour in my life, without which there'd be no life.'

As OnyChile said it, she knew the answer to the unasked question.

At the end of this confession, there was silence. Ndaba sat shrunken into the pew. OnyChile had no recollection of what she had said as she descended towards the sea of faces. She longed for a silent scream.

Marjorie priest stepped forward.

"Would anyone else like to say a few words?"

Nobody moved. A few necks craned backwards. Samson stood up. He eased past Ndaba and walked purposefully towards the altar-rail. He faltered briefly over the first few words, coughed and began again.

"I never expected to have to speak at Gogo's funeral, so you must excuse me if it doesn't come out prepared. My name is Samson and I am here from Simunye. I am not often in Mbabane, so I'd like to tell you what Mrs Kavnat did for my life because, without her help, I would probably not even be employed now. She was a second mother to me.

"It was my education she paid for, and her friends (he searched for a face) ... helped me with extra maths at school, and after a good matric, I went to see her because I wanted to see if I could go to the University. It was her writing on my application form to the University; I even still have the copy. I wasn't sure what subject to apply for. I thought I should do economics, and she asked me why. I said because money is what makes things happen, and she asked, 'Makes things happen for you?'...he smiled...

"And then she said, 'In this country, there are two things that are needed, food and education; if you want to give to your country, then what about teaching or agriculture?' I chose agriculture because of her, and I did my degree in horticulture. She told me that giving was the only thing to think about. I work in the sugar industry, the white gold industry we call it, so you could say I came to economics through the back way."

He had their attention. He smiled again and knew he had said enough.

"...So now I have a very good job, and some training in it as well, teaching other workers, and I get to travel to South Africa. I learn all the time. I just thought I would like to tell you we are burying a very great lady. She gave me everything, and she made me what I am." He turned and bowed to the altar and re-joined Ndaba, who looked at him with new eyes.

Marjorie priest, transfixed to the rail like a cabbage white butterfly, startled awake. After a brief pause, she ascended the pulpit and read two prayers and the requested poem. Silence reigned; somebody coughed. She took out a piece of paper from the folds of her surplice.

"Now we have the contribution of her granddaughters who will play the coffin out. I would like to say that only the family and close friends will attend the graveside. They will re-join you all in the Church Hall. We will now have the...pause...Andante from Bach's Concerto for two violins ..." she examined it again "in D Minor."

There was a collective slant of bodies forwards, curiosity almost choreographed. It seemed the instruments alone accounted for it; the craning necks equal throughout. Were violins entirely unfamiliar? The older raised her violin, and the younger followed. Jem gave the upbeat, and Kate came in, her long, sustained note shaking only momentarily before steadying. After the second higher entry, the conversation took over, the violins soaring and speaking to one another with perfect musical compassion.

OnyChile had never before heard Kate play like that, rising to meet her fastidious sister, who responded with every phrase shaped in the trust that it would be matched. In a packed church of almost two hundred, not a shuffle or a throat cleared. The roses seemed to exhale, the white light casting a glow on the girls' faces and on the roseate instruments, an altarpiece painted by music. OnyChile wondered whether any Swazi had ever heard a melodic rather than a harmonic communion and what it might mean to them. Was this spectacle or divinity? There was no way of reading the rapt attention. Bach just went on and on weaving, amending, refining...

As the movement tipped towards the final cadence, Jem gave the pallbearers a signal, and to the strains of musical harmony, the coffin left the church, down the aisle, and out of the door. The last bow left the string as the hearse drove off, followed by silence. Nobody moved. Even Marjorie, quelled, remained seated. OnyChile joined the girls, who quietly packed away. They left by the side door, followed by Ndaba and Samson.

Samson escorted the weeping old woman to his car, leaving OnyChile and the girls to travel alone.

It was not good manners to overtake a hearse at speed or to skid in the dust to an anxious halt. All three broke through the thorn trees together.

Perhaps Bach had strung it. It was a miracle. On a pile of soil, two gravediggers lay sprawled, their bare chests running with sweat and heaving with the agony of drawing breath. Around the grave, green carpets of astroturf were laid under the straps, ready to be rolled by a winch, gleaming in the low sun. To one side sat a canopied awning and, in its shade, chairs fitting for Ascot. All that was lacking was the ice bucket and champagne. Marjorie had somehow been teleported and was standing at the foot of the grave with a prelate in a purple stole, looking thunderous. Perhaps Marjorie had no licence for interment, and he had sidled in to complete what she had had no business to start. His irritation made clear he would make this as brief as possible.

OnyChile knew that her euphoria was endangering any remnant of dignity, but they were now into the home straight, and the effect of sublime Bach and blessed relief was champagne uncorked and fizzing. Even the bejewelled dowager enthroned under the canopy in her elaborate head scarf could not suppress buoyancy. The small file of people curtseyed to her as they passed, which she acknowledged with the merest inclination, and they stood well clear of her view. The coffin arrived beyond the thorn trees and waited.

Ndaba and Samson remained aloof from the small gathering, leaving OnyChile and the girls alone on one side of the miracle grave, heady with relief.

The coffin lurched aslant through the trees, the pallbearers ill-matched in height, staggering to counteract gravity; the flowers again imperilled. The incongruity caused OnyChile momentarily to laugh aloud until Kate dug her nails into her mother's arm.

They laid the coffin on the straps and were on the point of lowering it.

"I'm sorry. Could you turn her round?" OnyChile asked. They looked quizzical. "It's just that she would never put her back to a view.

Look at the view." She pointed through the blue gums to the distant Lobamba Mountains shrouded in haze, promising rain. They shrugged and did as asked, with a terrifying sideways tipping. All three closed their eyes, the collective imagination far worse than a blocked view. The winch began the lowering.

"Can you save the flowers? She wouldn't have wanted that, not such beautiful…"

The winch stopped. The flowers were retrieved and placed to one side. The winch resumed its slow whirring. As the coffin dropped below the ground, the loss of her mother hit her. OnyChile stifled a cry. The parting was like opening a vein and watching the blood of her life seep away. Her noble, self-denying mother was going, was going… was gone.

"You can refill the grave now," said the thunderous priest to the exhausted gravediggers. They looked disbelieving and remained sprawled against the mound. Samson took a step forward, grasped a handle and emptied in two spadesful, which thudded on her mother's thin belly. One by one the pallbearers followed, covering the small buttonholes of frangipani and fern thrown in with them.

When the gravediggers complied with reluctance, directed by the angry priest, the dowager under the canopy rose and, after a nod to Ndaba, proceeded towards an opulent four-by-four with bull bars and more chrome than Las Vegas. A chauffeur held the door; she was seated and departed in a slow scattering of gravel.

"I'll stay," said the priest. "You never can tell with these people…"

"I'm sure they can be left to finish?"

"Graves are robbed every day."

∽

The Church Hall lay deserted, rows of cups untouched, cakes under cling-film undisturbed, plates of sandwiches and virgin pyramids of koeksisters glistening with sugar. They couldn't have all gone already!

"What has happened? Where is everybody?"

From the kitchen, a young woman appeared.

"They've all gone. You've managed to insult the whole nation." She could barely contain her anger. "I stayed to make sure you knew what you had done."

"What on earth do you mean?"

"In Swaziland, we bury our dead. We don't pretend to. We all attend the grave, and we all together bury the body. It is the way we show our love. You have insulted our love; you have insulted us all…"

OnyChile clawed at words like grasses on a cliff face. Wordless horror was descending, but not comprehension.

"I had no idea. Nobody told me. I cannot begin even…"

"No, you can't."

"…but… but I was told there's another funeral due any minute. We had to be out in time. How was everybody to get to the cemetery?"

"You should have provided buses. That's what's usually done." Her lip curled with contempt.

"The priest never told me…"

"You come to Swaziland, and you listen to a white priest! I spit on you."

She heaved her bag over her shoulder and walked out, slamming the door. The echoes of oak and the clang of the fallen key were the muffled explosions in a distant quarry over which they hung suspended.

☙

In the days that followed the departure of both sets of daughters, Ndaba's without farewell, hers banking against the blinding sun in the twelve-seat plane bound for Johannesburg, nothing could soften the ostracism. OnyChile faced hostility and avoidance on every street corner and in every shop. Scorn was clear and expressed. With the lighting of the evening fires across the hills, the keening would begin, the nightly punishment from the flat above. Ndaba blocked her ears but could not conceal her misery that her OnyChile was so openly reviled. She was implicated and had failed. Her authority had withered; her lifetime of respect laid waste.

No suggestion was adequate; OnyChile's abject apology in the paper in both languages was inadequate. Her short article explaining the difficulties of Ncwala was ridiculed. Ncwala happens every year. She could not implicate the Jews or the priest, who escaped unscathed.

"Most people cannot read here. It can do no good, eva though you mean to help. In Swaziland, nobody can forget nothing. That big woman who came is family of the King. The whole country knows about it. They can remember forever. Eva they talk about forgiving all the time in church, nobody can listen. Ow, they can hold it forever in their hands like a warm stone."

∽

The invitation to the Clinic came as OnyChile was preparing to depart. Gogo's grave was planted and enclosed with low bricks. The furniture for Ndaba's house on the border had been roped on a bakkie and perilously driven into the hinterland. The flat was as empty as her heart. She would have to accept.

The Clinic, the nucleus of her mother's existence, stood on a hill surrounded by trees, a miniature of all the military hospitals she had waited outside as a child, doing homework on her knees. Wards cantilevered down the slope, open to the garden and refreshed by breezes caught in filmy white curtains. In the reception area, slow women slowly mopped, sweeping the clean floor with methodical strokes; open doors into wards made palpable the patients who had awaited her mother's visits in tilted beds and traction harnesses; a lifetime had passed in the blink of an eye. She was transported back into the lonely childhood of her mother's poverty and the curse of her own existence.

"You must be Mrs Kavnat's daughter?"

"Yes."

"Let me relieve you of those." The young receptionist took a pair of callipers and a neck brace from OnyChile. She handed over a packet.

"Milly thought you might be able to use these drugs, perhaps for someone who hadn't money. They were only prescribed recently..."

"Where would we be without Milly's supervision? Of course.

Thoughtful of you."

She loaded them over her desk and led OnyChile down the passage past the open wards.

"The Superintendent was anxious to meet you before you left. We've organised a staff tea. We were all so very sorry about your mother."

The Superintendent was standing with his back to the room, gazing out of the open door into the garden. Behind him, nurses were setting out cups and cutting a cake. He turned, a tall, stooped man with a distracted air, as though his case notes were being committed to memory; he seemed somewhat at a loss and scratched his head a few times, gazing out of the window. Suddenly remembering the occasion, he removed his white coat and came towards OnyChile with hand outstretched.

"I'm so sorry. I'm Bill Thorpe. Do sit down. First, I must tell you how sorry we all are about your mother. It was a terrible shock, so very sudden. I fully intended to be at her funeral, but unfortunately, I had to go to Johannesburg with a patient, and a migraine struck me down. I'm prone to them, and I simply couldn't travel back in time. To make up to her, I donated the airfare to the children's village, not that it made me feel any better... Everyone said it was a wonderful service, which, of course, makes it more regrettable that I couldn't be there..."

Bill Thorpe seemed to be talking to himself, rattling a résumé to mask the overall silence. OnyChile tried to make it easy. She made a pretty speech about how important the Clinic had been to her mother and how grateful she had been, year after year, that they had kept her on, and in case it needed saying, she undertook to forgive them on her mother's behalf.

"Of course, at eighty, she understood it couldn't go on forever. I think what grieved her was simply not being told..."

"Not being told what? There was conspicuous interest from the table.

"That you had advertised her position."

"What on earth do you mean?"

OnyChile clarified.

"Well, when I rang her on her birthday, a week before she died, she told me that you were advertising for a physiotherapist, and of course, she had been predicting it for years, but that you could have just warned her. She would have understood."

The looks around the table were aghast. Bill Thorpe covered his face with his fingers and dropped his head. "My God!" he said quietly, "Is that really what she thought?"

There was horrified silence. It took moments before he spoke.

"How could she have believed that?" He was still searching and kept shaking his head. The nurses and the Registrar exchanged glances as though they needed confirmation from one another repeatedly.

"So, you didn't advertise?" Bill straightened up and looked at OnyChile as though for the first time.

"Yes, we did. But it was for an assistant. I could never have let your mother go. She was a miracle worker. I have never seen a practitioner like her. She never gave up on a patient. Apart from her skill, I truly believe she was a healer, very unfashionable of me, I know, but there it is."

"So, she simply misunderstood?"

Bill's devastation now was personal. Why had he not thought to tell her, the miracle worker? His perplexity was developing deeper roots, and he seemed to need to dig them out.

"I can't believe she did not know how much we valued her. How could she not know?!"

"She was always very modest. She kept saying she needed re-training and was out of date."

"She was; very out of date. She never learnt that diagnosis is now supposed to be an exact science and that you allocate two months to paraplegia or four weeks to post-operative recovery and then sign off. She wouldn't listen to any of that. Did you happen to see a very tall man at her funeral, one who walks with a stick?"

"No, it was very crowded."

"Let me tell you about him. He had Guillain-Barré Syndrome. It's a dreadful progressive paralysis, and it needs constant massage, heat and exercise just to slow it up. There is no known cure or known cause. He was in here for six months and, by the end, almost entirely paralysed. Your mother treated him every day, but she realised that he was pining and wasting, as much out of despair and loneliness as his condition. He missed his children. She persuaded me to discharge him and let him go home. I had my doubts because I thought his family would never manage his care. Once your mother got an idea in her head, she was pretty determined. So, he went home. Every day, she visited him and treated him there, carrying heavy machines up the three floors to his flat. He recovered almost the full use of his legs and, apart from one hand, his arms as well. Someone said he walked into her funeral. That was entirely due to her..."

A nurse went to refill the pot. Bill resumed.

"So, you see, when I saw her with others like him— he was about six foot four, and others the same size, and watched your mother, so frail, trying to take their weight on her thin shoulders, I could see a single fall breaking every bone in her body, I had to get her an assistant, for those sorts of things... I would never have replaced her..."

Suicide by mistake.

OnyChile rose. Bill accompanied her to the exit. Just as they were parting, he hesitated.

"This is perhaps cruelly irrelevant now. Why we all wanted to meet you, was to ask a favour. We are planning a new ward for the Clinic, and we wanted to name it after her. It would be the Kavnat ward, and we wondered whether you might do us the honour...when it's built, of course...."

"Of course, I'll come. There is nothing on earth that would have meant more to her."

Bill was not much comforted and turned away.

OnyChile saw him watch her retreat in the mirror of the loyal Toyota.

She knew he would never be allowed to keep his promise. There would forever be that warm stone. Ow! Nkosiam.

CHAPTER 37

The Donga Divide

'I feel, too, that the terrible pain I have gone through in past years, partly from the defects in my own nature, partly from outward things, has probably been a preparation or some special work that I may do before I die.'

A bomb detonated in a quarry sends its dust high into the atmosphere. The immediate collapse is obvious: stone fractures and falls. The fine powder that for days, perhaps weeks, goes on silently falling is less obvious, yet it obliterates...

The lonely death of her mother was that detonation, the funeral and its insensitivity the immediate destruction, but the dust was the lives of all those that had contributed, now pulverised. It covered and blanketed. She would pick her way through the debris, stunned and staggering, holding on to any remaining habit simply to try to make sense of it.

There were others whose well-being called for first responses. Her own survival would take years, for what the dust had obscured were the foundations of all her certainties: the taut steel of Louie's misery, the perennial support of Ndaba's quiet service; both had braced her and prevented her from facing her own failures. 'You never regret the things you do, only the things you don't' and now the things she should have done, the letters not written, the holidays not planned, as they should have been, rose in jagged rebukes. They would speak forever. Those were the most obvious in the immediate aftermath, but there was a much deeper destruction, an existential one, the core of self-regard and self-acceptance.

Her inventive and conquering life she had built on the qualities she had judged worthy, derived from those she admired. Each had, in different ways, stood against the surrounding racism of indifference. The *crime of indifference deserved the deepest pit of Dante's Inferno, and she had seen it everywhere and believed herself free from its callousness. Her mother's desolate end had been a tungsten flash that captured her own glaring indifference when caring mattered most. There was no escaping it. Her failure to ask Ndaba how to manage the funeral or to discern the blatant racism of the priest exposed the assumptions that exposed her just as baldly as those whites who had taken all the front seats.*

The priest's dismissal of 'these people', the citizens of their own country, was also Nicolson's 'horrid pink palms' and Max's shouting for tea, the ripples from Cecil Rhode's rape of Africa, Cape to Cairo. By that single event, she was tipped into the donga, the black lightning that split her two worlds and streaked across the landscape of her life. She had not surmounted that divide, as she believed, but mixed it into the mortar of heedless survival, failing to attend to it. The shame was mortifying.

The greater severance from all the 'givens', including the illusions about herself, would take much longer.

∽

The ricochet from Louie's loss was cushioned by many things needing attention. Some were simply practical but the more important were all the obligations I had so long neglected, as well as those demanding remedy. Being with silent, desolate Ndaba and the girls together for a narrow window of Africa made imperative their introduction to my lost life, their past family, and the country of their birth.

The loss of my mother and the almost simultaneous loss of my two older daughters, neither of whom had expressed any sympathy for her or me, would take years. Both had undone knots too deep to be identified; that tapestry I had woven on the smooth shuttle of the belief that mothers and daughters were welded together. I was alone with loss and guilt and paltry gestures of remedy. All I had endeavoured to fill was my own lack and longings. Louie and I, matched in stoicism, constructed that net of silence. A single conversation revealed that it should never have been necessary.

Some transgressions can never be salved. There had not been a word of reproach from Ndaba. She suffered my disgrace with controlled misery. I would leave; she would stay. What my insensitivity had defiled were all the years of Louie's first loyalty: to the Swazis, to Africa, to its poverty, as Heli's had been. This conflict between the two worlds of my birth had pushed its splinter deep into the muscles of my immediate family. Jess and Ros had had numerous holidays with David and Carol in game parks from Sabie, where they lived with marauding monkeys, to the Okavango delta with its migrating herds of hundreds; this was our 'African pair', familiar with tents, land-rovers and long lenses, from weaver colonies suspended over water to the so-called 'big five'. With a wildlife photographer for a father, they were, by proxy, aficionados.

Jem and Kate were entirely ignorant of wildlife, cooking out, the sound of egrets or the dawn spilling honey over the morning quietude of grazing antelope. In the short space before Christmas and every reason to escape from Mbabane, I would begin to remedy that, not to offer a tourist attraction, but to seed an empathy with the country game inhabits, which had incubated us all and which I had so woefully neglected.

In Louie's tin Toyota we set off with rudimentary camping gear for Hlane game reserve, newly created near the Mozambique border. My expectations of campsites, where huts would be available, relied upon long-defunct memories. A shop of some sort would offer essentials, candles, matches, cold beer and a braai. 'Let me show you my Africa' was implicit in the thoughtless way I threw things into the boot.

Heavy heat sits over the kettle of the low-veldt, which simmers just below boiling. From Mbabane's median altitude, we dropped, dropped, down towards the furnace of still air. Unpaved roads had been churned into glutinous yellow clay by heavy rains. Wheels spun, axles danced, and twice we spun, facing back the way we had come. The girls looked anxious. I was not going to be defeated before we arrived. This is Africa; let me show you what it expects. Brace up, let's see resolve.

Luckily, there were no moving obstacles on the road, just the bleached bones of trees uprooted by elephants. At the gate, a man in a bush hat took the money and pointed ahead. We skidded, and swerved, dancing on in the matchbox car to reach the only camp, only just: the axles, the mudguards, the wheels jammed with yellow gloop. Nobody human thought high summer was the time to visit, so we had it all to ourselves with the resident ostriches who peered at us with their dowager disapproval, great hammy legs and crinolines of feathers fluttering indignation.

The guide showed us to the only hut left open on the rim of a shrunken lake.

"Ostriches, are they safe?" Kate asked, as the guide unlocked.

"Mostly they are, but if they approach, sit down. They might attack if they see your legs. They don't like legs."

"Great. No longer allowed legs," said Kate, giving me that look.

"Mind out for warthogs with young. They can charge."

"Even effing birds and pigs are dangerous. Why do we need to see anything else?" Kate swung on me. I was damned if I would be cowed by my daughter, whom I had de-fanged by bringing her here, far from cell phone distractions. The Scottish boyfriend, who had thought to gate crash the funeral, was relegated to panting for her in Johannesburg, which had not improved her temper.

"Will you want me to take you on a game drive? I can come back later if you like. The evenings are best." the guide asked.

I had not yet admitted, even to myself, that Louie's car would be no match for a rhino or an elephant if it couldn't cope with a quiet road. I accepted.

༶

We drove out in a short wheel Land-Rover, our female guide and a driver in front, we three abreast in the back. Within a quarter of a mile, the road was strewn by branches.

"Elephant. Not far. You are in luck," the guide said. The driver muttered in a low voice in Siswati. He stopped and very slowly began to inch back. A thunderous thumping joined a trumpeting cry as an enormous bull elephant broke cover and hurtled towards us in the road.

"Not a move. Not a sound," said our guide as the elephant stopped, swinging its trunk and raising it like a solo horn player preparing a concerto, parping twice.

"Jeez", Kate slid soundlessly down below the window. After a few minutes, the elephant decided to abandon his performance and turned off the road, crashing back into the strings of the singing bush.

We continued to back away until we could turn and slowly drive off.

"Not many see that," said the guide. Jem had managed a photograph of an angry elephant between two heads. Kate continued to hunker down, which is why she missed the start of the next act. Two rhinos and a calf stood sentinel, blocking the future.

"This could be dangerous." the guide whispered, "just stay very still." The driver cut the engine. "They can't see very well, so they may come close. Shhh..." They did. Very close.

After sniffing at us with their horns inches from the driver's door, the calf lost interest and wandered off, followed by the adults.

"That was lucky. They killed a ranger the other day when one just tipped his open top and punctured him. Have you had enough?" the guide asked.

"More than enough," said Kate. "Let's go."

Back in camp, it was the mother who did the cooking solo under a gas canister lamp outside, while the grunting of warthogs kept the terrified indoors. It was also the ageing mother who climbed a steep ladder onto a narrow shelf to spend the night below the thatch while the girls occupied the double bed below. Wimps. Britain breeds wimps.

"Imagine what the spiders are like. No way" said Jem, an arch arachnophobe. So much for their introduction to echt Africa!

Shortly after sunrise, the following morning, I found Jem sitting mesmerised by the African dawn., watching the impala visit the water hole.

"This is really something else," she said. After Kate condescended to rise, we drove to another reserve where unaccompanied walking was possible. Before the noon heat sizzled the day, we set off with a map to what it claimed as a 'python pool'. Kate strode ahead nonchalantly, bravura replacing yesterday's terror. Jem and I walked behind, along tracks through thorn bush alive with the singing cicadas and the odd violence of a beetle attracted by sweat. The relentless sun bore down. I could feel the infection of Africa sinking its grip as Jem glanced at me and rolled her shoulders in disbelief. Kate strode ahead, damned if she would catch enthusiasm.

We were crossing a riverbed with a few brackish pools when Jem asked

"What are these?" She had stopped to examine deep, crisp, fresh spoor: unmistakable, recent, sharp as three-toed tridents. Crocodile!

"Run. Out of the river. Back!" Kate was by now far ahead beyond the banks of buried killers. Panic did bring her back, reluctantly shrugging and flouncing. Panic held its breath until she was safe.

"I thought we wanted to see the python? Make up your mind!"

I realised that any instincts I once had had been obliterated. I was no longer a fit mother for the African bush. Safety here relied on familiarity and a wide awareness of the signals I had forgotten; careless ease was not appropriate. The flickering ear, the sudden scuffle, and the call of a kite needed sharp ears and a bristle sensitivity. For too long, I had lived in my head. It was all George Eliot's fault for substituting imagination for reality. I no longer had African instincts.

∾

"I'm outa here," said Kate when we returned to Mbabane. It was all the excuse a girl needed to join her boyfriend. Jem and I took her to the airport the following day and stopped for a last foray into the game at a small reserve, Mlilwane, with nothing more dangerous than a shy leopard. We hired a couple of horses and rode out amongst the herds of wildebeest and zebra, grazing disinterestedly, cropping the long-dried savannah, methodically oblivious as we rode through them. Four legs good, two legs bad: Animal Farm's wisdom was here on display. Impala gave us not a second look, except while vigorously chewing and the cries of leaping monkeys in the tall bamboo were the soundtrack from a distance.

I looked at Jem, who had not been on a horse since the violin had curtailed it. She returned the long look and said, "Now I really understand you, Mum. I think really for the first time. I never have until now." It was what I had longed for and needed to hear.

She left the following day, waving from the window of the small plane that coasted down to the bottom of the runway before accelerating over my head and the single conical windsock limply inflating. Matzapha International Airport: Gateway to the World.

∾

Back amongst people, my punishment met me everywhere: chatting backs turned, and pedestrians crossed the road to avoid eye contact. In the evening, the keening from the flat upstairs would start up and Ndaba would block her ears. In the swept naked flat, Ndaba and I sorted through the last remnants of her and Louie's half-century together. Photographs briefly resurrected memories of our life before I abandoned them. There was no other word for my oblivious, child-centred, music and building-dominated years that now haunted me.

"You must keep whatever you want, Ndaba."

She peered over glasses as I lay them before her, putting down her silver polishing to take up one and then another.

"Ow. This one I can keep, darling. I remember that holiday with Dr Randall, and you are still so small. Why Dr Randall never come for Madame's funeral? Maybe Mrs Randall never let him? Ow, terrible he is not come to help you. She took up another and turned it face down. "I like this one of Madam, but…"

"But?"

"Not that man." She could not bring herself to say his name.

"You can cut him out?"

"Ow! I can do that easily." She fetched a pair of scissors and, lowering her slow bulk into a comfortable chair, proceeded to remove Max from everyone. "Eva, Madam, never talk about him after he's gone. Did you find his grave? No. Why? Because Madam never eva make the stone. No name anywhere. Can a man live his whole life and nobody want to remember him? Me the same. I don't want to see him. Never!"

"Why did you never leave Ndaba?" She looked at me and shrugged.

"How could I leave her with him? She can be blind, but me? I cannot be blind."

It was perhaps the moment to raise the subject that had been difficult earlier. In all the sorting and packing, I had not seen the four volumes of Daniel Deronda. I wondered whether Louie had sold them to pay a debt.

"Ndaba. You remember those books Marna asked you to keep for me..." She halted, looking apprehensive. "What happened to them?"

She pushed all the photographs aside, clasped her hands, and pressed her lips together. "Eva, I must tell you now, I can find you not understand anything I say. Mrs Randall, she did take them. She comes after Old Madame's funeral, and I see her taking them from my Madam's bookcase. I say, 'Those are for Miss Phil; Old Madame did say so.' 'Nonsense', she says, 'Miss Phil is too young to have them anyway. She can lose them.' Mrs Randall did take them, darling, when my Madam was at work. When I tell my Madam, she says nothing. What can I do?"

There, bald and inescapable, lay the world of servitude. The same servitude bound me too; that failed to ask Ndaba's advice about Louie's funeral and remained silent when it must have screamed its claim to be heard. Would there ever be an end to this injury? Ndaba sought to console me.

"Darling, I never say before, but when that man came to live in Bramley after old Madam passed, he stamp every book with his name; all Madam's books have he name stamp, eva the ones Old Madame leave for you. You can see." She went into the kitchen and took down Marna's battered copy of Mrs Beeton's Cookery Book, and there, behold, Max had been; 'Libris Kavnat' smudged above the title.

That figured: Max would have been oblivious to an autographed inscription in George Eliot's last novel. I suspected the universal stamping had been deliberate, like a dog lifting a leg on his new territory.

Between them, Ursula and Max's jealousy had deprived me of the only thing I wanted, not for its value but for George Eliot's steerage on my life and her link to that portrait already shipped and that memory of my last meal with Marna. I was angry, deeply angry, but Ndaba's misery precluded showing it.

"Do you know what Ursula did with them? Did you ever see them again?"

After some thought and a puzzled reconnaissance, Ndaba said, "I not sure darling, but I think Madame maybe say something because Mrs Randall later say she gave them to a university. Maybe she did, maybe not. I think…"

Ah well! No doubt Ursula's bequest of my books earned the appreciation of a librarian in a country George Eliot knew nothing about, had never visited, to sit in a catalogue nobody would ask for! Damn, Ursula.

~

There was a fight I could still have. I invited Marjorie-priest to lunch. She had ruined more than the funeral and she needed to know it, if only as a final stab for Louie and for Ndaba, and before I went home to lick the wounds of suppurating disgrace. I was incubating an idea, which waxed more vigorous by the day. I decided John had to meet Ndaba while there was still time. This lunch would clear the ravages of what that white-surpliced dunderheaded priest had destroyed, if only in the fire of contained fury.

"Oh, I'd be delighted," she said, "quite like old times with your mother."

The Ezulwini (Heaven) valley road snakes down from the temperate elevation of Mbabane at over four thousand feet to the low veldt in a single decline, steep enough to block ears. Bordered by craft stalls and fruit sellers and the fluttering of the red, white, and black Emahiya cloths worn by both sexes, it is an open marketplace where tourists stop and wander, drinks sellers peddle, and women sit behind baskets, ankle rattles, grass mats and carvings.

Off the main spine are unpaved dirt roads leading to hidden lush places. One of these was the Swazi River Café, on the bank of a sluggish river, intermittently visible through the thorn trees. We were the only custom on the broad balcony, which lay like a peeled half-orange dried beneath a sloping roof. We perused a menu and ordered.

Conversations with strangers usually begin with dull details. I did not warm to this woman, with her careful hair and fussy gestures, whose 'calling' had come late in life.

"What did you do before you were called?"

"I was in nursing, first for years in hospitals, but then with a private agency. I took on home nursing full-time. It is much easier to cope with a single patient and much better paid. Well, not always easier… The last patient I ever had, a single man, was extremely difficult, although without the usual resources…"

"What would you call the 'usual resources?" I passed her the bowl of nibbles, sat back and sipped.

"I'd say speech was one, and an ability to move, if only to gesture his needs…"

"He couldn't do either? Was he paralysed?" I tried to visualise not being able to get rid of Marjorie by any means.

"He couldn't do anything! No control of bodily functions whatsoever…"

"Stroke? Parkinson's?"

"That was the strange thing. Nobody could find the reason. None of his tests revealed anything wrong with him. Mind you, I had my theories…"

"Do tell," I was delaying the intended conversation, waiting for a suitable opening. Her self-satisfaction was as impenetrable as a bank vault. I wanted to divine a combination that would open her eyes not just to her injury to Ndaba and me but to the entire country she believed she served impeccably. It was not going to be easy.

"Well," she began, "he was known as a kind of spiritual advisor before this affliction…whatever it was. I think he overstretched himself. It happens with these guru types. They take on all sorts of exorcisms, and in the end, something gets them. It's why I stick firmly to the gospels. You can't go wrong with the gospels. Anyway, he did recover, eventually, and rather wisely, in my view, he decided to seek the protection of the Church. He entered the priesthood, perfectly restored. Unbelievable really. I heard about that much later when I was training as a lay priest myself. He was still ill when some male nurses replaced me. Perhaps they knew tricks I didn't. But he was my last hurrah as a nurse. Something about him got to me…"

"Do you remember his name?"

"I do. Not anyone you would have heard of. Rather secretive, actually, although quite well off. He lived in a rather grand flat, which was a good billet for me since it was nicely central near the tube and all the buses. I could get to Harrods in a quarter of an hour. Have you ever tasted a Harrods cheesecake? My weekly treat with a good cappuccino. Oh, what I'd give now for a decent coffee! His name was, I shouldn't say really, but how can it matter here? Martin Israel, in fact, *Doctor* Martin Israel. Some sort of medic, though not in general practice. Funny cove. He didn't really like women, I sensed that; even when he was in extremis…he sort of flinched at any touch."

She rattled on.

I never did bring up Louie's funeral. She rattled on about that, too, but I hardly heard a word. I paid and drove her back.

The impossibility of this woman sitting amongst the thorn trees, accompanied by strident rasping of crickets, had stripped away not only speech but comprehension. I was so geared up to broach her damage to the legacy of Louie's life that this deflection had, initially, a 'Look, there's a squirrel' quality. The displacement was so jarring that I did glance sideways. It was no squirrel but a looming growling bear that upended all intentions with one swipe of her perfumed paw.

Only the captive to her 'random' rattling and you, the reader, know the circumstances. Only you and she hold the threads to interpret this extraordinary encounter.

No unlikelihood could more eloquently reveal the great gulf between the time-bound world and that of eternity. In eternity, the ever-present NOW brought together a man prepared to murder, his punishment by an inexplicable paralysis, and a nurse drafted in, who could not help and gave up nursing, to enter the Church. So far, not so remarkable. The improbability in the time bound, however, was mind-blowing! Thirty years earlier, the victim of that intended murder made a narrow escape and lived perplexed until the death of her mother brought the nurse, now a priest, to metaphorically murder her reputation on another continent. For that to happen, two of the principals changed their professions and moved metaphorical mountains to escape the circumstances that had originally brought them together. What bound them all was an evil that clamoured to be exposed.

Had the three — the murderer, a nurse and the victim—met in Cranley Place, Kensington, thirty years earlier, there would be no great story to tell. But that story needed to be told, and reach completion on a sluggish river in an unknown country, Swaziland. But not until the mistaken suicide of the mother, whose prohibition had perhaps set the entire sequence of events to unroll. Both time and place were contracted to this moment of revelation.

That great gulf between time and eternity was the one I had tried to bridge by allowing myself to go 'mad' and to live in both realities. It is also the gulf that explains Judith's dependence on 'chance' and Georgina's call for 'meat and two veg'. And why the sceptic can never make the jump across them, or mankind absorb the evidence of the divine surrounding us, no matter how purposefully it reveals itself.

So, what is time? Or place? Or story? Is story merely skittering actors in a greater play? None of us were what we seemed or understood what threw us together.

Not even his immediate neighbours in his 'rather good billet' knew the female-phobic Dr Martin Israel of Cranley Place Kensington. His brutality has steered this narrative, just as a murder steered Marna's story. Martin Israel, camouflaged as an inhibited spiritual mentor, turned executioner with a block and a sword.

Do you, reader, still think events are co-incidental? What are the chances of that?

It's about the same as getting attacked by a crocodile. It happens. For reasons...

That's exactly right. Martin Israel, buried in mud, heard my footfall and leapt out to take off my head! Perhaps her conjectures about 'over-stretching' were not far from the mark.

No, not far at all. Keeping up with you requires full torque elastic.

Are you still winkling me out? Plucking at my sleeve? You'd punched me in the stomach and finished off with this complacent woman telling me that Martin Israel was alive and well and wearing a dog collar? He who said that the Church had not 'begun to wake up' had adopted its well-brushed surplice?

Perhaps you should make that surplus? Another to add to the sleep-walkers. He knew what he had done to you. Perhaps joining the Church was his form of penance. Or a safe protection from any other like you!

Only because he was found out by me escaping and succoured by those he'd tried to warn off. So, he went all respectable to obscure his responsibility by preaching what he had never believed?

Everybody finds their consolation in their own ways...

Their well-camouflaged hypocrisies...Why did you arrange that?

Think it through.

Well, hearing about his paralysis-in-extremis was rather gratifying, but I should not dwell too much on that.

It revealed a great deal about what you had almost forgotten; some would call it karma. Martin had tried to kill you but was himself felled instead; he had despised the orthodoxy of the Church, and yet it was his only refuge when he had been stripped even of bodily control. It was a savage lesson for one as arrogant as he was. But there were lessons for you, too.

Yes. It certainly cut us both down to size.

Revealing what?

That I had been a gullible fool, investing so much in someone so small and now so transparent. But encountering this oblivious, complacent woman, unveiling, between mouthfuls, the likely causes and their consequences was another stark exposure of my blindness. Blind to everything. Including banality's powers of destruction.

Your longing always blinded you. Longing always does. You abandoned all sense of who you were, in deference to his imperious manner, one you mistook for privileged knowledge, throwing pearls before swine, if I may say so.

Who am I, then?

You have begun to find out. You thought I was persuading you to write a record. No, I persuaded you to write your path to discovery.

So, to make it all clear, you arrange a meeting with a woman who had no pearls —so could never make that mistake— on the banks of a sleepy river on a different continent. You went to a great deal of trouble!

All places, all time, are one to us. Thought travels as easily to Swaziland as to Kensington.

I still have difficulty seeing people as the emanation of thought!

The masks of thought. Actors. It becomes obvious when they interact. Israel failed to eliminate you. The priest eliminated your reputation, almost as lethal. But she also closed another profitless door to ideas you have not fully developed yet. Even very dark clouds have light behind them.

To teach me? How to see? Where not to place trust? And to read a sell-by date on life. Yes. I see—a thousand thanks.

Prego.

CHAPTER 38

Return: Facts are not Truth

'Scenes which make vital changes in our neighbours' lot are but the background of our own, yet, like a particular aspect of the fields and trees, they become associated for us with the epochs of our own history, and make a part of that unity in which lies the selection of our keenest consciousness.'

The imperative impulse to bind my two worlds had become inflamed by the guilt of my neglect and Ndaba's age. I was half wondering whether we might move back to help her and whether John would cope. He was so very English, and he was tired. So, my return was not alone but with an old man as excited as a boy. John's imagined Africa, stretching from Cape to Cairo, was woven out of Kipling, Rider Haggard and Sanders of the River, a smattering of Churchill's Boer War, all wired together on a reputed noble Empire. A continent without distinctions, a place of pith helmets and stout boots, as well as names he could not pronounce: Chaka, Dingaan, Moshoeshoe. It had called to him from his early boyhood, and the closest he had been was on his way back from Ceylon in a troop ship.

It was a mere six weeks after Louie's harrowing end. The rudimentary airfield, with its windsock hanging limp in the heat, was the first sign that Africa 'tout court' had not been entirely modernised and might still hold his antique dreams. The small jet deposited us onto baked clay, and we stepped out into a world of sweat and easy smiles. The luggage of six passengers carried on six pairs of shoulders, followed.

Because Louie's flat was no longer available, I accepted an offer of a small apartment on the grounds of what had been the European Union Ambassador's house. Perched high on a leafy hill, it overlooked the distant Lobamba mountains. When South Africa was ostracised, all the diplomats moved to Mbabane, just across the border. They built extravagant embassies and filled their boredom with the Golf Club, the Casino, and the occasional play. After Mandela's restoration, they had wasted no time in packing up and moving back, leaving behind shells of inappropriate opulence.

Virginia, half Swazi, had lived in the flats above Louie before she married Richard, an affluent white salesman, and they had bought the grandest. The couple met us at the airport. As we drove up Ezulwini Hill, they apologised that the apartment was not 'quite ready', but we could stay with them until it was, which would take 'only a few weeks.' Entry to their home, surrounded by high wire, required PINs and the raising of remotely controlled gates.

The glitzy, marble-floored, sliding door palazzo, with its pale squared sofas, its glass tables, its servants mopping floors in white overalls, its lawn sprinklers fizzing over spiky Strelitzia and Bougainvillea could have been any grand hotel, anywhere. John's disappointment was palpable. The room we were to occupy was comfortable, dark and confined, like a B&B in the suburbs of a sunny Aberdeen. We were free to make ourselves at home on the broad terrace with channelled music and their children on mechanised skateboards, but 'please don't smoke.' John's pipe would be pocketed for the duration.

The only hope lay in my retention of Louie's Toyota with which to escape. First things first: We would drive to find Ndaba.

Virginia was surprised at such urgency. "You'll need a driver. It's quite difficult to find." She called to a man raking gravel. "Eric has been there before. He'll take you in our Land-Rover."

Eric, a lean, dark man with an easy smile, seemed glad to be relieved of gravel. He waited at the supermarket while I bought Milly's favourites: lemon extract for adding to Rooibos tea, pumpkin to roast, a whole 'shicken', and anything I thought likely to be difficult to find in her remote rural area.

The outskirts of Mbabane and succeeding valleys, scarred with cement works and pumping stations, only deepened John's gloom. Dwalili lay close to the border with South Africa. We passed a deep lake where Eric said the King had installed a submarine! He laughed.

"The King has money for everything. Nobody told him you need the sea. It just stays here. It comes up, it goes down!"

The young King's education at Sherborne School, the brother school to John's girls' school, had proved a challenge. It was generally agreed that his bodyguards had received an expensive education that did not reach past them to the monarch. The submarine was an eloquent testimony to that.

The industrial areas petered out and gave way to narrow unpaved tracks, winding through occasional huts, a corrugated iron church, and a worn mud field: Children kicked a ball and stopped to watch us pass. It was impoverished, haphazard, but wholly African; not the mud-hut thatched villages of Lesotho with their swept arenas and peach trees but scattered dwellings of iron sheeting, clap-board, some patched with brick.

"Nearly there," said Eric.

I had a vision of finding Ndaba hoeing and her disbelief at our unexpected arrival. I couldn't wait for John to meet her and the musical stream of words to follow. We bumped down a heavily rutted road and stopped. All was quiet. Eric went ahead through a barbed wire gate. Suddenly, I saw our invasion as based on another white assumption that affection was enough. We held back. Eric would warn her. After a few moments, he came out.

"She's not here. But they say please to come in."

Two young men at a covered table rose politely. Eric did not clarify their relationship with Ndaba; neither was Samson. I put the box of food on the table. Eric explained. They nodded, looking at John, standing uncertain. No African-born man, white or black, would defer like that, looking lost, quelled in a dark mud room.

Ndaba had gone to visit her 'other house in Mayflower' across the border. What a shame we had missed her. When would she be back? They were not sure. Sometime. Eric told them to eat the food. They suggested something.

"They say you can see the house if you want?"

Ndaba's other room, across a stand of stunted mielies and cut stalks, was fronted by a narrow open mud balcony, protecting her bedroom with its two beds covered by familiar spreads and cushions. This home had been the labour of years, ferried on her head. How important it had been; how pitifully basic it was. The other house she was visiting, a brick square in a street of identical squares in a new 'township', was far from commerce or employment in a sea of grass, aptly christened 'Mayflower' for sailing into the unknown. Louie had bought that as secondary insurance in case the King of Swaziland changed his mind and reclaimed Ndaba's hard-won patch. Louie was hedging all bets. Suicide had made its last provision, the legacy of Louie's love for her life companion. Not enough, not nearly enough.

We drove back with Eric silent.

"She'll come and find you. I'm sure," he said as we pulled into the prison compound.

༒

Until Ndaba returned, we would escape to the Drakensberg. I would find some grandeur to rescue this misguided impulse. Liberty was an open window on an open road through the Boer War battle zones, Dundee, Glencoe, Weenen —Place of tears—Elandslaagte, Blood River, Spionkop, all evocative to me; only names to an Englishman. My wild commando forebears were long interred beneath the impervious veldt.

John wanted to be interested, but it was hot, and the journey had little variation. After a night spent in a rondavel on a farm, we found ourselves in the place of my birth, Harrismith, before any shutters were lifted. Cruising the quiet streets in search of coffee, we passed a library. I had another impulse. Was it possible that we might find the farm that had left its traces on the memory of a three-year-old?

We followed the librarian opening up. I would approach an absurd question circuitously and ask whether she had any old newspapers. If I could locate a murder report, I might find the farm.

"We have bound copies of the Harrismith Chronicle. Are you after anything in particular?"

"A murder. Of my great grandmother."

"How exciting. I don't often get asked for murder on our very own patch. You've made my day." She went to a low shelf and indicated heavy bound copies of the Chronicle. "Any idea when?" I did a quick calculation. Uncle Lynn, who allegedly witnessed it, was ten years older than Louie. He would now have been ninety. Legend had him in a cot at three or four, so eighty-six years ago? It was now the start of 2001.

"Let's look at 1916/17?" With help, the librarian heaved the great binder onto a table and opened it. 'The Late Mrs Barrett's Funeral' was headlined in a narrow column.

"There she is!"

"Well! Look at that! First page! What a memory you have. I never thought…"

"No. Me neither."

The legend that had followed me like a yellar darg is about to reveal its entrails. Myths are raw-boned until a storyteller puts flesh upon them. That Boer in his hat in Wiltshire had reignited this tale as though sheltering a guttering match.

This story had lurked throughout my life in a sepia wash, beginning at Marna's funeral when I was sixteen and twenty years later continued by that improbable farmer from this very town, propping up a bar in Wiltshire hawking apartheid. Here, it lay entombed, with the catafalque slid open by a woman in a floral blouse in a small deserted library.

The librarian slipped away. "I'll leave you to it."

What fragments did I begin with? Marna's mention of thirty-six stab wounds to Louie as a child, but no clarification of what they referred to; an embroidered nobility of a kraal-fireside drawing of short straws to risk all and kill; a child witness laid to sleep covered with a blanket by the murderer, and a promised grave on a farm. If I could find it? That was about it, factually.

Emotionally, it had penetrated deeper. The alliance between Marna and Lynn was of a different quality, a deeper bond than that which held her to Louie or Ursula. Lynn's quiet chain-smoking presence, his rising to anticipate 'Mother's' every wish, held solicitous care that took gentle pains over everything to do with her. Not knowing much about mothers and sons, I had assumed an oedipal reverence from an only son but came to sense they shared this experience that they never spoke of, something always buried but eternally potent. Her funeral had dug it out, but what it was, apart from a violent death, had never been fully unwrapped. All I knew was that nobody should awaken Lynn without prior warning, the single trace of this silenced legend.

Face to face with the reportage of a mythical murder in the wake of Louie's recent suicide, I collected facts without finding meaning. A clear reading was difficult because the pages were tightly bound, and half a column disappeared into the binding. Demeaning facts twisted a heroic event into the debris of a prosaic theft. Much did not align.

Some of the expectations tallied: mostly the absence of any expression of tribute or any real regret. There was mention of 'warm esteem' for the deceased Mrs Eeltjie Barrett. Her daughter, Minnie/Marna, with her younger brother Victor—twenty-three—and five-year-old son Lynn, 'Chippie', headed the long list of attendants. Her funeral brought out the whole town, listed informally by first or nicknames. The noble best of what I had heard diverged wildly. The most crucial change was that this murder happened in a suburban house, in this commonplace town, not on the farm I remembered. No starlit acres, with cattle kraal or barking dog framed a heroic dispatch of a sadist for the benefit of all.

Instead, the bald details emerged in several court sessions.

On the night of the 16th March 1916, Mrs Eeltjie Barrett, a 'woman of regular habits', was stabbed to death by John Mpondo. He was a servant she had dismissed for insolence two weeks earlier. Two suspected accomplices, Molooi and Sehoya, were charged along with Mpondo. The first hearing established the circumstances of Mpondo's dismissal and was given piecemeal by witnesses who knew Mrs Barrett. One was Alma Barrett Mandy, the sister of Aunt Nell, the reader of tea leaves, predictor of the murder, in whose garden this tale was first seeded. Witnesses clarified one 'regular habit': Mrs Barrett would leave a glass jar of sweets on the window sash to crash and warn of any intruder. For self-defence, she kept her son Victor's military truncheon by her bedside.

That ended day one of the trial.

As all were departing, a group of vigilantes immobilised Mpondo's guards and set upon him with 'appalling ferocity', leaving him for dead. He was dragged into the police station by his arms. Two hours later, he sat up and asked for water. Although none of his bones were broken, the attack and his injuries delayed the trial for over a month. The public was, after that, denied access.

Before the trial resumed, Mpondo said he wished to confess; the Prosecutor and Chief of Police attended to hear him. In that confession, Mpondo described meeting a man, Johannes, at a fairground earlier in the day, and Johannes suggested robbing Mrs. Barrett and killing her. What motives Johannes had for this were not clarified. Mpondo related all the details of his and Johannes' entry; how he removed the jar, climbed in, and passed out a metal box of valuables to Johannes. Johannes climbed in, lit a candle, and stabbed Mrs Barrett in the chest and neck. As he was stabbing her, she flailed with the club, but it fell, and 'as the missus sank, she cried out, 'Look at the face, Chippie, look at the face.' Mpondo also told the police that Molooi and Sehoya were not involved. On the advice of the prime suspect, the police released them!

The details of the described entry to the bedroom were already known to the police from forensic evidence but not previously disclosed in Mpondo's presence. The little boy 'Chippie', my Uncle Lynn, witnessed this horror, but Mpondo covered him with a blanket and told him to be quiet. Mpondo did this twice. He and Johannes raided purses for an insignificant sum of money and then searched the pantry for food.

Their search woke a lodger sleeping in another room, Helen Thorburn. In her nightdress, she crept out, saw a light, and heard noises. She hurried away to alert a neighbour, Mr. Dick, and they returned with his revolver. On approaching the garden gate, both saw glimmering candlelight in the bedroom and heard voices. The gate latch alerted the intruders, who extinguished the light and escaped through the back. Mr Dick and Helen Thorburn entered to find the blood-soaked Mrs Barrett and Chippie, but no matches to light or examine the scene. Without ascertaining whether Mrs Barrett was dead, they departed to get matches and call the police, leaving Chippie alone in the dark with his massacred grandmother.

Later Chippie told the police that he saw 'John fighting with Granny.'

On the face of it, it seemed an open and shut case. Mpondo's foot and fingerprints matched the forensic evidence. Chippie, who knew him and spoke Zulu, picked him out in an identification parade. On Chippie's evidence, Mpondo was hanged. Chippie was six, the youngest witness ever to send a man to the gallows.

Are you now contented? Have we tracked the truth of this fable by instalments?

Far from it. That chilling cry, "Look at the face Chippie' from a woman being stabbed, is the point that links the story, as first told, and the trial here reported. What depth of calculation already looks for justice while struggling for life amidst savage violence? Or draws attention to a child witness, thereby endangering him, too? This woman, pictured in black at Marna's first wedding with a face of relentless power, capable of anything, could have inspired murder without the trivia of paltry coins.

Money does not explain this act since an opportune absence, a broken window, a timely entry would have secured money with much less risk. More critically, given that Chippie knew John Mpondo, who had worked for his grandmother, was it not more likely that an unfamiliar 'Johannes' would have elicited that cry? Someone neither of them knew needing to be remembered? Would a man facing execution invent this cry as part of inventing another assailant, and why was Johannes never sought? After three witnesses heard 'voices', why was only one man charged? Was Mpondo talking to himself? How did Mpondo recount so accurately details already verified and known to the police but which he, beaten up and left for dead, had never heard?

The savagery of the stabbing with a 'pocket knife' of an elderly woman in bed certainly suggests a personal hatred beyond mere avarice. That is what rings loudly.

Marna's lifelong silence about her mother spoke louder than any words from the woman for whom pithy disdain was as natural as breathing. Her mother's demonic viciousness lay too deep for clever précis. Photographs of that face support the early story, and Marna's silence did it more eloquently. Nothing tallied with the tale told by the evangelist farmer roving through Wiltshire, so even Mrs Barrett's sadism had to be set aside.

In the aftermath of the town's collective frenzy to kill Mpondo, leaving him for dead, was there a collective shame that was content to silence him rather than pursue the other man, Johannes? Perhaps the clear identification by a child was all they needed to effect a swift conclusion that was far from justice.

'Look at the face Chippie' was all that was left to validate the story I had heard from others and the one from Marna that nobody had ever heard.

What did this discovery teach me? That the telling of tales is coloured by the storyteller and belief in it by the listener? Marna always said facts are not truth. Was this event the first splinter of that conviction? She suspected, perhaps, that Chippie's evidence had hanged the wrong man? As he grew up, Marna and Lynne silenced their misgivings?

I will never know.

This extraordinary story wound around a spindle that began with Marna's birth in 1883 and continued with mine until it ended with Louie's death in 2000. The scars of it were intermittent but winced to new heat, like old burns.

At nine in the morning, on a sleepy suburban street, the event had taken me far from a story into Marna's silence. The story, in all its contradictory instalments, had stirred my heritage back to the place I had begun, breeding new questions like maggots crawling out of a sand bucket.

It had not yielded the fond-remembered farm.

A parallel universe of different dimensions? It's a perfect depiction.

What do you mean?

This inconsistent, varied account of your great grandmother's murder, buried in Marna's silence, embroidered by a tea-leaf reader at her funeral, re-invented in an encounter in Wiltshire from a passing Boer is finally, prosaically interred by a press report. It does not clarify but leaves you only with questions and doubts. There is only one consistent thing. It haunted you and repeatedly— and, improbably, found you. That alone is trustworthy.

As did the legacy of Martin Israel through that priest who triumphed over me. Somehow, truth always finds me, even ugly truth, but facts belie, consistently…

So….?

For a would-be writer, it was a valuable illustration that sympathies shape a story, not the facts in it but its emotional truth. For a searcher after truth, it forced the necessity to seek behind the event for psychological integrity. You preferred the romance of the valourous dispatch on the farm because it made sense of Marna's injury and silence, so that is what you believed. Now, you centre yourself in the senselessness of a murder for insignificant money when theft would have carried less risk. But injustice, betrayal, and white men's insults to a black suspect would have also been recognised by any other and produced a group of 'hostile' witnesses. It makes the violence rational and explicable. Emotions explain and on emotions is memory linen-threaded. As you already know. Even the re-examination of new facts does not alter it.

New and contradictory facts sent to confuse?

No. the opposite, to warn and to train. No different from that woman priest telling you about Martin Israel being universally female-phobic.

She diminished the personal and began to incubate your deeper understanding of a small and vindictive injured man. Masks and pretension concealed him.

The insubstantial pageant faded, leave not a rack behind?

Quite the opposite. This murder echoed in all of you and down the years. The death of Victor and an unhappy marriage for Marna followed. All gave birth to you. Its inconsistent mystery prompted your search and emotionally haunted your life. Even Marna's tears for Victor while reading Jackanapes seeded your literary intentions.

I did not realise that then.

No. We are nearly there. Let's walk on.

CHAPTER 39

Taeke: Coming Full Circle

'The exact crossings of genealogies which had brought a coronet into a new branch and widened the relations of scandal- these were topics of which she retained details with the utmost accuracy, and reproduced them in an excellent pickle of epigrams...'

"Do you happen to know a family called van den Bosch?" I asked the librarian. Her smile reached teasing eyes.

"I know about…. six, no seven, families called van den Bosch. Which one did you want?"

"Whichever lives on a farm with a great cliff and a waterfall?"

"That would be Taeke. Maweni. Do you know him?"

I explained that my grandmother was his cousin and that I had memories of his farm. She picked up the phone and dialled. I heard half a conversation before she handed it to me. Incoherent early memories become more incoherent over the telephone to a stranger.

"Would you like to come out?" This Taeke offered. My heart leapt.

"Love to. When?"

"What's wrong with now?"

Nothing was wrong with now except the need for a quick shedding of all that English caution and time for the best china and a narrow window. Taeke gave directions and said, "When you get to the farm gate, there is no road. You just drive over the field, but you'll see some tyre tracks, follow them to Mark's Bridge over the spruit. Don't worry, it's quite safe. You'll find the garden beyond. I'll wait for you."

A farm without a track of any kind was unfamiliar—an omen of a direction without any prepared pathway. I assumed rocks had been cleared as we bumped over a lush grass field. I was driving on faith.

Mark's 'bridge' was two flat girders, an axle width apart over an eight-foot drop. I lined up what I hoped were the tyres and took it at pace. Taeke was standing beyond on the lowest lawn and simply waved us past towards…the house… exactly as remembered!

"You're a van den Bosch all right. Nobody else would take the bridge at that speed. I'm Taeke."

He was a male image of Marna, same strong nose and humorous eyes. Fifty-seven years have passed, and nothing, but nothing has changed. There are the oaks. Hear in them contented doves. Beneath the oaks, the ribs of all my rusty tractors! Only the tyre swings had gone. I said so.

"No children here now, sadly."

Here is the stoep still festooned by Catorba grapes, still bearing and now ripe.

"Pick as many as you like. Sour though. I'm not good at tea. Is coffee all right?"

Taeke goes inside. John and I stay on the stoep, shaded by striped blinds above. As they always were. The silver-stream waterfall still falls over the lip of the cliff and still feeds the spruit running along the perimeter. From here, we are facing north, so it is at our back, invisible, falling silently but renewing the garden and filling the water troughs.

This is coming home, wondrous impossible. I had never really had another since. I had occupied flats, had a bed in many a dormitory, and after Max, no welcoming home at all. I had built one for our newer family, mostly to provide what Maweni had seeded in me. My dreams of Maweni had resolutely built for my children what I had never had. Two had already rejected it and me utterly.

Ndaba had been my home, a person, not a place. Maweni's dream, nurtured for a lifetime, is no longer a dream or perhaps a deeper dream. Marna sails back in her floral dress, and the toddler still picks the sour grapes. John pulls a face. He cannot know how critical that sourness is. I feel giddy with the glory of the Maweni I had lost and now find. Preserved as perfectly as a book between covers, always handled with gloves, each leaf separated by tissue, all colours minted fresh as each memory turns from oaks, from honey fields to lawns.

Gardens are rare on Freestate farms, but here, an almost English garden dropped in terraces linked by rose arches, abundant with colour: roses, daisies, dahlias and banks of shrubs. It always had. By English standards modest; by Freestate standards, it is luxuriously extravagant, almost frivolous.

Taeke returned with a tray. "Rosalie, my wife, does the garden as my mother always did. She'll be sorry to have missed you. On Fridays, we go to town. Or she does. My day off, and the servants too, so you'll put up with my lousy coffee." He poured.

I gave him my ecstatic memories; he filled in the facts. His father, Tommy—another christened Taeke— whose brown knees I could still see, was Marna's cousin. This next-generation Taeke and his brothers, Eelco and William, had been away at school when we were there. "I expect my Aunt Zita would remember you."

Observing Taeke recovered Marna. I told him so. He jumped in with his memory.

"A formidable woman, domineering, or I thought her so."

"Formidable, I concur. Domineering? Only if you let her. That's why she was wonderful. She would have worn shoes that colour."

Taeke was wearing a sumptuous pair of dark red boots, soft calf, very expensive looking.

"My weakness," he said. "I love leather, especially red."

"Me too. Especially red."

All those pictures of English 'Start Right' red buttoned shoes I had so coveted in pictures! There were no such shoes in my childhood, only laced dull brown or black. Noel Streatfield knew what shoes meant to children and that owning the right ones, from white boots to ballet pumps, offered whole worlds of inclusion on a skating rink or Sadler's Wells. Red shoes meant Christopher Robin and going down with Alice. Jodhpur boots with elasticised sides were a world of horse-mad girls and National Velvet. Things were always literary in boundless metaphors. They say DNA shared is also tastes in common. Identical twin studies showed it repeatedly: twins, separated at birth, first meet wearing identical ties and doing similar work and both with fat wives.

Not only the physically preserved farm, but there were other spicules of familiarity: aesthetics, language, modest smiling, disparaging disbelief, and a man entirely at ease with himself, forever in the first place that was a place for me. As Marna always was. The longer we sat over reminiscence, the deeper it exhaled. The green lung of the garden breathed for the house. Beyond it, the golden grass of the fields gave onto a low hill, blue in the noon sun and hazed with heat. An African farm is an island empire with habits of laundry, seasons of preserves, and a tractor fired every day at the same hour. Hospitality is both obligatory and legendary.

"Taeke, I have a memory of a great cave somewhere nearby and a small rock room with gun brackets buried underground. You had to slither in on your knees or backside. Where is that?"

"That's on the next farm over. I wonder if the brackets are still there? You English would never credit us handing over guns to Basutos when we were on the same side, fighting against you.

"Only half of me…"

"I stand corrected. Sorry. Bad enough being a Boer. It must be much more difficult being half a Boer. I haven't been over to that farm for, oh, many years. Would you like to see the house?"

The door to the central hall stood open, and the rifles were lined up in the rack by the door, where they had always been when Tommy took one each morning. Given the rumours of violence against farmers, I asked about that casual security.

"Nasty things have happened, but mostly to the unwary tourists. I refuse to submit to fear. This is my country, too. When I have to lock my guns, we might as well leave."

To the right of the hall was the dining room. There, Marna had sat to write letters, the silver tureen with its bulbous cover still glimmered on the dresser, but something here had changed; there was more light at its end. A grille of what South Africans call 'broekie lace'—wrought iron fine enough to garnish women's knickers—separated the sunroom from the gloom of polished wood and glinting reflections.

"Yes, we built that garden room for the late afternoon to catch the last of the sun. You really do remember everything! Come and see if you remember the kitchen?"

He led us across the hall to the kitchen. It was larger.

"No. I don't remember this. I remember it as behind the dining room at the back, smaller."

He was pleased.

"Quite right. It was there, but we moved it to make room for the museum."

The 'museum' held glass cases of objects, veterinary implements used by his great grandfather, the first vet in the country, books, family trees, old maps of farms, photographs of Boer commandos, and pictures of Tommy on horseback—nothing of Marna. I was not ready for documents or to taint memory with objects, not yet. I wanted to know about people. I decided to risk it.

"Taeke, now I will probably embarrass myself, but my grandmother once said someone in our family was descended from the Romanovs, the Russian royals. That wasn't true, was it?" Taeke looked amused.

"You think it couldn't be true because the only royals live in Buckingham Palace? That's always been the British conceit. There were quite a few royals in Holland, and some of those were Russian. So yes, Grand Duke Nikolayevich, Tsar Nicholas the First's third son, fathered seven children, most of them illegitimate, with his actress mistress. He was known as a compulsive womaniser, so much so that he was thought mad and locked up for it. Our first Taeke was called Atzo Nicolai and was his direct descendent, and we have had a monotony of Nicolais or Nicolinas ever since. Nothing to boast of, really, since he was deranged, but if you want a splash of Tsarist blood, help yourself. Half of Holland is called Nicolai. Shall I show you the farm? We can take a walk."

I blew a quick apology to Marna for not believing her—again!

Taeke took a stout stick and gave one to John. We climbed up, above the house and to its right. From there, we could see the falls, a celestial tap ever running. We passed a fenced-in area with a couple of gravestones and room for many more. One was very small.

"We lost Faith, our little girl, very tiny. She is buried here with my father. Sadly, there were no more children. We have never managed any others."

We climbed higher. A group of young, dark brown bull calves backed away, then nosed forward, watched over by a young herdsman to whom Taeke spoke in Zulu.

"My hobby now," said Taeke. "Rare breed experimenting. It's a disgrace; we now sink to buying our milk. Not even a cow. No arable, no milking. No one left to take this on."

I sensed that he had probably had enough of painful reminiscence and unexpected guests.

We turned back.

"Before you go, let me give you a small gift."

He re-emerged from the house with several generous sticks of biltong wrapped in brown paper.

"Still a little wet. Put them in the back window to dry in the sun."

There were not tears enough for that completion nor for the man who had lost his only child in infancy. Nobody to bequeath Maweni Heights where he had grown up and grown old and I had been only young, and where Marna would be forever writing letters at that polished table. Maweni was immortal. We had found it just in time.

∾

John refused all suggestions of cities. As Maweni rewarded my vivid recollection, his anticipation would filter out those places that might smudge his expectations. He wanted no white sophistication and as little familiarity as possible, although a cold beer was welcome.

After Maweni, we arrived at the Royal National Park just as the gates were closing after dark. Shown to a hut with a torch, we braaied some steak by torchlight and went to bed. As the dawn broke, I drew back the curtains upon the curved cliff face of the Amphitheatre. Stone hung in a single sweep, suspended from the sky and lit gold. Peaked at each extremity as though being pinched upwards to stage another drama, it was cruised by a pair of golden eagles, wheeling with motionless wings, dust in the thermals.

"Now wake up! Look!"

John sat against the pillows, unable to respond.

"I don't believe it!"

Staggering to the window, he stood. There was nothing but shadow porpoising across the lower hills between us and that navel panorama, the Mont aux Sources, spilling its cloud precipitation to create every river of the country; the Tugela, the Vaal, the Orange, all sprang from this central fountainhead. Like Rio's benevolent Christ, the mountain rose with arms outstretched to pour forth life. It was an inverse to my first sight of the Victoria Falls, so epic, so implacable, so generous; one fell, the other rose.

"Will that do?"

"Incredible. Simply incredible."

A long day's climb up the Tugela valley over rock pools and water-weathered flat stones overhung with trees and leaping monkeys, where we paddled and ate, washed John through with his introduction to my childhood. The sound of tumbling water was a constant song with occasional solos from erupting birds whistling, chattering and flapping. This valley replenished the slower Tugela far off, which wound, looping like a dawdling pencil, experimenting with contour, sometimes narrowly confined, mostly broadly languorous. I remembered all those times with Sanie, riding this trail on holidays, swimming in icy pools, and leaving her mother in bed with gin. We had taken this land of plenty entirely for granted.

But our children had never seen it.

The omission was too late to remedy. Children never exposed to a dog will miss their critical constancy and sensitivity; so too do children who do not grow up in Africa miss its essence. Its infection must bite early to inflame that tragic, conflicted loyalty. John could perceive what it might have meant, but knowing it would elude him. Every moment of this journey brought me back to Marna. 'We can never leave.'

I had left and I had been starved.

Describing its call is impossible to those who do not know it and superfluous to those who do. It has much to do with privacy and acceptance, a country so at home with its wilds that humans are left to forge alone, supported by both its beauty and its gaze that rests on its skies, its storms and thundering surf. Africa does not interfere. Not yet conquered or regimented, but abundant as Eden was.

Tourism had overpopulated the wilds of my youth with cars and comforts, so I took John to Itala, a new reserve only recently set aside for game, with one campsite up a steep hill under a prominent stone pinnacle. Supercilious giraffes contemplated our invasion through their mascara-lashed eyes, peering over flat acacia as we ascended in low gear to the camp.

As dusk descended, we went on foot up the stony, narrow path to the top of the pinnacle. A three-hundred-and-sixty-degree landscape encircled. Where the Amphitheatre gave its dimensions to height, this was Africa's breadth: limitless. Below, diminished thorn trees threw shadows no higher than a stunted grass, and giraffes cropped in herds, loping along with some non-urgent collective intention to graze a distant tree. Scurries of wildebeest sent up impromptu dust devils swirled by a multitude of creatures no bigger than ants from where we were. It was John's first view of limitless Africa, where wildlife did not exist to be looked at but were the only tracking creatures that owned it. Here, Rider Haggard might have been.

A drive back through Zululand and three nights in a tree house gave John the Indian Ocean, its crashing rollers, its pounding, insistent energy and its surf. Since he had encountered that in Ceylon, it was already familiar, but oh, the joy of surfing again, after the pallid water England calls the 'sea' with its half-hearted shrugging onto stony pebbles, its tiny coves and modest tides. For a naval country, England's sea is worse than disappointing. Perhaps that's why it sought an Empire and expropriated other peoples' coasts.

I arranged a proper Highveld storm, with indigo cloud, 'dry rain', and blitzkrieg forked lightning bouncing from koppie to koppie. We drove through it, putting full trust that rubber tyres would manage an electric field, which filled the sky with sheet-lightning linen tossed and spread between the zigzag forked kettledrum interruptions. The storm had put out all the lights of the hotel where we were staying in Graskop and for a forty-mile radius. We had been there for three nights and were almost staff, much to the apologetic embarrassment of the manager who served the same lamb cutlets and mint sauce every night. All other guests simply came to see the Blyde River Canyon and bussed on.

A group of French tourists stood helpless with suitcases in the black-out, trusting there might be beds. The African barman, who doubled as the receptionist and head waiter, was grateful for my elementary French, gave me his torch and let me do the honours. He gave John the keys to the bar, saying, 'Please help yourself to anything you want. I'll be a bit busy.'

"So that's an African storm?"

"Yup. Also, an African response to a crisis. Mobilising resources."

"No need to be smug about it."

"Things are just more dramatic. It's the rock and the sky speaking louder than sponge clouds to soggy fields. I don't hold it against you. How was the whisky?"

"I took a beer from the fridge."

On our return to Swaziland, the biltong was confiscated at the border by the Swazi customs official, who no doubt enjoyed it, by then perfectly dry. Ah well.

∞

Ndaba had heard we were back in Mbabane, and sent word when she would arrive. We waited at the bus station where white Kumbis disgorged large women from every quarter of the country. All had bundles on their heads; many had babies on their backs. I looked for one well-stooped.

"I'm more nervous than when I met your other mother," John said.

A whirlwind of enthusiasm came from behind his back.

"Ow, this is Master John. I can give you a big hug. Darling so wonderful to see him. Maybe another hug. I so sorry I am away when you come to Dwalili. I think maybe you go back to the UK and maybe I never meet him at all. Doesn't he have a kind face, darling? Madam, she says this man so kind, Miss Phil, and I can see. Such nice eyes, eva. Ow. Isn't it wonderful you come back so soon? But darling, my table still has not come to Dwalili. Maybe you can talk to Miss Virginia. Let me see you now...." The flow flowed. John smiled and went on smiling. Ndaba kept shaking her head in disbelief at her own delight. We drove up to the embassy while she briefed us.

"I never before see this house of Virginia. Madam also never comes here. Madam say this house is not bought with money, eva it cost a lot. She say this house is paid with soul. She says Virginia she cannot recognise in this grand house. Ow, darling, for one family? This big place! Still, how can I tell you? Maybe Virginia can get some soul back now you are here?"

"What happened to Virginia?" Ndaba pulled her explicit, wry disapproval.

"Virginia, she live like us, in the flat upstairs, and my Madam is very good to her and her little girl. No father, that child. Every day, Madam gives Virginia a big talk about getting work, and I look after the child sometimes; such a sweet little thing, so good you wouldn't believe. Then Virginia marry this white man, and now she talk to nobody; no friends, no family. She lives in this rich eva a prison. Madam was very upset. She never come here, never, but what can we say? Nothing, darling. People can marry the wrong one like my Madam marry that man. What can a person do?"

The point told.

Within a day, back in her flowered overalls and matching doek, she was ironing John's shirt's and making soup. Ndaba's occupation of the garden flat conveyed her life with us and her central stake in everybody's doings. What was bought, what was forgotten, what should be considered, what was worn, all merited comment. While polishing the floor on her arthritic knees, she again filled the air with her musical humming. It was a short sample for John of more than a half-century of service, which never thought to cease.

It was where she was most at ease, in expert service, the platform of her authority. In Swaziland, Ndaba determined everything that happened. It was her home, and our respective roles were reversed.

Like Maweni, captured just in time, Ndaba's last weeks with us were enough to show what I had talked of. Yet John also met the residual hostility that still burnt in acrid gestures. Ndaba's misery had turned to contempt.

"These Swazi's, Master John, can never forgive, and you not even here for my Madam funeral! Nothing your fault, eva Miss Phil cannot know everything here. Ow Nkosiam, these people so stupid. Take no notice." So spoke the daughter of a Zulu chief, who always forgot she was half Swazi just as Marna had straddled her two cultures when it suited.

John had certainly met Ndaba.

~

Five years later, almost on the anniversary of Louie's death, I had an urgent impulse to telephone Ndaba. She now had a telephone, but connections were always difficult, and her hearing meant she seldom heard it.

"Thoko very sick. Can't come to the phone."

"Can you tell me what's wrong?"

"She just lies quiet. No eat."

I telephoned Ndaba's daughter Phyllis in Johannesburg, who drove to Dwalili and took Ndaba back to Baragwaneth Hospital—the hospital where Tom had laboured in those half-remembered days.

She was discharged but died not long after. Phyllis rang to tell me.

"How did you know she was ill?"

"I don't know how I knew."

Ndaba was buried in Dwalili. I sent money for the funeral, flowers and a speech for Samson to read, but I knew I would not be welcome to attend.

Darling Ndaba, my constant light, my perfect mother.

So ended the sixty-five years of an ordinary life.
Ordinary?
Yes. Ordered but semi-conscious. One step before another, pulled along by the threads of obligations, survival, duties, and other people.
The dominant thread of endurance? For what purpose were such tight bindings, such certain retention of each one?
To offer a vocabulary and perceive the invisible line twitching through pattern and repetition. You have the whole life, its pigments, its languages, and its characters that help you to distinguish the real from the false. Your recall has laid it all out for those willing companions still trotting alongside us. They will understand every link and what contributions were made by the seemingly trivial and by the great upheavals,
The time has finally come to use that vocabulary, or it will go to waste.

CHAPTER 40

Far Fetched

Was this my story? Or the journey of an instrument, deftly wielded by its Master, whetted and sharpened by loss and tempered by disappointment. To what end? Why, through all its mistaken roles of wife, teacher, builder and mother, did its steel remain unblunted but never laid aside? What compelled its driving search for something to cut clean or shape?

Should I answer?

I think it's time you did! I have sifted through every other source for insight: all those words from theology to literature, but returned hungry for the kernel, the seed to explain the force that through the green shoot drove the flower: one that has not opened but droops.

George Eliot was not enough? Had she not accompanied you throughout? She had trodden the same question and left her tracks for you to follow.

She cast a sharp shadow, but this is not her story. Her tracks kept me following, and what she endured, slander, betrayal, loss and loneliness, made her companionship natural, but, as was true for her, there was some great work that summoned. I knew it was there, waiting, but not what it was! No better than she, given how widely she cast her nets.

Her first dedication was to the translation of Das Leben Jesu, the life of Christ, after which she took detours through all the orthodoxies that derived from that life. She sifted through all the conformities that compelled belief and obedience, others that twisted His gentle suggestions into vehement prohibitions, but none of them held her. His life alone remained inspirational, as did her own. Like yours, her characters spoke loudly and lived larger than any belief or philosophy. Her life, like yours, was the book she read and drew upon for the answer to the question. What was I created for? It is the question everyone asks until they persuade themselves to cease asking and wait to die without an answer.

༄

Every 'hero's journey' involves a departure from the comfort of the family and the known, followed by some fresh wind of new understanding or a blinding Damascene revelation, which rewards the initial courage to strike out. But they almost always end with the Prodigal's Return. Jubilation culls the fatted calf; the journey is complete. The jubilation implies that sanity or conformity has returned; the impulsive folly is now sober and back where it belongs. What is seldom explored is the difficulty for the prodigal in reconciling his larger self, honed by his trials and solitude, with the pinched demands of an outworn shoe.

My slow return had met no jubilation but doggedly offered new things to master, a new subject to teach, a new family to provide for, a home to build, and music to foster. At each section of the journey back, I was unexpectedly gifted, succoured and saved, given a long rest on a ship, a job by telephone, a cello in a dream, a home by a passerby who heard the sound of a violin, and all the attendants who appeared to help. They simply appeared as they had on the journey away, with the unexpected professors, both benign and malevolent. The Master of my life employed the world in His service.

In my skeletal Theory of Involution, I formulated a concept of collective consciousness and a universal memory and suggested that each of us had our entry to it through our DNA. Nothing was lost, and all experience was preserved. In the months in which I was deemed 'mad,' I had ventured through the veils into wider and wider and more instantaneous manifestations of the linkages between thought and event. Until all I knew was love, unconditional, purposeless and all-encompassing. Love sat with me on a doorstep in Kensington and toasted my recognition in stolen milk.

But in my descent back to restricted, narrow, step-by-step awareness, the vision I had gained did not forsake me. Each improbable gift that guided my recovery reminded me of that. Each helped to clothe a skeletal theory with the musculature of the omnipresent ordinariness of God, a love capable of taking a car off the road, offering a name in a dream, a name to save my life. A life that still feels a debt is owed, if only to share the circumstances that led me to see it. These days, many pronounce that we are all God, part of, or participants in God. That still leaves Him as a remote connection, rather like a titled ancestor or behind a curtain. For me, after repeated gifts and glories, God is Life itself, and every encounter with man or creature has the potential to make that evident. Each of us is an instrument played by our Creator, and He asks for our consent or permits our imperfect instincts to prevail. If they are discordant, we will suffer the consequences as we should.

Originally, I wrote what wore the clothes of a scientific theory. Believing that science was most in need of an alternative to Darwin's red-in-tooth-and-claw portrait of human emergence and character, I thoughtlessly adopted its language and its dry, spiritless concepts. Naturally, it fell on the equally arid refusal of scientists and failed to root.

It was just as well that it did.

I needed to live this life first to corroborate its truth. To flesh out its instant timings, its intuitive guidance, its generosity. No theory can offer these; theory distils thin water from rich wine. Those who thrive on theory have water in their veins, criticism on their lips, and safe sponsors replenish their pockets. They were never natural companions, but I needed to travel home through the ordinary saints, the men with hammers, the saviours of trees and those who knew what enough meant. The Return was a new exile from the Exile.

Henceforth, whatever I would write would be for them.

༄

This Safari is close to its end. You, the reader, are legitimately expecting a wrap-up with a bow. That is because the convention of memoir—and this *is* a memoir without tidy limits—insists upon some kind of triumph. One that you can pocket to justify the journey you have so generously undertaken. The reason the Hero's Journey ends with his Return is to afford those he abandoned the satisfaction of always knowing he would have to. Their collective reality would prevail. Otherwise, what a pickle of chaos he would leave in his wake! All those outworn shoes cluttering up their straight and narrow path.

But which life ends with a curtsy to the wisdom of conformity? Which creator takes a knee to convention? You know the answer.

Because you know the answer, I can suggest that there will be a wrap-up at the end of this, one with a larger triumph than a problem overcome, and it is a triumph that includes you, a collective triumph that sends its bright shafts deep into your own life's mirror and its stumbling uncertainties. I feel sure, since you are still here, that no small 'mission accomplished' will satisfy you. Uncertainty is what we have in common; it is what keeps us reading and united. Let's ride it a little longer.

At the outset, the author warned that her life was snapped 'across God's celestial knee...and was only raggedly left linked.' Splitting this life into two gave you the mirror in which the ordinary was reflected: two continents, two cultures, one despising the other, one over-reverent of the other. The contrasts between them make each more clearly seen. South Africa's youthful immaturity built the belief in Europe's superiority. British chilly constipation re-heated the longing for innocence and warmth.

Two mirror families, identical in composition but choosing to live apart, and two of most other things, one each side of that mirror; two Jews with names beginning with M. two Margarets, two of almost everything; Alisons, Marthas, Georginas, alcoholics and two Morris travellers. When it came to devoted love, there was only one Ndaba, one Marna, one Heli, one Noel, and one Brother Paul, each threaded along the spine of affection and sustaining this search.

☙

With Louie and Ndaba now gone, and all my daughters absent, our last dog dead, outer life was becalmed. My heedless energy of a direction towards a significant contribution was amputated. So much patterning, so many interventions by timely academics, mythical serpents and birds, all small miracles— to what end?

I had probably ten years of lucidity left.

Before embarking on another fool's errand, I needed to understand my failures. I could do nothing about my children, or the misjudgement of musical retreats, or master the cello, but I still believed that my original Involution had been a groundbreaking hypothesis. It had made little impact and received no echoes. At the time, I believed it would offer a new matrix into which specialists would neatly slot their own insights. I now saw it as an artist's sketch, penned as an aide memoire, perhaps because the artist, busy whirling, falling and getting 'sectioned', had no deft brushes and had dislodged her varifocals.

I had to find another ladder, not the scientific scaffolding I had first erected against the great cathedral of light —which only cast shadows—but instead to rebuild the cathedral from all the materials lying about, genius, inspiration, and the mystics who knew better. What I needed was to immerse myself in a deeper history, plumbing below the factual surface to the longing that drove an obsession. An obsession to melt into rapture and return with knowledge. In short, the lives they led. How their circumstances shaped their longing, and how their triumphs were received.

I began with mysticism, the records of the saints. Through both time and clime, I found their universal perennial agreement: on the unity of creation, the validity of encounters with synchronous 'miracles', their injected energy to uplift others, and their indifference to pain or rejection. I had sampled something of that truth. I knew they knew. I also knew that those without such encounters would never know. So how might I bridge that divide between direct experience of the nature of creation and the scientific checker-play of ideas about it? The ideas that believed smashing virtual particles in a magnetic accelerator would yield answers?

I had to research the other bank of that unbridgeable river. To re-examine the history of science that had dug itself so immovably into clay. Science had its own quasi-saints, the genius forerunners whose inspirations led its cavalcade. Their ideas were the pennants that science followed. I began with the earliest records of such men in pre-Hellenic Greece, Pythagoras, Heraclitus, and Empedocles, moved on and kept going. The early scientists were philosophers, and conceptually, they were absorbed by the whole. The whole gave meaning to the parts. Later, science dealt only with the parts, matter and its interactions. The diminishing of the whole's meaning and the mastery of parts created the goliath of steel-plated, riveted science, at which my original theory had only flung pebbles.

It would be the education I had never had. Not so much better late than never, but better taken late, with a more discerning mind, than early. I had perhaps a decade to dedicate to it before the salty surf on Costa geriatrica swept in with sharp sand and broken shells.

∽

As for any intended travel, preparations are necessary. I need bookshelves; John needs a companion. The garden is simplified, stripped of herbaceous borders and laid to lawn. Outer life is limited to essentials. Milly is our third Border Collie, named after the recently dead original, whiter than black and with a large African posterior. She is the last of a farm litter abandoned by her working mother, already back with her flock, unconcerned about her lonely offspring curled on a rough blanket in a stone-flagged kitchen. Milly comes home on John's lap, looking hopeful with bright, intelligent eyes. She grows apace into a working dog herself, rounding us up by nipping ankles and circling to curtail the speed of any traverse of the garden by legs or the lawn mower.

Milly soon makes friends with a Jack Russell called Alfie, who calls from across three fields to chew her tennis balls and steal her supper before he scampers home. John and Milly walk the local woods daily; she pulls the ageing man up steep slopes like a huskie and shares his tea with an extra bowl for milk, both accepted habitués of the local tea room. Milly is our replacement Ndaba.

I am free to read and read, notate, cross reference and re-read. Silence makes of home a tranquil library until suppertime.

☙

Through this more intimate recovery of the history of science, I encountered the scientific mystics, those contemplative forerunners who grasped the larger vision. From Archimedes in his bath to Newton with his apple or Clark Maxwell observing the effect of a storm on water temperature, genius lay in innocence; the productive questions began with 'why'. The 'how' would follow. Those innocents who asked 'why' were free from received opinions or doctrines of any kind. It was they who had led the scientific cavalcade from ancient Greece to Quantum Theory. Just like the mystics, their inspiration fuelled a frenzy of productive work, heedless of health and indifferent to rejection.

The error I had made in my original Theory of Involution lay in accepting the scientific story without examining its episodes of inspiration or the authority of its guiding genius. I had also failed to record the sequencing of their succession. They travelled from their 'now' back to the beginning, in incremental steps, each standing on the shoulders of their predecessors, from the whole, through the parts, back to the whole—circular time.

But the scientific sequence was also the mirror of memory, recovered in reverse.

Was 'Eureka!' 'I have found it'—re-cognition? The knowing that I know? Was that what Socrates meant when he said, 'Know thyself'? Recognition can only happen when it has been known before, so recovered. From Eden through Babylon's centuries of combat and now reapproaching a longed-for Eden? Was that why the Christian Church suppressed belief in reincarnation? With prior experience Man might compete with its authority? And why science claims it *'discovers'* rather than *recollects*? So, back to Terry and his Chinese boxes. God undoubtedly re-enters if inspiration does. Since Darwin, science does not 'do' God.

Unrolling that scroll of 'spiritual' science— inspiration recovering the history of creation— also makes other languages visible; painting and music portray the concepts of science more explicitly, dating its advances. Flat cave paintings gain flesh and grow three-dimensional, adding perspective until they become photographic with the enlightenment, and then return to the flatness of modernism and abstraction. Music, likewise, goes from rhythm to melody, piped or strung, then adds depth with harmony and complexity with ornamentation and structure. Then both melody and harmony disappear, back to atonal, discordant, and rhythmic, until John Cage 'composes' silence in fixed (or dislocated) proportions.

All languages mirror the scientific journey, of man's recovery of himself, his history and lifetimes of experience.

Through them all, the mystics, scientists, painters and musicians, I traced the thread of Man's journey. From his diminished, lonely, meaningless solitude back through his memory to the glorious, integrated perfection of his world, Man is the mirror of the divine. Not merely part of it but able to comprehend and augment it. The inspiration of genius spun the web that linked us all, thread by thread, link by link. Spontaneous inspiration co-created; the book of Genesis was not a record of the past, but creation was continuously being written.

With regard to time, it circled back to reapproach the experience of the beginning.

∽

Like all my mystical compatriots, it was my experiences that lit the road to Damascus. No philosophical guide, no religious adherence, and no prolonged meditation would have given coherence to ten years of systematic study. The Key that linked it all was the individual life. My seemingly haphazard life of bare survival had sampled a working knowledge of the truths of mysticism and the disciplines of science. If I believed myself 'summoned'—and I did—it was to link those like me, both mystic and scientist, into a single skein of evidence that would plait both together as different ways of seeing a single truth.

Involution as a theory was very simple.

The experience of Mankind was stored and coded in DNA, a cellular memory from the beginning to the present.

That, at the time, was new; fifty years ago, DNA was believed to give instructions for protein assembly, not to receive or store anything at all, a dictator in ear-muffs.

Science appropriated only three per cent of DNA for that. I assigned the rest for the storage of universal memory; some call it the Akasha.

The gradual recovery of that memory had been through the inspirations of genius in moments of contemplation.

In a dream, the waft of a scent or a bar of melody can recover a whole landscape and evoke the delight when it was first seen.

In contemplation, the granular intellect sinks into the waters of memory and dissolves. It returns to the surface with corals of experience. The deeper they lay in time, the more universal they will prove. That coral is compared with others, similar, still alive, still responsive and obedient to principles and processes already understood. Being found consistent with the familiar— for creation is continuous— the recovered insight, newly bright, is annotated, on display and gradually accepted—ladelling memory, spoon by spoon, into the collective intellect, the museum called Scientia.

Contemplation is limited to the individual. Before his inspiration is wrapped in language and conveyed, it is almost universally shunned and resisted. The genius was the scientific mystic, alone with the blazing torch of certainty. He was often locked away for diving too deep or returning with a baroque pearl, not yet understood, not yet finding a place among others.

The journey of Involution has taken Mankind back to his origins in the garden of unity, love and perfection. The Pied Pipers that had summoned Man's following were individual heralds, the Heroes, never the group, the orthodox, or the doctrinal. Those had always worked to impede, extinguish or subvert the light of inspiration.

The history of science was a slow pilgrimage, initially by martyrs, to recover the experience of the Creator and the nature of His creation. As understood by the individual, but once shown to be valid, shared with every other individual open to the new.

∾

How best to serve a meal that incorporates all of history, all the scientific disciplines, all art and music, as reflecting the collective journey from the whole universe to the whole grain of sand?

Six attempts to write in prose stumbled and fell in chapter three. In prose, I had to supply factual evidence and experimental validation. The axles of the lumbering argument I hoped to turn through 180 degrees were embedded in the weighty mud of intellect's demand for factual underpinning and validation. It could go no further. As I was intent on diminishing the role of intellect, why would I feed its sceptical resistance? Vultures circled in the mind, picking at the carrion of argument. The Decline and Fall.

One night, I was reflecting on the burden of feeling called upon and the demands of obligation to a vision that was self-evident to me but had to be rendered intelligible to others. Why was a half-educated non-entity without disciples chosen for this sermon? These lines came unbidden.

Does Messiah part the cloud when man, his origin, forgets?
In another epicycle, another set of clothes?
To speak as is appropriate in the play upon the page
Rather, as a comet comes in periodic phase?

From that moment, the book began to write itself. Rhythmical poetic lines laid themselves page after page, alluding to the notes I had accumulated for nine years. For another two years, often through the night, I retook the Odyssey of Creation and Man's understanding of it.

You were behind this flow of words, were you not?

Maybe, but you had accumulated the vocabulary, the chronology, and the relationships between all of them. It was merely a matter of calling up what had long been laid down. You were demonstrating

Involution in practice, to yourself.

Music accompanied this creation, from the clacking of sticks and peasant clogs to the baroque instrumentation of courtly dances and the majestic symphonies of the romantics like Mahler. I felt music helped me to keep pace with science's stations of its cross until, after Beethoven's late quartets, music began to fracture. Harmony felt too tidy for the depth of uncertainty science was delivering. Post Darwin, science made the search for meaning meaningless: no God, no purpose, no spirit, no creator. Modernism's discords, rock and punk, and the rhythmic monotony of Steve Reich spelt that out.

Like the first heralded English vernacular and narrative poet, Chaucer —whose wife was also, pleasingly, called Philippa— I travelled with a caravan of the greatest thinkers and creators. We had a lot of fun along the way.

∾

The end came suddenly. I realised I had finished when I reached to check a reference in Bertrand Russell's History of Western Philosophy about Pythagoras refusing to eat beans. The fact was as I remembered. I knew my book was finished as I laid Russell's book aside.

"Can you come down quickly? Need help." John shouted.

I went outside to see Alfie barking, braced on his forepaws. Coiled before him was a grass snake rearing to strike. Alfie had tossed the snake out of a narrow flowerbed against a wall; the stand-off between dog and snake looked ominous for one or the other. I grabbed Alfie and shut him indoors. I returned and, with a broom handle, levered the snake onto a spade. It was injured near its head, but not seriously. I carried the snake to our large natural pond, and it slithered gratefully into the reeds. I let Alfie out.

Immediately, he returned to the same spot in the flowerbed and threw out an identical second snake!

A spiritual pun

So, Bertrand Russell was underlined by Jack Russell to confirm the conclusion; the sign to signify the uncoiling of the twin snakes of the

Caduceus, the wand of Hermes, the mirror coils of DNA.

Since the adder that greeted us on the day we moved in, we have never, in forty years, seen a single snake in our garden, let alone two, no longer intertwined.

∽

Yet the work did not light any blaze; it flickered brightly among a few, guttered and now lies dormant. I believed it the best of what life had bestowed, and like a Christmas pudding it was rich with genius— the best of all of us— and threepenny pieces of their glittering arguments.

> *Our life has been your Bible book,*
> *Forsooth your bell and candle, both…*
> *(For life is what this treatise probes)*
> *Other pages, other lives, here's the library interred.*
> *You read your memory's catacomb*
> *As a fluent blind man's Braille…*

I believed I had delivered my universal infant, and it had taken a great deal of painful contraction. I mastered book design, enjoyed designing its double-hinged cover to mark two places at once, managed to get reputable bookshops to accept a few copies, done a few tours of festivals, but it lay…. uncelebrated. There were a few who…

A Christmas pudding keeps for an eternity of ordinary time. Others will lend it a spoon and find it good. Remember Beethoven's last quartets and his audience's incomprehension of his harrowing new discords that cry out from his lonely wilderness and yet soar into heart-rending melody?

When the fireflies of Twitter go out, a man in slippers will find winter long enough to sojourn with your book, his feet upon a fender. Take heart.

CHAPTER 41

Milly-Polly. Finishing Touches

'An ass may bray a good while before he shakes the stars down.'

When a chef brings a dish to the table, he does not trouble his guest with the details, grinding flour, plucking herbs, the labours of the pestle. He only hopes that his choices are enjoyed in the mouth. So, I will pass over the disappointments, the modifications, the re-editing and the appeals to so many who might have helped, whose own works and professed interests closely dovetailed with my own. After all, I had served a voluntary apprenticeship in long years of study and even been called 'erudite'. That implied a mastery of ingredients, or that's what I hoped.

You will not hear the name of the Fellow of All Souls who asked for my manuscript, all four hundred and fifty pages, 'in hard copy' but uttered no opinion of it, although he kept it and the postage for its return. Nor of the Oxford Professor appointed to 'promote poetry in unusual contexts' who had 'no time to read the works of other people'. Nor the Director of an esteemed Institute founded by a poet for the promotion of the perennial philosophy who regretted 'that you so foolishly chose to write science in poetry. It was unwise to mention the approval of Koestler and Lorenz. People say things in letters they would not stand by in public. Of course, I have harboured similar ideas myself for many years…'

These were my hoped-for tasters; none prepared to lift spoon to lip. Instead, they fill out the bin, the discarded attempts to reach a readership. I did try in every way possible, and even a 'Runner up Book of the Year' award by one generous director cut no ice with others. Nor could it find a reviewer familiar with its span of arguments across science, art and religion. 'I would not have the temerity to venture any opinion on this. Sorry. Shall I save you return postage and pulp?'

These final nails in the coffin of hope buried further efforts among the gowned cognoscenti. I realised that I was combining ingredients that had no business being cooked together. Life itself as inspiration was suitable only in confessionals to a priest behind a screen or concealed as fiction. Do not name it science! Science takes its heavy tramp, left, right, left-right-left, along macadamed roads, not floating in the ether of dreams or synchronicity. Let alone underlined by timely nodding or slithering beasts.

Why do you imagine that we urged the writing of this work—to record the life and then —and only then— to show its relevance to the magnum opus? Why else record the ordinary details of an extraordinary life to match the lives of other passionate obsessives that have delivered us here? Why are you not finally at peace?

Because it failed to reach those I hoped would develop it, and my life is almost over.

Are you sure of that? It has value for those who find it. There are threads from the tapestry that hang loose. Perhaps we should stitch a simple hem before life folds you away?

ↀ

So, to grief. A year after publishing Involution, Milly, the dog of the book, the caretaker of the household, the companion for John, was fourteen and arthritic, wasting rapidly. It was many months since she had been able to jump into a car, the only place where she was afraid and aggressive. We had never understood what caused that fear, but it grew until she was happier travelling in the boot, protected from her own snarl that shamed her. Now she lay fur-matted and defeated. It took her three days of unconsciousness before she died, her tongue moistened with a sponge, like Jesus, stiffening on her mat and keening, emitting spasms of wolverine yelps as though to assure her pack on the other side that she was coming. It was time to let her go, so I left her on her final night.

In the morning, she was stiff, cold, and absent, her loss gigantic and indescribable.

I managed to bury her, before John saw the pitiable corpse, in a grave already dug before the winter frost. As there could be no more dogs, she wore her collar to her final bed, and I threw in the last two roses of the summer. Her mound was covered with bricks against a raiding fox. Her loss was like the death of music, the stave on which our habits were written, the walks, the mowing, the bright eyes watching for any hope of shared pleasure; Milly the second was gone.

Myths are peopled with creatures; they are the original Daimons and remain so. Throughout this enchanted life, we have encountered snakes appearing at the interstices of change through the joints in the wall of life, birds landing on the shoulders of a whirling woman deemed mad, and always a vigil dog for the decade-long spans of growth and change.

The devoted mongrel Windy spanned a childhood into adolescence, bridging patient absences with periods of ecstasy. Bella, the beautiful, honorary show-jumper, was ever attendant on Jem and Kate while I laboured on building and fell into exhaustion. Tara the timid beat the boundary in an unceasing frenzy to ward off the aggression of the neighbours, hell-bent on acquisition. She was the legal eagle for their years of oppression. Tara beat that boundary— back, forth, back, forth— to self-destruction and damaged a heart and a liver in that exhaustion of constant protection. She died at only six, sighing as she died by an injection. Envy had destroyed her; she absorbed it as clearly as poisonous vapour.

Dogs were the constant presence; other animals intervened selectively. A cat launched herself at a portrait and launched this story.

Many will sigh, imagining this is false or sentimental, but did Jung dismiss the improbability of a scarab beetle appearing at his window in Switzerland just as his patient was describing a dream of one in Egypt?

The Divine is the field of consciousness, in which animals are at home: Reach into it by the dissolution of boundaries, and they are summoned as a moth is to light. Animals lack self-importance; they just are. Being. They have no idea about critical appearances, how rare such 'attuning' is, or that their alignment with dissolved boundaries is significant. If they are 'messengers', they are unconscious of being so, drawn by their sense of safety, to one who has peacefully entered their instinctive dimensions. All animals are aware of one another and the boundaries between them. Alter those boundaries, and they find a man or a woman closer kin. Plants do it, too: flourish under loving looks, wilt and die to indifference.

> The wild is tamed by its consent
> to shaman out what we forget…
> They bide with us to educate
> the gift of giving, in full spate.
>
> She centred us long, yet sudden gone
> The call of the wild cried, cried her home…
> Three days she keened I come, I come
> My heart is strong, beats on, beats on
> but hear, I hear; I speak your tongue…
>
> Just give me a span while I prepare
> my absence from this loving lair.
> She returns to breathe the spreading tree
> of song in wolfish symphony.
>
> The sycamore its leaves release
> to trickle on a grave fresh filled
> against the wall of guarded ground

∾

Steadily and with punctuating regularity do the old lose friends. They take to reading obituaries. I have had very few close friends and few obituaries to prepare me for farewell, as obituaries must surely do.

The death of Milly, the collie, left a cavern, not merely of emptiness and loss, but a life of meaning with a day's routine of exercise into which to sandwich the discipline of a book I believed of value. Its value, if it existed, was unrecognised except by a few admirers. The accumulated boxes of unsold first editions act like a mocking rebuke of self-importance. The lash of time's chariot had driven the purposeful endeavour and propelled its direction. Both purpose and direction now lay loose, unattached to anything. No intentions survived.

We are back where we began. Into that void stepped my Daimon to exhort this record of my rich encounters. Perhaps to spin out my allotted span but mostly, I suspect, to force a re-examination. Having obeyed, in resurrecting people and finding inescapable patterns, I have met my ingratitude falling over itself in the heedless hurry to achieve. To achieve what? This distillation did reorder priorities and crayoned afresh the links I had never noticed at the time. Mostly the shadow of my stoic mother, Louie, and how firmly her unhappiness held my leash.

∽

A home without a dog is not a home. It has been three years barren. At our age we find we are denied a rescue animal. Those cadaverous starving creatures, picked up in the streets of Romania, cannot be adopted by people deemed 'too old', whose garden is not completely boarded with shiplap. No record of three dogs living out their lifespan and trained in road safety persuaded the do-gooders of the Nanny State. Strong Guidelines. Sorry.

A puppy is unwise and perhaps selfish? Yet, and on the other hand? Perhaps? An advertisement was tempting. 'Border Collie Female. 4 months, house trained, seeks home. £500.00'. She was expensive, but already house trained?

"Let's just go and look?" said Jem.

"You're not to let me buy. Just look. Then think. No impulsive decision. Okay?"

"Deal. Just look."

We found the bungalow on a busy highway, set back behind a chain link fence, and parked next door at a café. Outside the house, a caged trio of larger collies on a Land Rover snarled and barked, with real aggression clamouring to tear us apart, as we approached the door. Not promising. We knocked and were led through to a clutter-free, melamine kitchen by the owner. His wife shuffled out in slippers. Confined in a large metal cage, the puppy sat upright, straight-backed, as if in anticipation of release. You took your time, the beautiful creature seemed to say. A quintessential Border Collie puppy with symmetrical white stockings and white-tipped extremities, all the rest black but for the asymmetric streak down the nose.

Yes? Well? The puppy seemed to be expecting an answer, wriggling on her tail.

"What is there to think about?" asked Jem, "Just look? What at?" The puppy stretched up.

"Do you want to take her outside and have a chat?" asked her seller.

"I suppose so," I said as he put a lead around her neck. "Why are you getting rid of her?"

"I bought her as a working dog, planning to train her, but she doesn't want to know. Not disobedient, just not interested. She doesn't seem to take to the cows. I don't think she's a working dog, more of a pet." This was not said with convincing ease.

We watched her off the lead, run swiftly around his boundary and then return to sit at our feet. Good enough? How did I do?

"We'll have her," I said, putting the lead back on.

"Knew you would the moment you phoned," the seller said. He took out the breeder's notes, the pedigree, and the vaccination certificate. I wrote a cheque while the puppy waited.

"What's her name? I asked.

"She hasn't really got one yet. Her breeder registered her as Jan, but my grandchildren just call her 'puppy'. She's been micro-chipped," he added and handed me the registration.

"How is she in a car?" I asked, "Happy?" His wife gathered her up.

"She's fine in a car, but since she doesn't know you yet, I'll carry her out." Jem took the wheel while I received the puppy onto my lap on the rear seat.

"So, you brought a chequebook then?" said Jem.

"Well…"

"You old fraud!"

When we reached home, the puppy clambered up the front steps ahead of us, two paws at a time. Through our glass front door on the other side of the hall she spotted a ginger cat that I don't encourage. That cat murders birds. Puppy chased towards the glass; cat bolted towards the outer gate. Instantly, the puppy climbed the staircase and jumped onto my low upstairs window sill to bark at the cat. It is the only window in the house that affords a view of the gate! How did she work that out?

That was the first sign of her familiarity.

"We can't call her puppy?"

"Poppy?"

"Twee, for a dog."

"Polly?"

"Marna's favourite aunt was Petronella, called Polly. Yes. Polly resonates."

She was Polly by process of elimination, by default. What followed was never by default. We had kept Milly's sleeping mat, but Polly would only use it where Milly had; only eat from Milly's bowl where it was always placed, and take anything to chew outside, just as Milly had. She started direct signalling with shoes, placing a pair together, side by side on my low futon bed, and lugging them up, one at a time. She never chewed them, but there was always a pair, paired on my bed. Had she paired them on the floor, I probably would not have noticed. On the bed, they were conspicuous. I never saw her manage it; she waited until she was alone. It seemed a deliberate indication of a matching 'two halves of a whole' side by side.

On the old and Milly-familiar walk by the cricket fields, Polly set off as though she knew exactly where she was, always leaving the ball to be thrown where Milly's favourite drops were: in the middle of a slow stream, near the grass roller, on a bank near a particular tree.

She moved back as though Milly had never left. Arthritic Alfie resumed his weary stagger across the fields, although we had not seen him for three intervening years. He now needed a taxi home. So mature was this 'puppy' it was unnatural. She chewed nothing. But she was afraid in a car.

In the interim since Milly died, Kate had given me her discarded Mini. She thought I could use a more economical car, so the Mini had replaced the car with a boot. Polly would only come if I could keep one hand on her neck as I drove, and even then, she was fearful, quivering in the passenger seat. Not happy in a car: not really safe for either of us.

Involution, as a theory, presupposes reincarnation to explain the longevity and recovery of memory. I had never quite stretched to supposing it applied to more than Man as triggering conscious choice, although the hypothesis presupposed unbroken continuity. Polly's behaviour called that assumption into question. Her registration revealed that the seller had not bought her from her breeder in Norfolk. Another working dog trainer had been her first buyer. I rang him to ask why he had sold her so quickly. He was relatively local, far from Norfolk but close to us: real Somerset, well known as a trainer of working sheep dogs.

"Wha can Oi say? Oi wanted her along with er sister, an'er sister is the cleverest daarg I ever worked with, a she'da been the same. But Graham, when ee saw 'er, ee would 'ave her! On and on ee was, that ee 'ad to have er. If you don't moind me askin', Whaddya gi fer er?" I told him.

"Well, gi that kinda money! Course ee wanted er. Made a tidy packet, ee did. An ee tellin' me ee wanted to work er!"

"He said she didn't want to work."

"You don't ask a daarg. You make'em a workin'. You bring er to me; an Oi'll show yer. Moind you, pretty she was. Oi'll gi er that!"

Polly had passed through three owners in four months before she found us. The work of Ian Stevenson on human reincarnation provides much evidence that those humans who remember past lives were often reincarnated within the same or extended family. This had contributed to my suggestion, in Involution, that the long-lived traditions through certain families, and in certain countries, the luthiers in Cremona— Amati and Stradivari— the actors in England— Redgrave, Richardson, Fox and many others fired by the English stage—are those whose natural passions span generations of the same family. Could something similar be at work in a dog? Could the persistence of fear in a car— without any cause in her present lifetime — also corroborate another intuition, from my own travels through the realms of terror, that memory is threaded emotionally, even in dogs? Could that thread be strong enough to time an advertisement and the reading of it?

I wrote to Veronica, a collective 'entity' who, through an open-source channel called April, writes on such matters online. I asked her whether dogs were reincarnated and retained their identity. I mentioned a few of the indications that had prompted my question.

A few days after writing, but before I received any response, I drove to a local village in the Mini, but without Polly. When I returned to the car, I saw what looked like a coin in the passenger foot-well of the car. I picked it up. It was Milly's collar tag, from the collar in which she was buried!

Milly had never been in this car since we did not have it when she was alive, and the collar was long buried!

From the moment of finding that tag, all Polly's shoe-pairing ceased. I finally got the message, and she registered it. Polly's fear of the car gradually diminished when I exchanged the Mini for another with the familiar boot, with its luggage shelf removed; she was safely enclosed but part of any company, front paws over the back seat and a clear view.

Veronica's answer followed: 'Milly is very happy to be back at home with you. She waited until you were ready.'

A small recompense?

Recompense? For what?

Your book may have failed to achieve the recognition it deserved, but Polly recognised its truth just by returning. She validated its insights and came to tell you so. One of those insights was that affinities draw elements together, both love and hatred. You and she were bonded by love, but Martin Israel found you, equally 'improbably' in Swaziland.

We can never escape the adhesions?

Not if you belong.

CHAPTER 42

The Twitch upon the Thread

'May every Soul that touches mine- be it the slightest contact- get there from some good: some little grace; one kindly thought, one aspiration yet unfelt; one bit of courage for the darkening sky....to make this life worthwhile.'

Surely, a memoir promises to lead its reader to new revelations and deeper truths. At present, we paddle in a becalmed sea. After strife, endeavour and persistence, what do we recall but a catalogue of failures? Intentions, seemingly noble, all disappointed and rejected. Believe me, I am with you in that question, and because I have to find some, any, please God, reason, I look for a new thread to pull upon for an answer. No life so rich in synchronies, so led on a leash of next necessity, lavish with unexpected animals, so generous with gifts and opportunities can end like this? It shall not! Bear with me a little longer, and let us follow one, as yet unstudied, track.

There was one character, shadowed and silent, in the wings of my stage. I was never unconscious of her presence, but as her prompts were confined to books, I have neglected, upon this floodlit apron, to look squarely at the call of George Eliot. Her sharp claws intermittently hooked attention, like those of the cat that tore out the eye of Great Aunt Mary, and she was omnipresent. Rather than be accused of affectation or sailing my ship on the swell of her reputation, I have left her shadowed by perplexity and the passage of two hundred years. For a solitary, books are more critical than other people. They have to be. More than a literary inspiration, she was a driving influence before I felt compelled to discover why.

Without her, this life is incomplete. Indeed, it has a hole at its heart.

After 'Veronica' had confirmed the reason for Milly/Polly's return, I ventured to ask her another question. 'What accounts for the constant interruptions of George Eliot throughout my life? Why was she so insistent?'

Veronica's answer was enigmatic. 'You both come from the same stable.'

What did she mean?

She meant for you to find out.

Is this another of your Herculean detours?

If George Eliot has had a significant role in directing both the passions of my search, the country in which to seek them and the direction of my thinking, I needed to understand why, what and how. I had only two direct threads to pull George Eliot closer: the Great Aunt who 'knew her' and the books bequeathed to me but already stolen and given away.

༄

Great Aunt Mary was the first of Louie's possessions to be de-frocked of her crate, lifted out in her gilded frame and hung in the hall. She settled in immediately, pleased to be spared the clatter of cutlery and the smell of food, content beside a longcase clock of similar vintage. Here, her repaired eye's deep scarring could only be seen from one angle in an evening light. Hanging there, she was both metaphor and rebuke, her scar concealed, visible only when searched for. My last meal with Marna, the foreshadowing of Max, the undiscovered pull of George Eliot and the legacy of books already stolen—all the fibres of a covered wound were laced in that nearly invisible scar.

It was time to repair the damage my myopia had neglected, the close cross-stitching of my own family in determining my life. The aunt who 'knew George Eliot' had also read the succession of novels which punctuated that life, those works which had first drawn me to England. Through Aunt Mary, for reasons unknown, George Eliot travelled at my shoulder, not as a writer but as a forerunner of each decade. The slicing of those decades was as defined as a tight-fitting dust jacket, closing each before the opening paragraph of the next.

It was time to remedy my neglect of the woman whose direct intervention had plucked me out at sixteen and intermittently summarised my lessons. Why did she reach across two centuries and two continents to command my pursuit? I would begin with that gift of Daniel Deronda to my forebears. Through those, I would seek answers.

If Ndaba's memory served, I would begin at the universities to track Ursula's generous bequest of my books. I wrote to four of them. I also wrote to the librarian of Kew Botanical Gardens to track Great Aunt Mary's husband, John Sanderson, whose modernistic paintings of tropical trees now hang in my kitchen. How had this Sanderson couple encountered George Eliot since they never left Durban, and she never visited it? I also wrote to the secretary of the George Eliot Society in Nuneaton, who might have a hypothesis for the gift of the books. To the writing of letters, I added the reading of books, the nine volumes of her collected letters and what is called the 'magisterial' biography of George Eliot by Gordon Haight. From that, I acquired every precise detail of her life beginning at birth.

Fear not. I shall confine myself only to the magnetic parallels between her life and my own.

The 'same stable' began to declare itself immediately. It was the stable of ardent and stoical loneliness, both circumstantially and inwardly. Neither of us, its emergent steeds, could accept a bridle or be caparisoned with ribbons. We were both drays with large hooves and broad backs, hauling loads or ploughing unbroken ground to plant unfamiliar seed. Ploughing perhaps, but refusing any saddles.

Circumstantially, we might have been yoked together. Although Mary Anne Evans—as she was then—had a much-favoured, prettier older sister, Chrissy and an adored older brother, Isaac, she became an only child when Isaac went away to board. Mary Anne, at five, was also dispatched to a boarding school where all other pupils were about twelve. Like me, she trembled with night terrors; like me, she was named 'a three-cornered awkward girl'; like me, she attracted the attention of a young Irish spinster, Maria Lewis, who snaffled her interest in the pursuit of pious orthodoxy and religious works. She took to reading the bible daily as well as obscure theological tracts. Just as Judith lingered long into my adult years, so too did Maria Lewis cling to her most promising protégée for much of her life.

But, as a young child, when asked to draw a picture of God, she drew a single omniscient eye!

Her mother died when Mary Anne was seventeen, leaving her alone, responsible for her ailing father, Robert, and the entire care of his new home. The influence of some new older friends, the Brays, began to crystallise her doubts and her rejection of the narrow orthodoxy of her father's religion towards a naturalistic and less evangelical view of Christianity. Her suffering Christ could no longer be served by pallid Anglicanism. When she refused to accompany her father to church, it caused a harrowing and savage rejection. He banished her from his home—her only home.

Their 'holy war' lasted long.

Mary Anne had defied her father's great injunction, and he could not forgive her.

It was her first encounter with the conflict between parental morality and the call of her emotional and intellectual loyalty to herself. It would be as repeated and as absolute as my own. Repeated rejection became the theme of her life; her impulses and her call for a natural morality were honed and sharpened with every decision she made. The circle of rejection would widen until her end.

Our 'same stable' had padded stalls to insulate each of two rearing, 'strong-minded' women, both attributed with male brains, from any conformity to 'givens'. As children, we both preferred the company of adults, and we both were averse to joining any group, perhaps because rejection had become expected and could be avoided by limiting its opportunities. Even from a distance, a burnt child feels the fire.

As a young woman, now calling herself Marian, trying to establish herself as a writer in London, she fell for a charming roue; her 'Terry' was her landlord, John Chapman. He used her in every way, as a writer for his magazine, teacher, pianist, and perhaps intended more, along with other women, until his wife threw her out. Because she was critical to the success of his magazine, he helped her find alternative lodgings.

After Chapman, she 'walked out' with the arid and savage Herbert Spencer. He enjoyed her intellectually stimulating company; Marian and her friends assumed his attentiveness to have honourable intentions. Affronted by such romantic expectations, Spencer penned and published a savage description of Marian's ugliness. Having described her as *'one of the most admirable women mentally I ever met— ' the greatness of her intellect conjoined with her womanly qualities and manner keep me at her side'* —his essay on 'Personal Beauty' singled out all the features most characteristic of her — *'the heavy under-jaw, the large mouth, the long upper-lip, the long prominent nose, all so unlike the ideal Greek head.'* Just as Martin Israel began with my 'radiant spirit', which turned to letters advising people to 'steer clear' of my 'malign influence,' so Herbert Spencer made sure to convey the limits of his admiration to all her closest friends to whom she had introduced him! The parallels, admiration followed by betrayal, are unending.

I cannot but wonder whether if I had read her life before living my own, I might have made fewer catastrophic mistakes.

As I was over Terry, she was accused of insanity when she eloped with George Henry Lewes (GHL), a married man. GHL was caricatured as 'monkey-like.' Marian was taken, not by his looks, 'very unattractive looking…a miniature Mirabeau' but by his kindness, 'a man of heart and conscience, wearing a mask of flippancy.' Widely published in several fields, GHL was also a versatile playwright, biographer, linguist, and an engaging raconteur who introduced the blue-stocking writer to natural history. Marian found herself wading about rock pools with jars for his specimens. His scientific knowledge and natural philosophy gave a fresh perspective to her integrated ideas about God. Life and creation entered, briny together, at her wading feet and wriggling for inclusion into a wider spiritual religion.

I would omit the details of their marriage, but they have a direct bearing on why she and Great Aunt Mary encountered one another.

GHL was already separated from his wife when he met Marian, but his wife, Agnes, had given birth to children by his business partner, Thornton Leigh-Hunt. Three sons were born before GHL departed the marriage. The first was undoubtedly his own, but there is less certainty about the children that followed. To protect the second, Thornton and the third, Herbert, GHL had generously registered them as 'Lewes', so he was considered complicit in Agnes's adultery and could never legally divorce. His kindness of heart would condemn his relationship with Marian to eternal censure. Marian would be condemned for her courage in accepting GHL's generous morality and the liability of not only his reputation but also the dependencies of his three sons. She would support Agnes and the three boys for the rest of her life, even after the death of GHL.

Her decision to accept and live with the liability of GHL's reputation and the long-term demands of his sons, places a finger on the very pulse of her trust and integrity. It was another episode of pitting her own morality against that of respected society, and it would cost not only invitations to dine and back-room slander but also burial in Westminster Abbey. It would also require that she hid behind a male pseudonym, George Eliot, and permit GHL to navigate and negotiate the publication of her works. In Victorian England, men who defied were the butt of sly, almost envious jokes; women who defied were mad, or Jezebels and never forgiven.

Horrified by the scandal of her unmarried cohabitation, her brother, Isaac, refused any contact with her and pressured her sister to do the same. None of her original family was prepared to accept her love and loyalty to GHL, no matter what she did in care or generosity to others. She had made her bed and would have to lie on it. Louie's harsh rebuke on the day following my marriage floated back with the waft of a freshly lit cigarette.

George Eliot's life was a continual conflict between orthodoxy and liberty. She survived through her genius in transforming that life into art, the creation of characters in conflict between expectations and deeper moral commitments. Each book reflected each decade of her growing understanding. Her childhood relationships and the erosion of that back-lit innocence were examined first in *The Mill on the Floss* before she moved to the varieties of religions: from anaemic Protestantism (*Scenes from Clerical Life*) through ardent Catholicism (*Romola*) to intellectual hair-splitting (*Middlemarch*) she tracked, through fictional characters, her own search for answers. Some expressed her frustrations aloud. Love drove her, and she wanted to understand its driving nature and its perpetual renewal, as well as its doctrinal distortions in every promised and penned orthodoxy; each, in turn, was studied, embodied in fiction, and then discarded.

By the time she exhausted her tributes with *Daniel Deronda* and Judaism, George Eliot seemed finally freed of looking elsewhere for answers. Her final book, a series of observations, told through a fictitious character, *Theophrastus Such*, explores her difficulties with conformity and singularities of conviction across many fields. Nothing in her search, even its doubts, was left un-examined. However, the journey of that systematic search gave us unequalled literature and made her very rich. But even achieving wealth would expose her to new greed and frequent financial demands from those close to her, especially her demanding stepsons.

Her writing style, like my own, always straddles the divide between the observed and the observer, refusing 'singleness', ever self-critical of a too-exact depiction without reference to an alternative. I had never noticed that similarity until I read another biography called The Real Life of Mary Anne Evans, which laced that life into the boots of each new work. In each, she seeks but finds no answers.

Being essentially alone as a writer, perhaps the inner audible voice is both instructor and audience, the only way to 'hear' ourselves. I had never seen my compulsion for writing in dialogue or writing through 'voices' as symptomatic of this refusal of 'singleness' until I examined the life of George Eliot. At first, I read her as vitally alive fiction, but, through discovering more of her life, I realised each work was deeply biographical. Indeed, we are from the same stable as writers; life and literature are indistinguishable. Both of us directly break off to address the reader, to mirror back our invisible, silent listener, for we have no others. Even her intimate letters address her relations by their roles; 'Dear Boy', give news of 'The Pater', and sign off as 'Your loving Mutter'. She avoids names except for her characters. They were her true and only children.

No wonder she compelled me, and her works described my own life. Mine was neither as erudite nor as productive, for I lacked the breadth of her travels, her mastery of languages and, most importantly, a GHL, her devoted partner and amanuensis, who became her secretary, critic, editor, salesman and agent rolled into one. My searches flitted and flirted through the fields she had mastered; they had the same intent: to find or fail to find answers. Nor have I found a devoted publisher like John Blackwood. But in important ways, the search for meaning and a role to contribute, hers was my life, two centuries ahead!

A pressing question arose about the nature of this 'stable'. Did we both choose the circumstances of stoical solitude and the families that engendered it or did they scatter away from the demands of such driven intensity? Did we arrive to write adventurous and defiant views? Or were those views incubated by rejection and a resultant 'sod it, what's to lose?'

Write on. You may reach a conclusion, anon.

∽

The first breakthrough came from the secretary of the George Eliot Foundation, Kathleen Adams, who began her response, 'How I envy you the possession of an autographed first edition of Daniel Deronda...' In reply, how do I admit the vandalism of Max and add the theft by Ursula? Kathleen wrote the clue that would start an excavation. Dig here.

She wrote, *'Two of George Henry Lewes's sons had emigrated to Natal, where the youngest Bertie had fallen ill and died. It was a Mr John Sanderson, a newspaper editor who had informed George Eliot and her partner, George Henry Lewes (GHL), of his death and posted his last unfinished letter. The Sandersons had cared for the boy when he was gravely ill. This, no doubt, is why George Eliot sent the book to Marie Sanderson for her kindness.'*

So, Great Aunt Mary had become 'Marie' under South African skies?

At last! I discovered the shard of George Eliot, the childless stepmother, who had penetrated Africa itself and insinuated its call right within my own family. No longer a literary figure, the problematic stepsons of George Eliot are now gathered together in the singing tropics of Durban, a shared space-time capsule that I know very well. How had they encountered one another, this childless couple and these stepsons of the renowned author?

The volumes of her letters would be necessary, and many of the semi-literate, misspelt letters written by the youngest Bertie. Bertie's early death would leave a widow and two very small children, one he had never seen, to the care of strangers in my own family, great uncle John and great aunt Mary Sanderson. With George Eliot herself, they would share the godparenting of her (step) grandchildren.

No author has occasioned more biographies nor such impassioned devotion. Something about her brave and ruthlessly honest life seems to command more than literary appreciation. 'Those of Us Who Loved Her' was Kathleen Adams's title, putting herself and her society's devotees alongside those contemporaries who actually knew George Eliot and who sidled in or waited for the honour of a half hour in her company or wept at her grave. I wrote to a few in the hope of shared communion about my discovery—and my own devotion. None replied. It was as though each hugged her own George Eliot and wanted to hear nothing that might shatter the immaculate and exclusive vision.

༄

Discovering the circumstances of our temperamental kinship explained why George Eliot drew me and drew me to England, but similar outer circumstances were merely the canvas on which her compelling call was stitched. She described the people I knew. The irreverent Mrs Cadwallader was Marna immortalised; Casaubon was

Martin Israel to a watch-spring, convincing in appearance but empty, self-satisfied and ruthless.

But when I reached the end of her life of gentle defiance, walking alone and ignoring all the waggling heads, I discovered that after GHL's death, George Eliot, at sixty, had sought safety in a conventional marriage. I subsided like a wrinkled crepe balloon. She also married a John.

John Cross was not only a banker, twenty years her junior, but someone of conventional habits and a plain, square-cornered mind. In a grand, high Anglican Church in Hanover Square — hand-over, get squared! — it was an inversion of my fateful trip to see Martin Israel — 'Andover…this is hand over…all tickets please'—, an abdication, a descent from the pedestal of lonely courage which had inspired so many of her female friends, trapped by dependent marriages. For them, she had been a flag to the bravely possible! She had been that for me, too.

But imagining her on his arm, processing down an aisle, to approving nods, momentarily eradicated all I had believed!

Initially, George Eliot flirted with this young John Cross, signing herself 'Beatrice' and thereby signalling the chaste worship of a Dante. He was wealthy and had time to attend to all her practical needs, but marriage seemed— to her wide circle of admirers— both unnecessary and unwise, a betrayal of all they had thought she stood for. For twenty-five years with GHL, she had loved, and for love defied the convention of marriage, of necessity. Now, with great wealth, universal esteem, and the devoted attention of her eldest stepson, Charles Lewes, she needed no marriage.

News of that late marriage shocked me. The fact that Cross, on their honeymoon in Venice, threw himself off a balcony of the Hotel Europa into the Grand Canal suggests that it shocked him equally. The reasons for that should remain decently under the sumptuous velvet bedcovers. The gondoliere who fished him out and delivered a dripping man to the hotel porter were paid off and silenced. It was hushed up.

I see them clearly: those perplexed, small Venetians, faceless, slinking off, silhouetted in the undulating watery lights, counting coins.

What the conventional marriage achieved was a reconciliation with George Eliot's brother, Isaac, who had shunned her for twenty-five years during her cohabitation with GHL. Just as my marriage to John, a respectable schoolmaster, melted Louie's fierce rejection, my 'insanity' was forgotten in the balm of his respectability. The prodigal had returned home to her roots: her father's high rectitude, his Anglican Church and what remained of family, her once beloved brother. Her sister had already died.

She survived this decision for a bare seven months and died the same year, three days before Christmas 1880. That exciting house, first seen in Cheyne Walk when I was twenty-two, 'George Eliot lived here,' was not where she had ever lived. It was where she surrendered and died after moving in four months earlier with John Cross.

Almost the first person John Cross informed of that death was her long-estranged brother Isaac. Why, given that he knew all her close friends, would he choose Isaac? The hostile brother who had unequivocally shunned her? Why would he proceed to write a sanitised biography in collaboration with Isaac, ironing out all her wrinkled indiscretions? Intuitively, I feel something very disturbing happened in Venice, which made her new husband seek out the one person whose record of disapproval and rejection made him natural kin. Another Martin Israel seeking a corroborator to help excise his early affection and perhaps misguided marriage?

John Cross lived on for another forty-four years, giving literary readings which did not include her work nor did he ever mention her again. He refused invitations to any memorial of her. George Eliot, probably the greatest English novelist, was denied burial in Westminster Abbey and shunned to the last, even after death.

Hers was the classic hero's journey.

In returning to Maweni, I had done the same, looked again for the family I never had, the homestead that was the model of what I had tried to provide. In searching for George Eliot's link to my forebears,

I sought the shuttle that had woven us together. I was yet to find even tighter tension through that shuttle than I ever imagined!

∾

My return to Maweni not only echoed George Eliot's return to her roots but took me to where her stepsons would bind my life with hers.

Rhodes University in Grahamstown did indeed have the four volumes, still in their original bindings, kindly bequeathed by Mrs Ursula Randall. Could they perhaps be kind enough to send a photocopy of the inscription? With pleasure, they did. I revisited the inscription I had seen at sixteen and then disregarded when Marna could not enlighten. I realised why. She did not know.

On the title page, above the title, in the elegant small script of the confidently educated, discerning author was written:

> *From George Eliot,*
> *November. 1876.*
> *To Mr. Sanderson…*
> *In grateful remembrance*
> *of kindness shown to dear ones*
> *no longer living.*

Capitals were relatively large and free, tails shaped with small curves, and the alignment was clearly deliberate. The date, which was the date of first publication, was placed centrally; 'of kindness' was linked, as was 'no longer'. This writer wrote nothing unintentionally, not even to a stranger. But I have removed the wound.

There, at an angle, an eyebrow's distance above 'Eliot' was **LIBRIS -KAVNAT,** smudged! Stamp, stamp, stamp, Max had only just missed this most meticulous gift. Oh, the vulgarian! In case one was not enough, that stamp was thumped again at the bottom of the page. A fury rose. Although Ndaba had warned me, nothing could prepare me for the arrogance of that stamp signature that had taken over my books but also my mother's life and Milly's deep composure. Smudged, emboldened and expropriated was Max's oppression of everything. He, with his milk-fed ulcer, had dragooned the sale of our home and the abandonment of Louie's profession, gambled her pitiful earnings and insulted them both over half a century. In what lay betrayal? In what constancy? Marriage to that?

∾

The inscription on the books bequeathed to me was in commemoration of 'dear ones no longer living', George Eliot's stepsons dispatched, one after the other, to the land of my own birth. Somehow, Thornton, devoid of experience in anything, will run a store, whip a transport wagon, plant coffee or trade in ivory.

Prepare for him to enter your family. A passing mention of Marna's great aunt Mary provides an introduction to your Sandersons in Durban.

Here are Thornton's first impressions of them.

'I was soon quite at home with him and his wife. He is a very nice man and a great botanist—not a very scientific one, but the other kind—you know what I mean. —His wife is a charming creature, about 30, no children, and immensely fond of music, not that disgusting trash which is called music at home and here but Beethoven! Mendelssohn, etc... So you may imagine the evenings we have together, sonatas, symphonies, etc, while I howl German songs. Mrs S was delighted to find somebody as congenial as I was, for there is nobody in Durban or Maritzburg either, as far as I can find, who cares for anything but dance music.'

∾

You have now met your Great Aunt Mary through the eyes of George Eliot's (step)son, Thornton. The rarity of an accomplished pianist in the sweltering tropics was the finding of a rare curlew amongst the gulls.

A cat first drew attention to the connection, but a lifetime later you learn it was a flesh and blood link, not what you imagined, a compan-

ionable literary affinity. Not only a mental connection but a worldly one. Another confirmation that the world and the mind are single?

On the subject of flesh and blood, there is another parallel shouting for attention, the question of whose son he really was. Marna's early suspicion of her own father's illegitimacy was probably gnomic; she often was. Thornton bears the name of GHL's business partner, Thornton Leigh Hunt. Just as Marna's father, Charles Ashton Barrett, carried the name of *his* father's business partner, John Ashton. (Ashton and Barrett Farm Implement Manufacturers) No other Ashton hangs upon the Barrett family tree. Were both an identical smudging of paternity? Was Thornton Lewes dispatched to a country not likely to question? Just as Henry Joseph Barrett set sail for Africa and then abandoned his supposed son Charles, Marna's father, at sixteen, as soon as his wife Mary died. He then returned to Hull and remarried. Without any record of time spent or 'issue' left in South Africa? Perhaps, like Charles Ashton, the disgrace of Thornton was parked as far from respectable London as possible in the despised and disreputable South Africa of remote farms and ignorant population?

It is a perfect metaphor for a life of mistaken identity. 'Was I even the principal of my life?' was what you asked.

Illegitimacy was a serious stain, and people took pains to conceal it. Yet amongst those known to George Eliot, like Charles Bray, who fathered six with his mistress, and her close friend, Barbara Bodichon, who was herself illegitimate, as was GHL, it was flagrant and common.

Her life, like yours, was her bible. The conflicts of stepchildren, the selfishness of childlessness, and the legitimacy of inheritance were themes endlessly re-woven. An unmarried, childless woman of great wealth made books her infants, but found being 'up to our ears in boydom' exceedingly trying. The oldest, Charles, was adoring and tractable, 'Thornie' was wild and irresponsible, although when he was dying, she became devoted, and Herbert, who followed Thornton to South Africa, was plodding and dull.

But back to the land of my origins. On the slopes of the Drakensberg, the baking fields parched for want of rain, Thornie joins a Boer Commando to fight the Basuto. He writes, 'Who would have thought that by coming out here, instead of going to Poland I should have fallen from the frying pan into the fire, and instead of fighting an enemy I hate, I should have to fight one I despise….as with all my heart I am going now into a Basuto war.'

Sweating in the saddle, he picks his way up the stony trails. We can see him plainly, alongside the monosyllabic, weather-beaten van den Bosch Boer under a leather hat, forced by conscription to abandon his farm, riding silently alongside a jocular, naïve British mercenary, there to make his fortune. The two together portray the claims upon my own life. One to seek adventure, the other to preserve what had been hard secured and long worked.

They find partially buried bodies, but Thornie does not seem much troubled. Other game for sport might be *'Bushmen, who are almost the same as Chimps or gorillas'*. In another letter, he offers to *'procure and send home a baboon.'* The *'President has promised voluntary conscripts a farm of 5000 acres'*, and Thornie is expecting his allocation. After a number of skirmishes, in which the game is now black men, Thornie kills a 'dozen'—as he might number Warwickshire partridges. The Freestate Militia is disbanded, and the promise of a farm is rescinded.

Thornie is angry. Here, we meet the pragmatic realism of the Boer and the naïveté and callousness of a raw young Englishman.

I begin to resent this invasion without sensitivity. I already know of the disdainful attitude to my countryman's unlettered, abrasive voices, but here, the young blood is dispatched to milk opportunity from my country with scant respect for its courage or its hardships.

ᛜ

Was my esteem for the subtlety of George Eliot to be whittled away? There were no rebukes from her. Not directly to Thornton— of course, stepmothers need to be careful— but not any I could find in letters to her close friends where a stepmother *could* let rip and be forgiven. Clearly, her honesty was tied in knots over these boys. Their very existence troubled her more than their irresponsibility and constant demands for money. That was when the reciprocal devotion in her perfect liaison with GHL began to blur. I wondered why, given that their mother Agnes was still alive and hale, they had, after schooling in Switzerland, become so completely imposed upon his home with George Eliot.

I was in search of reasons for George Eliot's call upon me, but the more I read, the further from me she walked. The literary aspic, in which she had always been served as though in a fluted gel, began to shiver in doubt. I quelled doubt and persisted.

∾

Unlike most biographers who relegate these draining and demanding sons to a footnote, my interest in them has many strands. The simplest is that they provide my direct link to George Eliot personally, but also to the one arena of her life, enforced motherhood, she could never fully reconcile with the demands of her vocation. She tucked them, as she always did, into her characters and allowed Mary Garth in Middlemarch to voice her own rebukes about feckless horse trading and debt, a way to say what a stepmother could not say to stepsons about a failed attempt to buy ivory. I know the conditions too vividly not to see the harshness of dispatching two young Londoners with a gun to a sparsely inhabited country, its canny duplicitous farmers, sullen African servants, and the uncertainties of drought, disease and great distances, unrelieved by any culture or society. I cannot relegate the tragedy of their inevitable end as easily as she did.

∾

Bertie followed to join Thornie in 1866, but as Thornie was upcountry, Bertie was comfortably installed at the Sandersons. Shortly after their reunion, the brothers travel back to the Drakensberg. They find a farm on the eastern slopes, with abundant water, firewood, small game and wild birds which has a wonderful waterfall two hundred feet high. This paradise they procure for one hundred pounds and christen it 'The Falls of the Assegai.'

Another Maweni? Named just as Marna would? An echo in the same arena. The parallels fall two hundred years apart.

For two years, they farm together, selling and buying sheep that die and planting crops that fail. Early in 1869, GHL receives word that Thornie was in acute pain with a suspected kidney stone. He sends his son money and urges him to return home.

After a trip abroad, George Eliot and GHL return home to find Thornie 'pitifully wasted' and in excruciating pain, only able to lie on the floor 'writhing in agony'. George Eliot's doctor, the Royal Surgeon, Paget, does not initially diagnose tuberculosis of the spine but administers morphine over six months, and constant nursing offers little respite. Suddenly, George Eliot's serene world capitulates to the enforced motherhood of a helpless, dying young man.

She wrote that Thornie *'has more than ever the wizened look… instead of its old beauty… I cannot shake off the impression it creates in me of a slow withering."* It was clear he was drifting away. On October 19th 1869, he died in George Eliot's arms. *'It has cut deeper than I expected- that he is gone, and I can never make him feel my love anymore.'* The experience had affected her more explicitly than almost any other. *'I have a deep sense of change within and of a permanently closer companionship with death.'*

Thornie's death seems to have marked a turning point for her. The point at which reality spliced through imaginative sympathy and rendered her impotent. The woman of limitless emotional, creative power met her limitations. An awareness of mortality walked close thereafter.

∞

With Thornie gone, Bertie was left to farm alone. Within two months of Thornie's death, a letter announces his affection for a young woman, Eliza Stevenson Harrison. Her father opposes the match and has no intention of providing any kind of financial help. Eliza takes matters into her own hands and leaves home to join Bertie. He sells Falls of the Assegai because Eliza could never be safely left alone. Eliza's father, Mr

Harrison, is *'too stingy to part with anything. He could spare a span of oxen and some cows and never miss them...'*

This complaint must have struck gall in the woman whose discipline had provided for them all. Yet substantial monies follow.

What follows in Herbert's letters is a catalogue of bad judgements and reckless decisions: a speedy secret marriage to Eliza, the building of a two-roomed house on land that the seller from whom he had 'bought it' had never owned, then the demolition and transport of that house. He repents that he has never learned a trade. He thanks them for £200, and he hopes he will 'make better use of it' and asks for a hundred more!

By the time he writes again, he has a daughter named Marian after his 'Mutter' —George Eliot—for whose infant milk he must rely upon a goat but he is troubled with constant rheumatism. Bertie confesses he is *'quite a skeleton'* and reads because pain prevents him from sleeping, but his little daughter thrives. He is now taking Strychnia for pain. Eliza is again pregnant and due to be confined in May. It is now March 1875.

The pity of these cries from the wilderness is hard to read. Bertie was entirely out of his depth. His innocence and inability to read the seasons, the canny grasping farmers, the unpredictability of labour, the diseases of his stock, his wife pregnant too soon and again too quickly, all blows rain down upon him. His simplicity keeps him going and he fails to see the inevitability of his end. Seriously ill, and leaving his heavily pregnant young wife, he travels to Durban in the hope of sea air. She, alone on a farm, gives birth to a son he will never see. She names him George after GHL.

His end was, in all important ways, my beginning. His end inscribed those volumes, 'For kindness shown to those no longer living.' That same hand might now continue, 'And for those not yet alive!'

On June 29th 1875, in a Durban hotel, Bertie died holding the hand of

John Sanderson. It was my forebears who wrote the description of his tragic end to his parents, George Eliot and GHL.

'While I was there, Dr Taylor, who had been sent for, came in. He told me Herbert could not live many hours. On asking if he had made him aware of this, he said no; it was of no use; he was too far gone.

As I sat by him, holding his hands and supporting his head with my left, he seemed to make several attempts to speak without being able to articulate, and my endeavours to help him were of no avail. About five minutes to ten, his breathing became less violent, and as nearly as possible, at ten o'clock, with one or two slight gasps, he died so peacefully and without effort or struggle that I continued with his forehead resting in my hand, not sure he might not yet revive.

Of course, he had not many friends or even acquaintances here, but about a dozen followed him to the grave, which is under the shadow of the trees in the beautiful Episcopal Cemetery.'

This letter from John Sanderson to GHL was followed by one to George Eliot from Great Aunt Mary, who signed it 'Marie'. In it, after more details about the end of Herbert's life, there is an appeal, *'For his poor young wife, left with two babies, we feel the greatest sympathy and cannot help thinking of her constantly as I believe she is very weakly and this dreadful shock, coming so soon after her confinement may be very serious and then the desolation! Poor young creature!*

The pitiful parallel deaths of the two brothers were the tragic bondage that underlay my own with George Eliot—marked by that inscription and the gift of Daniel Deronda, which took a lifetime to uncover, a story written across two continents and two hundred years.

∽

Are you finally contented? Now you know the story of the stolen books and the reasons they were sent?

It's good to finally meet the woman who hangs in my hall after all her sojourns with Marna, who knew nothing of this, and Ndaba, who thought she had the evil eye! She writes with many dashes and no great concern for grammatical exactness; I like her instant sympathy and her candour to a famous author whose books she had read. These letters could have appeared in any of them. She was clearly accomplished as a pianist, as was George Eliot which forged the bond with the boys. So yes, many things fall into place.

But?

Two disappointments, perhaps disillusionments. The Sandersons wrote those letters five days after Bertie's tragic death on July 2nd 1875. They must have taken a month or more to reach the Leweses. Yet, on August 14th, George Eliot writes to her friend John Cross with some dispatch. *'We have lately had a sorrow in the death of our youngest son, whom you have heard us speak of as Bertie….From having been splendidly muscular and altogether vigorous, he had become reduced by what he reported to be neuralgic pains…He went to Durban for the sake of sea air and medical advice, but while there, an attack of bronchitis hastened his death…He has left a widow and two children, one of them an infant boy…He was a sweet-natured creature—not clever, but diligent and well judging…and we felt that a colony with a fine climate like Natal offered him the only fair prospect within his reach. The issue, which one could not foresee, must be borne with resignation—is in no case a ground for self-reproach, and in this case, I imagine, would hardly have been favourably altered by a choice of life in the old country.'*

Do you find that bloodless?

It is my first dent in the Thirty-nine Articles of George Eliot's perfection. I find it not only bloodless but specious and self-exculpating. Why wouldn't a dubious diagnosis have been altered by access to her 'Royal' doctor, Paget? Bronchitis is not a killer unless perhaps you have been systemically poisoned by Strychnine. Why was a 'not clever' boy better abandoned to a country where he knew no one and nothing? Why is there no grief, but grief speedily wand-waved to resignation? Why is there no mention of the kindness and intelligence from the Sandersons? Worst of all is the speedy dismissal of self-reproach.

I have a theory: Bertie had possibly contracted tuberculosis from Thornie. In some stages, it is contagious, and they had lived together intimately for two years before Thornie returned home to die. Tuberculosis was not treatable in 1875. Why was it never suggested that they return home together if Thornie was in such pain?

Do you have answers?

I have hypotheses. I suspect Bertie was rather unintelligent and perhaps dull company, unlike Thornie's quick humour. George Eliot does refer to the endless ways boys can be boring. What I never thought to find anywhere in George Eliot is double thinking, the excuse that access to doctors, nursing, and even small comforts would have made no difference. That is guilt speaking. Rather loudly.

Perhaps you could make allowances for the recipient? Not knowing Bertie?

Sorry. John Cross was fast becoming an indispensable 'nephew' and addressed as such. He had known George Eliot and GHL for about a decade, well enough to be a confidant to grief, if grief there was.

What is the other disappointment?

That cuts deeper. That mystery of my adoration of George Eliot is reduced to a prosaic explanation. A token of mere incidental gratitude triggered my life in pursuit of those books and their dedication…

It is only a fragment that could be labelled 'prosaic'. And you know better than to call anything incidental! Is this not a revelation? Saved as a bon-bouche to comfort you? Look at the arc of the whole sequence. An act of kindness to a dying young man causes books to be packed and shipped across the world to a stranger. Ten years later, that stranger dies and leaves them to her nephew, whose daughter, your grandmother, is but three years old. She nurses those books and the aunt's portrait throughout her life —the aunt who 'knew' George Eliot— without quite knowing how or why, until she comes to live with you and your mother. Your cat tears out an eye so that you hear the story that, for her, had neither a beginning nor an end.

After your grandmother tells the enigmatic story, she bequeaths books to a perhaps one-day writer, you, who remembers the name and reads the library of her own life through several volumes. Through those, she is seduced by literature, to another country, and to poetry; she shapes her own passions to the blueprint already lived, stepping in the tracks already left by the author. Meanwhile, your aunt steals the books that a step-father has defaced and gives them away, out of reach. Yet they are doggedly sought and located. Prosaic? I hardly think so.

Doggedly has another meaning. You did not know, did you? That 'Polly' was GHL's nickname for George Eliot?

No!

Like Great Aunt Mary, she came home to be re-hung. While you excavated her calls upon you, 'Polly' had already found you. She always did.

Hers were the prints into which you trod, and when the winds of your own blew them faint, they reappeared inexorably. Over here! Look again. Onward.

CHAPTER 43

The Full Picture. Uitspan

Just as Great Aunt Mary could not stop thinking about Eliza Stevenson Harrison, the young widow with orphaned babies, I couldn't either. She gets very chilly references in the few biographies that allude to her, and I understand why. Her letters to her husband's unmet parents, George Eliot and GHL, are sycophantic and sentimental, with little understanding of the recipients, two sophisticated people juggling the need for solitude to write, travel and a busy house with endless social claims upon them.

Eliza's letters show a self-absorbed, unlettered, simple girl, rough-edged but determined, as her impulsive elopement with Herbert had shown. She was also calculating, using her children's lisping quotations and kissing of portraits to solicit the sympathetic support of Herbert's wealthy parents. They are gruesomely inappropriate; reading them clenches the stomach, especially in one who knows only too well the great gulf that exists between the manners of both countries. She and Herbert had always received generous financial remedies for their endless errors from the Leweses and then, after Herbert's tragic death, from the Sandersons, who helped Eliza build a house. None of that was acknowledged or enough. On hearing of the death of GHL, Eliza took it into her head to board a ship to land, uninvited, in England.

Seldom was a decision more ill-judged or more ill-timed. George Eliot was not the frail grieving widow Eliza imagined would welcome her as a live-in helpmeet with longed-for grandchildren to fill her shortening days. She was an intending bride on the brink of a new life! Eliza and her 'little Africans' were speedily packed off. They would stay with Herbert's older brother Charles, his wife Gertrude and their much better-behaved children in Hampstead until a permanent arrangement could be decided upon.

George Eliot and John Cross had a honeymoon to catch.

After many months of Eliza's quoted complaints from Charles in letters, we lose sight of her and her children. They disappear into a frugal Brighton boardinghouse, which the family believed would suit her better. George Eliot advised Charles not to 'dissuade Eliza from returning to South Africa'. I see them quite clearly, three windblown figures on a lonely beach, throwing pebbles into the unending, shrugging grey sea.

They did not belong in England. None of us do, not quite.

∾.

In searching for her, I found my final jewel, a diadem to crown my long journey of perplexity. The story of my family's direct connection and role had been comforting. There was a reason for George Eliot's magnetism beyond the genius of her books. Discovering it was like a long exhalation after a lifetime's held breath, but, as I expressed to my Daimon, it held disappointment. Was that all there was to it, just a fortuitous happenstance that leaked across two centuries? 'Write on' was what he replied.

In seeking a last view of the pitiful family, 'Harrison', I opened the most blinding revelation. 'Harrison, Frederick,' appeared in a footnote in Haight's 'magisterial' biography. The footnote is to a letter addressed to a Frederick Harrison— no relation to Eliza. He was a positivist shunning orthodox religion, who had appealed to George Eliot to provide an alternative 'liturgy' for family prayer. He obviously believed she, too, was unsatisfied by any orthodoxy. In her reply, she demurs, '*that would hardly lie within my powers,*' but adds, '*I wasted some time…in writing…a poetic dialogue embodying or rather shadowing…the actual contest of ideas…it may* **promote and influence a different kind of presentation.**' (The emphasis is mine) That dialogue 'Symposium' was published as 'A College Breakfast Party' (1878) and was almost the last thing she wrote.

While I was standing imaginatively at the end of Brighton Pier, a coincidental name tipped its crucial significance into the sea that would take Eliza home to South Africa and do the same for me. In a different way. Home to the restoration of my self-belief.

In this long poem, the cast of Hamlet gathers for breakfast in an Oxford Common Room to dispute the nature of knowledge and the voices who claim the path to it. They speak in turn, some to celebrate Reason, some to raise the muse of Soul. Each argues the superiority of his way. A Priest argues for the authority of the Church and obedience to it in the face of science's 'see-saw' speculations. Guildenstern (Golden Star in German) shows contempt for science's 'air chariot' with its 'rainbow bridges.'

> He demands
> 'We settle first the measure of man's need
> before we grant capacity to fill. I demand
> Your Church shall satisfy the ideal man
> His utmost Reason and his utmost Love…still the Soul remain
> Larger, diviner than your half-way Church
> Which racks your Reason into false consent
> And soothes your Love with sops of selfishness.'

From her wide nets, cast through all the sciences, religious orthodoxies, academic philosophies, and literary speculations, Eliot distils, through the voices of argument, the inadequacy of any of them if given priority or dominance. Each mask upon the stage is Shakespeare's poor player: 'That struts and frets his hour upon the stage/And then is heard no more'. Only Soul remains… In this poem, she gives voice to each false claimant before reasserting the priority of the 'larger, diviner Soul,' unserved and unreached by any religion.

Why did you never venture into George Eliot's poetry?

I only discovered she had written poetry through this accident of name. I am glad I did not know and glad you never introduced this earlier, or I would not have attempted what I did. I would not have had the audacity, but finding it now rewards everything!

She began the dialogue you came to richly embroider; her actors were all spirits from the unequalled poet's greatest drama. Your Yorick was a woman with too long a nose, too male a mind. Your actors mostly sat behind a microscope, mapped the world or the heavens, or simply stayed home to pluck a lute. You write a similar dialogue between Reason and Soul to examine the nature of knowledge. She invokes Shakespeare's characters, known by name, to articulate her views; you invoke scientists and artists, known by name. Both of you sit above and make them dance before giving Soul the floor. What think you now? Horatia? Foreshadowed?

So, I was far-fetched to complete what was requested of her- a Religion for Humanity?

Perhaps. It is possible. George Eliot's Key to All Mythologies is re-assigned for you to newly fashion? Not for her world, but for yours? The conceptual understanding and the poetic expression could have been penned by the same hand.

Was it?

Time does not exist, but timing is another matter. The same stable, remember.

ɷ

Uitspan In Unison: In which two, hitched together, thread a song, 'The surrender of Reason to Soul' in minor thirds and reach their final cadences. The first was scored in 1878 (A College Breakfast Party) by George Eliot, and the second in 2012 (The final passage in Involution, Canto the Ninth) by the author. After all Reason's talk, the combined cadences fell silent on the 22nd of November 2019 on the 200th anniversary of George Eliot's birth.

> 'Good-bye, Horatio.
> Each now said "Good-bye."
> Such breakfast, such beginning of the day
> It is more than half the whole. The sun was hot
> On southward branches of the meadow elms,
> The shadows slowly farther crept and veered
> Like changing memories, and Hamlet strolled
> Alone and dubious on the empurpled path
> Between the waving grasses of new June
> Close by the stream where well-compacted boats

Were moored or moving with a lazy creek
To the soft dip of oars. All sounds were light
As tiny silver bells upon the robes
Of hovering silence. Birds made twitterings
That seemed but silence Self o'erfull of Love.

'T'was invitation all to sweet repose;
And Hamlet, drowsy with the mingled draughts
Of cider and conflicting sentiments,
Chose a green couch and watched with half-closed eyes
The meadow road, the stream and dreamy lights,
Until they merged themselves in sequence, strange
With undulating ether, time, the Soul,
The will supreme, the individual claim,
The social Ought, the lyrist's liberty,
Democritus, Pythagoras, in talk
With Anselm, Darwin, Comte and Schopenhauer,
The poets rising slow from out their tombs
Summoned as arbiters that border-world
Of dozing, ere the sense is fully locked.

And then he dreamed a dream so luminous
He woke (he says) convinced; but what it taught
Withholds as yet. Perhaps those graver shades
Admonished him that visions told in haste
Part with their virtues to the squandering lips
And leave the Soul in wider emptiness. '

George Eliot A College Breakfast 1878

We have reached the final furlong, nearly home. You hesitate. Do you want me to carry this story up to bed? Why don't I simply leave you with your other half?

I thought you were that?

Are you finally aligned, you and your matriarch? Both reconciled to your reflections and limitations, both home to self-acceptance? You have attained a shared philosophy, one she began and you completed— the religion of living life, not one dictated or interpreted, not one set in stone or script, but spontaneous in impulse, wise through error and occasionally joyful when affirmed by creation's accord?

Then lunch awaits, and I have an idea, perhaps a modest gift for your departure. You may unwrap it, for it waits...

∞

"Shall we have lunch?" There was no reply. John's hearing aids are not reliable even when in situ, and that is not reliable either.

"LUNCH?" I repeated.

"Good. Good. Back veranda? I'll lay," he said.

"Already done." I said, "So is the book, finally."

"Really? You think so?"

"I think so." We did sit and eat. Lunch is modest in our ménage.

"I have realised," I said, "that myths and fables are not meant to end. It's no good trying to find a final finial and screw it into this bed of my existence. It won't sit well."

"What are you saying?"

"I'm saying that I have realised my life was a fable. Things happened for all their own reasons, not mine. Trying to pith precise meaning is a form of distortion. I have finally arrived back where I started. I should have written it like Animal Farm, as a commentary of universal value, oink oink."

"I thought what you wanted was to show life itself, tripping the light fantastic…" John galloped his fingers along the table edge. He sometimes nails it when I least expect him to.

"Do you realise that today is the two hundredth anniversary?" I asked.

"Of what?"

"George Eliot's birthday."

It was very odd, that bird. It just sat there against the railings of the balustrade. It was attentive in a contented kind of way. Birds don't usually sit so still or so close. Not to a dog.

Polly rose to her feet and went to sniff at the pigeon. It tried a couple of lazy hops without fluster. Polly looked at me for an explanation—she is used to birds taking flight, not passive, nonchalant—but the pigeon just nestled down. So, Polly lay down too, with her chin on her paw and her eyes on the pigeon. Like her namesake, she is a most contemplative creature.

"Do you think that pigeon's injured?" I asked.

John peered at it." It looks all right from here."

I rose and went round closer to the pigeon and picked it up. It permitted that without protest. No bird has ever invited me to stroke its blue-green speckled feathers, the blended colours of sky and stone. Heavier than I had expected and warm to the touch, with its spiky claws wrapped around my finger. The friendly creature looked at me with an inquisitive red-rimmed eye. Then I noticed a yellow band around its left leg.

"It's tame. It's a homing pigeon. Perhaps it's lost?" I made a mental note of the numbers on the yellow band, then gently tossed the pigeon skyward. It flew off in a leisurely north-westerly direction. Perhaps that was inhospitable of me? It was hoping for a crumb?

The bird has flown?

The bird has flown!

I had clean forgotten that message which erupted impromptu at that hostile Kensington portico! I did not know myself, at the time, what it meant except to indicate that I needed nothing from him. From Martin Israel, 'That means nothing to me!' he spat, really angry. He had expected something else. Martin Israel, the man who sought my destruction. What? Forty-five years ago? My metaphor for liberty, both his and mine, had fallen upon flint.

It was a pitiful reaction, but Martin was being tested. We needed to know. It was also for you at the time and again now. Time has no significance; links ignite any dry tinder, behind or ahead.

The quest, known then, is now concluded?

Winging home. We're almost there.

We finished the meal after I had written down the numbers. John cleared the plates. I was wondering about the extraordinary appearance of a homing pigeon at this juncture.

"Perhaps I'd better tell its owner where it is?"

A search of registered pigeon fanciers identified the owner. His name was Terry! He lived in Wigan. Tel No………. email ……….

I rang the number.

"Voicemail is not available. Please try later."

I emailed a new faceless 'Terry' whom I visualised as short and whiskery among his coops of contented couriers, throating at their owner in some dim Midland's yard, all awaiting this final bird's return.

"This email address is not recognised."

You again?

How clever are you, really? Entwined snakes last time you finished a book. A homing pigeon for this one? Terrestrial to aerial. A Terry begins all this, and a Terry's bird finishes it. Birds were Terry's thing, no?

You clever thing! That's really witty. Super economical. Perfect.

You mentioned Orwell's Animal Farm. Remember his first book? You were talking about the writing of fable, and the master of fable says 'yes'.

Like the 'The Man from del Monte' to pineapples?

No, better than that. A sharp reference to Orwell's first vehement book, The Road to Wigan Pier. *You said it yourself. As your fable's finial, something that doesn't exist.*

Doesn't exist?

Wigan Pier is a music hall joke. Wigan is not by the sea and has no pier. Instead, it has a loading staithe for coal. Since nobody, for any reason, would stop among the black slag and brown-brack waters of Midland squalor, the citizens of Wigan put their fingers to their noses. To send up the pretentious travelling on to Blackpool, they called their wooden staithe against a sluggish polluted canal, 'Wigan Pier'.

Take a leaf from the writer of that fabulous fable. They turned the joke upon themselves, turning the cheek to those who did prefer to be beside the seaside. I suggest you do likewise.

Orwell took up their cause?

A compassionate man. His book was for them, the eaters of tripe sleeping four to a bed.

Tripe?

Yes. Tripe features.

Well, thanks!

Follow the citizens of Wigan. Thumb to nose. Wigan Pier. Tripe. Neither is accurate. Words can be spun. Fables survive without end. You already know that. It's important to have fun, stay awake and leave answers to find you, as our Ave Columba did. At the beginning and the end, complete with an olive branch of peace?

I have had so much fun thanks to you. Grazie mille.

Prego Cara mia. The quest was ours in you as much as you in ours.

The life of mind spans all of history; it knows no division and slices no time.

For now, I bid you all adieu.

༺

When you are ready, I shall pluck you
From brittle anonymity…
We'll meet where Petrarch first saw Laura
Abelard uncovered Héloïse.
It is your home, and only I shall enter,
All corridors and shadows I know well.
Did I not stand behind the pallid lover tracing
The blue transparent veins along your arm?
Was I not present when you recognised the absence
Of worship in his strategies of love?

Remember how you felt consoling fingers
Through your hair when you turned to me in pain?
When morning bright, you gathered up decorum
Did I not stand behind your straightened chair?
How often did I fill the glass you scarcely noticed?
While you were thinking of another love you knew?
How many were usurpers, and mistaken?

For each, in turn, I filled your mouth with song…
For each, prepared the bed with smoother linen…
The drawn thread-work of despair and disappointment
Made lace (and deeper longing) sharper creased.

Did I not walk beside you when, in anger,
You marched the stony road towards the hill?
The cloud and mists came cloaking round to hide you…
Recall the piercing sun that struck the water?
The medallion silver lake lay in your palm…
You were flooded with delight to be alone.

I know everything there is to know about you,
I thread your necklaces from all the beads of dream:
I feel your surreptitious itch to dance the Charleston,
I know the jingle that causes you to frown.
I am the rock that shapes your private dwelling,
The path through thrift you tread in barefoot sand…
I have placed my gifts daily on your doorstep…
The doe I sent to nibble at your roses?
The flight of starlings to salute your crown?
I have waited aeons for your recognition.
My perfect world requires your completion…
In your tossing bed, I lie beside you
To watch in sleep your quiet breathing fall…

I shall know the moment I may turn and lift you…
My hands will liquid-shape your acquiescence:
In the silent break of day, upon my shoulder
Upon dawn's clavicle, your happy cheek will lean,
Cradled in my neck, you'll breathe our essence:
I shall carry you entwined and carefully
Through the silver light and striding water…
Wade until we drown in salt-bright sea.

Involution Canto the Ninth.2013

AFTERWORD

The Refuge

There is a place to which my protégée repairs. I use the word deliberately, for it is the haven of repair. This life has been one of searing loss, boundless longing, and dogged duty, but underneath all that, one of deep solitude. To celebrate an acceptance of being alone, she created an imaginary refuge, complete with landscape. She has visited it often when there was nowhere to turn. Nobody has ever been invited to share it, for a sanctuary is secret.

I will take you there.

A pathway leads through chipped stone shingle towards a simple shack which has its back to any approach. Wildflowers, poppies, anemones, ground-hugging orchids, hyacinths, daisies, and small white lupins push through the arid ground and proclaim we are probably in Greece. The flowers wave their wind welcome, disturbed by small breezes. The windowless shack, dark painted, offers its back, elbows spread to shield the view beyond.

We must circle it to see the sea. Below us, a quiet bay is enfolded by the arms of earth. It lies like an undisturbed silver disc open on the horizon through narrow straits. Only wheeling birds know of its existence.

The shack has a wooden veranda, weathered to grey, where a hammock swings and a cracked table will take a glass. The interior is dark, seldom entered. This sanctuary communes only with the waiting sea.

To reach the shore, we descend a steep slope, where the soft sand covers footprints as soon as they are trodden. An arch of rock guards the beach, and the small salt pools at the rock's feet are alive with darting fish and the periscope eyes of crab. It is not yet the occasion to penetrate that arch. We may view the future from here.

On the far edge of the lapping sea, there is a small boat, attended by a navigator, who stitches a rust-red sail; one of us. He is cowled like a Franciscan monk in a brown habit and does not turn. He knows it is not time.

He is patient because he is certain that aloneness will be over when he turns.

If you have enjoyed this book, please consider leaving a review on Amazon (.com or .uk) Goodreads, iBooks, or on any platform on which you are active. It will help the author and the book, and will be much appreciated. The author can be contacted through her website or substack (see last page.) Thank you for reading!

GLOSSARY

Advocaat: a traditional Dutch drink made of egg yolk, brandy and vanilla. Traditionally made at birth, and opened for a coming of age.

Assegai: A sharpened spear used in hunting and warfare

Baganda: The dominant tribe in Uganda

Bechuanaland: now Botswana.

Biltong: Salted and dried meat, usually beef, but ostrich is also used.

Blerrie Engelse: bloody English people.

Blitzkrieg: Lightning Flash-war. Sudden eruption

Boerewors: sausage typical of farm produce and barbecue fare.

Braai: barbecue.

Calpurnia: The negro maid in 'To Kill a Mockingbird'

Caveat Lector: Reader Beware

Doek: Headscarf

Dompas: A contemptuous word for a passbook. Stupid pass.

Donga: A water-eroded, narrow, deep chasm in the earth.

Duiker: A small antelope.

Gogo: Grandmother; old woman, a term of warm respect.

Greats: The second part of a humanities course of Mods (Classics) and Greats (Philosophy)

Hex: Witch.

Himmel: Heaven

Impi: Zulu warrior

Kabaka: The traditional King of the Baganda

Kaffir-boetie: A derogatory word for a liberal. Black brother.

Kerel: a small boy

Koeksisters: Fried dough dipped in syrup or honey.

Koppie: a small hill

Kraal: Collection of rural housing, often mud and thatch.

Kumbi: Small buses or taxis

Lekker: delicious (food), great! (experience)

Lobola: Bride price, paid often in livestock.

Meisie: Young girl or woman.

Mevrou: Mrs or Madame

Mos: Somewhat, commonly.

Nederlandse Kirk: Dutch Reformed Church

Nkosiam: My God. Nkosi; Boss, chief. God

Ncwala: An annual holiday set aside in Swaziland for the King to choose a new bride.

Pondok: Derogatory for a shabby basic house.

Provis: A cover-name for Magwitch (a jailbird, a disguised mentor of Pip) in Great Expectations

Riempie: Thin strip of leather, commonly inter-twined for chair seating.

Rondavel: Round mud room, usually thatched

San: Indigenous small-stature tribe, once called Bushmen.

Siestog: Yuk, Disgusting.

Sjambok: A raw-hide whip

Spruit: Small running stream.

Stoep: Veranda

Stroompie: A small stream.

Swaziland: now Eswatini.

Tannie: Aunt, but used universally to refer to a mature woman.

Tiekies. Thruppenny-bit (Three pence) coin

Totsiens: Goodbye

Tshwala: Home brewed beer

Uitspan: unharness.

Umhlangano: collective discussion or large conference.

Umntwana: small child, infant.

Vrystaat: Orange Freestate, Province of South Africa

Wag n'bietjie: A long white thorn liable to snag a passerby. Literally, 'wait a bit'.

Wors: Sausage

AUTHOR'S NOTE

All quotations below the chapter headings are taken from George Eliot's novels or letters. Their relevance to this safari was more important than their specific source, so I have not cluttered the page. George Eliot owns them all.

All characters are real people and carry their own names. In the case of one or two incidental characters, whose role was needed but whose names I have forgotten, I have given them names that convey their age and 'atmosphere.'

All letters and journal entries are quoted verbatim. None are fictional; none are embroidered or edited. Some are verbatim extracts from longer ones.

Conversations and monologues are reconstructed as close to accurate as memory allows. I have a more acute auditory memory than a visual one. Recovering those conversations aimed to recapture their vitality but not to distort or dramatize their context.

Nothing in this book is fictional. Events recorded, happened as recorded, including the synchronicities and timings. It was, in small and extraordinary timing through the events of mundane life, that the larger patterns emerged. This is why this 'memoir' needed them and doggedly became a Life. Many others were omitted, but the important ones that moved revelation and action forward were retained. A leash was fixed on my collar to control direction but discourage diversions.

I have had an extraordinary, ordinary life. I hoped, by sharing it, that other ordinary lives would see their own extraordinary. All lives are extraordinary, and every one is precious in itself and as a fractal of a greater harmonious life in which nothing, not an incident, not even a thought, is irrelevant.

Seeing is not believing, but believing fosters clearer seeing.

OTHER WORKS

Involution: An Odyssey Reconciling Science to God. The book for which this life provided the vision and vocabulary.

It was nominated as 'Runner-up Book of the Year' (2013) by the Scientific and Medical Network. Published by CollaborArt Books in 2013. Excerpts may be read on the website https://involution-odyssey.com/. Reviews may be found on Amazon https://www.amazon.co.uk/Involution-Odyssey-Reconciling-Science-God-ebook/dp/B00DEKR01A/ref=sr

A Shadow in Yucatan. 'Recapturing the dying sixties, peopled by voices of her generation, Stephanie walks through pregnancy to pain, finding unexpected friends in unlikely places, and a growing instinct for truth and generosity. It tells Stephanie's story, but her story was also the story of that golden time. Its nostalgia sings like cicadas in the heat. https://www.amazon.co.uk/Shadow-Yucatan-Philippa-Rees/dp/0957500238/ref=monarch_sidesheet

Short Pieces, Poems and Stories

Can be found on my substack: Reflections https://substack.com/@philipparees?utm_source=user-menu

And on my website https://philipparees.me/

www.ingramcontent.com/pod-product-compliance
Lightning Source LLC
Chambersburg PA
CBHW051931290426
44110CB00015B/1943